FRANÇOIS
MITTERRAND

FRANÇOIS MITTERRAND

A VERY FRENCH PRESIDENT

Ronald Tiersky

ROWMAN & LITTLEFIELD PUBLISHERS, INC.
Lanham • Boulder • New York • Oxford

ROWMAN & LITTLEFIELD PUBLISHERS, INC.

Published in the United States of America
by Rowman & Littlefield Publishers, Inc.
A Member of the Rowman & Littlefield Publishing Group
4720 Boston Way, Lanham, Maryland 20706
www.rowmanlittlefield.com

P.O. Box 317, Oxford OX2 9RU, United Kingdom

Copyright © 2000 by Ronald Tiersky
First Rowman & Littlefield edition published in 2003
Reprinted by arrangement with Palgrave, an imprint of St. Martin's Press, LLC.

British Library Cataloguing in Publication Information Available

Library of Congress Cataloging-in-Publication Data

Tiersky, Ronald, 1944–
    François Mitterrand : a very French president / Ronald Tiersky.
        p.   cm.
    Subtitle of previous ed.: the last French president.
    Includes bibliographical references and index.
    ISBN 0-7425-2473-6 (pbk. : alk. paper)
    1. Mitterrand, François, 1916–   2. Presidents—France—Biography.
    3. France—Politics and government—1981–1995.   I. Title.
DC423 .T544   2002
944.083'8'092—dc21   2002031709

Printed in the United States of America

♾ ™ The paper used in this publication meets the minimum requirements of
American National Standard for Information Sciences—Permanence of Paper for
Printed Library Materials, ANSI/NISO Z39.48-1992.

To An Ping

TABLE OF CONTENTS

PART ONE
WINDING PATH, CONTESTED ITINERARY

PART TWO
THE DESIRE TO MAKE HISTORY, 1981 TO 1995

PART THREE

CREDO, MORALITY, LEGACIES

ACKNOWLEDGMENTS

THE FOLLOWING COLLEAGUES AND FRIENDS gave much appreciated help and advice in work on this book:

The archival research done especially for this book mainly concerned Mitterrand's presidential years, in particular the two subjects of institutions and foreign policy. Monsieur Hubert Védrine, today foreign minister and then secretary general (chief of staff) at the Élysée palace, was François Mitterrand's longest-serving aide and the key man in making the so-called cohabitation system work. He has my friendship and deep thanks for many interviews and for giving me access to the archives and office facilities in the rue de l'Élysée annex. Hubert Védrine's own book on Mitterrand's foreign policy, *Les Mondes de François Mitterrand* (1996), is by far the best and most complete book to date. Pierre Morel, a key Maastricht negotiator for France and a Mitterrand foreign policy advisor who was subsequently ambassador to Moscow and now to Beijing, has been a generous source of historical background, wise judgment and intellectual perspective. I also thank Pierre de Boissieu, de Gaulle's grand-nephew who was the permanent French negotiator for the Maastricht Political Treaty for a long interview on European integration.

Among academic colleagues my intellectual debts to, and friendship for Pierre Hassner and Stanley Hoffmann are very large and span many years. I want also to acknowledge the following French and European colleagues: M. Pascal Boniface, François Bujon de l'Estang, Yves Boyer, Roland Cayrol, Samy Cohen, Roger Cohen, Michèle Cotta, Jean Daniel, Bassma Kodmani-Darwish, Jean-Luc Domenach, Michel Faucher, Nicole Gnesotto, Pierre Grémion, Catherine Grémion, Jean-Marie Guehenno, François Houter, Josef Joffe, Jacques Julliard, Michel Kajman, Claude Kiejman, Georges Kiejman, Jean Lacouture, the late Georges Lavau, Anne Lauvergeon, Anne-Marie Le Gloannec, Pierre Lellouche, Christian Lequesne, Simon Lunn, Serge Mallet, Dominique Moisi, Maurice Gourdault de Montagne, Thierry Pfister, Marc Riglet, Jean Leclerc du Sablon, Dominique Schnapper, Françoise de la Serre, Mary Sills, Paul Taylor, Bruno Tertrais, Paul Thibaud, Dominique de Villepin, Pierre

Vimont, Martha Zuber, and also Anne Debaquié of the CERI staff. Many American colleagues also have my gratitude for recent or more ancient conversations: Norman Birnbaum, Avis Bohlen, Anton Deporte, William Drodziak, Joseph Fitchett, Julius W. Friend, the late Pamela Harriman, Tony Judt, Flora Lewis, Robert Paxton, Mark Kesselman, William Pfaff, Andrew Pierre, George Ross, Martin Schain, Vivien Schmidt, Simon Serfaty, Scott Sullivan, and Samuel Wells. Julius Friend, whose own book on the Mitterrand presidency is a standard reference, read the entire manuscript, saving me from many errors and giving excellent advice. Robert Thomson, U.S. editor of the *Financial Times,* read the beginning chapters, encouraging me to think that this was a subject that could interest a wider public.

Institutional support: The *Centre d'études des relations internationales* (CERI) has several times been my institutional home in Paris. During a semester in Washington, D.C., in 1996, I was a Woodrow Wilson Center fellow and an academic visiting scholar at the National Defense University (NDU). Sam Wells has my gratitude for his hospitality at the Wilson Center. At NDU Dr. Stuart Johnson made possible my stay, which allowed me to work with Dr. Hans Binnendijk, Ambassador Vernon Penner, Dr. Jeffrey Simon, Dr. Charles Barry, Dr. Patrick Cronin, and many others. I remember with warm feelings conversations with Ben and Ingrid Mast of "O" Street.

At Amherst College my debts are the most ancient. Let me thank presidents Peter Pouncey and Tom Gerety, as well as deans Ronald Rosbottom, Lisa Raskin, and David Ratner for various sorts of help, not only financial. In the Amherst political science department Victoria Farrington and Donna Simpter have been wonderful to work with, as was Sharla Franco, an excellent proofreader.

Susan McEachern, executive editor at Rowman & Littlefield Publishers, has been a wise friend to this book. Her expertise and thoughtfulness have been crucial at every step. Let me once again thank Michael Flamini of Palgrave/St. Martin's Press for his genial help with the hardcover version.

Because I am writing for the general reader, references to, or quotations from, my meetings with François Mitterrand are not footnoted. Readers must take my word, as with any interviewer without tapes, that Mitterrand did say what I attribute to him. Translations are my own, as are any errors or misinterpretations.

PREFACE

THIS PAPERBACK EDITION OF *François Mitterand: The Last French President* (New York: St. Martin's/Palgrave, 2000) has a new subtitle, revises a few judgments, and corrects a few misprints and errors.

One might think that the new subtitle means that I am abandoning the assertion that Mitterrand was "the last French president" in a recognizable and important sense of the phrase. What, in particular, of Jacques Chirac's presidential victory in May 2002 and the conservatives' parliamentary landslide in June? Chirac was certainly not well elected in the first round of presidential voting. His 20-percent score, though the best among a large array of candidates, was the lowest ever for an incumbent Fifth Republic president. And his 82-percent score on the second ballot resulted only from the fact that the extreme rightist, racist, and xenophobe Jean-Marie Le Pen unexpectedly beat out, 18 to 17 percent, the incumbent Socialist prime minister Lionel Jospin in the first round. It was of some significance in the second round that close to one-fifth of the French voters that day still chose Le Pen. Almost 40 percent of registered voters abstained, also a record for presidential second-round voting.

Chirac's unexpected electoral coattails dominated the parliamentary elections that followed. Jospin's lefitst government coalition—which had done a fairly decent job—was ousted and "cohabitation," when the president is of one party and the parliamentary majority and prime minister are his adversaries, was rejected. Three cohabitations—two during Mitterrand's fourteen years in office and another from 1997 to 2002 with Chirac and the Jospin government—had created voter dissatisfaction with cohabitation's governmental contradictions, blockages, and inability to resolve many issues.

The result of the 2002 elections is a conservative majority in the lower House and the Senate, along with a conservative tendency in the Constitutional Council (France's highest constitutional court). President Chirac has, in theory, more of the levers of government in his hands than any previous French president, including Charles de Gaulle and François Mitterrand.

Still, it is doubtful that Jacques Chirac has the ambition or the means to be the kind of *gaullien* president of which François Mitterrand, so I contend, was the last (de Gaulle, Georges Pompidou, and Valery Giscard d'Estaing being the others). These men were the founding presidents of a gaullist republic, focused on an immensely powerful president. Furthermore, during this period French political life was still strongly attached to the great ideological struggles of the twentieth century, increasing emphasis on control of the presidency still more.

The years 1958 through 1995 were, in short, the "heroic" period of the Fifth Republic, when the very nature of French society was continually at stake in each national election. The Fifth Republic was founded in catastrophe by de Gaulle in 1958 as a result of the Fourth Republic's collapse during France's Algerian war. Following the uncharismatic but gaullist Pompidou and the liberal-conservative but non-gaullist Giscard d'Estaing (the first non-gaullist president), the new republic arrived at the first *alternance* or alternation in government, when François Mitterrand and the controversial "union of the Left" Socialist-Communist coalition, whose program was "to change society," were elected in 1981.

The union of the Left tested the heroic republic's capacity for survival and stabilization. It passed the test, despite serious difficulties, due, in part, to Mitterrand's tenaciousness and Machiavellian-republican realism.

In 1986 the first cohabitation government arose, playing out the political-institutional options possible within the Fifth Republic's ambiguous presidential-parliamentary constitution.

Contrary to predictions that constitutional deadlock and crisis would ensue from an election producing cohabition, Mitterrand accepted the conservative parliamentary victory and named the conservative leader (none other than Jacques Chirac) as prime minister, on the principle that legitimacy to govern derives from the most recent national election. Consequently, his presidential powers were sharply reduced.

The 1995 election of Jacques Chirac to succeed Mitterrand thus initiated a revised Fifth Republic, and a less dramatic, more routinized governmental structure and political life. The president's powers have been curbed by a constitutional amendment that cuts the presidential term from seven to five years. Parliamentary elections have been rescheduled to coincide with presidential elections, increasing the chances that coinciding presidential and parliamentary majorities will again become the rule.

Is this a return to the overpowerful gaullist presidency? Probably not. There are few reasons to think that President Chirac could, or would want to, seize the full range of *gaullien* powers of his four presidential predecessors. The heroic-president period of the Fifth Republic is over. The decline of the old ideological struggles has turned political alternatives into a basically center right-center left contest as in other European democracies. The global context for French domestic politics is no longer a dangerous east-west cold war intensified by a large and powerful domestic Communist Party but rather the context is found in the less menacing, nonnuclear challenges posed by European integration and globalization. As for the pharaonic powers of a *gaullien* president to build monuments to himself in Paris, these too will be limited.

The contention that Mitterrand is the "last French president" remains valid, or so I argue, yet I have chosen a less controversial subtitle for this revised paperback edition: "A Very French President." "The Last French President" was misinterpreted or caricatured by some reviewers of the book. It was undoubtedly confusing to some general readers as well. Its genuine meaning was, however, nicely captured by the title of a review of this book in the *Times Literary Supplement* (April 5, 2002): "The Titan's Legacy."

◆   ◆   ◆

The hardcover edition of this book failed to reveal the extent of corruption during the Mitterrand presidency. Many new revelations have come to light since the hardcover manuscript was finished. These include the true extent of the Elf oil company corruption scandal and also the French government's purchase, with skimmed-off "commissions," of a chemical factory in eastern Germany, presumably part of illegal French government financial support for German chancellor Helmut Kohl's election campaigns. The Kohl-Mitterrand partnership was so central to the future of European integration that Mitterrand thought, again presumably, that the end justified the means. François Mitterrand, especially during his second term (1988–1995), tolerated an unacceptably corrupt political atmosphere among high French governmental officials, the details of which are still emerging.

Let me end with the usual author's affirmation that all judgments and reporting of the facts of the Mitterrand story are my own responsibility.

Amherst, Massachusetts
June 2002

PART

WINDING PATH,
CONTESTED ITINERARY

ONE

INTRODUCTION: FRANCE'S MOST CONTROVERSIAL POLITICIAN

He thought the success of his undertakings the more likely in that his actions had for setting a society in which he felt himself—by family origins, early experiences, the diversity of his gifts and culture, his disappointments, his mistakes and about-faces, the variety of his acquired roots [in various parts of the country], and even by the intensity of his successive sincerities—eminently representative. [François Mitterrand] seemed the most French of all the French of his time.

> —Jean Lacouture, *Mitterrand: Une Histoire de Français*

Some people must die in order to be missed and this was the case with François Mitterrand. Doubtlessly because, given how long he lasted, he became identified with France. He liked to say that he had become part of the landscape. He was right. When he died, France mourned for herself; fifty years of French history were sliding away. Alternately or simultaneously a pétainist and a résistant, a socialist and a liberal, a Catholic and a secular, a centralizer and a provincial, authoritarian and tolerant, François Mitterrand was able to embody the complexity of France.

—Franz-Olivier Giesbert, *François Mitterrand: Une Vie*

Fortunately—or unfortunately—I had experienced far more of the world than most . . . This did not mean increased wisdom on my part, but it certainly meant a broad knowledge of the complexities of a life in one's time and of the numerous and often dangerous opportunities, to be taken or avoided.

—Gore Vidal, *Palimpsest: A Memoir*

FRANCE'S REPRESENTATIVE MAN

FRANÇOIS MITTERRAND WAS, TO REINVENT A STEREOTYPE, a "very French" president. Paradoxically, he was also France's most controversial politician. He was, therefore, simultaneously France's most representative, and most controversial political man. The French people understood this intuitively; foreigners found France once again fascinating because of this French president's somewhat inexplicable allure.

Mitterrand was quite unlike Charles de Gaulle. General de Gaulle, despite his own extravagant personality, was an unquestioned national hero, a pure and intransigent embodiment of French courage, determination, and honor. De Gaulle was, in other words, anything but a representative Frenchman. François Mitterrand, on the other hand, was a remarkable president who stayed the course, whose presidency was, history will show, creative and in places illustrious, despite its scandals and Mitterrand's own imperiousness and shortcomings of character.

Thus Mitterrand should be thought of not as a pale imitation of de Gaulle. He commands interest in his own right and, if I am persuasive, will appear as a richer, more complex study of France and the French than de Gaulle. This bold assertion naturally does not mean that Mitterrand's career was a more inspiring story of leadership or morality. It was not. But Mitterrand's vicissitudes and transformations create deeper insights into France and the French—he as he was, the French as they are.

This difference between Mitterrand and de Gaulle as one focus of my book is tied specifically to de Gaulle's idea of himself and of the French. To connect de Gaulle and the French is not to begin with objective realities. It is to start with de Gaulle's "certain idea of France," his "exalted" conception of

France, France as "the Madonna in the frescoes," what the French *should* be, although they almost never are, in order that France might "be herself." De Gaulle, in the memorable drama he created in words and deeds, was the heroic leader whose only goal was service to France, and thus to the French State. To connect François Mitterrand and France is, by contrast, to begin with objective character and social structure, with the man growing up out of the boy, and with French history since the 1930s in all its light and shadows.

De Gaulle's type of pure Frenchness meant that he was in a certain sense not much else. De Gaulle was France was de Gaulle. This made for strength— de Gaulle didn't have a single doubt that he embodied France—but it also cut him off from other experience. He could not afford to be either too interested in the rest of the world or, above all, influenced by it.

On the other hand the equally French François Mitterrand was French in a different way. He was by temperament and by education a cosmopolitan as well as a Frenchman. His character and the results of rubbing up against the world hither and yon, inveterately on the road as opposed to de Gaulle's single-minded francocentric worldview, made him an unusually intriguing foreign leader to Americans and other non-French peoples. Thus, his biography can be richly rewarding because his worldliness facilitates translation of French mentalities and comprehension across cultures. De Gaulle felt *chez lui* only in the presidential Élysée palace in Paris and in his rural residence in the village of Colombey-les-Deux-Églises. Mitterrand was at his ease not only in Paris and various homes in the French provinces, but also in Venice, Jerusalem, Egypt, Prague, and several countries in North and sub-Saharan Africa. De Gaulle's political vocation was all-consuming, with the exception of family. Mitterrand, by contrast, led a versatile life combining politics with a full menu of unconventional, sometimes bohemian interests. He reveled in the diversity of his interests and savoir-faire, indeed in the diversity of life itself. Mitterrand was in many respects a dilettante, a specialist in several things, a great talent in one or perhaps two. De Gaulle, by contrast, had few outside interests; they would have detracted from his ambitions and goals. When de Gaulle died at home in 1970, he slumped over a game of solitaire, his wife in the next room. When Mitterrand died in 1996 in a small government apartment alone with his doctor, his "two wives" and his out-of-wedlock daughter were all, despite the years of "awkwardness," still devoted.

Mitterrand's savoir-faire did not, however, extend very much to the United States, a country that he referred to, formally and semiresentfully, as "les États-Unis d'Amérique," "the United States of America." Like so many Frenchmen (including de Gaulle), François Mitterrand had a love-hate relationship with America. In 1980, in his last book before becoming president, Mitterrand defined his attitude toward the United States and Americans: "I like the Americans, but not their policy. During the Fourth Republic [1946-58] I was exasperated by the climate of submission to their least desires. I didn't admit their right to set themselves up as the policeman of the world. . . . My relations with the American ambassadors in Paris always had a touch of trouble. . . . [Right now] I don't even know the current ambassador, who has been in France for two years."[1]

If he thought of America and its people as interesting, this humanistic feeling didn't hide from himself or others the fact that he knew rather little about the one or the other, as opposed to his genuine knowledge of several other societies. He felt very foreign, very French, in the United States, which surfaced sometimes in conversation. Once with me he tried out a not terribly successful comparison of the Far West in American history with the role of Siberia vis-à-vis Russia. There is a superficial parallel, having been made by many people, but not much more. I think the comparison helped him justify his very French argument that the United States and the Soviet Union were ultimately, in relation to France and to Europe, geopolitically two dominating superpowers. Mitterrand never denied America's democratic political and cultural life and all the differences between it and the Soviet Union. Nevertheless, in private he often referred to the United States, half-joking but half-serious, as "the most powerful empire in the world." This is typical de Gaulle–like thinking that boggles the minds of most Americans, yet is a viewpoint widespread around the world. It would take us astray to argue the issue out here.

No matter how many times Mitterrand visited the United States he remained basically a tourist, which contrasted with his feeling of familiarity—and paternalism and post-colonialism—in many other foreign lands. In the following passage François Mitterrand describes how he was bowled over by New York:

> The first time I saw New York, it was heaven, it was dazzling! We flew [the Atlantic] overnight and [on arrival] the rising sun hadn't yet dissipated the early morning fogs. Manhattan, gray and golden in its geometric relief, had a round sweetness. I thought of Botticelli. . . . Arriving by plane I've always had the same impression of entering into the future through a window. When I'm asked what cities I prefer, I put New York at a level with Venice, Ghent, Florence, Jerusalem. . . .[2]

Despite this bedazzlement, the roots and branches of American society were, and remained, hard to grasp. Europeans of his generation, educated in nineteenth century ideas of class and class conflict, naturally found it hard to understand a society that, whatever its genuine social class divisions, did not derive from feudalism. In Old Deerfield, Massachusetts, a well-preserved colonial New England village where I once took him on a tour, he looked at the large white houses, half-mansions, and observed that these "obviously had belonged to the early American grand bourgeois class." The early American *grande bourgeoisie?* The appropriateness (or not) of this concept sparked discussion of the possible meanings of "bourgeois" society, American, European, and other. Mitterrand said, "Ah yes, I take the point." But he really seemed a semiblind man touching the great American elephant. It was one of the few times in all our various conversations—which after all mainly concerned France and Europe—when I saw puzzlement plain on his face. Whatever else I felt at the moment I was impressed that this man could recognize, without loss of face, what he didn't know.

◆ ◆ ◆

There is of course a fundamental painful point in reckoning with François Mitterrand's record and the winding road of France's most controversial politician. Mitterrand's various incarnations and apparent shifts of character have always been seen as a lack of courage or honor. Some foreigners even think of Mitterrand's career as "very French" in this regard, certainly a wrong way to use the idea of Mitterrand as France's representative man. Even if these problems are intertwined in foreigners' perceptions of France they are different problems. One leader, whether Mitterrand or de Gaulle, does not define a nation. Moreover, where questions of honor or judgment are posed, as they were repeatedly in Mitterrand's career, the answers we can give today, with some hindsight, reveal an unexpected portrait of a French president and, in certain ways, of the French past as well.

"How many are the acts of one man in which we recognize the same character!" Ralph Waldo Emerson's exaltation of individual character gives us a starting point from which to measure Mitterrand.[3] A similar thought is expressed by the Frenchman Henri Michaux, poet, traveler, historian, and résistant: In *Un Barbare en Asie* he writes that "Every individual is born with a given character, a principle which doesn't need to be demonstrated, generally far from being transcendental and around which he assembles his ideas. . . ."[4]

Nevertheless, character is a complex thing all the same. To decipher a life means seeking the essence of character; but also highlighting our most meaningful experiences, those encounters that affect and develop us, "hurled into the world" as each of us begins life.

◆   ◆   ◆

"De Gaulle is not the only one in French history," François Mitterrand once told an interviewer objectively and disarmingly. If François Mitterrand was not a "great" leader (although I think he could have been in those moments of great crisis that elicit a great leader), he was a truly remarkable political talent, a leader of strategic vision who had immense influence in French and European politics. He achieved a great deal: Despite his failures, important as they were, he achieved much more than was conceded by his critics at the time. Therefore, to underline the contrasts between de Gaulle and Mitterrand, as I am doing in this introduction, does not eliminate Mitterrand. In fact the "merely" remarkable Mitterrand becomes all the more interesting because of what he did achieve in less dramatic times, without the crisis circumstances that allowed the larger-than-life Charles de Gaulle to play the role of France's savior and redeemer.

In sum, whatever the man's character flaws and whatever the questions that must be asked about his long march through French history since the 1930s, François Mitterrand was uncontestably the most impressive political man of his generation. And de Gaulle aside, he was unquestionably the leading French politician and statesman of the second half of the twentieth century.

Why there was so much ambivalence about whether Mitterrand was a substantial leader, both in France and abroad, is yet another interesting question we must ponder.

Part of the issue is that François Mitterrand, from his earliest entry into politics, was always a man for controversy. He was always drawn to the great issues of his time, tempted first by the challenges to his ambition, later by the substance of the matter. Polemic was one of Mitterrand's most natural and sharpest weapons. Irony, sometimes witty and sometimes devastating, was his characteristic mode of conversation. Overall his desire to fight the big political battles resembled de Gaulle's invocation of *Hamlet* in the *War Memoirs*: "To be great is to embrace a great quarrel." To engage himself in the "great quarrels" was a kind of courage that played to his strengths and served his own ambition well. But along the way his courage sometimes veered over into recklessness that got him not only into hot debates but also into the personal scandal which almost ended his career. The so-called Observatory affair of 1959, the subject of chapter 2, is a little-known episode even to the French of today. It is crucial because his role in the affair at first seemed to confirm that he was a basically fraudulent, corrupt politician. However, I believe that this extravagant moment in his career should be read with empathy as well as moral rigor. It was almost certainly a matter of illegal behavior on his part, but it was also a test of character. It became a crisis of identity out of which Mitterrand, the sort of game-playing Fourth Republic politician whom de Gaulle disparaged as a "politichien" (a play on words he loved because it combined politician and dog), emerged matured rather than destroyed. The Observatory affair was a crucible that forced Mitterrand's character development. It transformed a brilliant, hugely talented but morally unanchored Fourth Republic wonder boy into de Gaulle's successor as the dominant leader in French public life.

And if the French themselves had difficulty re-evaluating Mitterrand, if they continued to suspect him, this was partly because they were reluctant to re-evaluate themselves objectively in light of the successive revelations of their World War II, colonialist, and cold war past. Mitterrand was, so to speak, them. There was much they preferred to deny about themselves and it was convenient to displace the blame onto someone like him, all the more tempting in that they could then imagine themselves, as has so often been observed, as having been always de Gaulle–like permanent patriots and résistants. In reality, the various stages and stops along François Mitterrand's path had been the low points and high moments in their own political history. No other politician summarized so much of the French experience as it really had been, for better and for worse.

It was clear and thus fairly uncomplicated to assert in France, that de Gaulle was a hero. Not even the French Communists chose to deny it at the time. De Gaulle soared proudly, even arrogantly, above the disgraces of French history. But to ask today's French if François Mitterrand was *un grand président* is like asking them if they are still a great people. It is a vexing question, and not only because of globalization, because France has become only a medium-sized power and economy. Mitterrand's reputation at home was and continues to be a matter of the French coming to terms with their collective self-image. In a sense it is the soul-searing business of settling accounts with their own history as it really was.

How could a man with a Vichy past have possibly become a widely respected contemporary statesman in the world's leading international councils? How could a Fourth Republic politician, an ambitious cabinet minister in eight different governments in eleven years, possibly have metamorphized into an imperious Fifth Republic president who changed the face of contemporary French politics? It is not impossible.

◆   ◆   ◆

François Mitterrand was president of France for two seven-year terms, 1981 to 1988 and 1988 to 1995. His first term was a rocky but overall remarkable example of what I call "Machiavellian republican" politics. These first long years produced major achievements of political clarification and legitimacy, of intellectual disillusion, and political-moral consensus in French political life and political culture. While not historic in the weightiest sense of the term, they were deep alterations in French political life *at the level of* history.

Three changes stand out, watersheds in French thinking about *socialism, legitimacy,* and *Europe.* In Mitterrand's first term the long French intellectual romance with the idea of socialism was finally clarified, because Mitterrand's government finally tried it out in reality. Between 1981 and 1984 three governments, all led by prime minister Pierre Mauroy, carried out the most ambitious socialist program since the Clement Attlee government in Britain after World War II. Out of its failures and half-successes, French Socialist and Communist mentalities were unfrozen; they had to face up to reality. And a point of no return was reached in France even before Mikhail Gorbachev arrived in power in the Soviet Union in 1985. In the process of movement on the French Left, the once fearsome French Communist party was finally shrunk to a junior partner to the Socialists. The latter then were politically free to become a moderate left-wing governing party, as had the German Social Democratic party and British Labour before them. Even if success brought new problems for Mitterrand and the French Socialists, his strategy for modernizing the French Left had worked beautifully, a plan developed in the 1960s and even laid out publicly at a meeting of the Socialist International in 1972. How François Mitterrand's strategy trapped the French Communist party is a textbook lesson in Machiavellian modus operandi, in having good luck at the right moment, and in democratic goals.

In terms of increasing the legitimacy of French institutions, Mitterrand did not keep a promise to rehabilitate the historic French parliamentary regime as opposed to the gaullist presidential republic. To the contrary, on election day he did not hesitate to don the mantle of the over-powerful gaullist presidency. The justification, he once said, was that on coming to office "I was obliged to do everything at once." He needed the gaullist presidency to keep control of a risky situation. Whether or not this claim holds we will want to investigate. In any case, as if in return for the Left's acceptance of the gaullist regime, it, or at least the Socialist party if not the Communists, was accepted by the Right as the

legitimate alternative government. This second historical development provoked by François Mitterrand was surely remarkable for a man who had joined
the Socialist party only at the age of fifty-five!

The third and final change provoked by François Mitterrand was in the
character of France's commitment to European integration. Simply stated, his
presidency committed France beyond a point of no return. Mitterrand made the
French Left into equally experienced managers with French conservatives of
Franco-German partnership, the motor force of European integration. In his
European policy, Mitterrand showed that he could operate internationally at a
gaullien, that is, de Gaulle–like, level of policy and vision. He decisively updated
de Gaulle's own policy of the 1960s for a limited intergovernmental "Europe of
the peoples."

Like de Gaulle, Mitterrand began from France's national interest. But in
the new era of economic globalization, post–cold war politics, and a relatively
ever-smaller France, French national interests could be maximized only by
expanding European integration in a mix of supranationalism and federalism.
Neither an intransigent nationalist nor a dreamer of federalist utopias, Mitterrand's pragmatic "gaullo-mitterrandism" achieved such a wide consensus in
French society that it ended up being criticized domestically as a new form of
orthodoxy, a *pensée unique,* the one and only politically correct policy.

Mitterrand's second term was faced with major international movements:
the collapse of communism, German unification, the Soviet Union's long-
awaited metamorphosis, the Maastricht Treaty for a new stage in European
integration, and the descent into hell in former Yugoslavia. No European (or
American) leader got all these developments right, and Mitterrand's policies
were criticized on more than one front. These are issues that will receive detailed
analysis later on. In addition, during the last three years of his second term
Mitterrand suffered horribly from a devastating prostate cancer. Amazingly, the
cancer had first been diagnosed in fall 1981, when Mitterrand ordered his doctor
and the few others aware of it to keep it confidential. This is another controversial
decision that needs to be discussed as a problem in democratic accountability.
Mitterrand had promised to be honest with public opinion about his health: He
did not keep that promise.

Mitterrand's achievements and failures as president over these fourteen
years can be argued, and they will be. In addition, the fact that no other directly
elected president in a developed democracy can govern for so long means that
the unusual nature of French institutions counts heavily as well. Finally, from
de Gaulle through Mitterrand, the *relationship* between each president and the
French presidency, the interaction of the man and the office, must be measured.

CHARACTER, PRIVATE
BEHAVIOR, AND POLITICAL MAN

Who, then, was Mitterrand? And what?

Let us begin with three premises. First let us agree with Emerson that a single character is visible in the various acts of any individual. Behavior may be homogenous or wildly self-contradictory: It is always in character. Thus, there was only one François Mitterrand—there could only have been one—and biographers searching for multiple personalities are on a wrong track. There may, however, be a decisive moment in someone's life, a point when character is tested and reaffirmed or changed. This is captured in the psychological dictum that "all life tends toward a point." This was the case with Mitterrand in the bizarre 1959 Observatory affair detailed in the next chapter.

The second premise is that some people do, as Gore Vidal says, "experience far more of the world than others." This wider experience "does not necessarily lead to increased wisdom," just as travel does not necessarily broaden the mind. But wide experience does usually educate one to the varieties of existence and the complexities of life, to "the numerous and often dangerous opportunities, to be taken or avoided." In the case of François Mitterrand we have a political leader of extraordinarily large experience, someone not shy, for better or worse, of the numerous and sometimes risky opportunities that present themselves in a worldly life.

The last premise involves the relationship between the private and the public, that there is a need to examine, in Mitterrand's case, the apparent contradiction between the unconventional private man and his belief "in the force of institutions," of regularities and dependabilities, as the bedrock of social and political life. Mitterrand had thought seriously about, and in fact was obsessed with, the nature of human freedom in an existential, personal sense. One result was purposefully never to wear a watch: Let others worry about punctuality, to whose demands Mitterrand was not just indifferent but absolutely antagonistic. He was a contemporary bourgeois Frenchman, a modern man, who had "two families." He was a president who, even in the present age of terrorist attacks, regularly strolled Paris afternoons with friends, an inveterate *flâneur* stopping off at favorite bookstores to buy rare or best-selling volumes, and at preferred bistros, where he consumed dozens of oysters, which he no doubt believed were a source of virility and sexual potency.

But the conduct of his personal life was emphatically not his model for the political system and the structures of society. For citizens in a republic (and this line of thought appears first in Mitterrand's writings as a prisoner of war in Germany in 1940-41, discussed in chapter 10), it is institutions that are fundamental.

Mitterrand was (that is, he came to be) a classic republican democrat, not an idealistic or socialist Rousseauist direct democrat. For the "ardent republican" in French political history that was until recently the minority liberal opinion in French political culture, institutions create the very possibility of political and social freedom. Societies and governments, as opposed to private lives, exist only through institutions, just as justice can only exist through institutions. It is no accident that Mitterrand's main international legacy, European integration 1985-95, was a matter of building institutions. And it is no accident either that French and American democratic political concepts are less far apart today than at any time since the American and French revolutions.

Once he had become a bedrock liberal in the aftermath of World War II, François Mitterrand, despite his socialist rhetoric later in life, had no time for romantic ideas of "the masses" and "spontaneity" (whether left-wing or right-wing). His instinct was always to channel crowds toward institutions, the best case in point being the May 1968 great strike wave. De Gaulle seemed on the verge of being forced from office by the strikes that had paralyzed the country; indeed the Fifth Republic itself almost collapsed. At a high point of the anti-government anti-state activism, Mitterrand addressed a massive rally at the Charlety Sports stadium in south Paris. He did not encourage the crowd's enthusiasm for revolutionary slogans. Instead, he emphasized the strategy, assuming that de Gaulle would resign, of a new presidential election in which he would be the leftwing presidential candidate and Pierre Mendès France would be his choice for prime minister. The mainly student crowd, which had shouted "Power to the Imagination!," was roundly underimpressed with this so-called realism. And in truth Mitterrand the institutionalist *was* against "May 1968." which he thought, to use Raymond Aron's term, was a classic French psychodrama, which had in the past led to tragedies. He knew that this traditional "spontaneity" endangered much more than the youthful strikers could fathom.

A second case of Mitterrand's institutionalism was his response to the massive geopolitical changes wrought by the end of the cold war in Europe, 1989-1991, especially his hesitations and doubts regarding German unification, the collapse of the Soviet Union, and the disaggregation of Yugoslavia. Mitterrand in 1989 wanted to channel and slow down German unification, which was out of control and forced headlong by the East German people voting with their feet. Some accused him of hoping to prop up the East German state. Later, in August 1991, faced with the short-lived coup against Mikhail Gorbachev,

Mitterrand seemed in a press conference to accept its success much too easily. Some accused him of preferring preservation of the Soviet Union to the risks of a genuine political and social revolution. Regarding Yugoslavia, Mitterrand, inside the European Union's Council, argued that Tito's state, artificial as it was, should be kept intact, and that the German plan to give EU diplomatic recognition to the secessionist Croatian and Slovenian republics was too dangerous. The horrendous result here proved that Mitterrand was perhaps not right, but he certainly was not wrong either.

This "institutionalism" seems to have been more deeply woven into Mitterrand's political thinking than other values, and his controversial commitment to socialism doesn't even come close. The other basic values were European integration and his own ambition. I would say that he knew ambition by itself could not last. François Mitterrand's politics were thus a Machiavellian republicanism made up of his own ambition, expressed through policies that cleared away obstacles and built the institutions he believed were necessary and possible. European integration thus trumped socialism; France's national interest trumped any premature European federalist schemes.

The real question is whether institutions for him could have meant anything other than a republican democracy. As a young man in the 1930s, later as a POW, and at Vichy and under German occupation, he seems to have hesitated about democratic values. But as he found his feet, increasingly firmly, he came to know his own mind. His in many ways extravagant personality did not, in the end, have much significance for his political accomplishments. For Americans one only has to cite the case of Thomas Jefferson and Sally Hemmings to make this point.

The Austrian statesman Metternich, said a nineteenth-century contemporary, was "not a genius, but a great talent."[5] The same can be said of François Mitterrand, no mean appreciation.

CHAPTER 2

THE OBSERVATORY AFFAIR (1959): MITTERRAND'S DEFINING CRISIS

My critics seem to think that every time I leave through a door I come back in again through a window.

—François Mitterrand

EVERYTHING IN A LIFE TENDS TO A POINT

IN MANY SUCCESSFUL POLITICAL CAREERS, especially those of substantial leaders who have faced great adversity and stayed the course, there is an overwhelming crisis—a time of testing, a huge defeat or scandal, often totally unexpected. At such moments a politician learns that even the best luck is never permanent, nor is luck alone, or even great skill, sufficient for success. Machiavelli wrote that even if a prince possesses both skill and luck, sometimes adverse circumstances will still bring him to ruin.

How a leader reacts to crisis is a subject in itself, aside from whether the objective result is triumph or failure. The American Ralph Waldo Emerson and the European Friedrich Nietzsche had the same thought: What doesn't kill you makes you stronger.

That is, adversity and testing can be more than simple defeat and recovery. It becomes what psychologist Erik Erikson called an identity crisis. Beyond the normal disappointment of defeat, a leader is faced with an ordeal of character so severe that personal identity is shaken and fundamental self-esteem is put in doubt. In some cases such a personal crisis ends a career or even leads to breakdown, perhaps even to thoughts of suicide. In other instances, this sudden crisis and immense self-doubt is faced and surmounted. Adversity is transformed into a kind of rebirth of character, a crucible in which character is tempered and matures.[1]

Often an identity crisis is part of adolescence. In the case of Martin Luther, Erikson's famous subject, the crisis announced itself in a fit or seizure that occurred in the choir of the monastery at Erfurt, "sometime during his early or middle twenties." An identity crisis can occur even later in life, and, though less often, in middle age. "In some . . . people . . . this crisis will be minimal; in other people," Erikson wrote, " . . . the crisis will be clearly marked off as a critical period, a kind of 'second birth.'"[2] What counts ultimately in such times of testing is less what caused the crisis than the individual's response to it.

MITTERRAND, DE GAULLE, AND IDENTITY CRISIS

Comparisons with de Gaulle never ended for Mitterrand, and a large part of chapter 1 in this book has already added to the injury. In one sense such comparisons were flattering for Mitterrand, but they became intolerable because they were a terrain on which he could not win; in the shadow of de Gaulle, Mitterrand could only hope to be understood on his own terms and for his own achievements. Mitterrand once was quite candid:

> As for the [de Gaulle–Mitterrand] polemic . . . it has become a ritual. If I don't quote de Gaulle, I am accused of waging a battle against a shadow. If I do cite him, I am suspected of trying to steal a part of his heritage. De Gaulle played an immense role in our history. But that doesn't lead me to an attitude of perpetual eulogy. There are already enough people who are professionals at this. But I do have the greatest respect for him.[3]

The identity crisis concept is, without claiming too much for it, useful for understanding both de Gaulle and Mitterrand. It creates new insight and spotlights unfamiliar similarities and differences about moments of truth faced by each man in his own way at his own time. Almost everything was different in the personalities and situations, in the nature of the crisis and testing of identity. Nevertheless, both lives and careers are illuminated by it.

In the case of de Gaulle, the crisis and test of identity was obviously June 1940, the French defeat by Germany, symbolically focused on June 18, the day of his famous BBC speech of official "mutiny" against France's legal government at the time of the Nazi invasion. Rather than accept defeat, de Gaulle called for rejection of the Reynaud government's armistice with Hitler, for active resistance against it. He placed himself, "moi, le général de Gaulle," as leader of this mutiny, this resistance. In fact heard by only a few thousand French people who had no idea who the speaker was, the June 18 speech launched France's return from "the abyss." Four years later, on August 25, 1944, the hero General de Gaulle led a parade of Free France down the Champs Élysées to the Paris City Hall.

De Gaulle had nurtured an idea of himself as "hero" even as a young man. But the dramatic moment came late and the adult man, born in 1890 and already fifty years old, stepped into a new career as a mutineer and outlaw, a military revolutionary whose radical action could be legitimized only by victory in a cause that seemed hopeless. In his *War Memoirs,* written in the 1950s, de Gaulle wrote of what was at stake for France in June 1940:

> For me, what had to be served and saved was the nation and the state. . . . I thought, in fact, that it would be the end of honor, unity, and independence if it were to be admitted that, in this world war, only France had capitulated and that she had let the matter rest there. For in that case, whatever might be the issue of the conflict . . . its self-disgust and the disgust it would inspire in others would poison its soul and its life for many generations.[4]

But success of the June 18 speech and the decision to rebel was not divinely ordained: How would he make this tremendous gambit work in practice? Whatever he really believed at the moment, his *War Memoirs* give this exalted version:

> As for me, with a peak like that to climb, I was starting from scratch. Not the shadow of a force or of an organization at my side. In France, no following and no reputation. Abroad, neither credit nor standing. It was by adopting without compromise the cause of national recovery that I could acquire authority. It was by acting as the inflexible champion of the nation and of the state that it would be possible for me to gather the consent, even the enthusiasm, of the French and to win from foreigners respect and consideration.

De Gaulle justified the need for absolute intransigence, and explained where it had to lead him: "Those who, all through the drama, were offended by this intransigence were unwilling to see that for me, intent as I was on beating back innumerable conflicting pressures, *the slightest wavering would have brought collapse*. In short, limited and alone though I was, and precisely because I was so, *I had to climb to the heights and never then to come down*."[5] In one of his brilliant essays on de Gaulle, Stanley Hoffmann thirty years ago made a point similar to the argument here about the conjunction of national and personal identity crises: "The reason why de Gaulle's effectiveness began only in the midst of crisis [was that] only in the depths of crisis and despair does the fear of losing one's personality stir up millennial hopes of rescue. . . . But when the crisis came, and when the stakes were nothing less than a national community's survival in the world, then de Gaulle's peculiar message—that France must regain her greatness by saving her identity—struck the deepest chord."[6]

François Mitterrand's career and indeed his life likewise came to a defining moment, an identity crisis, a crucible of character. It could not have been more different from de Gaulle's, yet it was likewise a testing and tempering of character: neither virtue nor vice is simple.

Mitterrand's crisis should, at first glance, have been World War II. Life-shaking events fell on the young man: his short battle career, his wounding and capture, his eighteen months in German POW camps during 1940-41, a dangerous escape back to France followed by his controversial Vichy service, and, finally, his involvement in the Resistance followed by an official role in the French Liberation administration. The war years had to have been traumatic for Mitterrand, but from our knowledge of the period there was no great personal crisis connected with the war itself, though there did occur a great disappointment in love.

Mitterrand went off to the front leaving behind a seventeen-year-old fiancée in Paris. The story has the usual classic turn (see the following chapter). In the soldier's absence the sincere, too young, and less committed fiancée switched her affections to another man. Mitterrand's anguish was profound, and in the only deeply researched book on this period of Mitterrand's life, Pierre Péan concludes remarkably that "this failed engagement marked him more than either his war [experience] or his captivity."[7] This conclusion may be thought an exaggeration.[8] But given Péan's large documentation and the clarity of Mitterrand's obsession with this "dream girl," the impression may in fact be justified.

Yet disappointment in love is neither uncommon nor does it constitute an identity crisis, although it does indicate, contrary to Mitterrand's reputation and much behavior later in his life, that he was capable, at least then, of love, and thus dependence and vulnerability. It would be easy and plausible to speculate that Mitterrand thereafter shied away from emotional commitments that could turn out so painfully.

Mitterrand's identity crisis, if my judgment is correct, came in October 1959. It was the so-called "Observatory affair," a piece of very bad business that is either skirted or only half-explained in existing biographies. The Observatory affair shows Mitterrand as a caricature of his opportunist reputation, playing in light and shadows with his professional honor, his conscience, and, ultimately, it appears, with the integrity of his professional and personal identity. For this reason alone it certainly is worth laying out the matter in detail.

THE OBSERVATORY AFFAIR:
IDENTITY CRISIS AND UNEXPECTED LESSON

The gist of the "Observatory affair" of October 1959 was an apparent assassination attempt on François Mitterrand. The real character of the Observatory affair became clear only as investigation and surprise revelations showed that it had been faked and that Mitterrand himself was part of the machination, that he had willingly crossed a line between fearful or panicked behavior and a serious violation of political ethics and the law.

The event was dramatic, apparently straightforward. Even without the fakery, the attempted assassination of a major French political leader, a Senator from the Nièvre and one of the Fourth Republic's most traveled and energetic ministers, would have been a *cause célèbre*.

Driving home after midnight on the evening of October 15-16, 1959, François Mitterrand's car, a dark blue Peugeot 403, was trailed by a suspicious-looking vehicle. Mitterrand said he had recently received threats to himself and his family, apparently from Algérie française extremists. Sensing that he was in danger—a year earlier he had been followed in the same manner—Mitterrand, instead of going directly home to the rue Guynemer at the northeast corner of the Luxembourg Gardens, headed south a few blocks to the south end of the park. The other car followed and its purpose, said Mitterrand, was clear enough. Suddenly pulling his own car to the curb on the rue Auguste-Comte, at a square just near the old Observatory, he leaped out of his vehicle, ran toward the park, jumped a three-foot railing into the Gardens, and hit the dirt flat, hiding behind the cover of the hedge that followed the railing and the grating.

The second car drove by, letting fly a machine-gun burst at Mitterrand's car. It sped away leaving seven bullet holes in the right-hand door and one bullet lodged in the driver's seat. Mitterrand got up, crossed the street and rang at the door of the concierge at 5, avenue de l'Observatoire, to telephone the police. Neighbors, who had heard the gunshots, had already done so. The police arrived, Mitterrand was safe, and an investigation was begun.

So much for what seemed to be the facts in what seemed to be a simple story: François Mitterrand had barely escaped an attempted assassination by the *ultra* extremists fighting a counterterrorist war against decolonization and independence for Algeria.

But why Mitterrand in particular? The reason was not hard to figure. Mitterrand had become one of the Fourth Republic's stellar, emblematic leaders, a member of numerous governments (more than any other politician) during that twelve-year exercise in governmental instability. By the time of the Algerian crisis of May 1958, when de Gaulle was called back to power, François Mitterrand had moved to the ranks of likely premiers. This was dangerous for the *ultra* cause since Mitterrand, once a firm colonialist like most French politicians, had over the years moved toward a liberal position favorable to a new statute for Algeria.

Mitterrand had been a centrist in the Fourth Republic but had been seeking acceptance as a leader on the left. His hopes to become premier had been short-circuited by de Gaulle's return to power and he, along with Pierre Mendès France and some few other centrists (not to mention the Communists) voted against de Gaulle, against the new Fifth Republic, and, by implication, against a rigid policy of keeping Algeria French. To be against de Gaulle and increasingly liberal on colonial questions made of François Mitterrand a potential man of the Left. Mitterrand was, in short, an obvious target, and the assassination attempt seemed in the logic of *ultra* desires to bring France's "dirty war" in Algeria into the metropole, into Paris. It was the classic extremist strategy of intimidation and provocation: the use of terrorist violence to awaken public support for the French military (and its reluctant use of counterterrorist terrorism, including torture) and for the Algérie française policy.[9]

In responding to police questioning and to reporters, François Mitterrand said he had "seen little," and his account of what he thought had happened was minimal. He had seen a small, dark-colored car carrying two or three men; after leaping to his hiding-place he heard the shots but saw nothing else. He did imply, weakly, that he had indeed been set up by an Algérie française hit team: "I am, like my political friends, a patriot. . . . It is sad that campaigns should be whipped up to this extent, setting French people against French people. . . ."[10] What a weak denunciation of putative assassins—unless something else was being hidden!

Immediately there arose the predictable left-wing outpouring of support in his favor, a contradictory congeries of anti-colonialists, anti-fascists, and anti-gaullists and which saw in addition, a remarkable occurrence for France in 1959, the Socialists and Communists in step with each other. Such a collection of groups could only appear "Against" and "In defense of. . . . " There was too much disagreement and political hatred among them for it to be otherwise.

It seemed to be a straightforward affair and, out of the threat to Mitterrand, *a belle operation politique* for himself and the left. Suspicions ran toward vaguely defined counterterrorist squads, perhaps located in the French state's para-police forces, perhaps *ultra* gangs outside government and gaullist control. The latter hypothesis explained an otherwise puzzling statement by a leading gaullist politician, Lucien Neuwirth, made hours before the episode at the Observatory, warning that "Commando assassin groups have already crossed the Spanish frontier and a list of well-known people to be killed has been drawn up." This declaration by someone who was no friend seemed to support Mitterrand's version of events, or else it was a coincidence or even served as an unexpected trigger for the attack.

On the Left, the Socialist and Communist party leaderships, both normally disdainful of Mitterrand, announced the outrage of the "official" Left, and, somewhat more awkwardly, solidarity with François Mitterrand. The Communist daily newspaper *L'Humanité* for October 27, 1959 headlined "Unity Against the Fascist Plots." *France-Observateur* (predecessor of *Le Nouvel Observateur*) editorialized on October 29 that "We thought the operation against François Mitterrand directly threatened his life. We know now that above all else it was meant to attack his honor."

Mitterrand suddenly was a lionized leftist, with the massive memberships of leftwing groups about to go into the street in his support. At a press conference, Mitterrand hinted darkly that his assailants might actually be closer to the government in Paris than to the *ultras* in Algiers, lifting himself into a featured role as an opponent of de Gaulle's new regime and also indirectly implicating President de Gaulle himself. This was a big political movement for Mitterrand—from the center toward the left, from one of the Fourth Republic leaders to a rival of de Gaulle himself. But it was also dangerous; how dangerous was about to be revealed.

◆ ◆ ◆

The political bombshell in the Observatory affair arrived in the person of Robert Pesquet, a former gaullist, former Poujadist, right-wing populist deputy who had once held the official position of administrative secretary of the gaullist RPF in the National Assembly. With a great crash of drums and cymbals Pesquet announced to the French press that the entire assassination attempt had been faked, staged by Mitterrand with Pesquet's aid. As reported in the *Times*'s (London) less than elegant translation, Mitterrand's intention, according to Pesquet's press statement, was to "allow the Government to dispose of sufficient means to carry out searches of those Frenchmen who were the national defenders of *Algérie française* and to allow it to proceed to various political operations directed against the Parliamentary defenders of *Algérie française.*" Pesquet's invention was hardly convincing: Why should Mitterrand, in the opposition, have thought he could manipulate the Debré government? In any case, from Pesquet's unlikely story it was easy to extrapolate to the idea that Mitterrand hoped to look good to the anti-colonialist left, to gain notoriety in public opinion, and thus advance his standing as a leader on the French Left. Because of his opposition to de Gaulle, whose support was solid in the right and center, Mitterrand's ambitions for high office had to run on the left.

In further elaborations of his story, Robert Pesquet told the extreme right wing newspaper *Rivarol* that "M. Mitterrand chose a right wing accomplice rather than one of his leftwing friends, in case the accomplice was caught," then alleged, at a press conference held in the presence of his lawyer, that it was he who fired a submachine gun at Mitterrand's car, that he had in his possession matching cartridges to those picked up by the police in the Avenue de l'Observatoire. Pesquet then gave a *rocombolesque* account of the actual event:

> M. Pesquet said that when M. Mitterrand left the restaurant where he had dined he followed him in a car as had been arranged. He had a friend with him sitting in the back armed with a sub-machinegun. . . . When they arrived at the Observatory gardens M. Mitterrand jumped from his car as had been arranged. However, there was a courting couple sitting on a bench and M. Pesquet said he did not dare to fire for fear of hitting them. He drove round the gardens waiting for the couple to go. Then a taxi appeared. "Mitterrand had by then been lying on the grass for seven or eight minutes," M. Pesquet said. "I heard him say to me, 'O.K., go on, fire. ...' And I fired." [11]

Two further items in the *Times*'s report indicated the thick tension in the Paris situation. The well-known left-center and leftwing opposition weeklies *l'Express* and *France-Observateur,* both favorable to Mitterrand, had been seized early that day by the government because they contained accusations that certain military officers, cited by name, were part of subversive political operations. In addition the interior ministry announced that "leaders of the

Algerian nationalist 'justice committee' for the Paris region had been arrested in a 'vast operation' against the National Liberation Front (FLN) during the past 48 hours." The *London Guardian* commented it "seems almost incredible that a man of M. Mitterrand's position and political experience should lend himself to a fake attempt on his own life, taking an ex-Poujadist as an accomplice," adding that "unhappily it is not hard to understand the reasons that might cause a leftwing French politician not to tell the police that his life had been threatened."[12] Pesquet had to be lying, the newspaper's correspondent said, because the suggested *coup*—including no fewer than three alleged Pesquet-Mitterrand meetings—was simply too crude for the clever Mitterrand, and ultra-rightists had sufficient motivations to target him for real. François Mitterrand, at a press conference, made the point himself:

> Can anyone really believe that, for my personal publicity, I needed, one night in Paris, to fake an assassination attempt? I was a member of governments for seven years, nearly fourteen years a parliamentarian. . . . I have a comfortable professional [income] on the basis of my own work; I can write where I choose to, books or articles, I can go where I want, see whom I want. That is, I have a range of choices totally without any link to any ambition at this moment. . . . We are dealing with a masterpiece of provocation. It should serve as a warning, or at least an experience, for each of us. . . .[13]

But Pesquet held an astonishing trump card. A few hours before the "attack"— post office cancellations proved the timing—Pesquet had mailed two letters to himself, the first to his home, the second *poste restante* to the Lisieux post office in the Calvados. These letters, opened formally in the presence of a court official, described the faked assassination in detail and, obviously, in advance. Pesquet added that on Monday, October 22, François Mitterrand had even come to thank him at the "Cristal," a café-bar in the sixteenth arrondissement.

Mitterrand was caught out in a tremendous lie and a fraud. He now admitted that he had met Robert Pesquet before the assassination attempt— "fifteen minutes on October 7, another fifteen minutes on October 14, and forty-five minutes on October 15, at the Senate." Pesquet's initial story, he said, talked in general terms about Algérie française dangers to anti-colonialist politicians and Mitterrand said he was not very impressed. But Pesquet persisted and escalated the danger of which he was supposedly warning Mitterrand: "I have something grave to tell you . . . I'm an *ultra* but not an assassin. I've just come from Algiers, and I can tell you. There will be a wave of attacks. You are directly threatened. You are at the top of the list."[14] Mitterrand said Pesquet had told him, "I've become more and more involved in this business. The Algiers people have me trapped, and they also want to kill Mendès, Mollet, and Pflimlin. I don't want to be their accomplice. I'm risking my life to warn you. Don't denounce me, don't hand me over to the police."[15]

Mitterrand's story now was that, given Pesquet's warning, which he had come to believe, he agreed to be part of a faked assassination attempt in which he and Pesquet would escape danger. And this rather than alert the police, whom Mitterrand indicated he couldn't trust. Having conceded, he met Pesquet for forty-five minutes on the fifteenth, Mitterrand now said, "Thus the scenario took place within the pace of a few hours. I am convinced that people more alert than myself would have avoided the consequences of these hasty actions. But many others, not more alert than I, would have let themselves get ensnared."[16]

Mitterrand's new version of what happened was plausible, barely, and in any case very thin. Even his friends doubted that such an experienced politician would be so trusting of someone so obviously suspicious, a known scoundrel. In particular, Mitterrand had said nothing of Pesquet's warnings about this precise threat against him, not even to his closest associates, not even to Georges Dayan, a comrade from POW days who was Mitterrand's closest personal friend and political associate.

Mitterrand's story held precariously until his own need to keep amending it began to tilt the balance. In a long interview with *France-Observateur* magazine, Mitterrand was doubted as to how someone of his sophistication and experience could have been taken in by what he had called Pesquet's "mise en condition," by the warnings and pleas designed to soften him up. And why, during the "attack" itself, did he react exactly as the Pesquet letters indicated he would do. Why, for example, when he was followed by the second car, did Mitterrand drive to the Observatory, exactly as the Pesquet letter said had been previously agreed. Mitterrand explained weakly:

> That spot had not exactly been "indicated" to me. Pesquet had talked in detail about the route I normally take to go home. He suggested that I avoid my street, the rue Guynemer. "You'll get yourself caught in front of your door," he said, because there is no room to get away between the buildings on one side and the Luxembourg garden fence on the other. He added that the only spot where I would have the possibility to escape was the Petit Luxembourg gardens, with their stone walls and trees. In short, he "advised" me to go there. He in no way gave me a rendez-vous. Later . . . when I saw I was being followed, I naturally thought of the warnings I had been given that afternoon. I said to myself, so [the attack] is for tonight, and I immediately thought of the advice that I had been given by the one who warned me, that is Pesquet.

Mitterrand's account is hardly convincing, except if one imagines a distraught man, and this was not the claim he was making. And what about the Pesquet letters posted *before* the fact, telling what would happen? Didn't that prove complicity? Mitterrand's answer:

> This letter proves nothing. Pesquet gave me the point of departure that evening— the Brasserie Lipp restaurant, where I was to meet him toward midnight—and the point of arrival—the Petit Luxembourg gardens, the only possible refuge in case of attack. The route to get from the first point to the second was as if self-evident [*tracé d'avance*]. The letter would have been interesting [i.e., relevant or incriminating] if it had given the details of the attack itself. But on that it is completely silent.[17]

A VOCATION IN POLITICS CALLED INTO QUESTION

Being blindsided by the Pesquet letters and exposed publicly as a gross liar was what turned a personal crisis into a genuine identity crisis. We have to imagine the electric shock to Mitterrand of being caught out, the sudden realization of immense, unavoidable humiliation, and the personal affliction and dishonor as the scandal spreads across public opinion. To the extent that life tends toward a moment, this was Mitterrand's, the crucible of a career. In anguish he implored friends, "Twenty years of work, of efforts, are all down the drain!" Would pride and combativeness prevail over grief and threatened loss of career? Or would Mitterrand, shown up as a lightweight opportunist and a crass manipulator after all, be forced out of politics?

Isolated politically and cornered by evidence, Mitterrand defended himself as he could in the media and politically. On October 30, 1959 he published a desperate semiconfession, now no longer denying the previous meetings with Pesquet and "admitting" that he had been led into an Algérie française extremist trap sprung by him:

> Yes, I have been taken in by [the Algérie française extremists]. The have been stalking me for five years. For five years [since taking a liberal turn on colonial questions] I have been moving among traps and pitfalls. And on Thursday night, October 15, I fell into their ambush. . . . Because a man [Robert Pesquet] came to me, confided his hesitation about shooting, asked me to help him save himself, five years of prudence, analysis, and patience suddenly collapsed. . . .[18]

Mitterrand publicly accused several right-wing politicians by name besides Pesquet, among them the veteran extreme-rightist Jean-Louis Tixier-

Vignancour and his then-young disciple, a certain Jean-Marie Le Pen. In a press conference he accused the right-wing deputy Pascal Arrighi and others of doing the "work of assassins." Arrighi replied by exhuming an old accusation that in the 1930s as a teenager Mitterrand had been a *cagoulard,* a member of the extreme-rightist, violent pro-fascist organization known as La Cagoule, "the Cowl." (See the following chapter.)

Jean-Jacques Servan-Schreiber defended Mitterrand in *l'Express.* But it was François Mauriac, illustrious man of letters and long-time friend of the Mitterrand family from the Charente, who had the most effect, with an artfully contrived Christian plea for understanding. In his October 24, 1959, *Bloc-Notes* (Diary) column he wrote, "In this unworthy battle, to kill is not the point, to dirty [a man's honor] is the goal. . . . Even if François Mitterrand, against whom nothing is yet proven, were able to show that this is a complete machination, the smart crowd would only smile with a knowing tilt of the head." On October 30 Mauriac's column engaged the writer even further for Mitterrand:

> Mitterrand has paid dearly for being less strong than his enemies themselves believed him to be. And I am grateful for his weakness. It shows that he belongs to a different species than those who have tripped him up and who, no doubt, guessed his secret weak spot. Mitterrand was capable of trusting a corrupt man who pretended to be unburdening his heart to him. [Mitterrand] had been a christian youth, like the rest of us, in the provinces. He had dreamed and longed like us, gazing up at the hills and forests of the Guyenne and the Saintonge which stood there before him and which were traversed by the road to Paris. He had been that Barrésian child [Barrés was a writer] "who clenched his fists out of pain at his desire to dominate life." [Mitterrand] chose to sacrifice everything to this desire to dominate. He could have, like me, become a writer, to tell stories instead of living stories. He chose to live them. But this choice meant a hardening of his nature. He became hardened, I think, as much as would have been required in an earlier epoch. But today is the time of assassins.

Against appearances François Mitterrand could well have believed Robert Pesquet, Mauriac concluded; this apparently implausible act on the part of an experienced politician could be explained "by the christian wound which never heals completely in a heart apparently hardened."[19] It is hard not to be touched by Mauriac's christian sentiment; but it is harder still to believe François Mitterrand was acting only, or basically, to help Robert Pesquet. Mitterrand surely believed Pesquet but then tried to turn a good deed into a political coup. Mitterrand's fatal error was to overlook the possibility that Pesquet's hand-wringing was really a ploy to hide an intent to betray, trap, and discredit Mitterrand.

The French Left's man of integrity, Pierre Mendès France, also weighed in, telling his own experience of having been approached by an assassin who likewise warned him of the plot under a vow of secrecy:

> Perhaps [Mitterrand's accusers] would be less sure of themselves if, like him, like me, they had received over the years horrible letters of threat and blackmail; if their wives and children had also been harassed . . . if they had felt the fury and hatred of men hiding in the shadows, who day after day promised them the fate of a Jaurès or a Jean Zay [left-wing leaders who had been assassinated] . . . .

François Mitterrand's family, like those of Mendès France and other left-wing leaders, had indeed been threatened repeatedly in addition to the threats he had received. There could be no doubt that the danger his profession and political positions created for his wife and two sons was very real, perhaps felt even more because the Mitterrands had lost their first child, a son, Pascal, to illness at the age of two months in 1945.

In the first legal action regarding the faked assassination attempt, Michel Debré, de Gaulle's prime minister at the time, pushed for Robert Pesquet's indictment on charges of obstruction of justice and possession of illegal weapons. And Mitterrand himself brought a defamation of character lawsuit against Pesquet. But then the crushing blow against Mitterrand came, as the preliminary investigating magistrate in the case also formally requested that the Senate lift Mitterrand's parliamentary immunity on charges of giving false information in his original account of the assassination attempt, an offense of *outrage à magistrat,* or contempt of court, for having "concealed valuable evidence that was in his possession"; that is, Mitterrand had not spoken of his knowledge of the scheme, whatever his own part would prove to be.[20]

But Prime Minister Debré was himself no newcomer to the vicious politico-terrorism and counterterrorism of the Algerian war period. Just a few years earlier, in January 1957, two political-gangster types had accused him of complicity in the Bazooka affair, a bazooka assassination attempt against General Raoul Salan, commander in chief of the French paramilitary police force in Algeria. None other than François Mitterrand was justice minister in the Guy Mollet government at that time, the year before de Gaulle's return to power. After listening to Debré, Mitterrand decided against moving to lift his parliamentary immunity.

If Mitterrand then asked Debré for understanding or protection in October 1959, he in any case failed to get it. It was of course possible that the facts justified both decisions. In Mitterrand's case they seemed clearer or were less in dispute than in Debré's alleged direct involvement in planning the Bazooka affair.[21]

Deputies are given parliamentary immunity as a guarantee of independence and a form of protection against potential executive and judicial misuse of power against the legislative branch. It is rarely proposed and even more rarely voted. The lifting of Mitterrand's parliamentary immunity was thus a solemn act, a sign of dishonor that also makes a parlementarian susceptible to legal indictment. Mitterrand made an impassioned speech in parliament, emphasizing the threats to a considerable number of politicians who wanted a liberal evolution in France's colonial policy: Former prime minister Maurice Bourgès-Maunoury had been threatened a month before in exactly the same way as himself, and by the same man, Robert Pesquet. Pierre Mendès France had also been harassed and threatened with assassination. This was true, but even if this constituted mitigating circumstances, Bourgès and Mendès France had not behaved as he had, and their support could not gainsay the specific judicial infractions of which he stood accused. The accusation stuck that he had committed fraud and then lied about evidence to legal officials in an attempt to make himself a leftwing hero against Algérie française counterterrorists. The Senate result came down against him. The official report by Senator Delalande concluded that, whatever the mitigating circumstances,

> [The legal infraction] consists essentially in the false statement give by M. Mitterrand according to which he knew nothing about his attackers and had no suspicions about who organized the attack. The propositions which Pesquet may have made earlier to other politicians shed light on those made to M. Mitterrand, but, whatever the role of Pesquet and the nature of the attack, M. Mitterrand remained obligated to inform the police and the court of necessary facts which he knew, and which would assist the police in investigating and identifying his attackers.[22]

There was some question as to whether in the French law of that time "omission" of evidence, failing to tell authorities what he knew, was equivalent to "commission," lying about evidence. But it was quickly agreed that Mitterrand's concealment of his contacts with Robert Pesquet went beyond any such distinction, and that he had had a legal "obligation to inform the police and the court." On November 25, 1959, the Senate voted by a large majority, a crushing majority in both a legal and a moral sense—175 to 27, with 77 abstentions—to lift his parliamentary immunity with the purpose of enabling the serious accusations against him to be tried in a court of law. On

December 8 Mitterrand was officially indicted in what seemed the beginning of the end of a successful career.

But the matter never went further in legal process, and the Observatory affair took on another dimension from Mitterrand's ethical and legal violations. The key witness against Mitterrand, the former deputy and scoundrel Robert Pesquet, fled the country and went into hiding in Italy. Without Pesquet as chief witness, a trial of François Mitterrand was very unpromising and the court let the indictment lay unused. Michel Debré's government must have seen risks for itself if it brought Mitterrand to trial with the remaining evidence, and Debré himself must have been concerned about Mitterrand's knowledge of fact and rumor concerning his role in the Bazooka affair. The gaullist movement's fringes in 1959 were honeycombed with colonialist-gangster, counterterrorist *ultra* plotting of the Pesquet type and much worse. Neither the government nor President de Gaulle himself had influence or control of all the fringe groups who thought of themselves as colonialists-thus-gaullists, or gaullists-thus-colonialists. A trial of Mitterrand—in which the former justice and interior minister could start a chain reaction—could damage the Debré government's authority and the new regime's legitimacy. Pulling strings in a knot dislodges other strings.

Perhaps the explanation of government inaction against Mitterrand after a certain point lay in his earlier indulgence of Debré. Perhaps Robert Pesquet's flight from justice was a convenient pretext for Debré to look the other way after all. The indictment against Mitterrand then languished in a pre-trial investigatory phase, a reprieve but also a sword of Damocles that threatened for seven additional years, because Pesquet remained at large and/or because the gaullists were holding the indictment in reserve.

That the Observatory affair and its possible use against Mitterrand remained current knowledge in top gaullist ranks was recently confirmed in print by de Gaulle's then-spokesman Alain Peyrefitte in the second volume of his de Gaulle conversations, *C'était de Gaulle*. Peyrefitte records a conversation with de Gaulle of September 22, 1965, in which de Gaulle compares Mitterrand unfavorably to the mayor of Marseilles and alternative left-wing presidential candidate, Gaston Defferre, arguing that having Mitterrand as his adversary was preferable to Defferre:

> PEYREFITTE: So, you think that [Mitterrand's candidacy is] better for us than if [the left's candidate] had been Defferre?
> DE GAULLE: Oh yes! Defferre has a certain sincerity, a certain largeness, a certain esteem which Mitterrand doesn't evoke at all. Mitterrand is not liked. And then he has too much baggage, the faked assassination attempt, all that. . . ."

Then two months later, in a November 24, 1965, campaign discussion, the gaullist minister Roger Frey suggested to de Gaulle that the Observatory affair might be raised as an issue against Mitterrand in the presidential campaign—at forty-nine years of age and with little organized support, the junior man unexpectedly had ended up de Gaulle's run-off adversary. "Why not use the Observatory affair?" Frey suggested:

> It was dishonorable. He faked an attack against himself and tried to fool the justice system, the police and public opinion. It would suffice to resurface the Senate report, which resulted in a massive vote to lift his immunity. Everything is public, but everything is forgotten or hidden. . . . It's really astonishing that entire parts of the life of a public man can be hidden, that [Mitterrand] could have been inflicted with the moral condemnation of lifting his parliamentary immunity—very, very rare in the Senate. In a democracy, electoral campaigns are the time to air dirty laundry. . . .[23]

De Gaulle replied: "No, and don't insist. It would be wrong to demean the office of the presidency, since one day [Mitterrand] may have the job."[24] And de Gaulle's campaign stayed away from the affair.

In 1966 a judicial *non-lieu* or "no bill" was returned by the relevant court, quashing the indictment for lack of evidence and available witnesses. Probably the fact that he had been a presidential candidate in 1965 strengthened the pressure to drop the matter. Mitterrand's friend and lawyer Roland Dumas, later foreign minister and whom the former named president of the constitutional council in 1993, writes in his memoirs that it "took six years of effort . . . to undo the hold on the most visible and most feared opposition leader."[25] It was, he says, one of the last of a garish type of scandal typical of the nineteenth-century and the interwar period. Mitterrand was now legally, if not psychologically or politically, rid of the Observatory affair. He had survived the ordeal, an example of the maxim that what doesn't kill you makes you stronger.

As regards Mitterrand's guilt: It is more or less certain that he did not, despite Pesquet's accusations, originate the plot. (Twenty years later Pesquet alleged, without proof, that Michel Debré had been responsible. The matter cannot be resolved here.)

Nevertheless Pesquet's letters prove conclusively that Mitterrand had not simply been duped as he claimed. Apparently Mitterrand trapped himself because he believed Pesquet—one liar believing another, the severest critics could say. Mitterrand joined the plot presumably because he believed Pesquet's story that the latter was himself trapped and wanted desperately to escape becoming an assassin. For Mitterrand, "turning" Pesquet, using him against the colonialist *ultras* also meant revenge for the 1954 *affaire des fuites* (see chapter 4).

But all this depended on Pesquet's sincerity with Mitterrand. The latter, tempted by ambition and revenge and ignoring his own experience, was taken in by a man he should have realized was a scoundrel. Perhaps above any other motives, Mitterrand was too tempted by the possibility of a political short-cut, a public relations coup to build his prestige in left-wing politics, where, after his rejection of de Gaulle in 1958, he had confined himself but been rejected. Evidence for this is that during the few days when he was greeted as a new anti-colonialist left-wing heroic leader, he accepted the applause and took all the bows while continuing to conceal the truth.

Nevertheless, this book is no court of law and understanding rather than guilt or innocence, is the main issue. The key point here is to analyze the Observatory affair as a problem of character formation, as a time of testing, an identity crisis, a moment of maturation.

The causes of Mitterrand's actions were by and large in the circumstances of French politics in 1959 and in his own radically changed position. The debacle of French decolonization and de Gaulle's return to power in 1958 had altered Mitterrand's career and the focus of his ambition. De Gaulle's occupation of the Right and the center pushed Mitterrand toward the "real" Left made up of Socialists and Communists. Having rejected the gaullist "permanent coup d'état" that ousted the Fourth Republic and brought in the Fifth, Mitterrand, a centrist or center-left politician, now had no other strategy for seeking the highest office, still only forty-six years old, than on the Left. So he had to become a man of the real Left.

Despite the logic of all this, Mitterrand and other liberal and left-wing leaders genuinely feared being killed for their political views on Algeria. Perhaps Mitterrand thought that by dealing with Pesquet he was avoiding a real assassination attempt. But at a minimum, Mitterrand acted unethically in agreeing to his role in the faked assassination, and probably had acted illegally—fraud and obstruction of justice were plausible legal charges. Whether at a trial he would have claimed to have acted out of personal desperation or political misjudgment, Mitterrand never made a convincing case that his unethical/criminal choice occurred because he needed to conspire with Pesquet to save his own life. Other politicians—Mendès France, Bourges-Mounoury—had been threatened and reacted differently. Mitterrand's Resistance exploits had shown that he did not lack physical courage. Why would he now be so easily intimidated? The Pesquet letters showed that Mitterrand was lying, and given Mitterrand's subsequent lies and revised lies in what he told journalists and government officials, it is hard not to conclude that he knowingly committed a serious violation of political ethics and the law.

And the more Mitterrand "explained" the less convincing he became, even to his friends. One of the most damaging accounts of his duplicity was that of Pierre Viansson-Ponté, one of France's most distinguished journalists and editorialists. A Mitterrand friend since the war, he was a senior editorialist (later editor-in-chief) at *Le Monde*. The day after the attack Mitterrand gave his friend Viansson a blatantly false story:

> . . . I asked questions, worried, anxious, with the desire to be convinced. And I was convinced by your answers, your story, your detailed explanations. . . . Sincerity and emotion visibly dominated any attempt at calculation. Still under the shock of that crazy night, you told all, to the comprehending friend even more than to the prudent and tempered journalist. . . . You told me everything, didn't hide anything . . . a sign of esteem and confidence. . . . "There, you know everything," you concluded.
>
> . . . Everything except the most important thing. Because you had not said a word, even by allusion . . . about this sinister Pesquet, about your dealings with this provocateur. . . . And four days later, after I had sworn in writing to *Le Monde*'s readers and in conversation to ten, twenty, fifty people, that you had been the unwitting target, the innocent prey, the victim of another machination and that your life had genuinely been in danger, the bullets too real . . . for it to have been otherwise, I was the most surprised person of all at [Pesquet's] "revelations."

Being taken in was not, Viansson said, a question of "wounded vanity or of humbled pride," because "a journalist with thirty years experience who has been lied to so often has experience and is armored. . . . But simply I felt pain for you, and in spite of all the marks of attention and even esteem you have made towards me since that time, I am still marked by it."[26] From then on, François Mitterrand's reputation, already damaged by scandal and innuendo, was characterized as not merely opportunistic but as fundamentally shady, corrupt, and fraudulent.

In what sense, finally, was the Observatory affair an identity crisis for François Mitterrand, a turning point in character development and in his career?

The Observatory affair involved François Mitterrand's dark side, and it unexpectedly became the kind of personal crisis where identity is redefined or restructured. It was precisely because Mitterrand was caught out that the Observatory affair became a crucible of character, threatening his career and even his life. One insightful biographer makes this summary: "[The Observatory affair] left deep marks on Mitterrand and had a decisive effect on his political development. Those close to him at the time noted two very different attitudes in him. After Pesquet's revelations, he was dejected, distressed, almost prostrate.

Several people saw him in tears. Some, such as his best friend and closest associate Georges Dayan and another close friend, André Rousselet, were frankly worried he might attempt suicide *(même un geste désespéré)*."[27]

The Observatory affair is, in short, a "missing link" in Mitterrand's biography, the connection between the Young Turk and the Old Lion, the moment of transition between the immature, grasping Mitterrand and the mature Mitterrand. This immaturity/maturity dichotomy is the only sense in which there was ever more than one Mitterrand, as opposed to the often-caricatured "man of many faces"; he was in fact a single man of great versatility. The identity crisis concept gives an explanation, in other words, of the central unanswered questioned about his political development, the two careers of Mitterrand: how M. le Ministre of the Fourth Republic, a well-established forty-three-year-old man of great talents and equal flaws but not clearly superior to several others, acquired in full middle age the *gravitas,* depth of character, and breadth of viewpoint to become the man who dominated French politics for a generation. The precocious Mitterrand of the pre-1958 years reacted not by becoming a "new man"—he could not—but by becoming a politically and morally wiser, more mature one. He grew not into a fundamentally different man but into a more self-aware, less reckless, more prudent and cautious, more hardened, and more determined version of himself. Mitterrand in his prime was a man in his fifties and sixties, not his thirties and forties. The youthful high-flyer developed into a tough, intelligent veteran politician whose presidency, when it finally happened twenty-one years after the Observatory crisis, was anything but a fluke. It was the culmination not of tactics but of a transparent, patiently pursued long-term strategy, a victory prepared by sensible, if occasionally daring, risk-taking over time.

Paradoxically, without his self-immolation in the Observatory affair, François Mitterrand never would have "become himself," would never have reached his full potential. He was able to turn adversity into growth, to grow up rather than to give up. He behaved better, with more judiciousness and cunning, while still remaining the same person. He reorganized and rebalanced the Machiavellian and other elements of his character.

Fighting his way out of the Observatory affair, Mitterrand needed someone to blame and somewhere to go. The obvious candidates for blame were the *ultras,* along with the capitalist, colonialist bourgeoisie on whose fringes Algérie française terrorism grew. "The Observatory affair was a social break for him—he isolated himself, then reconstructed a character for himself," said André Rousselet. Georges Beauchamp, another close friend and POW comrade said, "Danielle [his wife] kept telling him: 'You've nothing in common with those people [the bourgeois].'" Danielle Gouze Mitterrand, from a militant

Socialist family, probably played an important role at this time in keeping Mitterrand afloat both emotionally and ideologically. Acknowledging that he had "been part" of them, that he and they "came from the same origins," Mitterrand wrote bitterly that "for ten years, ten years too many, I was part of the Tout-Paris milieu . . . I was seduced, oh yes!, by what now exasperates me, that is the cocktail of little drugs" that allows the bourgeoisie to survive.[28]

For him the diatribe was in any case an explanation of who had placed the trap, justifying more than ever moving leftwards where hatred of the bourgeoisie and of gaullism reigned. Mitterrand had discovered the theme for his political future: "Socialism," he now announced, "is the only political choice against gaullism."[29] He would never be the Left's most genuine Socialist, but he could still be its most genuine anti-gaullist. The Observatory affair, by whatever detours, ended therefore by marking François Mitterrand as a man of the Left.

Mitterrand, the Fourth Republic's man-in-a-hurry, spent no less than twenty-three years in the opposition, 1958-1981. This long march is good evidence that the Mitterrand of the Fifth Republic was no longer the man of the Fourth. Becoming the "recordman" of the opposition, as he once put it, was neither in his nature nor past. But his psychology had been changed in the personal crisis of the Observatory affair. "One must know how to give time to time," became a Mitterrand motto.

A last issue is why the Observatory affair was for so long common knowledge among politicians and the French media, yet remained so little known in the country at large. That such a significant, bizarre event in a French president's past was undiscussed, covered up for so long, is similar to the silence that camouflaged François Mitterrand's Vichy past before it was exhumed by an intrepid journalist in fall 1994. These silences resulted from a whole series of complicit relations between French politicians and the press, and among the politicians themselves, which surfaced again and again.

CRISIS AND THE MAKING OF MITTERRAND

To have focused Mitterrand's identity crisis in the Observatory affair doesn't mean, far from it, that its memory or its lesson determined everything he subsequently did, nor even that it was the main factor in any particular decision or undertaking. It is a background explanation, defining a changed man, a politician who, because of his internal resources, finally was not destroyed but changed and tempered by the Observatory affair. Thereafter for several years cries of "Pesquet! Pesquet!" greeted him when he spoke in the National Assembly. And when he made his first run for the presidency in 1965, there was much irony on the Right that "the man with the

Francisque medal, the man of the Observatory" was going to contest de Gaulle. Commentators such as Raymond Aron, Jean-Jacques Servan-Schreiber, and Pierre Viansson-Ponté predicted disaster for the Left. François's brother Robert, however, emphasized how each insult or dismissal became an incentive to gain political rehabilitation, to climb out from the pit of the Observatory affair. Two commentators, Jacques Derogy and Jean-François Kahn, even drew a parallel with Clémenceau's disaster in the Panama Canal scandal, suggesting that Mitterrand's later audacities were a kind of recurring psychological compensation for his one-time disgrace.[30] This view from three decades ago converges with the analysis made here.

Mitterrand survived the Observatory affair rather than being destroyed by it. Having come through the crucible of where his bad inclinations could lead him, he gradually attained *gravitas,* a maturity of judgment that had been lacking, a serenity about his own nature and his capacity to survive as a combination of player-of-the-game and nonconformist. Mitterrand was now armed for the long term—he had learned what would become a tenet of his philosophy: that in politics nothing is ever permanently won or lost. Whereas Charles de Gaulle, so certain so early and for so long, was knocked off his pins at the age of seventy-eight by the unexpected events of May 1968, François Mitterrand, who matured late, was never again radically destabilized at the personal level, standing up to both political controversies and mortal illness. Instead the primary issue of modern democratic leadership opened out before him: how democratic leaders can balance the conflicting demands of what is necessary and what is good, of Machiavellianism and republicanism, and how, afterwards, they will deal with the problem of their own "dirty hands." In the campaign of 1965 de Gaulle acidly told an aide that Mitterrand had only one thing going for him—ambition. As much as this was true before the Observatory affair, after it François Mitterrand gradually became, not entirely different, but a much larger and substantial leader, a man of personal authority and prestige. If many people continued to perceive him in the old way, this was a necessary if frustrating price to pay for the winding road and shortcuts he had attempted.

If a Machiavellian must learn only how to lie better (to "lie well rather than badly"), then the Observatory affair merely showed Mitterrand that he had to become a more skillful liar. But if as a Machiavellian *republican* Mitterrand had learned the difference between permissible exaggeration and impermissible lies, between acceptable and unethical behavior in a democratic system, then the Observatory affair shows the potential good uses of bad behavior and adversity.

CHAPTER 3

MITTERRAND'S WORLD WAR II: BETWEEN PÉTAIN AND DE GAULLE

When I think of my future, I see only uncertainties. I only know one thing: to live outside the usual and to take to its maximum the intensity of living. Yes, I once saw the Marshal at the theater. I was seated just in front of his loge, and I was able to look at him from close up, at my ease. He has a magnificent allure, his face is that of a marble statue.

> —François Mitterrand,
> letter to a friend, dated March 13, 1942,
> having recently arrived at Vichy

Q. You opposed General de Gaulle from the time of your Algiers meeting in 1943.

A. I refused to become part of his network of power.

> —François Mitterrand, interview

INTRODUCTION: A VERY FRENCH YOUTH

FRANÇOIS MITTERRAND'S YOUTH AND WORLD WAR II were as representative yet unique as the man he would become. Born October 26, 1916, Mitterrand was a combination of quintessential French habits, experiences, and beliefs, yet he was also a special kind of work in progress. The undiscerning eye could view him as a typical young French bourgeois from the provinces; yet, the eye that saw deeper would notice a young man in whom the desire for an outstanding destiny burned fiercely.

Origins, geographical, social, and psychological, remained always at the center of Mitterrand's mentality:

> The place where I come from exists today only in the minds of a few survivors. These last inhabitants, these last witnesses, are disappearing one after the other, according to the law of the species. But the shape of the cities and the layout of landscapes have changed less than the human reality, than the way of life. War, technological revolutions, changes in habits and mores, the demographic explosion, the abandonment of the countryside—modernity has more surely and more definitively decomposed and then buried the world of my childhood and my youth.

In these poignant, anonymous *Memoirs for the History of My Life,* a talented pseudomemoirist imagines Mitterrand looking back on a long life, remembering a world being lost before his eyes. "In the year of my birth, more than three hundred thousand Germans and more than three hundred thousand Frenchmen died at the battle of Verdun. I thus opened my eyes, then grew up in a small provincial town, in the heart of rural, immobilist France, still stunned by the great carnage which had exhausted it, bled it white, left amputees."[1] Always Verdun, for his generation the permanent scar of Verdun.

François Mitterrand's "ascent" from the provinces to Paris followed a classic French trajectory; it had long been the path of ambitious young men. Numerous nineteenth-century French novels have given us protagonists who resembled the talented, ambitious Mitterrand. A not unimportant observer, Charles de Gaulle, disparagingly referred to Mitterrand as *le Rastignac de la Nièvre,* for example, Rastignac being Honoré de Balzac's personification of crude ambition, success, and corruption, while the Nièvre was Mitterrand's adoptive electoral district. "Mitterrand?" said de Gaulle dismissively during the 1965 presidential campaign, "He has absolutely nothing besides ambition."[2] Julian Sorel, the innocent but ambitious hero of Stendhal's *The Red and the Black,* was, in his initial uncertainty and then in his fatal corruption by power, another often-used model for making sense of Mitterrand, as in French biographer Catherine Nay's 1984 account of him, *The Black and the Red.* Going "up" to Paris was, all in all, something like heading for New York or ancient Babylon.

The Mitterrand family inhabited the small but vibrant town of Jarnac, in the Charente region in southwestern France near Bordeaux. Somehow productive of more than a few national talents, Jarnac had already launched, among others, the careers of the writer François Mauriac and General Guillaumat, a World War I military victor. In Mitterrand's generation, the writer and résistant Claude Roy was also from Jarnac. Thus when a French youth of that time went up to Paris, in addition to making what Flaubert called his "sentimental," that is, moral education, he (and sometimes she) remained imbued with the psychological outlook of the village, province, and region: In Paris-centered France, "Provence" designates the much-beloved Mediterranean region, whereas "la province" means all of the country outside Paris, all the provincial areas, including Provence. One of young Mitterrand's heroes was Georges Clemenceau, "the Tiger," a victorious prime minister in World War I and France's demanding negotiator with Woodrow Wilson, Lloyd George, and the Italian Vittorio Orlando in making the ill-fated Versailles peace treaty. Clemenceau's home town was Mouilleron-en-Pared, a *bled,* a tiny village in a far-off corner of the Vendée.[3] By comparison, Jarnac was almost urban.

Jarnac, with a population of about 4,000 then and now, lies dozens of kilometers from the Atlantic coast in the Bordeaux region, far enough away so that it is an inland agricultural town, not much directly influenced by an ocean that was much farther away then than today. Jarnac's defining economic industry was the production of wine vinegar. This made for a rivalry, an inferiority complex and resentment vis-à-vis Jarnac's famous sister town of Cognac, which lies about ten kilometers away. Cognac had long been a center of wealth and social prestige due to its eponymous, coveted brandy, whereas Jarnac's wine vinegar industry made for prosperity but produced nothing like Cognac's social pretensions. The "vinegar families" of Jarnac were middle bourgeois, as compared with Cognac's upper-class agricultural bourgeoisie of "cognac families." The Jarnac-Cognac relationship embodied a kind of class structure which, while it expressed a mere nuance in the Marxist scheme of things, was a large part of social and political culture to the families of these areas. To these people, certainly not Marxists, the phrase "class struggle" did have a recognizable meaning, both between workers and owners and within classes.

The Mitterrand family, according to the French biographies of him, could not help but share in the Jarnac resentment of the monied snobbishness of

Cognac's brandy makers. As Jean Lacouture says, in Charente, "Cognac ruled, along with those who produced and sold it." In addition to this social class resentment, François's mother, Yvonne Lorrain, taught her son the venerable Catholic suspicion of money; or, rather, she gave him the pious Catholic's disdain of the greed for money and of money's social power; the influence of inherited wealth was seen as the worst form of money's capacity to deform lives and corrupt beliefs.

Born at Jarnac, at the family house 22, rue Abel-Guy, François Mitterrand was the second son (of four), and fifth child in a family of eight siblings, not including two first cousins who lived with them. His father, Joseph, rose to the well-paid position of train station master at Angoulême, when, late in life, at the age of fifty-four, his father-in-law, "Papa Jules," gave the family vinegar factory over to him. François's mother was, all accounts agree, a pious and devoted woman whom he venerated. She was a rather open-minded person in a rather closed-minded milieu. Yvonne Lorrain was, beyond her religious influence on François, the one most responsible for the humanistic, tolerant attitudes he acquired in a community otherwise much given to right-wing, *bien pensant,* conformist prejudice.[4] Her unconventional combination of contradictory attitudes seems to prefigure the adult her son would become.

The Charente was a region with no heavy industry to speak of, thus no industrial working class. The largest fortunes were Protestant, and the Protestant ethic, if the general view of it is correct, made them unashamed of success. Mitterrand, a fine connoisseur of France's sociology, observed that "The natural alliances of the (Charente) Protestants were made with the porcelain of Limoges or the châteaux of Bordeaux."[5] The Charente Protestants were also republican; the Catholics often were still monarchist, or in any case anti-republican and opposed to the Third Republic.

Origins, as said, mattered enormously in the France of 1920, long before the arrival of television or "the American challenge," let alone globalization. If the Vendée thought of itself as the bastion of counter-Revolution, and if Provence was "red," the Charente could be described as part of the Aquitaine, of *douce France,* a sweet-earthed, sweet-climated, rural, agricultural bourgeois society, steeped in the habits and the culture of a conformist-conservative right-thinking reverence for "France." Anti-Dreyfus feeling had, not surprisingly, been strong in the Charente of the 1890s and 1900s. Following World War I and the Bolshevik Revolution, extremist right-wing thinking in most of rural France became inflamed. This added new anti-Socialist and anti-Communist thinking to anti-Semitism, anti-secularism, and anti-republicanism.

The Mitterrand family was of its time and place; socially conservative and politically right-wing, but not far-right wing, not monarchist or fascist.

Yvonne Lorrain appears as a cherished saving grace in this milieu, and, while she had support from her own side of the family, she had much to stand against. On one hand her brother, Robert Lorrain, was, with Marc Sangnier, one of the founders of the socially engaged and tolerant "Sillon" ("the furrow" or path) movement that developed into French christian democracy and the MRP party after World War II. Further, it was Yvonne Lorrain's friendship with François Mauriac that led him to be interested in her son in Paris. They saw each other many times during François Mitterrand's student days, beginning the benevolent relationship that again came to the younger man's aid during the Observatory affair. (Yvonne Lorrain died in January 1936.)

On the other hand, several other Mitterrand/Lorrain relations were hard right-wing nationalists, xenophobes, and even fascist-inclined, attitudes more common to that time and place.

François Mitterrand attended local public schools until, at the age of nine, like many boys of his background, he was sent to a Catholic Christian Brothers' boarding school in Angoulême. The College St. Paul was seen by families like his as a safe haven on the road to Paris. Robert, François's older brother, had been enrolled there the previous year. The College St. Paul was not a Jesuit school, but some of its teachers used a Jesuit model while others, according to Mitterrand, "had remained rural priests. It was not a school of doctrine, unlike the Jesuits."[6] It was much frequented by boys of his Catholic yet energetic and not entirely closed-minded milieu because their parents liked its unusual combination of religious authenticity and serious piety, plus a genuine intellectual opening onto the larger secular world. The young Mitterrand was seen as a *bon jeune homme catholique,* and he in turn was marked especially by two St. Paul teachers, the Abbey Jobit, his confessor and professor of philosophy, and his history professor, Monsieur Irigoyen. François Mitterrand later told an interviewer that the Abbey Jobit was much more than a banal religious teacher: "I typed his thesis on Kraus, a German philosopher. I had the feeling of approaching something extraordinary and mysterious." Irigoyen, said Mitterrand, had "a very strong influence on me." After his teaching time at St. Paul, Irigoyen became an archaeologist. Mitterrand maintained a correspondence with him for years, and talked deferentially of his book *La Pierre et la Pensée* (The Stone and the Thought).[7]

François Mitterrand was a fervent, practicing Catholic still at this time. He joined the Jeunesse étudiante chrétienne (JEC, the Catholic Action's youth organization). And his first intellectual distinction, at the age of sixteen, came when he took part in a public speaking contest sponsored by a group, "Religious War Veterans," founded by a Jesuit priest after World War I. Although he didn't win, he represented the College and got to the finals held in Bordeaux.

And if Mitterrand later arrived at agnosticism, he never lost a deep and genuine spiritual element in his character; sometimes, in respect of this, he would call himself "near to being a deist." The upshot was the same.

PARIS 1930S: FIRST POLITICS, FIRST LOVE

Succeeding his Angoulême days, François Mitterrand continued up to Paris, where he began college. Once again he was following beaten tracks with high hopes.

Rumors persisted throughout Mitterrand's career about his right-wing opinions as a young man during his Paris days. He most certainly was, we have seen, of conservative background and temperament, what politically had to be called a rightist. But he was alleged by some critics to have had fascist sympathies, even to have been a monarchist. The most precise of these accusations held that he had joined La Cagoule ("the Cowl"), a violent extreme rightist group of the 1930s. These issues deserve our close attention.

Mitterrand arrived in Paris in October 1934, not quite eighteen years old. Following his brother and many friends and acquaintances, he boarded at a religious *foyer* ("hostel"), the well-known Christian Marist Institut called, then and today, the "Cent-Quatre," because of its address at 104 rue de Vaugirard. He immediately joined the Christian Student Youth organization at the Cent-Quatre, as he had at St. Paul. As for his university studies, he again followed a common practice. The public university was undemanding, basically large lecture courses in which the professors read their preprinted lessons. Because the halls could not accommodate all the students, students could study up these polycopied lectures at the end of the term, getting, if intellectually able, first-rate grades on the exams. So like most students at his main school, the prestigious and private Institute of Political Science ("Sciences po'"), in the rue St. Guillaume on the Left Bank, Mitterrand registered simultaneously at Sciences po' and at the University of Paris undergraduate law faculty. He graduated from both institutions in 1937, proving, with many others, how the French system made life less inconvenient for its elite students.

As for Mitterrand's politics at this young time, he certainly was a conformist right-winger, but, although he expressed favorable opinions of the Action française and of the nationalist writings of Charles Maurras, he was hardly the proto-fascist.[8] For one thing, his temperament, whatever his ideas, was not extremist or violent. He was a dutiful fellow with a bon vivant character. He had a definite literary sensibility as well, and rather than settle on a single flavor was curious about a variety of things. He was not much of a political militant. Indeed, his curiosity led him to meetings in order to hear left-wing leaders such as Léon Blum as well as right-wing leaders such as Colonel de la Rocque.

And then there was his "careerism," an ambitiousness that seemed in no way searching for the exotic; it was rather a desire to excel in the familiar. Mitterrand instinctively wanted respectability and legitimacy, both of which would have been compromised by a leap into right-wing extremism. If he was going to be a political leader, it would not be of a sect.

Two photographs of this period show François Mitterrand in street demonstrations of rightist students. The first is an anonymous crowd photo that—a pure coincidence—made the front page of several newspapers. Mitterrand is shown in the midst of a February 1, 1935 crowd of medical and law students who were demanding official measures "contre l'invasion métèque," that is, against the "invasion" of "mixed-race" (i.e., foreign students, meaning Jews) who were allegedly occupying the rightful places of "true French" students. Then, on March 5, 1936, standing with Bernard Dalle, a friend and brother of one of Mitterrand's closest friends, François Dalle, Mitterrand could again be spotted in a photograph of a demonstration against Professor Gaston Jèze, known as the advisor of the Négus, that is of Emperor Haile Selassie of Ethiopia. Gaston Jèze was, not surprisingly, Jewish, and a law faculty professor whom the students detested for his harshness. He had advised the Emperor in his appeal to the United Nations against the Italian invasion of his country by Mussolini's army. Right-wing students had, to the contrary, applauded Mussolini and the Action française called Professor Jèze an anti-national traitor, an "Anglo-Ethiopian" guilty of prostituting intelligence, a "Negroid Jèze against all patriots." Mitterrand joined at least some of the anti-Jèzist demonstrations that prevented Professor Jèze from teaching his classes.

The first picture, reprinted countless times against Mitterrand, in fact shows a very well-coifed eighteen year old with a writing notebook under his arm, standing among a group of civilians and police. People are standing around, some unmistakably yelling, some unmistakably smiling. Mitterrand himself has a charming or sly smile on his face, seemingly good-natured and quite happy with himself. The second photo shows two well-dressed law student friends. Bernard Dalle told an interviewer in 1994, "Yes, we demonstrated against Jèze, like most of the law students. You have to remember that colonialism was [still] well regarded, and that we didn't see why Mussolini should be prevented from taking Ethiopia." But the journalist Pierre Péan, in his book also excerpts a report for other students by François Mitterrand on a lecture on Ethiopia on March 18, 1936, which includes one personal comment: "It is always useful to know the history of peoples at once so different and so much the same as others; because, at bottom, it is not the color or the form of one's hair which gives value to the soul." While the anti-fascists thought of François Mitterrand as a rightist, he felt himself to be, and wanted to be, anti-racist.[9]

Interviews of his friends and acquaintances of the time indicate that Mitterrand was more a literary type than a political activist. At the same time as the Jèze affair, for example, he was publishing a great deal in student and youth organization newspapers. He wrote a long, eloquent, metaphysical review of François Mauriac's *Les Anges Noirs* (The Dark Angels), in which he dissected *bien pensant,* conformist hostility to the book's depiction of human weaknesses, of the dark folly of a man who dares to commit "an act not in the normal progression of a life." Describing his own outlook on life, the young Mitterrand wrote, "It is difficult to judge the value of an act. A life can take its whole orientation from a single act, or a particular desire. The total and decisive formation of a human character can result from the consent of a single instant. 'Le damné est un saint manqué,' wrote Jouhandeau: Exactly right. They are of the same nature. . . . They haven't tried to bet on both God and Mammon; they wanted no half-portions. But will God forgive those he loves? . . . Mauriac answers, 'so long as a person does not despair. One wants to believe him.'"[10] Was Mitterrand affected by the Jèze affair, by the spectacle of crowds of strident students (including himself) ganging up on a single professor because he was Jewish and dared to defend the unpopular Ethiopian cause against European brutishness? And could anyone have imagined a more prescient intuition of the separate roles of François Mitterrand and François Mauriac in the Observatory affair twenty-three years later? While the Mitterrand of 1959 was anything but Professor Jèze reincarnate, he was still nonetheless the young literary critic who had understood Mauriac's dark hero in *Les Anges Noirs* with uncanny empathy.

Pierre Péan's research also settled the nagging rumor that François Mitterrand had sometime in this period joined the infamous Cagoule and/or the Action française.[11] He did not. But he did join, for a short time—meaning several weeks or a few months—a patriotic/nationalist, rather xenophobic but not fascist group called the "National Volunteers" that was the youth organization of the Croix de feu ("Crosses of Fire"), headed by a charismatic leader, Colonel de la Roque.[12] This soft spot in the young Mitterrand for dramatic leaders was to show up soon again vis-à-vis Marshal Pétain.

Mitterrand's familiarity with the far-right milieu was constant. Through family connections, he knew Commandant Jacques Le Cordbeiller and also Colonel Paul Cahier, a founder of the Cagoule and leader of the extremist Revolutionary Social Movement (MSR). That the Mitterrand family as a whole was connected is shown in the fact that Cahier's daughter Edith, who was a niece of rightist Eugène Deloncle as well, married François Mitterrand's older brother Robert. Mitterrand in short found himself placed next to dangerous fires (as well as the Christian Brothers) throughout his student days, and naturally enough he played with some of them. However, the fires were everywhere: the late 1930s were also the time of the French Communist movement's rise, of the Socialist-Communist Popular Front, and the grand cause, on the Left and the Right, of the Spanish civil war. Would François Mitterrand, like several of his friends, take a wrong turn, become a fascist sympathizer, an anti-Semite, later on a collaborator?

Mitterrand seems to have been quite alive to exciting times. He wrote to a friend, "I like risk, otherwise [I get] bored," adding in a dialectical flourish, "The real risk would be the absence of risk. . . . My great regret is not to be able to get involved in everything. I wish that the destiny of all those I meet were a sort of prey on which I could have the influence I wanted." Pierre Péan, reading this and other personal letters that he was the first to see, observes that a "secret Mitterrand," revealing himself to only a few friends, had begun to demonstrate "that insatiable appetite vis-à-vis the world," the wide-ranging, versatile curiosity that marked him out.[13] At the same time, the wish to determine the "destiny" of others indicates an intense, almost avaricious desire for the leader's role, which is a worrisome kind of motivation.

Young Mitterrand didn't have to choose between the classroom and mass demonstrations. Street politics, fists in the air, barricades, and, occasionally, actual fights with the police, were then (and, until recently), a normal part of Paris student and worker culture, reaching irrepressible intensity in the interwar period that the British historian E. H. Carr memorably called "the twenty years' crisis." No doubt a certain kind of grand fun and great excitement, the 1930s Paris culture of politics in the streets was still a fool's paradise played out while Hitlerite Germany rearmed. The actors of French politics—governments, unions, capitalists, parties, students, workers—took themselves and their causes seriously, and rightly so. But they danced to a tune of willful ignorance or insouciance, whose orchestra was about to switch from French to foreign.

Unfortunately there is little indication that the youthful Mitterrand was particularly perceptive about the cataclysm that would soon befall France. Among those few French who were aware was a certain Colonel Charles de Gaulle, a young professor at the National War College desperately lobbying the Léon Blum government to adopt an aggressive national military policy rather than appeasement. De Gaulle had one meeting, in 1936, with the pacifist-leaning Blum, who claimed to agree with him but said the government was too divided. Another sober observer was Raymond Aron, a Jewish graduate student destined to become France's leading liberal intellectual. Aron had returned to France in 1933 from his doctoral research in Germany, where he had witnessed the beginning of Hitlerite power. In his first published article, in 1936, Aron warned it was a colossal mistake for the French government not to oppose, with force if necessary, the Nazi regime's remilitarization of the Rhineland. Later it was learned that the German military had orders to withdraw if they were resisted. The French government's timidity was fatal.

In spring 1938 François Mitterrand began a doctorate in public law, which he obtained in due course with honors ("mention bien"). He and a partner also won the tennis doubles championship that year at the Cent-Quatre. He was still a practicing Catholic. He went to mass often and made a pilgrimage to Chartes with Father O'Reilly.

In September 1938 Mitterrand began his military service in the "colonial infantry" army corps. One of the truly important events in his service was meeting the closest friend of his life, Georges Dayan, then twenty-two years old, in the barracks. Dayan, with whom Mitterrand had been slightly acquainted at the Law Faculty in Paris, was the first real "man of the Left" Mitterrand had befriended, and Dayan was Jewish besides. The military—as usual, and more than most people realize—was an opening to new social and cultural worlds.

In September 1939 Mitterrand was mobilized and sent near to the Maginot Line. He did his duty, watching and waiting, during the "phony war" of June 1939 to June 1940. Although France and Germany were officially at war, their frontier was quiet. Adolf Hitler's armies were conquering and plundering in Eastern Europe where Joseph Stalin's monumental lack of preparation had produced the scandalous August 1939 Molotov-Ribbentrop Nazi-Soviet Non-Aggression Pact, which led to the Soviet Union splitting up Poland with the Third Reich.

The French government hoped, full of fear, internal divisions, and ignorant of history's lessons, that Hitler's ambitions would be mollified by "Lebensraum" in the east and that France, by complicitness in German expansionism, would be able to avoid war. The Maginot Line fortifications, as de Gaulle and a few others had the courage to say, expressed the lack of French will in the face of German determination to undo the Versailles treaty. It was a purely defensive strategy of appeasement, featuring a spectacle of fortifications built to "show" what human costs a German invasion of France would incur. Bereft of offensive capabilities, the Maginot Line's real aim was not to "provoke" the Third Reich with a show of French "aggressiveness." The French strategy was a combination of classic appeasement and defensive deterrence. On the one hand, they were saying, we won't interfere with your aggression elsewhere if you leave us alone; our declaration of war against you is only the result of an inconvenient formal treaty commitment to Poland. On the other hand, we hope our massive fortifications and artillery will dissuade any thought of invading us; but this big show of stationary force has precious little of the new weaponry that would be crucial if a real invasion were to happen, that is, tank armor and a war concept based on strategic movement, just as de Gaulle had so strongly argued.

This weak French response in the face of national danger was of course abetted by French right-wing sympathies with Nazism and with the Hitlerite idea of the strong leader. The upper-class French preferred Germany, however dangerous it was to France, to their greater fear: Soviet communism and its local French adjunct. This was the choice as they saw it. This was the "spirit of Vichy," similar to their attitude in defeat in the 1870-1871 Franco-Prussian war, when the Paris Commune presented a "Red" threat at home. The French propertied classes were more concerned for their wealth and privilege than for their country, prepared to sacrifice national independence in the vain hope of preserving their privileged places.

At any rate, the wealthy classes had been losing confidence in right-wing and centrist parties and politicians, who had been unable to hold off the arrival of the Left to power. The Popular Front coalition of Socialists, Communists, and Radical-Socialists—led by the Socialist Léon Blum in tense rapport with the Radical Edouard Herriot and the Communist Maurice Thorez—won a parliamentary majority in June 1936. "Better Hitler than Blum" was the stupefying rallying cry of reactionary newspapers, which thought it a scandal that France was "defaced" by having a Socialist Jew as prime minister and Communists in the government.

Indeed, within four years they did get Hitler rather than Blum. Hitler was in Paris by the summer of 1940, the memory of which is preserved in a notorious newsreel film of him parading down the Champs-Élysées. Léon Blum ended up in a German prison, where he wrote his minor classic, *On the Human Scale*. The book was moving, yet exasperating for all it failed to recognize concerning his own and the French Socialists' failures during the 1936 to 1938 period.

As for François Mitterrand's military service, his older brother Robert said that he didn't ask for a deferment, which would have sent him back to the provinces as a reserve training officer. He wanted to stay in the Paris area, the reason being an extraordinary first love. He had met Marie-Louise Terrasse in January 1938 and they became engaged on March 3, 1940. Robert remarked that "François would pay a high price" for refusing deferment, because "there is a great difference between cannon fodder and an officer candidate in training."[14] In September 1939 François was mobilized and sent to the front.

The great sentimental disappointment, the great rejection in love of Mitterrand's life, occurred at this time—the loss of his fiancée to another man while he was at war, a prisoner in Germany. The evident depth of his attachment to Marie-Louise Terrasse appears to contradict his lifelong reputation as a ladies' man. But logically, even emotionally, the one explains the other: François Mitterrand's later refusal or inability to seek the emotional depth of commitment of his first love can plausibly be explained by this initial, crushing disappointment. A deeply scarred man might well avoid, if only unconsciously, the situation that had once proved so damaging.

Marie-Louise Terrasse was a woman who was going places on her own, a quite intelligent, attractive young woman of ambition.[15] Mitterrand once spoke of their first meeting, on January 28, 1938, to a prisoner-of-war comrade. She was fifteen years old, Mitterrand twenty-two, an odd, exciting couple. There was surely an extra fascination because of the age difference combined with Marie-Louise's maturity beyond her years. It was, Mitterrand recalled, "love at first sight . . . I saw a blond who had her back to me. She turned toward me. My shoes were nailed to the floor. . . . Then I invited her to dance. . . . I was crazy for her." Marie-Louise Terrasse, now the television personality Catherine Langeais, told an interviewer in 1994, "You may be surprised, but François was a very good dancer."[16]

Marie-Louise, probably both intimidated and amused by this love-crazed older man, at first ran from the student-soldier Mitterrand. Her mother prohibited her even from talking to, let alone taking up with, him. Not knowing her name at first, Mitterrand, à la Dante, called her "Béatrice," and he became increasingly infatuated. His long-time friend, François Dalle, recalled how François found out the girl's identity and learned her route between the Lycée Fénelon and her family's apartment near the place Denfert-Rochereau, in the thirteenth arrondissement. Mitterrand was a romantic; his enthusiasm had traces of obsession.

In April 1938 Marie-Louise overrode her mother's prohibition and began to date François Mitterrand. Her family was more intellectual and more open-minded than his was; her father and her brother were *normaliens,* alumni of the philosophically oriented École normale supérieur. At the Terrasse family country house François met literary types, such as the well-known Georges Duhamel, and political types—Marie-Louise's father was the personal secretary of leading Third Republic conservative politician Pierre-Etienne Flandin.

François wanted to become engaged to Marie-Louise, who, despite the mutual passion of the affair, resisted. François Dalle said of this situation, "It didn't happen easily. Béatrice resisted a long time before accepting to become engaged to François. He was assassinating her with love letters! His love was really violent. . . . I had the impression that this love would not pan out. He talked to me about it all the time, and if my attention flagged he bawled me out: 'You don't care about my situation!'"[17]

Mitterrand nonetheless maintained the facade of a larger social life. At Easter 1940, he went, with Dalle and friends Pol Pilven, Bernard Duprez, and André

Bettencourt, on a lark that Dalle had been able to arrange through his brother-in-law to visit the Count of Paris, pretender to the French throne, who was living at Anjou Manor in the suburbs of Brussels. "None of us," recalled Dalle, "was royalist, but we were very happy to meet the Count of Paris. . . . He asked about what we read, about our life and our opinions. . . . François talked a great deal, about French and international politics."[18] This incident seems to be the sole source of the silly rumor that François Mitterrand was at one time a monarchist.

On March 3, 1940, during the "phony war" period, Marie-Louise and François were finally engaged. They spent two months in this blissful condition before Mitterrand's subject turned from love to war. Marie-Louise was left in Paris when the phony war ended, and Sergeant Mitterrand was sent to the front, near Verdun. The Wehrmacht's blitzkrieg defeated the French Army in a mere six weeks. It was one of the great military routs of the twentieth century, a disgrace for France.

On May 29, 1940, François Mitterrand wrote to Georges Dayan about the violence of the German attacks, the bloody combat. Many men had been lost from his company and he was astonished he had not been hit himself. He said that he had lost all his letters and photos in the confusion.

Mitterrand was wounded on June 14, 1940, near the village of Stenay, by an exploding shell fragment that lodged in his back. (Earlier he had written to his father, "If I am wounded, inform Marie-Louise.") He was evacuated by French medics in a harrowing stretcher ride interrupted by strafing from a fighter plane, which scattered his bearers into a trench, leaving the incapacitated Mitterrand completely in the open, looking up at the bullets raining down.

> Night and day the Foreign Legion and the colonial infantry (of which I was part) took turns trying to stop the German forces who, having broken through at Sedan, collected themselves in the Lorraine. Having left [the town of] Stenay in the Ardennes, we reached the famous Hill 304, near *Mort-Homme* just before Verdun, on June 3. From the Meuse river heights we saw the German assault units in shorts and lightweight shirts deploying in the great plain which, at the horizon, loomed up to Montfaucon. For our part, we dragged our pack of twenty to 30 kilos, our legs tight in calf stockings.
>
> Night came and it was silent. Edouard Morot-Sir, a philosophy professor in civilian life, who commanded our unit, looked out, standing, over what remained of the parapet of a trench still there from 1917. I was sleeping in a shell hole ten meters behind. Suddenly at five o'clock, machine guns and artillery let us have it, with an impressive combination. I went to Morot-Sir's side. The Germans marched toward us, singing. Hostilities began at ten o'clock. Our command shifted us to Mort-Homme. The weather was admirable . . .

> Morot-Sir and I had only to stretch out our hand to collect the wild strawberries which littered the ground, when a shrapnel shell exploded above us. A metal piece got me on the right side: It's still there, in the shoulder blade.[19]

So he survived. He was captured a few days later by the advancing Germans while being taken to the rear for treatment.[20]

FRANÇOIS MITTERRAND, PRISONER OF WAR

Captured, a prisoner of war, François Mitterrand was sent to nearby transit camps before being shipped in September 1940, crowded with other French prisoners in cattle cars, into Germany. He was later asked in which camps he had been held:

> First in stalag IXA, southwest of Cassel. Then, in October 1940, in stalag IXC, in Thuringia, not far from Rudolstadt. From there I was sent out as part of a [work detail] *kommando,* a small unit of about 250 men. I belonged to kommando 1515, in the village of Schaala. It was a very mixed group. It was made up of what were curiously called "intellectuals," Spanish republican refuges, French army volunteers, Jews, priests, grade-school teachers, etc. I still have an excellent feeling about this Schaala kommando, in which a spirit of fraternity prevailed. Above all in my barracks. Things went really well among us. It was there that I recognized the French vocation for cooking and law. Ah! the time spent cooking potatoes stolen from the fields, which, soaked in shoe grease, browned on the coal heater which gave us warmth.[21]

Making sense of François Mitterrand's later politics and career requires measuring the ways these eighteen months as a prisoner of war counted in the long term. They were crucial in his own evolution, and his enduring friends—Patrice Pelat, Jean Munier, Bernard Finifter—often were comrades from the *stalag.* In Mitterrand's posthumous *Interrupted Memoirs* (1996), one chapter reemphasizes his war experience: ". . . it was in captivity that I began to rethink fundamentally the criteria which had guided my life until that point."[22] Let us simply note this point in passing, to return to it later, especially when we discuss Mitterrand's mature political and moral ideas in the third part of this book.

In his *Memoir in Two Voices,* conversations with Elie Wiesel published in 1995, Mitterrand recalled the intensity of his feeling of isolation when held in a strict security prison after an escape attempt:

> In prison in March 1941 I felt horribly isolated. I said to myself, "We're in 1941, I'm in a cell in a medieval prison in the heart of Germany, under the regime of a man, Hitler, who says—the Russians were not yet in the war—that this Europe will last a thousand years. My family doesn't know my location and the army to which I belonged has no idea where I am, nor my comrades. In the town where I find myself, apart from a jailer and perhaps a policeman, my existence is unknown." I had nothing other than my escaped comrade's bible to read. That was my only social relation. . . . Never would I know another such destitution, such isolation, even more so in that I had no reason to believe this wouldn't last all my life.[23]

But prisoner comrades before this period of high security incarceration remember a vigorous Mitterrand, dealing well with the hard life of even the first months of captivity. He was very active in organizing prison events, an animated conversationalist who gave literary "lectures" in an improvised prison adult education effort. (Several particularly remember his improvised talk on *Lady Chatterly's Lover!*) Mitterrand also wrote copiously in prison camp newspapers and fabricated his first set of false papers while there, a skill he soon used again at Vichy.

Mitterrand was successively assigned to several jobs: first he was employed as a gardener, then as an unloader, a driver, a handyman, and, finally, a carpenter for six months. Of this last task, Mitterrand wrote an article, "The Carpenter of Orlathal," for the Pétainist prison journal *France, Revue de l'État Nouveau*. What French prisoner of war newspaper would not have been Pétainist at that moment? But the *Revue*'s "publisher," it is true, was Mitterrand's friend and former Cagoule member, Gabriel Jeantet, one of his several contacts with extreme rightist groups from before the war. (Chapter 12 discusses in detail the range of issues in Mitterrand's Vichy past.) Mitterrand wrote touchingly of his relation to his German "employer," an old man from the local village.

> We were lined up in the middle of the local square as the people from the village approached to examine us. Then came the choices. Someone said "that one there," and I docilely followed my new master. . . . [Arriving at his house] my boss indicated, without saying a word, the tool shed . . . and put a meter and a saw in my hands. I knew that, now, I was a carpenter. . . . About 3 P.M. a loud *"Komm her"* reminded me of my condition. . . . Then he took a large board and put it up on two saw horses. He took a large red crayon . . . from behind his ear and wrote. First two dates, then two names of cities: 1806-1813, Saafeld-Leipzig, and, next to it in capital letters, NAPOLEON. Then he indicated the horizon with a circular motion and said: *"Über alles,* Napoleon" . . . I have often

thought since of this adventure. For six months I continued to cut rafters, to measure slats and to saw boards. We never talked again of these things.[24]

Mitterrand's comrades in the camp later recalled the common wisdom about him. Not yet known as "the Florentine," he was already nicknamed "Janus," sometimes "the Emperor." He clearly thought of himself as superior to the mass and had already developed his habit, kept even in the camps, of addressing people in the formal form—the "vous" form and using family, rather than first, names—whereas prison normally flattens class distinctions, creating informality among prisoners as a form of solidarity.

Mitterrand's loyalty to friends, his physical and moral courage, and his intelligence were repeatedly emphasized by his comrades. His three escape attempts attest to determination and courage. They were complicated maneuvers, meticulously planned to a point, then subject to improvisation, chance, anxious encounters with some locals, and near-miss captures.

The first two attempts failed, but they were extended and nearly successful. The first, on March 5, 1941, ended 550 kilometers from the camp, only about thirty kilometers from the Swiss border when Mitterrand and his comrade, a certain Pastor Leclerc, exhausted, hungry, and passing themselves off as Italian workers since neither spoke decent German, made the cardinal escapee's mistake of traveling by day. The second attempt, this time with two other prisoners, was launched November 28, 1941. Of the three men, one was caught immediately; the second, Levrard, got safely to Paris. The third, François Mitterrand, made it across the "former" French-German border to Metz, then an occupied German city, only to be denounced to the Gestapo by a hotel manager in a small establishment where he took a room near the train station. Taken to a camp for escaped prisoners at Boulay-en-Moselle, where tough cases were vetted, there was a good chance that this time Mitterrand would be sent far away to a yet tighter-held camp in Poland.

Before this happened, less than two weeks later, on December 10, 1941, Mitterrand's third escape attempt succeeded. He climbed the barbed wire out of the transit camp at Boulay and was briefly hidden in a nearby hospital by nurses who passed him on to Marie Baron, a woman in town who, it was known, had already helped several escapees. She hid and fed Mitterrand, and, knowing she was watched by the Gestapo, sent him on to the Stenger sisters. Mitterrand stayed two days with them before Marie Baron, gathering a group of escaped prisoners, collected him for the trip to Metz by train. Mitterrand and the three others all leaped off about fifteen kilometers before Metz. They crossed the frontier "on foot, at night, in a storm, and they dispersed."[25] Mitterrand went to Nancy, where he sent a postcard to Marie Baron saying, "Package arrived safely." There he met a Christian Brother who gave him a false identity card. On December 16, Mitterrand passed the internal north/south, German occupation/Vichy French demarcation line, near Chamblay.[26]

BACK IN FRANCE

François Mitterrand was thus back in France, having survived eighteen hard, extraordinary months as a prisoner of war in neighboring Germany. In context, at the pace of events, eighteen months was a long time. Everything had changed, and yet much in French political culture was still the same, but for the worse: *Plus ça change, plus c'est pire.*

Mitterrand, understandably exhausted and worn down after his imprisonment, first spent several days, perhaps a week, in the Jura mountains, which, if not a safe haven (they were German-occupied) were at least French territory. Then ensued three or four months in hiding, recuperating from his ordeal and getting back in touch with events. But the idyllic location of his hideout was of some disadvantage. Mitterrand was in the small town of St. Tropez on the Mediterranean, then still a fishing village with a few luxurious residences. Mitterrand's guardian angels in St. Tropez were, ironically, a well-known Jewish family, the Lévy-Despas, family friends from Paris and part owners of the original French Monoprix "five-and-dime" store chain.[27]

Despite his bad health and the danger, Mitterrand soon interrupted his convalescence and went to Paris to see Marie-Louise Terrasse. He was desperately worried about her commitment to him, having heard in prison letters from family and friends that she was wavering. By this time Marie-Louise had already met with some of their common friends to decide how best to break the bad news to François.[28]

Nine days after crossing the German-Vichy frontier, Mitterrand arrived unannounced in Paris on the day before Christmas, 1941. Seeking a safe moment and place to reveal his presence, he followed Marie-Louise around during the day and caught up with her at midnight mass, at the Saint-Dominique church, on Christmas eve. Marie-Louise had to confirm to François the devastating news. While he had been in Germany, in the camps, things had changed. She was already linked with another man.

Later Marie-Louise told a biographer, "I was torn apart. I had a lot of tenderness for François; but the new man in my life was so handsome. . . ." A few months later they had one last encounter—"We both cried"—and she gave him back his engagement ring. François had earlier asked his brother to try with her father, "a very good and just man," to get her to hold off any definitive decision. In a letter to

Robert, François had written, "You believe perhaps that it would be better for me if everything were to end, but I have complete confidence in you." The biographer Franz-Olivier Giesbert observes that François's letter was "pathetic—with love, grief, and indulgence." François had recommended his brother, "If she seems faithless or careless about the pain she is causing me, you should know above all that she is suffering intensely, with a violence at which you can only guess. She deserves much comprehension and friendship."[29]

According to one version of events, François Mitterrand bitterly threw the engagement ring into the Seine. Another story has it that Mitterrand had the ring in his pocket when he arrived as a Resistance leader in Algiers, two years later. What is not in doubt is that François Mitterrand was sentimentally crushed by this rejection in a relationship that had lasted, on his side, nearly four years and to which he had committed himself profoundly. [30]

MITTERRAND AT VICHY

The beginning date of his Vichy time is clear; it is the end that is murky.

Mitterrand signed up at the Pétainist "French State" in April 1942, first as a *contractuel* or contract-hired lower-level post, and soon thereafter he got a regularized, civil servant position. He remained working at, if not always for, Vichy until sometime in the second half of 1943. Like most Vichy employees who later joined the Resistance, François Mitterrand did not leave in an instant but gradually disappeared from view in the oddly transformed spa city, living a double life for several months as he gradually melted into the underground.

The obvious question is, What were his motives in going to work at Vichy? Banal as it sounds, he needed a job. It was wartime. He also wanted a position, even in wartime, that had some kind of a future. There was nothing promising in Jarnac. Occupied Paris was no place for an escaped prisoner. He could not know whether the Vichy regime would last or not, but it was the existing French State on French territory, and Mitterrand as yet had no idea of turning against this government, of joining the Resistance. Thus Mitterrand's decision to head for Vichy was in one way perfectly plausible, despite its apparent culpability in retrospect. (See chapter 11 for more on this matter.)

War, defeat, and occupation had exploded any idea of a traditional, smooth bourgeois career ascension for the French youth of his generation. Who now, even in April 1942, could be sure what would happen, how France would survive and be governed? Except for the French Communists: In June 1941 they became *résistants en bloc,* not out of patriotism but out of orders from Moscow when Hitler treacherously attacked the Soviet Union, violating the Nazi-Soviet

Nonaggression pact. Apart from them, few people in the French population as yet had gauged de Gaulle's importance and the claim of Fighting France to be a legitimate French government in exile.[31]

The Vichy regime had been established by a legal, although desperate and extorted, delegation of powers from the Third Republic parliament. It began when Hitler accepted French government requests for an armistice, that is, a cease fire, which is not the same as a peace treaty. The Germans took the northern three-fifths of French territory as a military occupation space, leaving a somewhat autonomous but not independent "French State" in the southern third of the country. The peace treaty sought by Vichy was withheld by the Nazis, one main reason being to justify holding in Germany the almost 2 million French prisoners of war. What effect would this mass of released French soldiers have if allowed to return to their homeland? Although many French soldiers had become defeatist themselves, accepting the idea of prolonged German hegemony in Europe, many others might again take up the fight against Germany if returned to France. Still, from 1941 to 1943, a significant number of conscripted French workers, in the Service du travail obligatoire (STO), were brought to Germany in exchange for some prisoners of war.[32]

François Mitterrand's first Vichy job, in early 1942, was a temporary clerk's post in the "Legion of Fighters and Volunteers for the [Pétainist] National Revolution." Through connections he got a permanent civil servants job in April with the Commissariat to Aid Returning Prisoners of War, those who escaped and also those released in small groups under the above-mentioned agreements between the Germans and Vichy. The Germans' release of bunches of POWs against newly conscripted French workers was a strategy of tempting Vichy further into collaboration by creating the possibility of achieving ever greater "successes" in getting its soldiers back.

The now twenty-six-year-old Mitterrand was, despite his youth and modest status, connected to Marshal Pétain's personal entourage through always active family relations and friendships. At Vichy he often saw Gabriel Jeantet as well as another old friend and new Vichyite, François Méténier. Jeantet, editor of the POW magazine Mitterrand had written for, had become a key aide to Pétain. He was simultaneously violently anti-German and anti-gaullist, plus a fervent exponent of Pétain's "National Revolution" ideology. Jeantet founded the "Association of France," a propaganda mouthpiece for National Revolution ideas. In June 1942 he refounded the journal, *France: Revue de l'État Nouveau,* whose cover bore the *francisque,* the Frankish battle-ax that was the Pétainist symbol.

In seeming contradiction with these friendships, Mitterrand at the same time became active in clandestine Vichy networks that were in contact with French prisoners still in German camps. Mitterrand's profile—a talented organizer, a POW, a successful escapee—quickly allowed him to stand out in official Vichy prisoner-of-war activities but also in clandestine, semisponsored networks trying to take care of French POWs.

Thus the crucial fact emerges that, for any particular individual, going to work at Vichy, despite the evil it had done and would do, implied no necessary allegiance to collaboration with fascist ideas or Nazi subordination. Looked at only with the faces of Marshal Pétain and Pierre Laval, Vichy's nature seemed clear; but looked at from below or within, Vichy was indeed a *pétaudière,* a cauldron of confusion.

For example, the dilemmas of French POWs were deep and cut several ways. Pierre Péan explains "the significance of the traumatism provoked by the captivity of a large part of the French army":

> Since summer 1940 a substantial part of the nation's active population was to be found behind barbed-wire. At the end of 1941 slightly less than 1,500,000 young men were still interned in *Stalags* or *Oflags.* The problems posed by this captivity were numerous. . . . All of French society was affected by it, to which was added the more or less avowed feeling among those at home that these prisoners had a certain responsibility for the defeat, thus for the country's disastrous situation. The prisoners, for their part, felt forgotten, abandoned. Except, they thought, by *le Maréchal.* They bore a grudge against the political class. Resentment, frustration, shame, guilt, characterized everyone's approach to the principal stigma: the defeat.[33]

The Commissariat to Aid Returning Prisoners of War had originally been created by Vichy in autumn 1941 to deal with the approximately 350,000 soldiers who had been repatriated by agreements with the Germans or had escaped, having generally not yet found jobs or regularized living situations. An eventual Mitterrand sponsor, Maurice Pinot (whose real name was Pinot de Périgord de Villechenon) had been appointed chief commissioner at that moment. His competitor for the job had been a former Third Republic prefect, the later notorious René Bousquet, who lost out despite the support of Pierre Pucheu, Vichy's interior minister.[34]

In this Vichy period, François Mitterrand personally made about fifteen sets of forged papers for himself and for others. A friend, Marcel Marivin, said it was Mitterrand "who taught me to forge an official seal using a half potato. It was a good imitation."[35] But by itself this anti-Nazi activity did not give Mitterrand particular prominence. Such "illegal" work, fighting the war by means other than rifles, was natural to almost any former prisoner, including, and especially, at Vichy. There was anguished solidarity among these men, born of shared suffering and also a shared shame. Mitterrand was devoted to helping his former comrades still languishing in German camps. In any case his sense of responsibility for French POWs, his forgeries, and his escape networking indicate, against the suspicions that he was somehow a collaborator and a fascist, that the Mitterrand working at Vichy was anti-German, anti-Gestapo, and anti-Nazi.

Mitterrand, as was said, quickly became an important figure in the Vichyite world of escaped and returned prisoners, rising in the bureaucracy. Toward the end of May 1942, Jean-Albert Roussel, an official in the returned prisoners administration, offered his friend Mitterrand a choice of two positions. One was in the Commissariat for Jewish Questions, the other was a promotion in the prisoners of war Commissariat. "Mitterrand chose the second without hesitation, although it paid three times less."[36] What significance should be attached to this choice? Was it forbearance, taking a lower-paying job because it was morally preferable? Probably. Did it show that Mitterrand was not anti-Semitic? Almost certainly, and especially for the POW whose best friend was Georges Dayan and who had been hidden by the Lévy-Despas family. Or did it show simple political caution? This is also probably true. But was a devious Mitterrand already calculating how things might look later on? The most cynical explanation has the least plausibility.

With a job and an assured salary, at the beginning of June Mitterrand took a week's vacation at Mantry at the home of friends, really distant cousins, the Sarrazin sisters. Péan, with access to Mitterrand's personal letters of the period, tells us that his disappointment in love was still very much on his mind, but that "the 'Beatrice wound' was beginning to heal." Mitterrand wrote in a letter with seeming existential willpower, "I loved her because I loved her . . . I am not suffering and I can love beyond her. . . . She was one of those allegorical goddesses which are described in Proust."[37] He began to spend time with Marie-Claire Sarrazin, whom he called "Clo." Surrounded by women for that week, Mitterrand's temperament began to reacquire its old moody character. His female hosts nicknamed him "the tyrant."

At Vichy, Laval's fascist views were now trumping the ambiguities and confusion of Pétain's thinking. But enough confusion persisted that French people could still see Pétain as the "shield of France." The "National Revolution" would replace the weak, despised parliamentary republic with a strengthened, "pure French" government. France would become a "national" country, taking an appropriate place in a German-dominated Europe that Vichyites and Pétainists believed was the inevitable future.

François Mitterrand at this time, there is no question, still intensely admired Marshal Pétain. Pétain was the "hero of Verdun," whose significance for that French generation's collective memory could hardly be exaggerated. In addition to his reverence of Pétain, a typical French attitude, young Mitterrand also disdained the Third Republic. The French rout by the disciplined Germans seemed proof that the weak parliamentary republic, the French form of democracy, deserved to be thrown into the dustbin of history.

Of Philippe Pétain, Eric Hobsbawm, the dean of British left-wing historians and himself a Jew, wrote remarkably:

> Marshal Pétain was certainly not a fascist or Nazi sympathizer. One reason why it was so difficult after the war to distinguish between wholehearted French fascists and pro-German collaborators on one hand, and the main body of support for Marshal Pétain's Vichy regime on the other, was that there was in fact no clear line. Those whose fathers had hated Dreyfus, the Jews and the bitch-Republic—some Vichy figures were old enough to have done so themselves—shaded insensibly into the zealots for a Hitlerian Europe.[38]

According to other writers, whether Pétain was himself a fascist is less clear. His crude anti-Semitism showed already during World War I, but anti-Semitism alone doesn't equal fascism. In any case Pierre Laval and so many others were such fascists and Nazi sympathizers that increasingly these aspects of Vichy's nature and policy began to stand out. Nevertheless, for long months people could believe much of what they wanted about the Pétainist "French State." Eugen Weber, a learned and empathetic foreign historian of modern France, makes this judgment:

> Between 1940 and 1944, more than one in four of the 330,000 Jews living on French territory [i.e., both foreign and French Jews] were deported. The majority were identified, arrested and shipped off by French administrators and French policy, without whose zealous cooperation German forces in France would have been unable to carry out the job. In a time of want, fear and national humiliation, few of the French cared about what happened to the Jews. While many individuals helped them (otherwise three in four would not have survived), many also denounced, pursued and robbed them. The drumbeat of official Vichy propaganda presented Jews as noxious parasites, and the church went along, fearing godless Communists more than godless Nazis. Some bishops . . . had other priorities. Objectively, the church, like its Vichy allies, shared in the vicious anti-Semitic policies of those dark years.[39]

Vichy appears, to Weber, more like the Nazi regime itself than as a Pétainist "shield" of the French people against the German occupying forces. And Péan recalls the sad truth that "some of France's most prominent Jews pressured their Government to limit the influx of [foreign Jewish] refugees," trying to prove their French loyalty by sacrificing fellow Jews in danger. Trying to save themselves by emphasizing the distinction between French and foreign Jews was a desperate legalistic claim akin to Vichy's own insistence on its "sovereignty" while it willingly did what the Nazis wanted. But the French citizenship itself of French Jews was precarious: Vichy soon started to "denaturalize" French Jews, taking away their French citizenship. This was homegrown Vichyite anti-Semitism, profiting from defeat to attack a small minority, hopefully to create a new sacrificial lamb. Vichy's guilt had grown as the war both forced and tempted it into increasingly dirty hands.

MITTERRAND BETWEEN PÉTAIN AND DE GAULLE

As for the Resistance, the first fact is that only a few people made a single decision early on to oppose the Nazis and join the Resistance. The usual path to the Resistance was little steps, beginning with small acts and proceeding to full engagement. It was also not unusual for people to come to the Resistance from the Vichy regime, for that is where politically active people and government officials before 1940 often went if they had stayed inside France. Mitterrand biographer Nay is right to say,

> It was by no means odd for Resistance activity to develop within a Vichy organization. Elsewhere, in the army of the armistice, in the youth camps, and so on, others struggled as best they could against the Germans, although they continued to [believe in] the Marshal. The earliest Resistance newspapers often revealed the same duality. But the gap between the Resistance and Vichy [widened] slowly—above all, after the occupation of the southern zone on November 11, 1942. "We were fighting against the Germans, but nobody was overtly against the Vichy regime," says Pierre Coursol, a member of the Commissariat to Aid Prisoners of War.[40]

In his book, *Ma part de verité* (1969), François Mitterrand wrote laconically of his own road after his escape: "Back in France, I became a résistant, without any major dramas."[41] Laconic is quite an inadequate word to describe the total omission of Vichy! Mitterrand the presidential candidate wanted to avoid discussion of the complexities of Vichy and his own past.

At other times Mitterrand said that literally during his first days at Vichy he launched into fabricating false identity papers and counterfeit official cachets, to be sent to prisoners of war through the mail. French prisoners in Germany could receive packages, because the German-French armistice agreements allowed such communication with people at home. Allowing packages was a compromise on both sides. The Germans couldn't take the risk of releasing the prisoners, and by keeping them with mail and other privileges, they could hope that some would accept, either directly or through the filter of French domestic defeatism, the idea that a Nazi-dominated Europe was inevitable.

Indeed, anti-German aid to French prisoners was helpful to Vichy itself because, however much Vichy collaborated with the Germans, the Pétainist government wanted French prisoners back, if only to bolster its legitimacy at home. This was a part of Pétain's image as France's "shield." But this anti-German undercover work gradually led some people toward the Resistance, as it did Mitterrand. Unlike an unemployment office or a university, the Resistance had no official sign-up days or procedures. Of Mitterrand's beginning work a friend commented, "Manufacturing false papers may not have been very heroic, but it showed his state of mind."[42] So Mitterrand's unofficial Vichy work—helping French POWs escape from Germany—was part of Vichy's mixed political culture. Some of the Vichy cadre was pro-Nazi, some was survivalist and collaborationist, and some worked against the Germans. Activity such as Mitterrand's illegal work was intrinsically anti-German and anti-Nazi, a kind of resistance if not part of the still small and localized Resistance movement.

Mitterrand's hesitant first step toward the organized Resistance came in June 1942. This was soon after his arrival four or five months earlier at Vichy, although it was a full year before he defected completely and went underground.

This first step was brought about when Jean-Albert Roussel asked him to attend a clandestine meeting of ex-prisoners, called by a man named Antoine Mauduit, to discuss resistance. Mauduit was a little-known but apparently quite charismatic industrialist scion (though some people thought him slightly mad), from northern France. Before the war he had left his business and signed up in the Foreign Legion "in order to rediscover man." A mystic, whom Mitterrand later called "one of the most remarkable men" he had ever met, Mauduit died later in deportation.[43] The meeting, held on June 11 to 13, 1942, at a fifteenth-century chateau at Montmaur in the Hautes Alpes, was to set up a permanent secret network against the Germans, although not necessarily against Vichy.[44] In any case, Mitterrand, by attending the meeting, took his first step into what was recognizably a Resistance group.

A dangerous, tumultuous year ensued for Mitterrand, from June 1942 to June 1943. He led an increasingly double life, continuing to work at Vichy but increasingly active in Resistance activities. His passage into the Resistance moved in three steps: from his initial work as a counterfeiter of papers and official stamps, to regular contacts with Resistance groups in ad hoc jobs, to quitting Vichy, ending the double life, and joining the Resistance outright.

During this year, the fate of France's prisoners of war became a larger and larger issue. Although repatriation was first of all a humanitarian task, the political implications of so many returning soldiers came increasingly into focus. The French prisoners in Germany were, or could become, a huge political stake. The human mass involved was, to give a comparison, bigger than the largest pre-war labor union, the left-wing General Confederation of Labor (CGT). Many POWs believed they had been betrayed by the military hierarchy on the battlefield. Most of them had hardly had a fair chance to fight, although de Gaulle believed that many of them, especially their battlefield commanders, had hardly fought. Some also felt themselves to be abandoned by their government, first by the Third Republic and then by Pétain as disappointment grew. If a significant number of them went over to the Germans or just gave up on Vichy, it would be another disaster for France.

Like others in the POW commisariat, François Mitterrand, knowledge-able and deeply affected by his own experience, worked against the prisoners' constant temptation to collaborate. More so than in other Vichy administration, the mood in the Commissariat for Prisoners was decidedly anti-German, even if still Pétainist. And it was on a collision course with Pétainist resignation to the idea that France would do best to make its peace with a permanently dominant Germany.

The sudden November 1942 invasion by the Germans of Vichy's "sovereign" third of France did not push François Mitterrand into the Resistance per se. But it did reveal the Potemkin village character of the "French State" and the *fantoche,* puppet character, of an increasingly suspect, disdained Pétain. Mitterrand did not so much plunge into the Resistance as go step by step, the single most important motivation being, Mitterrand always said, a sense of solidarity with his fellow prisoners.

THE PHOTOGRAPH AND THE MEDAL

François Mitterrand's passage at Vichy remains a controversy, despite the history of it discussed above. The causes of controversy are based on symbols rather than deeds. That is, there exist two emblems of apparent confirmation of a "Vichyite" character, seeming evidence that Mitterrand must have had collaborationist and/or fascist leanings.

The first of these two symbols is a photograph of himself, another man, and Marshal Pétain. It shows the young Mitterrand listening in evident rapture to Pétain, a sepia snapshot of a rather dimly lit Vichy salon in 1942. The second emblem is the *francisque* medal, Vichy's highest civilian decoration, which was awarded to François Mitterrand in March or April 1943. It is certain, moreover, that Mitterrand himself had asked two well-connected Vichy sponsors, Simon Arbellot and Gabriel Jeantet, to nominate him, probably early in February. Several witnesses recall him wearing the medal in summer 1943, seemingly to show it off.

What is to be made of these two "proofs" that Mitterrand was "a man of Vichy?"

As for the photo, there can be little doubt that it depicts Mitterrand's admiration for Marshal Pétain. This was indicated in the Mitterrand letter of March 13, 1942, quoted as an epigraph to this chapter. Mitterrand was, no doubt about it, a *maréchaliste,* one who believed in Pétain's special role, perhaps as late as early 1943. Mitterrand's *pétainisme,* his espousal of the National Revolution's ideas, was, however, very thin and episodic. (See chapter 11.)

The *francisque* medal is a different kind of story. It was initiated October 16, 1941. But the evidence is overwhelming that by 1942 it had become, at least for anti-German Vichy cadres heading toward Resistance, an aspect of camouflage in their double game, part of a disguise for anti-German activity. Other later French leaders of consequence were also awarded the *francisque*: Michel Debré on November 13, 1941; Alexandre Parodi on August 19, 1941; de Lattre de Tassigny and Raymond Marcellin; and Antoine Pinay was for a time a member of the Council of twelve officials who voted on nominations.[45] Mitterrand's friends and associates in the Commissariat for POWs, who had originally all been *maréchaliste* like him, had all gotten the medal, and in fact were nominating each other for it, as Péan's research verified. Several witnesses testified that Mitterrand at the time had told them that it would be "useful for us," would "serve as an alibi." He even wore it, according to Pol Pilven, at the Cintra Bar, a Vichy "watering hole for collaborationists and Gestapists," as a kind of dare.[46] The one inaccuracy in Mitterrand's account of the *francisque* was the date that he actually got and wore the medal: summer 1943 according to witnesses, the end of 1943 according to his own account, perhaps a fault of memory, perhaps so that the date of receipt would fit better with what Mitterrand wanted it to show.

Pierre Péan in any case judges that "The award of the medal in no way contradicts his [increasingly Resistance-oriented] action and ideas in the first half of 1943."[47] Though not yet a full-time résistant, Mitterrand was taking steps in that direction and taking distance from the Vichy regime.

In January 1943, Pierre Laval was reappointed by Pétain as premier, and placed his own man, André Masson, at the head of the Commissariat for POWs, pushing out Maurice Pinot, Mitterrand's patron and friend. In response Mitterrand and a group of others, altogether seventeen men including Jean Védrine and Paul Racine, resigned collectively in solidarity, not against Pétain whom they still admired, but against Laval.[48] This was a significant act of independence, moving from total outward conformity at Vichy, as well as a sign of a growing anti-Vichyist sentiment in Mitterrand, who then got a sinecure position as national delegate in the National Student Administration.

On July 10, 1943, Laval and Masson organized a meeting at the Salle Wagram in Paris, near the Étoile. Using a friend's invitation, Mitterrand got into the room to make a gesture of open defiance. Masson's speech, focused on the POWs, nevertheless criticized "the treason of de Gaulle and the felony of Giraud." At that moment François Mitterrand leaped to his feet and shouted, "France is not with you! Whom do you represent? Nobody! You don't have the right to speak in our name!" Doing this was risky for Mitterrand in two ways. Not merely did he draw public attention to himself, but he contested the legitimacy and representativeness of Vichy's POW administration, thus of Vichy itself. This concern with "representation" would turn out, we shall see, to be a recurring Mitterrand theme. From the floor, he added a further denunciation, of Vichy's agreement to send French workers to Germany in exchange for POW returns: "We don't accept the shameful exchange which you call *la relève* [changing of the guard], which uses our comrades still [in Germany] as a means of blackmail to justify the deportation of French people. Getting the return of one prisoner in exchange for sending three French workers, what a pitiful policy!" Six months later, in a January 12, 1944, BBC speech, Maurice Schumann, de Gaulle's spokesman, saluted the young man's exploit: "An immense majority of the 3,000 French present supported the valiant patriot [i.e., Mitterrand], against the government minister of anti-France. . . . The spirit of this young man who, in the center of Paris itself, made this public challenge to treason, this was the true spirit [of the former POWs]."[49] And indeed he was.

Thus by early 1943, July at the very latest, François Mitterrand was in the Resistance. "Beginning in February-March 1943, François Mitterrand, well known by his real name at Vichy, began also to be called Morland, Purgon, Monier (or Monnier), Laroche, capitane François, Arnaud, Albret and other names. Elusive vis-à-vis the Gestapo and [Vichy's] Milice, he seemed so also for those who thought they were his friends. . . . Behind a paravent of Vichysois respectability he played a double or even triple game in which he alone knew the points of connection with his true personality."[50] Mitterrand most often used the Resistance name "Morland," and his activities increasingly resembled a star—of which one point only was his *maréchaliste* facade.

On November 15, 1943, he left France representing his "interior" (i.e., metropolitan) POW Resistance network in order to contact the "external" Resistance organizations headed by de Gaulle and Giraud. Mitterrand considered himself entirely a man of the "interior" Resistance, but insofar as he had an external allegiance he thought of his organization as part of the Giraud network. He wanted to reach Algiers, where "Free France" had relocated from London in order to be on French territory. He transited several days in London, where he was extensively interviewed by the British Secret Service, whose archives contain the minutes of his debriefings.[51]

His mission, in addition to making other contacts (he met the legendary "Colonel Passy" for example), was to meet with General Giraud, de Gaulle's rival for leadership of the Free French. But by the time Mitterrand arrived in Algiers, de Gaulle had bested Giraud, and on December 5, 1943, the young metropolitan résistant Mitterrand/"Morland" met the General. This date indicates that by December 1943 Mitterrand had become a full-time résistant important enough to merit an audience with de Gaulle.

His path had quickened during 1943. By February he and Maurice Pinot already were the recognized leaders of a so-called Pin'Mitt' (Pinot/ Mitterrand) Resistance network, whose members were recruited mainly from the prisoners' administration. By the beginning of March, "François Morland" was in a position to contact the main leaders of the interior Resistance. The three main Vichy zone Resistance movements (Combat, Libération, and Franc-Tireur) had just accepted de Gaulle's leadership and had confederated in the so-called *Mouvements unis de la résistance* (MUR). Henri Frenay, the founder of Combat and one of the very first résistants, oversaw the MUR leadership; he also became Mitterrand's sponsor, leading to the young man's first government position.

It was during these months in the first half of 1943 that various Resistance missions led Mitterrand to meet up unexpectedly with old friends, among others a certain "Lahire," who turned out to be his old school pal and later gaullist, Pierre de Bénouville; with a certain "Rossini," that is, Jacques Baumel, also a later gaullist leader and defense specialist; and Bertie Albrecht, Henri Frenay's assistant. In Péan's 1993-94 interviews with Mitterrand on this subject, the French president went back repeatedly to two points. The first was Frenay's remarkable performance as an "interior" Resistance leader and his unfortunate conflict of personalities with de Gaulle's delegate from the "exterior," Jean Moulin. The second point was the larger struggle between interior and exterior leaderships. Mitterrand told another interviewer that, "[De Gaulle] kept in Algiers all the important leaders who were rivals. There was truly a continuous gaullist effort to put aside all the interior résistants who were not politically on their side."[52] In this conflict between the interior and exterior Resistance, we see the germ of François Mitterrand's anti-gaullism.

Mitterrand's Vichy service altogether lasted from early 1942 through the middle of 1943, when he and his comrades resigned from the Commissariat for POWs. He spent less time at Vichy, in other words, than he did as a prisoner of war in Germany. His Resistance career was slightly shorter than both, happily so, because the war ended. But measurement of commitment by length of time is misleading. When he joined the Resistance, Mitterrand did not—could not—know the date the war would end.

Thus Mitterrand arrived in Algiers representing his own Pin'Mitt' Resistance group. Along with his battle with General Giraud for leadership of the exterior Resistance, de Gaulle was having trouble uniting the various Resistance groups, the POW groups, and many others under the National Liberation Committee (CNL) and his own authority.

Mitterrand's Algiers meeting with de Gaulle is folklore in Mitterrand's biography, because in this first encounter of supposed allies, the young "Morland" resisted de Gaulle's authority to decide the young man's place. For de Gaulle, on the other hand, Mitterrand was just one minor problem to deal with, at a time when he was having stormy contacts with giants such as Churchill and Roosevelt.

"Morland" met de Gaulle in the Algiers "Free French" headquarters. The interview went badly. De Gaulle proposed unification of the POW movements under his nephew, Michel Cailliau, the son of Marie-Agnès de Gaulle, the General's sister. Cailliau was the head, with Philippe Dechartre, of the "Charette" group. His own *nom de guerre* was "Michel Charette," although he was also called "Vergennes." But "Morland" refused consolidation and the associated promise of weapons and money, because fusion would weaken his own organization's independence and would give Cailliau undeserved authority. The "Pin'Mitt" group had little respect for "Charette."

Another reason gradually loomed even larger, lasting decades beyond the Liberation: Mitterrand/"Morland" rejected de Gaulle's assumption that he, de Gaulle, the "exterior" Resistance leader of Fighting France, should command the interior Resistance as well.[53] This conflict between the exterior and interior Resistance movements, not much apparent outside France then, or even now (Washington focused on the political struggle between the two generals, Giraud and de Gaulle, for control of the exterior Resistance), would have long consequences, both in Fourth Republic parliamentary animosities toward gaullist groups and in Mitterrand's battle with de Gaulle in the Fifth Republic. The meeting in Algiers was thus, on Mitterrand's part, the beginning of a long and stubborn resentment, a resistance to de Gaulle's charismatic authority, personal prestige, and assumed authority. Rightly or wrongly, Mitterrand said later of the meeting in Algiers: "I refused to become part of his network of power." Mitterrand wrote twice, in 1969 and 1971, of this important first meeting with de Gaulle. In *The Wheat and the Chaff* (1971), written after de Gaulle's death, his tone was serene:

> There he was in front of me with his funny head, which looked too small for his tall body, that face of a *condottiere* knocked into shape at some Catholic school. . . . He was pleasant enough. . . . He questioned me about the state of the Resistance, its methods and mood. . . . He wanted the [fragmentation] of rival groups to cease immediately. After their merger, which he expected to be carried out under Michel Charette [Cailliau], his own nephew, they would get weapons and money, not before. . . . I replied that, useful as such discipline was, the Resistance had its own laws and could not be reduced to simply carrying out orders coming from outside—that as far as the [rival organizations] were concerned, his instructions remained inapplicable. The interview was brought to an end.

The earlier 1969 version indicates a very different atmosphere:

> As I hesitated to agree to merging the three POW organizations into a single formation under the authority of one of his nephews, as he had ordered, he coldly took leave of me. Afterwards I had difficulty getting back to France. . . . Much later, I learned from a document that during my stay in Algiers it had been suggested to General de Gaulle [by Michel Calliau] that I be sent to the front in Italy. . . . I learned . . . that it was best [not to say] that the Resistance and Gaullism were not exactly the same thing.[54]

The only notes of the meeting were put on paper by Henri Frenay, someone whose opinion de Gaulle took seriously. Despite the tension the younger man was allowed to say his piece, and the upshot was that de Gaulle, who began the meeting archly by noting that "Morland" had arrived on an English plane, "gave absolution for the Vichyism of the young, impertinent visitor."[55] Frenay, one of the few first-hour résistants who remained in France, someone who himself had briefly accepted Pétain, added that in his own view many Frenchmen who had believed in Pétain had done so in good faith, and then been disappointed: "[E]ven if they made an error," he wrote, "one can't make of it a crime." To cut the Resistance off from such people would be a human misjudgment and a bad political error.

Michel Cailliau did in fact want his uncle to keep Mitterrand outside France. "Morland" would no longer pose a challenge to himself, and this would serve de Gaulle's aim of getting loyalists into the interior Resistance leadership. Mitterrand, faced with such difficulties, showed both determination and courage. After all, in addition to doing battle with de Gaulle, by returning to France he would place himself once again in danger, once again a man hunted by the Gestapo. After failing several times to get a seat on a Free France plane out of Algiers—Mitterrand believed he was being deliberately hampered by gaullist influence—"Morland" was able to get to London by catching a British military flight to Morocco, then to London. From there he returned to France by sea.

Mitterrand/"Morland" spent his few weeks in Algiers, it is true, leading a full social life in addition to business. He made the rounds in *le Tout Alger,* and was seen in the company especially of a certain "Louquette," the daughter of a senior French officer.

In Marrakesh on his way back to London, using the name "Captain Monier," Mitterrand had other remarkable chance encounters. Met at the airport by a pretty young Resistance junior officer, Mlle. de Geoffre, he was lodged, in another fantastic *coup de chance,* in the sumptuous Resistance residence of Josephine Baker, the famous American-French singer. Since September 1939, Josephine Baker had been living off and on with Jacques Abtey, a captain of the French Intelligence Service in a mansion belonging to H. E. Si Mohammed Ben Mennebi, second son of the Grand Vizir, in the medina of Marrakesh. Baker, a French and American patriot who had a spotty political record (she had supported Mussolini, among other things), had two jobs at that time. As before the war in legendary Paris settings, she was a nightclub and music hall variety entertainer. But she was now also an agent of the French Resistance's intelligence arm, the "Second Bureau." Recruited by "Fox," that is, Abtey, the couple's function in Morocco was to maintain liaison between the Free French counter-espionage service and the Intelligence Service station in Lisbon.[56]

A few days after Mitterrand was ensconced chez Josephine, Mlle. de Geoffre returned to give "Captain Monier" his transit orders. Extraordinary coincidence yet again! He was put on the plane carrying General Bernard Law Montgomery, returning from El Alamein after defeating Rommel![57] Among the passengers that day were several other English officers, two Frenchmen, and, bizarrely, a German soldier, whose significance Mitterrand/Morland/Captain Monier was not told and did not need to know. Montgomery, shortly before landing in England, told Mitterrand: "I don't know who you are nor how you found yourself on this plane. In any case we won't be landing in London. You will debark at Preswick and you'll be on your own."[58]

But despite the lucky star hovering over Mitterrand's transits on this voyage, he had failed in the key mission: to convince the gaullist Resistance leaders that they misunderstood the attitudes of French prisoners of war vis-à-vis Vichy and the Resistance alike. The gaullists took for granted a psychological availability and determination that, unfortunately, was not present among the former prisoners back in France as a whole. In other words, the gaullists were seeing the prisoners as versions of themselves. At war's end Mitterrand's first published book appeared, an analysis of the French returned prisoners. Mitterrand wrote that these men were a sort of "walled-in France, an isolated France, a France doubly captive," and that "this particular France was in itself a front of the war distinct from the others. . . . "[59] In this debate, Mitterrand was not wrong, or was at least as knowledgeable as de Gaulle. But thereafter the factor of "de Gaulle," the General's charismatic personality, would change the psychological equation.

De Gaulle never abandoned his suspicions of the prisoners' movements and their leaders. Maurice Pinot, co-leader of the Pin'Mitt' movement, later recalled how they first heard of the creation of the gaullist National Council of the Resistance (CNR):

> In May 1943, we learned of the establishment of the National Council of the Resistance (CNR), led by Jean Moulin. The CNR and various Resistance movements brought together all the political parties and trade unionists hostile to Vichy. We decided that if the POW groups were not represented in that body, they would run the risk, at the Liberation, of being undervalued, forgotten, and excluded. And, in any case, continuing the struggle against the occupying forces meant we needed means that only General de Gaulle and his men could provide. So it was of the utmost importance to make contact as soon as possible with the various groups within the CNR.[60]

So Pinot and others of the Pin'Mitt' leadership arranged to meet several gaullist CNR leaders: Claude Bourdet, Emmanuel d'Astier de la Vigerie, Jacques Baumel, and Eugène Claudius-Petit. "These men did not conceal the fact that General de Gaulle was not entirely well-disposed toward the prisoners of war. . . . The general had many grievances against them and could not understand why the escapees or repatriated men wanted to form a group of their own instead of joining the various Resistance movements on an individual basis." To de Gaulle this seemed a kind of corporatism, a syndicalism of former POWs. It was the very group egotism that had undermined French parliamentary republican regimes, a political sociology for which he used the metaphor of a "cracked mirror," a splintered representation of French society by its political parties and pressure groups. But according to Pinot, de Gaulle, despite having been a prisoner of war himself in World War I in Poland, "knew little of the conditions and consequences of [this] captivity. . . . He believed that most prisoners of war had surrendered without fighting. . . . The general openly despised us and regarded the *oflags* and *stalags* as so many despicable Vichys."[61]

Even if de Gaulle had been willing to recognize one prisoners' organization as separate (and it would have been the gaullist movement headed by Philippe Dechartre and Michel Cailliau), he certainly didn't want to recognize two, the other being the Pin'Mitt' organization, let alone three of them, meaning the Communist-controlled "National Front." De Gaulle therefore "ordered" merger talks, and the conflict between the three groups was launched into heavy waves. Dechartre explained the gaullist group's view of the Pin'Mitt' movement as Pétainist: "Between François Mitterrand's movement and ours was a fundamental difference of outlook. For us gaullists, captivity represented failure and, to expiate that sin, we wanted to take part in military action. On the other hand, for the [Pin'Mitt' group], whom we regarded as Pétainists, defeat represented a sort of judgment of God. They felt the unfortunate prisoners had paid for the mistakes of others and therefore had a mission to purify the country, enabling it to rise again. We found them a rather sentimental lot and disdained what they called the 'prisoner of war mystique.'"[62]

A basic issue lies hidden here. The gaullists were holding the POWs responsible in a certain way for their own situation, and were exhorting them to more sacrifice. The Pin'Mitt' leadership was taking the POWs (by implication the French as a whole), as they were, and asking for what their "country" (now the Resistance leaderships) owed them. Meanwhile, Pinot and Mitterrand did not blame the soldiers, the people, for the failures of France's leadership, the Third Republic, the military General Staff, the Vichy regime. If de Gaulle's was a call to duty, honor, and nobility, the Pin'Mitt' leadership wanted understanding, compassion, and perhaps some indulgence. De Gaulle's was an idea of permanent rigor, discipline in society, whereas Mitterrand's was an idea of peace, or at least normalcy, of taking people as they are. Each has its truth.

"MORLAND'S" NETWORK

The Resistance was not only a military affair that could bring one death or victory. It was, for many of those involved, a great adventure in courage, in generosity, and also in romance and betrayal.[63] François Mitterrand's Resistance network was extraordinarily rich in this regard. One episode suffices to indicate the combination of dangers and passions in the Resistance, all the more interesting because it involves a certain Marguerite Antelme. Later she became internationally famous as the novelist Marguerite Duras, author of many works including *La Douleur*, about the war, and *The Lover*, an autobiographical novel about growing up in Indochina, then still a French colony. The successful film version touched a wide public outside France.

The Mitterrand/"Morland" network was continually worried about spies inside the group, and particularly so in spring 1944. The new MRPGD (Mouvement républican des prisonniers et déportés de guerre) leadership, headed by Mitterrand, had been gravely damaged when a Gestapo assassination squad caught members of the group in a small hotel in the rue Saint-Jacques in Paris in the middle of April. "Valentin" (whose real name was Steverlinck) was killed and Rodin fled; then Marcel Barrois was arrested at the end of April, raising suspicions of penetration by Gestapo spies. Three more Gestapo raids at the beginning of June created a full alert. Three of the movement's hiding places had been quickly found out, and five MRPGD members had been arrested. Mitterrand suspected a certain Savy, the pseudonym of Barrois's former assistant, and a man named Bourgeois. On July 7, yet another comrade, Henri Geérin, was arrested and taken to the infamous rue des Saussaies, fourth floor, where the Gestapo interrogated its victims.

At about the same time, Dionys Mascolo, a close friend of Marguerite Antelme, told the MRPGD leaders that she was pursuing a bizarre strategy to obtain the release of her husband Robert Antelme, interned at the Fresnes jail. She had gotten to know a French agent of the Gestapo, a man who promised to help her, perhaps due to a personal interest in her. François Mitterrand decided that Marguerite should continue this relationship with the French Gestapo agent, seeking the release of her husband but also to try to find out how the Gestapo got its information about the MRPGD.

The French Gestapist, Charles Delval, became increasingly intimate with Marguerite Antelme. They dined together in high-class Paris restaurants, such as Marius, Les Capitales, and Le Cardinal, and they saw each other every day. Delval knew all about the death of "Valentin" in the hotel in the rue Saint-Jacques. He said his job concerned only arrests, that he didn't know much about the Gestapo headquarters, rue des Saussaies. He claimed to be interested above all in painting and art books and wanted to open an art bookstore or become an expert appraiser for the courts when the war was over.[64]

Marguerite offered Delval jewelry and silver to save her husband. He, on the other hand, asked her repeatedly about Mitterrand-Morland's whereabouts, saying that this information would free her husband in a day. Marguerite gave daily briefings to Dionys Mascolo who, through a contact, kept the MRPGD leadership informed. The leadership, including Mitterrand, debated whether Delval should be killed to stop him from doing damage. There was also discussion as to whether Savy and Bourgeois, the two suspected spies, should be killed as well. Edgar Morin, a French Communist résistant at the time, later a well-known sociologist, also wanted to be part of the discussion about getting rid of Savy and Bourgeois. According to Morin, he and Mitterrand talked in practical terms about orders to kill, and gave the go-ahead to Commandant Rodin who designated Michel Grilickès to do the job.

"Let us imagine the two men," writes Piere Péan, "François Mitterrand and Edgar Morin, walking around the Pantheon and taking the decision to liquidate Savy and perhaps Bourgeois. . . . A banal decision in these times of the hunt and fear."[65] It is no glory to decide life and death. But it is of consequence for an understanding of his character and political life that François Mitterrand, just as he himself was on a Gestapo hit list, had responsibility in such decisions to liquidate, or not, French Gestapo agents. One example was Henri Marlin, head of the French Gestapist organization in Clérmont-Ferrand, assassinated on Mitterrand's order by Jean Munier and Alain de Beaufort. The planned execution of Savy was overtaken by events—Paris's insurrection and the Liberation in August 1944.

Tragically, Robert Antelme, Marguerite's husband, had been deported to Germany just days before the Liberation. In the meantime, many in Mitterrand's network thought that Marguerite's relation with Delval had been scandalous and treasonous, or both. Like the MRPDG men, Marguerite Antelme-Duras in August-September 1944 took part in Resistance interrogations and torture of Gestapist collaborators. Later in *La Douleur* she wrote that she had tortured "like a job, like a duty . . . ," and she then became the crucial witness against Delval. "[It is] I who will kill him," she wrote of her motivation; "He had tried to get rid of the head of the movement, François Morland."[66] It was still war. On September 21, 1944, Charles Delval was turned over by the MRPDG to the judicial police; his wife, Paulette Delval, was released. Charles was executed in the Frèsnes prison courtyard in the first days of 1945. His wife Paulette and the handsome Dionys Mascolo (a.k.a. "Lieutenant Masse" and already Marguerite Duras's sometime companion) were at that point lovers as well. It was not a ménage à trois but two separate, unmarried relationships full of jealousies and lasting several years, a not uncommon situation after the war had removed so many French men from a generation. Paulette Delval had a child by Dionys Mascolo in June 1946; Marguerite Antelme did likewise the following year.[67]

The "Morland" network's exploits concluded in an astonishing François Mitterrand–Marguerite Duras–Robert Antelme coincidence, which seems too much to be true only to those who have never read the history of war or experienced it.

When in March 1945 François Mitterrand arrived with the military-civilian delegation to open the Dachau camp, as he walked through the fields of the dead and near-dead, a voice from one of the piles of bodies called out his name. It was none other than Marguerite's husband, Robert Antelme, desperately ill with typhus and placed in a triage pile with prisoners deemed sure not to survive. Mitterrand wrote later of this moment, "And from a pile of bodies apparently with no movement, a weak voice arose calling me by my first name. ...I didn't know who it was...."[68] He reacted immediately, breaking procedures for quarantine. He called Paris to have false papers made and sent to him overnight, hand-carried by Georges Beauchamp and Dionys Mascolo. Robert Antelme, dressed in a soldier's uniform and passed off as drunk, was released without the usual hygiene procedures.

Mitterrand brought Antelme back to Paris the next evening. Marguerite Duras, on seeing her husband being carried up the stairwell, "screamed no, that I didn't want to look. I turned, ran up the stairs. I screamed, I remember . . . I found myself in the neighbors' apartment. They made me drink rum. They poured it into my mouth. Into the screams."[69]

Mitterrand and Marguerite Antelme-Duras were, after all this, forever old comrades, whatever bad feelings they had experienced at the time. Mitterrand saw her many times, even when president, although most people were ignorant of what really linked the president and the novelist. And Marguerite was far from the only person whose past with Mitterrand looked one way on the surface, and quite different deeper down. Some friends, who were mainly aware of her *mauvaise fréquentation* with Delval, thought that Mitterrand was making a mistake. Those who arrived much later in the story and knew little or nothing about all these tangled relations wondered mainly how the French president seemed to know so many interesting people so well from so many walks of life.

DANIELLE:
A MARRIAGE MADE IN THE RESISTANCE

It is plausible that François Mitterrand was still on the rebound of his rejection by Marie-Louise Terrasse when he married Danielle Gouze in October 1944. It was a marriage made during the war and within the Resistance ambience. François, according to family lore, announced his intention on the spot to marry Danielle Gouze after seeing her face in a photograph at her sister's home.

Danielle was the younger sister of Christine Gouze, who, besides her job as an employee in the occupation regime's Administration for Cinema, was a Resistance activist herself, a "mailbox" for the MRPDG network. Christine was romantically involved with one of Mitterrand's stalag comrades, Patrice Pelat, who was then Mitterrand's bodyguard. Christine, later the movie producer Christine Gouze-Rénal who married the *pied-noir* actor Roger

Hanin, confirms the story but denies that Mitterrand was serious. In February 1944, "Morland" was at her apartment, rue Campagne-Première in Paris, with some of the movement's leaders, Patrice Pelat, Bernard Finifter, and Jean Munier. Their scheduled meeting place had had to be changed because of Gestapo surveillance. Noticing a photograph of a young woman, François Mitterrand asked who she was. Christine replied, "My sister." "What is she doing?" "She's preparing her 'bac-philo' exam at home in Burgundy." In a flash Mitterrand exclaimed, "She's ravishing, I'll marry her!" Whatever the meaning of all this, that's what he did. Perhaps it was a fortuitous witticism, or perhaps he wanted to get himself settled.

The twenty-seven-year-old François and the nineteen-year-old Danielle (like Marie-Louise, a younger woman) were introduced a few weeks later, at a restaurant in the Boulevard Saint-German. Mitterrand/"Morland" arrived wearing a soft wide hat that covered half his face and accented his Resistance moustache. Danielle said "He looked South American" and that he talked "in an ironic manner" she didn't always get and didn't like.[70] She was not bowled over, clearly, but François Mitterrand's determination and charm won her over, and in fact ended by dazzling her. They were married six months later, October 28, 1944, two months after the Liberation of Paris, in the Saint-Séverin church on Danielle's twentieth birthday.[71]

Danielle Gouze Mitterrand came into François's life a politically engaged, plain-speaking girl from a left-wing, secular, socialist family. Her father was a résistant. Principal at the Villefranche-sur-Saône secondary school, he had been fired by Vichy. He thereupon took the family to live in their small vacation cottage at Cluny, surviving economically by giving private lessons. The house became a safe place for Resistance activities. Danielle must have been impressed with "Morland's" Resistance reputation even if she knew little of the man, seven years older, she was engaging her life with. François himself could not have been sure exactly who he had become and where he was heading.

MITTERRAND'S ANTI-COMMUNISM
AND THE RESISTANCE STRUGGLE

One of Mitterrand's later accomplishments as leader of the Left opposition and then as president of France was to outmaneuver the French Communist party and to shrink its electorate. But in the 1960s and 1970s, many people were confused by his strategy of trapping the Communists by allying with them; people didn't know that anti-communism had from the beginning been Mitterrand's clearest political conviction. It was central to Mitterrand's whole background and political culture at home in Jarnac, and then to his Catholic student days in Paris. In intergroup Resistance negotiations Mitterrand continuously deflected Communist proposals to amalgamate the POW groups, already well aware of the Communist tactics of entryism and white-anting, that is, of joining with others and then gaining control from inside. The Communists were dangerous partners, and circumstances pitted Mitterrand and his group against both them and the gaullists. It was a formidable training ground in the politics of maneuver.

Around the end of February 1944, Mitterrand, back from his trip to Algiers, found that Michel Cailliau had started negotiations to fuse with the Communist "National Front" organization. Cailliau justified this with his recurring theme—that the Pinot-Mitterrand POW organization was Pétainist. But everyone knew the gaullist goal was to amalgamate all the interior Resistance movements under de Gaulle's authority and orders.[72] One of the PCF's negotiators was Edgar Morin, who in the 1950s was kicked out for defying party policies and wrote a celebrated *Autocritique* describing his disillusionment and exclusion. At that later date, Morin freely admitted that he had in fact been a Communist "submarine," an "entryist" whose task was to lull the Cailliau leaders into allowing Communists to penetrate the gaullist organization.[73]

On March 12, 1944, the first meeting took place to discuss fusing the three organizations. Mitterrand couldn't prevent the merger, and thus the MNPGD was created, made of gaullists, Communists, and the Pin'Mitt' movement, which de Gaulle's nephew continued to brand "a Vichy-oriented" organization. Henri Frenay strongly advised de Gaulle to remove Cailliau, who was not respected. De Gaulle finally agreed and Cailliau, furious, quit the POW organization.

Soon the French Communist hopes for revolution were betrayed by Stalin, when in the summer of 1944 Moscow ordered PCF leaders not just to accept de Gaulle's authority but to give up their weapons according to his order that the Resistance militias should disarm. The Yalta Conference and its implicit recognition of spheres of influence was still six months away, but Stalin was certainly signaling his policy by ordering a French Communist stand-down and disarmament. Moscow's instructions disappointed and con- fused many French Communists, but they obeyed.[74] French Communist leaders such as Maurice Thorez and Jacques Duclos sacrificed PCF interests, as always, for the Soviet motherland (and their own prestige inside the international communist movement). Socialism for France must, they said, await Soviet expansion into Western Europe, a trend which, like the rest of their story, was "inevitable."

CONCLUSION:
FRANÇOIS MITTERRAND AT THE LIBERATION

Mitterrand was twenty-eight years old in spring 1945, but was infinitely more worldly than the colonial infantry sergeant of 1940 and a world removed from the up-to-Paris provincial of 1934.

Mitterrand was politically precocious, one of fifteen Resistance leaders designated by Alexandre Parodi, in de Gaulle's name, to staff a temporary Liberation "government of secretaries general" of cabinet ministers still to be named. These deputy ministers would launch provisional government administrative structures in liberated France.[75] This responsibility was given to him, moreover, in spite of de Gaulle's unpleasant contacts with him (Mitterrand was not the only one to have been subjected to acerbic treatment from de Gaulle!), and in spite of letters from the persistent nephew, Michel Cailliau, seeking the position Mitterrand was given. Henri Frenay, set to be Mitterrand's boss as the minister for war veterans and prisoners, strongly recommended Mitterrand to Parodi.

But there is some evidence that Mitterrand tried to get the position of minister at the last moment for himself instead of Freney. According to this version, Mitterrand even organized demonstrations against Frenay by members of the latter's own POW movement. In a well-known confrontation, de Gaulle convoked Mitterrand, telling the ambitious young man that he had a choice: If he was unable to stop these disloyal demonstrations, he must resign; if he could stop them, that indicated that he was their organizer, and he had to sign an agreement on the spot to end them. Otherwise, de Gaulle said, Mitterrand would be arrested for insubordination upon leaving de Gaulle's office! It was still wartime, after all.

Mitterrand was given three minutes to decide. After a brief discussion with two aides he had brought along, he signed a statement literally dictated by de Gaulle.[76] Mitterrand's version was that he wanted to appear to criticize Frenay, so as to seem at equal distance from Frenay and the Communists, thus underlining his independence. But in either case he would be in an advantageous position to be named minister.

Péan concludes benignly "that Mitterrand had political ambitions which conflicted at least in part with those of his former protector." This seems too kind to an ambitious young man. In a POW movement newspaper, Mitterrand editorialized that Frenay's shortcoming was that "too often he has refused to give our organizations responsibilities which we were ready to shoulder. . . . We want to be understood: We don't want to substitute ourselves for the minister

[Frenay], we want to help him."[77] This seems a disingenuous justification for turning against a remarkable Resistance leader to whom Mitterrand personally owed a lot.

No further conclusions are necessary now. Chapter 11 discusses deeper political and moral questions that arise from François Mitterrand's wartime record, in the context of the great and scandalous "revelation" of his Vichy past in 1994, through Pierre Péan's book. Let us at this point just take note of what a wealth of experience this young man had acquired. At twenty-nine years old François Mitterrand had, by the end of 1945, made all the stops in his age's turbulent history and had experienced, for better and worse, far more of the world than most of his compatriots. What was the road forward?

CHAPTER 4

GOVERNMENT AND OPPOSITION, 1945 TO 1981: ODYSSEY OR STRATEGY?

I had been the minister and friend of Robert Schuman and of Pierre Mendès France, two Fourth Republic government leaders who tried to give it style and ideas. De Gaulle certainly had more style, perhaps fewer ideas, but no one spoke the language of the State as did he. Mendès France burned with the desire to be right. The same scruple existed in Schuman who always feared that he might be wrong.

—Mitterrand, *La Paille et le Grain*

François Mitterrand's reception [as a presidential hopeful in 1965] was cold. As Pierre Viansson-Ponté said, had he not for ten years [in the Fourth Republic] "been part of all the combinations, all the governments or almost?"

—Franz-Olivier Giesbert

[In] the alliance Mitterrand agreed to with the Communist party he locked himself into a choice: Either he would betray his Communist allies, or he would betray all the promises made in his speeches to be

the president of social peace. No one could imagine in 1974 that the
Socialist party [by the next election in 1981] would be able to win an
absolute majority alone in the National Assembly.

—Raymond Aron, *Mémoires*

AN ALMOST PERFECT
FOURTH REPUBLIC, 1946–1958

FRANÇOIS MITTERRAND WAS MADE TO ORDER for the French Fourth Republic
political game, and it was made to order for him.

The Fourth Republic, which lasted from 1946 to 1958, was a parliamentary regime with paradoxical institutions. The French state was centralized in
the French tradition going back through Bonaparte to the Bourbons, but it was
now too weak a state to govern a highly fractured society in which no class or
group could attain hegemony or hold things together. Administration by
executive bureaucracy was more decisive than the constantly changing governments produced by parliament. Administration was, in classic French fashion,
a *dirigiste,* or tutelary "guiding" of society. The prestigious, highly profession-
alized bureaucracy produced by the *grandes écoles,* the top schools, had huge
self-regard. Governments were, by contrast, weak multiparty coalitions. The
constant changes were debilitating but they were also a means by which an
ambitious new political man might quickly rise: *Ecce* Mitterrand!

Small parties could play decisive roles in building government coalitions—
there were twenty-four changes in eleven years—by adding the few deputies
necessary to constitute a majority in what was then called the Chamber of Deputies.
The just-thirty-year-old François Mitterrand could thus avoid the big parties and
their leadership competition, for fear he might be held back, by becoming a key
leader of a small but crucial "hinge" party. In July 1945 he had written of his options
in a letter to his closest friend, Georges Dayan. Given his diverse political
inclinations, his first thought was to join the Socialist party, then called the SFIO,
"but there are crowds of dead-wood veterans in the leadership." Naturally he would
have nothing to do with the Communists, although, he said, he felt some sympathy
for their putative goals. "But my relations with them are tough. . . . Their sectarianism
is unlimited. Either you fight them or you are swept up by them. They call me a
Vichyite [*sic*]." Of the MRP (Christian Democrats), he said, "They are too Catholic,
even though I am a Catholic too."[1]

This breadth of possibility indicates an openness that smacks of either
superficiality or refusal, by this formerly religious Catholic, of the collectivist
discipline of party churches *tout court.* It seems also clear that by World War II's

end Mitterrand, despite his right-wing youth, could already have been a leftist. In any case by this time he already had high ambitions for himself, although he avoided advertising them too loudly. But Maurice Schumann, himself a high French and European official, told a pertinent story recounted by the female English driver dispatched to drive Mitterrand/"Morland" from the Heston military airport on November 16, 1943, to Carlton Gardens in London, headquarters of Free France: "This guy called Morland wanted me to stop the car. I first thought he had sex in mind, that's the case often enough with your boys. But instead he got out of the car and said, 'Take a look at a man who will soon be in power in France!'"[2] Was the Englishwoman not getting a look at two complementary facets of "Morland"?

THE DELIGHTS
AND POISONS OF HIS BRILLIANT CAREER

Mitterrand had to join a party if he was to have a parliamentary career. With his older centrist colleague René Pleven, and a few others, a small party was created with a large name, the Union of Socialists and Democrats of the Resistance, or UDSR. This put Mitterrand no longer on the Right but not yet on the Left, and he would not be smothered in a mass of competing leaders in a larger party. The UDSR did become a hinge party, "a small party too weak to be feared but too strong to be discounted," as the sagacious English observer Philip Williams said. This would suit Mitterrand so long as the Fourth Republic lasted and the premiership was to be rotated. But when de Gaulle's Fifth Republic created a president-oriented system with direct election to legitimize it, Mitterrand would see the benefits of fighting for leadership of a large party.

Mitterrand emerged quickly as a Fourth Republic rising star. He shared in more governments than any other politician—eight of the total fourteen from 1946 to 1958. He held some of the highest positions. He was minister for colonies in the Pleven government in 1951, interior minister in the 1954 Mendès France cabinet, and justice minister in the Republican Front government of Guy Mollet in 1956. He also represented governments in more pleasant duties, such as escorting actresses Martine Carol and Simone Signoret at the Cannes Film Festival. Several famous photographs depict a dashing and still romantic Mitterrand locked in intense eye contact with Brigitte Bardot. A women's magazine opinion poll named him one of "France's ten most attractive men." It was a full menu for the young "Mister Minister."

After de Gaulle resigned as provisional president in January 1946, the gaullist RPF lost ground in the first Fourth Republic elections and went into systematic opposition to the new regime. On the Left the Stalinist yet large and

TABLE 4.1

FOURTH REPUBLIC POLITICAL PARTIES

COMMUNISTS	"THIRD FORCE"	GAULLISTS	EXTREME RIGHT
	Socialists		
	Christian Democrats		
	UDSR		
	Radicals		
	Independents		
	Soc Dems/RGR		

popular French Communist party was ejected from the government in May 1947, and it moved into "splendid isolation," anti-system opposition as well.

The Fourth Republic lived as it had to, restricted to the Center, its so-called third force governments composed of shifting coalitions of centrist parties in which small parties like Mitterrand's UDSR had an unusually large role.

Given Mitterrand's later Union of the Left alliance strategy with the Communist party, it seems contradictory that his Fourth Republic political career should have been built on anti-communism. But if we place ourselves in 1945, with the experience of his interior Resistance struggle with the Communists behind him and premonitions of the breakup of the wartime alliance among the United States, Britain, and the Soviet Union, Mitterrand's anti-communism during the Fourth Republic makes perfect sense.

Beyond anti-communism, Mitterrand's Fourth Republic career was posted under the sign of personal ambition, of making a career. Max Weber made the distinction between politics as a vocation and politics as a profession, a way of earning a living and reputation. In Mitterrand's case, we have a profession that was not yet a vocation.

The Fourth Republic began its legal existence on January 1, 1947, after two years of rule by a provisional government. A Socialist president, Vincent Auriol, presided over the return of parliamentary government, with the old political parties back in charge. The Fourth Republic quickly resembled the Third, a regime of weak foundations and incoherent policies.

There was a brief interlude of tripartism, an alliance of Christian Democrats, Socialists, and the French Communists. Stalin had gotten a free hand in Eastern Europe in 1944 and 1945, whereas the West European communists had had to disarm. Loyally, if resentfully, the French Communist militiamen obeyed, and the PCF became one part of this three-party coalition that lasted until 1947.

In late 1944 and early 1945 Mitterrand worked at various jobs—as a journalist, writer, and editor. Among other things he became editor of the POW magazine *Libres* (meaning roughly, "We are Free"), which the Communists had made a failed run at taking over. He was writing his first book, *Les Prisonniers de Guerre devant la Politique* (The Prisoners of War and Politics), in which he accused the Communist party of trying to "colonize" and control the POW movements. Searching his way forward, Mitterrand was a jack of all trades. And there were also two personal tragedies: His first child with Danielle, a boy named Pascal, died from an infectious disease at three months, and Mitterand's father was diagnosed with prostate cancer, the illness that would later strike down Mitterrand himself.

His editor's position at *Libres* didn't support the family, and Mitterrand contacted his friends with "supplicant, almost begging letters" about a job.[3] His first full-time civilian position turned up, a temporary sinecure that was controversial because his employer, the cosmetics company L'Oréal, and its director, the former *cagoulard* Eugène Schueller, had a record of collaboration with the German authorities. Quite possibly Schueller was thinking of how he might be able to use Mitterrand's Resistance reputation. In any case, Mitterrand's friends François Dalle and André Bettencourt, former résistants and now executives with L'Oréal, got him the position of editor-in-chief of the company's women's magazine, *Votre Beauté*. The idea was to establish a beachhead in publishing from which Mitterrand could move to create a literary review, still one of his ambitions, inside L'Oréal's general publishing house. Mitterrand needed, however, to stabilize his financial situation. In spite of his family's bourgeois situation at Jarnac, his marriage with Danielle Gouze, whose parents were schoolteachers, was, in Jean Lacouture's words, a construction *sur le sable,* built on sand.[4] Mitterrand stayed, with much frustration, at *Votre Beauté* until 1946, trying to give the magazine a more serious viewpoint and some political content. Dalle and Bettencourt have said that Mitterrand dealt only with them and may never have met Schueller at all.

Mitterrand decided to run for parliament and was a candidate for deputy in the two Constituent Assembly elections of 1946. Their purpose was to write a constitution to be put to the people in a referendum. Mitterrand was defeated in the Seine department in the June 1946 parliamentary elections, his first test in universal suffrage. Thus he didn't have a deputy's salary until November, when, in the second parliamentary elections of the year, he won in the Nièvre, a district he was "parachuted" into from outside.

The first Constituent Assembly constitutional proposal offered to the French people was a left-wing plan for a single house parliamentary system with a weak president, in the spirit of Resistance unity and the hope for a new socialist France. The French Communists had dragged the Socialists into this project, which could have given a single party, perhaps eventually the Communist party, virtual control of French politics. In other words, this was another example of French Communist intimidation of the French Socialists (We've made mistakes, but you've never made a revolution). The French Communist strategy was to make possible a "peoples' democracy" regime in France.

Not even de Gaulle had been able to control the first Constituant Assembly's constitutional proposal. After his resignation he left Paris for a kind of internal exile in his village of Colombey-les-Deux-Églises, where he waited, eventually for twelve years, for a new national emergency to bring him back to power. But this first, potentially dangerous constitutional proposal was unexpectedly voted down in the referendum, the first time the French had ever said "no" to a referendum or plebiscite.

In the Second Constituant Assembly, the Socialists shifted from a left-wing alliance with the Communists to a centrist alliance with the new MRP, one of the Christian democratic parties springing up across western Europe. The SFIO/MRP second constitutional proposal was a recipe for an only slightly reformed Third Republic regime, with all the "poisons and delights" of its parliamentary games inside the Palais Bourbon, literally and figuratively "the house without windows."

The context in which François Mitterrand launched his political career in 1946-1947 was the beginning of the cold war. Mitterrand, a leader of a small party, campaigned on his opposition to Christian Democrat/Socialist/Communist tripartism as a form of hegemony. He also criticized de Gaulle's nationalizations of 1944-1945 (contrary to what he said and did in 1981 as president!), as well as excessive centralist French government bureaucratization.[5]   Unlike most politicians, who wanted to exclude and isolate the PCF, Mitterrand, believed the Communist movement had the legitimacy of its popular support, about 25 percent of the electorate in 1947. The Socialist leader Léon Blum, in *On the Human Scale,* had branded the French Communist party as "un parti nationaliste étranger," a party that was nationalist, but in favor of a foreign country, the Soviet Union. Mitterrand accepted this but added: "The Communist party is on the Left if one looks at its five million voters. It is not on the Left if one thinks of its methods of action. Without communist voters there is no left-wing majority."[6] Mitterrand was already one of only a few French politicians who dared challenge the PCF's pretension to be the party of the Left *par excellence.*

TABLE 4.2
FRANÇOIS MITTERRAND'S
FOURTH REPUBLIC GOVERNMENT POSTS

1. War Veterans, in the Paul Ramadier government, January–November 1947
2. War Veterans, in the Robert Schuman government, November 1947–July 1948
3. Junior Minister (secrétaire d'état) for Information in a reshuffled Schuman government.
4. Overseas Territories (overseas departments and territories, plus Algeria), in the René Pleven government, July 1950–August 1951
5. State Minister in the Edgar Faure government, January–February 1952
6. Minister Delegate for the Council of Europe in the Joseph Laniel government, June 1953–September 2, 1953, when he resigned in disagreement over French policy in Morocco and Tunisia and France's war in Indochina
7. Interior Minister in the Pierre Mendès France government, June 1954–May 1955 (July 1954: the *affaire des fuites,* military secrets scandal)
8. Justice Minister in the Guy Mollet "Republican Front" government, February 1956–May 1957

Mitterrand was first elected deputy in the Nièvre on a center-right platform in November 1946. In January 1947, Paul Ramadier called him to be minister for war veterans, the position he had worked for since the end of the war and his first regular government portfolio. He was the youngest member, *le benjamin,* of this government, something he was still repeating at the drop of a hat to interviewers twenty and thirty years later. Of the young *ministrables,* the likely government ministers, of the Fourth Republic, Mitterrand recalled later that Félix Gaillard was generally thought the "most brilliant," and that he and Gaillard, who turned out to be the last regularly chosen Fourth Republic premier before de Gaulle's return, were the two leading figures. Gaillard got to the top in 1958, but was hardly heard from again; Mitterrand's coming turn was cut off by the appeal to de Gaulle, yet it was he who lasted.

In short, in French Fourth Republic politics there was always, as in Italian politics, "another slice in the salami," always another possible cabinet reshuffle to keep things the same under an appearance of change. Table 4.2 (above) shows a list of François Mitterrand's Fourth Republic government posts.

THE CHARACTER OF A PROFESSIONAL POLITICIAN

The Fourth Republic's reputation as a miserable failure, as a mere replay of the Third Republic's characteristics and deficiencies, was all the more regretted because France failed to cultivate a new politics on the bitter but fertile soil left behind when the Nazi occupation regime was kicked out. In the late 1970s, however, after de Gaulle's return and departure, the Fourth Republic received revisionist study that showed it had been a launching pad for French economic modernization, a "French economic miracle" like the German and Italian experiences. The special French state economic planning system, *le Plan,* was widely watched. And in terms of cultural renewal, France, or at least Parisian France, was exhilarating. There was distinctive philosophical thinking (the existentialism of Jean-Paul Sartre, Simone de Beauvoir, Albert Camus; the existentialist "personalist" theory of Emmanuel Mounier); film noir and cinematic "realism"; and the marvelous French *chanson* era (Edith Piaf, Yves Montand, Juliette Greco, Georges Brassens, the Belgian Jacques Brel, and Charles Aznavour).

De Gaulle affected Mitterrand's life, as he did so many others. "A good leader," the proverb says, "inspires men to have confidence in him; a great leader inspires them to have confidence in themselves." De Gaulle's return to power in 1958 in a way gave François Mitterrand an example he needed: that of a leader unlike other Fourth Republic politicians, someone more than a party politician, a leader ultimately above party politics. Perhaps one can say this was the kind of character that Mitterrand had been developing in wartime conditions, when life literally was at risk and the highest stakes propelled certain people to their full potential. The Fourth Republic's advent, by contrast, was an invitation to political decadence, which it failed to prevent. De Gaulle, who already had the character of "General de Gaulle" to uphold, was able to do so. François Mitterrand succumbed to the Fourth Republic's poisons and delights. How could he know there would one day, soon enough, exist a different regime susceptible to his deepest ambitions, to his desire for a special "destiny"? So François Mitterrand, after making an almost perfect navigation of the Fourth Republic, had, like de Gaulle, to make his own long march before returning to the promised land of power.

SCHUMAN, PINAY, AND MENDÈS FRANCE

For Mitterrand and many other rising Fourth Republic politicians, three men stood out as role models in this period. Robert Schuman, because of his

Europeanism and his crucial influence in founding the first European institutions, inspired all those who, like François Mitterrand, thought that only European integration could replace European wars. The second widely respected figure was Antoine Pinay, a provincial man with the *France profonde* cachet of honesty and simplicity that implies (and provides a rare example of) French hard money conservative rectitude. The "Pinay bonds" of the 1950s remain a reference for monetary success, and his reputation was such that still in the 1990s, before his death at 100, new finance ministers, both conservative (Edouard Balladur) and Socialist (Pierre Bérégovoy) made a ritual pilgrimage to seek his blessing. This blessing came to be seen as an endorsement of 1980s and 1990s promises guarding a "strong franc."

The third and most important of the three leaders for François Mitterrand was Pierre Mendès France. Mendès France was also a financial and economic specialist and a policy conservative, but became above all else an example of the courage to govern by principles. He said in 1954 that he would not count Communist parliamentary votes in his parliamentary investiture even if he failed to gain office because of it. This was moral principle vis-à-vis the "foreign nationalist party" stigmatized by Léon Blum, a model for Mendès France. And it was also good strategy. It would be foolish for Mendès France to put the Communists in a position where they could blackmail him politically because they might defect from his parliamentary majority. His decisiveness—"to govern is to choose" was his motto—led to his daring resolution of France's Indochina war. Mendès France promised to go to Geneva to met Ho Chi Minh's Viet Minh representative and negotiate an end to the conflict within thirty days, or else he would resign. Mendès met the deadline, by doing what no other Fourth Republic had the courage to do: accept France's military defeat and political departure from Indochina. The 1954 Geneva peace agreement did extract France from hopeless colonialist agony in Vietnam, where, after the disastrous outcome of the battle at Dien Bien Phu, French forces were on the verge of being driven into the sea. Unfortunately, to Americans' ultimate great sorrow, the Geneva agreement led soon enough to the United States taking over the French "responsibility" in Indochina.

MITTERRAND'S MISSED
CONNECTION WITH MENDÈS FRANCE

Pierre Mendès France's government lasted only seven months and seven days before the players of the parliamentary game succeeded in overturning it. Nonetheless, because of his moral stature, Mendès emerged from his quick trip through the Fourth Republic's firing line as the potential "providential" leader of the non-Communist French Left in the Fourth Republic. He remained so through the 1960s even though he, like Mitterrand, was pushed into permanent opposition by de Gaulle's success. Mendès France never returned to power and his reputation came to mean both the French Left's lack of political acumen in addition to its sense of moral superiority. François Mitterrand finally supplanted Mendès France in the 1970s by making the Machiavellian bargain Mendès had rejected in 1954: alliance with the Communists, rather than rejection of the PCF and its voters as untouchables.

But Mitterrand was very much intrigued by Mendès France. From the time of his university days prior to the war, Mitterrand had been attracted to the then-youngest French deputy trying to modernize the old Radical-Socialist party. Mendès France was a model, if not the only one, for Mitterrand's own ambitions.

When in June 1954 Mendès France got his chance at the premiership, he called on Mitterrand to help him put together his government, in which Mitterrand took on the important and risk-filled ministry of the interior.[7] Just how risky would soon become all too apparent.

In the important debate about creating a European Defense Community to facilitate Germany's rearmament, Mendès France was more skeptical than Mitterrand about the idea, though Mitterrand thought it a mistake to try to create a military Europe before there was a political Europe. Both Mendès and Mitterrand believed the EDC would be an appendage of the Pentagon, although German rearmament was necessary. Mitterrand, seeing that Mendès France's cabinet contained gaullists and Europeans alike, accepted Mendès France's instruction that government ministers were to abstain on the EDC vote.

THE *AFFAIRE DES FUITES:*
MITTERRAND FACES OFF THE EXTREME RIGHT

The so-called *affaire des fuites,* or military secrets scandal, was a damaging, unfounded, and politically vicious allegation that Interior Minister François Mitterrand was leaking national security secrets to the Communists. It was, especially during the height of the cold war, a witch-hunting accusation by far Right political forces. It became the first of several scandals that threatened not only Mitterrand's ministerial position but his entire political career.[8]

The story can be quickly recounted. As interior minister in the Mendès France government, Mitterrand had acted firmly against Paris police chief Jean Baylot, a focus of extraconstitutional, ultra–cold war intrigues. Only two weeks after taking over as minister, Mitterrand fired Baylot because he was using his police position for often illegal anti-Communist activities. Baylot had been Paris police chief for ten years; a close associate of pro-Americans and Atlanticists, he was a French "equivalent of J. Edgar Hoover."[9] Baylot was notorious for illegal wiretaps, and he had infiltrated the Communist party with spies, some of whom were former Vichyite collaborators. In 1952 he had ordered the sensationalist arrest of the Communist deputy leader Jacques Duclos in a far-fetched accusation of using homing pigeons for espionage (although no one doubted Duclos might have been engaged in pro-Soviet work), and he authorized the use of forged leaflets to provoke Communist party militants into a violent demonstration.

Baylot considered the Mendès France/Mitterrand government to be a proto-Communist dupe against which direct action was justified. Mitterrand, not for the first time in his life, seemed to be on all sides, paradoxically acting against the Communists but also as their protector. He remembered that a year before, while still in the Laniel government, North African and Vietnamese demonstrators had been unscrupulously attacked by Baylot's police. Ever since then, Mitterrand had wanted Baylot removed, and now Premier Mendès France gave him the authorization. President René Coty asked Mitterrand to back down, but the latter threatened to resign and denounce the president. Mendès backed Mitterrand and Jean Baylot was fired.

The Baylot network sought immediate revenge by falsely accusing Mitterrand in the military secrets affair, the *affaire des fuites*. Two days before the cabinet meeting that was to endorse Mitterrand's decision to fire Baylot, the minister for Tunisian and Moroccan affairs, Christian Fouchet, a gaullist, was tipped off by police inspectors that someone in the government, supposedly Mitterrand, had leaked the minutes of a recent National Defense Council meeting to the Communist party politburo. The meeting had concerned French military operations in Indochina. Inspector Jean Dides, a controversial Baylot lieutenant in charge of monitoring the Communist party for Baylot's office, was Mitterrand's accuser.

The leaks were real, but Mitterrand was not the culprit. He was cleared for the simple if stupefying oversight by Dides that the Defense Council meeting at issue had occurred a month before Mitterrand became interior minister and thus a member of the council! Nevertheless, the scandal was extremely damaging to Mitterrand, who said later that "I found myself in the middle of an imbroglio created by a police inspector who was marching around in political circles showing [allegedly compromising] documents, including the list of regiments leaving for Indochina, a list posted on the docks at Marseille port!"[10]

Especially wounding was the fact that Pierre Mendès France had initiated an investigation of his interior minister without telling Mitterrand of the accusation, creating the impression that he himself had believed that it might be true. This machination showed how the colonialist ultra-Right operated: It wanted to avenge the firing of Baylot and, in the process, to discredit the Mendès France government for "giving away Indochina" at Geneva. In addition, Mitterrand, although his anti-communism was well known, was being smeared and hopefully unhorsed for dismantling illegal police operations that the Baylot-Dides police command had put in place against the Communist party.

Was Mitterrand perhaps a Communist dupe after all? Clearly not, but his image in public opinion was confused by the fact that ultra-Right adversaries, ferocious anti-communists, had chosen him as a target. French political scientist Roland Cayrol wrote in the first biography of Mitterrand in 1967 that, even though Mitterrand was completely cleared, "there would remain a doubt" about his character. "Once slandered, there would always remain something. This was probably the reasoning of the extreme right-wing people plotting [against Mitterrand]. And in fact their propaganda was intensive enough that, despite everything, some people continue to believe there was 'something' wrong about Mitterrand's character in the military secrets affair."[11]

Mitterrand thus survived the *affaire des fuites,* but with considerable political damage. In addition to a permanent suspicion about his character, his relationship with Mendès France, the recognized "man of integrity" among non-Communist left-wing leaders, suffered because the latter had appeared to doubt his integrity. Although such a procedure was plausible in a national security matter, Mendès France, a senior colleague who had given Mitterrand an important position, seemed now to lack confidence in him.[12] Mendès's action was all the more unfortunate because Mitterrand, given the discrepancy in dates, could have acquitted himself quickly had he known of the accusation and the investigation.

Mitterrand in any case now knew that he was a prominent target for the ultra-colonialist Right. He had begun making enemies earlier as minister of French overseas territories and needed to be permanently on guard. In light of France's debacle in Indochina, he now seemed a "liberal" on France's remaining colonial problems, especially in North Africa. By no means did Mitterrand favor immediate independence, but he saw that the old colonialism in North Africa was moribund. Different solutions were needed for Tunisia and Morocco, as opposed to an Algeria that was constitutionally part of France, but change was, he thought, vital. "Mitterrand," an American biographer rightly says, at the time "appeared to be one of the few politicians with a vision of the future."[13] However, his growing influence in succeeding French governments meant also that the counterterrorist ultra-colonialist circles would continue machinations against him, dirty tricks culminating in the Observatory affair.

MITTERRAND, MENDÈS FRANCE,
AND THE COMMUNISTS

Mitterrand's complex position with regard to the Communist party and its supporters in the Fourth Republic, which became his electoral strategy in the Fifth Republic, placed him in opposition to the clarity of Mendès France's position. Mendès was an anti-communist on principle, rejecting any contact with them, and excluding them from non-Communist Left strategies. Mendès France was even against any electoral alliance with the Communists for mutual support, another disagreement with François Mitterrand.[14]

The latter, by contrast, had seen in the Resistance how the French Communists could be used, just as they tried to manipulate him. Mitterrand thus had learned not to reject out of hand the possibility of certain dealings with the Communist party, but most of all not to exclude Communist voters from the nation. He recognized, rightly, that the ideologically Communist electorate was much smaller than the PCF total vote, and that 50 percent or more of the Communist voters were casting protest ballots and could be won away from the Communist party. Thus the opinion of one biographer about Mitterrand in the 1950s is not wrong, yet must be explicated: "A man of the left? Certainly not. His trajectory developed between center right and center left with one constant: a visceral and militant anti-communism."[15] When Mitterrand allied the Socialist party with the Communists twenty-five years later, most French people had forgotten or perhaps never knew about either his long-standing anti-communism, or his 1946 rejection of tripartism that involved the Socialists and Communists alike. Yet, unlike other French politicians, anti-communism did not prevent Mitterrand from hard-nosed engagement with Communist leaders (going back to Robert Paumier, Waldeck Rochet, and others he encountered in the Resistance). Nor did it keep him from certain actions, such as dismantling the Baylot-Dides illegal police apparatus used against the PCF, which some people took for procommunist although his measures were republican and civil libertarian.

Mitterrand's Fifth Republic Union of the Left strategy rested therefore on the assumption of the naturally competitive, combative nature of all alliances, all the more so in an alliance of a social democratic Socialist party with a Stalinist Communist party. The Communists never forgot that, despite any coalitions, François Mitterrand was a permanent enemy in a way that the hands-off Mendès France could never be. Mitterrand endangered their existence by ensnaring the PCF as a party and by siphoning off masses of Communist votes. But to much of French and foreign opinion Mitterrand's behavior would appear to be reckless or inscrutable, his "soft spot" for the Communists unfathomable. And Mendès France's rejection of any policy of engagement with the French Communists resulted in huge moral disapproval until the early 1970s when, under Mitterrand's new leadership, the refounded Socialists (the PS) began to reverse the balance of power with the Communists.

MITTERRAND THE EUROPEAN, THE ATLANTICIST, THE CENTRIST

The enduring commitment in Mitterrand's political career was, as we shall see, his Europeanism, understood as the best policy for the French national interest. By Europeanism I have two concepts in mind: *positive* integration of European states continuing beyond postwar reconstruction, and European integration leading to at least some *federalist* structures and institutions beyond a purely intergovernmentalist or confederalist approach.

Mitterrand attended the European Hague conference in 1947, and as a member of the government he voted in favor of the European Coal and Steel Community (ECSC) treaty in 1950, and later, in 1957, for the Rome Treaty, creating the European Economic Community (EEC).

In addition to his Europeanism during the Fourth Republic, Mitterrand's Atlanticist orientation was also clear. He displayed realism regarding the danger the Soviet Union represented for France and Western Europe and voted consistently in favor of NATO, although always cautioning about the various prices of alliance with the American protector. Even during the Fourth Republic before de Gaulle's return there was some resentment in the French center parties against American "hegemony," in addition to gaullist and Communist policies.

Already in the 1950s Mitterrand was arguing that exclusive American control over the alliance's nuclear weapons was "one of the essential points" of concern between America and the European allies. "It is intolerable," he said, that Washington by itself could take such fateful decisions. Mitterrand also called for redefinition of American and European responsibilities worldwide, in Asia, Africa, and in Europe. He warned, in reaction to American talk of a "rollback" of communism in Eastern Europe, against NATO's mission becoming offensive, as opposed to a defensive alliance.[16] Mitterrand's policy statements in the 1950s were too demanding for France's and Western Europe's weakened positions, but they do show his gaullien geopolitical outlook and policy mind-set. Domestic support for de Gaulle's foreign policy of independence in 1958 was much wider, it is clear, than just his own supporters. The

Communists were anti-American, thus semifavorable to de Gaulle's policy; and in between the gaullists and the Communists were Mitterrand and other centrists like him. François Mitterrand's Fourth Republic career showed that it was possible to be simultaneously European, Atlanticist, gaullien, centrist, and willing to engage the domestic French Communist movement in a test of strength on its own terrain, the French Left. Mitterrand, both the admirer and the critic will say, was nothing if not versatile.

MITTERRAND THE AFRICAN

In 1950-51, Africa first appeared on the young Mitterrand's political horizon when he became minister of overseas territories in the government of the centrist René Pleven. Later, Mitterrand always emphasized that it was this experience that began to broaden his view beyond Europe. It was also one reason Mendès France named him interior minister in 1954. Algeria was still nominally part of French national territory, and thus within the interior ministry's jurisdiction. This put Mitterrand in charge of France's Algerian dilemma. By contrast, the foreign ministry was responsible for Tunisia and Morocco, and a special ministry was in charge of Indochina. In 1953, with France heading toward defeat in Indochina, Mitterrand published *Aux Frontières de l'Union Française* (At the Frontiers of the French Union). In 1957 he followed this with the more incisive *Présence Française et Abandon* (French Presence and Withdrawal). This book was, among other things, an exposé of Communist policies on national liberation for the colonies. Mitterrand argued that Black African nationalism was being sidetracked and manipulated by Communist propaganda, both Soviet and French. The French Communist party was wrapping its Soviet-inspired colonialism—the colonies should shift from being American influenced to Soviet controlled—in a nationalist banner. The Communists demagogically asserted that French colonies should remain French for the time being, because their true freedom could come only when socialism came to France itself, at some undefined point in the future. Immediate independence for the colonies would lead not to socialism but only to new bourgeois regimes subservient to world imperialism. Waiting would put new post-colonial states in the Soviet camp, supposedly the side of fraternal independence and brotherhood. Mitterrand's book was a quite cutting dissection of Communist hypocrisy, and he was one of the few centrist politicians with the courage to call facts facts.

Mitterrand's progressive, liberal credentials developed in the 1950s, not because of any movement toward socialism per se, but because of his conclusion that the old colonialism was dying, that a new relationship with its African *pre carré*, or sphere of influence, was brewing. Mitterrand appeared increasingly in the national limelight as an expert, or at least a specialist in the problems of colonialism and demands for independence.[17]

But Mitterrand's policy on the colonies couldn't avoid the differences in constitutional statute, meaning that Algeria had to be a special case and that his call for reform had to be balanced by a policy of continued presence. Thus on November 1, 1954, speaking of violence in Algeria, Mitterrand, in a portentous declaration, told the National Assembly that "Algeria is France. And who among you would hesitate to use any means to preserve France? There is a tremendous difference between Tunisia and Morocco, on the one hand, and Algeria on the other, which is part of the Repubic."[18] Contrary to legend, Mitterrand did not utter the notorious phrase, "Algeria is French. The only negotiation is war." But, unfortunately, the sentence was in his written text.

In any case, during the Fourth Republic a new set of questions, those concerning African development, was added to Mitterrand's political personality and his intellectual interests. Other politicians and French business people had equal knowledge and ties in Africa—Jacques Foccart, de Gaulle's *éminence grise* in Africa, and Jean-Baptiste Doumeng, the French Communist agro-business "red millionaire," were two of the most famous and colorful. But no one could contest that after his apprenticeships in the Fourth Republic, "Mitterrand the African" had become a politician to reckon with. And since Africa was so much a part of France's own history, Mitterrand, in his development of an African "life" and expertise, came to embody French interests and passions. (The careers of some of his African colleagues ended grotesquely: One thinks of Houphouët-Boigny's lavish construction in his native Ivory Coast village of a Catholic basilica larger than St. Peter's in Rome. But in the Fourth Republic they were young, fighting the good fight.)

President René Coty told François Mitterrand in May 1958, "I would have gladly named you [premier], M. Mitterrand," but for two problems: Mitterrand's liberal policy on Algeria would have provoked more chaos in Algiers, and he would have broken the French political taboo against dealing with the French Communists.[19] An almost perfect Fourth Republic, but not quite.

Mitterrand later deprecated his Fourth Republic posts: "As for me, I only had posts of second-level responsibility in the Fourth Republic. Important, but on the second level. When the Fourth Republic began, I was thirty years old. When it ended, it could be said that I had hardly begun my political life. And there are so many people who are already finished at the same age."[20] Yet whether Mitterrand would have been a great success as Fourth Republic premier is doubtful. Besides a vague "liberal" attitude, he offered no fundamentally new directions in a period when new beginnings were desperately needed, at least politically. There was only his own cleverness and daring as a leader. But skillful game-playing is not true leadership, and Mitterrand in the Fourth Republic was more admired, or rather envied or resented, than loved. François Mitterrand in 1957 was, it can be said, brilliant in rather ordinary ways. He would have had his turn at the helm, but we do not yet see in Mitterrand the man of stature who, in the Fifth Republic and after a long march in the opposition, would break up old political patterns and move France decisively forward.

The key to understanding the turning point of Mitterrand's fifty-year political career lies in the Fourth Republic's collapse, as a result of uprising in Algeria; the consequent return of Charles de Gaulle to power; and the infamous Observatory affair.

MITTERRAND IN
THE FIFTH REPUBLIC, 1958 TO 1981

Mitterrand's rejection of de Gaulle's return to power in May 1958 and of the Fifth Republic in October were acts either of courage or of recklessness. He, Pierre Mendès France, and a few other deputies stood alone between the massive gaullist wave on one side and the rock-solid Communist party monolith of deputies on the other. Where was the political future in this positioning?

Of necessity, Mitterrand's search for a way forward was not straight. A theme of being an outcast, an untouchable, runs through the years after the Observatory affair. Even de Gaulle sometimes had despaired of ever finding a road back into national life, and Mitterrand's detour into the Observatory affair probably resulted in part from a secret worry that his "no" to de Gaulle's return to power and the new constitution had ruined his career. That is, Mitterrand had to fight to maintain the courage of his anti–de Gaulle convictions, and the Observatory affair seemed a shortcut.

The PCF's leaders realized that in the changed conditions of the Fifth Republic, with the massive gaullist movement on the Right, François Mitterrand could well be useful, even necessary to them. In spite of his anti-communism he was open to dealing with the PCF. This was important because in cold war Europe and particularly cold war France, Western European communist parties were having great difficulty maintaining themselves because it was clearer and clearer that they had no potential of gaining power and that the Soviet Union was unlikely ever to "march down the Champs-Élysées as an army of liberation" as the PCF leader Maurice Thorez, in a slip, had imagined in 1949. Mitterrand recognized the French Communist movement's legitimacy because he recognized its representativeness, the fact that 25 percent of the electorate voted Communist and the Communist-controlled CGT trade union was France's strongest.

But the French Socialists, at least the majority, rejected Mitterrand. The disgrace of the Observatory affair, as shown in chapter 2, was immense. And lurking behind that was, as always, the suspicion about Mitterrand at Vichy. Mitterrand's willingness to negotiate with the Communists was therefore the third of three black marks against him, even if the Socialist leaders knew he was less likely to be intimidated by the Communists than any of them. None of the Socialists had a strategy for dealing with the "Communist problem." The French Left was just stuck, divided in two, with one-half (or two-thirds) of it, the Communist party, possessed by a superiority complex. The Socialists, moreover, had to accept the cold war, which meant enrollment in NATO and the patronage and protection of American "capitalism." But they didn't even get the benefits of this fact, since the conservatives didn't need the Socialists to govern, and the latter were thus consigned to permanent, practically voiceless opposition. French political scientist Maurice Duverger quipped at this time that "the Socialists are like the slice of ham in a sandwich, and getting thinner all the time." In Italy in this period the ruling Christian Democratic party won the Kennedy administration's approval to make the so-called "opening to the left"—a daring expansion of the ruling coalition, which allowed not the Italian Communists but only the Italian Socialists into the government! Woe to be a continental European Socialist party in the 1950s and 1960s!

François Mitterrand himself was, in 1960, still far from an "official" Socialist, let alone a member of the Socialist party, then still called the SFIO. His UDSR party had been named for socialism, but also for democracy and the Resistance; and ecumenism was the Resistance movement's hopeful view of the future. Its long name was, however, the inverse of its social reality. The UDSR was a club of notables with a small electoral base. Mitterrand, disdained as the culprit of the Observatory affair and *persona non grata* among SFIO leaders, approached the new Autonomous Socialist party, the PSA, which had been created in 1959 by SFIO dissidents who rejected the party leadership's acceptance of de Gaulle. The PSA also boasted a few Radical-Socialists and other notables, above all Mendès France. With Mendès came Charles Hernu, a young Mendèsiste who was to become an important Mitterrand loyalist. Like Roland Dumas and later Robert Badinter, Charles Hernu was a Freemason, and freemasonry became another source of later recruits to Mitterrandism, people sympathetic to the cause of a nonideological leftism, secular but not anti-Catholic, anti-Communist but willing to negotiate with them, anti-gaullist while respecting de Gaulle's historic role as savior of France. In all of this was the possibility, still only a glimmer, of a French left-wing majority not blocked by gaullism or by French communism.

Mitterrand's attempt to join the PSA was rebuffed, which just indicated how severe was his loss of prestige and his semipariah status after the Observatory affair.[21] Alain Savary, an SFIO dissident who had rejected de Gaulle as well, blackballed Mitterrand. Himself a "Free France" veteran of impeccable reputation, Savary "could not accept," he said, "the man who had worn Vichy's francisque." Mitterrand's Vichy past was reproached anew, although Savary's cause was dubious, as he must have known.

The early 1960s were thus for François Mitterrand a time of re-creating credentials and credibility, building networks of loyal friends and new contacts in the political, business, and trade union worlds. Because of his disgraced reputation these efforts were discreet, often organized by Charles Hernu: private meetings, round table conferences of centrists and Socialists in the "non-communist Left" and travel.

In January 1961 Mitterrand visited China with a Lyons sugar manufacturer named François de Grossouvre, who had been introduced to Mitterrand by Mendès France. Grossouvre became a longtime friend to Mitterrand and a personal advisor in the Élysée. Unfortunately he was also one of two shocking suicides in the Mitterrand presidency during the second term (former prime minister Pierre Bérégvoy being the other).

One goal of the meetings and conferences was to test the terrain for possible negotiations with the French Communists, as part of a Union of the Left party coalition strategy, which was in effect a plan designed for Mitterrand, aiming at the new directly elected presidency. In China, Mitterrand was fascinated, but was no more ideologically seduced by Mao Zedong's Peoples' Republic than he was entranced with the French Communists.

Mitterrand talked with Mao in a two-hour private meeting. In Mao the Frenchman found a mixture of ideology and realism, a peasant and military experience of things as they really are, and, the most evident thing in him, a ferocious willpower to build a new China with a Chinese people that had "stood up" (as he said in his memorable proclamation from the Tiananmen wall upon taking power in Peking in 1949). Mitterrand wrote about his experience that China was "mixing the absurd and the admirable." Although repulsed by the extreme propaganda of the regime and the Maoist cult of personality, Mitterrand was misled enough by Mao's conversation (this was the horrendous Great Leap Forward period) or indulgent enough as a guest to write in an editorial, on his return to Paris, that "Mao is a humanist."[22] Most likely he was also thinking of his need to justify a Communist alliance on the French Left.

Back in Paris he produced a forgettable book, *La Chine au Défi* (China Under Challenge), and espoused the idea that France should break with Western policy and open diplomatic relations with Communist China. President de Gaulle was moving to the same conclusion, an instance of French national interest beyond Left and Right. In his famous press conference of 1963, de Gaulle surprised the allies and the Communist states alike by announcing diplomatic recognition for the Peoples' Republic, as well as rejecting the British application for European Economic Community membership.

To recognize China was a mutual de Gaulle–Mitterrand conclusion that went deeper than tactics. Mitterrand saw a margin of maneuver for French diplomacy and his bold foreign policy proposal could bolster his presidential ambitions. De Gaulle's decision to recognize China was part of his attempt at a French-led East-West détente. He was attempting to take advantage of the margin of maneuver available to France in the post–Cuban missile crisis standdown, based on the judgment that East-West war had now become extremely unlikely. In de Gaulle's calculation, a French détente with China and with the Soviet Union would be good for peace, for the European equilibrium, and for France. Not least, it was also a way to reduce American leverage on French freedom of diplomatic maneuver. For Mitterrand, recognition by the French Communist leadership, despite the cold war and despite their animosity toward him and what he was attempting, was necessary for any non-Communist Leftist to win the French presidency.[23]

Mitterrand had quickly understood the electoral implication of the 1962 constitutional amendment creating a directly elected French president. The return to majority voting in two rounds would lead to bipolarization, as opposed to the fragmentation effect of a proportional representation electoral law. This was because each party could run its own candidate on the first ballot to "count its troops," with a justifiable Left and Right rally around the best placed candidate to win on the second ballot. Thus a non-Communist leftist well ahead of the Communist candidate after the first ballot (i.e., Mitterrand) could get most of the Communist votes at the runoff ballot. Since a Communist candidate could never win the presidency at a general election, Mitterrand's strategic problem was, so to speak, minimized while still remaining enormous. The problem was, first, to become the leading non-Communist Left candidate and, second, to come in ahead of the Communist candidate on the first ballot. In 1962 the gaullists had also changed the system for parliamentary elections to majority voting, reinforcing electoral bipolarization by obliging Left and Right to ally for majorities on the second ballot just as in the presidential election.

In this calculation, Mitterrand's unusual combination of anti-communist credentials and experience in dealing with them rather than writing them off became an increasingly important card in his hand. His commitment to exploring a Socialist-Communist alliance distinguished him from other potential left-wing unity leaders; in fact it made him the only likely winner among them because no one else, not even Mendès France, had the audacity (the Communist alliance) and the authenticity (his proven anti-Communism combined with the belief that many Communist voters were winnable) of his strategy.

A few years later he wrote of his situation at this time, "From 1962 on, since it had been decided that the presidential election would be by universal suffrage, I knew I would be a candidate. But when? How? I couldn't know. And I was [politically] alone. I had neither an organization nor a party nor a Church, a counter-Church, a newspaper nor public support. I had no money and could expect none of the traditional . . . sources of finance."[24] Exaggerated, yes, for effect, but it was true enough of a protean politician, a rightist become a centrist become the man of the Observatory scandal, en route to his next incarnation.

1965–1981: FROM OUTSIDER TO PRESIDENT

In 1965 Mitterrand made his first run for the presidency. It was the first direct election under the constitutional change that de Gaulle had won in order to legitimize the superpowerful presidency he had created. Mitterrand's candidacy had to rise above his own controversial reputation, Socialist party disarray, the total Socialist-Communist lack of communication, and the fact that, since this was the first direct presidential election in the history of France, nobody knew how it would work.

De Gaulle expected to be an easy winner; however, he was less good at sniffing out electoral politics than at war. The Socialists and the center-Left struggled to find a viable candidate. The Communists controlled about 20 percent of the electorate, but their pariah status, the "splendid isolation" they were proud of, made them apparently impossible alliance partners for a Socialist. The left-wing dilemma was examined by the magazine *L'Express,* which searched editorially for "Monsieur X," meaning a left-wing candidate who would surely lose to de Gaulle but could start rebuilding the Socialist and center-Left parties. The magazine's "Monsieur X" turned out to be Gaston Defferre, a respected Socialist SFIO politician, a former résistant, and the powerful mayor of Marseilles, but a man with frighteningly little charisma and a marked meridional southern accent, which displeased the ears of Paris. Furthermore, Defferre's policy brooked no alliance with the Communists. This reassured the other Socialist leaders but made of him an even more certain loser, and by a greater margin.

However, Defferre's candidacy ran quickly into trouble, and in early 1965 he aborted his "unity" candidacy, which left the Socialist party divided and demoralized. François Mitterrand's opportunity for resurrection was at hand.

Pierre Mendès France and Mitterrand remained the two leading left-wing, anti-gaullist politicians outside the Socialist party. Mendès France refused on principle to run for the presidency, as a parliamentary republican still unreconciled to de Gaulle's 1958 "coup" and change of regime. By contrast, Mitterrand, who in 1958 had infuriated de Gaulle with his warning that "after the generals might come the colonels," that is, the possibility of a military coup against de Gaulle himself, accepted presidential politics. Presidential politics was becoming an established fact which Mitterrand, as opposed to Mendès, knew how to reckon with, while still safeguarding his belief that the parliamentary republic was the best regime for France.

As a matter of principle Mitterrand continued to denounce de Gaulle's rule as a "regime of personal power." His 1964 book, *Le Coup d'État Permanent* (The Permanent Coup d'Etat), was an ideological anti-gaullist diatribe, but at the same time it was his most substantial book (see chapter 7), full of astute historical analogies and constitutional law arguments.

Mitterrand entered the presidential race on September 9, 1965, by simply declaring himself a candidate and producing sufficient petition signatures by national and local government officials, as the constitution allowed. The SFIO Socialists made a fateful decision to support Mitterrand's candidacy when the Communists—who opposed a direct presidential election because they would show worse than in parliamentary elections—signaled through back channels that they would not obstruct his way. Mitterrand and the new PCF leader, Waldeck Rochet, had first met each other in the Resistance and had continued to consider each other as comrades and friends. A former small farmer, or *paysan,* Waldeck Rochet nonetheless had an openmindedness unusual for his origins and his Communist party training. Touched by the ecumenical spirit of the Resistance movement, he, in the few years he was at the PCF helm between 1964 and 1968, showed that even in the most Stalinist West European Communist party, some humanistic rejection of total ideological "democratic centralist" thinking was possible. A Communist need not reject everyone else as impure and unredeemable. Friendship across partisan lines was not unthinkable, especially since the Left's failure to stop Nazism from going all the way to Götterdämmerung was a lesson no humanist could ignore.

The fact that Waldeck Rochet was succeeding the French "little Stalin," Maurice Thorez, who had led the PCF for thirty years and was finally retiring, was thus another favorable circumstance for François Mitterrand's presidential hope. Last, the small but ideologically potent PSU first said no to Mitterrand, then changed its decision.

By 1965, then, François Mitterrand had become clearly positioned on the Left, if not yet fully a "man of the Left." As a presidential unity candidate daring to accept Communist support and thus for the first time showing the way to a possible left-wing majority, he was starting to lift a moribund Left, at least in electoral terms, on his shoulders. His strategy showed further that Mitterrand's second national career, after being Mister Minister in the Fourth Republic, would be based on presidential opposition to de Gaulle and gaullism. Mitterrand, in one writer's image, was becoming a kind of antithesis to and left-wing double of de Gaulle, like Mozart's Don Juan defying the statue of the Commander.[25]

Mitterrand's 1965 electoral program was a mixture of the hard, the soft, and the new. The hardest-hitting aspect, as in his television address just before the first round of voting, was his denunciation of de Gaulle's regime: "that of a single man . . . [who] will designate an unknown successor who will appoint his friends, a faction that will be worse than a party, an anonymous collection of interests and intrigues." The soft or ambiguous part of his program was his leftism, neither Socialist nor Communist but the generic historical European social democratic left of "generosity," of "fellow-feeling" and the goal of "happiness."

Mitterrand, in contrast to de Gaulle, claimed to be a genuine European, openly favorable to integration with France's neighbor and partner countries. The innovative part of his agenda was a call for repeal of a 1920 law that banned the sale or advertisement of contraceptives, at this point meaning acceptance of "the Pill," which recently had been introduced on the market. He was the first major French leader to take up this cause in what was then a still very-practicing Catholic country. Being in favor of birth control made of him a secular, modern, humanist, and even pro-feminist candidate. He also called for abolition of France's death penalty and of independence of the judiciary from (gaullist) political influence. Mitterrand's positions ironically may have lost him more women's votes than he won in this particular election, since 90 percent of practicing Catholics, most of them women, voted for de Gaulle.[26]

With 45 percent of the total first ballot vote, President de Gaulle did not win outright in the December 1965 election; there would be a second ballot. A centrist, Jean Lecanuet, took enough votes from de Gaulle, along with Mitterrand's left-wing candidacy and several splinter candidacies, to deny de Gaulle a first-ballot majority. Mitterrand's 32 percent on the first ballot was a surprisingly strong showing, especially considering the shadow on his reputation and his late start (and even then at only 11 percent). De Gaulle's victory over Mitterrand, 55 to 45 percent at the runoff, also was seen as surprisingly close, as a kind of moral victory for the latter and as proof of voters' encouragement of left-wing alliance, including the Communists or at least their electoral support. This, in the cold war years, was an unexpected radical statement from French public opinion.

Nevertheless, during the campaign Mitterrand and the Communist leader Waldeck Rochet did not risk even a public handshake, or even one public meeting. The electoral agreement for the Communists to call for a Mitterrand second ballot vote by their supporters was done in private conversations among intermediaries.[27]

◆ ◆ ◆

Mitterrand's unexpected relative success in 1965 began a decade in French politics that, broken by the still more unexpected crisis of "May 1968," saw the decline of gaullism, the non-gaullist Giscard d'Estaing's election to the presidency in 1974, and the rise of the Union of the Left alliance of Socialists, Communists, and a tiny center-Left Radical Socialist splinter grouping. François Mitterrand, heretofore a marked and "outdated" man of the Fourth Republic, now seemed destined for a significant role in the Left's struggle against de Gaulle, gaullism, and the "regime of personal power." The 1965 election had, as French journalist Serge July wrote, made of François Mitterrand definitively a man of the Left. He was now persuaded that he was the providential leader who could unite the Left's disparate forces in a challenge to gaullism, thus carrying the Left to power.[28] Even if he was not an ideological Socialist by being true to his genuine convictions, a liberal parliamentary republican such as Mitterrand was on the Left. In the pure logic of politics, de Gaulle's very strength, gaullism's hegemony, and the majority voting of presidential government pushed the "enemy brother" Socialists and Communists together, in spite of all that still divided them.

Did François Mitterrand become a genuine Socialist in some sense at this time? Was it Saul of Tarsus's conversion or Henry IV's cynical calculation that "Paris is worth a Mass"? Two views coexist. The first one portrays Mitterrand as a shameless opportunist acting hypocritically out of personal ambition. It stresses motives and origins, emphasizing where Mitterrand had come from, his right-wing youth, his Vichy passage, and his own words: "I was not born a leftist," he once said, "much less a socialist."[29] Or, as he said another time, "At the university I was intimidated by my socialist classmates. I was familiar with scholastic talk but put off by their vocabulary. It took me some time to see in their dialectic the kind of medieval recipes that I had been taught [as a Catholic and Frenchman]. It bothered me hearing the marxist left speak a French translated from German. Words ending in 'ion' and 'ism' scorched my ears, while I flattered myself with a classicism that seemed supremely revolutionary to me."[30] Origins and education, so this first view asserts, are everything or nearly so. Where you come from is what you are.

The other view of Mitterrand's socialist authenticity, an existentialist view, begins not from psychology but behavior. Whatever the genuine or self-deluding motives, one is what one does. Mitterrand's socialism is attested to by his left-wing strategy and his socialist experiment as president. Whatever the questions about his origins, in deeds he was ultimately more of a socialist, or perhaps a better phrasing would be a more effective socialist, than longtime Socialist party leaders with better ideological credentials.

Americans, focused on the cold war struggle between liberal and communist regimes, rarely knew much at that time about the huge differences between socialists and communists and often didn't know there were differences at all. But wherever there was a European-style struggle within the Left, meaning nearly everywhere else in the world, the conflict was a part of history. In Russia from 1917 to 1921, in Weimar Germany, in post-war Eastern Europe and elsewhere, the internecine struggles of communists, socialists, and fascists ended in murderous outcomes.

In short, the French Left's electoral cooperation and then political program alliance in the 1960s and 1970s was always deeply ambivalent on both sides. On the one hand, there was the common goal of defeating gaullism and going to government; on the other hand was the permanent struggle between Socialists and Communists for dominance on the Left. The domestic geopolitics of this struggle were clear. So long as an East-West cold war continued, and so long as the French Communists were Stalinist and stronger than the Socialists, the French Left was unelectable. Indeed the French Communist leadership *preferred* their "splendid isolation" in opposition because, first, they hesitated to govern a capitalist country and, second, they couldn't attempt revolution, blocked by France's position inside the NATO bloc and by Moscow's cold war bargain with Washington not to disrupt the European equilibrium. The Soviets, in other words, reliably accepted the tacit cold war arrangement in which each superpower and each military alliance kept its hands off the other's half of Europe (e.g., Western nonintervention in East Berlin in 1953, Hungary and Poland in 1956, Czechoslovakia in 1968). The French Communist threat to French society was thus full of dual strategies, doubts, and paradoxes.[31] So, therefore, was necessarily the strategy of alliance with the

Communists proposed by Mitterrand. Double-dealing on both sides, seeking a common victory leading to the other's defeat, was the name of the Socialist-Communist game.

Encouraged by the 1965 results, in December 1966 the loose grouping of parties that had supported Mitterrand a year earlier (called the Fédération de la gauche démocrate et socialiste, or FGDS) signed a new agreement for reciprocal electoral standdowns in the 1967 legislative elections. The SFIO Socialists, under Mitterrand's influence (though he was not yet a party member), were breaking their refusal to deal with the Communists. Mitterrand's growing importance for the Socialists indicated the means of his advance—he offered electoral success.

The payoff was prompt. The FGDS parties won twenty-eight additional seats; the Communists, who benefited a bit more than the others from having allies in the majority voting, thirty-two seats. Besides their mutual rejection of gaullism, however, almost everything still separated the two camps: NATO, the Common Market, and underneath both the chasm of political and ideological culture that separated liberals and communists.

Mitterrand and the Socialists did promise to abandon the *force de frappe,* the French nuclear deterrence force de Gaulle was building. Here they agreed with the PCF, which defined French nuclear weapons demagogically as just another expression of capitalist imperialism, to which Soviet nuclear weapons were only a just response. Mitterrand, who understood little about strategic matters at this point, may genuinely have believed that the French nuclear force was a bad thing, or at least an unnecessary thing. In addition the Socialists themselves had an anti-capitalist and partially pacifist political heritage, which led to rejecting the nuclear force. In any case Mitterrand, by the late 1970s, would revise his ideas about strategy and the nuclear force.

MAY 1968: POPULAR REVOLT, MITTERRAND'S MISAPPREHENSION

That François Mitterrand's Vichy past and the Observatory affair had been so buried when he emerged as a presidential leader is remarkable. Even more so is the collective amnesia in France's political memory of the monumental student-worker revolt of May 1968, the "elusive revolution" as the French thinker Raymond Aron called it.[32]

The very meaning of the social rebellion of May 1968 remains a great but almost forgotten controversy in French political culture even today. No one discusses it anymore, and someone should. Its ethos was left-wing, anarchist, anti-gaullist, anti-authority, and often generous and joyous; nevertheless, many, probably most, of its student rebels and striking salaried workers were, strictly speaking, bourgeois, people who were carried off in a political whirlwind. But even those responsible for the historic rebellion have seemed reluctant ever since to take responsibility for the events of May or to speak about its long-term significance. The French, to adapt Tocqueville's well-known phrase from *The Old Regime and the Revolution,* often seem as surprised as are foreigners by what they do. In the end, with almost no one to defend May 1968, it is as if its great "events" had been an immature, embarrassing, and even shameful French "psychodrama," the classic French susceptibility to civic irresponsibility analyzed by Aron and Tocqueville.

May 1968 was in essence a totally unexpected rebellion of society against the French state, meaning both against de Gaulle and gaullism, and against the insufferable sense of superiority of the French *étatiste* bureaucratic elites and government civil service administrations. May 1968 began coyly as a student strike over limited parietal visiting hours in the dormitories at one experimental university, Nanterre, in the northwest working-class suburbs of Paris. The student revolt caught fire, spreading all through the public university system and then tempting huge numbers of workers to join in by occupying factories and other workplaces.

Half of France's entire salaried work force, over 9 million people, including the great mass of "bourgeois" employees, not to mention much of the government-run radio and TV network news staff, and nearly all of the universities except for the natural science faculties and the *grandes écoles,* were soon striking. The country was brought to a near stop for two weeks. Although student strikes and worker rebellions occurred also in the United States, Japan, Mexico, and in other countries, the French rebellion of May 1968 was, in its extent, duration, and intensity, the only episode of its kind in an advanced western industrialized democracy since World War II. It was conceivable only in France, not quite finished with its two-century history of rebellions, revolutions, and counterrevolutions, and with the cycles of French political "exceptionalism."

François Mitterrand reacted characteristically and thus unsuccessfully in this crisis. Guiding mass social movements and crises was not his talent; he distrusted them too much.

He acted precipitously to try to take political-electoral advantage of a social rebellion. Stretching his role of unofficial neoleader of a united Left, he called a press conference on May 29, at which he announced demagogically that "the state no longer exists" and that a "provisional government" to replace de Gaulle was necessary, which should be formed by the Left. The degree of social dislocation did make it seem for a time that de Gaulle was undoubtedly finished, but to imagine a revolutionary situation and a provisional government in the prosperous, post-industrial, NATO and EEC-ensconced France of 1968 sounded like a man in a self-indulgent dream of 1848, which was one of Mitterrand's favorite historical references.

Mitterrand suggested that Pierre Mendès France could be prime minister in the provisional government, although he had not discussed the matter with Mendès. The latter reacted badly, as was to be expected. He, Mitterrand, would prepare to run for the presidency, "which would not be long in becoming vacant," referring to the demands for de Gaulle's resignation. If Mendès France seemed once again to be letting the train go through the station, François Mitterrand's comportment seemed to be sheer opportunism, or at best an attempt to pursue the right move at the wrong time.

Despite Mitterrand's desire to appear sympathetic to slogans such as "Put the Imagination in Power!," he disdained the utopian young "revolutionaries" of 1968. In a savage passing remark he said that, whatever their revolutionary pretentiousness of the moment, one could see in them "future barristers." Always preferring institutions to movements, François Mitterrand almost completely "missed" making something of May 1968's massive energy and rejection of de Gaulle. He felt enthusiasm neither for its anarchism—genuine or hypocritical—nor for the generous bread-and-butter "Grenelle Agreements" that induced the trade unions, and especially the Communist-led CGT, to wind down the factory strikes, which took some hard disciplining of Trotskyite and anarcho-syndicalist strike leaders. The Communist reputation was further tarnished when journalists learned soon after that the CGT leader, Georges Séguy, had been secretly negotiating early on with Pompidou government representatives for an end to the strikes in exchange for huge pay increases and other benefits. This moment closed a two-decades old argument over whether the French Communists remained revolutionaries or not. It was unlikely that they would ever see a more propitious situation for seizing power than May 1968, and instead they acted conservatively. Even CGT participation in the strikes was extended more by mass enthusiasm at the working-class base than by orders coming from the Communist hierarchy above.

De Gaulle and the gaullist apparatus survived this near-death experience, although at one point the government ministers actually packed up their files in preparation for abandoning their offices. Wiretaps showed the Communist party leadership was discussing, quite ambivalently, whether to try to seize the Élysée palace; they decided against it. (They were heavily restrained by secret contacts with a highly cautious Moscow.) De Gaulle himself, disoriented like this for the first time in his seventy-eight years, feared that he and his family would be taken hostage in the Élysée palace. He seemed to have lost his nerve and believed the situation was irretrievably lost. On both grounds France's president disappeared from the Élysée suddenly for twenty-four hours. Later it became known that he had fled to the French military headquarters in Baden-Baden, West Germany, where he was persuaded to return to Paris.

De Gaulle gave a television address on his return, the "chienlit" speech, which sparked a mass response from the French people, many of whom had not been on strike, and others, again to use Tocqueville, who were surprised at what they had done and who were anxious now to call the whole thing off. Even the Communists, above all the Communists, who needed to show that they still controlled the labor movement, wanted a settlement, and they had the juicy "Grenelle Agreements" as the sign of supposed Communist intransigent bargaining.

De Gaulle, abandoning an earlier idea for a referendum, his typical reaction to a crisis, instead called snap legislative elections for June 1968. In a classic French paradox, the revolutionaries of May turned around in June to give the gaullists an electoral triumph, with the gaullist party itself handed an absolute majority, the first time any single party had won such a majority in the Fifth Republic. Because of the demobilization of left-wing voters—out of political fatigue, disappointment at not having "changed society," and out of shock and embarrassment at having destabilized the country and risked its booming economic situation—the French Left was badly beaten. The non-Communist Left FGDS parties, Mitterrand's coalition, held only 57 seats, as opposed to its outgoing 118, and the Communists were cut from 73 to 33. In a way, the French Communist party at 33 seats was in itself a kind of revolutionary change! The PCF would have a hard time controlling left-wing strategies if it had such little parliamentary strength. Perhaps the Communists would even lose the veto power they held by virtue of being necessary to any Socialist strategy.

Nevertheless François Mitterrand continued to pursue the strategy of left-wing alliance. Socialists and Communists found their common electoral interests increasing as the two parties became more balanced. Believing that his legitimacy had been lost in May 1968, Charles de Gaulle found confirmation a year later when he resigned the presidency in April 1969 after losing a referendum. He was not constitutionally obliged to resign, but de Gaulle wanted to quit the stage of French politics in a memorable way, leaving an example of a man not bound to power and office, but to the interests of France. After the rescue of de Gaulle and the gaullists in June 1968, a decline of gaullist enthusiasm during Georges Pompidou's succession of de Gaulle led to the election of the first non-gaullist president of the Fifth Republic, Valéry Giscard d'Estaing, in 1974.

For the 1969 presidential election, which Pompidou won, the Communists had suggested to the non-Communist Left a joint candidate, François Mitterrand, who was still not a member of the Socialist party! The Communists preferred not to run their own candidate because a presidential election, which focused on single candidates, was the least advantageous for them. They were a party of party politics, so to speak, not a grouping built around a leader like the gaullists or Giscard d'Estaing's coalition.

But the Socialists refused the Communist offer, and the Socialist Gaston Defferre, L'Express magazine's "Monsieur X" of 1964, ran a "third-force" noncommunist Left campaign, meaning no official alliance with the Communists. Mitterrand remained out of the election. The Communists were obliged to run their own candidate for the first time in a presidential election. Jacques Duclos, a Comintern-trained Stalinist who had begun his career as a pastry chef and had been the target of the "homing pigeon arrest" in the early 1950s, on the first ballot won a surprising 22 percent against a disastrous 5 percent for the SFIO Defferre.

This 1969 result seemed a historic defeat for the Socialists, at least for those who refused an alliance with the PCF. The catastrophic loss only fortified François Mitterrand's arguments for a united Left strategy. The 1969 result showed that left-wing voters were endorsing unity, and that Socialist voters who favored a united Left strategy would vote Communist to punish the SFIO Socialist party leadership for refusing to accept what the rank and file wanted.

The fact that left-wing unity was such a popular idea with the voters had, it goes without saying, much to do with the attractiveness of Mitterrand as a candidate and as a strategist. The Socialist leadership was being forced, willy-nilly, to look increasingly to Mitterrand as their potential leader. In any case Georges Pompidou won the 1969 election easily, serving until his untimely death in 1974.

In 1969 the SFIO, its resolve strengthened by defeat, began the transition from elephant to thoroughbred. It changed its name, from the SFIO to the simpler, modernized PS, Socialist party, and began to look toward the future rather than to argue about its past. The new PS was, in program terms, not much advanced over the SFIO, but under its transition leader, Alain Savary, the policy of electoral alliance with the Communists was accepted as permanent. Defferre's 5 percent result had made even the most complacent old Socialist "barons" admit the need for change.

It took two more years for Mitterrand to win the new PS over to his cause. At the June 1971 PS party convention in the town of Épinay, Mitterrand, by using thoroughly prepared networks and classic party factional tactics, ousted the transition leadership and merged his own small organization with the Socialist party. The "Épinay party" was born.

Mitterrand bested Alain Savary in the contest for election to the position of first secretary, in effect the leader's title. The contest had a personal as well as political feud in it: Alain Savary was the PSA leader who in 1959 had blackballed Mitterrand from the small party's membership, saying he "wouldn't accept anyone who had worn Vichy's francisque medal."

Mitterrand at Épinay had the support of factions led by future ministers Pierre Mauroy and Gaston Defferre, as well as the left-wing CERES, a very French operation of semi-Marxist, statist Jacobin republicans, whose leading figure was Jean-Pierre Chevènement. The presidency, the former small party man Mitterrand might have said, would be worth years of factional fighting in a large party.

Under Mitterrand's influence the Épinay party soon adopted a much more socialist-sounding policy menu than its old party documents. *Changer la vie* (meaning "To Change Society" or "To Change Our Way of Living"), the 1972 book-length full party program, contained all sorts of proposals for economic democracy, empowerment of citizens, decentralization, workers' self-management, quality of life changes, and a new internationalism.

This party document is important for two reasons. It shows that François Mitterrand immediately led the refounded Socialist party leftward, whether or not he genuinely believed everything in the new, more socialist program. Second, *Changer la vie* was quite clearly a more ideological socialism than the old SFIO's brand. This made possible joint policies, even a common program, with the Communists, not just mutual electoral help.

THE PARADOXICAL
CONSERVATISM OF FRENCH COMMUNISM

Obviously interesting is the question "What did the French Communists, still Stalinist, still tied root and branch to the Soviet Union, want in their alliance with the Socialists?" Essentially they, exactly like Mitterrand, wanted to manipulate any united Left coalition to stay on top, while at the same time rebuilding the Communist party's internal erosion during the last phases of the cold war. Georges Marchais and the other Communist leaders knew that underneath a facade of false statistics, party membership and other forms of Communist politics—trade-union, newspaper circulation, attendance at cell meetings—had been declining for years. This was not surprising for a party that had no real strategy for power, only its "seige" position of defiant isolation in

France, obliged to defend the Soviet Union and to act as an arm of Soviet interests in a radically hostile environment. The PCF's revolutionary credentials were being questioned by extreme-left Trotskyites, Maoistes, "Situationists," and the like; the party was increasingly dependent for its political and electoral prestige on an intimidating but frustrated trade union, the CGT, and on the PCF's "fortress" municipal governments. Signs of erosion through the movement's domestic isolation and containment were everywhere.

Since the end of World War II and their ouster from the Ramadier government in 1947 at the outbreak of the cold war, the French Communists had husbanded their electoral capital, preventing the socialist Left from the kind of place in national politics held by the German SPD and British Labour. For decades the golden rule of French politics had been that the Left could win power neither with the Communist party nor without it, and the French Right and French business maintained good enough relations with Moscow to keep a Soviet blessing on this arrangement. Moscow literally "advised" the French Communists that international communist interests were better served by French conservative governments than by the "destabilization" of France that a Left government would create.[33]

What was to be done by the French Communists, situated "in," but not "of" French society?, as French sociologist (and former French Communist official) Annie Kriegel put it. They were the most significant political force still contesting the Fifth Republic's legitimacy (and capitalism as a whole), yet their own illegitimate nature meant that a left-wing alternative government seemed to be impossible. In other words, the PCF's conservative, in some ways reactionary, strategy thinking kept the Left at bay; there was a tacit, objective alliance between gaullists and Communists, in which the former ruled the country while the latter ruled the Left.

In their own minds, the naive French Communists, essentially the majority, played a revolutionary waiting game, acting conservatively while earnestly expecting either the crisis of French and Western capitalism or some sort of Soviet arrival, whose manner they couldn't predict. In the 1970s the idea of growing Soviet power in the world seemed quite obvious. One only had to look at various parts of Africa (Ethiopia, Somalia, Mozambique, Angola), and the "decade of ungovernability" and "crisis of democracy" in the Western world to see portentous signs of Western decline and world communist expansion. The Soviet invasion of Afghanistan in 1979 was seen at the time as the beginning of yet a new phase, perhaps the achievement of world hegemony by the Soviet superpower.

The PCF strategy of tacit alliance with French conservatives could work, however, only so long as the French Socialists remained moribund. But if the

Socialists could revive themselves, the French Communist strategy of "splendid isolation" would no longer work. The French Communists would either have to evolve or wither; Stalinist protection of the Soviet Communist "bastion" was no longer a sufficient motivating force to maintain French communism's "assets," first of all the enthusiasm of party activists.

François Mitterrand's arrival as PS leader thus gave the French Communists a chance at evolution, while simultaneously posing a very dangerous threat to them. The rest of France could only hope that however events turned on the Left, the consequences would not be disastrous for the country.

Did Mitterrand, one of the few politicians who realized French communism's paradoxical conservatism, prefer its decline, or, if it were possible, a democratic, so-called "Eurocommunist" evolution? That is no easy question. The answer is probably that, while he had to prefer his own party, he was prepared to deal with either Socialist supremacy or a Socialist-Communist balance. While the Communist party leadership was on the whole mediocre, demagogic, and had been educated all their lives to disdain social democrats, the Communist voters and party activists at the base could, in certain circumstances, become a vital support of left-wing policies and governments. These people at the rank-and-file level were often the Communists who remained true to the initial motivations— the desire to move forward with historical progress, and to help others. The tragedy was that when Communist activists were taken up into the party apparatus, their initial enthusiasm and energy to do good was twisted, as they moved into positions of responsibility, into a ruthless compulsion to do what the party said, and not to ask themselves questions.

Certainly so long as the Soviet Union remained neo-Stalinist, Mitterrand preferred the PCF's decline. But a genuine democratic, liberal evolution of the Soviet Union and of the PCF would permit genuine left-wing alliance in France, perhaps even "organic unity," the classic left-wing code word for refounding a single, unified left-wing party. A single Left party, which the SFIO had been from 1905 to the Communist breakaway in 1920, would repair the historic split of French socialism at the Tours party convention in that year, over whether or not to accept Bolshevism and to join Moscow's Third International. For a few years, say 1973-75, talk of "organic unity," of a potential fusion of the PS and PCF, was not irrelevant.

Mitterrand himself was given a boost in prestige at this time by his election as vice president of the Socialist International. In early 1971 he had paid a solidarity visit to Chile, and met Salvador Allende Gossens, a center-Left politician who had been elected president with a plurality (i.e., not a majority), and who was leading a radical experiment for a "Chilean road to socialism," based on a coalition of Socialists, Communists, and his own small center-Left

Radical Socialist party. Mitterrand observed the Allende experiment with admiration for its daring and worries about where it was headed. Indeed it ended in disaster with a military coup (eventually producing Pinochet), and Salvador Allende himself dying under a military attack of the presidential palace, in what was alleged a suicide. Off and on François Mitterrand wondered whether he would become the French Allende, a victim of the "American imperialism" (including CIA help to the military putschists) he believed was responsible for Allende's destruction.

In the Socialist International his closest sympathies were with moderates such as the German Willy Brandt (who was conducting an audacious West German "Ostpolitik"), the Austrian Bruno Kreisky, and the Israeli Shimon Peres. Mitterrand's willingness to deal with the French Communists was understood and accepted by these associates, so long as his anti-communism was unquestionable in principle and vigilant in practice. An exception was the German defense minister and later chancellor Helmut Schmidt, who believed Mitterrand to be a dangerous politician. When they worked together in 1981-82 as staunch NATO allies in the Euromissile crisis, however, Schmidt's view of Mitterrand was altered.

The years 1972 to 1978 were dominated in French domestic politics by three factors.

The first was Georges Pompidou's sudden death on April 2, 1974, which meant a new president would be elected in May. Valéry Giscard d'Estaing, finance minister to both de Gaulle and Pompidou, though not himself a gaullist, won the candidacy on the Right when the gaullist Jacques Chirac supported him unexpectedly against his fellow gaullist Jacques Chaban-Delmas. The deal was that Giscard d'Estaing would name Jacques Chirac prime minister if Giscard won, which is, indeed, what happened. On the Left, Mitterrand had expected to run in 1976 with, he thought, a good chance of winning. The year 1974, he said later, was just too soon. The political stage was not quite set. This was correct. Giscard, the first non-gaullist president, won by the narrowest of margins on the second ballot in 1974 against Mitterrand, 50.81 percent to 49.19. For Mitterrand and the Socialists, Pompidou's unexpected exit from the scene had shifted the strategy from a highly likely Mitterrand presidential victory in 1976 to a parliamentary election in 1978, when, in the case of a left-wing victory, a left-wing prime minister (Mitterrand) would have to contend with President Giscard d'Estaing in the as yet untried situation of "cohabitation." The cohabitation question was not yet answered in French politics: If the president and the prime minister are not of the same political tendency, who will ultimately rule? What will happen to the overpowerful presidency when a parliamentary majority can overturn his chosen candidate as prime minister?

Second, President Valéry Giscard d'Estaing's domestic projects were deflected by the 1974 recession, which resulted from the first of two 1970s oil price spikes inflicted by the Organization of Petroleum Exporting Countries (OPEC) on Western economies. As opposed to German and Japanese deflationary policies, Giscard maintained relative domestic prosperity through monetary and fiscal policies that put off the moment of reckoning. Giscard hoped the international economy would bounce back, saving him from taking responsibility for the fact that a man of supposed financial conservatism was really governing the money with a political mentality. The second oil price spike in 1979 wrong-footed him, however, and his defeat by Mitterrand in 1981 had as one cause the economic problems which could no longer be kept away from the French economy.

The third factor was a series of significant developments on the French Left. In summer 1972 a radical "Common Program of Government" was negotiated between the Mitterrand-led PS, the Communist party, and the splinter so-called Left-wing Radical party. It was supposedly a statement of what a Union of the Left coalition would do in government. The program began naturally enough with the need for electoral cooperation in order to oust the gaullists (Pompidou was still president).

The Common Program went on, however, to add an agenda of socialist policies. The most daunting were large-scale nationalizations in banking and industry. Nationalizing corporations sounded to most French conservatives and allied governments like a plan for Sovietization. The plan for nationalization of banks was less-well understood but more significant. Taking control of the remaining private investment banks in France (75 percent of the banking sector already belonged to the state in the form of the "big three," the Crédit Lyonnais, the Banque Nationale de Paris, and the Crédit Agricole) would give the state near total control of French domestic investment, thus loans to industry and business.

And since the state could control or regulate what it did not own outright, a macro-socialist economic plan would be possible. This was yet another Marxist-sounding element of the Common Program.

However, the French Communists, at least for the present they said, agreed in the program not to challenge the Common Market and France's membership in NATO. This Communist concession was hinged on the goal of "democratization" of the Common Market and the reduction of NATO and the Warsaw Pact.

At first the Common Program was hardly taken seriously outside the Left. It was laughed off as irrelevant, if only because the Socialists and Communists hated each other. An exception was Raymond Aron, the dean of

French liberal intellectuals and a man whose own memory stretched back to his studies in Weimar Germany, when Hitler's writings had been laughed off. Aron regularly criticized the substance of the Common Program:

> The Common Program is a typical example of an attempt at a kind of socialism between social democracy and Soviet-style socialism. The social democratic governments which have been durably successful have all subordinated nationalization of the means of production to the more important criterion of effectiveness. . . . In a less-developed country, state ownership of an industrial sector, often narrow, can be justified. In France, with its present level of development, the nationalizations listed in the Common Program go far beyond the level which is tolerable for a country which wants to remain inside the European Community, itself an integral part of the Atlantic community. To use a Marxist formula, after a certain point quantity is transformed into quality. . . . Desirable or not, the nationalization of a firm in a sector which remains competitive doesn't compromise the sector as such. The nationalization of gas and electricity industries provided, at the beginning, technical and economic advantages. The state-owned sector has a tendency to overinvestment, and in that there is a risk of lessening capital available for the private sector. As for the Common Program, it foresees first nationalization of the entire banking and credit system, then that of nine big industrial groups, then a threat of nationalization of any other enterprise, of whatever nature.[34]

In 1977, Aron predicted what would happen if the Left alliance won the 1978 parliamentary elections with Giscard d'Estaing still as president: "A government led by François Mitterrand, under the presidency of Valéry Giscard d'Estaing, will inevitably fail. One of the two presidents will chase the other out. If François Mitterrand succeeds in chasing out the president of the Republic, his experiment will last longer and cost more."[35] For once Aron was wrong. He might have been correct about what would have happened if the first cohabitation had confronted Mitterrand and Giscard d'Estaing in 1978, but he was undeniably wrong about the Mitterrand-Chirac cohabitation that occurred in 1986.

Rank-and-file activists were enthusiastic about the left-wing parties' joint program. Party leaders, however, distrusted each other's intentions.

What did François Mitterrand really want? What did he really plan? At a Socialist International meeting in June 1972 in Vienna, only a few days after signing the Common Program, Mitterrand quite clearly revealed his game to his social democratic associates: "Our fundamental objective is to rebuild a great Socialist party on the terrain occupied by the Communist party, showing that of the five million Communist voters today, three million might vote Socialist. This is the reason for the [Common Program] agreement." Inside the secrecy of the PCF Central Committee headquarters, Georges Marchais that same month warned, in a speech kept secret for three years, that the Communists were not fooled by Mitterrand and the Socialists. They were, he said, "still fundamentally social democratic and reformist," which is, or was, the worst communist insult of a fellow leftist.

Mitterrand's own commitment to the Common Program was a subject of controversy. His motives were complex, it goes without saying, and not entirely Machiavellian.

The 7 percent economic growth rate used in the program was already high compared even to the roaring sixties. It became a mockery after the 1974 oil price hike created a recession in the West, yet it had the undeniable virtue of making the Left's social promises and nationalization plans work out on paper. So the Common Program was never revised after the 1972 negotiations, either in its economics or in other respects. It remained a sort of white elephant that Socialists and Communists used for different purposes.

Mitterrand emphasized that state ownership in industry and business was a venerable French tradition, from Colbert to de Gaulle, and the Left would nationalize in order to create an economic plan, not to collectivize society. He asked how he could be thought unpatriotic or crazy for proposing what de Gaulle had done at the Liberation—nationalizations of electricity, gas, rail transport, and the Renault auto works due to Nazi collaboration. If new nationalizations were necessary to prevent French enterprises from being bought up by foreign capital, this should, he argued, be a consensus policy that all French patriots could support. Party factions struggled over whether nationalizations had to be done at 51 percent (the Rocard "second left" position), or 100 percent (the Communist position and that of the PS left wing, the CERES).

Mitterrand surely doubted the realism of *autogestion,* a vague, May 1968–type idea for which the Socialist-leaning CFDT trade union was responsible. It meant some modernized version of old ideas for self-management in factories and self-government in neighborhoods. The long LIP watch factory takeover by its workers had enthused Socialists who still believed in May 1968, and *autogestion* was an attractive ideological concept that the Socialists could use against Communist concepts like the centralized socialist command economy and the hoary "dictatorship of the proletariat." Mitterrand's delegation of the Marxist-leaning Chevènement to lead the PS Common Program negotiating team also served to ensure a radical-sounding document. This bit of Machiavellianism indicates not that Mitterrand himself was being radicalized but rather that he believed that a quick, radical agreement between Socialists and Communists would foster left-wing activist enthusiasm for coming elections and for renewal of the Socialist party. That was the main point. To put all the disagreements on the table right at the start in order to fight the Communists to the finish would be self-defeating for the non-Communist Left and for him. Mitterrand had to have not only the courage of his convictions, but also that of his strategy.

The key years were 1972 through 1977, during which time the Union of the Left as a whole made constant electoral gains and party memberships soared. In spring 1977, the left-wing coalition seemed well on its way to ousting the conservatives in the parliamentary elections of 1977.

But this period was also the time of the most bitter struggle between Socialists and Communists to dominate the Left. The Socialists under Mitterrand's leadership were reviving, and thirty years of Communist hegemony on the French Left were at risk. Mitterrand's strategy worked, and precisely in the sense that nearly all the electoral gains for the Left were gains by the Socialists. In the 1973 parliamentary elections, the PS got 21 percent, a brilliant rebound from the dismal 5 percent score for the 1969 Defferre presidential candidacy. More importantly, this was a mere point behind the Communists. The two left-wing parties were equalized for the first time since 1936, that is, for the first time since before World War II, when the Communists, who had been a splinter group in the 1920s, grew along with the fascist menace and when Soviet prestige was in the ascendant. The usual Socialist level for two decades had been around 15 percent. The Communists were frustrated and worried.

In local and regional elections in 1976-1977 the PS broke through, shattering the myth of a natural Communist superiority on the Left. But the Communists still dominated France's factories (Communist party cells), the trade union movement (the CGT), and local governments (especially the Red Belt working-class suburbs around Paris and the "Red" agricultural areas in central France and the Mediterranean region). Socialist CFDT factory organizing was a success, its "self-management socialism" doctrine gaining ground quickly against old-school Communist ideas of Soviet-style central planning.

The Socialists were on the move at the Communists' expense. Alliance was working, but mainly for one party at the expense of the other. The Communists in the 1930s had talked aggressively of "plucking the Socialist chicken"; now Mitterrand's Socialists were nicely plucking the PCF chicken. The Communist leaders faced a decision: whether, if the current trends continued, they would accept a left-wing victory that would put themselves in a subordinate position, or fight in what could be the historic defeat of French communism.

So Mitterrand's strategy for victory depended on one element he couldn't control: how the French Communist leaders would react to falling behind, to losing their much-vaunted "vanguard" role and becoming a junior partner to the Socialists. The Communists had tried all sorts of political face-lifting to become more attractive to the voters. They had tried "Eurocommunism," meaning liberalized new doctrines fixed up with the Italian (PCI) and Spanish (PCE) communist parties; warming up to liberal democracy, to the European Community, and even to NATO. They said the party's goal was no longer Soviet-style socialism but "socialism in French colors." The Soviet Union had been irrevocably revealed in Aleksandr Solzhenitsyn's *Gulag Archipelago,* the French translation of which in the mid-1970s confronted French left-wing intellectuals as never before with their illusions regarding communist society, a reckoning that political scientist Pierre Hassner called the "Solzhenitsyn effect." The facade of "really existing socialism" in the Soviet bloc was lifted even in the fashionable arrondissements of left-wing Paris.

For the first time "the Party," as the Communist party had always been designated, criticized Soviet political repression. Its leaders, its newspapers, and its journals for activists began to notice the costs and injustices in Moscow's rigid control of society. In 1975 the PCF had endorsed the Portuguese Communist party's Leninist strategy in the Revolution of the Carnations, but in January 1976, at the time of the PCF's twenty-second party congress, General Secretary Georges Marchais announced a new view of socialism: "There is no democracy and liberty if there is no pluralism of political parties, and if there is no freedom of speech. . . . We consider that the principles we enunciate concerning socialist democracy are of universal value. It is clear we have a disagreement with the Soviet Communist party about this question."[36]

The French Communists even boycotted a few meetings with the Soviet Communist party, and on the eve of the 1976 party congress Georges Marchais announced a bombshell: The French Communist party was dropping the "dictatorship of the proletariat" concept. Whether all this was tactics or strategy was probably unclear even to the French Communist leaders themselves.

Mitterrand's view of the Communist leaders was frank disdain. "My great luck," he said, "is the intellectual mediocrity of the Communist leaders. Look at them: Marchais, Plissonnier, Laurent and the others. Not one of them is better than the others. They are easy to manipulate. All their reactions are predictable. They're programmed. If I had to deal with leaders like the Italian Communists things would have been much more difficult." As for Marchais on Mitterrand, the former told dinner guests, "Every time I see Mitterrand I'm tempted to put my hand over his mouth."[37]

The French Communist leaders then made a secret decision. Since the Union of the Left was profiting the Socialists more than them, the Communists would break it up, sabotage it, and ruin the Left's chance to win the elections of

March 1978 in order to save themselves. The Communists, constantly raising the ideological stakes by updating the Common Program, would maneuver the Socialists into a split in the name of realism, then blame them for destroying the alliance. This would damage the Socialist party's credibility and the Communists could reappear as the only "serious" socialist party. In other words, the Communist leaders had to ensure that the Left did *not* win the 1978 elections, because otherwise they would be obliged by their own rank and file and by their own past promises to join a Socialist-led government as a junior partner.

Inside the Socialist leadership, Mitterrand had always warned that the Communists might do something unpredictable if and when they were cornered. In Franz-Olivier Giesbert's words, "The Communists became convinced that their salvation required breaking the alliance." But with Communist secrecy of decision-making and "democratic centralist" party discipline against leaks, the reason for the sudden new Communist intransigence was not perceived immediately.[38]

Thus in 1977 the Communists insisted on "updating" the Common Program. For the Socialists, not to redo the Common Program's economic promises would, given the recessions of the 1970s, have been irresponsible. But to open a new negotiation with the Communists was politically dangerous, because it made keeping the alliance hostage to a Communist strategy. The new balance of forces, with the Socialists leading the Communists in votes and in parliament, meant a bidding war to see who could appear the most generous and radical. The Socialists wanted no new negotiations, no new program. They wanted to maintain or increase their new electoral superiority and then pick and choose in the 1972 Common Program if the Left formed a government.

But the Communists threatened to walk away from the alliance and so the Socialists had to begin a renegotiation of the Common Program in April 1977. Representatives of the PS, the PCF, and the small Radical-Socialist party began talks, which lasted off and on for five months. The Communists insisted on the hardest-line positions and totally unrealistic goals—demanding, for example, 100 percent state ownership of nationalized enterprises, instead of 51 percent, and, a mindboggling new demand, nationalization of all the subsidiaries as well as parent companies of the target corporations. This "detail" was a subject not even broached in 1972!

Left-wing public opinion, not privy to the secret PCF game, thought the Communists were just being themselves—tough, militant, Sovietized. Few could imagine the PCF leaders were out to sabotage the alliance.

François Mitterrand had a firm response: "Yes to the Common Program, no to a Communist program!" But the Socialists, though stronger electorally, were in the weaker negotiating position this time. The Communists wanted out, but they remained necessary to a left-wing, that is, a Socialist-led electoral majority. The Communists, Mitterrand perceived, wanted above all to avoid a possible historic defeat by the Socialists and were fully capable of treachery in an attempt to cut their losses. Communist leadership betrayal was the one element Mitterrand could not control.

At a negotiating meeting on September 22, 1977, the Communists achieved their goal, a crack-up of the Union of the Left in which they seemed no more responsible than the Socialists. They painted the Socialists as having "turned to the right," an old Communist point of attack against social democrats. Mitterrand appealed to Communist voters and activists, many of whom were convinced that a Communist and Socialist alliance was the only solution to the French Left's problems, each one to correct the defects of the other. "Many Communists understand," said Mitterrand, "that their leaders don't want alliance. But they believe in it, and they don't accept either that the French Left should be sacrificed to foreign interests."[39] This latter allusion was clear to the PCF's members. It referred not only to the PCF leaders' Stalinism but also to Moscow's desire *not* to have a left-wing government in France that would pursue a liberal socialism endorsed by the local, that is, French, Communists. For Moscow, Soviet-style socialism had to remain ideologically sacrosanct.

So the left-wing parties, which had seemed sure winners a year earlier, went to the 1978 parliamentary elections in conflict with each other, with hardly any contact at all between PS and PCF leaderships. Left-wing voters were disoriented, and the electoral support of each other's better-placed candidates was disrupted. The Communists paid the bigger price, with their worst showing since 1945. But the Socialists failed to surpass the 23 percent they had won at the previous election in 1973, a score much below the 28-30 percent the polls had forecast for them in the halcyon days of 1976-1977. Communists sometimes even voted for conservative candidates on the second ballot. Paul Laurent, one of the top PCF leaders, was overheard exclaiming with glee, "We have put together the conditions for a beautiful defeat!"[40] In context, the oddness of seeking defeat rather than victory was perfectly congruent with French communism's paradoxical conservatism; it was one local example of the failure of the entire Stalinist movement worldwide to reform itself before the collapse.

The conservatives were thus returned to power in parliament in 1978. Valéry Giscard d'Estaing was still president and François Mitterrand was again the loser. His political career even appeared over for good when a new, dynamic Michel Rocard openly challenged him for the Socialist party leadership, beginning with an election night speech questioning "archaic" socialism, a reference to Mitterrand and to the Common Program's anachronistic formulas.

For two years after the 1978 loss, Mitterrand maneuvered hard to stay in control of the Socialist party, attacked by openly arrogant Communist leaders and put into question by Rocard's early announcement that he would be a candidate for the 1981 presidential election. Rocard hoped with his quick start off the blocks to deter Mitterrand from running again. But after keeping his silence so long that he seemed to be abandoning the field, Mitterrand announced in November 1980 that he intended to be the PS presidential candidate in the spring 1981 elections. Rocard, disappointing his supporters deeply, then withdrew his own candidacy. Mitterrand's campaign program was a list of 110 Goals, many of which came from the "Common Program," although a few were new. With little prospect of winning or of resurrecting the Union of the Left, which he would have to do in order to form a government in his image, none of it seemed to matter very much.

VICTORY IS THE GREATEST UNCERTAINTY

In January 1981 Mitterrand's candidacy still seemed a loser. His own Socialist party was demoralized and ambivalent about his new run for the presidency. The French Communist leaders were gloating, having escaped the trap of his strategy. And he himself seemed, at sixty-four years old, a man whose time had past. However, by the time of the election three months later, Mitterrand's victory over the incumbent Giscard d'Estaing had become a foregone conclusion in the polls.

The first ballot, April 26, 1981, showed that Mitterrand had been able to take one-quarter of the Communist votes away from the Communist presidential candidate, Georges Marchais, who got only 15.5 percent instead of the party's usual 20 percent. Mitterrand himself even broke through the 25 percent barrier, beating the Socialist scores at the Liberation (23 percent) and in the 1956 Republican Front (18 percent), not to mention the 1978 score of 23 percent. And on the second ballot, May 10, 1981, he got a clear victory of 52 percent, despite more secret treachery inside the Communist party, urging its activists on to a cynical so-called "revolutionary vote for Giscard" to beat Mitterrand on the runoff ballot! For months, one close observer testified, "Georges Marchais had followed the same strategy of apparently seeking the defeat of Giscard but working underneath to sabotage Mitterrand."[41]

Giscard d'Estaing had seen the tide turn against him because of economic conditions, foreign policy miscues, and personal scandal.

The second oil price spike in 1979 caused renewed international recession in the West. It hit France, as well as other countries, hard this time, showing that Giscard d'Estaing could no longer insulate French economic conditions from those in France's partner countries. Mitterrand also took away Giscard d'Estaing's natural advantage of foreign policy in two new east/west crises: He savaged Giscard d'Estaing's naive reaction to the Soviet invasion of Afghanistan in late December 1979. Giscard made a hasty agreement to meet Leonid Brezhnev in Warsaw where, hoping to burnish his image as an international peacemaker, he took the bait of a vague Brezhnev reference to a Soviet pullback (that never materialized). Giscard touted this Brezhnev "concession" at the June economic summit in Venice. But the Soviet leader had only been referring to a rotation of troops, which actually meant a total increase in Soviet troops. Indeed Giscard had thought Brezhnev's agreement to the Warsaw meeting was a tacit reelection endorsement from Moscow, and thus extra French Communist votes at home, similar to what had occurred in the 1974 electoral campaign when the Soviet ambassador called on him during the electoral campaign. Mitterrand scathingly called Giscard d'Estaing "a little telegraph delivery boy" doing Moscow's work.

The second foreign policy issue was the rising Euromissile crisis, focused on the new Soviet SS-20 missiles. As opposed to Giscard's conciliatory statements consonant with his clear desire to court Moscow, François Mitterrand unexpectedly took a hardline against the Soviet missiles and endorsed the NATO plan to answer the Soviet challenge. All of a sudden the French Socialist candidate seemed to be stronger on defense than the conservative!

A third issue was the aura of scandal that had settled over Giscard d'Estaing's personal behavior. Titillating gossip in *le Tout-Paris* discussed the details of a 3:00 A.M. minor auto accident on the Champs-Élysées, involving a car with the president of France at the wheel and a female companion beside him. There were also more serious stories of sumptuous private vacations and hunting safaris in the Central African Republic. These included tales of personal gifts of diamonds from Emperor Jean-Bedel Bokassa. Bokassa's reputation combined unconscionable violations of human rights, personal acts of torture, and even, allegedly, acts of cannibalism. The French president, with his wife, was said to have illegally kept the diamonds. Several years earlier Mitterrand had written about the character of the president he would replace: "From a letter by Voltaire to his niece, Mme. Denis, I note this passage: 'I much resemble the man who dreamed he was falling from a bell-tower and who, finding himself in the middle of the air, said: "If only it lasts!" I don't know why the image of this sleeping fellow makes me think of Valéry Giscard d'Estaing.'"[42]

In the end, Giscard d'Estaing lost the campaign because he lost his reputation. François Mitterrand, against all logic, had seen victory drop into his lap. Carrying the cross (and the double-cross!) of French Communist support, thus was François Mitterrand elected president of France. Since most Communist voters chose Mitterrand against Giscard on the second ballot, as they had to if he was to win, having been counted out only a few months earlier he had now literally defeated the entire Right and the French Communist leadership simultaneously!

Truly nothing is ever permanently won or lost in politics.

Would François Mitterrand as president of the Fifth Republic prove to be of greater stature than the Fourth Republic's man about government? Did the shadow of the Observatory affair still lurk in his conscience? Would Mitterrand, as promised, take his Communist "ally" into the government? Could he survive a decade of left-wing policy promises for which the conditions no longer, by any stretch of the imagination, existed? And what about the reactions of France's European partners, of the United States, of the Soviet Union?

And the problem for Mitterrand was, in addition, that he had to do everything at once.

PART

THE DESIRE TO MAKE
HISTORY, 1981 TO 1995

TWO

CHAPTER 5

SOCIALISM

After it's over the Socialists will either put a monument in front of my house or they'll burn it down.

—François Mitterrand, 1982

MITTERRAND'S SOCIALISM:
AN UNCONVENTIONAL FAILURE

WHY FRANÇOIS MITTERRAND ACTUALLY WENT THROUGH with the "socialist experiment" upon his election in 1981 is an immense question. If there was a single answer, this author would give it, and we could go on to the next subject. There had to be many answers, of course. When there are more causes than are necessary to produce a certain end, social scientists call it an "overdetermined" result. A human fist causing someone else's broken nose is direct and sufficient causation of the given result. Social and political life is rarely, theoretically speaking, so simple and elegant.

Posing some of the pertinent questions about Mitterrand's socialist experiment will give an idea of the complexity of the analyses and answers to be suggested. Would it have been tried at all without Mitterrand, or was his presence a sine qua non condition, a factor without which it would not have occurred? And why, after all the often-disastrous socialist attempts to create qualitatively new and better societies had failed, did François Mitterrand and the French Socialist party keep their promise to test yet again this nineteenth-century dream? Why did Mitterrand and the Socialists risk domestic political and social peace, the equilibrium of a complex advanced economy, and France's international position in Europe and among the big Western allied countries?

Answers to such questions are found not in logic but in history. Not hindsight from the year 2000, with market economics having spread over the globe, but historical perspective is necessary to explain why, in 1981, France had a Union of the Left government composed of Socialists and Communists launching a new experiment in an old socialism. Looking forward from historic left-wing turning points—in 1917, 1920, 1936, 1947, 1958, 1972, and 1978—the Mitterrand experiment seems eminently comprehensible, if not inevitable. Could France and the French still make history? Could the Left in France still deliver on its historic role, or would its heroic self-image have to go quietly into a newer world than that in which it was born? Could France, despite everything, once again be a beacon to the world?

My own somewhat unconventional judgment of Mitterrand's socialist experiment has two points of departure. The first is not to overemphasize the failure, but to stress the various meanings in the fact that he and the French Socialist party actually kept his promise to try. The second is to examine why disillusionment was accepted so quietly by the Socialists and Communists, as if expected, which was surely the case for many of them. There was no hint of a revolutionary radicalization, unlike what happened to the Allende experiment that was outflanked by the MIR peasant revolutionaries in Chile in 1970-1973. Allende's fate and that of the "Chilean road to socialism" were, as already stated, still much on Mitterrand's mind when he arrived in power himself.

By its end, Mitterrand's socialist experiment had lasted barely eighteen months. In 1983 he took the final decision to break with socialist economics, and in 1984 he quietly replaced the Union of the Left government and its Job-like prime minister, Pierre Mauroy. The demoralized and diminished Communists quit the government. In Julius Friend's term, François Mitterrand "tiptoed away" from socialism, which he rarely spoke of again other than to explain to journalists why he wasn't speaking of it anymore. The French Left's great socialist experiment ended with a whimper, rather than in polarization or violence. That in itself was significant.

The financial and economic costs of the first two years were so high that only the most ideological anticapitalists among Socialists and Communists could protest its abandonment. The Socialists conceded failure without any formal public explanation from the president or the prime minister about what they were doing and what had gone wrong, let alone apologies for the miscalculations and risk-taking.

It was a costly way to dispel an illusion. But if realism came at a high economic price, the nation had avoided political violence and, in addition, finally dealt with the Left's lasting attachment to utopian thinking. In the process, France's "Communist problem" was dealt with in French (that is, democratic) terms through elections and the freedom of association, which also meant the freedom to exit. Internationally, the French Left's misadventure became an example for Socialist parties in other European countries—Spain, Greece, Italy—about to come to power. From today's viewpoint, the Mitterrand experiment, over by 1984, does not stand out as a prelude to the end of the cold war, let alone a preview of Gorbachev's misadventures. The collapse of Eastern Europe's communist regimes and the Soviet Union are unrelated to the problem of France between 1981 and 1984. The initial Mitterrand years seem a passing episode, a well-intentioned mistake in a much longer presidency. Yet historically what happened on the French Left had been much more than background noise in modern European history.

◆　◆　◆

In electing Mitterrand as president in May 1981, the French voters did not explicitly give a mandate for radical change. They were quite familiar with François Mitterrand's Union of the Left strategy, but Socialist and Communist leaders had hardly spoken to each other since the falling-out and defeat in the parliamentary elections of 1977-78. No one could be sure what result a new parliamentary election would give, if, as was likely, Mitterrand dissolved the sitting conservative parliament and called the voters quickly. Moreover, Mitterrand's presidential victory over Giscard d'Estaing was solid but not overwhelming.

But Mitterrand's presidential victory and snap dissolution of parliament brought the possibility, steadily stronger, of a left-wing victory in elections scheduled for June 1981. The voters, faced with the likelihood of a left-wing victory, performed as François Mitterrand had long predicted: They would not put the Left in government without making certain that the Socialist party was stronger than the Communist party. Thus, despite the dismay of the past three years on the Left, a huge number of voters switched to the Socialist party from the Center and Right. Even some prudent Communist voters voted Socialist! The overwhelming left-wing majority, and the near-unprecedented absolute majority for the Socialist party alone, had everything to do with the voters' desire to put the Socialists in a position of strength so that they, and Mitterrand, couldn't be taken hostage by the parliamentary strength of Communist "allies." The PS majority was obtained by a 15 percent jump in Socialist votes, from 23 percent in 1978 to 38 percent in 1981, an extraordinary gain for one election. It was because of the majority voting system that the Socialists could gain an absolute majority of parliamentary seats with only 38 percent of the vote. In most constituencies their candidates were better-placed than Communist candidates, so the latter had to stand for Socialists as the "unity" candidates in the second round of voting.

Mitterrand's socialist presidency began, as it had to, in controversy. There was apprehension on the part of his "bourgeois" adversaries and his own supporters as well. Here was a man who had become a Socialist belatedly in the 1960s, in full middle age, in his fifties. He had joined the Socialist party and become its leader in 1971, at the age of fifty-five, then led the party to three defeats (1973, 1974, 1978). Now, in his unexpected comeback, he was suddenly France's "elected monarch" president and the contested leader of an unlikely left-wing coalition of chalk and cheese.

Mitterrand never was an ideological socialist. While he had learned the history of French socialism, he remained a dilettante in socialist theory (which suited him fine, one should add). His blood boiled, however, at "the social power of money," "the injustice of the social power of money in society." Much of this went back to Jarnac and his Catholicism. Some of it was more recent (including the lessons he drew from the Observatory affair). Mitterrand especially disdained inherited wealth; a tax on wealth as such, in addition to a stiffer and more progressive income tax was always high on his list of policy priorities. The French state got, and still gets, most of its revenue not from income tax, but from consumption taxes, VAT (value-added tax), and the like, which weigh more on the less well off. Mitterrand wrote and said (as had de Gaulle) that "a class struggle will always exist." But neither believed in a class struggle in the Marxist sense, or that state ownership of industry and banking was a recipe for a higher order of society. For both, the human problems of human beings are eternal, however much technology can change the sorts of advantages and disadvantages from one society to another, or one epoch to another. Both were what we would call realists.

◆   ◆   ◆

After the Union of the Left parties signed the 1972 Common Program, "many Socialists," wrote an American observer, "feared the United States more than the Soviet Union. Mitterrand worried in 1974 that if he were elected, the United States might try to destabilize him in the way Henry Kissinger had tried to destabilize Salvador Allende."[1] This may seem implausible, looking back from today. But at the time left-wing movements worldwide were hoping to follow the "Chilean road to socialism," a so-called "third way" socialism between Stalinism and social democracy. A Socialist party alliance with a Stalinist Communist party in a major NATO country was hardly a situation Washington could put on a back burner.

François Mitterrand met with the U.S. vice president, George Bush, right after the first Council of Ministers of the Mauroy government, and provided Bush one of his most candid and full accounts of how he conceived the Communist problem:

> Joining the Socialist party was in no way for me a rally to Marxism; it was the means for the left to win power, and also the means to bring communism back to its genuine level. In France, communism attained an exaggerated level of support, partly because of its heroic attitude during the war. But, politically and historically, the most important moment [in France] since the Liberation was when the Socialist party surpassed the Communist party. We got to a situation then in which, for a left-wing voter, to vote "useful" no longer meant to vote Communist. To have them inside the government takes away their originality, since they are associated with the Socialists in all decisions. They should therefore be less and less capable of getting votes beyond those of the Communists [i.e., of sympathizers and protesters].[2]

Mitterrand surprisingly said that he thought the Communists would stay in the government a long time. Rather than defect if things went badly, they would hang on to the posts they had finally obtained because they had no replacement strategy and would suffer further losses if they opted out. (He was wrong about the Communist leaders' tactical wisdom but correct about the consequences.) Mitterrand even argued, surely reflecting on his own background, that France's Catholic tradition, which had gotten people used to unquestioning obedience, paved the way (as in Italy) for Communist discipline. Communism, he said, had introduced a "totalitarian poison" inside socialism, which was "incompatible with 'humanist socialism,' the tradition of Jaurès and Léon Blum."

Bush was impressed by Mitterrand's sense of responsibility about the Communist issue as far as the United States and the other allies were concerned, and also by his arguments that the situation would be managed, could even produce the long-awaited reduction of the French Communist party. Meanwhile the Reagan administration, while Bush was still in Paris, had issued a hard-nosed declaration saying that "the tone and the content of our relations as allies will be affected by the arrival of the Communists in this government." Bush promised he would get the White House to think again, which he did.[3]

As for "France's independence," Mitterrand commented in a gaullien mode as to American displeasure: "I didn't ask myself whether my decision corresponded to the wish or will of this or that country, and I will not ask the question. The American reaction is their affair, and my decision is mine. The more France's decisions are independent, the more France will be respected, and thus I will act the same way in the future."[4] The implication was that if the Communists did prove to be a problem, it would be a problem he and the Socialists, that is, the French government, had chosen to risk and one that French voters accepted. American leaders naturally tried to influence the French, but resistance to U.S. "diktats" was understandable in return.

Other American visits followed, including that of Henry Kissinger to Mitterrand's country home at Latche on August 3, 1981. If nothing else, this signaled that the Reagan administration was engaged seriously with French developments. Kissinger reported back to Reagan his impression that Mitterrand could be counted on, even with Communists in government, to be a reliable ally and to handle the various aspects of the "Communist problem." Mitterrand told his own people that his major foreign policy emphasis in the first few months would be "to cut off at the beginning any attempt by the major liberal countries to marginalize a Socialist France" in pending discussions—the first Franco-German summit meeting of his term, then the European Council, and the Group of Seven summit.[5]

As for the Communists, to refuse to join the Socialist government would only have made a bad situation worse. The PCF's leadership realized that it had been trapped by Mitterrand after all, a resounding vindication of his two-decades-long strategy. To have given an overwhelming absolute majority in parliament to the Socialists was all the more wisdom by the electorate, because the Socialists were so notoriously a fragile, disunified party. Success, power, and, as the anchor, Mitterrand's personal authority, all bolstered the untested Socialists. And in this regard, the Socialists' internal party factionalism also had a positive aspect. Given a severely factionalized party, a top leader can employ the strategy of divide and conquer.

A hardline, Soviet-schooled PCF official, Etienne Fajon, had summed up the increasingly ragged situation for the French Communists in a 1975 tract, entitled *Alliance Is Struggle*. By June 1981, French communism's situation was collapsing all round.

And Mitterrand made particularly sure to take a firm line toward the Soviet Union, to eliminate any doubts about his control, intentions, and his reliability. For one thing, in April 1983, Mitterrand ordered an extraordinary mass expulsion of Soviet "diplomats" from France for political and industrial espionage. But the initial and most critical episode was the Euromissile crisis, which was marked by Mitterrand's full solidarity with NATO. (See chapter 6.)

POLICIES AND RESULTS

Mitterrand won the presidency May 10, 1981. He took office on May 21 after a series of unpleasant skirmishes with outgoing president Valéry Giscard d'Estaing over dates and protocol. On May 22, Pierre Mauroy, the mayor of the northern industrial city of Lille and a classic social democrat, was appointed prime minister. Mauroy and his finance minister Jacques Delors immediately had to fight a collapse of the French franc in the markets. François Mitterrand opposed an official devaluation because he didn't want to signal weakness, either his own or a typical left-wing "incapacity to manage the money." On June 3, the government announced a first series of left-wing measures for aid to the less well-off: the minimum wage (SMIC), subsidies for families with children, and the minimum income for senior citizens each were raised substantially.

Not all policies of the Mitterrand-Mauroy government originated in socialist thinking. As said above, nationalizations in industry and banking were also defended as the basis of a modern industrial macroeconomic plan and a tool of national independence. Decentralization was another example of a policy that was as much French as Socialist. Reform of the overcentralized "Napoleonic state" was a century-old goal of French liberals. Not yet the dominant mentality in French political culture, French liberalism in its various forms had been mainly a Tocquevillean, provincial, and middle class aspiration to lessen the role of the state in French society. The positive program of French liberals in the 1960s and 1970s, talked up in political clubs and discussion groups, had emphasized the need for a renaissance of civil society in France's localities, regions, and provinces, which would fill political space vacated by a decentralized state. "Nothing is truly destroyed," said the nineteenth-century French sociologist Auguste Comte, "until it is replaced."

In terms of foreign policy, for worriers among France's allies and adversaries Mitterrand's election was an alarm bell following the left-wing Portuguese and Spanish revolutions of the 1970s. Realists believed, however, that French foreign policy would remain basically the same because French national interests hadn't changed given France's geographical and geopolitical positions.

It is not much remembered that significant amounts of "worried" French money were in fact sent abroad in a classic reaction to left-wing governments arriving in power, just prior to, and after, May 1981. The French bourgeoisie, at least the skittish parts of it, saw a "red menace" and took evasive action. The run on the French franc began near the end of the presidential campaign, as Valéry Giscard d'Estaing's lead over Mitterrand evaporated, due both to the red menace fear and also to market operators betting against a Mitterrand government. A small number of the French grande bourgeoisie actually moved to homes abroad, often to New York, where for a few weeks there were agitated debates about what might happen.

But once the mood passed and people saw that Mitterrand was indeed in charge—and calmly so—the money and the people returned, taking up their previous situations as investors and rentiers and doing quite well as socialism became Mitterrand's "new realism," the decade of the "strong franc," the second phase of his presidency.

SOCIALIST KEYNESIANISM:
GOOD INTENTIONS, UNTENABLE RESULTS

The overall program of the Mitterrand/Mauroy government was based on several principles: (1) a socially generous, that is, left-wing Keynesianism; (2) large-scale nationalizations in industry and banking; (3) decentralization of the centralized state; (4) *autogestion,* meaning workers' participation and control in industrial management; and (5) industrial policy and planning by the state, a combination of *planification* and *le Plan.* But the Socialist plan to be produced by a Ministry of Planning headed by Michel Rocard became impossible because of financial collapse. Planning, decentralization, and self-management went together poorly, and perhaps only rhetorically.

Mitterrand believed, on taking office in May 1981, as he and his advisors had thought for years already, that if they reached power it would be necessary to move quickly. The political momentum and popular enthusiasm of electoral victories can quickly evaporate. In this case it would allow anti-Socialist and anti-leftist opinion crucial weeks to organize, to raise shields, and to put sticks in the wheels of the new government's agenda.

However, given the relative unexpectedness of victory, the Mauroy government's laws on nationalizations, planning, self-management, and decentralization would require a few months to draft and longer to pass. But the government could almost immediately vote up uncomplicated bills to put money in the pockets of left-wing voters and supporters, to launch the Keynesian, demand-side reflation. Mitterrand solemnly asserted that "It would be morally unacceptable, as well as politically damaging, if the new left-wing government did not do something for working people right away."

The very first cabinet meeting saw a debate among Mitterrand's advisors (in the French regime, Prime Minister Mauroy acted more as chief counsel to the president than in charge of the government himself), which recurred regularly: Was the national interest best served by Europeanism and Franco-German solidarity, or by going it alone in a politically motivated monetary and fiscal policy? "Although some of his advisors urged an immediate devaluation and protectionism," American political scientist Peter Hall wrote of this discussion, "those he most trusted suggested that reflation should be possible without isolating France from the international economy." [6]

A similar question of judgment arose later in 1989-91 inside the French government, when the European Monetary System (EMS)—effectively, though indirectly, because of the need to match high German interest rates—turned France and other EMS member states into payors for German unification. The same national versus European arguments recurred when President Mitterrand negotiated the Maastricht Treaty's outline for full monetary union and the single European currency with German Chancellor Kohl. The nationalist position remained a weak minority, but its policy—that France could have a more national interest-based, gaullist, Thatcherite outlook—was intellectually and politically important beyond its numbers.

Mitterrand's optimistic advisors turned out to be wrong in predicting that France could buck its environment and conduct a countercurrent, demand-side reflation of the French economy against deflationary policies in the United States, Britain, and Germany. One of Mitterrand's key economic advisors, Jacques Attali, notes that on July 5, 1981, the Organization for Economic Cooperation and Development (OECD) revised downward its forecasts for the international economy. Growth would be lower than predicted, even if interest rates would also start down. The Western recovery, now discounted for the current year, would not come until 1982-83. For France, the Mauroy economic stimulus program would therefore disastrously worsen the balance of payments, because imports would increase. And the Socialist government's reduction of the work week plus the addition of a legally mandated fifth week of paid vacation would weaken employment. In a thunderous understatement, Jacques Attali explains the French government's calculations: "We would have preferred to have these [OECD] numbers before announcing our stimulus package. Now it's too late. The excessive initial optimism of the OECD makes us appear to be excessively generous in a stimulus which is really very modest. Everything now depends on the State's industrial dynamism and the 'reconquest of the domestic market.'" [7] This meant import substitution; that is, replacing imports into France with French products. One signature ostentatious stand was to block Japanese VCR exports into France at Poitiers in order to encourage a French manufacturer.

Mitterrand's optimistic decision for a generous, Keynesian stimulus package to relaunch French economic growth had been risky but not implausible at the time, as Attali says. The American Federal Reserve's deflationary policy, under Paul Volcker's tenure, was about to produce expansionary effects internationally (or so many economists predicted). This international expansion would float the French left-wing government's Keynesian domestic pump-priming. France would merely reflate a bit in advance, accepting a temporary balance of payments deficit, on the assumption that new demand among France's trading partners would soon elicit more French exports, righting the trade balance.

In retrospect, economists explained Mitterrand's risk in relation to German policies: "When Germany set its monetary and fiscal policies to grow slowly, it was impossible for the rest of Europe to grow rapidly. If governments tried to stimulate their economies, as the French did at the beginning of the decade, they simply produced large trade deficits that could not be financed. The restrictive macro-economic policies of Germany effectively forced every-one else in Western Europe to adopt similar policies."[8]

But besides purely economic calculations, there was a long history of left-wing political struggle in Mitterrand's approach, with which any explana-tion much reckon.

A policy of immediate reflation by putting money in the pockets of working people attracted Mitterrand for three reasons. First of all, he had long promised to act immediately for working people. Keeping promises, as we have seen and will see again below, was far from politically and morally negligible, especially at the beginning of his term. Second, this generous, risk-taking economic policy united the Socialist factions among themselves. It is always easier to achieve consensus in increased spending than in making cuts, and keeping the president's party unified was very important, especially when the PS was fighting a two-front war in parliament, against the conservatives and also against its putative Communist ally. Finally, French business, although it was for once being made to wait in line after working people, could believe that increasing consumers' purchasing power first would create new domestic demand, benefiting French industry.

Immediately after the Left took power, therefore, a flurry of government bills to benefit working-class people passed. The most significant law raised the minimum wage 15 percent in real terms in eighteen months, between May 1981 and December 1982, benefitting 1,700,000 workers. Family allowances increased sharply over two years—81 percent for two children, 44 percent for three children. Health insurance was expanded to part-time workers and the unemployed. Housing allocations for low-paid workers went up by 25 percent in 1981. Old-age pensions increased modestly as well. Altogether government social transfer costs rose by 4.5 percent in 1981 and 7.6 percent in 1982, very large amounts.

In July 1981 the legal workweek was reduced from forty to thirty-nine hours (with employers "encouraged" to pay at the forty-hour rate), with, as said, the fifth week of paid vacation. This was not supposed to be a simple benefit but part of the Mauroy government's plans to reduce unemployment. Only a small 20 percent of French businesses added new employees in 1981-1982, and how much was due to the shorter workweek was unclear. Perhaps 28,000 new jobs at most were developed due to this scheme.

While there were other programs to reduce unemployment, the main new employer turned out to be, as usual in France, the state: 200,000 new government jobs were created in 1981-1982, almost all with the civil service prerequisites, including tenure, that jobs in private business did not offer. "In distributive terms," says Peter Hall, redistribution of national wealth and help to the disadvantaged, the "position of the poor, aged, and lower-paid was substantially improved. When most other nations were trimming transfer programs and workforce privileges, France took a dramatic step forward."[9] Initial employment results boded well. The 1981-1982 percentage increase in unemployment was held down, only 4 percent in France versus 29 percent in West Germany and 22 percent in the United States, both still at the end of their recessions. And the French economic growth rate, 2 percent over two years, looked good against the last years of stagnant growth rates in Germany, Britain, and America.

But positive judgments and comparisons hid the fact that nearly all the "forward" movement derived from using the state treasury and the government's budget as a substitute for economic growth and productivity increases. It was deficit spending of a huge kind—the 200,000 new government jobs being the most flagrant case in point. Good deeds give satisfaction, but the government and Mitterrand were about to be held responsible for mismanaging the money. Using government debt instead of promoting growth meant a massive balance-of-payments crisis loomed in the fall of 1981, less than six months after Mitterrand and Mauroy took office. The French trade balance had plummeted and the French franc was under attack in the markets.

In July 1983 President Mitterrand finally made a frank avowal, a mea culpa, about his demand-side dash for growth in 1981-1982, against the international business cycle: "I was carried away by our victory, which intoxicated us. Everyone . . . was predicting that economic growth would resume by 1982. Honestly, I lacked the necessary expertise to be able to contradict them."[10] This wasn't a confession of incompetence (although

Mitterrand's lack of background in economic matters was well known). He meant that his own advisors, in line with an international consensus, forecast an imminent upswing. He relied on expert advice that turned out to be wrong. That the upswing arrived "late" was not only a French miscalculation. But Mitterrand's high-risk experiment foundered on the too-clever-by-half strategy of trying to use an international capitalist upswing to float the French Socialists' experiment. Interdependence was not so easily manipulated. France was now deeply integrated in the world economy, which made reflation in one country a high-risk bet.

French trade, about 13 percent of gross domestic product in 1953, was now over 20 percent. French industry was more vulnerable to international trends, especially recession, and domestic reflation would generate more imports than before. French energy dependence was also high, and increases in the price of oil could wreak immediate havoc with the balance of payments. The second sharp oil price hike, in 1979, Giscard d'Estaing's last year, left a $12 billion deficit when the Socialists took office. Almost 40 percent of France's imports were paid in dollars, thus exchange rate movements also could put a French government into difficulty, a circumstance aggravated by the fact that membership of the EMS almost eliminated the old French safety valve of devaluing the franc to regain competitiveness and slow down imports. By this time, the export benefits of a cheaper franc were just about balanced by higher prices paid for imports. Unemployment, way beyond that in comparable partner economies, was becoming a structural dilemma for every French government, now including the Socialists. The French baby boom of the 1960s was expanding the number of newcomers on the job market by well over 200,000 per year. But the oil price spikes of 1974 and 1979 meant hundreds of thousands of lost jobs at a time when nearly 250,000 new jobs per year were necessary just to keep pace. Despite pump-priming domestic demand, the Mitterrand/Mauroy government was unable to keep unemployment from rising sharply, which contradicted a central Socialist promise.

French business was also lagging. Under Giscard d'Estaing the government's industrial policies emphasized "diplomatic exports," such as weapons, airplanes, and turn-key plants, and the so-called grand projets, meaning massive infrastructure export projects—telephone systems, nuclear plants, metro systems—which improved French trade balances overall but left the French consumer goods market very vulnerable to import competition.

> While France sold arms to the OPEC nations, the Germans and Japanese
> penetrated French markets for automobiles, electronics, and consumer durables.
> Only too late did the attention of [Mitterrand's government] shift from the

"challenge of the Third World" to the "reconquest of the domestic market." By
this time, small and medium-sized firms producing for domestic consumption
were [endangered].[11]

Giscard d'Estaing's economic policies intentionally insulated salaried workers
from the 1974 and 1979 oil price income effects, a short-term benefit that
eventually had to be paid for. Corporate profits declined, and a major rise in
unemployment occurred, rising from 2.6 percent to 7.6 percent. Household
spending rose by 3.5 percent per year between 1975 and 1980, and the cost of
social benefits went up twice as much. A Socialist government could hardly do
better in this area, although the Giscard policy was storing up problems the
Socialists would have to face.

The specter of increased unemployment was one issue, obliging all
salaried workers, middle class as much as working class, finally to share the bill
for the oil price hikes—altogether equivalent to about 8 percent of GDP. At the
same time, corporate profits had dropped from 17 to under 10 percent of value
added, which had produced a sharp drop in business investment. Between 1973
and 1981 private investment fell 14 percent in volume. All this limited the
capacity of a Keynesian policy to stimulate investment by expanding demand,
in that low profit margins and high debt meant that French firms would be slow
to respond to a demand-side stimulus.

> The Socialists faced an acute policy dilemma for which conventional economic
> theory left them only two options. They could use traditional Keynesian
> techniques to stimulate demand, although this might well cause balance of
> payments problems before it began to affect investment. Their second option
> was to raise profit levels directly by depressing wages or cutting corporate taxes,
> but to do this the Socialists would have to discipline the workforce or cut social
> spending. The first tactic was economically dangerous; the second politically
> unpalatable. In large measure the history of the Mitterrand years is the story of
> how the Government gradually moved from the first option to the second, all
> the while seeking a third way out of the dilemma.[12]

The "third way" could not be found, and Peter Hall's judgment, while a model
of clarity, doesn't convey the sense of history, the hopes and fears of an entire
French Left generation at stake.

The agonizing retrenchment came in 1982-83. Barely six months in
office, a massive and unsustainable balance of payments deficit was about to
hit. The government's budget deficit increased from 0.4 to 3 percent of gross
domestic product in 1982. Real disposable income increased twice as fast as the

increase of GDP. State spending grew by over 11 percent in volume in that first year, and French industry was saddled with huge wage and benefits increases.

Most of the increased disposable consumer income was spent—contrary to the "plan"—on imports. In 1982 automobile imports went up 40 percent; electrical appliances, 27 percent; and consumer goods, 20 percent. In 1981-1982, the French trade deficit went from 56 billion francs (then about $10 billion) to 93 billion francs (then about $18 billion). French inflation, though falling, remained well above partner country levels. The French franc, naturally, was under strong pressure. The need to switch from Keynesian reflation to classic deflation had to be considered. The French franc was devalued against the Deutschemark three demoralizing times in three years.

Worse yet, since much of French imports, as opposed to exports, were denominated in U.S. dollars, the Socialist government wanted to maintain a strong exchange rate against the dollar in order to cut the bill for imports. But this was confounded by devaluing the franc against the mark, so the opposite occurred, with rising interest rates in the United States and market speculation against a weak French franc completely exploding the franc's trading ranges. From 4.2 francs to the dollar in 1980, the franc collapsed to 8.6 by 1984, when Mauroy resigned, and went over 10 to the dollar for a short time in 1985 before the run was exhausted. The extra counter-cyclical French economic growth was now finished as well, and the increase in unemployment accelerated. Inflation went up by 3 to 5 percent in France, as it was declining elsewhere. The government's budget deficit headed straight up; the trade deficit simply headed off the charts.

François Mitterrand, facing disastrous financial and economic results, faced a pivotal choice: either to reverse his Keynesian Socialist experiment, or, in the name of Socialist going-it-alone, to choose economic isolation, closing the French monetary frontiers and throwing up new trade barriers by invoking the EEC's "escape clauses." In effect, this would mean declaring a national economic emergency. Although the situation was not entirely of Mitterrand's making, it had been a great risk to head the French economy downstream to easy money when France's main partners—Germany, Britain, the United States—had been turned upstream on a deflationary course. As the international recession ended and growth picked up in partner countries, France had to put its own house in order or else build fences to avoid even worse trade deficits and currency devaluations.

Debating the October 1981 devaluation of the franc against the mark, Chancellor Helmut Schmidt made the extraordinary demand that the French cut about $3 billion from their 1982 budget. At the end of November, the French finance minister, Jacques Delors, announced a "pause" in any new progressive measures. This announcement sounded ominous to leftists with historical memory, because Léon Blum's "Popular Front" government had been forced to the same avowal in February 1937, and was still unable to prevent its breakup and ouster soon thereafter.

The obvious sign of a rout came on June 13, 1982, the day following the second devaluation of the French franc against the Deutschemark. A hard austerity plan was announced, aimed at compressing the government's budget deficit to 3 percent of gross domestic product by a huge cutback in government spending. A wage-price freeze, a radical disappointment to leftists, was decreed until October 1982. Business social security payments were frozen for one year, the business tax burden was reduced by 10 percent, and accelerated depreciation rules were announced, all to lighten the balance sheets of French enterprises. This wage freeze and abolition of indexation can be seen as a, if not yet the, turning point away from socialist policies.[13]

The measures were accepted, however, with quietism and resignation within the Union of the Left coalition, that is, from the Communists and left-wing Radicals, and in the Socialist party itself. The Left had created an economic and financial situation fast getting out of hand. The Mauroy government, giving up its rhetoric of "reconquering the domestic market," talked in conservative tones of reestablishing the *grands équilibres,* the major structural equilibria in the French economy. Pierre Bérégovoy, President Mitterrand's chief of staff and later finance minister and prime minister, was named minister for social affairs, with a mandate to reduce the cost to businesses of fringe benefits and to lower deficits in the unemployment insurance funds.

Over the next months the French financial situation nonetheless contin-ued to deteriorate. A somber debate took place among François Mitterrand, Prime Minister Mauroy and various official and unofficial advisors. The question was whether a second, more draconian austerity program was unavoidable, or whether a "nationalist," protectionist policy was possible, both to save the French financial situation, and, conceivably, to save the socialist experiment in which the French Left's historical credibility had been invested.

In March 1983 Mitterrand took a fateful decision to keep the French franc in the EMS, in effect abandoning remaining Socialist plans. A new sense of reality, disabused and, like it or not, more business-oriented, characterized the Laurent Fabius government that replaced the Mauroy government on July 17, 1984.

Would the Communists be part of the Fabius government? The answer was no. The PCF's leadership declined Fabius's offer to maintain the Union of the Left. It had had enough of the disadvantages of junior partner status, being held co-responsible for Socialist policies without having much voice in them. The Communist leaders, who had to reckon with the taste for left-wing "unity" they had instilled in their own rank and file, hoped that a distanced support of the Socialists in parliament would give some new political advantage. It did not. The Communist exit marked the official end of the Union of the Left, and it also disproved Mitterrand's forecast to George Bush that the PCF would want to stay in the government "for a long time," in order to reap the benefits of being in government. But the Communist leadership, it was being shown, had little capacity for continuity. Since the beginning of the cold war it had had only one real strategy: defense of French communism's "splendid isolation." French communism was a "counter-society," in, but not of, the larger French society. By the end of the 1950s Communist thinking had become a profoundly conservative theory of managing the huge expansion of membership and prestige achieved, with Soviet help, in the Resistance and the cold war. Beyond that, the French Communist party's leaders had for three decades been short-sighted and self-interested. With little perspective, lacking the convictions either for genuine democratization or even for sticking with a "party line" beyond the short term, they squandered the movement's historic human capital in neo-Stalinist games. By the time the Marchais group in charge of the PCF decided to jump ship, as opposed to taking up Fabius's offer in July 1984, even among its own members few believed that the leadership knew what it was doing or had faith in its explanations of why it had carried the party from defeat to defeat. The average Communist's belief in the party, its most formidable asset, had been destroyed by years of cynical manipulation from the top. Abused too often, great numbers of French Communists felt emotionally and politically orphaned.

As the Fabius government took office, still based on the Socialist party's absolute parliamentary majority of 1981, it inherited the March 23 decision for austerity taken by Mitterrand and Pierre Mauroy. This plan raised taxes on the middle class by 40 billion francs and cut public spending again, this time by 24 billion francs. A 1 percent surcharge on taxable income was imposed on about 70 percent of taxpayers, and about one-third of the taxpayers were required to make a compulsory loan (!) to the government of 10 percent of taxes, repayable in three years. This was a signal of genuine desperation, hardly recognizable, in fact humiliatingly unrecognizable, as the policy of a country such as France.

In addition, the prices of goods made by state-owned industry went up an average of 8 percent; taxes on tobacco, alcohol, and gasoline were increased sharply. In another desperate measure, French people leaving for abroad as tourists were prohibited by a currency control from taking more than 2000 francs out of the country. People were very angry, though such measures did alert leftists to how dreadful circumstances had become. Some strikes and demonstrations occurred, and President Mitterrand's popularity fell from its early highs of around 60 percent to 32 percent.

Keynesian socialism in one country had, in short, failed. Pierre Mauroy stated a chastening fact about the possibility for independent national policies of this dimension: "a genuine left-wing policy can be applied in France only if the other European countries also follow left-wing policies."[14] Interdependence and European integration were limiting the freedom of action of *every* country, not only France, to go it alone, with the partial exception of Germany. And Germany's allergy to inflation was the main limit on how much any French government could use the old policy of creeping devaluation to stimulate growth and exports.

The fateful moment had been reached in the third week of March 1983, between the two rounds of voting in local elections across the country. The Socialists took heavy losses in the first round, and the runoff ballot promised worse. The franc, still in free fall, could no longer hold its relation to the mark in the European Monetary System. The Bank of France had been obliged to spend about $8 billion to defend the currency.

Mitterrand took advice on two options: the "Europeanist" and "neo-protectionist" strategies. It was a Hobson's choice, a choice among bad alternatives. Finance Minister Delors negotiated for help from the Germans, who were loathe to be seen as paying France's bill. But the Kohl government finally agreed to share the costs, revaluing the mark by 5.5 percent, thus making German exports more expensive, against a much smaller 2.5 devaluation of the French franc. Otherwise, Delors had argued plaintively, France would have to take the franc out of the EMS, a worse outcome for Germany's interests because the future of European integration would be involved.

Fundamentally, François Mitterrand was agreeing to a deflationary program that everyone realized marked the end of Socialist policy. It was no longer a pause, but a choice for conservative finance policies and austerity budgets that would take years to see through. Mauroy, who had sworn he "would not be the prime minister of a third devaluation," fell on his sword and announced the devaluation on March 21.

In the next few years wages were compressed and the corporate tax burden was lightened in the hope of finally producing the élan in French industry that had failed to appear in 1981. Increased corporate profits, the Socialist government now said, would lead to higher levels of investment, growth, and, in the end, jobs; in other words, exactly the reverse of the 1981 strategy.

But, in March 1983, there was an alternative strategy to collapsing back into mainstream conservative economic and financial policies. Based on neoprotectionism, this strategy was urged on President Mitterrand by various advisors invited to evening meetings at the Élysée, who thus were dubbed "night visitors." The metaphor conveys "the incredible hysteria which [then] surrounded the question of the French franc among the Socialists."[15] These "night visitors" advocated unilateral withdrawal from the EMS in order to be free to devalue unhindered by German demands for French government budget cuts. A new regime of mandatory deposits by importers would improve the trade deficit by reducing imports, thus avoiding recourse to deflation. This was a nationalist-autarkic policy, as risky—or more so—than the 1981 strategy. The key was to retake monetary independence from the markets and from German monetary policy, a return to the neomercantilist, nationalist monetary policy of using devaluation as a weapon. New economic expansion, the logic went, would be created behind lower French interest rates and rising trade barriers.

This would not have been only a change in economic policy. The "night visitors" strategy meant a second great counter-current political risk on top of a first that had already failed. It would have been perceived as a no confidence vote in relations with Germany and in European integration. Moreover, this national policy was hardly guaranteed to succeed. Why believe that French industry, historically fragile and recently pulled this way and that by Socialist strategy, would suddenly respond vigorously to a new jerk of government policy? And a second radical policy debacle after that of 1981-82 would have permanently compromised François Mitterrand's presidency. Mitterrand must also have recognized that since a second experiment might well fail as had the first, there was little political or moral justification to impose large new burdens on the French people. In the name of what? The people had not really elected him to make a revolution in 1981; to go even further now would be simple political adventurism.

These "night visitors," on various days and to various extents, included Pierre Bérégovoy, Laurent Fabius, the CERES leader Jean-Pierre Chevènement, and the industrialist Jean Riboud, François Mitterrand's closest confidant among French businessmen. This kind of nationalist, neoprotectionist opinion was out of character for ministers such as Bérégovoy and Fabius. However, younger, aggressive policy intellectuals among the government's informal advisory groups still had the taste for risk because they believed European integration, and the EMS in particular, constrained the French government's room to maneuver. Integration, they argued, gave German policymakers an unacceptable lever on French decisions.

But Mitterrand recognized that, even if the "night visitors'" neoprotectionist policy worked, government deflation would be necessary if suddenly diminished French purchases of imports (because of devaluing the franc and

other anti-import government measures) were not simply to produce domestically generated price inflation instead. Mitterrand realized that his choice for
back-peddling and austerity was no mere technical shift to financial conservatism. The March 1983 decision ended any hope that the socialist flame would
be relit. The Mitterrand experiment was history.

THE SOCIALIST EXPERIMENT'S
MENU OF NATIONALIZATIONS

All the other elements of the socialist experiment, nationalization, the Plan,
better working conditions, and *autogestion,* were disabled by the quick failures
in 1981-1982 of the government's business cycle policies. Soaring trade and
budget deficits, a fast-weakening currency, and the promise of more of the same,
meant that, for those who remained believers, the chances of successful
"structural" reforms were ruined, or, for the disillusioned, the Socialists had
created the self-contradictions that Raymond Aron's warnings against the
Common Program had forecast.

The signal Socialist and Communist policy was the nationalization of
key parts of industry and the banking sector. This was a historical goal that still
united most Socialists with the Communists.

Nationalization had two purposes. First, by taking ownership of huge
French industrial groups, the government could physically guide a significant
part of the French economy toward social goals, or at least its own definition of
them. In terms of percentage of gross domestic product, percentage of
investment, numbers of employees, and so on, an increased public sector in
French industry was to be the main lever in Socialist planning of the economy.
In addition, by nationalizing banks, the French government would be able to
control the direction of loans to industry, to give investment at the macrolevel a
social character. Peter Hall commented, "In a sense the policy was designed to
overcome one of the classic structural constraints of capitalism—the dependence of investment on 'business confidence.' No matter how low that level of
confidence and the truculence of French business under a socialist regime,
investment would continue because at least half of it would be provided by the
state through aid to the private sector and the nationalized industries."[16]

Laws implementing the first Mauroy government's nationalization
program were voted by parliament in February 1982, which meant that they
were still being implemented as the French trade deficit was ballooning and the
franc was being decimated in the markets. At the time, Socialists and
Communists still debated whether 51 percent control was sufficient, or whether

the ideological number of 100 percent was required. In retrospect, the simple fact that Mitterrand kept to his promise to nationalize on this scale seems by far the more significant point.

The three largest French banks—the Crédit Lyonnais, the Banque Nationale de Paris, and the Société Générale—were already about 75 percent under state ownership, a legacy of post–World War II reestablishment of the French economy. But nationalizing the remainder of private ownership of French banking, argued the conservatives, would give the French state an unacceptable dictatorial hand in controlling business investment in the entire country. Nationalizing industries, as Jacques Chirac said at the time, was a large detail. Nationalization of the rest of French banking, of the remainder of the credit sector, was in itself the possibility of a collectivist-style state control of investment.

The Mitterrand-Mauroy government went ahead in any case, although neither man wanted a collectivist economy, let alone a Soviet-style command economic structure. The remaining 25 percent of private shares in the big three banks was taken by the state, along with two significant investment banks, Suez and Paribas, as well as thirty-six smaller banks. However, foreign branch banks in France were not touched. This meant that, had the Mitterrand government's policy headed, despite everything, toward collectivism, foreign branch banks could have become important and politically suspicious sources of loans for French industry. But, to repeat, Mitterrand and the Socialists had nothing like this in mind. However, they were painting themselves, at least ideologically, into this sort of corner. The collapse of France's monetary situation, the shift from a strategy to the tactical filling of holes in the dike, allowed for no planning at all, let alone a socialist plan. Thus the left-wing government never used its new ownership of the banks for political goals; it merely replaced some of the old managers with new ones.

On September 9, 1981, parliament voted up the Mauroy government's law for 100 percent takeovers of six industrial groups: the Compagnie générale d'électricité (CGE), the Compagnie générale de constructions téléphoniques (CGCT), and Thompson-Brandt (all three in electronics and telecommunications); Rhône-Poulenc in textiles and chemicals; Péchiney-Ugine-Kuhlmann (PUK) in aluminum and chemicals; and St. Gobain-Pont-à-Mousson in glass, paper, and metals. The law also converted into majority, but not 100 percent shareholdings, the French state's debt holdings in Sacilor and Usinor, two huge steel enterprises. In addition, 51 percent state shares—all at very generous prices to private shareholders—were taken in Dassault and Matra, the two largest airplane and defense contractors in France. Finally, Honeywell-Bull, in computers, and Roussel-Uclaf, in pharmaceuticals, were also taken over.

By February 1982 the nationalization policy wound up its expansion of the public sector. The French state now owned thirteen of the twenty largest firms in the country and had controlling majorities in all sorts of subsidiary companies. State holdings now stood for 24 percent of the employees, 32 percent of revenues, 30 percent of exports, and 60 percent of investment in the industrial and energy sectors of the French economy.

Yet French society was not much changed. How could this be? Mitterrand and the Socialists never wanted social collectivism or full state control of investment; they wanted state guidance and planning in the economy. But what was this to mean? When the ambiguities of Mitterrand's electoral platform, the so-called "110 Proposals," and the Socialist and Communist programs became matters of public policy decisions, the sentimental-ideological strategy of "opening the road to socialism" proved to be as chimerical as ever. In retrospect, the nationalizations of 1981-1982 were not necessary in any economic or sociological sense. But in the eyes of leftists they were necessary politically as the justification of the entire project of Socialist-Communist coalition government. The years 1981-1984 in French government proved to be an amazing concatenation of cross-cutting delusions and self-delusions, of double-dealing and slipping up on banana peels, some of which were one's own. Many left-wing sympathizers were still utopians, but even idealists count like anyone else in a democratic society.

Of course, not all idealists are alike. The various parties and factions within the Left assigned different purposes to the nationalizations.

Inside the Socialist party, various factions each had their own conception of the purpose. The small but influential neo-Marxist group pushed its combination of statist republican and anti-capitalist ideas. The "second left" of Michel Rocard and the CFDT trade union intellectuals wanted to try *autogestion* self-management "experiments" in state enterprises, hoping for private businesses to follow successful examples. In the Mitterrandist center of the party were more cautious or realistic hopes that an enlarged state-owned industrial sector would produce a recognizably socialist economy, although they were fuzzy on what that economy might be. Others in the Mitterrand faction were particularly concerned with taking the initiative on the Left away from the Communists. A successful Socialist-led nationalization program would defeat the Communist claim to be the only "serious" left-wing party, and would attract Communist supporters to the Socialist party.

A last purpose served in going through with the nationalizations was political and moral. François Mitterrand had long promised to nationalize if he won the presidency. And despite the reasons not to nationalize in the manner he did—so many and at 100 percent instead of 51 percent—he was keeping his promise to the voters, a moral commitment, even if an economic mistake.

Furthermore, keeping the commitment legitimized Mitterrand among the Communist voters. He was, after the nationalizations, less contested than ever as leader of the Union of the Left, and, after its breakup, of the Left in a more general sense. Since Lenin's denunciation of "the renegade Kautsky" in 1917, communist activists worldwide had been taught that social democrats could never be more than opportunists and revisionists. The French Communists had viciously denounced French socialism's historic leaders such as Léon Blum and Guy Mollet in this manner as "social traitors," "social fascists," and "social revisionists." To be a French Socialist had, for a long time, not been pleasant in intra-left ideological struggles. Those days were now ended.

For a few years after the 1981 nationalizations the big losses run up in the newly nationalized industries were treated as if the French state was merely subsidizing temporarily loss-making firms. This impression seemed to be validated by the strong American, British, and German economic recoveries beginning in 1982, which presumably would soon spill over into France. By 1985, some of the nationalized firms (Péchiney, Rhône-Poulenc, Saint-Gobain) indeed began to turn profits. But by then the socialist experiment had been abandoned, so that what might have appeared as a modest success had no political-ideological significance.

The policies of 1981-82 had, in the end, little or no socialist impact. They basically extended and restructured the longstanding statist role in the French economy. Taking into account Giscard d'Estaing's insulation of the French economy during the 1970s, France had, in effect, been put through not one but two economic experiments under two successive presidents, each costly in its own way. The Mitterrand experiment cumulated the effects of its own spending spree *and* the Giscard d'Estaing policies. By 1983 Mitterrand's line was "Industrial competitiveness is now the priority of priorities."

The idea of a "socialist" industrial policy and macroeconomic plan went through a brief vogue in 1981. Two cabinet ministers, Pierre Dreyfus, a well-known industrialist and former head of state-owned Renault during its heyday, and Michel Rocard, for the Plan, conceived ambitious projects. The goal was to avoid having to choose priority sectors of industry; instead there was to be a *politique des filières,* which meant building up the range of products in every sector so as to minimize losses to imports. France, according to this view, could, in principle, produce everything it needed, though perhaps not at the cheapest cost. The plan would buy time to save firms in difficulty and stave off potential Communist ideological harassment of the Socialists for "abandoning" French firms. But in only a few months time, the collapsing financial situation made industrial policy impossible.

TABLE 5.1

COMPARATIVE ECONOMIC RESULTS UNDER
GISCARD D'ESTAING (1976–80) AND
FRANÇOIS MITTERRAND (1981–85)

	Average 1976–80	1981	1982	1983	1984	1985	Average 1981–85
GDP growth (% volume)	3.3	0.5	2.0	0.7	1.6	1.3	1.2
Unemployment (level)	5.4	7.3	8.1	8.3	9.7	10.5	8.8
Price inflation (annual %)	10.5	13.4	11.8	9.6	7.4	5.0	9.4
Investment (GFCF as % GDP)	21.7	21.4	20.5	19.6	19.8	20.0	20.6
Exports (% volume change)	7.1	5.1	−1.7	3.4	6.9	4.3	3.6
Imports (% volume change)	9.3	1.8	5.8	−1.5	2.3	3.1	2.3
Labor productivity (% change)	3.0	1.5	1.9	1.1	2.4	3.0	0.0
Current balance (billion F)	3.5	−26	−79	−34	−0.8	0.0	−28
Budget deficit (% GDP)	0.7	2.6	2.9	3.1	3.2	3.0	3.0
Real disposable income (% change)	2.6	2.9	2.7	−0.3	−0.7	1.1	1.1

Source: Peter Hall, *Governing the Economy*, p. 223. Reproduced by permission of Blackwell Publishers.

The idea of a socialist plan, because it required more lead time and a longer implementation, died even more quickly than socialist industrial policy. Under Michel Rocard, the ministry quickly drafted an "Interim Plan" for 1981-83 and set up a new National Planning Commission, aided by all sorts of sub-committees and working groups, to prepare a full five-year Ninth Plan, to run in 1984-1988. But with growing budgetary chaos in 1982-83, any kind of planning, let alone socialist planning, ended. Rocard's Ninth Plan document ended up endorsing Mitterrand's decision to end the socialist experiment and replace it with conservative, market-oriented tax cuts for business to encourage new investment and job creation. Rocard, the president's adversary since leaping toward his own presidential candidacy in the Socialist defeat of 1978, mocked the job Mitterrand had made for him, calling the vague Ninth Plan "a theatrical exercise in collective psychodrama." In March 1983, the Ministry of Planning was quietly abolished.

A last aspect of the Mauroy government's socialist program was a series of four bills—the "lois Auroux, " or Auroux laws, named after the labor minister, Jean Auroux—voted in fall 1982. This new legislation covered French private sector business, based on a report of Auroux's team (which included Martine Aubry, labor minister in the 1997 Jospin government and Jacques Delors's daughter), a comprehensive review of the thin and backward French legislation of labor-management relations and workers' rights.[17]

Two "false good ideas" finally excluded during the discussion indicate the initial radical mood of the drafters. The first was a right of veto by enterprise committees on hiring and firing. The second was authority to be given to hygiene and security committees to shut down a production unit or a machine if the committee deemed it dangerous. Labor Minister Auroux told Mitterrand that during the disastrous economic situation the veto on hiring and firing would probably lead workers' organizations to put safeguarding jobs ahead of saving businesses. As for the right to stop machines, which existed only in Sweden and was hardly used, a different "right of absence" was substituted: A worker who believed himself in danger could leave his work station without reprisal.

As for the four Auroux laws finally voted by parliament, the first (August 4, 1982) created legislation protecting salaried workers from reprisals if they organized and guaranteed the right of unions to discussion on the nature and organization of working conditions. The second (October 28, 1982) formalized the system of representative workers' organizations in the workplace, fixing the functions of unions, workplace delegates, and enterprise committees. The third law (November 13, 1982) formally obliged collective bargaining and created a system for resolving enterprise conflicts. It instituted legally binding negotiation, that is, it obliged management to negotiate in industrial sectors and in individual enterprises. The fourth Auroux law (December 23, 1982), provided expanded authority to hygiene and security committees, especially in making changes to prevent workplace accidents.

French private business organizations reacted initially with hostility, making hard declarations about the violent history of French labor conflicts and citing fears about "soviets" being created in their businesses. They didn't say much about the French private sectors' own "savage capitalist" practices, as they were called, or the hardships workers endured.

In the end, the Auroux laws were absorbed without much problem by French businesses, showing that social democracy was quite possible in France. This was not surprising given the fact that these laws, with the extreme proposals cut out, basically brought French labor relations standards up to something like the standard of Germany. The French Communist leader and transport minister Charles Fiterman recognized their mainstream character: "Using a purely juridical and formal approach, [the Auroux laws] contained nothing like a taking of power by salaried workers in the enterprise."[18] Fiterman could have added that the junior partner Communists had supported the Auroux bills, had agreed that the situation wouldn't stand more radical undertakings, and that they themselves saw the point of facing economic and financial realities.

The old SFIO had died a good death. The new PS was establishing, albeit with much disquiet, a modern sense of purpose. And the neo-Stalinist Communist party was moving toward a final choice between obsolescence and disabused practicality. All this was not nothing.

DECENTRALIZATION

The one permanent success in the Mitterrand experiment was the long-sought-after decentralization of the French state, but the struggle for decentralization long predated socialism. Was decentralization "socialist," or was it a good reform of an overcentralized French state finally accomplished by the Socialists? Pierre Mauroy said that, in retrospect, decentralization of the state administration—not nationalization, not the failed planning effort, and not the never-tried *autogestion*—was *la grande affaire,* the most important reform, of his three governments. How can this be?

Parisian centralism was no new invention, of course. *Étatisme* (statism), *dirigisme* (state guidance of the economy's major sectors), and the *tutelle* (the state's tutelary role vis-à-vis civil society) had characterized the shape of French society from Louis XIV through de Gaulle.[19] And even in regimes of weak governments, such as in the Third and Fourth Republics, the French administrative bureaucracy impassively continued to "guide" French society's evolution. In the nineteenth century the historian Jules Michelet was the voice of French passion for the state when he said that the Bourbon centralization of power had been "a great historic undertaking" and a "great achievement." Charles Pasqua, when he argued in the 1991 Maastricht referendum debate that in France the state has more influence on the nature of society than in other countries, was speaking from a French historical perspective, not as the semi-authoritarian he was often considered. For de Gaulle, France's "greatness" was possible only with a strong state capable of unifying the French people in respect of common undertakings. Unlike the American example, in which private entrepreneurs continually force the evolution of civil society, in France the number of risk-takers has been historically small, whereas the appetite for state guarantees has been unusually high and has been met, albeit at a cost of citizen autonomy.

For François Mitterrand and the Socialist party, minus the Jacobin-Republican-centralist-CERES left wing, decentralization was vital to reinvigorating French civil society, what Americans call the economic private sector, public opinion, and local government, and the realms of civil and political rights. Decentralization would lift the rigid Napoleonic iron corset from the statist French bureaucratic government administration and subsidy-driven, "guided" economy.

French Socialist thinking met up, on this matter, with French liberals, meaning the center-Left and center-Right as organized in the left-wing Radicals, the Radical-Socialists, and the UDF coalition of Giscardist Republicans and the Democratic Center, to form a broad bloc favorable to decentralization. The gaullists and the Communists opposed what they described as "dismantling" the French state. For the gaullists, in France only the state could guarantee a vigorous society, as had been true, they argued, for centuries. Against them, Socialist decentralization was presented as an idea whose time had come. Against the typical Communist attachment to an all-powerful state, the autogestion doctrine in Socialist party ideology was an effective ideological rebuttal. Here the Socialist party was imposing its new, postindustrial idea of socialism on old Communist shibboleths directed at an industrial society rapidly being transformed.[20]

What was the decentralization? In a law guided through parliament by minister for decentralization Gaston Defferre, venerable Socialist mayor of Marseille and a staunch Mitterrand/Mauroy associate, the Napoleonic system of Paris-appointed prefects was simply abolished. For 150 years the prefects had been the highest source of public authority in the French departments, having replaced the Old Regime's similarly appointed and similarly powerful *intendants,* or governers. The powers of the prefects were divided between the departmental and regional councils and their presidents, that is, to elected as opposed to centrally appointed officials. The days of "Paris and the French desert," of Parisian centralization of everything, were to be ended. Local governments were authorized to raise part of their own revenues through local taxes, as opposed to dependence on money distributed by Paris. Putting the party heavyweight Gaston Defferre in charge of decentralization signaled that Mitterrand meant to get this done. Pierre Mauroy, who remained mayor of Lille in addition to being prime minister, also wanted power to the provinces.

Was decentralization, however, really a "socialist" success? Was it part of a new socialist structure of society?

In one sense, yes, given the Socialist party's program commitment to devolution and self-management. But the Communist party was certainly against weakening the central state, as was the Jacobin-Republican Chevènement CERES faction inside the Socialist party leadership. The CERES had, understandably, to accommodate the PS majority on decentralization. But successful decentralization would be another political defeat of the Communists by the Socialists; another step forward in Mitterrand's strategy of winning over PCF voters and sympathizers to the belief that Socialists are effective but compassionate, Communists minus the Stalinism.

Even so, the Socialists' successful decentralization reform is to be noted in history more as a victory over Napoleon than over Stalin, more a French than a socialist reform. And it is not surprising that decentralization is one Socialist change that conservatives do not talk of undoing.

If decentralization was, as Mauroy said, the biggest Socialist party success of the Union of the Left years, it showed a basic lack of clarity, an eclecticism in PS ideas about what socialism meant. Decentralization fit awkwardly with the PS policy of nationalizations as well as the idea of a national economic plan and a state industrial policy. The question was raised again, for those who attached importance to it, as to whether Mitterrand and the Socialists were authentic, serious socialists in theory and in ideology, or whether they— not just François Mitterrand but all of the leaders taken as a whole—were flying in practice by the seat of their pants, carrying a regilded left-wing banner.

There were ultimately more significant practical issues in decentralization beyond ideological struggles among the PS and the PCF. In multiplying the places where government money is raised and spent, the decentralization reform has been criticized for increasing the number of sites for, and the ease of, corruption, especially in terms of campaign and political party financing. Parties have lucrative opportunities to skim money, more or less illegally, from local and regional government institutional budgets, or to receive kickbacks in awarding contracts. This is to some extent the case, but evidence indicates that French decentralization is nonetheless one of those rare instances of a reform that solves a bigger problem than the ones it creates.[21]

Ten years after the Defferre decentralization law, which Mitterrand had vigorously endorsed, Edith Cresson, again with Mitterrand's support, took on the so-called "delocalization" of various Parisian institutions to the provinces. Delocalization transferred institutions, jobs, and elites out of Paris as a part of a second phase of decentralization, coupled with plans for regional development schemes in which the relocated Paris establishments would be central. All this was unpopular with the powerful groups who saw themselves as victims, and involved political risks that added to Cresson's already troubled term as prime minister.

At the end of 1991, Cresson announced that she would be the prime minister to finally bite the delocalization bullet. Thirty thousand *fonctionnaires*, that is, civil service positions, would be transferred to the provinces, 15,000 by 1996, the rest before the year 2000. Many of the office buildings freed up in Paris would, Cresson added, be transformed into low-cost housing. This was a big part of Cresson's stipulated role of turning Mitterrand's second term leftward in social policy issues.

By 1994, however, only about 3,000 jobs had been or were being transferred, and of this reduced total 1,000 were military jobs moved out by the Army 2000 plan launched in 1990 before Cresson's arrival in power. After her departure from office in 1994, a Delocalization Public Mission government office and an Interministerial Committee for Regional Development still existed, attached to the Interior Ministry; but there had also been several successful rejections of government orders to relocate and twenty more ongoing appeals to the Council of State to reverse delocalization orders.

One was the Goeblins tapestry manufactory, whose highly skilled weavers didn't want to leave Paris. It was allowed to stay in Paris rather than moving to Beauvais. The state cigarette company, SEITA, supposed to go to Angoulême, was saved because, as a private corporation, its Board of Directors had the legal right to refuse the state's orders. The Caisse nationale des monuments historiques likewise refused successfully to go to Nevers. Other companies found ways to obtain partial, if not complete, immunity. For example, the Voies navigables de France (French Navigable Waterways) company had to accept delocalization to Bethune, but traded its centrally located Paris building for a lesser building near the Gare du Nord, where top management still stays and "important meetings" are held.

In addition, as civil servants with job rights and guarantees, Paris government workers could refuse to move to the provinces, in which case the government had to find new positions for them in Paris. By 1994 perhaps one-third had accepted the move to the provinces, meaning that most often delocalization meant shifting around "empty eggshells," bureaucratic structures with few people to run them. The unhappiness of some obviously became the good fortune of others. Locals hired to fill empty positions were delighted, as were, in some cases, civil servants from other parts of the country who were happy to move to a choice location, for example, in the South of France.

The cost to the government was significant. Delocalization of one job cost between 30,000 and 1 million francs, nearly 1 billion francs altogether so far. And some of the vacated buildings and offices in Paris took a long time to sell, since in the 1991-94 recession office vacancies in Paris were extremely high.

The unpopularity of delocalization fell mainly on the one who had the temerity to risk such controversy, to take on the powerful groups that it antagonized. Edith Cresson, adding to her other adversaries, even took on the "enarchs"—the holy ENA (the École nationale d'administration) was sent to Strasbourg.

◆   ◆   ◆

With Mitterrand's decisions for austerity policies in 1982 and 1983, the confusing period launched in 1981 was slowly brought under control. The government's budget deficit was to be kept below 3 percent of GDP, a target reached by sharp budget cuts and some fudging of figures. Lower taxes, especially for business, were scheduled by the end of the Left's five-year parliamentary term in 1986. The end of socialist-leaning policies in employment came in spring 1984, with plans for restructuring the entire steel, shipbuilding, and coal industries. The Mauroy government, with Mitterrand's support, had dug in for three years against any large job layoffs. The new plan in 1984 openly acknowledged that 60,000 jobs would be lost within a few years by closing plants in these traditionally left-wing, highly unionized industries. Coal in particular had been an industry fighting declining competitiveness for many years; shipbuilding and steel were more recent victims of foreign competition. No less than one of every four jobs in the steel industry was to be eliminated by 1987, and Creusot Loire, a French champion, was allowed to go bankrupt, the largest bankruptcy in French history.

In July 1984, on Mauroy's departure and the arrival of Laurent Fabius, the Communist party quit the government, taking up an ambivalent parliamentary role. Generally the Communists supported the new Laurent Fabius cabinet, although occasionally they voted against it and sponsored sporadic street demonstrations against government policies. Total opposition to the Socialists was obviously too risky, as the Communist rank and file was still very much committed to left-wing unity. Yet the PCF's leaders needed to try something to regain their credibility as a hard-line worker-based force, which three years as junior partners in Socialist governments had done so much to weaken.

Nevertheless Fabius and the new finance minister, Pierre Bérégovoy (the successor to Jacques Delors, who soon after his resignation became president of the European Community Commission), kept the financial lid tightly closed. The government's budget deficit was held to the 3 percent President Mitterrand had promised, and taxes were cut for individuals and, more importantly, for business, to encourage investment and the creation of new jobs. The Socialists' new pro-business orientation was flagrant, making permanent the "pause" of late 1982—like the French Popular Front in 1937 and the Attlee Labour government in 1947. In January 1995, Mitterrand spoke of the dilemmas he had faced at the time:

> The first accusation against a Socialist is that he won't know how to manage things, that he'll cause a collapse in the value of the franc, because the franc is not his strong point. And if a Socialist did create a currency collapse, then the poorest worker, the fellow who doesn't even have wool socks, would never forgive him. Many [commentators] have emphasized the turning-point in the choice I made in 1983. But how could I have done otherwise, once I knew I didn't want France to be isolated, that instead she be even more linked to the other European countries?[22]

But stabilization was not enough to keep the Socialists from losing the 1986 parliamentary elections to the conservatives, especially since unemployment continued to rise, from 7 percent to 10.5 percent overall in 1981-1985. The French franc hit historic lows, with the dollar, as said, in mid-1985 buying over ten francs. Foreigners with French mortgages or just a tourist's view of international economics were delighted.

The first "cohabitation" situation resulted from these elections, with a formerly all-powerful Socialist president facing off with a newly powerful conservative parliamentary majority and prime minister. Would the RPR/UDR government coalition led by Jacques Chirac seek a total rollback of Mitterrand's socialism? Would it seek revenge?

THE SOCIALIST EXPERIMENT ON BALANCE

François Mitterrand, in his final interviews in 1994-1995, emphasized his constant concern with persistent social inequalities, a theme he wanted associated, justified or not, with any discussion of his legacies. "I don't have a feeling of guilt about it, but I profoundly regret that circumstances prevented me from reducing social injustices in a significant degree. Valéry Giscard d'Estaing and I took the economic crisis in the Western industrial full in the face, a twenty year crisis."[23] Perhaps he was sincere (although it was odd for François Mitterrand to associate himself with Giscard d'Estaing in any way); but how genuinely had he tried? How important had reducing inequalities and lowering unemployment been for him, compared with "making history," compared with his ambition for a socialist experiment and then, a story we are coming to in chapter 6, a relaunch of European integration? Even if socialism was impossible, had two or three fewer percentage points of unemployment been so? We will return to the issue of punitively high French unemployment and continued inequalities at several points, especially in the next chapter where the higher range of unemployment appears as a price paid in France, as elsewhere in Europe, for meeting the economic criteria set out in the Maastricht treaty for creating the single European currency.

Yet the priority given to the socialist experiment, even its failure, had certain virtues in their defects. To have actually tried, to have failed in practice rather than have remained in the illusory comfort of hopes, finally *clarified* the whole question of socialism in modern French history. Socialists and Communists alike were forced to face themselves in an unforgiving mirror, each with the cherished glories, true or false, of their respective pasts and in the reality of what they had become. What had happened in France, furthermore, taught lessons learned in the nick of time in neighboring countries where the Left had just, or was just about to come to power. The Mitterrand experiment legitimated realism and pragmatism across the West European Left. Amidst a new silence among French intellectuals as a political force, the left-wing parties and their activists were inoculated against the grand and dangerous rhetoric of "changing society" and of a "peaceful transition to socialism."

The Mitterrand experiment neither brought socialism to France nor France to socialism, and it is legitimate to ask whether Mitterrand didn't give up too easily. The answer must be negative. In his March 1983 decisions, he knew that there were no economic or political reasons to believe that a re-radicalized policy would be more successful than had been the case in 1981-82. Nor did he have the moral right to impose a second, more dangerous radical experiment on the French people, who would pay the price. And there was, third of all, the fact, ideologically inconvenient as it was, that economic expansion had been relaunched in the United States, Britain, and West Germany, with Mitterrand's France dancing out of line, and looking poorer and confounded for the effort. Spite was hardly a sound basis for the next step in Mitterrand's approach to the economy.

The Mitterrand experiment, however all this may be, was the most genuine, practical attempt at democratic socialism in Western Europe since the Attlee Labour government in Britain tried in 1945-1947. Why hasn't it been given more credit for its *intent,* especially by leftists themselves? This lack of recognition is as enigmatic as the not-unrelated amnesia in the Left's historical memory of the barricades of May 1968. Is it disappointment? disillusionment? intellectual embarrassment? lack of gratitude? or, more prosaically, only the need for time to do its work? If the Left just tiptoes away from its history rather than confronting it, a duty to itself will remain undischarged.

A further issue is the psychology of the central leader. It is more than curiosity to ask how it was possible, psychologically and ethically, for a fundamentally conservative and classical political man such as François Mitterrand to have kept his radical promises, to launch such social changes from the pinnacle of the state, using the presidency and parliamentary majority as the kind of political steamroller he had long criticized, sometimes even getting his way by decree. The answer lies, hardly noticed, in Mitterrand's concern with institutions. (See also chapter 7.) Nationalizing significant parts of the economy and decentralizing the state were major alterations in society. But, done in an orderly way and with fair compensation to owners, they were in effect a change from one order to another, legitimate if radical, radical but legitimate. The economy was being made more statist, more "French," but it was not, as was clear very early on, being collectivized. This was not revolutionary expropriation; the state paid, if anything, too much, a political premium for nationalization. Nationalization and state ownership of industry and banks was radical in terms of liberal economics, but, in France, it was a well-established practice historically and politically. French conservatives who admired de Gaulle could not claim seriously that Mitterrand was a bolshevik! In the decentralization reform, some of the central state's powers were reallocated within a continuing, and very French, respect for the state, even among Socialists. Foreign judgments of the current Socialist government of Lionel Jospin attest to this.

To attempt the impossible, it can be said conclusively, leads necessarily to failure. A practical explanation of the 1981-1983 disasters of the socialist experiment is obvious, and we have given it above. However, for ideological Socialists and Communists, the intellectual and emotional issue was existence itself, literally to be or not to be. A sympathetic foreign author observed sadly that, "The rule of the Left in France ended without drama," the Socialist-Communist split-up greeted with "indifference."[24]

What follows indifference can, however, take many forms, and even disappointed former enthusiasts should not be indifferent to the future.

◆   ◆   ◆

When François Mitterrand took leave of his Union of the Left prime minister on July 17, 1984, he told the loyalist Pierre Mauroy, "This is the most painful day of my term in office." Mitterrand, knowing there could be another day for Mauroy, was also being liberated from their joint failure, which Mauroy would take with him while Mitterrand went on. Detractors might have preferred that he had failed in a conventional way, going down with the ship, rather than breaking the mold to show that there was life and new roads to try even after a left-wing train crash. Mitterrand survived, and the Socialists governed from 1984 to 1986, and again from 1988 to 1993. And the first post-Mitterrand Socialist government, installed in 1997 under Lionel Jospin, began with much less historical baggage to carry because of his efforts.

François Mitterrand asserted that the French people had in any case legitimated his instincts and policies:

> Some people think I have acted as a right-wing president. That's extraordinary! They attack me in particular about my monetary policy decision in 1983. But after 1983 there was 1988, and in 1988 I was reelected. I am thus allowed to believe that left-wing people accepted what happened. And in any case, not to take those particular decisions would have killed Europe and blown apart the [French] currency, and even people on the Left didn't want that. I had therefore to choose. But I regret that I was obliged to make this choice. We have on the whole carried out a left-wing policy. How can this be denied today?[25]

Mitterrand often returned to the subject of changing camps: "Most young people begin on the left and end on the right. I myself went in the opposite direction. My conscience is absolutely clear. Jaurès was not born a socialist. As for me, I was a young man a bit slow in evolving, but on the other hand, some don't evolve at all."[26] His experiment in socialism would, he realized, leave no grand socialist legacy: "Socialists must live in their epoch; and the demands of a post-2000 world will not be the same as those of 1981. The term 'Mitterrandism,'" he said, "has the significance only of irritating me. I represent one variety of socialist."

But what was that variety of socialist? Was it a positive model, a negative one, or both? To define socialism is necessary before handing out bona fides and medals of good conduct. The problem remains that socialism is a fundamentally ambiguous concept. At least until today, it is clearer as an intention than as a reality. Mitterrand's socialism was a variety as complex as almost any other—complicated by origin, by doctrine, by result and by legacy. The extreme-Left satirical magazine *Charlie-Hebdo* sent out a questionnaire to politicians asking "What is left, which way is left?" Mitterrand, one of the recipients, unexpectedly replied, and it was published. To be on the Left, said Mitterrand,

> It's to be in power, the political man will say. It's to be in opposition, the *contestataire* will retort. It's through a lifetime of commitment, day after day, week after week, with the patience of a struggle recommenced a hundred times, the battle-hardened activist will say. It is through creative enthusiasm, the

rejection of dogma and conformism, adds the adolescent impatient to shake the established order. It's by loyalty to basic values, meditating on the lessons of experience, will say those who know that nothing lasting is built without points of reference. It's by adapting to the terrain, by permanent renewal, the capacity to act always a step ahead, will conclude those for whom "left" means movement. I have met all these types. Perhaps I have been each of them, and each, in its way, is part of the truth.[27]

This reply can be mocked, but it is surely a genuine summary of Mitterrand's existential experiences, of his own road to socialism.

France in any case would have a new government, whose watchwords would be not socialism but "modernization" and European integration, a government in step with, rather than rowing against, its major European and Atlantic partners. It might, for François Mitterrand, still be possible to make history, or at least to succeed. This was the lie in Mitterrand's other genuine evocation, to Mauroy, of "the most difficult day" in his presidency.

"Truth, like light, is blinding," wrote Albert Camus. "A lie, however, is a beautiful twilight which illuminates every thing in its proper measure."[28] An existentialist thought appropriate for a Machiavellian republican. Mitterrand's "socialism" had been, of course, Machiavellian. Otherwise it couldn't have worked.

CHAPTER 6

EUROPE

I will tell you what my plan, my *grand projet* is. It is to turn the whole
of Europe into one space. Today [in 1990] the barriers and the walls
have collapsed. The storm is not over . . . but we are getting there. One
space, a single and vast market, and, at the same time, constant and
structural links established among all the European countries. This is
why I have talked about a Confederation. Within that [Confedera-
tion], I would like the [Union] to forge its own economic, monetary
and political structure. In other words, within the single European
space I would like to see a strong nucleus, [the European Union]
capable of making political decisions collectively. . . . I would like to
make of France—we are working at it and it isn't easy—a model of
economic development and social cohesion. That is my plan. Why
complicate the issue?

—François Mitterrand interview, July 1990

On January 26, I phoned Helmut Kohl, who liked our proposal. He
thought Thatcher would have problems with it but that Mitterrand
would probably agree, if sufficiently consulted. "You know my old
rule. . . . Salute the German flag once, but the Tricolor three times!"

—George Bush, *A World Transformed*

I was struck again and again on a daily basis during these fourteen
years [at Mitterrand's side] at seeing the huge gap between, on the

one hand, the reality of the world, that is interdependence among states in the world community and, on the other hand the idea people have especially in France of France's power and of the power of the president of the republic. . . . The Franco-French domestic polemic about the policy to adopt toward [German] reunification . . . reflected our self-delusions, as if France were at the center of everything.

—Hubert Védrine, *Les mondes*

FRANÇOIS MITTERRAND'S EUROPEANISM

FROM CHARLES DE GAULLE THROUGH FRANÇOIS MITTERRAND, moving Europe "beyond Yalta" was a historic task for French policy.[1] To end Europe's division and to achieve German unification was what France, along with the United States and all the allies, had long claimed to seek.

Already at the end of 1944, after the Liberation of France but before the Third Reich's actual downfall, de Gaulle announced to the French that there was no alternative to reestablishing relations with a rehabilitated and pacified postwar Germany. Before war's end they must conceive to live again as neighbors with a people who had committed unspeakable wrongs, who had done damage beyond despair, whose country would, at its defeat, be the most hated in the world.

A German shadow hanging over France was not new. Since its unification between 1866 and 1871 by Otto von Bismarck, Germany had been too big, too powerful, and too close for the French not to obsess. In 1926 the German diplomat Gustav Streseman had said objectively enough that, following Berlin's World War I defeat, "The fear of seeing Germany rise again paralyzes the will of French politicians and prevents them from thinking objectively." Germany after 1871 loomed as a perpetual danger to a France in geopolitical decline; Germany had become a mirror in which the French people and policymakers saw their own fears. De Gaulle's goal was, naturally, to change France's view of itself and thus to think objectively about Germany.

World War II finally taught at least courageous French political leaders the fundamental lesson that close engagement with Germany was unavoidable and in France's own interest. "The great German people," as de Gaulle called them in a sign of French confidence, were too dynamic to be treated (as had been the case at Versailles in 1919) as an object of revenge, to be confined and made to pay exorbitant reparations. This Germany was a tinderbox that would explode sooner or later. Fourth Republic politicians began the process of dealing with post–Third Reich Germany. The European Coal and Steel Community

(ECSC) and the Rome treaty creating the European Economic Community (EEC) were the essential Fourth Republic agreements involving Germany. Projects for a European Political Community (EPC) and a European Defense Community (EDC) failed. Political union and a rearmed Germany with its own general staff, even inside NATO, were ideas too advanced to be attempted with a Germany no one, especially the French, was prepared to trust so soon again. So German rearmament, necessitated by American dispatch of military forces from Europe to fight in Korea, was accomplished without an independent German general staff. The German military was re-created directly as an arm of NATO's integrated military command.

De Gaulle, in power again in 1958, was faced immediately with the Rome Treaty, signed in 1957. He implemented the Treaty, that is accepted the EEC, for three reasons: it benefited France economically; it was subject to French national sovereignty and veto; and it yoked Germany to a common wheel that would have permanent consequences and be difficult to escape. His *Memoirs of Hope* put the point revealingly: "I told Adenauer that from a strictly national point of view France, unlike Germany, had no real need of an organization of Western Europe, since the war had damaged neither her reputation nor her territorial integrity."[2] The EEC was for France a huge economic benefit, especially subsidies to agriculture and a competitive stimulus to lagging French industrial entrepreneurship. It was also an indirect, unconventional means of national defense: to be in a military defense organization with a divided Germany watched by an American overlord calmed French worries about Germany. At the same time the French were all the more swept up (and rightly so) into the cold war, seeing the Soviet Union as a danger internationally and the huge French Communist movement as a threat domestically. Finally, as collective psychology, to be Germany's senior European partner would begin to exorcise the German specter lurking in the French mirror. How could a divided Germany be as dangerous as it had been before the war? How could Germany be the first enemy when the Red Army might, as the French Communist leader Maurice Thorez blurted out in a press conference in 1951, "one day arrive on the Champs-Élysées as an army of liberation?"[3]

By the time of François Mitterrand's presidency the logic of the special Franco-German partnership inside the European Union had evolved. France still benefited economically from European integration, but national sovereignty had been fragmented, with areas of decisionmaking "pooled" into collective sovereignty. As for France's own political need for Europe, the fear of damage to France's prestige and territorial integrity had faded, replaced by the new menaces of globalization and Americanization. France, whatever continued independence had been possible for it in de Gaulle's time, now needed an organization of Europe for France's own sake, and the basis of Europe's organization was Germany's economic power and France's political leadership. Franco-German entente was useful in itself but got all its meaning only to the extent that it was in the service of building an independent, peaceful, and prosperous Europe.[4]

On the German side, French acceptance of unification remained crucial. Former chancellor Helmut Schmidt sometimes said, not only to win points, that "France was more important for Germany than the U.S." In the tumult of German unification in 1989, Schmidt's successor, Helmut Kohl, had to defuse international worries about unification with reassuring declarations and economic sidepayments. But Kohl's attention to France among Germany's European neighbors reflected Schmidt's: "The French nation," he said, "is the only one which, in the eyes of all our neighbours, can legitimize German unity." The American and Soviet superpowers had to *accept* German unification; France, along with Poland, were the contiguous once-victimized nations that could *legitimate* it.[5] In addition, a Europe "beyond Yalta" would free Eastern Europe and liberate Soviet-dominated countries elsewhere.

Communism's demise and the cold war's end should have freed Europe *as a whole* from the need for American protection. What the French and others saw as American hegemonistic tendencies should therefore logically have disappeared, at least in Europe. "The key issue," wrote Hubert Védrine, however,

> lies in relations with the U.S., above all after 1989 when existing counterweights [to American] hegemonic behavior disappeared or no longer dared to resist. In military matters it remains impossible to act without them or to oblige them. One could denounce this situation and François Mitterrand sometimes did, though in general he avoided useless rhetoric. His refusal of Americanization took the form of passive resistance, rarely a direct quarrel. It is possible to try to convince or constrain the Americans, if one has built a relation of forces which resists the first shock, and if one knows how to work with the different centers of power—the presidency, Congress, lobbies and the media.[6]

Facts are facts, and even the French ultimately face up to them. When American secretary of state Madeleine Albright ironized that "In order to understand Europe you have to be either a genius or French," she gave homage only to the French stereotype.

France paid real prices in the passage to a post–cold war Europe. German unification created an even-larger neighbor than before, and French autonomous influence and room for diplomatic maneuver were reduced by that, as well as by the collapse of the Soviet Union and cold war diplomacy. Gone was the

French ploy of holding out the U.S.S.R. as an alternative diplomatic partner if America pushed its advantages too far. Lest this point be misunderstood, I hasten to add that no Frenchman would have chosen to keep the Soviet Union and a divided Europe even if France's "losses" could have been avoided. To see this does not require being either a genius or French.

PUSHING AND PULLING EUROPEAN INTEGRATION

In 1981 European and international geopolitics were still locked into a bipolar framework produced by American and Soviet superpower. Europe, in this schema, was simultaneously the most militarized and yet most stable area of the world. Precisely because of overarmament, the actual danger of war in Europe was close to zero. No one could have wanted it because no one could have won. For the same reason—the effectiveness of nuclear and conventional deterrence—not a single square meter of European territory had changed hands since the end of World War II. So in spite of the ups and downs of détente, and despite momentary positive local developments such as the Prague Spring, the Europe of Yalta, divided Europe, was still in place when François Mitterrand became French president in 1981.

Mitterrand's international outlook was very European in the sense that he believed in, or made use of, the "myth of Yalta." This myth was the idea that the Soviet Union and the United States agreed implicitly at the Yalta conference in early 1945 to divide Europe and rule over it.[7] Whether Mitterrand believed in the myth of Yalta or in its reality—that the United States couldn't have prevented Soviet occupation of Eastern Europe without launching a third world war before the second was over—his view of European geopolitics, like de Gaulle's, looked beyond Europe's most disastrous century to encompass what the continent had once been and what it might become again in the future.

Geopolitical in the grand classic European sense, Mitterrand's diplomatic outlook focused on maintaining the European equilibrium. His own historical memory began not with the 1930s but with the causes of World War I. Like de Gaulle, he thought in terms of long historical developments in which ideologies were fleeting. Even as a young Fourth Republic politician, François Mitterrand could have signed de Gaulle's famous statement that "communism will pass, but Russia is eternal."

However, his federalist inclination about the end point of European integration differed very much from de Gaulle's, it goes without saying. Yet the two leaders had the same sense of a French president's duty in European politics: to serve the French national interest.

Mitterrand's European policy was based on two fundamental premises. The first was that continuing European integration was necessary, as opposed to de Gaulle's belief that deeper integration would be bad for France and bad for the European peoples. "More Europe" was necessary to foster peace and prosperity, but in the longer term also to create a European power capable of balancing the United States and other world powers in the "multipolar world" that France wanted. The second premise was that realism and idealism—national interest, not some vague European interest—remained the top priority. National interest, not an ideological or utopian view of the future, was the reason why France should support more European integration. Thus Mitterrand's federalist inclinations regarding the long-term future of European integration arose out of French patriotism, from an absolutely traditional, in a sense gaullien, idea of national interest. It was no abstract internationalist, let alone socialist shift of loyalty from France to a supranational "Europe," the caricature invoked by Mitterrand critics on the extreme Right and extreme Left. Mitterrand was a very French president. More supple and less intransigent than de Gaulle on the international stage, he was nevertheless as French and as firmly national-minded as the General.

From time to time there was a scurrilous criticism of Mitterrand's policy as "Vichyite." It titillated because many were aware of the president's Vichy past. But more than that such criticism meant, as when directed as well at Valéry Giscard d'Estaing, a sell-out to foreign interests, namely German. The allegation recalled the anti-national behavior of the French upper classes in the Franco-Prussian war, when peace with the invading Germans was made on the backs of the Paris Commune and "the people." For a few domestic critics claiming to be more patriotic than the president this seemed a plausible explanation of Mitterrand's enthusiasm for tying French monetary policy to German practice in the 1980s, and for Mitterrand's support for a single currency with the Deutschemark as its centerpiece. This attack on Mitterrand as "Vichyite" is worth mentioning only for completeness. It is a conspiratorial view of history and of his motives that merits little attention.

For Mitterrand as for de Gaulle, then, France's main European problem, that is, France's German problem—how to deal with Germany's strength—required a European-level solution. France alone could not balance Germany, nor could it match Germany's economic strength, above all unified Germany's economic and demographic size, by itself.

The solution was not to organize with other countries against Germany but to organize European integration around Franco-German cooperation, a Franco-German tandem or special partnership whose leadership would be the political fuel and the economic engine of European development. The first steps were, as mentioned above, the European Coal and Steel Community and the European Economic Community.

His own experience—"I was born during one European war and I fought in the second"—convinced him that some structure beyond the nation-state was necessary to Europe's domestic peace and wider place in the world. He was proud to say that he had "voted for Europe the first time in 1947 at the Hague," at an initial European integration conference. And he remained committed to the "European idea" even when, as a minister in various Fourth Republic governments, he negotiated, generally defensively, for France's national interest. French worries about the German renaissance brought down the first attempt at German post–World War II rearmament, the European Defense Community of the early 1950s. Rather than a joint foreign policy and security organization, it was the European Economic Community, launched on January 1, 1958, and renamed the European Community in 1967, which produced the framework in which German strengths and dynamism seemed somewhat less overwhelming. The EC worked both to soften the pressures of German economic superiorities and to harness Germany indirectly as France's diplomatic partner.

The Franco-German duo thus became the core of a "small" integrated Europe, essentially Western Europe. Since Eastern Europe was under Soviet domination, there was no question of expansion at that point. This little Europe fit France's German worry, not merely its cold war security situation, well. From these geopolitical facts arose the impression, or anti-French insinuation, that the French benefited so much from the cold war that they were happy to see divided Europe persist because it magnified their influence, held West Germany in check, and kept the Soviets far away. Objectively this may have been true. But the French were neither responsible for the cold war nor could they have prevented it from ending even if they had wanted to. Nevertheless, the controversy about France's supposed satisfaction with Yalta Europe was a continuing, bitter slice of cold war diplomacy.

François Mitterrand's second premise about Europe's future—the need for realism rather than idealism—guided his reaction to the collapse of communism and the Soviet Union. The Soviet collapse peacefully produced the kind of changes that historically have come about only as a consequence of great wars. Historians will have much to say about why so few Soviets, so few Russians, so few Communists in Eastern Europe fought for regimes to which their lives had been fixed. For West European leaders such as François Mitterrand, the issues were different. What would happen if large communist states, powerful but rigid and fragile, broke up quickly, on the principle of national self-determination? Would the result be democracy or wars? The answers were not obvious. Europeans and American leaders alike debated whether to try to channel communist disintegration, thus to support national communist states while encouraging democratic evolution, or to endorse secessionist and other new national tendencies in the former Soviet Union and other ex-communist countries.

In either case a new European policy was needed by the French and other West Europeans. The liberated Eastern countries would require integration into the European equilibrium and connection to the European Union in some fashion. But how? And at what price? How could the EU deal with the problems of new poor countries when the problems of the existing poor countries had not yet been resolved? For example, what about Poland, with its 35-40 million people and large number of inefficient farmers? If Poland joined the European Community structure, its farmers would have to be subsidized by the already extravagant Common Agricultural Policy. Would the wealthier EC countries pay for Poland when in the last enlargement they had just agreed to subsidize the inefficiency of Spain's agricultural producers?

Faced with the complexity of the new post-Yalta Europe, François Mitterrand advocated the advantages of a "European confederation." A confederation would englobe the European Community, a larger and looser pan-European integration structure with many more members than the "small" EC. The confederation could accommodate various groupings of countries participating in different aspects, creating a stratified community at "several speeds," a departure from the "everyone participates in everything" principle. The confederation as envisioned by Mitterrand could be connected in various ways to the European Community (which the 1991 Maastricht treaty subsumed in the European Union). And the principle of a "variable geometry Europe," Europe "à la carte," a "two or three-speed" Europe, would be accepted such that the European Union would not be diluted by a surrounding confederation.

Mitterrand defined his view of Europe's future in the July 1990 interview quoted as an epigraph to this chapter. His "overall plan" was the attractive view that Europe should be thought of as "a single space." The Single Market created by the 1987 "Single Act" treaty would be completed by monetary union, a single European currency (the euro), and a European federal reserve bank (the Eurofed), making the European Union area into a true single economy. The European confederation, which he had first mentioned in a New Year's speech on December 31, 1989, would attach ex-communist and other new participant countries to the Union without the burdens and responsibilities of full membership in the EU's single market. Associate status with the EU would link the two layers of membership, whose eastern and southern boundaries (Turkey? North Africa?) Mitterrand didn't specify.

This vision was what I would call the voice of the genuine Mitterrand speaking, the statesman taking a long-term view that was realistic enough to acknowledge that not everyone would get everything, yet filled with enough ambiguity to encourage hopes and different possible outcomes for the general project. It was still unsatisfying, even frustrating, in its generality and emphasis on *les lenteurs de l'histoire,* history's usual slowness to unfold. A German minister of European affairs had expressed a similar point of view when asked to define the EU's exact goal: "To give a precise institutional definition of the term 'ever closer union'" used in the Maastricht treaty as Europe's goal "is not absolutely necessary." Events on this scale must take their course, although a *forcing,* as the French say in Franglish, is sometimes necessary. One example was Mitterrand's own demand for a cut-off date for establishing the euro, in order to be sure it would happen. Sometimes things were called by their names, at other times vague expressions hid what was being done, in order to diffuse political opposition, as when the term "an ever closer union" replaced "federalism" in the Maastricht treaty.

Foreign minister Roland Dumas once explained the French view of the Maastricht Treaty with unusual precision: "The treaty creates the basis for a European Union with a federalist tendency, which in turn would be the backbone of a pan-European confederation still to be created which will unite twelve states and 340 million citizens, making of Europe the leading world power." "That," says Védrine, who was close to the core of French policy discussion, "was really the basic concept."[8] French policy under Mitterrand knew what it wanted, even if getting it was anything but certain.

The newly democratized former communist states wanted to join the European Union right away, however. They felt it was their right, after having paid the price of Yalta Europe, in the form of Soviet domination, for so long. They objected to Mitterrand's confederation idea, with its stratified memberships and the appearance of a new "class" distinction. The confederation idea seemed to draw invidious new lines of division between haves and have-nots across a Europe that could become the kind of "single space" Mitterrand claimed to want.

And François Mitterrand's view was, in fact, one from within the "club," based on French and European Union interests. It was an "establishment" conception for post-communist development of the European continent. In a notorious unguarded moment during an interview, President Mitterrand even said that it would be "decades and decades" before the ex-communist countries would become economically and socially developed enough for full membership, that is, without putting the Union itself into an untenable position vis-à-vis the tax burden on it own people.

Mitterrand also liked the federation-within-a-confederation idea because of a necessary pending decision about "widening" versus "deepening" the EU, meaning the problem of whether expansion of membership should precede or come after reform of decision-making structures to prevent stagnation. Decision-making reform, deepening, would be all the more important in a European Union of twenty or twenty-five members, that is, with ex-communist and other countries included. Practically speaking, deepening meant more supranational, majority-vote decisions as opposed to unanimous decisions, in which each country, even the smallest, has a veto.

But the former communist countries did not want to hear about anything less than full EU membership. They feared that a "temporary" associate membership would be merely a cover for prolonged second-class status behind what they called an "economic Iron Curtain." Resentments even led to a bitter public debate between old friends François Mitterrand and President Vaclav Havel of the Czech Republic at a grand meeting of intellectuals and public figures in Prague in 1991.

Mitterrand's idea for a federation-within-a-confederation was thus eliminated from French policy declarations, at least for a time. But it, or some other concept allowing a "variable-speed" Europe, is already apparent in the European Union as it functions today, in the Social Charter membership list (Britain opted out, leaving eleven of twelve members), in the single European currency membership (eleven of fifteen countries signed up initially), and in various defense and security policy structures (e.g., not all EU countries belong to the defense talking-shop known as the Western European Union).

Looking back at his fourteen-year presidency as a whole, "Europe" in any case stands out as François Mitterrand's enduring and significant policy commitment. "Europe" survived Mitterrand's ideas for historic changes, first among them the socialist experiment. If he was tardy and ambiguous in his arrival at socialism, Mitterrand was no latecomer to European integration. If one "message" is to be associated with Mitterrand's name in the history books, it is not socialism but the "European" message: Integration is a necessity, the requirement for the world's original nation-states, those in Europe, to invent, in their own national interest, the first successful supranational political structure beyond the nation-state. Mitterrand, in the end, was more of a European than a socialist, more a statesman pursuing French national interests than a man of the Left or a Machiavellian.

No one was really surprised that Mitterrand could have abandoned socialism so rapidly and completely in 1982-83. He had been expected to jump ship with few second thoughts if pushed into a corner. By contrast, he came to the cause of European integration in an entirely different way and was bound to it differently. "Europe," to him, was a cause of the future whereas socialism was a great idea of the nineteenth century.

Mitterrand never could have given up the cause of Europe as he did that of socialism precisely because "Europe" was a *cause* to him just as socialism was to others. European integration had become, in his judgment, a permanent French national interest. There remained domestic "Euroskeptics"—the right-wing of the gaullists and the National Front, the left-wing Socialist party minority and the French Communist party, and some of the Ecologists. But Mitterrand's presidency produced a center-Left/center-Right consensus that "more" Europe was good for France. All the rest became policy questions about how much and at what speed.

MITTERRAND, FRANCE, AND EUROPEAN SECURITY

European security must be discussed with its sister subject, European integration. No French president, especially the one who had to deal with the end of the cold war, could separate the revolutionary transformation of the European geopolitical system from the basic policy decisions about expanding European integration. Problems of war and peace were intertwined with problems of prosperity and development; issues of European security and problems of European integration overlapped, even were, to some extent, the same thing.[9]

The difficulty had long been how to deal with the fact that France was no longer a "great power" even in Europe. There is no European great power, unless it is Germany in economic terms, leaving France the second power. De Gaulle had been a master at the fine art of playing from weakness, emphasizing the French trump cards: diplomacy, surprise, and intransigence. Mitterrand showed he had learned the gaullien lessons well.

Mitterrand's geopolitical views and his European security views were, somewhat surprisingly for a veteran politician, largely unknown or misunderstood when he took office in May 1981. Foreigners and even the French themselves had known him since 1965 primarily as a left-wing leader, Socialist party first secretary, and the presidential candidate of the fractious Socialist-Communist Union of the Left coalition. Mitterrand's socialism and above all his alliance with Communists focused everyone's attention. "It's a fact," he wrote, "that when I was a candidate the Americans [and] the Russians were not favorable, rather worried; the German government was not favorable either. Happily the French thought differently!"[10] To me in more than one interview in the 1970s he said jauntily: "But M. Tiersky, you really are too preoccupied with the Communists!" My academic specialty, the study of "Eurocommunism" being then a growth industry, was obscuring a larger, more important picture. "Happily," even an American professor could open his eyes wider.

The Soviets, contrary to the common wisdom that they would rejoice at a left-wing victory in France, were worried lest a successful Socialist-led left-wing government cast doubts about their "vanguard party" doctrine, the justification of communist single-party legitimacy everywhere. And Moscow knew that the French Communist and the Soviet reputations of "vanguard" invincibility would surely be diminished by a disappointing PCF participation in government in France.

Helmut Schmidt had said in February 1981, two months prior to the French vote, "Mitterrand might be elected? Don't wish me bad luck!"[11] And even though Margaret Thatcher and the Japanese disliked Giscard d'Estaing, whom they thought had acted in an insulting manner toward them, they were not favorable to Mitterrand either. The ruling Algerian FLN party, then an important French partner after being its enemy in the Algerian war of national liberation, believed it would have chits to call if the French Socialists formed the next government. And the Algerians early on were indeed given a favorable deal for export of natural gas at above-market prices by Mitterrand under the guise of third-worldist development aid. The Israelis knew François Mitter-rand's concern for Israeli security and his long-standing interest in Jewish civilization. The Socialists of Felipe Gonzalez in Spain and Mario Soares in Portugal, the first soon to come to power, the second the leader of Lisbon's ruling party, were sympathetic as well.

What a mixed bag! Mitterrand had been in opposition for so long that he was seen, as noted, largely through his anti-capitalist rhetoric and socialist program and through contrarian commitments such as his promise to destroy the French nuclear deterrent, the *force de frappe,* as a contribution to peace. Once in office, Mitterrand turned out to be a pragmatist, a classic European statesman in the French style, imbued with a sense of history and geography more than with the desire for a crusade.

In May 1981, in short, foreign governments as well as the French Socialists saw a left-wing-sounding leader rather than the man who had already spent three long centrist decades in French politics before joining the Socialist party at the age of fifty-five. When Mitterrand became president at the age of sixty-five, remarkably few of his foreign partners or adversaries could say they knew either his personality or his policy orientations. His past, we have seen, contained changes of orientation and certain episodes that he didn't want reopened. But on the other hand, the uncertainty about him incited an obsession in Mitterrand, according to the testimony of Hubert Védrine, to avoid the least irresponsibility, especially in security affairs. François Mitterrand in 1981 had a lot of convincing to do in a short time.

Fortunately or not, Mitterrand's presidency began in 1981 with the Euromissile crisis moving toward its height. He would have the opportunity to show what his fundamental orientation would be.

THE EUROMISSILE CRISIS:
MITTERRAND'S SURPRISING DEBUT

The Euromissile crisis refers to the Soviet/NATO conflict over the SS-20 medium-range missiles the USSR had installed at home and on the territories of East Germany and Czechoslovakia in the 1970s. These were a new generation of ballistic missiles whose medium range threatened Europe but not the United States. Their purpose was the old Soviet goal of driving a wedge between the United States and Europe in NATO's defense. New missiles that threatened European but not American territory reinforced American temptations to back away from insuring the security of the European allies.

The issue was really political, however, an attempt to intimidate the West Europeans. Other Europe-based NATO weapons—American, French, and British air- and sea-launched missiles—negated any plausible new military threat represented by the SS-20s. The real European fear was therefore a "decoupling" of American security from that of Europe, through the excuse given to Washington to weaken its guarantee of its allies' territory. Zbigniew Brzezinski defined the conflict persuasively: "Soviet leadership decided to elevate the [Euromissile] issue into a new test of will, again making the Atlantic security connection the ultimate stake. [The Euromissile crisis] is," he concluded, "the functional equivalent of the earlier Berlin crises."[12] Not surprisingly, it was the defense-focused German Helmut Schmidt who first officially "noticed" the existence of the SS-20s and brought them to NATO attention in 1977.

Washington, surprisingly, did not demur but instead made the famous 1979 "double track" decision—simultaneously to arm and negotiate disarmament—with the European NATO allies. Either the Soviet Union would remove the new SS-20 missiles or NATO would build and deploy its own Euromissiles, the Pershing II and Cruise missiles. The U.S. ambassador to Germany Richard Burt said that the American decision was remarkable since putting American land missiles capable of reaching the USSR back into western Europe (all but short-range missiles had been removed in the 1950s and not replaced) was to consciously accept anew a risk the United States had unloaded twenty years earlier. Eventually there were 572 new missiles, consisting of 464 slow Cruise missiles and 128 fast, accurate, and powerful Pershing IIs, which were comparable to the SS-20s in quality if not in number. All the Pershings were bound, significantly, for West German territory.

France had sometimes been a wild card in east-west diplomacy, pursuing a distinctive position while remaining inside the alliance. How would the new French left-wing government, led by President Mitterrand, behave as it arrived untested in office? Would Mitterrand make trouble for NATO out of anti-capitalism, neutralism, pacifism, or by his Communist partners in the government? Would he behave with de Gaulle–like maverick independence to demonstrate autonomy and to cultivate the Soviet leadership? Or would Mitterrand's France prove to be—the least likely view according to expectations of him—a staunch NATO partner, sharing allies' views of what was at stake and what had to be done?

For the next two years until the Euromissile crisis was over, Mitterrand in fact proved to be the staunchest European leader standing against Soviet intimidation. The test of wills ended with no agreement with the Soviets, a miscalculation on their part. The NATO Euromissiles were consequently deployed. Ronald Reagan's administration called him America's most reliable ally in European security matters and his behavior in the Euromissile crisis became the founding act of Mitterrand's entry into European politics. Fears were calmed about France's Union of the Left president.

His policy was also quite a remarkable French gesture of solidarity in transatlantic partnership, given that European confidence in American leadership in 1981 was still at the nadir it had reached in the late 1970s, compounded by new worries about Ronald Reagan's steadiness. Vietnam, Watergate, and Richard Nixon's resignation, plus the shaky foreign affairs performance of the Carter administration, all made for Western demoralization when placed against the Soviet Union's expansionism of the same period, culminating in its invasion of Afghanistan in late 1979, which deeply worried western capitals.

West German domestic trends were worrisome as well, to both Washington and Paris. A broad peace movement had arisen, pacifist, anti-nuclear, and neutralist, not only in West Germany but also growing, under protection of the Protestant churches, in East Germany. As the Euromissile crisis expanded, the West German and East German peoples became obsessed with the possibility of a war in Europe, which would certainly hit them first. The Soviet invasion of Afghanistan and the arrival in office of Margaret Thatcher and Ronald Reagan, reputed as warmongers, brought home to German minds that any danger of war in Europe was a danger for them before anyone else. A war that began on German soil could (as President Reagan had said in a moment of ill-considered geniality) conceivably be limited to Germany, or at least to Europe. Tactical nuclear weapons made a "war-fighting" superpower strategy, at the expense of the Germans, at least thinkable. "The shorter range the missiles, the deader the Germans!" became a peace movement mantra.

French editorialists pondered ominously the risks German pacifism created for France and the other allies, while the German SPD political intellectual Richard Löwenthal, in a much-remarked *Foreign Affairs* essay, showed how the "German problem" had been unexpectedly transformed by nuclear weapons. Being the first target of the most damaging weapons, Germans now saw themselves not as the benefactors but the victims of power politics. "For the first time in modern history, then," said Löwenthal, "what appears as the German question has taken the form of an almost desperate desire for *peace* by the German people west and east."[13] The Euromissile crisis made manifest the historic change in Germany's geopolitical situation in the nuclear age. The corollary was that France's policy could and must change.

It would be a considerable achievement if François Mitterrand could influence the German debate on whether to accept deployment of the Euromissiles. The hardline chancellor Helmut Schmidt, who had been defense minister, fell from power in 1982 when many of his own Social Democratic deputies, sympathetic to the peace movement, repudiated his leadership. The SPD's moderate coalition partner, the small Free Democratic Party (FDP) led by Hans-Dietrich Genscher, then shifted alliances, joining the conservative Christian Democratic party led by Helmut Kohl. Kohl became chancellor and the new German government was committed to NATO's "double decision." But German public opinion remained heavily neutralist and pacifist.

Given the Union of the Left domestic coalition and the issue of having Communist government ministers, Mitterrand's plan had always been, for a first stage of his presidency, to emphasize strict French solidarity within NATO. He knew he had to give guarantees to the allies, that he would find little tolerance for de Gaulle–style maneuvering. A firm anti-Soviet line, and an extra effort to "disintoxicate" French opinion about a Soviet Union many French people had long admired, was necessary.

On April 5, 1983, a tough, sudden, unprecedented mass expulsion of forty-seven Soviet diplomats was ordered by Mitterrand, for alleged espionage. Thirty-seven were clear KGB operatives, the rest had ambiguous commercial jobs.[14] The Soviets, then in the midst of crises of leadership succession, responded weakly. At home the French Communists, who had been pondering whether to quit the Mauroy government coalition over the March austerity plan, were trapped. Quitting the Union of the Left at that point would seem like they were following a Soviet lead, just like the bad old days. Mitterrand's comment was that, "with the Soviets there is nothing better than pressure applied at the most sensitive spot. France demands to be respected."

A strong anti-Soviet policy required strong control of the French Communists within the French government. Instead of being moved by them, Mitterrand demanded and got a historic endorsement of NATO's "double track" decision by the French Communist government ministers. This banging of heads had the additional advantage of disorienting the French Communist rank-and-file, which saw that their once-vaunted party really was only a junior partner to the Socialists. Communist government ministers endorsed government policies that the party-as-party rejected! This was also a blow to the doctrine of "democratic centralism," according to which Communist party elected and government officials took strict orders from the party apparatus.

Mitterrand backed the 1979 NATO Euromissile decision at his first meeting with Helmut Schmidt, on May 24, 1981, only a few days after taking office. He was warning the Soviets not to count on France dancing out of NATO's line, and also, incidentally, assuaging Schmidt's doubts about him and his domestic political strategy. Védrine concludes that Mitterrand's policy in this last great military-political crisis of the cold war was "neither that of his predecessor, nor that of the [German] social democrats, nor, without a doubt, that which the French Socialist party would have chosen without him."[15] It showed the originality that François Mitterrand's presidency was assuming: leftist and socialist, yet also anti-communist and anti-Soviet; rejecting Reagan administration demands that the west Europeans abandon a controversial gas pipeline project between Soviet supply and Western European consumers, because Washington feared European dependence, yet showing NATO solidarity where it counted most. "Allied but not aligned" was Mitterrand's motto for France in NATO, meaning fundamental solidarity without automatic acceptance of American policies.

In fall 1982 Mitterrand met immediately with the new conservative German chancellor Helmut Kohl, now a Franco-German diplomatic custom. He got on better with the congenial Kohl than with his incisive, argumentative predecessor. Among other agreements, the never-implemented military clauses of the 1963 Franco-German treaty were resurrected and plans for joint strategic discussions were announced with an eye to the Euromissile crisis. Mitterrand also would speak to the German Bundestag in January 1983, shortly before crucial West German elections which would determine whether

Kohl would still be chancellor when the German parliament voted on the Euromissile deployment.

In the face of huge "peace" demonstrations in Germany, Italy, Britain, and other NATO countries, Mitterrand's policy was enunciated on Brussels TV in October in one of his more memorable statements: "I myself am also against the Euromissiles. Only I observe that the new missiles are over on the other side, while the peace demonstrators are on our side." This took conviction, and to make it stick as French policy required a leader of unconventional courage.

Mitterrand's Bundestag speech on January 21, 1983, was meant to be a solemn warning to German parliamentarians and to the German people. It "was not rhetorical. It expressed a strategic decision which had important consequences for himself and for France."[16] All of Mitterrand's various European projects—to alter relations with the United States and the Soviet Union, to deepen Franco-German partnership, and others—were blocked by the Euromissile standoff. Mitterrand's problem was to convince the increasingly pacifist and neutralist German populace that the Soviet Union had unilaterally broken the European "balance of terror," an act that required a firm NATO response, not appeasement of Soviet intimidation. The stake was, in other words, political, not military, although it appeared to be another step in the arms race. To reestablish a balance of weapons would be to reject any sort of Soviet right of veto of Western security decisions, with Germany to benefit first of all. NATO's missiles thus had to be American and they had to be stationed on land. The political "recoupling" would be achieved because any Soviet attack, however far-fetched, would mean destroying or capturing U.S. land-based nuclear weapons capable of hitting the Soviet Union.

Mitterrand told the German parliament in plain words, "The Soviets with their SS-20 missiles are unilaterally destroying the equilibrium in Europe. . . . I will not accept this and I recognize that we must arm ourselves to restore the balance. . . . Whosoever is staking a bet on decoupling Europe from America jeopardizes the . . . balance of power and thus the preservation of peace. . . . Our peoples must remain assured that they will not succumb to . . . foreign domination." German commentator Josef Joffe explained exactly how NATO's Euromissiles would affect Soviet thinking:

> The ultimate logic of the Euromissiles was the destruction of sanctuaries. If all are going to be entangled in a war, all are going to be equally vulnerable. If all are equally vulnerable, all will be equally safe. . . . Euromissiles point both ways. . . . They are poised to carry nuclear destruction into the territory of both superpowers, promising to defy any traditional distinction between "small" and

"big" wars; that is the murderous foundation on which the safety of lesser allies thrives. It is hard to exaggerate the political, if not historical, significance of the missile deployment. By stationing Pershing II and cruise missiles in Western Europe, the U.S. accepted a burden that few great powers have wittingly shouldered in the past.[17]

So the Soviets, as they themselves later admitted, lost a momentous battle of wills, when in 1983 the Pershing IIs were quickly and quietly deployed in West Germany after the conservative coalition, led by Kohl and Free Democratic party leader Hans-Dietrich Genscher, won the elections.

As for France's policy toward the Soviet Union, "the Bundestag speech," Mitterrand said, was "not a [nonnegotiable demand] but a psychological stage in Franco-Soviet relations," a show of determination to the effect that a French left-wing president would not, any more than a conservative president, be intimidated by Soviet power.[18] In that speech François Mitterrand had addressed not just German deputies (against the policy of his supposed SPD comrades!), but also the whole history of West European Socialist thinking about defense and security. He had also spoken to the West German people, reckoning with what Richard Löwenthal called their "almost desperate desire for peace," which to many of them meant above all not provoking the Soviets.

> Only an equilibrium of forces can bring good relations with the eastern countries, our neighbors and historical partners. This was the basis of . . . détente; it allowed you to implement your *Ostpolitik;* it made possible the Helsinki Agreements. But this balance . . . like it or not is a matter of deterrence. In order for [deterrence] to be remade—remade and not maintained since the SS-20 missiles unilaterally were responsible for upsetting it—a convincing threat to deploy [the Pershing II and Cruise] missiles is the only hope for negotiation.[19]

President Mitterrand's speech was not too controversial in France. Nuclear deterrence was a consensus policy after the Left accepted the *force de frappe* in the late 1970s. Moreover, the new missiles were not heading for French territory, reducing even more the effect on French public opinion.

But the French president's defiant stand was an electric shock in German opinion. Few European leaders had ever dared speak so openly about the logic of deterrence and especially about the link between nuclear balance and *political danger* from the East, which was the real issue hid by the otherwise senseless arms race. Helmut Kohl was grateful to Mitterrand for political education of German opinion and for advising the West Germans that their national interest was to vote the CDU-FDP conservative coalition back into power in the imminent elections, rejecting social democratic, Green party, and peace movement appeals for "sanity."

The Soviet ambassador Yuri Rubinskii later guessed at Mitterrand's thinking:

> I don't think François Mitterrand thought the SS 20s were much of a military threat to western Europe. What he wanted was to deal with German fears, the rise of a pacifism which would have detached Federal Germany from the west. . . . It would have destroyed the European Community and the Franco-German co-leadership so useful to France. It would be the end of the German buffer zone, France's projection into the first line of battle, in a certain way reducing France independence, making it no more than the staging area for the USA in western Europe.[20]

The Soviets retaliated against Mitterrand's hard line by playing a card they had held in reserve: a sudden demand that French and British nuclear forces be included in east/west strategic arms control negotiations. The exemption had been bait, its annulment was punishment. The French Communists, leashed by their promise of "flawless solidarity" in the Union of the Left government, said little or nothing, at least publicly.[21] Mitterrand was beginning to be known by the quality of his enemies, establishing credentials as a statesman and showing that a Socialist president could take a hard line when necessary. The stereotypes of Left and Right were more misleading than ever.

It was only two months later that Mitterrand ordered the expulsion from France of Soviet diplomats charged with espionage, the so-called "Farewell" affair. He overrode expected Quai d'Orsay foreign ministry anxieties about Soviet retaliation. In ten years under Pompidou and Giscard d'Estaing the personnel at the Paris Soviet embassy had risen from 200 to 749 people, with neither conservative president having kept Soviet presence under control. Mitterrand was apparently different.

The outcome of the Euromissile crisis was a great gain for transatlantic solidarity. The NATO Euromissiles were deployed, albeit with varying degrees of difficulty in different countries. It was easier at the end in West Germany than in Britain and Italy. The Soviets began to recognize they had overestimated their ascendancy in European affairs (as elsewhere). Ronald Reagan's "Star Wars" SDI proposal began to weigh on their calculations. Henry Kissinger evaluated the Euromissile episode in this way:

> Whenever Germany seemed tempted by neutralism, which, in the French mind, spelled nationalism, French presidents attempted to provide Bonn with a

European or Atlantic alternative. In the 1960s, de Gaulle had been a staunch defender of the German point of view on Berlin. In 1983, Mitterrand emerged unexpectedly as the chief European supporter of the American [Euromissile] plan.[22]

The peace movement, continuing to demand partial reductions in medium-range land-based weapons, was outflanked and astonished a few years later by Gorbachev's and Reagan's negotiation of *total* elimination. With the 1987 Intermediate-Range Nuclear Forces (INF) treaty and its "double zero" options, all Soviet and U.S. Euromissiles were withdrawn.

French domestic policy and foreign policy were evolving in similar ways. The Euromissile crisis peaked more or less at the same time as Mitterrand's Socialist domestic experiment was abandoned with the decisions in 1982 and 1983. His shaky domestic financial and economic situation was an added incentive for a strong alliance policy.

The Euromissile crisis was the equivalent, all other things being equal, of what the Cuban missile crisis had been for de Gaulle. It took political and moral courage for a French president to be so candidly anti-Soviet and pro-NATO, thus pro-American. Just as de Gaulle had, in October 1962, told President John F. Kennedy's emissary that he "didn't need to see the photographs" of Soviet installations to convince him he must support Kennedy, Mitterrand had no second thoughts on alliance solidarity once he had decided a fundamental east/west standoff had been reached.

The French president failed nevertheless to make the Euromissile crisis into a pedagogical exercise for French opinion, above all French Left opinion. The all-powerful gaullien president had decided, but he offered precious little explanation as to why French policy was doing the right thing. This lack of attention to pedagogy would, in the long run, turn out to be characteristic of Mitterrand and have an effect on his legacy. (See chapter 12.)

EUROPEAN INTEGRATION, ACCELERATED SPEED

Denouement of the Euromissile crisis and the crash and burn of the socialist experiment meant a new start was possible and necessary for Mitterrand's presidency. The next phase would be *un forcing Européen,* a decisive relaunching of European integration in tandem with Federal Germany and Mitterrand's conservative partner, Chancellor Kohl. The third man would be

Jacques Delors, a French Socialist and Prime Minister Pierre Mauroy's finance minister. Delors was selected in 1985 to preside over the EC Commission, which he revivified as it had not been since the 1950s and early 1960s under Walter Hallstein.[23]

The policies of Europe's states in European integration negotiations are no longer, if they ever were, simple choices for or against Europe. Even for the most nationalist governments, for example, that of Margaret Thatcher (who, it is often forgotten, finally accepted the 1987 Single European Act), the question is not whether to be for or against Europe, but what kind of European integration is necessary.

European policies in the Mitterrand period separated roughly into two sorts of opinions: those which stressed national autonomy, seeing economic integration as beneficial but not much else; and those who saw a larger "Europe" as a national interest, who wanted economic integration to lead to political institutions, foreign policy, and a joint defense. In France both types had their heroes: Jean Monnet and Charles de Gaulle were both Frenchmen. Jacques Delors had a reputation as more of a European than Mitterrand, but Delors's Europeanism as president of the EC commission was a version of the rule that "Where you sit is where you stand." After he left the commission to return to French politics in 1995, often Delors sounded little different from Mitterrand. He muted his federalist inclination and even accepted as inevitable a "multi-speed" EU, as he once told a group of interviewers including this author.

Mitterrand, by contrast, as president of France, always had to put the French national interest first when dealing with EU decisions. But precisely because he saw integration as good for French national interests, he was pro-European. Integration was overall not merely good for France, it is necessary, even if in certain respects also dangerous. A statesman's alternatives are rarely black and white.

This interplay of national interest and European integration explains why even "a federalist in the long run" like Mitterrand wanted to keep fundamental authority for now in the inter-governmental European Council. Composed of national representatives and operating with a veto provision, the Council is the forum of national interests in the EU structure. Mitterrand, Kohl, Thatcher, and other big-country leaders, and even certain smaller-country representatives thus held the supranational Commission and the politically messy European parliament to defined roles. Wind could be blown in their sails when desirable, for example to support Jacques Delors's Commission and the Single European Act project. But the wind could disappear when it was a matter of avoiding dangerous extensions of federalism, such as awarding more powers to the not yet politically mature European parliament.

◆ ◆ ◆

Beyond general premises the most difficult part was to determine *which* French policies will bring *what kind* of Europe within *which conception* of France's national interest.

One gaullist leader whose evolution has illustrated the consensus around Mitterrand's combination of national interest and European integration is Philippe Séguin, a neo-gaullist, RPR leader and, with former interior minister Charles Pasqua, one of the main figures of the nationalist-oriented wing of French conservatism.

Séguin originally criticized the Maastricht treaty as harmful to France. He denounced Mitterrand's willingness to pay any price in unemployment for "slavish" national government budget cuts and high interest rates so that France could fulfill the Maastricht convergence requirements for membership in the euro-group, especially the need to cut the annual government budget deficit to 3 percent of GDP by the end of 1997. With echoes of the "night visitor" advice to Mitterrand in March 1983, Séguin proposed what was called "the other policy." It would unilaterally lower, not raise, French interest rates to encourage economic growth, thus more jobs and more tax revenues. Renegotiation of the convergence criteria agreements were also an issue: Why, Séguin asked, should the right number be 3 percent of GDP and not 4 or 5 percent budget deficit limits? Why lock the French franc, or for that matter other weaker currencies such as the lira and the peseta, so strictly to the German mark? The social pain of Maastricht's imposed economic austerity was too great, he concluded as the "social gaullist" he was.

The other neo-gaullist leader of the anti-Maastricht movement, Charles Pasqua, interior minister in both the 1986 and 1993 conservative cohabitation governments, took another critical viewpoint. He stressed the danger European integration posed literally to the French state and French society. In France, state and society were more tightly intertwined historically than in other European states. In France the state historically had been the architect itself of social structure, so French society would be profoundly affected if abandonment of French autonomy to the EU's "pooled sovereignty" went on. This was not merely a dilution of sovereignty and national independence; diminution of sovereignty is in France an attack on the very character of society. In France the state is, or was, everything, or almost.

In this sense, Pasqua argued, European integration forces greater changes on France than on other EU societies. To oppose the Maastricht treaty, with its increased European centralism and the crush of Bundesbank hard money morality, was therefore a kind of French patriotism, a refurbished gaullism for the 1990s.

Pasqua and Séguin were allies until 1998-1999, when they split over whether the constitutional amendments necessary to ratify the Amsterdam treaty of 1997 should be accepted. In June 1996, a year after Mitterrand had left office, Séguin, then president of the National Assembly, addressed a room full of business leaders and academics. "Perceived wrongly as anti-European," Séguin said he was only opposed to a Europe that was "too passive," especially faced with capital and currency markets. His European thinking was based on certain ideas, several of them gaullist to the bone: solidarity, social protection, the social market economy, even including a German-style cogestion that would be an innovation in French "class struggle" industrial relations. This European "model," distinct from U.S. and Asian habits and an example that Europe could offer to other peoples, was also France's geopolitical hope: "France knows," Séguin said, "that a European destiny is the condition of maintaining its influence in the world. She therefore wants Europe, resolutely. But this Europe must signify something much more decisive than simple commercial gains. France believes in grandeur; she thus wants a Europe which counts in the world and is a model to offer to other peoples."[24]

Séguin in 1992 had already accepted the Maastricht referendum's legitimacy, despite being narrowly on the losing end. And in late 1998 he accepted the constitutional amendments, voted by the Assembly and Senate in "congress" at Versailles, necessary to implement the Amsterdam treaty. For the sake of party unity and perhaps his own presidential ambitions, Séguin seemed to accept President Jacques Chirac's pro-Maastricht, pro-euro, pro-Amsterdam treaty line.[25]

In the Séguin-Pasqua debate and parting of ways, one sees how François Mitterrand's choice of Europe became a consensus in French politics that permitted the Séguinist neo-gaullists to find a way to the future: "The greatest possible French influence in the most powerful possible Europe."

FRANCE'S INTEREST IN THE "SINGLE INTEGRATED MARKET" 1992 PROJECT

Even adding all the Euroskeptic oppositions together, Mitterrand's presidency had resulted in "Europe" becoming a mainstream policy across the old Left-Right abyss in French politics. This "recentering" of French policy had its counterpart in domestic politics, whose vagaries no longer unexpectedly upset the French and European apple carts. France under Mitterrand had become a less unpredictable partner in European negotiations and nowhere more so than for Germany. The "Franco-German motor" of European integration would continue to run, piloted by Mitterrand and Helmut Kohl, more confidently than ever in the direction laid out by Giscard d'Estaing and Helmut Schmidt. This fork in the road toward Europe was clearly in part one result of the Socialist experiment's failure. The Socialist party's Jacobin nationalist left wing and the Communists didn't like that. But Mitterrand would have headed France toward more European integration even had socialism been less of a disaster.

In December 1985 a new constitutional document was added to the EC treaty, the awkwardly named *Acte unique,* which was translated into English as the (equally vague) Single European Act (SEA). The term signified putting together various existing agreements in a single document, to "complete the single market" within EC territory. This would be a market comparable to the national market of any member country or the American national market. Going beyond the EC's "customs union," which had abolished formal barriers to trade, meaning tariffs, the SEA would bring down informal barriers to trade as well— quotas, paperwork, content standards, and the like. By December 31, 1994, there would be a true single, unified market throughout the EC members' territories on which there would be completely free movement of goods, workers (but not yet people as citizens), services, and capital.

Among the major EC leaders, Jacques Delors, Helmut Kohl, and Mitterrand argued strongly in favor of the Single Market project. Margaret Thatcher and the Danes opposed it. Kohl and Mitterrand told Thatcher that if there was no agreement of twelve members, the ten who agreed would go ahead anyway. This threat of going around the veto of a major country had wide implications, but the two leaders didn't shy from it. "At three minutes from the deadline for talk, failure seemed certain," says Hubert Védrine, because of British/Danish opposition. Thatcher, after a last moment of hesitation, accepted. The Single European Act, the second constitutional document of European integration after the Rome Treaty of 1957, thus was voted up with the British and Danes accepting it. Later Margaret Thatcher cleverly cited her vote in favor of the SEA as proof that she wasn't "anti-European." For Mitterrand the goal of eliminating informal barriers to trade and thus completing the single market was a minimum step ahead. He wanted further structures to complete and balance the single integrated market: monetary union (the euro and the Eurofed), common business cycle policies, "deepening" the institutions of decisionmaking, and, finally, the "political union"—legal structures for citizens' rights, police and judicial cooperation, and a common foreign and security policy.

The SEA's preamble announced that a European Union would be built in two parts, the existing European communities (EC, ECSC, and Euratom, the atomic energy agency) and a separate foreign policy agreement. The European Council meetings were institutionalized, the areas where majority voting applied were increased, and an economic and monetary union was announced that would transform the European Monetary System (EMS), creating the ecu, the precursor of today's euro, the Single European Currency. Negotiating the Single European Act was a huge and complex business, and its effect would be larger than foreseen by its godfathers, François Mitterrand included.

From 1985-1986 on, European events were swept up in the maelstrom in the East European countries and in Soviet-American negotiations between new Soviet leader Mikhail Gorbachev, two American presidents, Ronald Reagan and George Bush, and the German leaders Kohl and Genscher.

GERMAN UNIFICATION
AND FRENCH DILEMMAS

When the Soviet Union collapsed and, along with it, divided cold war "Yalta" Europe, a French diplomat summed up the situation for France: "For we French," he said, sighing ruefully, "now there is only Germany, only Germany." This was the old defeatist attitude, so hard to overcome.

The great question about François Mitterrand's policy toward German unification, and Margaret Thatcher's, was whether they welcomed the quickest end of divided Europe, or whether they sought to slow things down, to channel reunification through solid institutional pipelines to prevent an out-of-control reunification pushed at breakneck speed by East Germans moving to the West. Perhaps German unification even might be elided by maintaining an East German state in confederation, not federation, with the West, in order to avoid a new German-dominated Europe.

Did France, did Mitterrand's policy, really want the end of the cold war? Or was French policy guided by old fears? These fears added up to what were called Mitterrand's "hesitations" about German unification.

In the vocabulary of classic 1850 to 1950 European geopolitics, the Soviet collapse, leaving a weakened Russia and subsequent confusion about NATO's purpose, meant there was no powerful state in the East as an objective French ally in confronting potential German dangers. One geopolitical price France paid in the end of the cold war was, in other words, to see the emergence of a unified and perhaps newly ambitious Germany in principle free to pursue German national strategies. Realist commentators therefore opined that France had lost something valuable with the cold war's end—a certain geopolitical and diplomatic leverage on Germany. Zbigniew Brzezinski even argued that there were two big losers in the end of the cold war: the Soviet Union and France. France had lost the geopolitical advantages it derived from a divided, straightjacketed Germany and a strong, vigilant Soviet Union. While in principle France's adversary in east/west conflict, the Soviet Union was objectively France's ally in keeping Germany corseted.

But this doesn't mean the French would have preferred to prop up a totalitarian Soviet Union, a divided Europe, and a divided Germany. With Russia weakened and the United States more committed to the new larger, more powerful, and more central Germany than to French worries, France's policy was really of second consequence in negotiating the end of the cold war.

How would the French cope with post–cold war, post-Yalta, post-Soviet Europe? What would be their strategy vis-à-vis a Germany that contained not 62 million people as against 57 million French, but 80 million—or over 90 million ethnic Germans counting, as Mitterrand and others did in private conversations, Austria and German communities in Poland, Czechoslovakia, Russia, and elsewhere?

KOHL'S TEN-POINT PLAN,
MITTERRAND'S REACTION

In October-November 1989, Chancellor Kohl was not yet clear about how quickly events would go and what form unification, or reunification, would take. He felt he had to propose some organizing plan concerning steps, pace, and framework. On November 28 came his "Ten Point Plan," quickly put together in secrecy without even his own government—not even Hans-Dietrich Genscher—being informed of it. Nor were foreign officials forewarned; not Mitterrand or other EU partners, not the Bush administration. Kohl felt the plan couldn't wait and that he couldn't risk delay or allowing others to mobilize in a debate. Events were moving too quickly on the ground in East Germany.

At first seen as some kind of unilateral West German "breakout" move given the speed at which East Germany was disintegrating, Kohl's Ten-Point Plan was soon recognized as a plan for prudence. It was not a move to accelerate events, already proceeding too quickly from the West German point of view, let alone a ploy by Kohl to put his Western partners into a corner. Kohl was facing what was not-so-jokingly called the possibility of "reunification on West German soil," that unification of the two Germanys would occur by all the East Germans moving to the West! The Ten-Point Plan's overall goal was to contain the East German collapse and slow a population movement in danger of spinning out of control, the result of which would be human disaster in East Germany and domestic political disaster in the West. After all, Chancellor Kohl faced West German nightmares of the damage unrestricted East German arrivals would inflict.

Mitterrand's policy of slowing down events and gaining German reassurances was widely criticized. In his rapidly written postpresidential book, *Of Germany, of France*, he reckoned with his critics.[26] Mitterrand, with Thatcher and Gorbachev, it was said, secretly opposed German unification. German bad feeling was especially bitter concerning Mitterrand's demand, as a condition for accepting unification, for an incontestable international legal document, not just a German policy declaration, confirming the Oder-Neisse border between Germany and Poland as permanent. Kohl, to the contrary, delayed even a German parliamentary declaration on the boundary because he needed nationalist votes for his CDU party in upcoming elections. In a February 15, 1990, private dinner conversation at the Élysée palace, Kohl's irritation showed: "The Oder-Neisse border issue became inflamed. The issue never should have been posed [as a prior condition of unification]. For the Germans it remains a large wound. To treat wounds with boiling oil rather than with balm doesn't help healing!"[27]

Mitterrand's response was always to say that he never was against German unification, which was "a German right" as a matter of national self-determination, no matter how uncomfortable it might prove for neighbors. The Germans were not somehow guilty, vis-à-vis France or anyone else, for their large population or economic dynamism! Nevertheless, appropriate institutions could create a peaceful European framework for unified Germany—"We can create communities, European institutions" to resolve border problems and other issues—whereas overoptimistic, naive solutions to issues created by past conflicts would only create the next German, thus European, self-immolation. Mitterrand's goal was, he argued, only to get unification done the right way, to channel it with "communities" and "institutions."

The French president's policy was plausible. The problem was that, as critics said, there was another possible French policy, not merely defensive and precautionary but, as in the American policy crafted by President George Bush and Secretary of State James Baker, a rapid, full endorsement of German unification once Kohl had made clear where he was headed.

A gaullist French ambassador who had been Prime Minister Chirac's political advisor in 1986 quickly improvised for this author in an interview the de Gaulle–like speech Mitterrand might have made. The moment the Berlin Wall was breached in October 1989, the French president should have seen that unification was inevitable. He would have immediately gone on television with a solemn, forward-looking speech congratulating the Germans on the imminent achievement of their destiny to be unified again. He would have announced "France's joy" that "what Germans and French had sought for forty years," that is, the "end of the Yalta system," was on the horizon. France, by virtue of history and geography, would "of course" be at the cutting edge of diplomatic negotiations with its allies, at the forefront of Germany's friends and partners.[28]

Why did Mitterrand not make such a speech? Clearly he did not have confidence enough either in France's situation geopolitically or in the meaningfulness of a Franco-British strategy that, however pursued and sweetened, would wound the West Germans terribly. Geopolitical inequalities and the demons of the past still outweighed, he implied, a full confidence even after four decades of postwar German evolution. But this lack of confidence was as much within his own mind as in the German, French, and international contexts. All of these were signaling acceptance of the incipient European revolution. Given the immense risks Gorbachev and Kohl themselves were taking, given the risks even Ronald Reagan and Margaret Thatcher had taken, at home and abroad— especially with Gorbachev—François Mitterrand seemed to lack confidence and political imagination. Having thought all his life in the mold of World War I (of which World War II in Europe was a second act), and then of cold war Europe, Mitterrand's "caution" and concern for international guarantees, the boundaries of states, and the need not to overload institutions, was really a lack of vision. Had he launched a French public debate on German unification instead of deciding essentially alone with the advice of his entourage, he might have learned that his judgment of the French people's worries was exaggerated.

With a vision of a "postgeopolitical" Europe, a hopeful term the Germans used, one in which European integration was both deepened and widened, Mitterrand might have hesitated less and encouraged more in October-November 1989. French friendship with the emerging unified Germany would have benefited had he not just supported Kohl's policy but spoken on its behalf internationally and welcomed the former East Germans into the West and into the European Community.

Later on, Helmut Kohl's memoir, *Ich Wollte Deutschland's Einheit* (I Wanted German Unity) said openly that Mitterrand's attitudes at this time were disappointing and personally wounding. But the moment passed, and, diluted in the greater success of German unification, the Mitterrand-Kohl Franco-German leadership collaboration on European integration soon resumed as before.

But nevertheless, had not the French or some other important government raised the issue of border guarantees, history—there is always the possibility— might one day have rued the absence of new guarantees to Poland and

Czechoslovakia. Was Mitterrand not correct, even if the possibility was unlikely, that France and other European states might one day be called on to defend agreements on German unification in 1989-1990 against a more assertive Germany? For example, if the United States one day disengaged from Europe on its own, could France—and Britain and others—react with strength and self-confidence vis-à-vis unified Germany?

Védrine gives the positive interpretation of Mitterrand's outlook: "This vision anchored far in the past permitted François Mitterrand to see far ahead," although it did lead to "an excess of worries."[29] But no one, says Védrine, has shown that this excess of precautions did practical damage. On the contrary, it "inspired all the proposals that have worked out," including a more substantial Maastricht Treaty. "No one has explained," Védrine says, "what else would have needed to be done."[30] But there is a difference between what is necessary and what is possible, and Mitterrand, concentrating on the first, missed chances to do more. Neither France nor Britain was at the center of events once the East German people and the West German chancellor, with American blessing and Soviet concession, were at full throttle. France and Britain had some room to maneuver, but could not delay (Mitterrand) or stop (Thatcher) German unification in the near term.

Quite in character, Mitterrand's worry about seeing a unified Germany born too quickly was twin to his subsequent concern over the implosion of the Soviet Union. He obviously had no love for communism—"Do you think we should cry over communism's demise?" he said in a television interview, "Not me!" But he exuded a somber disquiet about preserving European stability, meaning preserving existing states in their boundaries or else accepting changes only when all the pieces were firmly in place. His main concern was, as always, for peace and the European equilibrium, not necessarily first of all for national self-determination. Desirable as it was, what effects would German unification have on the European equilibrium? What would the Soviet Union's collapse and disappearance, however good for its people, do to Europe's stability? The German people had the legitimate right to unification, the Soviet people to change states. But what about the time frame and stages and methods? What about the effects on others countries and peoples?

As for Soviet positions, Gorbachev and Schevardnadze were playing from a weak hand and losing more trumps all the time. Often they insisted that if unified Germany was to be a member of NATO, then the alliance would have to change its character. Perhaps both NATO and the Warsaw Pact could evolve into political alliances with friendly relations. Gorbachev said he wouldn't object to American military forces remaining in Germany and could see advantages for European stability; but he did not expect more than five or ten years because the next generation of Germans wouldn't want them. Bush argued that a unified Germany, which would be either a member of both alliances (one Soviet suggestion) or of none (another Soviet proposal), could shift its weight with more dangerous effect than a Germany inside NATO and tightly bound.[31]

Mitterrand finally accepted Kohl's accelerated timetable, which sought the most rapid possible unification of the two Germanys. Delay had become, in Kohl's view, the most dangerous alternative. The overriding French goal then became to embed German unification in the Atlantic Alliance and in the European integration process. German unification, European unification, and a strong Atlantic Alliance were three integral parts of a framework to make certain that German unification worked out positively. Thus France insisted on unified Germany's full membership in NATO and Mitterrand several times rebuffed suggestions (not very serious and half-ironic) by the Soviet leaders Gorbachev and Foreign Minister Eduoard Schevardnadze that unified Germany should have a "French status" in NATO, outside the integrated military command while still a full member of the alliance.

From the German side, to assuage French concern that unification might lead German policy eastward, away from plans for EC monetary and political union, Helmut Kohl joined Mitterrand's proposal that German unification and "deepening" of European integration must go together. It was well understood, by the West Germans most of all, that legitimacy for German unification required embedding the new Germany in the European Community. German unification and European integration were two sides of the same coin. Védrine's judgment is balanced and judicious, especially because a mistake by one leader at a given moment could be compensated by the determination of others:

> Gorbachev, Kohl, Bush or Mitterrand may have wavered at times or committed errors. But the stakes were high. Each of them, in conscience, acted as a true statesman: Mikhail Gorbachev in renouncing any use of force and in comporting himself democratically in consequences of this policy; François Mitterrand in concentrating on things that would guarantee future stability and cohesion of the continent, plus relaunching European integration; George Bush in avoiding any over-aggressive wielding of Atlantic superiority against Gorbachev; Helmut Kohl in taking the "one-for-one" [currency] decision at the right moment and in co-sponsoring the [Maastricht] Treaty with the French president. Only Margaret Thatcher walled herself up in a double refusal—no to reunification, no to relaunching European integration—therein losing any possibility of influence.[32]

MAASTRICHT: GERMAN UNIFICATION, EUROPEAN MONETARY UNION, AND EUROPEAN POLITICAL UNION

French and German leaders had to show unity rediscovered after the dramas of German unification. This they did. In April 1990 Mitterrand and Kohl proposed together a combined next stage for European integration. A treaty on "political union" would accompany the already planned monetary union treaty for a single European currency. This would show German unification had not derailed but was in fact a new stimulus for deepened European integration. By accepting not only monetary but political Europeanization, unified Germany could show still more that it was not a destabilizing factor in the European equilibrium.

The "Maastricht Treaty" thus was actually *two* treaties, one for monetary union (the "euro" and the European Central Bank, or Eurofed), the other for political union (internal and police affairs, and the plan for a common foreign and security policy). The Maastricht treaty (named after the beautiful Dutch city where the Frenchman d'Artagnan died in the siege of 1673), was concluded December 10-11, 1991, and initialed on February 7, 1992, by the then twelve EC members. Ratification, according to the various national constitutional requirements, was then necessary. In some cases, as in France, amendments to the national constitution were required. Ratification was by no means a foregone conclusion in all countries, and in France it became unexpectedly risky.

To link European integration and German unification was to blunt the worries about unification by increasing the Europeanization of Germany. Kohl and Genscher, all through the heady months of rejoining the two German halves, stressed that the new Germany would be "embedded" (their word) in European integration, a guarantee for Germany's neighbors and for the nervous Germans as well.

NATO's role was also vital as an overall guarantee to the geopolitical results of German unification and the European equilibrium. German leaders told the Soviets that neutrality for unified Germany, a historic Soviet proposal made first by Stalin in 1952-1953, and that Gorbachev and Edouard Schevardnadze suggested again in 1990, was out of the question. No German chancellor from Adenauer forward would have accepted German neutrality and it was no more acceptable to Helmut Kohl, now the "chancellor of German unification." Genscher stressed that neutrality, leaving aside the geopolitical significance of asking West Germany to leave NATO, would "isolate" Germany into an unanchored, independent position that the Germans themselves didn't want. Worried enough by their own history, the Germans remembered what happened whenever Germany found itself hanging independent between East and West.

They wanted to be bound and tied up in NATO and European integration. To save themselves from temptation was their proposal! The combination of German strengths and anxieties could, if Germany were independent, be dangerous. The noted American journalist Elizabeth Pond described Germany as the first "post-national" European state, beyond nationalism not out of altruism but self-interest rightly understood. Gorbachev and Schevardnadze finally agreed that Moscow, having accepted German unification by East German collapse into the arms of the Federal Republic, would also agree to the former GDR's five states being absorbed into West Germany's NATO member-ship, albeit with a few face-saving details.

It remained to resolve Franco-German views about what the Maastricht treaty would say concerning the proposed "European defense identity" and its relation to NATO. NATO meant continued American military presence in Europe, which was the backbone guarantee of European and German stability.

During the summer of 1991, French negotiators Pierre Morel and Caroline de Margerie met regularly with their German counterparts to settle differences. The French side wanted an independent "European defense identity" specified in the Treaty; the Germans wanted above all to avoid anything that would weaken American commitment to remain in Europe. Finally the Germans agreed that the Maastricht Treaty would speak of a "European defense identity" in addition to the goal of a common foreign and security policy. In exchange, the French, "not wanting to give U.S. secretary of state James Baker a pretext to smash European defense autonomy even as a goal," Morel said, agreed that European defense projects had to work within NATO, not outside. This agreement showed once again how the Franco-German tandem arrived at solutions that then could be put to the other partners as joint propositions.

Unification would not affect West Germany's external policy. The former east Germans would have to accept this, and few of them were in a mood to contest it. Unified Germany's national interest in the European equilibrium was clear: a European Germany, not a Germanized Europe. Helmut Kohl's chief diplomatic advisor summed up the chancellor's views:

> . . . that the security of all sides should be increased and German unification should become the cornerstone of a stable European peace order. All thoughts of neutrality, demilitarization, and alliance or bloc disaffiliation he described as "old thinking." Kohl founded his position in the experience of German history, that peace, stability and security in Europe had always been guaranteed when Germany—the country in the middle of Europe—had lived with all its neighbors in firm ties, with contractual equality and mutually beneficial exchanges.[33]

The next issue was the significance of German unification for enlargement of the European Union, for new memberships. German unification was itself the first expansion of the EU into ex-communist Europe, through the absorption of East Germany by the West. This "precedent" tempted the new democratic governments in Central and Eastern Europe (CEE) to quicken their own case for membership, with accompanying financial and development aid. Mitterrand said that a too rapid incorporation of the former Soviet satellites would drown the EU budget and paralyze its decision-making, with excessive numbers and unresolvable new claims and disagreements. But his own proposal of a European "confederation" that would create levels of membership by associating the eastern countries with the EU but put off their full membership for many years, failed completely at the time. Vaclav Havel angrily reproached Mitterrand's confederation concept as a "small Europe" view of a problem that should have been posed in terms of Europeanism, humanism, and generosity by the advanced European countries. Havel talked of historically just recompense in dealing with peoples who had suffered so much during the period of Soviet imperialism in their countries. Delay could even permit a Russian backlash against those who had "lost" Eastern Europe and demoralize the Czech and other East European nations who had paid such a high price for WWII. Many Eastern Europeans alleged that Mitterrand and the West European leaders were perpetrating a new "Yalta," excluding Eastern Europe again in order not to risk the rich, privileged situation of the European Community.

One can imagine Mitterrand's view of Havel, an old friend and a man for whom he (with his own Resistance record) had extraordinary esteem. In the past, on visits to Czechoslovakia Mitterrand had always insisted courageously on meeting with the dissident Havel and his friends. Now president of Czechoslovakia, Havel, in his position, had to want immediate membership of the EC, had to denounce Mitterrand and France as he did. But membership in the near term for Eastern European countries would cost too much, and had to be squared with "deepening" the decision-making institutions. Czechoslovakia, and after its breakup the even smaller Czech Republic, was one thing. But the rest of Eastern Europe's poor millions with their huge and inefficient agricultural systems would break the bank by overloading the Common Agricultural Policy's subsidy budgets, two-thirds of the total Community budget. Putting the newly liberated Eastern European countries into a waiting room of "association" relationships was the kind of practical choice about "what" and "how much" Europe a French (or German or British) leader such as Mitterrand faced. It shows how choices "for" and "against" Europe at any single point are never simple alternatives, but dilemmas to be partially resolved, with time bought, and eventually surpassed or altered by changing circumstances. East European economic and social development alters the issue of full membership and permits an order of accession to be justified.

Among the worries about the new Germany was that it might resist "deepening" European institutions because its government would decide tacitly to shift Germany's foreign policy agenda to national German expansion of influence in the East. A geopolitical German strategy would have two goals: (1) avoiding EU institution-building that would further tie Germany's hands; (2) using new East European member states to create a German sphere of influence inside the EU with German-controlled votes resulting from historic ties and German financial and economic largesse.

"Our policy," writes Védrine, was "held in a single phrase, logical and chronological: Deepening first, widening after," which meant reinforcing EU internal coherence first, and only then allowing new members in. The Germans understood French worries very well, realizing French policy was not anti-German although it had to focus on reining in Germany's freedom to maneuver.

In fall 1989, the *annus mirabilis* of German unification, President Mitterrand had told the European parliament that "deepening" had to precede "widening," more institution-building before new members. In late October Mitterrand added the idea of a European bank to underwrite East European development, focused on privatization of state-owned industry in the former Eastern communist countries. The political logic of the European Reconstruction and Development Bank (ERDB) was to multilateralize the political weight of German wealth by channeling it with other country donations through the bank. The French could claim credit for the idea (Mitterrand's aide Jacques Attali first of all), and they and the other member countries could weigh in together against Germany's advantages. The German response, once again accommodating, was to adopt the same policy as the French about expansion. "Deepening" would indeed precede "widening," continuing institution-building would come before new members.

So a second, political union treaty was added to the original monetary union treaty to be concluded at Maastricht. The Franco-German tandem was on track again, having righted itself after having been unbalanced by the unexpected speed and character of German unification. The Germans were, as usual, listening hard to French recommendations. French diplomacy was seen as a leading force in the Community.

The only question was whether, despite "losing" or accommodating on each specific issue, the Germans were not fated to dominate European integration anyway. Could Germany *avoid* hegemony in Europe?

The upshot of reacting to German unification was to advance the previously projected calendar for European political union. More majority voting, as opposed to unanimous voting, plus other decision-making changes would be in place along with the single European currency when new members arrived.

Near the final Maastricht negotiations, the British, according to Mitterrand's diplomatic advisor Caroline de Margerie in an internal memo at the end of October, "opposed all new points of progress. They are opposed to the single currency and the European central bank, opposed to qualified majority voting in foreign policy matters, opposed to a common defense even in the long term, opposed to a European parliament more influential in the legislative process. They are dealing very well," she wrote admiringly, "making exchanges and various alliances to arrive at the least possible movement."[34] As for Bonn, besides monetary union the Germans also wanted a stronger European Council (the locus of national state, and thus of German, influence) and more German deputies in the European parliament to reflect unification. They supported the French goal of a written commitment to a future common foreign and security policy with some sort of European defense commitment, while specifying it should not conflict with NATO and the Americans. (In July 1999 Britain and Italy, saying the Maastricht methodology had worked, urged their EU partners to set Maastricht-like "convergence criteria" for reforming their militaries and defense industries.)

France clearly wanted monetary union more than the Germans, who would have to give up the Deutsche mark with its solidity, prestige and patriotic value. At the end of negotiations and faced with only a vague commitment to launch, President Mitterrand demanded and won a precise date, 1999 at the latest, with an automatic trigger for launching the single European currency and the Eurofed. As opposed to the Bundesbank model, the French, reflecting their historic situation of a government-influenced monetary policy, wanted the Eurofed open to the political sway of the European Council, what the French called an "economic government." The Germans, whose politically independent Bundesbank had been modeled on the American Fed, stood firm. This Franco-German difference persisted, and the German position finally won out in the Treaty.

The French wanted a strong European Council, thus primacy of national governments in EU functioning, even more than the Germans. The French resisted the German idea to give more powers to the European parliament. The Germans, not as enthusiastic in Brussels as they sounded at home on this point, quietly agreed. Given huge unemployment and its left-wing commitment to a "workers' Europe," France's Socialist government, working with the French Socialist president of the Commission, Jacques Delors, asked for a "Social Charter" that would give workers and unions an increased stake in European integration, increasingly perceived as basically a corporate and politically elitist operation. European integration lacked popular sentiment, it was failing to legitimize itself. Or, as Jacques Delors said memorably, "One doesn't fall in love with a single market."

In another internal memo two weeks before the Maastricht summit, Pierre de Boissieu, French negotiating representative at the preparatory conference, described prospects for the Political Union treaty. The Germans, he said, rhetorically emphasized enlarging the European parliament's powers to show German public opinion and the strong German *land* governments that "Europe" was being made more parliamentary, that is, more like the German system. As for the Dutch, "The less defense and intergovernmental agreement, the more there will be of the European parliament and of the Americans, and [Ruud] Lubbers [the Dutch premier presiding as president *pro tem* of the European Council] will be happy." François Mitterrand was infuriated by Lubbers's chairing of Council meetings. Several times Mitterrand asked for the floor in the last session, but Lubbers instead recognized John Major or Britain's non-federalist-minded allies. The European Council's collegial procedures, though Mitterrand complied, were not "very French"! Spain, de Boissieu continued, "will follow France on Political Union and the Common Foreign and Security Policy, but it wants unanimous voting [i.e., a veto for Spain] on questions concerning it particularly." Greece "wants financial aid and to become a member of the WEU [military consultative organization], in order to be equal to Turkey." De Boissieu, in a style for which he was known, concluded that the Delors Commission was floundering in the political union negotiations, that, as opposed to its EMU work, "it has neither understood nor mastered."[35]

The delay in expanding EU membership surely contributed in indirect fashion to Balkan disintegration of the past decade. Membership or even mere association in the European Union is a kind of security guarantee, and Bosnia and Kosovo clearly suffered because they were not attached to the EU. But this can only be mentioned here.

In the last year of Mitterrand's presidency three new members were accepted: Austria, Finland, and Sweden were admitted January 1, 1995. Norwegians decided in a referendum, as they had once before, against membership. So the twelve were now fifteen. Poland, the Czech Republic, and Hungary soon joined the North Atlantic Treaty Organization, but ten years after the European revolution of 1989-1991 there are still no new ex–communist country members of the European Union.

It must be remembered, on the other hand, that the bargain struck at the time of Maastricht in December 1991 was concerned with dangers seen in German unification. The collapse of former Yugoslavia was in the future, not to mention the human tragedies in Bosnia and Kosovo. The failure to begin eastward EU expansion, that is, preempting a special German zone in the east, in retrospect might be seen as yet another instance of fighting the last war, or learning the wrong lesson from history. This malady is French, but not only French.

THE MAASTRICHT MONETARY UNION TREATY

The monetary union treaty was, according to sympathetic experts, a gem, well prepared and negotiated, orderly, and with a clearly defined if risky purpose. Experts on the other side were certain that the old European nationalism would prevent the euro from ever seeing the light of day. Because the EC Commission had competence and time, the result was polished. The political union treaty was, by contrast, rushed, unfinished, and overambitious; in this sense its very vagueness was a virtue. "Political union" was set in a more flexible time frame, as against the fixed 1999 deadline for launching the euro.

On the decisive day of the monetary treaty negotiations, when Mitterrand and Kohl had the final confrontation with Thatcherite and Lubbersist resistance, Mitterrand said to Kohl at their ritual breakfast together: "The day's going to be difficult." The German replied, "Well, then, François, we must go do battle together."

When Mitterrand insisted on fixing an automatic starting date for launching the euro, without requiring new authorization even if the target date for economic convergence was not met in 1997, a turning point was reached. To have such a cut-off date for launch would oblige lax monetary policy countries to change in the interim (Italy proved to be the most spectacular adapter) and would short-circuit reasons for backsliding sure to arise in the meantime. Kohl immediately supported Mitterrand's proposition, as they had agreed beforehand. "This was one of the most important moments of the European Councils of these fourteen years," according to Hubert Védrine, "perhaps it was the most important of all."[36] Monetary union, a European currency, was that important to the French.

But why, it is reasonably asked, did the French and Mitterrand, so jealous of France's independence, not see monetary union as a loss of French sovereignty? The answer is less complicated that it seems. French monetary policy, as well as that of other EC countries, had nearly *always* tracked German Bundesbank monetary policy because the mark was so much the dominant EC currency. In the European Monetary System, in place since 1979, French interest rates had been obliged to follow German interest rates, as if French monetary policy had been a secondary economy in a Deutschemark zone. When German interest rates were raised or lowered, the French rates had to match and then some. Otherwise capital would flow massively from France to the more stable German monetary environment, which was also normally more profitable. A Eurofed governing board, with equal votes for German, French, and the other Euroland members, would therefore not be a worse situation for the French and could even help it regain a part of influence, if not sole sovereignty, in the "pooled sovereignty" of governing board decisions. No longer would the French be subject to interest rate decisions taken unilaterally by the Germans for German reasons. The "discovery" that pooled sovereignty could provide more genuine French monetary influence than a fictive national monetary sovereignty was a milestone in European integration.

The number of countries permitted to join was determined by meeting certain "convergence criteria" set out in the treaty: low inflation rates, low interest rates, and low budget deficit and public debt levels. When Maastricht was signed, with Germany suffering the financial burdens of unification, France was ironically the only one of the four big EC countries that would have met these criteria, a point of pride for the French Socialist Bérégovoy government. But the hard-money convergence criteria were, as already said, blamed for adding to unemployment. Recent studies indicate that 1 or 2 percentage points were added by the Maastricht criteria to France's 11 to 13 percentage unemployment rate over the period.

Finally, the limited "Social Charter" was agreed upon, listing workplace and benefits regulations. But the accord was signed by eleven countries rather than twelve. Britain, in the form of John Major's conservative government, successor to Thatcher's, was allowed to opt out, which meant the Social Charter couldn't be part of the text of the treaty. At the same time Britain agreed it wouldn't try to use its theoretical veto to stop the others from proceeding at eleven.

The monetary union treaty and plans for the euro were, in retrospect, a resounding success for Mitterrand, for French policy and for European integration. A series of French governments had been pursuing monetary union and a common currency since the first European summit hosted by Georges Pompidou in 1969, when Chancellor Willy Brandt had said Germany might agree to abandon the mark in the service of integration.

RATIFICATION:
ONE CLOSE CALL FOR HISTORY

For President Mitterrand, ratification of the Maastricht Treaty began with an apparently firm majority at home. But the national referendum he called for September 20, 1992 almost ended in a disaster for his entire European strategy.

French ratification of the Maastricht treaty could have occurred with a parliamentary mechanism alone. Both houses of parliament—the national assembly and the senate—meet in "congress," with a 60 percent vote required for assent. Mitterrand decided to add a referendum to the purely parliamentary process. Why?

On June 2, 1992, the Danes rejected the treaty in a narrow majority of no votes, 50.7 percent. This was not unexpected given historic Danish Euro-skepticism, but one country opting out could start a chain reaction in other nations where majorities in favor of integration were weak. The Maastricht process could have unraveled.

Mitterrand had two kinds of reasons for moving toward a referendum in France. At the domestic level, public opinion had been insufficiently consulted on "Europe" all the way along. Parliament alone had ratified the original Rome Treaty in 1957, and Georges Pompidou's 1972 referendum on British membership was voted up with so weak a majority and high abstention that a doubt about European integration's legitimacy in French opinion was posed. The Single European Act of 1987 had been seen as a highly technocratic business and French public opinion had hardly noticed it. For Mitterrand the occasion seemed right, and it seemed politically good to relegitimize "Europe" in France through a referendum in addition to parliament's assent. To those who questioned taking the risk, Mitterrand replied that a referendum could reduce the "democratic deficit" in Europe's institutions, which many of the same critics had previously emphasized. As for the Danish rejection of Maastricht (they reversed their judgment in a second referendum a year later), Mitterrand's answer was that Europe "would do with Eleven what was not possible to do with Twelve." Moreover future new members in the Union would have to accept Maastricht's conditions beforehand.

Many French and other pro-Europe politicians were worried about François Mitterrand's decision to go to a referendum. Valéry Giscard d'Estaing, Helmut Kohl, and John Major—plus Jacques Delors privately—thought the risk too great, that Mitterrand was playing unwisely with the future of European integration, that he would give all the French anti-Europeans on the extreme Right and Left reason to unite and multiply their strength. And in truth Mitterrand's attempt to reverse the flow of doubts about Maastricht would do much either to reforge Europe's legitimacy or to smash it. The "democratic deficit" card was played by Mitterrand: "We are paying the price today of forty years of silence about Europe. This is one more reason for the referendum." European affairs minister Elizabeth Guigou said the referendum would "break down the wall of [technocratic] silence" about Europe's true benefits and costs.[37]

The first opinion polls gave about 55 percent favorable to the Maastricht referendum. Among the neo-gaullists, Jacques Chirac, who had originally demanded a referendum on Maastricht in typical gaullist style, ended speculation about the possibility he would answer with a gaullist *non* when on July 4 he announced he would vote in favor, "without enthusiasm, but without doubts." Chirac obviously had a future presidential candidacy in mind and had not failed to notice that "Europe" was a majority issue in the electorate. At the end of June the French national assembly and senate voted up the necessary constitutional revisions for the treaty. But in the field, opinion polls began to show the percentage of yes votes declining. Guigou noted that people were sounding angry about the "Europe of the technocrats." The anti-Europe tone was gaining ground. People felt the pro-Europe parties, especially the governing Socialists, were not in touch with their problems or their feelings on the question of more integration. Toward the end of the campaign, some Mitterrand advisors even suggested he cancel the referendum, whatever the political cost, since the larger damage to European integration would be worse. Chirac, Giscard d'Estaing, and other anti-Mitterrand conservative politicians were ironically obliged to campaign on the theme that the French "had to say yes to Europe before saying no to Mitterrand." It was a lovely paradox.

Since the French anti-Maastricht voters saw Europe as a danger to national sovereignty, culture, and prosperity, the theme of Europe as "protection" was now stressed by the pro-Europe forces, protection against "globalization" and "Americanization." Mitterrand's standard campaign speech said it was a matter of "a strong France in a strong Europe . . . capable of resisting outside aggression." People were "illogically projecting all sorts of imaginary threats onto Europe when it in fact protects us against very real dangers" stemming from the United States, from Japan, from world instability. Clearly Mitterrand was also reaching for arguments.

Finally on September 13, one week before the balloting, Mitterrand directly addressed French fears of Germany: "I am personally wounded when I see how the 'yes' voters as much as the 'no' voters justify themselves with arguments about a German danger. First of all it shows a lack of confidence in oneself. Then it implies that there are demons which are specific to Germany, when the fact is that every people must be vigilant about its own. To understand Germany and the Germans demands more respect of them."[38] How not to see this courageous argument as penance for Mitterrand's own lack of confidence in Germany and the Germans (and in France and the French) at the end of 1989?

September 20, 1992, the day of reckoning: The Maastricht Treaty was approved 51.05 to 48.95 percent. By a narrow margin of French voters,

Mitterrand's European policy, in a sense the core of his presidency, was not overturned. In August Mitterrand's dormant prostate cancer had rebounded full force, and the last weeks of the referendum debate were pure agony because he put off surgery in order to campaign. Victory was painful but all the better. In spring 1993 the conservatives won the parliamentary elections, launching the second cohabitation that, along with worsening illness, basically cut Mitterrand's influence until the end of his term.

Still, Helmut Kohl had final months with his "old French partner," for better or worse, in sickness and in health. And François Mitterrand's presidency had refounded French domestic politics on the European question. Differences between French conservatives and Socialists on European integration and the value of Franco-German partnership were now marginal. A superconsensus, the *pensée unique,* was so well established that it in some ways had become the problem as well as the solution in French partisan politics.

The Maastricht agenda crowned François Mitterrand's outstanding contribution to European integration over the decade of 1984 to 1995. It was a great policy success for him personally. Helmut Kohl, by accepting monetary union, took the greatest political risk that could have been asked of him vis-à-vis German public opinion: sacrificing the Deutschemark, postwar West Germany's national treasure, its most potent symbol of legitimacy. Mitterrand gave what he could in return. He "sacrificed" gaullist-style military sovereignty by accepting the Eurocorps integrated command structure and also the goal of a common European security policy and defense structure. In January 1992 he added a surprise: European defense could not be limited to conventional forces only, thus the French *force de frappe* would inevitably, "and rightly so," become part of a common European defense. This didn't mean sharing the trigger on French nuclear weapons, but rather some Franco-British nuclear force cooperation within a European defense framework. Such was the outline when Mitterrand's project was reborn at the Franco-British St. Malo summit of December 1998, which brought together President Jacques Chirac and British Prime Minister Tony Blair.

Metaphorically speaking, then, the Maastricht negotiation exchanged French promises of openness regarding military sovereignty for a much more important German abandonment of monetary sovereignty. The overall issue remains, in any case, whether one thinks, as I do not, that German hegemony in Europe is a foregone conclusion.

As for Mitterrand's *grand projet* of turning the whole of Europe into one single space, this truly separates him from de Gaulle. De Gaulle never would have tied German unification to producing European monetary union and the euro, because he didn't want it. Mitterrand said of de Gaulle, "If you put aside his insistence on France becoming a nuclear military power—and after all, he was a soldier by profession—he never understood the importance of Europe, of this continent conceived of as a single entity."[39] The contrast couldn't have been clearer.

FRANCE'S BROADER INTERNATIONAL ROLE: LESSONS OF THE GULF WAR, BOSNIA, AND RWANDA

To put the Gulf war, Bosnia, and Rwanda in a section at the end of a chapter on France's international policy is obviously inadequate. I want only to offer short summaries and conclusions about François Mitterrand's role in these events, in line with the purpose of this book.[40]

THE GULF WAR

Saddam Hussein's army invaded Kuwait on August 2, 1990, and the Iraqi government announced it was annexing it, or, as they argued, "returning it to the Motherland." Foreign affairs ministries remembered that Iraqi policy had never accepted the 1961 independence of Kuwait, which Iraq considered an illegitimate and artificial creation of British imperialism. Baghdad thus annexed Kuwait as a returned Iraqi province. Despite any sympathy that may have existed for this claim, a forcible destruction of the independence of a sovereign state, a member of United Nations, was contrary to the UN Charter. Allowing it to stand would be an unacceptable precedent.

The Iraqi invasion came at a time when international attention was focused on the problems of making a success of German unification and the imminent Soviet dissolution. Saddam may have thought the Soviets, and perhaps the Chinese, who were facing withering Western criticism for the Tienanmen massacre in June 1989, would protect him with a veto in the UN Security Council if the issue arose there. Did he believe that France was another possible ally, at least a neutral in the affair, because of a purely industrial and oil-based view of French policy, linked not only to Iraq but also hostile to American and British oil competitors, because of previous Franco-Iraqi arms sales contracts, and because of advisors who thought they instinctively knew what French policy had to be? Perhaps he thought that Mitterrand, having honored contracts signed by previous governments and having sought an Arab/Iranian equilibrium in the Iran-Iraq war of the 1980s, would not risk seeing the Saddam regime fall.

In any case the contrary occurred. With good relations among the major leaders, George Bush, Margaret Thatcher, François Mitterrand, and Mikhail Gorbachev, working intensively in the space of three weeks, August 6 to 25, approved UN resolutions 661–665, setting in place the commercial, financial, and military boycott of Iraq, and authorizing the use of force if necessary to implement them.

In fall 1990 a multicountry coalition constructed by American leadership tried to get Saddam Hussein to withdraw or, perhaps, to accept minimal border changes. At the same time the Bush administration raised the threat of a full-scale military invasion to liberate Kuwait with a military operation organized on Saudi Arabian territory. "Desert Shield," the protection of Saudi Arabia from possible Iraqi aggression, would become "Desert Storm." Bush had vowed that the invasion and annexation of Kuwait "will not stand," not a threat an American president makes lightly. The 28-country multinational, multiethnic, and multireligious Desert Storm military force was a rainbow of flags, but American at the core.

In September, Mitterrand felt that the Americans were shifting from the agreed objective of liberating Kuwait, the stated goal of the UN resolutions, to a plan to bring down the Iraqi regime. On September 24, in a UN speech he tried to provide Saddam with a step away from confrontation by saying that, "If Iraq affirms the intention of withdrawing its troops and if it frees its hostages, then everything can become possible." By speaking only of intentions rather than accomplished acts, Mitterrand drew justifiable criticism; he was moving away from the spirit if not the letter of the agreed resolutions. In January, French diplomacy was still furiously trying to avoid war by repeating offers that would allow Saddam to say only that he *intended* to pull out of Kuwait.

George Bush's memoirs specifically cite Mitterrand's UN speech of September 24, 1990. Another problem with it, says Bush, is that Mitterrand was offering Saddam the unjustified "carrot" of taking credit for starting a peace plan for the region as a whole if he would evacuate Kuwait. This reward was unacceptable, as was Mitterrand's innovation of calling for a "democratic choice" for the Kuwaitis on restoration of their independence. The meant not to return the ruling al-Sabah family to power but instead to install a democracy. Restoration of the prior legitimate government was part of all the key Security Council resolutions, but it was "conspicuously left out" of Mitterrand's proposals, which were supposed to attract secular Arab regimes such as Saddam's. Bush argued that "We could not allow a dictator to be the one to alter [Kuwait's] domestic political structure." In a letter to the American president Mitterrand wrote grandiloquently: " . . . I would not risk the death of one single French soldier if it was exclusively in order to restore an absolutist system." Bush notes that Mitterrand nonetheless responded to his request to stop raising the issue, perhaps because Saddam, trying to exploit the French disagreement, at the end of October released about 250 French hostages, alone of all the western hostages he held, saying it was a response to Mitterrand's UN speech.[41] Saddam was clearly testing to see if Mitterrand was a turncoat, open to blackmail.

Despite all efforts at a diplomatic solution—Mitterrand's were the most active among the NATO European allies—Saddam Hussein didn't move his forces and went on with the "Iraq-ization" of Kuwait. This involved, among other things, destroying Kuwaiti official records and citizen identity cards. On January 16, 1991, after a last failed effort of diplomacy at the United Nations, Desert Storm was unleashed. On January 16, François Mitterrand made a solemn declaration to parliament: "At the end of the allotted time, we must recognize that no [satisfactory] response has come from the Iraqi leaders. The time has now come for us . . . to apply the principles which we say are ours. I say with regret but determination: recourse to armed force to oblige Iraq to get out of Kuwait is now legitimate. This is why I will order the use of military means . . . as part of the application of United Nations resolutions."

Weeks of intense bombardment softened up Saddam's tank armies that had been dug into sand bunkers, then the land war began on January 17. Contrary to predictions of fierce Iraqi resistance, the Desert Storm forces won quickly— malnourished Iraqi tank drivers ran toward the invading forces in order to surrender. Kuwait was retaken.

The French were full partners in the military operation, although the British fielded 36,000 troops to the 16,000 French. One revelation of Desert Storm operations was European military deficiencies plus French difficulty relating to the NATO-integrated command structure given France's post-1966 self-exclusion from it. (Similar technological lags were revealed in the Kosovo operations in 1999.) The French military contingent was sited on the west wing of the allied disposition, at Hafar el-Batin, where its interoperability problems would have the least consequences. On September 18 Mitterrand had given a revealing brief to defense minister Jean-Pierre Chevènement, a Socialist of quirky convictions who opposed French participation but whom Mitterrand needed politically: "Our troops shouldn't be too far north because they would be too much in the front line. They shouldn't be in the south because they would be too much in the rear. They shouldn't be too mixed with the Americans either, in order to keep their autonomy."[42] If France had had a more self-confident military and a less-checkered history with NATO there would have been no need to continue playing such games.

The Gulf war had double importance, beyond a specific response to a specific problem. Saddam Hussein has, since his defeat, been governing a rump of former Iraq, two-thirds of his country out of his control, a diplomatic and personal pariah. He has made no foreign diplomatic trips to receive the plaudits he thought would be his for defying western power. And his police state will look from an historical perspective just like so many others of the same type once he is gone. His dream of portraying himself as a miraculous leader, the rebirth of Nebuchadnezzar, will seem farcical.

But there was a more general meaning in the successful building of the Desert Storm coalition. It was in the grouping of so many countries east and west, and in the inclusion of Muslim countries disciplining a Muslim brother country. In the post–cold war world, coalitions of the strong and the willing are replacing the bipolar alliances of the cold war decades.

George Bush's diary for October 17, 1990, speaks of Mitterrand in cordial terms: "As I look at our allies in the Gulf: the Brits are strong, and the French are French. Mitterrand himself has been great. The Quai d'Orsay [their foreign ministry] is off wanting to compromise and get their own [agenda]. The rest of the Europeans do not want to use force."[43] Bush said that overall he found dealing with Mitterrand easy and direct: "I liked the way François made decisions. When I would call him about difficult problems, he would give me a straight answer. He told me what he was going to do; then he went ahead and did it."[44] This is far from Margaret Thatcher's description, in her memoirs, of Mitterrand telling her one thing privately and then saying another publicly in discussions on German unification. Leaders of states dissemble and mislead just as they tell the truth. The lesson is not a moral judgment but an exhortation to remember to analyze with whom and on what occasions François Mitterrand played it straight, and what he thought of the way other leaders dealt with him. Statesmanship is an existential exercise.

A second lesson is that unlike what happened in the Euromissile crisis, Mitterrand's policy in the Gulf crisis combined overall alliance solidarity with traditional French solo attempts at a special diplomatic role, deriving from French historical relations with governments in the region. Third, after French (and other) diplomacy failed, Mitterrand resolutely gave the order to go to war. Perhaps not every French president would have done this.

The Gulf war action also provoked the first great debate, at least in France, over the international community's so-called *droit d'ingérence,* or right to intervene, in a country where the government or civil war factions are committing massive war crimes or crimes against humanity. The sovereign right of states to be free from outside intervention can legitimately be overridden— (the question is by whom and under what rules of determination. Warring governments are summoned to give immediate access to victims in danger on all sides. Inside the French government the leading advocate of the right to intervene at this time was the minister for cooperation Dr. Bernard Kouchner, one of the founding members of Doctors without Borders. Kouchner's view spoke not merely of a right to intervene, but an *obligation* of the international community to intervene.[45] Mitterrand thought the right of intervention premature and risky as official policy, although its moral standing was irrefutable. About intervening against the Serbs a few years later Mitterrand and Kouchner had the following exchange, reported by Hubert Védrine:

> KOUCHNER: Intervention—the word makes people nervous—is only preventive action.
> MITTERRAND: The right of intervention doesn't exist. . . . We're not there yet. . . . No action without the United Nations.

Pushed by Bernard Kouchner and also by Danielle Mitterrand's advocacy, Mitterrand reexamined his position concerning Iraqi treatment of its Kurdish minority. Thus France agreed, finally, to participate in setting up "security zones" for the Kurds in northern Iraq as part of Operation Provide Comfort. France should have been in the lead on such a human rights matter, but the French reason of state interest in post-Saddam relations with Iraq, political and commercial, is more compelling for them than for, say, the United States.

A last conclusion is that the Gulf war also showed indirectly how French geopolitical and military policy has become increasingly expressed through and constrained by European integration. It is increasingly difficult for France to go its own way in opposition to German and British policy in a major crisis. France's limited military power, its inability to project force alone, won't permit solo actions of any scale. And any solo action risks disrupting intra-EU relations which are now a kind of French "near abroad."[46]

MITTERRAND AND THE SOVIET AND YUGOSLAV IMPLOSIONS

Mitterrand's policy moved case by case, pragmatically. But it did begin with a predisposition in favor of the maintenance of existing states and against unbridled national self-determination which produces "just" but weak and threatened tiny states. In the most important case, this meant Mitterrand's support right up to the end for Mikhail Gorbachev and, more surprisingly, for the retention of some kind of Soviet "center" against the final breakup of the Soviet Union.

During the August 1991 coup against Gorbachev, Mitterrand's preference for state continuity even led to a huge diplomatic blunder. It was an uncharacteristic error of precipitous reaction, in which Mitterrand assumed right away that the long-dreaded coup against Gorbachev had been successful. In a television interview Mitterrand called the perpetrators "the new leaders" of the Soviet Union, and read, with forlorn, forced hopefulness, from a quick letter he had received from their spokesman, Gennadi Yaneyev, to the effect that "Soviet reform would continue." It was as if Mitterrand wanted to reassure French opinion that the worst had not happened and that France had a special diplomatic status, since the coup leaders were explaining themselves to Mitterrand. This was surely a misjudgment masquerading as serenity.[47]

With the outbreak of a complex civil war in former Yugoslavia—among Serbs, Croats, and Bosnians (among the latter were Croats, Serbs, and a majority of Muslims) who wanted a Greater Serbia—the French once again advocated maintaining the established Yugoslav state and counseled negotiations for autonomy of the republics within it. The newly unified Germany, under Kohl and Genscher, fiercely advocated immediate diplomatic recognition of the secessionist Slovenians and Croatians. The German position won. To the now-unified Germans, national self-determination, as in Germany, demanded recognizing secessionist republics as separate states.

In retrospect Mitterrand's "centralism" and prudence regarding Yugoslav dangers was as correct as his bad reading of the Soviet situation. No single policy, obviously, fits all cases at all times. Sometimes national self-determination is the only good policy; at other times it is self-destructive because untenable. Circumstances are crucial and recognizing circumstances is the statesman's specialty.

Immediate German recognition for the secessionist Croat and Slovenian states did unwittingly feed the slide into war because of Serb reactions to the demise of a Yugoslav state that had been built on Serbia. German policy, by justifying the breakup of Yugoslavia through secession, inflamed not only ethnic hatreds but the Serb sense of geopolitical amputation. Serbian political leadership dreamed of a greater, not a smaller, Serbia.

As for French policy, Mitterrand, Balladur, and the foreign ministry were, in opposing secession and advocating a continued but decentralized Yugoslavia, stuck in "history," as the criticism went. This meant a supposed French fatal attachment to centralism as the solution for state-building, because centralism was the French way. A second criticism was the inflamed view that Mitterrand's policy was hostage to French prejudice in favor of "Serb friends." Since World War I, when a French-led Allied eastern army had delivered Serbia from a German-Austrian-Turkish invasion, France allegedly saw itself as the main partner in a tacit but real anti-German, anti-Vatican, anti-Croatian coalition, in which Serbs were crucial.

The very creation in 1918 of the Yugoslav state, built on Serbia, was a French diplomatic victory, a new permanent bulwark against German expansionism into geopolitically weak, *Lebensraum* areas in Europe's East and South, that is, the Balkans. World War II, with the arrival of Marshal Tito's partisan Communists, added new complexity to an already complex situation, above all the Croat Ustachii fascist state, allied with Nazi Germany and fascist Italy, fighting the Serbian-Communist partisans led by Tito.

In any case, a pro-Serb sentiment was no doubt very real in French diplomatic thinking, to which Mitterrand was not indifferent. Mindful of Europe's twentieth-century disasters in the Balkans, Mitterrand was in a general sense pro-Serb and favorable to a Yugoslav state that, while centralized but weak, might rein in the notorious Balkan separatist passions and hatreds. But this general view of Franco-Serbian mutual interests did not necessarily mean a preference for the Serbs as a people. Nor did it dictate what any French president, Mitterrand or other, would do in practice, faced with a particular problem in given circumstances. Did French historical memory prefer Belgrade to Sarajevo? Did the French prefer provincial authoritarian Damascus or the cosmopolitan tolerance of Beirut?

Critics of his alleged Serbophilia who worried first about the Bosnian Muslims or even the Croatians quoted Mitterrand as saying in private, "So long as I am president, France will never make war against the Serbs!" This seemed a damning indication and became a widely repeated "explanation" of Mitterrand's policy. But what he actually said was that "France will never make war against the Serbs *alone*," which is something radically different.[48] Mitterrand had geopolitical sentiment for France's World War I alliance with Serbia, the latter's invasion by the Third Reich and suffering at the hands of the Croatian fascist regime in World War II. But Serbian-inflicted carnage on the Muslims and Croatians, and Croatian carnage combined with Bosnian Muslim intransigence, which made their own human suffering worse, incited Mitterrand to rule out any independent action by France to stop the Serbs, *not* to rule out stopping the Serbs. The French army, lacking logistics, intelligence, and other military capabilities, could not have done the job alone against a well-equipped, hardened Serb army whose young men believed they were fighting to avenge historic injustice against them. Any land war against the Serbian army, whether European or, later, American, would have resulted in huge casualties. Serbia soldiers were eager to prove their honor in combat with Western military forces. When Slobodan Milosevic gave up the standoff and withdrew Serbian forces from Kosovo, many allied deaths were averted.

Besides, critics of Mitterrand can't have it all ways. The idea of some overpowering pro-Serb loyalty in his thinking contradicts yet again the image of Mitterrand as a cynic incapable of loyalty. Critics would have to agree that were Mitterrand the pure geopolitician and Machiavellian they often claim, he would hardly have made policy on the sole basis of pro-Serb feelings regarding historic alliance. Mitterrand and Helmut Kohl had the following conversation on December 3, 1992:

> MITTERRAND: Do you intend to send German troops [to Bosnia]?
> KOHL: No.
> MITTERRAND: Then let us be realists and speak frankly. Izetbegovic is pushing for the internationalization of the war. It is our interest that all of it stops as soon as possible. . . . The Serbs are in the wrong from A to Z, but we don't have the material means to use force to stop them. . . . The solution is a consensus of the three ethnic groups.[49]

So much for the assertion that Mitterrand was blinded by sentiment about a "historic French alliance with Serbia." This is one factor in the equation but statesmen are not generally asked to make decisions involving only one factor.

◆ ◆ ◆

In practice, French policy in the Bosnian wars began with the principle that national self-determination, while fundamental, must be limited. Without reasonable, practical limits, national self-determination becomes self-destructive by creating economically unviable, politically threatened states in dangerous neighborhoods. It is no service to small or tiny nations to condemn them to precarious existence, even if it is no justice to ignore their claim to self-determination. Intermediate solutions are the right road between, on one hand, subservient minority status in a larger state and, on the other, dangerous independence. Federalism, decentralization, regional autonomy, and other such structures can achieve what will always be less than perfect solutions. Mitterrand had argued in this vein in EU meetings against German desires for immediate recognition of Croatian and Slovenian secession from Yugoslavia.

Mistakes made by well-meaning outside powers damaged further the already worsening situations in former Yugoslavia and in parts of the ex-Soviet Union. Both French and German (and American) leaders meant well, even though their recipes contradicted one another.

Mitterrand's policy was to keep the Yugoslav state intact while providing genuine autonomy and decentralization for ethnic populations. This was, in retrospect, wisdom, as German policy was just well-meaning. Mitterrand's conception was realistic and forward-looking, albeit to the unhappy dangers of more ethnic conflicts in the new, post–cold war Europe. It was emphatically not an atavistic reflex in favor of the Serbs or Serbia's historically central position in the Yugoslav state.

In Washington, the conflicts in Bosnia put an end to a momentary rise of "bring the boys home" feeling after the Soviet Union collapsed. Bosnia became the first European security crisis that the Clinton administration could not avoid, and the United States headed back into European military problems. For much of 1993 the French were concerned that Clinton, oriented strongly toward domestic affairs, would indeed disengage from close European attachments. De Gaulle forecast that America would eventually disengage from Europe in any case, and that the Europeans, led diplomatically by the French, must prepare for this likelihood. Ergo the logic of French attempts to foster a "European pillar" of NATO, and, through the force of French attitudes, to inspire the taste for independence among its European partners. The paradox of France's policy was, obviously, that American thinking was incited by French suspicion to seek the very return across the Atlantic that the French—despite everything—did not want!

NATO's failure—the failure of both Europe's governments and America—to do better in Bosnia between 1992 and 1994, especially in the months-long siege of Sarajevo, demoralized Europeans and Americans alike. But a surprising new Franco-American concord developed in early 1994.

Against the background of the Bosnia war, the larger issue of remaking NATO for post–cold war challenges led to the American proposal that NATO offer a "Partnership for Peace" (PFP) to the Eastern European countries. The Partnership for Peace policy would be a way to associate Eastern European countries with NATO, without dealing with their desire for full membership (and protection from the East) right away. But the PFP program would also act as a double stabilizer and peacekeeping element in the region. Bringing NATO's political and military conceptions into the Eastern European countries would be a guarantee of domestic peaceful development. And it could also, by bringing various Eastern European representatives together regularly in transatlantic cooperation, be a force for regional stability. But the PFP was initiated amid another Franco-American skirmish.

Initial descriptions of American thinking by Secretary of State Warren Christopher and National Security Advisor Anthony Lake indicated that the Clinton Administration might go far in remaking American policy in Europe. So far as the French were concerned, it was progress that Clinton would remove the Reagan and Bush administrations' resistance to a free-standing European pillar of NATO. But on the other hand, early discussions about the Partnership for Peace in summer and fall 1993 indicated that the Clinton team was seriously considering offering *full* membership in NATO—including the key Article 5 guarantee specifying that an attack on one is an attack on all—to the so-called Visegrad countries (Poland, the Czech Republic, Hungary, and Slovakia who, in 1991, signed a cooperation agreement in Visegrad, Hungary).

President Mitterrand, joined by the conservative cohabitation government of Edouard Balladur, thought this would be reckless. Even if the United States was willing to take on such a responsibility, the French didn't want to make a military guarantee of the borders of Poland or Ukraine, given unstable Russia. Thus the French, as one concerned official said, were "almost relieved" when the Clinton administration's Partnership for Peace proposal in the end offered no more than associate membership in NATO. The Partnership would not have Article 5 guarantees, but those of Article 4, which, while a guarantee of sorts, do not pledge NATO allies without fail to aid a country under attack. Article 4 is essentially a country's right to "consult" NATO if its security is threatened.

This Franco-American deal on Articles 4 and 5 took months to ripen. Simultaneously, NATO's threat to use air strikes to lift the Bosnian Serb strangulation of Sarajevo had stood unused since August 1993, when NATO threatened air power if attacks against civilians continued. The Clinton Administration constantly deferred to the allies, who, with troops on the ground, did not want to risk Serb reprisal attacks for air strikes. This was the situation Mitterrand left to his successor Jacques Chirac in May 1995. To Chirac's great credit, in his first year he had the key European role in negotiating the Clinton administration's decision to launch the allied military operations, which ended, after a few month's resistance, in a Bosnian Serb standdown.

◆   ◆   ◆

The single most historic decision of the end of the cold war was Mikhail Gorbachev's rejection of force to maintain the Soviet empire in Eastern Europe, an empire that had been erected by Josef Stalin from 1944 to 1949. That François Mitterrand, for his part, didn't get everything right in dealing with the end of the cold war and German unification was understandable and many criticisms were made and suggestions offered later for how he could have acted differently.[50] And François Mitterrand, like almost everyone else, including Bush and Kohl, overestimated the capacity of the Soviet Union to endure. Even the strategist who overturned French Communist strength in France did not see how fragile was the Soviet leviathan on its own pedestal.

◆   ◆   ◆

As for France's German problem, the continuing Franco-French debate is revealed by the large sales of a 1999 French book emphatically titled *On the Next War with Germany.* The author, Philippe Delmas, enriched his success with a teasing title. The book in fact argues that France's only conceivable policy for the future is precisely to *avoid* another war (thus gaining economic, financial, and diplomatic influence) with unified Germany:

> There is no policy of equilibrium of powers [in Europe] that can accommodate German power left to itself. . . . France must therefore adopt the strategy that it alone can fulfill, proposing to Germany the creation of a joint power. This goal puts against itself all the conformisms and traditions as did, in its time, the Single European Currency. The euro violated French sovereignty and German self-centered discipline. It bothered the United States which happily long didn't believe it was possible, and it worried the British. . . . Today no one would believe in [a Franco/German union], just as yesterday no one believed in the euro or in German unification.[51]

The goal of a joint French-German power is, Delmas estimates, no more ambitious than were European monetary union and the euro, remembering that most commentators for most of the 1990s thought success was unlikely. Nevertheless, positive signs were accumulating. Already by the time of the French presidential election of Mitterrand's successor in 1995, the *Economist* magazine observed that the convergence criteria "define a decade of economic practice. European budgets now are not only justified by reference to the Maastricht criteria; they are designed around them and the criteria themselves are repeated endlessly like a mantra, until the numbers become suffused with magic significance. All the leading candidates in France's presidential election this spring competed to assure voters how solidly they stood behind the Maastricht orthodoxy."[52]

Having moved European integration forward so much in the 1985 to 1995 decade, in the process navigating the demise of Yalta Europe, is a crucial Mitterrand legacy. One must also stress the domestic social pain inflicted by the choice for Europe, the additional unemployment and damaged lives produced in the process. Successful launching of the euro in 1999 has international commentators now analyzing problems such as the strategic implications of the euro, the euro as a competitor for the dollar as a reserve currency, and "Euroland" as an "equal partner" with the United States in the world economic balance. A well-known American economist has even judged that "The economic integration of Europe over the past half-century, culminating in the euro, represents history's most dramatic success in institutionalizing interdependence."[53]

MITTERRAND'S AFRICAN POLICY
AND THE 1994 GENOCIDE IN RWANDA

"Africa is different." As much as people want to elude problems of distance, climate, and topography, the difference between outside action in the Balkans and what happened (or rather didn't happen) in Rwanda is structural. It is a question of circumstance and personalities.

This said, if there is one policy area where François Mitterrand needed to make a *mea culpa* at the end of his two terms, it was Africa. But in his last press conference on Africa he continued to take the self-justifying line that he had done what he could, that the problems were so great that no individual leader could have made a significant difference in a short period of time. He said to the assembled journalists, "I am not leaving office with the impression of a failure."

But Mitterrand's African policy had indeed been largely a failure, at least compared with the "Third Worldist" ambitions it announced for itself on coming to office. In 1981 Mitterrand nominated Jean-Pierre Cot, an activist personality, as minister for cooperation and African affairs. He announced, in a rhetoric-filled speech at the flamboyant 1981 Cancun development conference, that democracy and economic development "must go hand in hand" in Africa. The rich countries cannot just demand democratization but must help the poorer countries prosper. The one reinforces the other. For the rich countries, poor country economic development will create new markets, increasing trade and keeping potential illegal immigrants at home, as well as incubating local democratization and respect for human rights. A decade later, at the Franco-African summit meeting in France at La Baule, in Brittany, June 19, 1990, Mitterrand made a second rhetoric-filled speech calling again for a more enlightened rich country policy in Africa. But he also stressed that it was time for Africans to take better charge of their own government and their security problems as well. The end of the cold war allowed France and other states in principle to ask African regimes for more democracy and less corruption, because threats of increased ties to the Soviet Union no longer functioned as blackmail. He also suggested creating a multilateral African Rapid Action military force "to serve the interests of democracy."[54]

Despite the facade, the reality was that Mitterrand and France were continuing to retreat from Africa; maintaining the old policy of French influence was too hard and too expensive. His promises to change French neocolonialist relations, to unmake corrupt alliances with the Mobutus and the Bokassas, and even with the relatively benign Houphouët-Boigny sort of African politician, quickly collapsed into the "Francafrica" system that de Gaulle had refurbished after 1958.[55]

These failures in France's African policies under Mitterrand's lead can only be noted in passing here. They were not begun by him, but he did not do much better than his predecessors and he should have.

RWANDA

Any evaluation of Mitterrand's responsibility as France's leader must deal specifically with the terrible question of French responsibility in the 1994 genocide in Rwanda. The Rwandan problem must also be seen in light of French and European mishandling of the Bosnian agonies of 1991-1995. And Mitterrand's worsening illness must be taken into account—his first operation came in 1992. Whatever the circumstances, however, Mitterrand was still president and still in charge.

As an explanation from the French side, the best version is a bipartisan report from a French parliamentary committee issued in December 1998. This investigatory committee, an innovation in French politics, was led by a Socialist former defense minister, Paul Quilès, and contained deputies from both the government and opposition parties. It was first established to examine allegations that French military advisors had helped train the Rwandan Hutu Government army and paramilitary militias that did much of the killing.

The report concluded, to no one's surprise, that successive French governments had made serious errors of judgment, but that France could not be blamed for the genocide committed in April 1994 by what were called "Hutu extremists." At least 500,000 people died, mainly of the minority Tutsi ethnic group.

The French report blamed the United Nations for delaying military action once the mass slaughter began. French troops, in what was called Operation Turquoise, formed the core of a very small UN force authorized on June 22 by the Security Council with the mission of protecting civilians. But by this time the killing of the Tutsi was over, with bodies buried or laying around much of the countryside.

The basic delay, said the French committee, had been in the international community, especially the United States, which, despite being the only country with the possible military force to act, had been traumatized and made wary by the killings of American soldiers in Somalia in 1993.[56]

But the committee also blamed successive French Socialist and conservative governments—Edouard Balladur took over in 1993—for failing to see the danger of the situation, after the first thirty French military advisors went in to train Rwandan police and army personnel in 1991. This involvement had been provoked by attacks in 1990 by Tutsi rebels using bases in neighboring Uganda. The French had orders not to get involved in Rwandan government military actions but President Juvenal Habyarimana believed that Paris would support him politically and militarily if necessary.

The French government was worried, as international observers said, that the United States was trying to supplant French influence in Rwanda. But the parliamentary inquiry found that while the Americans had trained some rebel commanders, there had been no supplying of their organization. The French worries about American intentions blinded Paris to how their military aid of Habyarimana against the Tutsi rebellion was strengthening the Hutu militias for the mass killing being planned.

In material terms, the French, from 1990 to April 1994, sold about $24.5 million worth of arms to Rwanda, essentially mortar rounds, bullets, and three Gazelle helicopters. The French later provided three more Gazelles. This seems like small military potatoes but it was significant on the Rwandan scale. The report concluded:

> While France did not participate in battle, nevertheless on the ground it was extremely close to the Rwandan armed forces. It continuously participated in the working out of battle plans, provided advice to the general staff and to sector commanders . . . [and] taught mining and ambush techniques, suggesting the most appropriate emplacements.[57]

Paris ignored occasional warnings from French advisors in Rwanda that their work might be put to bad use. But finally, the report said, "France in no way incited, encouraged, aided or supported those who orchestrated the genocide and began it in the days that followed the assassination [of the Rwandan president, Habyarimana]. . . . [But] France maintained its presence and developed its military cooperation against a background of ethnic tensions, massacres and violence, *as if impervious to a context whose seriousness it underestimated"* (emphasis mine).

Hubert Védrine gives an insider's account of how the French government saw the tragedy build up and occur, and what, according to him, is to be made of the violent criticisms of France's policy. Some people

> directly accuse France of having *deliberately* supported a Rwandan government
> that was readying a genocide! . . . The obsession of French policy was the
> contrary. France was the only country in the world, with Tanzania, to worry
> about what might occur in Rwanda—even if no one expected massacres that
> were so extensive and so systematic. How could French policy have abetted such
> a horror, consented to it, even tacitly? Do [critics] understand what this
> defamation means for [French government leaders such as] François Mitterrand,
> Édouard Balladur, François Léotard, Alain Juppé, Michel Roussin, Bernard
> Debré, Jacques Lanxade, Pierre Bérégovoy, Roland Dumas, and for the
> diplomats and civil servants of the ministries of defense and cooperation?[58]

A Tutsi minority government based on only 14 percent of the people could not have gone to democratic elections with any hope of winning. It would have had to become more repressive to stay in power. The least bad conventional political solution, which the French tried, was to get Hutu toleration, under French, American, and UN pressure, of the Tutsi and respect for minority Tutsi rights in government. But this unrealistic French policy unwittingly destabilized the situation further, bringing the massacres closer. It is true that France did remain to some extent involved when the rest of the international community, as UN secretary general Kofi Annan and American president Bill Clinton said publicly later on, basically looked away.

In late 1999 the United Nations issued its own report, which mentioned French responsibilities very little. The UN blamed itself and Security Council states for failing to act preventively or more effectively. Secretary General Kofi Annan allowed himself to be blamed personally along with other high UN organization officials.

Soon thereafter a *Foreign Affairs* article conducted an extensive review of the responsibilities involved in the Rwandan disaster. Its conclusions paint a picture in which French actions, or lack thereof, are relegated to the background.

The first point is that only the United States, with its superpower military might, could conceivably have intervened to stop the killing. The "oft-repeated claim was that 5,000 troops deployed at the outset of the killing in April 1994 could have prevented the genocide."[59] But careful review of what happened shows that even a large force sent at the first reports of attempted genocide "would not have been able to save even half the ultimate victims," and perhaps many fewer.

The Hutus blamed the Tutsis for alleged murder of the Rwandan president in a mysterious plane crash on April 6, 1994. This was the signal for extremist Hutu incitement of their people to take revenge on the Tutsis. Between that moment and April 21 the genocidal killing of Tutsis, and also "moderate" Hutus by the extremist Hutus, was "the fastest genocide rate in recorded history." Perhaps 250,000 Tutsi victims had accumulated by April 21, a crucial date because it was not until April 20, at the earliest, that firm evidence of genocidal killing became clear. "Most early death counts were gross underestimates and never suggested genocidal proportions." Only on April 20 did Human Rights Watch estimate that "as many as 100,000 people may have died to date." A January 11, 1994, cable from General Romeo Dallaire to UN headquarters conveyed a Hutu informant's warning of Hutu plans for genocidal killing, but General Dallaire also expressed doubts about the informant's reliability and, significantly, there were no further telegrams from him to increase credibility of the information.

The largest possible deployment of American force with maximum speed might have spared, after April 20, about 275,000 Tutsi. Instead 150,000 actually survived. But this is a theoretical projection which ignores whether President Clinton could have gotten consent to such a vast, swift operation. In reality the 125,000 extra Tutsi dead were victims of distance, geography, and other limitations. But what if there had been more time? What if Rwanda were a country in Europe and its population white? Unanswerable but vital questions.

Where does this leave France's—Mitterrand's—responsibility? In practice, Rwanda was not being watched closely, not even by the French. And the French were without the military capability to send a huge deployment had they even known of the Hutu plans for genocide. France, and Mitterrand, wrapped their own lack of action in the inaction of the international community.

Nevertheless, the French had a special responsibility and experience in the area. It would seem that if anyone should have known what was being planned by the extremist Hutus in Rwanda, it was the French. The French government, if not any one individual personally, can perhaps be faulted for disastrously inadequate intelligence about Rwanda. But the Hutu ringleaders hid their plans and preparations well, and the killing was accomplished frighteningly quickly with rudimentary weapons. In the face of hundreds of thousands of dead people, helpless victims in a landlocked country on an inaccessible part of a rough continent, excuses offered about the practical difficulties of intervention seemed plausible yet totally inadequate.[60]

CONCLUSION

French ambitions from de Gaulle through François Mitterrand are "to be part of the *directoire du monde* [to be among the great powers' world concert], whatever its name [the UN Security Council, the G-7, etc.]. Therefore France has a *general* interest that the international system be better regulated, but a *national* interest not to find its own place lessened by expanding [international groupings] just any which way."[61]

France must be present in all the world's major power groupings, including NATO, but at the same time will work for a more multipolar world, not out of anti-Americanism but because a multipolar world is better for the French and better, they think, for international equilibrium. The American Gulliver's tendency to play "the world's only superpower" and "the indispensable nation" must be constrained in larger groupings, not unlike the strategy to "embed" German strength in European integration. This is classic power realism, mitigated by always remembering who your friends are as opposed to those who are just partners or, when unavoidable, adversaries.

For French policy this means, first of all, moving international security politics into a reinforced, more decisive United Nations Security Council. Mitterrand's motto, and today's French foreign policy, might be summarized as: "As much European Union, NATO, and American alliance as necessary; as much national sovereignty and multipolarism in the international system as possible." Recognizing that it is impossible to have all of all good things, this recipe, as a guide to goals, is not at all self-contradictory.

François Mitterrand's combination of patriotism, Franco-German partnership, and pooled sovereignty in the European Union—rather than de Gaulle's heroic but outdated intransigence—is the future of French international policy. But France needs to produce new leaders of Mitterrand's talents, stature, and subtlety at playing the game, which is by no means certain. A new de Gaulle is out of the question and would in any case be out of place and time. So much the worse for political dramaturgy, so much the better for Europeans glad to leave behind the century of total war.

CHAPTER 7

LEGITIMACY AND INSTITUTIONS

Nothing is possible without men, nothing is lasting without institutions.

—Jean Monnet, 1992

I believe in the force of institutions. Societies exist only through institutions. There would be no freedom without institutions. There would be no justice without institutions. There would be no nations without institutions, just as there would be no Europe without institutions. Institutions create a framework for living to which one gets habituated.

—François Mitterrand, 1994

[T]he conviction [de Gaulle] had of embodying France, of expressing her truth, of embodying a given moment of an eternal destiny, itself immutable, moved me more than it irritated me. I never found that pretension laughable.

—François Mitterrand, 1994

A RECONCILIATION OF LEGITIMACIES

FRANÇOIS MITTERRAND'S ELECTION AS PRESIDENT overthrew the quarter-century cozy arrangement of a French Right permanently in power and a French Left permanently in opposition. Or, as French political intellectuals defined it, the Right was in charge of the government and economy, while the Left dominated the culture, marked by ideology and literary-political fashions. Mitterrand's arrival in office with the Union of the Left in 1981 therefore posed questions not just of a change in government but more fundamental ones of legitimacy, of institutions, and of reconciliation and mutual acceptance (or not) between the Right and the Left.

Would Mitterrand and the Left be tolerated by the "big bourgeoisie" and its managerial class and by long-entrenched political and bureaucratic elites? That is, by the French Establishment? Could *l'alternance,* the replacement of the Right by the Left as the government of France, occur without creating a political and constitutional crisis? Would the Right, in parliament, in the streets, and in the financial markets (including Swiss banks), accept the Left's radical policy, its socialist experiment?

Today the answers may seem obvious. But 1981 was only thirteen years after the events of May 1968, which had shaken the assumption that the era of France's unpredictable revolutionary upheavals had ended. The shock of a "Socialo-Communist government" in the presidential Élysée and the prime ministerial Hotel Matignon was more traumatic than is usually thought of today in retrospect.

A second encounter with the issue of legitimacy arose in the cohabitation of 1986. For the first time the test would occur as to whether a divided government, whose president was of one side and whose government and parliamentary majority was of the other, could, given the constitutional ambiguities and room for maneuvering, avoid political-constitutional civil war. The answer for France, unlike the American case of full presidential government, in which a combination of presidential/congressional cooperation and gridlock is common, had still to be given. Would an overpowerful French president fight to keep his customary but largely unwritten, thus extra-constitutional powers? Would the new parliamentary majority, opposed in principle to the president, demand that he either "submit or resign"? Finally, could the new alternation of Left and Right in government become an established institution, made banal? Could the odd French cohabitation form of government be accepted, that is, made normal? Would French politics, folding up the tent of its unique political history, as historian François Furet put it, finally join the ranks of ordinary, pacified liberal democracies? Was the French Revolution finally, so to speak, over? François Mitterrand's presidency created, partly by strategy and partly by coincidence, a historical moment. The stakes of today's partisan issues were suddenly once again at the level of a turning point in French history.

LEGITIMACY, FRENCH AND REPUBLICAN

To raise the question of legitimacy tends to be a conservative concern, at the political level and also in the realm of concepts. To speak of legitimacy presumes the idea or norm of an accepted order and governmental authority that is voluntarily and widely accepted, because it is perceived as legally and normatively justified. A legitimate government is, to the conservative mind, both possible and desirable, and should be thought the normal state of affairs, except when it is tyrannical. In fact no government, including an originally revolutionary party, survives without legitimacy, which means the principle by which its right to rule is willingly agreed. Yet to emphasize legitimacy can, at times of great contestation and unresolved struggles for power, for example in May 1968, seem or actually be a reactionary position.

De Gaulle and Mitterrand were both conservatives by background and instinct, yet each had a capacity for acting the radical. Both, however they differed, believed in the virtues of stability, that legitimate political authority was, or should be, the normal case. But each also had the capacity to conceive of themselves in radical opposition, for example, de Gaulle in 1940 and each in his way in 1958. Mitterrand also acted the radical in 1981. And just as de Gaulle did after 1940 and 1958, Mitterrand left a larger, broader sense of political legitimacy in society than the one he had challenged. Mitterrand brought the French Left into the Fifth Republic consensus. With Mitterrand's success and legitimacy as president, the Left accepted the political institutions created by its adversaries and from which it had been excluded, and they ceased to challenge very strongly the liberal society and economy.

Both leaders, in extending the basis of acceptance of the regime, had to survive a crisis of legitimacy vis-à-vis their own supporters when forced by circumstances to abandon a vital position. On one hand, de Gaulle, by accepting Algerian independence (thus making a virtue of necessity), infuriated those who had carried him back to power precisely in order to keep Algeria French. Similarly, Mitterrand, according to his most ideological followers, was considered to have betrayed socialism. In combination, the two "treasons" amounted to cross-cutting disappointments, thus creating, by this fact of mutual disillusion, less ideological intolerance and more mutual tolerance. Common defeats can create legitimacy just as well as common victories. It is precisely great, self-sacrificing leaders who can in turn ask their people for great sacrifices.

De Gaulle, as a military man and a natural advocate of a strong executive regime, came to power with the natural support of the Right on institutional questions. But he made decolonization, diplomatic independence from the United States, and a strong if costly autonomous nuclear deterrent into founding policies of the Fifth Republic. After his acceptance of Algerian independence in 1962 in the Evian agreements, he had to win over the French Right to the new Fifth republic a second time.

The General had returned to power in 1958 with a historical legitimacy that his shift on Algeria put in question. He regained some legitimacy after Evian, by convincing many French diehards that decolonization was a world trend and unavoidable even for France. The best version of it for France would therefore be to act as if the French, under de Gaulle's inspired leadership, had become the anti-colonialist leader par excellence among the western powers. And so it was: of the richer countries de Gaulle and France became Third World government favorites because they spoke, or appeared to speak, truth to power. That meant de Gaulle criticized the United States especially for neo-colonialist, neomercantilist economic policies, and for its policy in Vietnam. De Gaulle could get away with condemning America's Vietnam War, of course, only because he had been out of power during France's own Indochina war in the early 1950s.

In a similar sense Mitterrand began in one direction but shifted sharply. Overcoming the disappointment of his followers over the abandonment of socialism, he cemented the French Left into consensus on the constitution and the institutions (although he regularly talked of some uncompleted major revisions, e.g., increasing parliament's powers and guaranteeing political independence of the judiciary from the government), as well as basic policy orientations, giving up socialist economics and accepting the French nuclear force. Mitterrand's retreat from socialism was comparable, in other words, to de Gaulle's decision to give in to Algerian independence. Each was an example of political courage, and each man cut a political Gordian knot that had been tied for a century. Both were granted, because of a change in mentalities inside their own camp, an extension of political legitimacy through ideological disillusionment of their own. After de Gaulle, frank colonialist attitudes hardly dared speak their name in French politics. After Mitterrand, the same is true of socialist ideology.

It is tempting but excessive to assert that François Mitterrand was "the de Gaulle of the Left," Yet there is something important in the comparison, not so much in the men but in the political effects, above all in the production of political legitimacy in the French common life. The left-leaning newspaper *Le Monde,* originally sympathetic but later increasingly critical of Mitterrand after his retreat from socialism in 1982-1983, in 1988 editorialized about the Mitterrand/Chirac presidential contest: "On the eve of a new presidential term, and after the parenthesis of the first cohabitation government [of 1986-1988], one wonders, rather positively, whether it would not be a good idea to keep in place a president who has revealed himself to be a reconciliator among the French"[1] The pinched tone of this endorsement was typical of *Le Monde,* but it did express the sense of many left-wing voters about Mitterrand's significance on the verge of his reelection. For observers with a long historical memory, this amounted to absolution for the man of the Observatory affair and of the recent retreat from socialism.

MAKING A SUCCESS OF THE ALTERNATION IN POWER BY THE LEFT

MAY 21, 1981, THE ROSE AT THE PANTHEON

For a century the Socialist Left in France had been ambivalent about whether it really wanted to go to government. If revolution was impossible, should the Socialists (or Communists) exercise power "in a bourgeois republic," thus to become "reformists"?

Faced with the historical residue of this ideological fastidiousness, which really hobbled the Socialists in the Popular Front era and even at the end of World War II, François Mitterrand quickly guided events upon his election so that the Socialists at least, if not the Communists, would be quickly vaulted over the old worry about contamination by "bourgeois" power. The left-wing government had more than enough to do (first of all to avoid capital flight and financial-political isolation) without worrying about whether it really should take office. The Socialists, Mitterrand knew, had to not merely take possession of the state's offices and buildings. Their psychology had to quickly accept, internalize, and believe in the symbols of the French State. At that point they *were* the French state.

Inauguration day, May 21, 1981: the photograph on this book's dust jacket. François Mitterrand, a red rose in hand (the Socialist party symbol, a brilliantly successful contrast with the Communist hammer and sickle), led a huge crowd of *le peuple de gauche,* left-wing supporters, to the Pantheon, resting place of France's great men, a national symbol and a symbol of the nation. In a carefully orchestrated ceremony, Mitterrand symbolically took possession of the Pantheon by the left-wing government, in the name of that half of the French people who had been permanently excluded from national power since the beginning of the Fifth Republic. This ceremony meant that the Left was as much at home, as much caretaker at the Pantheon, as the Right.

François Mitterrand reversed a feeling of permanent inferiority on the Left. The Pantheon ceremony, despite and because of its obviousness, was effective political psychology. Those who opposed the Left began to accustom themselves to its occupation of the national institutions and its responsibility for caretaking the national memory. The Leftists, *le peuple de gauche,* had to feel the psychology of the state enter their minds. If they worried the old worry about being coopted, they also felt satisfaction and determination. Newsfilm and photographs show more than a few in that crowd quite in tears.

Mitterrand demonstrated that a policy of national mutual recognition had begun with the French Left acting not as *demandeurs,* as those who must ask, but as the new legitimate government. "De Gaulle is not the only one in French history," said Mitterrand, stating the obvious, and left-wing parties, voters, and sympathizers had to now realize that the Right was not the only legitimate government. May 1968 had shown that the Left could still rebel; it had also shown precisely that the Left was not yet government-minded.

It was de Gaulle, absolutely in character, who at the end of World War II had resumed the state's rite of entombment of the country's most extraordinary minds and courageous heroes in the Pantheon. That Left Bank monument, originally a neoclassical church patterned on the Roman Pantheon, was created by the Revolutionary government of 1791. Turning first to the Pantheon was more evidence that Mitterrand intended, despite his socialism, to be the most gaullien successor to de Gaulle. Neither Georges Pompidou nor Valéry Giscard d'Estaing had thought to add to the collection of patriotic tombs there.

The new president entered the building's chiaroscuro walkways alone. He placed a rose on each of three tombs, those of Victor Schoelcher, who had led the nineteenth-century fight to abolish slavery in the French colonies; Jean Jaurès, the venerated pre–World War I French socialist leader assassinated in August 1914; and, in a sign of reconciliation, Jean Moulin, de Gaulle's envoy to the interior Resistance, who had been horribly tortured and killed by the Gestapo after refusing to divulge information. Mitterrand's beau geste expressed a desire not for revenge on the Right but for national unity that, notwithstanding fourteen years of ups and downs, in the end stood out as one of the main themes in his presidency.

The Pantheon inauguration day ceremony underlined Mitterrand's psychological-political fineness of perception and deftness of touch. It incited the Left to the moral courage of its sudden victory and huge parliamentary majority, the courage to launch, on the basis of this legitimacy, the risky experiment to "change society." Pierre Nora, editor of the renowned *Lieux de mémoire* historical series, a vast fresco of the places, rites, and symbols of French national memory, commented: "Mitterrand's passage at the Pantheon amounted to the Left's finding itself again, its re-enracination in one version of France's history." Nora added that Jacques Chirac's October 1996 sponsorship of the transfer of André Malraux's tomb to the Pantheon underlined a commonality of perception between Chirac and Mitterrand: "In both cases it is a return to origins, an appeal to founding and legitimizing tradition."[2]

During his two terms President Mitterrand transferred seven of France's eminent citizens to the Pantheon. The first was the eminent jurist René Cassin. The second was Jean Monnet, one of the founding fathers of European integration. The third entombment consisted of three figures, celebrated at the French Revolution's Bicentennial in 1989: the philosopher and politician Condorcet, the mathematician Monge, and the Abbé Grégoire, a hero of the Great Revolution and author of the revolutionary *Civil Constitution of the Clergy*, which the church held responsible for the martyrdom of priests who refused to abandon it. Mitterrand's last addition was Marie Curie, the great scientist who became the first woman enterred in the hallowed place of France's "great men." Marie Curie's family, however, refused to agree to her enterrement unless her husband and scientific partner Pierre Curie was placed with her, and this was done.

A LEGITIMACY ISSUE OF A PRACTICAL KIND: RESOLVING FRANCE'S "COMMUNIST PROBLEM"

François Mitterrand often had to deal with objections to his alliance with the Communists. This was of course during the heyday of the Union of the Left and Common Program years in the 1970s. But knowledgeable observers in Paris, Washington, Moscow, Bonn, and other capitals agreed with each other that the Socialist-Communist alliance in France was important and risky business. French political intellectuals such as Jean-François Revel; the former French Communist and now fiercely anti-communist Annie Kriegel; the Russian specialist Alain Besançon; and above all Raymond Aron kept up constant pressure in the media. Yet even Aron, my own mentor and the teacher of numerous American intellectuals, one day expostulated, referring to American preoccupation with the Communist problem, "Of course it's serious. But it doesn't keep us from sleeping at night!"

As things turned out, François Mitterrand, through strategy, determination, and luck, had ended up in a very good position vis-à-vis the "Communist problem" when he took office. The legitimacy of the Left as a governing coalition and of the Socialists as its organizing force had been prevented for years by France's "Communist problem." How would the French Communists behave inside a government of the Left in France in 1981? True, 1981 was not 1947 let alone 1936. Nevertheless, entry of the Communists into the French government was an alert for France's allied governments, both in the European Community and in NATO.

Those who had worried about the Communist party's potential damage to French politics if they got into government were not wrong. Great battles in domestic politics to outbid the Socialists (e.g., in nationalizations) and also in foreign policy (the PCF would want diplomacy and economic cooperation to be reoriented eastward) could result. On the other hand, it was necessary to ask in the name of what principle had such a large number of French voters been formerly disenfranchised, their votes consistently nullified, and their representatives a priori excluded from national power? French conservatives, it was clear, had no strategy other than exclusion for dealing with the deficit of democratic legitimacy represented by the Communist electorate. A "containment" policy was legitimate internationally, but it was a different matter nationally where Communist voters were presumably nationals and citizens like others.

Mitterrand gave various reasons why his policy of alliance with the Communists was justifiable and would surely weaken them. He regularly cited the example of de Gaulle, whose reasoning was laid out clearly in the *War Memoirs*:

> . . . of course the Communists could not be excluded in this period when the very substance of France would be seriously compromised if . . . social upheaval lacerated the nation. Not that I permitted myself any illusions as to the Party's loyalty. . . . But its participation in the Resistance, the influence it wielded over the workers, the desire of public opinion, which I myself shared, to see it return to the nation, determined me to give the Party its place in the task of recovery. Veering, biting, rearing but strongly harnessed between the rails and submitting to bit and bridle, it was to help draw the heavy wagon. It was my job to hold the reins.

What about the Communists who had fled France, General Secretary Maurice Thorez in particular? De Gaulle continued,

> This policy of unity had led me, since Algiers, to invite Communists to become members of my government. I [did] the same thing in Paris. . . . And now in

November 1944 I approved the proposal of the Minister of Justice granting M. Maurice Thorez, condemned for desertion five years before, the benefit of amnesty. . . . The Party's general secretary could henceforth leave Moscow and return to his country. . . . [His] return . . . would involve more advantages than drawbacks at the present moment. . . . Of course . . . the Communists multiplied their intrigues and invectives, although they attempted no insurrectional movement. Better still, so long as I was in office not a single strike occurred. . . . As for Thorez, while making every effort to advance the interests of Communists, he was to serve public interest on several occasions. . . . [He] brought an end to the last vestiges of the [Communist-led] "patriotic militias" [and] he continually urged maximum work effort and production at any cost as national watchwords. Was this out of patriotic instinct or political opportunism? It was not my job to unravel his motives. It sufficed that France was served.[3]

There could hardly be imagined a more pragmatic yet more anti-Communist rationale for doing business with the French Communists.

François Mitterrand thirty-five years later put the matter almost identically: It was "not my job," he said, "to ask whether the Communists were sincere, but to create conditions in which they had to act as if they were sincere."[4] But Mitterrand was not de Gaulle, and this was not the end of war and the tacitly agreed division of Europe. Was taking the PCF into the government too big a risk in 1981?

Mitterrand quickly declared after the elections that the Communists would be invited into a Union of the Left government. This put the PCF leaders back into the trap they had escaped by defecting from the alliance in 1977-1978. Having for a decade proclaimed publicly their devotion to "unity," the Marchais group at the top of the Communist party saw that if they refused to join the Socialists in the government—nothing stood in the way—their rank and file, which had held together since the 1977 split in spite of confusion and bitterness, was likely to bolt. The hypocritical Communist policy of 1977-1978 would be exposed.

So the Communist leadership had to join, as a junior partner, the government being constituted by the Socialist Pierre Mauroy. The Communists were obliged by the Socialists to sign a formal, humiliating agreement promising "flawless solidarity" within the government. They were, to their consternation, in a much weaker position than they would have been in 1978! The Communists marched under Georges Marchais from error to error, shrinking all the time.

The PCF had been the electoral equal of the Socialist party only a few years earlier and could have demanded parity in the government. Now they were given but four ministries, all of second or third importance, for a total of forty-two. The most significant of these was Charles Fiterman, a deputy PCF leader, as minister of transport. The three others were the health, civil service, and vocational training ministries, plus some patronage jobs: director of the Paris Metro network, director of the national coal board (the *Charbonnages*), and head of one division of the national health services administration. There was some fear that these ministries and bureaucracies might be as packed with party activists as in the old days, available for use in strike actions and street demonstrations. But in fact, as Mitterrand calculated, these jobs put Communists in charge of government administrations where they would have to negotiate constantly with unhappy workers and trade union organizations, obliged to share the responsibility for "management" decisions. Sweet irony! At times Communist ministers and administrators in these areas were pitted against the Communist party's own trade union people. The PCF leadership was in effect obliged to "deliver" certain constituencies in exchange for being in the government, a position they had not wanted but felt politically unable to refuse. And the Communists could not avoid shared responsibility for the unwelcome economic and financial results that began to flow in after Mitterrand had been six months in office.

Yet the ministerial Communists tried hard to be pro-government and above reproach. Fiterman, for example, seemed an honorable man making the best of a bad situation. He took a politically courageous decision authorizing Air France to buy American-made Boeing 737 planes, following years of stalling by the French pilots' union, which objected to a reduction in cockpit staff from three to two.

As expected and as promised, François Mitterrand and prime minister Pierre Mauroy kept the Communists entirely away from foreign policy and military and security affairs. Any national security leaks from cabinet discussions were eliminated simply by never discussing such matters in cabinet. In another humiliation, Communist members of the government were further controlled by putting Socialists in backup positions to watch for classic practices of flooding ministries with militants or doing business only with Communist-controlled firms. The Communist party leadership in turn worried, naturally enough, about dual loyalties developing in their own people, so they created an informal network reporting on "opportunist" and "bourgeois" tendencies of Communist government officials. It was, in retrospect, quite an absurd show for 1981, but historical experience obliged exemplary caution on the Socialists' part.

With insignificant exceptions the Communist ministers endorsed all Mitterrand's controversial, hardline, and anti-Soviet foreign policies of the period. They were held to support, like it or not, Mitterrand's unexpectedly firm NATO policy in the Euromissile crisis. They also accepted anti-Soviet French government declarations over the crackdown on Solidarity in Poland and in respect of the Soviet war in Afghanistan. The PCF as a political party, it is true, occasionally took a different line from its government ministers, which gratified hard-line Communist rank-and-file activists and created a certain degree of political static for Mitterrand and the Socialists. However the key fact remained that a still rather Stalinist communist party was allowing its government ministers to vote in opposition to party policy. This was, as already said, a perverse communist "democratic centralism": The party hierarchy, which controlled the ministers, ordered them to vote with the government's policy, against the party's policy! The historical wheel had turned from 1917 to 1947-1948 to 1981. "Flawless solidarity" was now imposed by a socialist party on a communist party.

The French Communist leaders were boxed in, seeking somehow still to escape their historic defeat by the Socialists.[5] PCF general secretary Georges Marchais did not have a ministerial position himself, and his occasional bullying from the sidelines was only a nuisance to Mitterrand and the Mauroy government. In parliament the main Communist goal was to avoid the impression that the party had become a doormat for the Socialist absolute majority. In this regard refusing to attack Mitterrand's hardline policy against the Soviet Union in the Euromissile affair was a huge dent in their ideological armor. The PCF did make an issue of the Mauroy government's switch to austerity economics in 1982-83, but after minor histrionics about the "anti-worker" policy of Mitterrand and Mauroy in spring 1984, the Communists voted unanimously with the government's policy on April 2.

The "flawless" Communist alliance behavior had to extend to the trade union movements as well. It was crucial to prevent the Communist-dominated General Labor Confederation, the CGT, from going into the streets to outflank the government, as the Communists had done during the 1936 Popular Front and again in 1947. But the PCF's control of the CGT was used by the Socialists to inhibit strikes and demonstrations, once again making Communist discipline complicit with the Socialist's.[6]

◆   ◆   ◆

In short, in 1981 the French Communist movement suffered the historic defeat by the French Socialists that the Communists, through political treachery, had avoided in 1977.

But had Mitterrand been justified to take the Communists into the government when the Socialists had an absolute majority alone? Was this the best way to solve France's "communist problem"? Had he behaved like a gambler, even though he had won?

In *A World Transformed,* George Bush recalled voicing U.S. concerns, and noted Mitterrand's reply, that he "would put a few Communists in ministries which would not be of major importance," that in five years the Communist vote would be halved. "I got the distinct feeling from that meeting, and from subsequent ones, that Mitterrand felt we were unduly obsessed with communism. . . . [The Department of] State was skeptical that his tactics would have the intended effect, believing he was being duped by the Communists. But Mitterrand was proved right."[7] The French president said of Americans that they "don't detest those who resist them, and they don't stay angry for very long."

The answer would have been less clear had the Left come to power in 1978, in a cohabitation situation, with Mitterrand as prime minister, trying to prevail in between Giscard d'Estaing as president and a then stronger Communist party. In 1981 he held all the cards: the presidency, a huge parliamentary majority for the Socialists alone, and a demoralized, cornered, increasingly unpopular Communist party. "I'll take the Communists into the government," he said after learning of the Socialist absolute majority, "precisely because I don't have to!"[8] Thus spoke the voice of Machiavelli.

There was no Socialist leader but Mitterrand to do what later seemed obvious, to find a way to deal with the Communist party without being suckered by them. Mitterrand in this sense played the classic statesman's role of expanding the sense of the possible. In a like manner, few American statesmen of the 1960s and '70s, with the notable exception of Richard Nixon, proposed that Russia's *transformation,* as opposed to its containment, should be an American goal.[9] Here was one example of a Machiavellian morality.

A smaller and wiser French Communist party is the result today, one that, on the whole, is helping to solve France's problems rather than to exacerbate them. Mitterrand's coup against the Communists legitimized the French Left and at the same time returned the Communist voters and activists to the nation.

ACCEPTING THE INSTITUTIONS

The legitimacy of French institutions was a second issue Mitterrand faced beyond the Communist problem. His reputation was not that of a beginner in constitutional matters, far from it. One British specialist of French affairs noted that "Mitterrand's parliamentary debate with Pompidou in 1964 on the relative powers of the president and the prime minister helped to establish Pompidou as de Gaulle's dauphin and Mitterrand as the Left's challenger even before the 1965 election. Pompidou's description of Mitterrand, 'neither a man of the Left nor a man of the Right, but an adventurer,'" was the still dominant perception of the man of the Observatory affair."[10]

On arriving in the Élysée in 1981, Mitterrand, even had he planned a return of the gaullist institutions to parliamentary government, which is doubtful, had to recognize that the French people had endorsed the gaullist arrangement of institutions: the overpowerful presidency, the total subordination of parliament to the executive, and the combination of a presidential and a parliamentary legitimacy through the direct election of both. In an interview early in his first term, Mitterrand, the new president, former parliamentarist, and scathing critic of de Gaulle's "regime of personal power," said blithely that, "The institutions were not created for me, but they suit me extremely well."[11] He added, in the manner of Edmund Burke: "Experience has taught me that institutions are good or bad according to the person or people who apply them."[12] He once even claimed that, "If I voted against the constitution, it was more against the context than the text."

As the most overtly partisan of the first four Fifth Republic presidents, Mitterrand "was least inclined," says Jack Hayward, "to hypocrisy and equivocation over the dual role of the office." Mitterrand gave a realistic description of the situation. "The President of the Republic is improperly but in fact the head of the executive, and has always been the leader of the majority. He attempts to combine the role of presidential-president that he is in reality and the role of arbiter-president that he pretends to be."[13]

Why did he so quickly accept the presidential role he had long criticized? The simple answer is that Mitterrand needed the overpowerful presidency. Of course, there was the sheer attraction of being in such total control. How much this played in his mind is hard to calculate "to the millimeter," as he would have said, but given his history there can be no doubt of it as a general proposition. As a practical matter rather than a matter of ego, Mitterrand was obliged, as he had said, "to do everything at once" from the day of his arrival in office. He had to break in a national government controlled by the Socialists, only a few of whom were old enough, like him, to have had government experience. He had to launch the socialist experiment quickly: delay, he thought, meant nullification, according to the experience of other governments that had attempted radical reforms. At the same time, he had to demonstrate his government's loyalty to NATO and France's European Community obligations. But after 1984 Mitterrand delegated more or less full policymaking to the prime minister and the cabinet in domestic policy. Of Jacques Chirac's aggressive expansion of the prime minister's office during the first cohabitation in 1986-1988, Mitterrand quipped that "M. Chirac often thought he was snatching from me powers that I had in fact already shifted!"[14]

Mitterrand nevertheless, throughout his two terms, regularly came back, as said above, to his intent to reform French institutions away from the "personal power" presidency, that is, to increase parliament's role and to increase judicial independence and the role of judicial review. But he never launched the major constitutional reform he promised. This, with him, was not an oversight. Questioned repeatedly in the last few years of his term, Mitterrand had no convincing explanation for his inaction. Perhaps illness prevented him from shouldering another controversial reform, or he thought that institutional reform as an issue needed still to ripen. Wholesale reform of the gaullist institutions became, in any case, moot.

THE TWO COHABITATIONS:
LEGITIMACY AND EFFECTIVE GOVERNMENT

Cohabitation—the peculiarly French governmental form that opposes a president of one side with a prime minister of the other in a hybrid parliamentary/presidential constitution—is a fundamental issue in the remaking of French legitimacy. Four years out of Mitterrand's fourteen as president involved the first instances of cohabitation in the Fifth Republic's history. And in a larger sense, the viability of cohabitation government is the institutional aspect of the question whether the French Left and Right have learned to live together within a single political system. If institutional cohabitation implies the acceptance of permanent political cohabitation, this would signal full legitimacy of the regime and would explain why revolutionary ideologies have lost their credibility in French public opinion.

Mitterrand in 1981 began immediately to prepare the terrain for treating the opposition as adversaries but not enemies. The newly elected president asked for a strong left-wing majority in the parliamentary election he had precipitated. But he also talked, in a new tone for France, of conciliation with the former government parties: ". . . I expect that the opposition be respected and associated, as it should be, in the responsibilities which are necessary for parliament's good functioning."[15] In 1981 the outgoing Giscardist government, in the old French spirit of resentment and revenge, had, according to the new prime minister, Pierre Mauroy, "systematically emptied the ministries, . . . even files of general documentation. . . . For men who claimed to have a sense of the State, there was, at this level, a serious failure of duty." Mauroy praised the secretary general of the government, Marceau Long, and the governor of the Bank of France, who promoted continuity in the government transition.[16] In the same vein, French television viewers remembered Giscard d'Estaing's spiteful post-election au revoir, in which he castigated the French for making the wrong choice, and then ominously walked away from the presidential desk, leaving the camera staring at an empty chair. It was not a good sign for *l'alternance* or for the possibility of working together later.

Mitterrand formulated several rules of cohabitation conduct, which, despite certain ambiguities, have become precedents if not constitutional rules.

- MARCH 2, 1986: "A majority which would contest the powers given to the head of State by the Constitution, . . . which would try to squelch the president's powers, would commit a very large error. . . . I am here, I am president of the Republic whatever happens. I assume my responsibilities and I will watch over them whatever the political majority and events may be. . . . I would prefer resigning from my office rather than renounce the powers which the Constitution gives me. There is no question of me becoming a president on the cheap, but I must also allow the government to govern."

- NOVEMBER 10, 1986: On economic and social questions, "The last word belongs to parliament and, if it is necessary, to the people." On national defense: "He who has the ultimate responsibility for the use of our weapons . . . is the head of State."

- DECEMBER 9, 1986: The president "is an arbiter and, to be more precise, a judge-arbiter. It is up to him from time to time to make judgments, as well as be a recourse."

- FEBRUARY 9, 1993: "The rules of the game are what is written in the Constitution. . . . There is no [presidential] 'reserved domain,' an idea which I have always contested. . . . The government has authority in security affairs and diplomacy. The President does too, it seems to me. Who would take the initiative to violate the constitution? Not me."

- FEBRUARY 18, 1993: "I have no intention of resigning, whatever the size of the change in the [parliamentary] majority in March. I will stay until the end of my term."

- MARCH 24, 1993: At the last Socialist Council of Ministers meeting before the conservative Balladur government arrived: "I will remain in place, I won't give in to an offensive made by a strong majority of the Right, because that is my duty as a statesman. . . . I will not allow myself to be isolated, caught in a rat-trap, nor strangled in the shadows."[17]

No one wants cohabitation government, except the French people, it seems. The politicians are obliged to accept it. Cohabitation is everyone's second choice, because the alternative may be to be out of power.

In the ambiguous constitutional issue of what influence the president would have in naming the cabinet of a prime minister of the opposing tendency, Mitterrand, as president, imposed a veto on Chirac in 1986 in the reserved domain areas of foreign minister and defense minister, refusing Chirac's candidates in favor of men he felt he would find less aggressive (Jean-Bernard Raimond at foreign affairs and André Giraud at defense). Mitterrand and Chirac had to deal together with the problem of French hostages in Lebanon, with the American request for overflight rights—on the very day the cohabitation government was launched—en route for the air attack on Libya. The two agreed that the American request had to be denied. Another issue was whether France should accept Washington's proposal to take part in the Reagan Strategic Defense Initiative (SDI) program. Chirac was in favor, Mitterrand against. There were in addition various protocol disputes over whose "sherpa" (Jacques Attali for Mitterrand or François Bujon de l'Etang for Chirac) should have pre-eminence in negotiating France's part in the G-7 summit in Tokyo. All of these disputes were settled in Mitterrand's favor, results Jacques Chirac would later reproach himself for as showing a lack of sufficient combativity on his part.[18] In foreign policy the president, by the constitution in ambiguous terms, but more surely by the precedent of actual cohabitation experience, retains a major voice. In matters of war and peace, above all in nuclear matters, the president has final authority. Elie Wiesel recounts that, when Mitterrand came to his home in New York as a friend for a visit, the nuclear black box and the telephone came with him. The telephone was put in the childrens' room and Wiesel joked that, if it rang, he would answer, "Sorry. Wrong number."[19]

Gradually even in foreign policy and high politics, what used to be a "reserved domain" for the president (no matter Mitterrand's denial) has become a "shared domain." Nuclear weapons authority (see below) is one of few remaining unambiguous instances of sole presidential power even in a cohabitation government.

The first cohabitation, involving President Mitterrand and Prime Minister Jacques Chirac, was a permanent contest for control, to occupy terrain in this untried situation. In the second cohabitation, there was less of a contest between Mitterrand and the conservative prime minister Edouard Balladur. During the first cohabitation Mitterrand declared that, "If foreign

policy were taken out of my hands, it would be tantamount to a coup d'état."
With Edouard Balladur as prime minister in 1993, however, a different pattern
ensued. Mitterrand's chief of staff, Hubert Védrine, claims there was not much
difference, as compared with the homogeneous Mitterrand/Socialist government practice, as to where presidential authority ended and government
powers began.[20]

French foreign policy in the first year of the second cohabitation was
marked by several significant changes. As a result of the wars in former
Yugoslavia, there was a partial French rapprochement with the NATO command
and with the American role in European affairs. France's perennially controversial African policies came into question again, especially in Rwanda, where the
disastrous intertribal genocide was being prepared. A hard line was taken with
the United States in the General Agreement on Trade and Tariffs (GATT)
negotiations, and on bilateral commercial affairs. Balladur's foreign minister,
the gaullist Alain Juppé, had a key part in several difficult negotiations: in the
several French "victories" in the GATT negotiations, including allowance of a
protectionist "cultural exception"; of the controversial devaluation of the Central
African franc, which was good for French finances but devastating to
francophone African economies; and of the turnabout of Franco-American
cooperation in early 1994 regarding the NATO ultimatum to the Serbs and
military intervention in the Bosnian wars.

Despite leaving foreign policy largely to Mitterrand and Juppé, Prime
Minister Balladur traveled extensively abroad in his first year in office—
nineteen foreign visits, half of them without the president.[21] He was obviously
preparing to run for the presidency, in an unexpected challenge to his neo-
gaullist associate and patron, Jacques Chirac. Balladur's vague "Security Pact"
proposal, concerning a range of security agreements between the West and the
Eastern European and former Soviet countries, was his major attempt at a
diplomatic profile. But it did not generate much interest, either at home or
internationally.

At the Élysée, François Mitterrand's aides insisted that foreign policy still
was run by the president. Even though the Quai d'Orsay foreign ministry
bureaucracy, run by the conservative Juppé, had enlarged its role considerably,
especially in operational matters, the government was, say the president's aides,
carrying out a policy "along lines laid down by the president." Since most foreign
policies were consensual to begin with, and since Mitterrand and Balladur agreed
to negotiate differences while leaving unresolvable issues in abeyance, this
explanation was plausible. The key points were, of course, that this cooperative
cohabitation required the prime minister's consent and that foreign policy to some
extent became a hostage to political cohabitation in the government. For Balladur

the cooperative approach, with its soft handling of an increasingly ill François Mitterrand, added to his popularity prior to the presidential campaign in spring 1995. Jacques Chirac, to distinguish himself from Balladur, then more popular in the polls, had already taken his usual combative stance, alienating himself from public opinion and irritating Mitterrand. A cooperative cohabitation could only enhance Balladur's presidential chances, given that there was no plausible post-Mitterrand Socialist candidate at the time.

Mitterrand had already begun a rapprochement with NATO in 1992. He accepted the principle of NATO peacekeeping missions out of area, and that the multinational "Eurocorps" would be under NATO command when on peacekeeping missions. In addition, France's activist policy to rein in the Serbs in Bosnia also had begun before the conservatives took office in 1993, with the use of force to protect humanitarian operations and to enforce no-fly zones.

Balladur emphasized cooperative cohabitation government in order to stress the difference between him and Chirac, and also so as not to add a political crisis to France's increasing economic difficulties and social tensions—unemployment especially—as the 1990-91 recession took hold. Some politicians, including Balladur himself, even worried that a May 1968–type upheaval might be in the works. So Balladur took care to keep Mitterrand informed, to consult him before every foreign visit, and, not least, to stick punctiliously to diplomatic protocol that highlighted the president's constitutional preeminence over the prime minister.

Balladur seemed to have the good role and Chirac that of frustrated outsider. While it was clear that the conservative government would run domestic policy, Chirac, not least to distinguish himself from Balladur, now argued that the government should run foreign policy as well, exercising its "full responsibility" in all sectors, including the GATT negotiations and the wars in Bosnia. The problem in Chirac's new doctrine was that it rejected the presidential "reserved domain" in foreign affairs and security policy, which he had earlier espoused and which, if he were president, he would want to preserve.

Before the 1993 parliamentary elections Chirac had even asserted for a moment that President Mitterrand should resign if the Left were to lose. But this was the flimsiest partisan thinking, since a presidential resignation over parliamentary elections would have turned France's regime onto a clear parliamentary direction, not something the neo-gaullist Chirac wanted for the future. "No one is contesting François Mitterrand's constitutional right to finish his term," Chirac finally said to get himself out of a ridiculous spot. Mitterrand replied to Chirac by threatening not to choose a prime minister from the gaullist RPR party, even if it emerged as the biggest single force after the elections.

The potential for instability and crisis in cohabitation situations was clear. Chirac said that, although the conservatives had no right to force

Mitterrand to resign, "the defeat of socialism, perhaps even its rout, will also be [Mitterrand's] defeat. . . . Whatever happens, France will have to be governed so as to break with socialism without delay."[22]

What are the lessons to be drawn from the two cohabitations and Mitterrand's role in them?

The lesson of the first cohabitation was appropriately dialectical. The one who lost political power in the parliamentary election, that is, the president, could, with sufficient skill, turn his new institutional weakness into future electoral popularity. Cohabitation had originally been thought a certain political death for the incumbent president. But contrary to its apparent logic, it worked for Mitterrand such that the weakened president could beat the prime minister both in the skirmishes of cohabitation and in the next presidential election. Most French constitutional experts had predicted that an activist, aggressive Chirac would, as a strong prime minister in charge of government business, emerge from the two years of cohabitation in a commanding position for the presidential election. The result was the contrary. French opinion now found Mitterrand to be much more sympathetic and trustworthy, especially compared with an "agitated" Jacques Chirac, than the superpowerful pre-1986, pre-cohabitation, elected monarch Mitterrand.

The lesson of the second cohabitation was equally nuanced. Early on it became clear that the president's strategy was very different from that pursued in 1986-88 in the struggle with Jacques Chirac. As opposed to regular confrontation, Mitterrand found Edouard Balladur, who had a moderate, bureaucratic, often unctuous, and delicate temperament, "interesting," as he said, to work with. According to Le Monde's editor, François Mitterrand "this time around produced a brilliant theory of the ideal cohabitation based on a simple principle: Not to turn disagreements into conflicts. At most they can serve to express a difference, to launch a criticism, but they should no longer be the weapons of a struggle for power as in 1986."[23]

Mitterrand supported the conservative Balladur government on unemployment, for example, endorsing the prime minister's forecast that an economic decline would appear by the end of 1993. But he "advised" the conservative government to remember the need for social measures as well, including no change in the jus soli nationality principle—the automatic right of nationality for anyone born on French soil, whatever the nationalities of the parents—as opposed to the stricter line being suggested by Balladur's interior minister, Charles Pasqua. Mitterrand also seconded Balladur's conceit that a harmonious cohabitation of conservative and Socialist leaders constituted a "French example" to others, in a favorite phrase of the prime minister's. The "spirit of 1993" should not, in other words, be like that of 1986, "when each watched the other in the hope of seeing him make the first mistake."[24]

Anyway, Balladur's program had shown more continuity than change compared with the departing Socialist government's agenda. While under different slogans, the economic and financial priority remained the strong franc, associated with the former Socialist finance and prime minister Pierre Bérégovoy. Franco-German compatibility and alliance would continue at the center of European integration. This consensus was the so-called *pensée unique*, or unemployment-tolerant "politically correct policy," that came under heavy criticism a few years later. Even Balladur's "European security pact" proposal, which Mitterrand could have taken as an incursion on the president's foreign policy supremacy, was accepted by him under the new concept of a "shared sphere" in foreign and security affairs, as opposed to the old "reserved domain" monopoly of initiative for the president.

Unlike Chirac, Balladur took great pains to avoid being unpredictable where the increasingly ill Mitterrand was concerned. Especially good relations between Élysée chief of staff Hubert Védrine and the prime minister's aide Nicholas Bazire undergirded the smooth, courteous working relations between president and prime minister. Mitterrand reassured Balladur that he had "no intention of trying to exceed his authority," let alone to form a "second government" in the Élysée. The prime minister in return did not seek to make Mitterrand's job, or his existence, more stressful.

Marking the difference between himself and Jacques Chirac, with the next presidential election in mind, Balladur said that the intrinsically "delicate" cohabitation situation could have the virtues of its defects. In international relations, a two-headed government need not weaken French diplomatic influence or prestige, "because it shows to our partners that when France's institutions or its leaders defend a position, it is obvious that all of France is supporting it. So . . . in fact [cohabitation] represents an element of added strength."[25] Even when the prime minister and president do not begin from the same premises, Balladur added, joint policies are worked out to avoid open intra-French conflict when an issue can't be put off. All this sounded plausible, but the truth was that even France's closest negotiating partners felt the hesitancy in French policy. Chancellor Kohl commiserated, "We know very well how to deal with the French cohabitation system," but this just underlined its odd character.

COHABITATION AND CONTROL
OF FRENCH NUCLEAR WEAPONS

"Cohabitation," as French security policy analyst Pascal Boniface says, "doesn't lend itself to big strategic decisions."[26] With regard to the special problem of nuclear weapons, Boniface has argued eloquently "against revisionism" in control of the French *force de frappe*. In nuclear matters, it should be clear that the president alone decides, even when there is political cohabitation at the top of the government.

In the 1986-1988 period, Prime Minister Chirac on several occasions opposed President Mitterrand on nuclear issues. Chirac, for example, wanted France to take up Ronald Reagan's offer of participation in the SDI research program. He, like Margaret Thatcher in Britain, said that since France couldn't mount an SDI research effort on its own, France couldn't afford not to join in an American-led project. Chirac also wanted to change—he said "enlarge"— the role of tactical nuclear weapons in French deterrence strategy. They should no longer be limited to a "warning shot" role announcing a full launch if an invading enemy did not heed—the theory of "pure" deterrence that refuses any notion of limited nuclear warfighting. Instead, French tactical nuclear weapons should, said Chirac, have a role that didn't totally exclude their use in battle. This would be a French rapprochement with the American and NATO "flexible response" doctrine, an abandonment of the gaullist concept that the French nuclear force would only be used to protect France (the so-called "sanctuary" doctrine). The Germans wouldn't have liked such a French evolution any more than they liked "flexible response," since a war-fighting plan with small nuclear weapons would be carried out on German territory. Third, Chirac, following another Reagan administration idea, advocated a single-warhead mobile land-based missile, altering the purpose of the land-based, silo-based missile field on the Albion Plateau in Provence by giving the French more strategic capacity to survive a first strike and retaliate. In the paradoxical logic of nuclear deterrence, the Albion Plateau strategic missiles, being stationary, were vulnerable; their purpose was not first strike, but to be a necessary target for the enemy on French soil, thus justifying a total retaliatory strike by French submarine and air-launched missiles. Jacques Chirac, in short, wanted France's nuclear force posture to appear more proactive, more NATO and American-oriented, than the gaullist idea of a French position separate from NATO, which made efforts by French diplomacy to deal with the Soviet Union more credible.

Regarding the Reagan administration's SDI project, President Mitterrand refused any French participation, saying that this would mean accepting a role of "subsidiary producer" to the United States. Washington, he argued, would certainly keep the essential projects closely held for American benefit. Moreover, for France to accept the logic of an anti-missile defense system would be to countenance a strategy that ultimately would make the French nuclear deterrent irrelevant. On tactical nuclear weapons development and the mobile-based land missile, Mitterrand wanted to keep the "pure" deterrence strategy, that is, no war fighting, as well as to avoid continuous costly upgrades of battlefield weapons. The Reagan administration's mobile missile project was controversial, of course, and was soon dropped even by Washington.

Although uncertainty had prevailed about how conflicts over nuclear policy would be resolved, in all these confrontations the president, François Mitterrand, prevailed over the prime minister, Jacques Chirac.

In the 1993-95 cohabitation government, Prime Minister Balladur did have several disagreements in security policy with Mitterrand: the size of the defense budget, relations with NATO, reducing the period of military service, and above all Mitterrand's April 1993 announcement of a moratorium on nuclear testing and the related reconceptualization of French nuclear deterrence. Yet on none of these matters did Balladur openly challenge the president. Where there was open conflict, it rather "opposed the prime minister and his own majority, notably on [the desire of Chirac and members of his own party for a] resumption of nuclear tests, where [Balladur] was sharply reproached with having caved in" to Mitterrand's refusal to conduct new French nuclear tests.[27] A controversial Chinese nuclear test in October 1993 created new pressure on the French government to resume testing, to upgrade the French deterrent. But Balladur signed a joint communiqué with the president saying that France would not do it. One good deed deserves another: When the Balladur government produced a defense white paper in February 1994, Mitterrand, after a few changes on nuclear subjects, that is, those within his range of authority, endorsed the whole document despite Socialist criticisms. In Balladur's own neo-gaullist RPR party (headed by Chirac), its defense specialist Jacques Baumel called the Balladur white paper "an adulterous child of cohabitation."

This gives a general idea of the confusion within parties generated by the peculiar French cohabitation system! There was a new pacification between the historic adversaries of Left and Right, but there was also a new kind of conflict within each side, and within each big party, whether it was the gaullists, the Socialists, the Communists or the loose UDF coalition of Giscardians. Only the National Front, armed with its mock-heroic leader Jean-Marie Le Pen, held together. The new mutual tolerance between Left and Right in France meant more disagreement among one's own. That's logical, as Mitterrand might have said!

The fact is that no written constitutional rule obliged the Balladur government to do what President Mitterrand wanted on nuclear testing or on nuclear deterrence strategy. But if precedent guides the future development of French institutions, the 1993-95 period creates constitutional custom in favor of clear presidential superiority in nuclear matters.

In Mitterrand's May 5, 1994 speech on nuclear matters, a valedictory on defense, he predicted that, because of the growing capacity for computer simulation of testing, as shown by American results, his moratorium would endure beyond his departure from office. He implied it would be permanent. However, when Chirac came to office as president in 1995, he launched a controversial series of new tests on the Mururoa Atoll, defended as necessary to get the last data necessary for French computer test simulations. In a second step, he declared the tests would be France's final series. The issue is still contested as to whether Chirac's tests were necessary in technological terms.

No doubt the tests were, for Chirac, also a posthumous vengeance on his nemesis Mitterrand. To the extent this was so, Chirac's order was a thumping use of overpowerful, autonomous French presidential power, which is still theoretically available whenever there is a loyal majority in parliament. The presidential institution remains in that sense dangerous.

COHABITATION AND
DIPLOMATIC NOMINATIONS

Conflicts over nominations to diplomatic and administrative positions, which involve political loyalties and patronage as well as competence, were a final and fiendish aspect of cohabitation games, even with Balladur.

In late October 1994, for example, the nomination as ambassador to India of Thierry de Beauce, a close aide to Mitterrand in the Élysée, was contested by the conservative government after Mitterrand had thought it done. The Indian government had been advised and had accepted it. De Beauce was scheduled to replace Philippe Petit, one of the few openly Rocardian ambassadors whom Mitterrand might target for replacement. The reason for trouble was that foreign minister Alain Juppé decided to link the de Beauce nomination to that of François Bujon de l'Estang as the next French ambassador to the United States, where Jacques Andreani was reaching retirement age. President Mitterrand opposed a formal veto to Bujon's nomination, for largely personal reasons.

Bujon had begun his career in the 1960s as a young counselor in de Gaulle's entourage. This was not necessarily a demerit, even in Mitterrand's eyes! But during the conflictual Mitterrand/Chirac cohabitation, Bujon had run the rough-and-ready advisory group that conceived many of the aggressive challenges to the president's authority. Furthermore, just prior to the 1986 elections, Bujon published an article arguing that in a two-headed cohabitation government the president and prime minister should have co-responsibility in foreign policy and defense matters. The presidential reserved domain should be contingent, not a permanent fact of institutional life.

Fighting Bujon's nomination on this basis was one of Mitterrand's pettier moments. "This gentleman will have to wait until I'm dead to go to Washington!" he joked sardonically, "But let him know that it won't be very long!" The journalist Jacques Amalric noted that cohabitation conflict in this instance had nevertheless made two people happy, "Andréani, who gets extended in Washington, and Philippe Petit, likewise in New Delhi!"[28] François Bujon de l'Estang arrived in Washington, it must be noted, very soon after the end of Mitterrand's term.

SECULARISM AND RELIGION: THE WAR IS OVER BUT THE BATTLE CONTINUES

A renewal of historic conflict in France over state aid to parochial schools occurred at this time. This issue over public finance of religious schools is the last battle in the two-century war in France between seculars and clericals, the last gasp of the French Revolution.

Why was state aid to private schools, mainly Catholic but also some Muslim and Jewish institutions, so explosive an issue, in 1984 and 1994? Why did the issue spark the largest popular street demonstrations in France since May 1968?

The Falloux law of 1850 stipulated that regional and municipal authorities could fund no more than 10 percent of private school infrastructure budgets. The Debré law of 1951 created a distinction among private schools, allowing some to get higher levels of public finance because the state could also pay teachers' salaries and administrative costs of those private schools that pledged to follow the state syllabus and exams in addition to dispensing religious instruction.

The Socialists had created a fiasco with the 1984 law sponsored by Alain Savary, the Mauroy government minister of education. This was the law to create what the Socialist program had called a "single, unified and secular" public school system, an apparently anondine phrase that was perceived as a mortal threat by parochial schools. Passage of the law would surely mean a seriously diminished private school population. Huge demonstrations against the law, first of half a million in Versailles, and then the same number in Paris, occurred. In the face of a rebellion by public opinion, President Mitterrand himself suddenly withdrew the bill from under the education minister's nose, an exercise of "elected monarch" fiat. Savary and the prime minister both resigned, the first to protest his old adversary's disrespect of him and the deeply worn-out Pierre Mauroy seizing the pretext to make an exit he had sought for months.

The stalemate on private school funding continued until the end of 1993. Then the conservative Balladur government tried to *enlarge,* not diminish, the possibility of state financing of private schools. President Mitterrand, in one of his rare clashes with Balladur, refused to put the government's bill on the agenda of an extraordinary end of summer session of parliament. His reason was the objection that "such an important matter" needed a full parliamentary debate; more likely Mitterrand hoped to derail the conservative move. Mitterrand's blocking maneuver, based on the president's real constitutional authority to oversee parliament's agenda, turned it into a partisan political matter, another example of Mitterrand's skill at employing every bit of his written constitutional powers to effect.

Balladur's attempt to quickly force through parliament a law for enlarged private school financing by the state was also his first test in which the Socialist opposition had popular backing. Confrontation would not be avoided.

A quick party-line vote by the conservatives lifted the Falloux law's cap on government subsidy of a private school's budget. But the Constitutional Council, on appeal by the Socialists, ruled that this violated the constitution's regime for balancing treatment of public and private education. Once again half a million people turned out to march, this time *le peuple de gauche,* along the historic working-class Parisian route from Place de la Bastille to Place de la Nation.

Balladur saw that left-wing opposition to the new bill was motivated less by hostility to private education as such than by worries about public school budgets. Seculars in France long ago accepted that Catholic and other religious schools should have some financial aid. The Socialist and Communist programs had essentially raised a red flag by proposing a totally secularized school system, which they presented, dubiously, as democratization. Balladur therefore quickly produced an extra $420 million for public schools and an amended version of the bill was voted by the conservative majority.

The outcry against the Socialist and conservative bills on state aid to private schools showed the existence of one continuing blank spot in the consensus rules of the game established in contemporary French political culture. But religion and parochial school state aid is an atavistic issue of the old France, different from new problems of race, immigration, religion, and citizenship—issues of an evolving French identity in the year 2000 world of European integration and globalization.

CONCLUSION:
"QUI T'A FAIT COMTE? . . . QUI T'A FAIT ROI?"

"Who made you Count?" So said the newly elected king, Hugues Capet, to the man holding him siege. "Who made you King?" replied Adalbert of Périgord. This well-known and probably apocryphal bit of tenth-century French political history has always been a metaphor for the problem of legitimacy: Who has authority, and by what right? François Mitterrand's career in French politics turned out to be a series of passages, linked like assorted staircases in the vaults of French legitimacy. He began his career in the midst of a collapse of legitimacy; he ended his time in office having done much to remake it. Having begun with a lurching, counter-current socialist experiment, François Mitterrand's long presidency ended up as an arsenal of legitimacy.

Mitterrand's presidency was, without doubt, the continuation of de Gaulle's presidency. There was a marriage of two legitimacies that, in effect, ended France's political civil war since the Great Revolution. The result is not some new version of "the regime which divides us least," as Adolphe Thiers said of the Third Republic, nor some new version of French "exceptionalism." The result is the first unquestionably legitimate French regime since the Revolution. Unlike the four earlier republics and unlike the empires and Marshal Pétain's Vichy state, the Fifth French Republic does not seem to call for a Sixth.

The Fifth Republic would have remained an incomplete success had not Mitterrand shown that the French Left could win its highest offices, and would in turn accept its institutions and premises. The socialist experiment would not have been possible without the all-powerful gaullist presidency to run it and guarantee it. Without de Gaulle's presidency and the Fifth Republic's elected monarchy, François Mitterrand could not have played "Mitterrand" nearly so well. And the French Left would not have so easily digested gaullist institutions, had it not been enabled by them to try its ill-starred experiment.

As leaders, de Gaulle and Mitterrand each survived a crisis of confidence among their own supporters when forced by circumstances to abandon a vital position. When he accepted Algerian independence, de Gaulle made a virtue of the necessity of decolonization. In doing so he disappointed—can one say betrayed?—many of his original partisans and was nearly assassinated for it at Petit-Clamart. Likewise, François Mitterrand in 1982-1983 was clearly giving up the cause, under constraint, when he abandoned socialism for economic realism. In combination, however, the two "treasons" were cross-cutting disappointments. And this double disillusionment promoted legitimacy, mutual acceptance, and even some humility by exposing the superficiality on both Left and Right of feelings of superiority. The lesson is that mutual defeats, as well as common victories, can create the sentiment of a shared past and future, of political community, of legitimacy.

Mitterrand's legacies are, in short, hardly conceivable without de Gaulle's legacies.

But there is also a worrying tendency in the new consensus besides the good of legitimacy. It is the possibility of excessive consensus, the decline of healthy pluralism, a *pensée unique,* a conformism of ideas and values. This is not American-style bipartisanship or gridlock *à la francaise,* but the dilution of Left and Right to the point where a politically neutered government in the Center tends to develop. Prophets of decline in the year 2000 see in this routinization of French politics a resurrection of political confusion, and an incapacity for reform and decisive decision-making. It is not yet possible to say they are wrong.

Was François Mitterrand the "last" French president? Just after leaving office in 1995, he talked of one sense in which this might be true:

> In fact I am the last of the all-powerful presidents [*grands presidents*]. Well, I mean the last one in the gaullien line. After me there will be no others in France, . . . because of Europe . . . because of globalization . . . because of the necessary evolution of the institutions. In the future, this regime may still call itself the Fifth Republic. . . . But nothing will be the same. The president will become a sort of super-prime minister. He will be [politically and institutionally] fragile. He will be obliged to cohabit with an Assembly which will have accumulated much rancor and rivalries, and which, at any moment, will be able to rebel. And it will then be permanent cohabitation, a sort of return to the Fourth Republic.[29]

The man who wrote *The Permanent Coup d'État* had, it seems, come to value de Gaulle's institutional legacy. He had found along his way that both the Fourth and the Fifth republics were made for him, but that his country, and he himself, were better off with the second.

Yet Fifth Republic developments have begun a "taming of the prince," to use an American political theorist's phrase.[30] The overpowerful gaullist presidency is being reined in, not by strokes of the pen, which could be artificial if done without public debate and consent (i.e., by referendum), but by the evolution of partisan and electoral trends, which is the solid ground of socio-political legitimacy. Mitterrand's forecast early in his first term that the Fifth Republic's institutions "were dangerous before me and will be again" seems a warning from another time.

To sum up, the most durable and characteristic achievement of François Mitterrand's political career was in matters of institutions and legitimacy. His legacy is to have restored an alternation of parties in power, to have made a success of partisan cohabitation and mutual tolerance when the voters chose it, and, finally, to have overseen the normalization of both. In a word, his long presidency, for all its defects, created a widespread sense of the legitimacy of French institutions.

Concern for institutions, procedures, and representation was, along with abolition of the death penalty, Mitterrand's most characteristic political combat as an "ardent republican." However these were, it might be said, questions of means rather than final ends. He may be thought deficient for not having, or at least not leaving, some grand substantive vision, a precise theory of "France," of "socialism," or of "Europe." In Mitterrand's writing and thinking there is no equivalent of de Gaulle's "madonna in the frescoes." His response would surely be, to adapt Edouard Bernstein's idea of socialism, that one can sketch a goal (e.g., the European confederation), but the end means little or nothing; the substance is in the process itself. And in the year 2000, could even a de Gaulle succeed in speaking for "Europe"?

Mitterrand's acceptance of cohabitation in 1986, of the near total diminution of his power as a result of the voters' choice, was a masterstroke. It was the last piece in the puzzle of remaking republican legitimacy in France. Mitterrand accepted institutional emasculation of the presidency rather than trying to save his power through resignation or other conceivable constitutional procedures and tricks. Had he acted otherwise, public respect for the constitution and the institutions, not to mention the politicians, would have collapsed.

"The defining moment of American democracy," an American commentator says, "didn't occur in 1776 or 1787, as commonly supposed, but in 1801— on the day that John Adams, having been beaten at the polls, quietly packed his things and went home. Only then did we know for sure that the system worked."[31] Likewise, the successful cohabitation of 1986, following on the alternance of 1981, meant full legitimation of the 1958 constitution. It all, let us remember, could have failed. Instead, the argument over de Gaulle's "permanent coup d'état" was put to rest.

But what of personal power and glory in all this, especially for a man, Mitterrand, so often said to live only for them?

In retrospect, the most important result of Mitterrand's socialism was not its disaster as policy; it was the survival after failure of the Socialist party in government with Mitterrand as president. The Left had tried its program, kept its promises to its rank and file, and launched a new focus on European integration. Mitterrand had been elected for seven years and had three to go; the Socialist party had been elected for five with two to go. That the Socialists accepted taking a new tack in 1984-1986 was an acknowledgment of humility about "changing society," and was also a justification for staying in office rather than collapsing or calling for new parliamentary elections.

To take an even more elevated turn, one can argue that the French Revolution finally ended in the now very French institution of cohabitation and that the international match for domestic cohabitation was France's acceptance of pooled sovereignty in European integration. Marriages of Left and Right, of France and Germany, of the nation-state and the European Union: This constitutes a formidable legacy of France's longest presidency.

As for Mitterrand himself, his acceptance of cohabitation and the reduction of his power was an act of genuine republican statesmanship. Of the hero in French history, Mitterrand wrote:

> It is so easy, so tempting to expel a people from its own adventure. . . . A great man appears, and everything begins and ends with him. This is a suspicious simplicity which allows us to avoid looking elsewhere for the laws of human societies. I believe in the importance of General de Gaulle, not in his necessity. A given situation produced him, not the contrary.[32]

So far from being obsessed with power, Mitterrand's willingness to enter into cohabitation was the purest moment in a controversial career, a republican apotheosis that redeemed the otherwise permanently tainted man of the Observatory affair.

CREDO, MORALITY, LEGACIES

CHAPTER 8

THREE

THE MACHIAVELLIAN REPUBLICAN

Chirac asked, "Looking me straight in the eye, do you deny that we discussed this at length in your office, that you knew about [the release of Wahid Gordji] and approved it?" Mitterrand without hesitating replied, "Looking you straight in the eye, I deny it."
> —From the French presidential debate, May 1988

The humble lie by necessity, the powerful by cunning and arrogance.
> —Giorgio Bocca, Italian journalist

If there really was so much abuse of authority on my part, what servility on your part to have accepted it!
> —François Mitterrand to other Socialist leaders[1]

I made it possible for the Left to be in power in a country which is in a majority on the Right. The Right resented me. That's logical. The Left did not show any gratitude. That's normal.
> —Attributed to François Mitterrand[2]

THE MACHIAVELLIAN REPUBLIC

FRANÇOIS MITTERRAND HAD, LIKE DE GAULLE, long pondered the qualities of leaders and leadership. From de Gaulle's youthful *The Edge of the Sword* to innumerable passages in *War Memoirs* to the wistful parts of his unfinished, posthumous *Memoirs of Hope,* the latter's writing was always a meditation on leadership. De Gaulle wrote about the subject constantly, openly, in a didactic manner. Mitterrand by contrast wrote less about the nature and qualities of leadership. His views, perhaps because on the Left speaking openly of leadership is suspect, are found here and there, in odd bits of his various books and in maxims he culled along the road of a career.

In one of his diary-form books, in an entry for Saturday, February 26, 1971, appears a discovery that became a leitmotif for him: "This thought from Thucydides: 'Every being exercises all the power which it can muster.'"[3] He repeated this Realist view of power at every occasion, yet he was a republican. Was there a contradiction? Can the ubiquity of power and the politics of a republic coexist? Is there such a thing as a "Machiavellian republican"?

Mitterrand was regularly described as an Italianate combination of Machiavellian and Florentine, the former entailing an amoral policy in which the end justified the means, the latter indicating a cunning yet elegant manipulation of people and things to power's ends. To what extent did Mitterrand truly answer to the stereotype? Is not every democratic leader, every chief executive, some combination of Machiavellian and republican?

Mitterrand's Machiavellianism as president was, seen in retrospect, highly exaggerated and his republicanism underestimated in my judgment. As president he was less amoral than his detractors alleged and more attentive to the character of republican political institutions and the rule of law. Because of his legal education and parliamentary specialty in constitutional questions, he was surely the most knowledgeable and experienced constitutionalist among the French Socialists' political leaders. The issue is whether he abused the rule of law to the extent his detractors alleged, or whether the degree of controversy, corruption, and scandal during his fourteen years in office was not exaggerated because of his own past, his controversial reputation, and his continuing nonconformism.

◆   ◆   ◆

Political leadership needs to be studied in the context of its institutions, so some discussion of characteristics of the Fifth Republic is useful before turning back to Mitterrand as president.

The Fifth Republic from de Gaulle through Mitterrand was generally characterized as a sort of "republican monarchy," what I am calling, more clearly I think, a "Machiavellian republic." The Fifth Republic before cohabitation sidetracked it into normalization that was a peculiar combination of Machiavellian and republican aspects, a constitution "which was," said a parliamentary republican critic, "authoritarian and of Bonapartist inspiration," whose rules, customs, and also ambiguities could be used by the president to transform parliament into a rubber stamp for executive bills and to create and sustain an overpowerful president, the most powerful in any liberal democratic regime of our time. "It was no accident," says French constitutional historian Claude Nicolet, "that the 1958 constitution . . . revived the referendum, when the nation is asked to vote by a leader who poses the question as he wants and who can mobilize all the resources of the administration."[4] From 1958 through 1986 French Machiavellian republican presidents were able to act alone on their own initiative, as *uno solo* in Machiavelli's term. This produced the strengthened government necessary for policymaking regarding France's crises in the 1950s and early 1960s. But the trouble with effective but irregular regimes is that they almost always live on past their usefulness.

The French people's political history was also, however, one of episodic, highly ideological, and thus inconsistent republican regimes.[5] Since 1958 they have experienced the overpowerful president not so much as an abuse but as a return to effective state authority and collective French prestige in which they share. To the extent that Jacques Chirac's presidency has not met the Mitterrand standard, his personal, national, and international prestige, as opposed to his popularity, is lower.

The people want a president who "counts," thus France counts, in international diplomacy. *De Gaulle, c'était quand même quelqu'un!* De Gaulle was really somebody! Mitterrand, keeping a sense of proportion, was also somebody. With Mitterrand, France counted, still or once again.

In domestic politics French presidents were criticized for what was called the "dérive monarchique," the slide toward a monarchical tendency whose aspects, as said above, ranged from omniscient oversight of government to the president's own great architectural, cultural, and building projects to the reserved domain in high-politics foreign policy and security affairs. The elected monarch wielded excessive powers and wide, unchallenged discretion.

In 1986 the first cohabitation, in which Mitterrand faced a conservative majority in parliament and thus a conservative prime minister and government, showed that the constitution could take a dramatically less presidential form, a unique and sudden shift, through a "mere" electoral result, of most constitutional authority from the president to the prime minister. But even during the four "elected monarch" presidencies of 1958 to 1986, French presidents were republican officials as well as overpowerful presidents, accepting and enforcing what was, despite its peculiarity, a liberal democratic constitution. The key to the French Machiavellian republic was not so much the president's institutional and customary legitimacy to decide policy *uno solo,* but to decide where he would decide. The differences between de Gaulle, Pompidou, Giscard, and Mitterrand were significant but still in the details. Each president played the combination of Machiavellian prince and republican president in his own fashion.

◆ ◆ ◆

The Fifth Republic constitution is a bizarre founding document. What is written was for three decades not the way government worked. Like a giraffe, what exists could only have evolved; no founding fathers would have conceived of it just so.

On paper the 1958 constitution looked parliamentary. De Gaulle's entourage designed its veneer to resemble that of the Fourth Republic so that the old republic's partisans could accept it while feigning to ignore crucial ambiguities allowing for a "de Gaulle republic." Article 20, for example, says clearly that "The Government," which can be ousted by parliament, "shall determine and direct the policy of the nation." Article 21 adds, no less clearly, that "The Prime Minister," appointed by the president but who also can be ousted by parliament, "shall direct the operation of the Government" including specific responsibility "for national defense." But de Gaulle, although he delegated most domestic policy to his prime minister, ran a presidential government that was consecrated by the 1962 constitutional amendment making the president directly elected. In the "reserved domain" of foreign and domestic high policy the president might ask for the opinions of his prime minister or foreign policy and defense ministers in cabinet. But decisions were his alone if he so chose. The "syndrome of presidential omniscience" allowed him to intervene and oblige a decision in domestic policy as well.[6] Parliament, under the president's thumb, was a rubber stamp institution and had almost no real powers of scrutiny, investigation, and government oversight. The French press from an earlier time lacked an investigatory tradition and was excessively deferential to authority, leaving the executive branch free of another republican constraint. Public opinion, never habituated to believe itself a partner in government, felt in its proper place ruled by the French bureaucratic and political elites, who also believed themselves in their proper role. One of France's best specialists on institutions puts the danger of overpowerful presidential government in terms Americans will find familiar:

> This "monarchical" inclination is not limited to France alone. But in no other democracy does there exist such a risk of political dysfunction, which is explained by the almost total absence in France of institutional counter-suffrage powers. In no other of the large democracies is the president elected by direct universal for a seven year term, renewable without limit, is endowed with such complete political and constitutional lack of accountability, does he benefit from a large indulgence on the part of parliament. The only difficulty a French chief of state might encounter is potential negative media judgments leading to a decline in his popularity.[7]

The monarchical bending of the Fifth Republic's institutions had occurred, in other words, long before Mitterrand arrived at the Élysée. There had already been three elected monarchs or republican Princes in this Machiavellian republican regime.

However, Mitterrand probably was the last Machiavellian republican president. Due to two factors—the mainstreaming of Right and Left and the need for French institutions not to be so different from their European partners—the overpowerful presidency is fading along with French political and historical "exceptionalism" as a whole. The end of matching presidential and parliamentary majorities has not resulted in constitutional crisis but, partly due to the Mitterrand legacy, rather in mutual acceptance, institutional legitimacy, and policy rapprochement of Left and Right. The downside of cohabitation is even beginning to show, to wit, whether it is not a politics of the lowest common denominator, whether this new lack of alternatives is really good for France.

Also affecting the gaullian Machiavellian republic's supercentralized structure is, as pointed out above in chapter 7, the ever-greater practical significance of European integration in French government policymaking. The European Union is now France's major international policy realm, external without being foreign any more. The range of autonomy of French presidents has dramatically decreased because of expanding European Union rules and structures, and integration has eroded the Machiavellian republic, the environment where *uno solo* can act independently. Obviously there is a similar, if less drastic effect in every other EU state, where chief executives increasingly find their own prerogatives, whether *uno solo* or governmental, reined in by EU collective decision-making.

THE MACHIAVELLIAN REPUBLICAN PRESIDENT

With false modesty François Mitterrand called the French presidency *la fonction,* what in American parlance would be called "the office" of president. He meant to advertise that he understood, despite his imperial reputation, the republican character of the presidency: a delegation of authority from the people, through universal suffrage and for a limited period, with defined and limited powers in the context of other institutions. True, François Mitterrand in opposition had from 1958 on been the most violent critic of de Gaulle's "regime of personal power," and parliamentary republicanism such as his had long historical roots in French political history, as the fact of four previous republics illustrated. For his 1964 anti–de Gaulle book, *The Permanent Coup d'État,* Mitterrand not by chance took his brilliantly à propos epigram from Chateaubriand, one of de Gaulle's favorite authors: "Liberty," Chateaubriand had written, "can look glory in the face." Mitterrand witheringly denounced de Gaulle's "emptying the Constitution of any substance":

> To attack gaullism on the level of its acts is no longer sufficient because gaullism is more a mythology than a policy. . . . One can persuade public opinion that de Gaulle governs badly but still not convince people that he ought to be replaced. Public opinion still prefers the myth of the Father (de Gaulle takes care of everything), the myth of Happiness (de Gaulle drives away bad luck), the myth of Prestige (the world is jealous of France which has de Gaulle), and the myth of Prosperity (thanks to de Gaulle we will soon be 100 million French and the franc will vanquish the dollar), to the cold reality of the facts. But the republicans are not without their response: . . . a new world where law . . . will make the people its own master. [Republicans] have on their side liberty and justice.[8]

The intellectual substance and gut vehemence of this book leave little doubt about its genuineness. But the fact is also that once in office, this same man used de Gaulle's overpowerful presidency as had his conservative predecessors, Pompidou and Giscard d'Estaing. Was Mitterrand always an emperor in republican clothing? Or did he fall victim to temptation upon election as president? Or, as I believe, were there not continuously "two souls in his breast," the Machiavellian republican's dilemma that inhabits every democratic leader and is played out according to temperament and circumstances?

The republican idea in France has many sources and no single founding, no equivalent of *The Federalist Papers* or of the American Constitution and Declaration of Independence. There are various French republican traditions, thus at key moments republicans have been heavily divided among themselves as well as opposed to the motley array on the Right—Bonapartists, monarchists, Vichyites, and other anti-republican mind-sets.[9] In France the republican idea has at various times emphasized the rule of law as opposed to arbitrary executive power, decentralization of the state, secularism as opposed to church-controlled education, parliamentary institutions, egalitarianism, and democratic legitimacy.

No regime is pure, and even in a democratic age certain avatars of monarchical government persist. Certainly this is true in France. *Homo politicus gallicus,* the French political man, is always some combination of French history and geography, the rainbow of the country's political culture. The mature Mitterrand's political culture was an eclectic composite of French ideas: realism steeped in a skepticism tinged not only with cynicism but also a certain romanticism and hope. Mitterrand's political character expressed, to say it differently, shifting balances of Machiavellian instincts and republican reactions. Or yet still another formula: He grew up as a Machiavellian and became a republican, and he remained both, and both were sincere. Very different he was from his predecessors—from de Gaulle the military man, from Pompidou the banker and *éminence grise,* and from Giscard d'Estaing the finance specialist, brilliant product of the *grandes écoles.* But as a political leader Mitterrand fit the Fifth Republic's institutions and they fit him like hand and glove. However chastening to leftists, Mitterrand's Machiavellian republican brilliance allowed the French Left to reorganize itself as a credible party of government.

"MITTERRAMSES": BUILDING MONUMENTS AND THE MONARCHICAL TENDENCY

"Culture" is intangible, but cultural artifacts and monuments are visible legacies of the power that built them. A prince in certain circumstances must know how to be frugal, or at least how to appear to be frugal, how not to build monuments to himself. But French elected monarchs in the Fifth Republic up through François Mitterrand felt not just a right but a public duty to build. The creation of a legacy in stone was part of the president's function; it was seen as an addition to the national identity. Public support of presidential stonework was a sign of the people's legitimation of the gaullist French presidency. The imperial French president was also, historians will quickly remind the political scientist, for the French people a sign of past glory. But presidential superpower within the contemporary French political culture allowed great undertakings (even if only in Paris) to provide the semblance of *present* glory.

Thus on coming to office François Mitterrand inherited a Fifth Republic tradition of *grands projets,* monumental public architectural and cultural projects initiated and defended by the president. What else would have justified such monumental presidential building as that by François Mitterrand— *"Mitterramses"* he was sarcastically nicknamed—in a democratic regime? "My ambition," he pompously said about the building projects, "is not for me but for France."[10] It was the appropriate Machiavellian republican note to strike. The French people loved or hated this or that project as they pleased, but they were in any case enthusiastic that Mitterrand was continuing the tradition. France was still France. The projects, some successful and some dismal, were a great success taken as a whole.

The one president who didn't build monuments was, oddly enough, Charles de Gaulle. De Gaulle, a British commentator wrote, had in reality a modest idea of the state's proper involvement in culture. He "made just three major decisions on cultural matters, but they were of great importance: to create a full-scale Ministry of Cultural Affairs, to appoint André Malraux head of it with the rank of Ministre d'état, and to maintain him at this post throughout his presidency." But de Gaulle did watch over Paris closely, even considering moving the presidency from the cramped Élysée palace to the grand Château de Vincennes on the east end of the city. De Gaulle restricted himself to Malraux's democratic project of *maisons de culture,* regional and local cultural centers around the country, and the inspired sandblasting of Paris's national buildings. Georges Pompidou launched the controversial museum posthumously given his name. La voie Pompidou, the lower drive along the Seine's right bank, was Giscard d'Estaing's doing, as was the public park and underground shopping mall complex in the center of Paris to replace Les Halles, whose markets had nightly contained Paris's food supplies and a high-low nightlife, including the rue St. Denis red-light district made famous in the Billy Wilder film *Irma la douce.*

It was presidents Giscard d'Estaing and above all Mitterrand who became pharaonic builders, reestablishing the city's reputation as the most innovative yet traditional and manicured city in Europe.[11] The reality of political power operates inside offices invisible to public opinion, so the state's symbols are from time to time put on display—with military parades, motorcades, fireworks, and the Marseillaise intoned stirringly by the mounted Republican Guard. But the most visible, most permanent imprint of the contemporary French state is found in the monumental building efforts of France's presidents. François Mitterrand, "Mitterramses," marked Paris deepest with his stone legacy.

Mitterrand acted the role of a *mécène,* a great patron, but not always to general acclaim. Some of his projects were widely regarded as of dubious taste or as outright architectural disasters. The new National Library (Jacques Chirac named it posthumously for Mitterrand in 1996), La Bibliothèque Nationale de France, François Mitterrand, which replaced the quirky but cherished old Bibliothèque Nationale in the rue du Richelieu, has been said to display both defects. The original plan had to be largely revised during construction, and an imposing, technologically much improved design comprising four towers, resembling four open books at the angles of a large square, now stands along the left bank of the Seine in the thirteenth arrondissement. The location is, not by chance, the Quai François Mauriac, named after the venerable writer and family friend who had sponsored Mitterrand's debuts in Paris on his arrival as a student in 1934 and who supported him at key moments in his career, especially in the Observatory affair.

Mitterrand, like Pompidou and Giscard d'Estaing, had a serious personal interest in cultural matters, though his tastes were eclectic and his attention was sketchy. Above all interested in books, he was not much interested or knowledgeable in painting or music. And of his architectural sense he himself said, "In the end I believe my tastes are fairly classical and that I am attracted by pure geometrical forms."[12] Several of his building projects reflected this, including the Louvre Pyramid, the National Library, and the Arche de la Défense. All this added up to a modernist bent, but didn't have much to do with any kind of "socialist" inspiration in art and architecture, whatever that might have been.

Jack Lang was a dynamic culture minister and regular companion of the president in forays into the human comedy. As opposed to Malraux's classicism, Lang was tuned in—the word fits—to contemporary trends, including the postmodern and the anti-hegemonic French sensibility that was (or was just mistaken for) anti-Americanism. Jack Lang was also a mover and shaker, a crafty bureaucratic player who accomplished many projects successfully. A British observer even says that in terms of practical accomplishments, Jack Lang's relative success can be opposed to Malraux's relative failure.[13] Lang successfully played the game of courtier with Mitterrand, who, according to other facets of his personality, should have dismissed his culture minister's poses and attitudes. But he strangely enjoyed Lang's company, which says something about the president himself.[14] In this mood and role as a sort of Renaissance patron, Mitterrand once intoned in a cabinet meeting: "There can be no great policy for

France without a great architecture." Taking this laudable sentiment to excess and with an attention to detail reminiscent of Valéry Giscard d'Estaing (and Jimmy Carter), Mitterrand himself even chose the color of the seats for the Opéra-Bastille![15]

Socialism was supposed to be a cultural change as well as an economic and political change. Mitterrand, putting money where his ideology was, therefore doubled the state's budget for culture and stuck to it even in hard times. It went from 0.44 percent of the budget to 0.76 percent in 1982 and reached a high of 0.94 percent in 1991. Less than 1 percent of the government budget may seem paltry, but compared with that of other national governments (and for culture!), this was serious business and France played its role as a beacon to other governments.

That Mitterrand was going to be preoccupied with his legacy in stone was made clear at his very first news conference, at which he announced changes to old projects and several new projects. The plan for La Défense, the business district of skyscrapers scheduled by Giscard d'Estaing for western Paris—final plans that were only eight months old—would be scrapped and redrawn. The Institute for the Arab World, an important political as well as cultural building, would be constructed on a different site, a curving narrow patch of land on the Seine next to the Jussieu University just east of the Latin Quarter. The huge La Villette park project in northern Paris would be cut back, but a City of Music would be added. For young people there would be the Zénith, a 10,000-seat hall for pop and contemporary music in the reconfigured La Villette park, a postmodern urban design for a park heavily strolled by neighbors and visitors.

The new Musée d'Orsay, under construction in the disused railroad station on the quai d'Orsay, would also be reconceived. It would begin with 1848—the year of revolutions—and emphasize realism in art and social history, combining neoclassicism, Impressionism, even including fin-de-siècle Art Deco objects. (A mint condition freestanding Art Deco metro entrance is a familiar sight to second-floor visitors.) Two final announcements, both on the grand scale, were the plan for a grand exhibition for 1989 to commemorate the Bicentenary of the French Revolution, and the long-disputed Ministry of Finance's removal from a wing of the Louvre, to make possible the so-called Grand Louvre renewal and restoration.[16]

Less than a year later, in March 1982, eight new Paris projects were added plus several less ambitious ones for the provinces. There would be an Opéra Populaire or People's Opera at the Place de la Bastille in Paris, where the infamous prison had stood. Its left-wing symbolism fit nicely (until the ticket prices became known) with the plan to build up cultural life in Paris's less well-off eastern neighborhoods. At La Défense the centerpiece would be a new building of radical design called the Arche de la Défense. A monumental rectangle, it would recall the Arc de Triomphe's outline, but its bulk, its substance, would be only the outline of a building housing an International Conference Center. The entire middle of the structure would be empty, missing. The idea was that the huge, open rectangular center would extend to La Défense the Louvre-Concorde-Arc de Triomphe line of vision. The Arche was a remarkably audacious architectural conception for a government project, conceivable only in a Machiavellian republic such as France's whose president had the self-possession of a François Mitterrand.

New projects for provincial areas were less ambitious—a school of dance at Marseilles, a national comic-strip museum at Angoulême, and a museum of photography at Arles. Making up only 4 percent of the total budget, the implication was that the provinces were yet again being awarded crumbs, the Socialist party's concern for decentralization notwithstanding. Being perhaps too explicit on this score, Paris ought to be, Mitterrand said, "a model for the city of the twenty-first century."[17] Paris was still to be Paris, and France still France, whether the Right or the Left was in power.

Mitterrand himself selected winners of design competitions for some of the projects, another unusual aspect of republican monarchy. His choices were criticized, his taste disdained, even the now-acclaimed pyramid complex conceived by I. M. Pei for the central Louvre courtyard. Mitterrand was megalomaniac to a greater extent than Giscard d'Estaing, it was said. His "fiat" was, he replied, limited to selecting among finalists chosen by committees of experts. But Mitterrand's wishes were pretty well known inside the committees, which tended to present him with congenial alternatives. As to the choice of I. M. Pei, it was because the Louvre project was a renovation rather than a new construction that Mitterrand by law could personally choose the architect and the design. The pyramid's aesthetic success is, today, the main thing; Mitterrand's tendency to build monuments to himself is important in his biography, but his biography is now history.

◆   ◆   ◆

A presidential defeat in the election of 1988 would mean, as it had with Giscard d'Estaing, that the fate of Mitterrand's architectural ambitions would end up in the hands of his successor. Therefore, Mitterrand sought to make his projects irreversible. Jacques Chirac, in 1981-86 still the gaullist conservative mayor of Paris, generally cooperated because new cultural attractions enhanced the city's attractiveness and because he knew that the 1986 parliamentary elections could make him prime minister with Mitterrand as president. Chirac also agreed that public building projects should be shifted eastward to the less prosperous parts of the city, especially to revitalize riverfront sites there such as Bercy and Ivry.

Chirac did become prime minister from 1986 to 1988. He combined this role, as was possible according to French law, with his office as mayor of Paris. Skirmishes and larger battles between the prime minister and president took place over Mitterrand's cultural projects. Building was usually behind schedule, giving Chirac time to affect the president's wishes.

Jacques Chirac wanted to stop the Bastille Opera project completely and to leave the Ministry of Finance in the Louvre. He proposed giving some of the freed-up space at Bercy over to the International Communications Center scheduled for the Arche de la Défense. But Mitterrand's great projects emerged basically intact from the cohabitation struggles with Chirac. For example, the Bastille Opera went forward mainly because of sunk investments, although Mitterrand, Lang, and the Finance Ministry did not find the architecture satisfying. Controversy erupted soon enough about the salary and overpriced productions of the first conductor, Daniel Barenboim, whose contract was bought out. Mitterrand's friend Pierre Bergé, a businessman and bon vivant with serious cultural interests, was brought in as business and artistic director, and a very young, unknown Korean conductor was engaged to replace Barenboim. To unexpected acclaim, Myung-Whun Chung, who served as the Opera's musical director from 1989 to 1994, proved a great success.

When the Socialists returned to power in 1988, Jack Lang was returned to the culture ministry. (He had asked Mitterrand for promotion to a key ministry but was disappointed.) To the large list of cultural projects under way was added a renovation of the Tuileries Gardens and, most important, the huge new National Library. Mitterrand decreed that the Très Grande Bibliothèque (TGB), the "Very Large Library," which was its temporary name, would be "an entirely new kind of library," the most advanced technologically and in design in the world. In fact, experts knew that this was a wish. No one had an idea what the TGB would look like when finished.

To beat the date of Mitterrand's departure from office in 1995, the architectural competition was held and he chose the winning design even before it was decided what the library's holdings would be or what other services it would provide. Then a 300 percent increase of the projected holdings, from 4 to 12 million books, created the need for major architectural changes. But even this added complication was dwarfed by the astonishing thoughtlessness of a design that planned to store most of the library's collection aboveground in glass towers. Neglected were the "minor" facts that books weigh a lot and are damaged by sunlight. A blue-ribbon commission was given the job of getting the design right. Mitterrand quickly accepted its first advice to put much of the collection in underground levels.

◆   ◆   ◆

In short, there was much sense in characterizing François Mitterrand as "Mitterramses." Mitterrand took advantage of the Fifth Republic's tradition of presidential building to the hilt. What was the meaning and the legacy of Mitterramses? There are several points to make, both about French institutions and about Mitterrand.

No doubt, as said above, François Mitterrand is the last French president to be able to build as he did. The sheer scope and audacity of his cultural projects will be difficult for future presidents even to consider, for several reasons. Any attempt to continue the tradition of grand presidential projects in Paris will encounter a simple limit: the lack of new sites and the financial burden of running the existing new monuments and buildings. This will be a good thing, because the Machiavellian republic needed to be narrowed, in cultural as in institutional powers. Monumental building became for a time an accepted part of the "very French" Fifth Republic presidency, but the very notion of it clashes with the values of republican government.

The balance is likely to be righted with its decline, due to the diffusion of powers in cohabitation but probably also by a sense that such an over-powerful presidency was a good idea whose time is past and should not return. No president or government should, in a republic at least, be able to leave such an architectural imprint. It smacks of other kinds of regimes. Mitterramses, like other aspects of the Machiavellian republican regime in Mitterrand's presidency, was the end of a line.

At the same time, the talent and determination required to achieve the extraordinary Paris park of monuments should not be underestimated. Good or bad for the people, as Parisian renaissance or, on the contrary, Parisian decline into a living museum of ostentatious and self-indulgently political cultural artifacts, as a matter of sheer audacity and (often) aesthetic success, the *grands projets* of Mitterramses show in yet another way that this was a president far out of the ordinary.

A last point is a mitigating circumstance against the accusations of imperious character and political-cultural dubiety. François Mitterrand could justify his Mitterramses complex by telling himself that in his *grand projets* the French Left finally would be getting equal historical-monumental patrimony with the Right. The French Left, excluded from power not merely since 1958 but for most of French history, should have parity in weight and prestige in stone. The French Left's holy sites would no longer be a building that existed by its absence (the Bastille) or a cemetery wall (the Mur des Fédérés where Paris Commune defenders had been executed). This successful debut in stone has added to the achievement of legitimacy and mutual acceptance within the French political class. The Left, in this way as in others, is no longer a permanent opposition, no longer disdained and intimidated, equally responsible for the republic's business and that much more separated from its old temptation by utopian thinking. Mitterrand very consciously began this process of symbolic incorporation of the French Left into the Fifth Republic with his inaugural day ceremony at the Pantheon, continuing not only in the *grands projets* but also in small but very important sentimental projects such as commissioning statues of historic left-wing leaders—Léon Blum and Pierre Mendès France—which have been placed in neighborhood squares carrying their names. Mitterrand's effort in stone, bombastic at the top, was, when considered top to bottom, a subtle policy of equal dignity.

REASON OF STATE LIES AND BETTER LIES

François Mitterrand was accused of being an exceptional liar. Was this true and if so, what was the type of lie at issue? How does this question fit within the conception of the Machiavellian republican?

"The prince must know how to lie," said Machiavelli. The question for him was only lying well or badly. Lying—deception, dissembling, misleading, conscious falsehood—is normal and ordinary; that is, present, in all political regimes, despite its being morally objectionable.

The most objectionable lies for the Machiavellian are those that are unnecessary. The most acceptable lies for the republican are the "noble lies" of modern democracies, for example, de Gaulle's creation of the myth that the French people as a whole were résistants, or the moral-useful lies of the contemporary democratic state, which may deny an intention to devalue the currency in order to fool speculation or may announce misleading military plans. There are other distinctions between kinds of acceptable lies, extent of lying, and those kinds of lying that are unacceptable, illegal, and unconstitutional, those in which the difference between regimes is found and justified.

In a democracy there are lies and lies, the "white" political lies of flattery and promises, and the lies of policy, linked to government and administration. Then there are reason of state lies, those reaching beyond narrow policy to national security, to threats to survival of the state, however hard to find an acceptable definition of the term. For example, to swear that "Our state will never negotiate with terrorists" can never be taken as an ironclad promise. But it is a fruitful lie insofar as terrorists and domestic public opinion believe in it.

François Mitterrand was a representative French president in this matter of lies, although with him, so went the criticism, the degrees and occasions for lying were exceptional. Overall he surely was less candid and straightforward in political relationships than other presidents. He often lied to preserve compartmentalization of his political and personal lives, among his different "networks" of friends and political associates who hardly knew of each others' existence. But it is not certain—and this is the important matter—that François Mitterrand's official dissembling, his reason of state lying was more egregious than those of his predecessors. Certainly that was his reputation among his domestic critics, yet leaders in other countries did not consider Mitterrand unreliable in general. Margaret Thatcher on German unification believed, and wrote publicly, that the French president was not as frank in public about his reservations as he was with her in private. Helmut Kohl tended to say that Mitterrand, if consulted solicitously, would be solid. George Bush found Mitterrand surprisingly solid, given his original expectations.[18] In general, Mitterrand behaved collegially and was respected. In the crunch (the Euromissile crisis, the Gulf war, European integration negotiations with the Germans) his partners never gave the impression they were dealing with a scoundrel or that he behaved like the foreigners' stereotype of Quai d'Orsay diplomacy.

In lesser matters Mitterrand was a past master of political dissembling. He was an inveterate liar, but not compulsive, that is, he lied often, daily, hourly, without compunction, in a Machiavellian way to keep his freedom of action politically or personally. But he seems never to have become a slave to his lies, whether in policy or about his past. He knew truth from lie, and lying was often a kind of game for him, as when he told different stories to different journalists and biographers to please or confound their biases. Calculated lying for a political end—putting his own strategy before truth—became part of Mitterrand's reputation. As a Machiavellian, truth, while important, was not an absolute value to him, but then, neither was lying. There was, and is, much hypocrisy among French political elites on this score and it remains to be shown that Mitterrand was qualitatively more culpable than other French politicians.

The moral issue for politicians is not purity versus devilishness; it is a matter of balance and of accountability.

REASON OF STATE
AND THE RAINBOW WARRIOR AFFAIR

The *Rainbow Warrior* affair has many aspects, including a death no one wanted. From Mitterrand's point of view, it is about the exercise of reason of state policy and how the prince deals with the blunders of his subordinates.

France's "green" political groups are, as everywhere, a combination of the best and the worst. They fight the good fight, but can be impassioned single-issue groups that, on their fringes, lean toward intolerant fanaticism. They have shown themselves capable of violence to people and to property, sometimes even an anti-industrial, anti-humanist irrationality in the guise of defense of animals, plants, and the Earth as a whole.

The 1970s saw the first international limits-to-growth hysteria, which was set off by two events: the first oil price crisis launched by OPEC and the Club of Rome's famous report on the coming exhaustion of world resources. "Green" parties made their appearance everywhere, and the French Verts won 3 percent in the 1978 parliamentary elections. Support was about equally divided between men and women. The party got 6 percent, double its total percentage, of the 25 to 34 age category, and almost nothing among people over 65 years of age. In 1988 the party got only 1 percent, but in European Parliament elections the following year, held on a proportional representation basis, which tends to increase the votes of small parties, the Greens suddenly got more than 10 percent. This was somewhat misleading since the overall abstention in this "irrelevant" election was 51 percent, and a right-wing populist "Hunting" party got 4 percent in protest of a European-wide ecologist campaign to ban hunting!

The most intense episode opposing Mitterrand's presidency and the ecologists was the *Rainbow Warrior* affair of July 1985. It seemed to show a heartless reason of state French government brutally crushing the international Greenpeace movement's hindering but peaceful anti-nuclear protests.[19]

In July 1985 the Greenpeace ship *Rainbow Warrior* was on a mission to frustrate French nuclear testing at the Mururoa Atoll in the South Pacific. The *Rainbow Warrior's* tactic was to sail into target areas so that tests could not be carried out, or at least would be put off amid sensationalist international publicity while the French government removed the obstacle. In this case, French intelligence agents, acting under orders to take a harder line, actually blew up the forty-eight-meter reconverted trawler sitting in the harbor in

Auckland, New Zealand—a violation of national sovereignty since it was the territory of another government. A Portuguese photographer, Fernando Pereira, who went back for his camera after a first "warning" blast, was unintentionally killed by a second explosion.

Journalists found out rather quickly that the saboteurs were not terrorists but French DGSE (secret service) agents, a man and a woman not married but working together posing as a couple called Turenge, thus their nickname *les faux Turenge*. It was also learned that Mitterrand's Élysée military advisor General Saulnier had authorized funding, indicating that the president had either known about the operation or that his staff had acted without his specific knowledge, no doubt to preserve "plausible deniability." Either case was bad, and in addition, the New Zealand government protested vigorously this blatant violation of its national sovereignty on the part of a state that was supposedly one of the world's vigilant guardians of sovereignty.

Mitterrand of course deplored the death of the photographer. But he insisted as president that DGSE dissuasion of Greenpeace was legitimate because nuclear testing was necessary to maintain the French nuclear deterrent. No citizens' group, however well-intentioned, could be allowed to block the French government's military security needs. There ensued a bitter internal debate at the highest French government levels about who would take responsibility for an act that, unwillingly or not, had caused a death. The president's personal involvement in the action against Greenpeace—did he specifically authorize blowing up the *Rainbow Warrior*? Did he know in detail what was planned?—was probably that he gave a general instruction to stop interference with France's nuclear testing but was astonished at the methods, the clumsiness, and the tragedy of what was done. Defense Minister Charles Hernu, one of Mitterrand's oldest allies, finally resigned, rather than General Saulnier. The loyal comrade, observers unanimously agreed, fell on his sword for the emperor.[20] "Is not the best way to save several guilty people to sacrifice one of them?"[21]

French biographer Franz-Olivier Giesbert lists lies and alibis proffered by the Élysée and the government. The operation may have been, one government official said, a British secret service scheme to weaken France's image and political credit in the South Pacific. This absurd allegation was Hernu's explanation. Another hypothesis was a possible neo-gaullist machination designed to discredit the left-wing government. Shades of the Observatory affair and the *affaire des fuites!* The truth is that it was quite simply a remarkably bungled French secret service operation. The *faux Turenge* couple was responsible for the actual sabotage. The two were apprehended, tried, and convicted. They spent a few years in a New Zealand minimum security prison before being discreetly pardoned and returned to a French island for "medical reasons."

So the *Rainbow Warrior* episode did not affect French nuclear testing policy. But then, in 1992, François Mitterrand declared his unilateral French testing moratorium. This allowed France to take the moral high ground internationally in negotiations that led to France's signing of the Comprehensive Test Ban Treaty (CTBT). But this came only in 1997, after Mitterrand's departure from office, and only after his successor Jacques Chirac broke Mitterrand's pledge to conduct the final, controversial series of tests on Mururoa Atoll.

The *Rainbow Warrior* affair showed that even a Socialist government may have to choose against well-meaning grassroots activists in favor of national defense traditionally conceived. Yet the clash did incite a debate on the limits of reason of state behavior and on acceptable rules of engagement faced with popular common cause organizations. Are activists responsible for the danger they face if they disrupt a government action as grave as nuclear testing? Could destroying a protest ship be legitimate, at least if no lives are put in danger? Or is the correct, if unsatisfactory, conclusion that both parties were responsible, that both had dirty hands because no one wanted the death, and that therefore no moral rule was confirmed or refuted but only a warning issued to each side for the future?

MITTERRAND AND LE PEN'S NATIONAL FRONT: WHAT PRICE ELECTORAL MANEUVER?

In 1984-1985, looking at a probable Socialist defeat in the 1986 parliamentary elections, Mitterrand's consideration of changing the electoral law had much to do with the rising electoral strength of the far right National Front, led by the demagogic Jean-Marie Le Pen.

The dilemma was complicated. To keep a system of majority voting, as in the United States, would minimize the FN's success, whereas a change to proportional representation would maximize it. Mitterrand opted to change the law, and the FN entered parliament for the first time, with a large group of thirty-five deputies. It was a political scandal, in fact the act of "corruption" that some commentators reproached him for more than any other in his term.

What was Mitterrand's electoral gaming here? Did it make sense politically? Was it morally justifiable?

Proportional representation, as said, maximized the National Front's proportion of the vote and thus its number of deputies. PR meant all National Front votes would be "useful"; they would not be wasted whereas in a majority system the FN would lose almost everywhere because it had no allies with whom to seek majorities. A far-right party would rarely or never get the majority necessary to win a constituency seat. With 15 percent of the votes in a proportional representation system however, a party gets 15 percent of the seats. With 15 percent in a majority system a party with no allies will be beaten in every district.

Why did François Mitterrand knowingly give the National Front an electoral success, putting it in parliament with a significant group of deputies? There were several reasons, not one of them being that he had any sympathy for FN policies and values.

First, he hoped that the proportional law, by maximizing the National Front's success, would split the right-wing vote enough to prevent an RPR/UDF victory. This failed, although the size of the RPR/UDF parliamentary majority in 1986 was considerably less than it would have been under a majority voting system. The result was a slightly less undesirable situation for Mitterrand in the first cohabitation regime.

Second, Mitterrand knew that a proportional system would minimize the Socialist party's losses. Finally, because the National Front's popular support was a growing social fact that had only partially to do with electoral laws, it would be safer to have the FN and Jean-Marie Le Pen inside the parliament, constrained by responsibilities, rules, and customs, than having them outside in charge of the streets, free of institutional accountability.

Mitterrand was nevertheless demonized for "legitimizing" Le Pen and his nationalist/anti-foreigner/racist demagogy. In private conversation with his Socialist associates Mitterrand had, in a Machiavellian lesson in electoral gaming, summed up the 1985-86 alternatives as follows:

> We have four objectives, which we have to put in priority if we can't have them all: no absolute majority for the RPR; no absolute majority for the RPR-UDF; help the center to emerge; give the largest number of seats possible to the PS.
>
> Majority voting in two ballots favors the RPR. It must be eliminated. If the left has only 41 percent, whatever the electoral law, the last three objectives are unattainable. As result, given that all the possible electoral laws will give an UDF-RPR majority, they are identical for us. And we shouldn't try to work it so they have a narrow majority. The narrowest are the strongest. Except for national proportional representation, with every other electoral system you get a majority of seats with 45 percent of the votes. . . . Our choice [as the PS] is thus between having national proportional representation or having 60 deputies more [through a system of remainders], knowing that in any case no system will stop the RPR-UDF coalition from a majority.[22]

A change back to majority voting was, not surprisingly, a priority of Chirac's cohabitation government's upon election in 1986. The goal was the old game of reducing the far Right's ability to weaken the moderate conservative coalitions of RPR and UDF, and pressuring the left-wing Socialist and Communist parties by forcing them to try to ally, thus highlighting their differences and the Communists' illegitimacy.

But cohabitation worked out poorly for the Chirac-led conservatives. The Socialists two years later looked unexpectedly to achieve another smashing absolute majority in the wake of François Mitterrand's big victory in the May 1988 presidential election, defeating Chirac, and his renewed dissolution of the Assembly. The June 1988 parliamentary elections, to be held on the basis of the majority electoral law, looked likely to produce such a large Socialist majority that Mitterrand, in a display of republican wisdom, deliberately urged voters to consider that the Socialists could be too strong: "It isn't good when one party rules alone," he said.

Be careful what you wish, for you may get too much of it! These 1988 elections produced neither the predicted Socialist party landslide nor even a majority. The PS had only a plurality, and as a consequence a weak Socialist minority government led by Michel Rocard, named by Mitterrand as prime minister. The Communists had been downplayed as a possible coalition partner for the Socialists in favor of an attempted new "opening to the center" that Mitterrand much favored. But the left-leaning Centrist group Mitterrand had tried to encourage failed to win enough seats to provide a Socialist/Centrist majority. The good news in this relative setback was that, due to the reinstated majority voting system, Le Pen's National Front was reduced again, from its previous thirty-five deputies to a single deputy, one in Vitrolles, a politicized district outside Marseilles.

Had Mitterrand committed a grave, immoral act by changing the 1986 electoral law, increasing the FN's parliamentary representation and its legitimacy? Or would the FN's social base have prospered regardless, whatever its number of deputies? And if Mitterrand had committed an error, was it political (a miscalculation of the outcome) or constitutional (is it wrong to manipulate institutions for partisan purpose) or moral (is it wrong to abet a racist political movement even if other good ends are met)? Finally, were the errors of 1986 (and which of them) repaired in 1988? The analysis of this problem must include more factors than simply the effect of an electoral law on the National Front.

Mitterrand's attitude about electoral laws was not constitutionalist. "The tendency," he said, "should be toward proportional representation and in any case there is no good [electoral] system. It should be changed from time to time."[23]

The 1986 decision to change the electoral law was one of Mitterrand's most criticized actions because of the positive effect for the National Front, even though Mitterrand as a candidate had always promised electoral law changes toward some form or degree of proportional representation. Mitterrand always began with the idea that the Left was not a majority in French society, that the Socialists tended to be divided, and that the collapse of the Communist vote after 1981 put all the electoral pressure on the Socialists if the Left was to govern. With the Communist electoral collapse, "the current electoral law [majority voting in two ballots] is close to a single ballot majority system."[24] During his second term Mitterrand sometimes talked of a "German system" for France, proportional representation overall with half the seats decided in majority district elections. But this slid away, as did other promised institutional reforms.

In a pragmatic accounting, errors are weighed against successes. Changing the electoral law in 1986 seemed overall a failure. True, it gave the Socialists 31 percent and kept the pressures reduced on Mitterrand. But it didn't keep the conservatives from winning, it allowed the National Front to win enough seats to constitute a parliamentary group, and it seemed to put Jacques Chirac on the road to winning the presidency in 1988. At most the electoral law shift held down the size of the Socialist defeat. In the longer run, Mitterrand and the Socialists had blackened their own reputations. Because the change benefited the National Front, some critics, at the time and later, considered this the absolute worst of Mitterrand's sins.

Was the electoral law change legal, was it legitimate? In France electoral laws don't have the semiconstitutional status and permanence that they do in the United States. It is legal and considered legitimate by both Left and Right to alter electoral laws, although naturally each change is accompanied by allegations of mere partisan goals. Mitterrand was reproached in 1986 for abetting the racist, xenophobic National Front. Did increasing the number of deputies through the shift in electoral laws really increase the FN's political strength? or did it also channel that popular pressure through parliamentary representation?

Whether this maneuver was justifiable depends, as said, on more than the effect on the National Front alone. As Table 8.1 shows, while the FN may have benefited, the Communist party decline continued. The PCF was even surpassed by the FN in 1993. Indeed, the disappointing 1986 results did not alter French politicians' sense of the legitimacy of changing electoral laws. In 1993 Mitterrand reproached himself for not having imposed his will on recalcitrant Socialist leaders to introduce a German-type system that would have obtained a better result for the incumbent Pierre Bérégovoy government. And Mitterrand's attempt to use proportional representation to increase the Left's chances—increasing the "unacceptable" National Front vote weakens the conservatives—resembled the fundamental

FIGURE 8.1

RESULTS OF NATIONAL ASSEMBLY ELECTIONS
(PERCENTAGE OF VOTE)

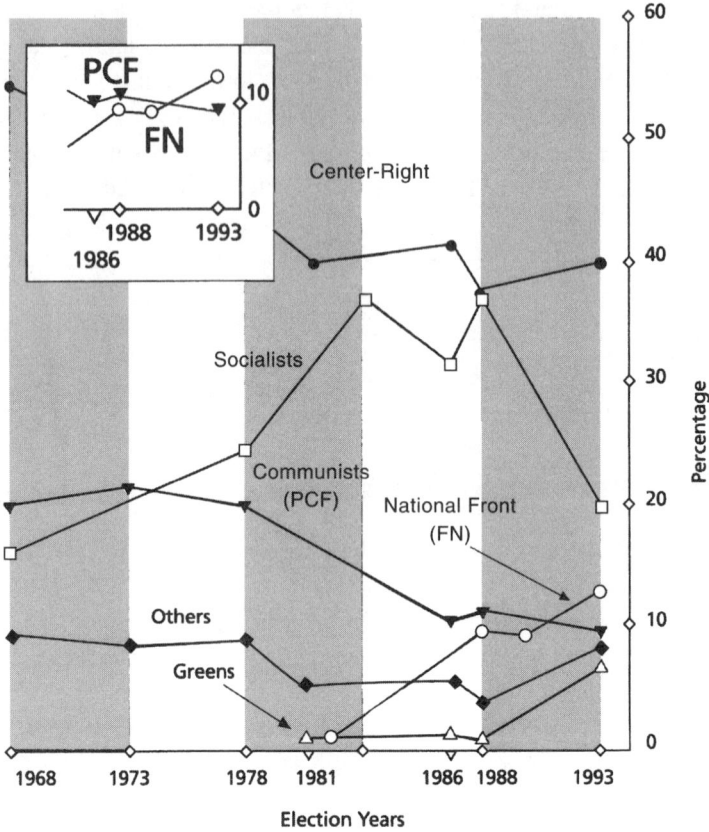

Figure from *France in the New Europe: Changing yet Steadfast* by Ronald Tiersky, copyright © 1994 by Harcourt, Inc., reproduced by permission of the publisher.

conservative electoral strategy from 1958 to 1981, majority voting to keep the Right in power and the Socialists in permanent opposition, because of the Communist party's illegitimacy as a coalition partner.

CORRUPTION, SCANDAL, AND "LES AFFAIRES"

What was François Mitterrand's attitude toward the more venal sorts of corruption? To what extent was he aware of it, involved in it, how much did he tolerate or condone what he might have stopped? Is the allegation correct that his presidency was unusually corrupt and that much of this was due to Mitterrand's own character?

During the first Socialist-dominated parliament of 1981 to 1986, "two scandals had created a sensation: that of the 'Vincennes Irish,' the arrest by the Élysée's special anti-terrorist cell of an alleged IRA terrorist group in August 1982, which turned out to be based on bad information and was followed by fabricated proofs, and the *Rainbow Warrior* affair. Neither of these cases had been politically exploited by the opposition however."[25] The Vincennes Irish affair later was linked to more general allegations of unjustified telephone taps by the director of the Élysée anti-terrorist cell group, Gilles Menage, in connection with danger to Mitterrand's own life and also to a possible kidnapping of his daughter Mazarine. In addition to the illegal telephone taps were rumors suggesting that the personal life of a well-known actress (Carole Bouquet was mentioned) was being monitored. Prurient rumors indicated that the president was interested; intelligence gossip suggested that a relationship between the woman and a suspected terrorist was at issue. The special Élysée anti-terrorist cell, which had mixed its government business and protection of Mitterrand's family, was dissolved in 1984. Many believed the excesses and unwarranted invasions of privacy had resulted from the president mixing in a single institution his own personal protection and a national security function.

In the 1986 to 1988 cohabitation years, the well-intentioned *Carrefour du développement,* or Crossroads for Development, became a tar baby. Cooperation minister Christian Nucci, the holdover Socialist director of this semigovernmental agency that had the goal of funneling Third World develop-ment aid, was accused by the new conservative Interior Minister, Charles Pasqua, of skimming money for Socialist party use and for himself. Although Mitterrand tried to protect Nucci, it was clear that this was a case of Socialist corruption. In November 1987 the Socialists were accused of having violated, when in office, the embargo on arms sales to Iran, of having granted licenses to the Luchaire company to sell arms in return for illegal Socialist party finance. The Socialists in return attacked Justice Minister Albin Chalandon, who had made money in an illegal financial institution that suddenly collapsed into bankruptcy, one run by the well-known jewelers the Chaumet brothers.

These scandals were eclipsed, however, by a series of sensational *affaires* that arose in succession after 1989. An accumulation of scandal allegations added to the woes of the floundering Edith Cresson government, giving Mitterrand and the Socialists in general a reputation for corruption, a label that detractors believed defined the Mitterrand presidency as a whole. One American observer with a particular feel for Socialist party insider debates and sensibilities put it this way: "François Mitterrand had always advertised his contempt for money. The Socialists had always felt themselves morally superior to the Right, suspected of all manner of deals and corruption. Accusations and indictments for corruption thus affected Socialist morale and the public view of the party even more than did scandals past and present attributed to the Right."[26]

The first episode was the snaring for insider trading of Mitterrand's presidential pal, Roger-Patrice Pelat, "the Colonel" who had been Mitterrand's bodyguard in the Resistance and had become a wealthy businessman. Pelat had the run of the Élysée palace. He and a few associates had turned several million francs profit from a deal involving the 1988 purchase of Triangle-American Can by the state-owned French Péchiney company. With insider information apparently from Socialist government Ministry of Finance officials, they had bought American Can stock just before the Péchiney takeover was announced, at five times the share price. Pelat was indicted in February 1989. As with Charles Hernu, Mitterrand vouched for his friend's character and friendship, but added, pushed by aggressive journalists, that "if [Pelat] had committed a crime," he, as president, "would have to reconsider their relationship." François Mitterrand was being obliged by public opinion and a more aggressive press to take precautions now that were unlike his "religion of friendship." The case of Charles Hernu had been one lesson; the much worse problem of René Bousquet (see chapter 11), occurring in the same period, was another. Roger-Patrice Pelat died of a heart attack just a few weeks after the indictment was announced. François Mitterrand was a sadder, wiser president in more than one respect.

Several other insider trading and local government budget skimming allegations involving the Socialists surfaced in the next few years, but the biggest corruption issue for Mitterrand and the Socialists in this period was political party and election finance.[27]

Why was this scandal so damaging, or thought to be so, for the Socialists? Almost all major democratic political systems—the American, German, Italian, and others—have had serious scandals involving money in politics over the past two decades of skyrocketing expenses, even in those European states where electoral campaign funding is in principle public. The problem was again that the Left, so long in opposition and so hopeful about its own goodness, had come to office assuming it would be different—better and cleaner—than the other side.

Electoral campaign costs had increased greatly in France as in other countries throughout the 1970s and 1980s, whereas the supply of free labor and enthusiastic propaganda in the form of party activists, upon which left-wing parties especially depended, was in decline. Television time is free and equally distributed among major parties at election time, but all other campaign expenses, especially opinion polling, increased at a rate the old fund-raising methods could never have handled.

In order to find a substitute for big-business contributions, which went to the Right, and significant labor union contributions, which were not available, the left-wing parties found a way to support themselves by commissions and side payments from largely dummy consulting firms set up at the local government level wherever a party was in power, with the ostensible purpose being urban design, architecture, provision of services, and so on. The French Communist party had long used such town hall consulting firm deals to finance itself, in addition to its other major sources of money, party members' dues, and "gold from Moscow." In the new PS created in 1971, Pierre Mauroy first set up these consulting firms in the Nord and Pas-de-Calais departments, where the SFIO had long been entrenched (he himself was longtime mayor of the Nord's capital city, Lille) and the terrain had long been bastions of the Socialists and later Communists. The consulting firms, or *bureaux d'études,* were soon made national in scope, with the most significant called "Urba." The 1982 Defferre law decentralizing French national state administration offered them another opportunity to hang a bid on. Public works investment was rising and the decentralization reform gave cities and towns new responsibility in urban development. The result, not surprisingly, was that decentralization, in addition to reforming the centralized Napoleonic state, created a new location for financial corruption. Kickbacks and sweetened contract bids increased enormously. "All political parties were involved in similar operations and, in the absence of public funding, considered them necessary, hence not immoral."[28] When police turned up cases of graft connected with party finance, the judiciary customarily did not follow up. So politicians became accustomed to an "immoral but necessary" system of party finance.

Campaign money was made into a reform issue by the Michel Rocard government (Mitterrand was still president, beginning his second term), which in March 1988 passed the first law to control it. The rather weak effect was not to break the old rules but to add some public financing to the previous system of occult financing. In 1991 a group of investigating magistrates suddenly began to dig into party finance corruption, somewhat on the model, at a much-reduced scale, of the Milan magistrates who broke the "Clean Hands" investigation in Italy, that brought down the entire old Christian Democratic political class. Police officials raided party headquarters and offices, finding evidence of fake billing for consultants' work in Marseilles, and, astonishingly, raw notes of meetings from the Socialist party internal committee that oversaw the whole network of semiconsulting and dummy consulting firms connected with

Socialist local governments. Ultimately the police officials involved calculated that a total of about 100 million francs per year ($17 million) was involved, about two-thirds of which went to the Socialist party.

The justice minister under Socialist prime minister Rocard, Pierre Arpaillange, thought the situation had become a red alert politically. He didn't want to have to order arrests of members of his own party. He suggested that immediate passage of an amnesty law was the way to avoid a wave of indictments of Urba officials and PS officeholders. In May 1991 President Mitterrand, who surely had been consulted all along, announced that French democracy needed a new campaign and party finance law, from the national to the local level.

The issue quickly became the question of an amnesty for previous wrongdoing. Prime Minister Rocard's first reaction (some said it was his Protestant upbringing!) was that the PS should collectively admit its guilt. Other leaders such as Pierre Mauroy and new party secretary Henri Emmanuelli, stressed how important an amnesty would be for the Socialists. Rocard finally acquiesced and when word leaked of the amnesty proposal, naturally the Socialists were condemned for whitewashing themselves. Mitterrand tried to interest the conservative parties, now in opposition, in a general amnesty. All of them, he knew, were involved in illegal financing. The amnesty idea was refined: included were the businesspeople who paid off and the Urba staff, who were not responsible for the system; excluded was anyone who got rich personally and also all parliamentarians. The law was adopted, by a narrow margin and with only Socialist votes (the others abstained to look half-white). All campaign finance infractions of the above kind committed before June 15, 1989 were amnestied.

The Socialists were nonetheless attacked for hypocrisy because the clause leaving deputies still vulnerable to prosecution meant that amnesty had been granted to other probably guilty actors outside parliament. Five magistrates from the High Court of Justice publicly denounced the amnesty of Christian Nucci himself, whose particular case they had been investigating.

The amnesty law did visceral damage to the Socialist party, which at the end of the day was said to have given amnesty to itself. This series of scandals convinced the French public that the Socialist party, contrary to its self-righteous self-image when it came to power in 1981, had become thoroughly corrupt. Exactly half of a 1995 list of 100 elected officials accused or indicted on corruption charges was made up of members of the Socialist party. As Saint Just said, "No one governs innocently."

Mitterrand's reaction was typical in two senses. In a January 24, 1992, discussion with a few television journalists came the realism and the Machiavellianism: "When one is very rich it is always a little bit suspect. Large fortunes are not made on the roads of virtue. But [people] should stop pointing the finger at the PS. It isn't guilty, it's the victim of a few low-life types. Urba is a clumsy business, but it is not dishonoring." This is both realism and self-indulgence. Nevertheless, only a year into Jacques Chirac's presidency a wave of similar corruption scandals implicated the conservatives—illegal party finance, fake jobs with state-owned companies to pay political appointees' salaries, cronyism, and misattribution of government resources, including choice rent-subsidized apartments. The conservative prime minister himself, Alain Juppé, actually had to vacate his own choice, rent-subsidized apartment. And Chirac's replacement as Paris mayor, Jean Tiberi, and Tiberi's wife, were also indicted in ongoing cases. The Socialist party seemed indeed guilty but not excessive in its misdeeds. By comparison, in Britain twelve ministers from John Major's government had to resign because of financial or sexual scandals, and in Tony Blair's second year no less than four ministers were forced likewise to resign in a short period of three months. And all this is not even to mention the various scandals of the Clinton administration.

The second issue, the amnesty, was another matter, and it seems to have been not a crime but a blunder. Mitterrand, the master politician, was remarkably pessimistic: "This business of the amnesty will cost us to a point which we don't yet imagine, I think. It will be worse than all the rest, than all our failures and all our errors. It will be the stigmata."[29] For once he overstated the downside of things. Because of the scandals that overtook the Chirac presidency in 1995-1997, Socialist disgrace faded as rapidly as the Socialist rose faded in 1982-1983.

Further Mitterrand scandals continued to surface, not unexpectedly, after his departure from office. Fourteen years in power allows a long accumulation of *affaires*, even had the Mitterrand presidency not been especially noted for them. To date, none of the new postpresidential accusations concerns Mitterrand himself in more than a peripheral way, though it would be naive to exclude the possibility of revelations yet to surface.

The most typically Mitterrandian of these postpresidential *affaires* concerns his former foreign minister, Roland Dumas, a close friend and associate for decades, and a well-known international lawyer whom Mitterrand, in 1993, had named to the lofty position of president of the Constitutional Council.

The episode began in January 1990. Thomson CSF, then a state-owned company, hoped to sell six warships, worth $2.7 billion, to the government of Taiwan. But the Edith Cresson Socialist government, in which Dumas continued his service as foreign minister, vetoed the sale because of concern that Beijing, more important to French interests, would be angered. Elf, the formerly state-owned oil giant, was asked to lobby on Thomson's behalf and it hired a certain Christine Deviers-Joncour to contact French government officials to permit the sale. The French government's veto was lifted in August 1991. Typically, no explanation was given for the change in position.

Ms. Deviers-Joncour, as Elf officials had known, was Roland Dumas's mistress. Dumas, however, insisted he had nothing to do with the government's reversal of course to permit the sale to Taiwan. He said that French agreement came from President Mitterrand and Prime Minister Cresson for essentially commercial reasons. Dumas claimed only later to have been made aware of a gigantic illegal $500 million commission paid to Elf by Thomson, approved by Mitterrand and the Ministry of Finance. Christine Deviers-Joncour received a separate commission, about $11 million, which Dumas also claimed not to know about, and which she said was perfectly legal remuneration of her work as a lobbyist.

Mme. Deviers-Joncour was arrested and spent months in prison under formal investigation for corruption. Her bitter 1998 book, titled *The Whore of the Republic,* claimed that despite their romantic affair she failed to get Dumas to change his mind on the ships for Taiwan.[30] Dumas was, up to even late 1999, fighting the allegation, but he has since resigned from his position as president of the constitutional council. He objected that political adversaries, by attacking him both directly and indirectly, as director of the Mitterrand Foundation, are trying to destroy Mitterrand's political legacy.

However plausible, Dumas could not provide convincing explanations for large cash deposits, hundreds of thousands of dollars, into his Paris Crédit Lyonnais bank account in the relevant period.[31] Dumas claimed these funds came from private sales of art objects with no paper trail, from old lawyer's fees not yet deposited, and other unusual but not illegal sources. In February 2000 Dumas's troubles worsened when prosecutors recommended that he should go to trial on the charges contained in a report submitted by the investigating magistrates Eva Joly and Laurence Vichnievsky. The specific charge was that he had personally benefited from the FF. 66 million of commissions paid to Christine Deviers-Joncour in the sale of French military ships to Taiwan. Deviers-Joncour then accused Dumas of being the ultimate beneficiary of a FF. 17 million apartment in central Paris that she purchased in June 1992 from funds drawn on a Swiss bank account fed by the Elf commissions. And this was only one part of other scandals involving Elf, which had lost FF. 20 billion overall in the last years of the Mitterrand presidency. Elf has come under scrutiny as one source of newly discovered French government and state enterprise illegal funding of Germany's Christian Democratic Union party during the Mitterrand-Kohl years. If proven, this

French funding of German electoral politics would give new meaning to the term European integration.[32]

Regarding charges of personal corruption made against Mitterrand himself, his worst accuser made allegations of four kinds:[33] That the president was complicit in the illegal party finance; that he tolerated, or was not vigilant enough about corrupt dealings by friends who used their relationship with him; that he defended the presumption of innocence beyond what was appropriate to the presidency; and that he was involved in certain questionable arrangements that set up Anne Pingeot, his longtime companion and mother of his daughter Mazarine, in a small real estate business in the town of Gordes in the Luberon, near Sarlat, and that Anne lived in Mitterrand's government-provided apartment on the Quai Branly. (See chapter 10.) Jean Montaldo also alleged that Mitterrand was paid relatively small sums in unjustified legal fees in the 1970s by Patrice Pelat through his Vibrachoc firm, and that this extra income was inherited by Gilbert Mitterrand when his father became president.

Mitterrand, responding to such accusations, said that he had "the standard of living [meaning the yearly income] of a high civil servant," that he "didn't own a single share of stock, and I would be incapable of the knowledge necessary to buy it." The public reading of his will didn't reveal any scandalous wealth, although it did indicate the extent to which he had lived over the years from his literary works in addition to his government salaries. This explained why he had published so many "unnecessary" books, and perhaps also explained his notoriety for letting others pick up his tabs. Mitterrand's worst or most characteristic abuse (along with certain of his ministers, Left or Right wing) was the occasional use of government resources for private benefit, often involving women. One such usage was to conduct side trips in the presidential airplane or questionable use of government houses and châteaux.

DEALING WITH TERRORISTS:
HYPOCRISY OR REFUSAL TO YIELD?

Foreigners tend to believe that French authorities, despite their vigorous denials, have repeatedly done deals with terrorists. Did François Mitterrand, against French declared policy, negotiate with terrorists? Unfortunately, there were occasions to be tested during his terms in office, and perhaps other French leaders did even if he did not. Let us not be concerned here with anyone but Mitterrand and Jacques Chirac, for a sharp and aggressive clash over the two leaders' responsibility for French dealings with terrorist cases became the bitterest moment in their presidential debate of April 1988.

Jacques Chirac, the cohabitation prime minister and then runoff candidate against Mitterrand, accused the president of irresponsibility for his part in having freed Jean-Marc Rouillan and Nathalie Ménigon, two founders of the Action directe group. They were freed during the Mitterrand-Mauroy government, whereupon they committed two brutal assassinations that violently shocked public opinion. The two dead were the immensely respected industrialist Georges Besse, head of Renault, and the high military-security official General René-Pierre Audran. Mitterrand objected that Rouillan, at the time of his pardon, had not yet committed murder. "It was only later that he became a terrorist assassin." Rouillan had also been freed under an amnesty voted by parliament, not a presidential pardon, for offenders with prison terms less than six months. For her part, Nathalie Ménigon was freed by a court, not by a political decision. "[These accusations are] unworthy of you!" Mitterrand told Chirac in the debate. "As for me, I've never freed terrorists."

The president then accused Chirac of having, during the latter's 1974-1976 conservative government under Giscard d'Estaing, freed a Japanese terrorist after a bombing at the Publicis Saint-Germain department store, of having let go Abou Daoud, a Palestinian terrorist implicated in the Achille Lauro hijacking, and, finally, during the ongoing cohabitation government, of having sent Wahid Gordji back to Iran "after having explained to me, in my office, that the proof against him was overwhelming and that his complicity was certain in the killings that bloodied Paris at the end of 1986." All this was, supposedly, linked with Chirac's attempt to solidify French ties to Arab governments.

Chirac replied first by remarking solemnly that he had never divulged any conversations that he had with a president. He then said quite unexpectedly, "Can you look me in the eye and tell me I told you that we had proof that Gordji was guilty, when I consistently told you that this case was a judge's responsibility and that I was unable to find out what was in the dossier and thus it wasn't possible to say if Gordji was guilty. And the judge in the end replied in the negative. . . . Can you really contest my version of these things in looking me in the eye?" Mitterrand did indeed reject Chirac's version, although the latter has maintained ever since that Mitterrand did not look at him in doing so, even if the viewing public could not have discerned this.

Chirac was absolutely correct to reproach Mitterrand for having violated the secrecy of official conversations between the two men. But on the substance of the matter, according to Jean Lacouture,

> Jacques Chirac knew the "Mitterrand dossier" in the matter of terrorism. He knew that in this domain the head of state had held firm above any suspicion, that more than anyone else he had refused to buckle, that the amnesty accorded

Rouillan et Ménigon concerned two people who had been arrested for carrying illegal weapons, for which they received limited prison time. To accuse the president, on this solemn occasion and with a huge election at issue, of being responsible for the subsequent assassination by these two of Georges Besse and General Audran was in fact an unworthy attack by the sitting prime minister.

Lacouture adds, "Regarding the substance of the Gordji case, Mitterrand was in the right against those who allowed this dangerous man to go back to his country." Whatever Mitterrand's mistake in revealing the conversation in his office with Chirac, wrote Edwy Plenel in *Le Monde*, "the facts plead in favor of Mitterrand."[34]

CONCLUSION: WHAT SORT OF MACHIAVELLIAN REPUBLICAN?

Representative democracy is a moral and democratic antidote to the amoral regime of a Machiavellian prince. But representative democracy is itself beset by internal contradictions, unresolvable choices of values.

A first contradiction is that democracy, in one sense, is intrinsically a permanent struggle by the people against their leaders. Public opinion must always check and balance even a democratically elected government. Second, fox and lion strategies are both necessary even for democratic leaders. Personally ambitious despite a democratic mind-set, leaders live an unavoidable contradiction inside their own minds.

"This reckless and mendacious man knew he would have to be held to account eventually." Is this yet another *Le Monde* or neo-gaullist or Communist comment on François Mitterrand? On his successor Jacques Chirac? It happens to be *The Economist* magazine, commenting at the end of 1998 on U.S. President Bill Clinton's hope to escape impeachment but vulnerability to criminal prosecution for perjury and obstruction of justice after he leaves office.[35]

That nearly all national leaders (many Americans would include even Ronald Reagan) might answer to some degree to such a description indicates strongly that François Mitterrand's "corruption" was no unique case but an example of a category, the Machiavellian republican leader. But in Mitterrand's specific case the alleged mountain of evidence against him was magnified by a further issue: the sensational revelations in 1994 about his Vichy past. (See chapter 11.) The issue from a disengaged point of view as observed from several years' distance is whether Mitterrand was more or less reckless and/or mendacious than other French or foreign leaders. My general answer is that he was not, and that this impression is increasingly clear as his presidency recedes into history. A study in comparative mendaciousness is out of the question at this moment!

Mitterrand played the role of both the lion and the fox, and his political intelligence was generally not at all inscrutable but close to basics, based on matter-of-fact calculations.[36] As he once put it to me, again in his friendly sarcastic tone, "The obvious is not condemned to fail just because it is obvious." Mitterrand, unlike most other French politicians, was not above the obvious. He knew that if the obvious were played with confidence, others, even French sophisticates, usually reacted in expected ways, enraged as they were at being had by basic good psychology. Much of Mitterrand's strategy and "Florentine" tactics were simply the realistic advice of the classic books of political power, obvious to anyone but overlooked by those searching for nonexistent, mysterious complexities of a leader they had decided was a sphinx. A few examples:

- Don't make a decision until you have to. Mitterrand's much-scrutinized "indecision" and "waiting game" tactics were essentially this simple well-known rule.
- Encourage adversaries and challengers to fight each other or to confound themselves looking for signals from you that don't exist, are misperceived or are camouflaged.
- Never overestimate your own control over circumstances, events, and other people, even when you seem to be in total control. The fact is that you are never, even as top leader, in total control. But others will assume you are, giving you yet another advantage.
- Remember that nothing in political life is ever permanently won or lost. This diffuses triumphalism in victory and despair in defeat, breeding a permanent moderation of reaction that, with distance and a sense for silence, raises your prestige as leader.
- It is better to proceed by addition than by subtraction. This is true generally, but intrinsically more applicable to democratic politics, which are electoral and coalitional.
- One must learn how to give time to time. This banal Spanish proverb counseling patience, and the need to extend patience with more patience, struck the imagination of French politicians and journalists, some admiring of Mitterrand's use of time (and disregard of the hour) and others resentful of the same.
- Situations and relationships must ripen to be harvested; thus avoid haste, play for the long run, let others agitate themselves, contradict, nullify, and destroy each other.

- Dominance or victory is attained by patience combined with decisiveness at the key moment. The versatile politician, the lion-fox, combines patience and the capacity to seize the day.

François Mitterrand had the classic gift of playing the political game on several boards at once, seeing the interconnections and holding in his mind a set of calculations revealed entirely to no one, not even closest political associates. The essential point is that behind the curtain of his facades and deceptions, Mitterrand was no Wizard of Oz attempting furiously to hide mere stage effects. And the mature Mitterrand, like de Gaulle, knew what he wanted in politics: not merely to win and to command (the Mitterrand of the Fourth Republic), but to have responsibility for the national interest, for the policy of the state. Each man showed the ability to reverse field, to play against type, for the national interest. De Gaulle became the master of decolonization, Mitterrand the modernizer of French socialism—both, it is true, in haste and obliged by circumstances. Each had hoped for something else, yet they adapted. Both were destabilized by events, de Gaulle by the events of May 1968, Mitterrand by the "end of Yalta" and German unification.

Altogether François Mitterrand was no sphinx, politically or personally. On the contrary, a certain hiding of intentions, some misleading by omission and commission, even at times deliberate deception of associates as well as adversaries, are routine aspects of even democratic leadership, necessary to the function and all the more so because others behave similarly. Mitterrand if anything was surprised that others, especially his own Socialists, found him so hard to read, but naturally he used this to his advantage.

The "mystery" appeared largely because he was so good at so many aspects of the profession that his dominance seemed artless. He was skilled especially at masking the weapons in his dominance of others (playing the waiting game, which could seem to be indecisiveness; letting impatient rivals exhaust each other, leaving only the last battle to fight). He did at times give way to violent argument and rebuke (e.g., with Michel Rocard and with certain journalists), but on the whole he did not appear as dominating and intimidating as actually was the case. The need to hide his skills was particularly necessary precisely because his superiorities were (unlike de Gaulle's) so conventional, because he was in many ways a very conventional politician, and because, except in Napoleonic portrait profile, he looked like one. Mitterrand was a representative man with typical skills honed to high force, whereas de Gaulle could call on his historical role as savior, his military sense of command, and his sheer overwhelming physical presence. Underlying everything else in Mitterrand's dominance was, by contrast, not mysterious magic but a banal psychological superiority—a talent for reading others, for playing to their needs, for giving them what they want but at the right time, for leadership in the sense of constructing networks and networking factions, his own capacity to learn, his determination, and an extraordinary power of will, which magnified the other talents beyond their normal reach.

Michel Rocard, the main leader of the so-called "second Left," was Mitterrand's main rival for party leadership over the years, especially at two points: when the Union of the Left strategy seemed bankrupt after the Communists sabotaged it between 1976 and 1980, and in 1987, before the president decided to run for reelection. Mitterrand's faction won out at Socialist party congresses, and Rocard, often more popular than Mitterrand in opinion polls and who was twice declared as a presidential candidate and then deferred to Mitterrand's own candidacy, ended up with a poisoned gift, the prime ministership, in 1988-91. Whether it was poisoned by the circumstances or whether Mitterrand poisoned it himself can be argued. The Rocard government was in any case a trial of "quiet hatred" between the two in which Rocard felt not only a lack of support from the president but politically misused and personally disdained.[37]

Mitterrand's behavior with Rocard was a classic example of Machiavelli's caution on using "cruelty" well or badly. There is little doubt that in dealing with Rocard Mitterrand behaved with a certain amount of cruelty. Some was explicable in Machiavellian terms as useful to dominating a rival through intimidation. But some of it was unnecessary, producing what Rocard called "execrable personal relations."[38] Mitterrand was much the stronger personality psychologically and even had to take care of Rocard in his personal quarters when the latter had a moment of collapse at the beginning of his first cabinet meeting. When Rocard in 1991 was trying to hang on as prime minister, Mitterrand experienced the former's "obsequiousness" and "outdated, ingratiating language" as "increasingly insuf-ferable."[39] Three years after Mitterrand's death, in November 1998, a still-bitter Rocard said in an interview that the former president "had not been an honest man." He "conducted his relations with others on the basis of ruse and violence. . . . Mitterrand named me [prime minister] in order that I fail. . . . [He told his advisors that] 'This way we'll dispose of the Rocard challenge . . .' referring to the fact that I was better than him in the opinion polls, which was perceived as a crime of lèse-majesté."[40] Rocard's attack on Mitterrand seemed a desire for revenge by a second leader who was constantly outdone by the top leader and who had been hurt psychologically as well as politically by this relationship. Mitterrand's cruelty with him stemmed in part from the great left-wing defeat in 1978, when Michel Rocard brashly reached for leadership by defining Mitterrand as "archaic."

As for the charge that François Mitterrand was "not honest" with associates and adversaries, the answer is, of course he wasn't, or at least in tactics, he knew how and when to be dishonest. Otherwise he could never have become Socialist party leader, kept the ambitious, ideological, and warring factions together, led the party to power and governed through all the crises of fourteen years. The Socialists, other politicians, and commentators in general disdained him for this but realists appreciated his skills at the same time. "One can't do politics with clean hands," Mitterrand would say. A French journalist agreed: "The eternal dialectic of the means and the end. In politics, one doesn't survive without some Machiavellianism, even cynicism. One is not elected president of the Republic by being a model of virtue and altruism."[41]

How much dishonesty is realistically compatible with democratic leadership? The question is complicated and there is no precise answer. It is hard to disagree entirely with Montaigne: "All this brings to my mind the ancient saying: That a man must do wrong in detail if he wishes to do right on the whole, and commit injustices in small matters if he hopes to deal out justice in great."[42] Republican government is different, but human beings, as James Madison wrote in *The Federalist Papers,* are still not angels, which is why government is necessary in the first place.

What then is the right question, as raised by the case of François Mitterrand?

The problem of corruption in contemporary democratic politics is not its presence or absence, but the degree and, above all, the kinds of corruption. An English commentator made a similar but more indulgent point: "The portrayal of Mitterrand as an adaptable, flexible leader should not be equated with his being an unprincipled charlatan. . . . His adaptability made it easier for Mitterrand to assume the consequences of policy reversals with some degree of conviction," as opposed to a Margaret Thatcher, whose credibility depended on being a "conviction politician."[43]

A different reproach was that Mitterrand never or too rarely admitted errors or apologized for his own mistakes and policy changes. In France more than in other countries, above all the United States, confession of error or regret tends to be not merely bad form, but it is interpreted as a sign of weakness and invites attack. Yet Mitterrand did acknowledge some important errors on the record. To go back to the Fourth Republic, his decision, as interior minister in the 1956 Guy Mollet government, to give over civil justice investigations and trials in Algeria to military courts, which resulted in death sentences and executions, haunted him forever he said.[44] He blamed his own economic policy inexperience and the "intoxication" of his 1981 victory for the costly mistakes of the Socialist experiment. He regretted not obliging the Socialist government into yet another electoral law change for the 1993 parliamentary elections, which allowed a devastating defeat for the Pierre Bérégovoy government and the Socialist party.[45] And in his *Memoir à Deux* conversations with Elie Wiesel, he acknowledged having "fallen short of his own expectations overall" for his presidency. But it is true that none of these was a formal apology given by the president in a public forum as a political act.

Mitterrand's adamant avoidance of formal regrets or apologies was, like de Gaulle's, a point of principle as well as a kind of armament that contributed to political durability. But this existential refusal, a husbanding of independence (not the same as arrogance) came at a price. Machiavellianism clashed with republicanism more in Mitterrand's *style* of leadership than in the substance. A certain candor of conscience is one aspect of democratic leadership in the open society. Mitterrand, while believing the common cause, gave priority to his own cause.

Constitutional democracy and institutional accountability of leaders is, like every political arrangement, beset by internal contradictions. Representative democracy has been and will be a permanent struggle, a "soft" war of the people against its leaders, and the reverse. There is no end, no perfect or permanent resolution.

The Machiavellian republican leader is, nevertheless, fundamentally more republican than Machiavellian. This is the saving grace. Often the republican leader is known by his acceptance of being out of power. "I believe that I hold the record for being in the opposition," Mitterrand regularly reminded his interviewers. "Twenty-three years straight. I was even called 'the loser.' . . . One might believe that politics is made up only of manipulation and of 'Machiavellianism,' that you have to be 'Florentine' in order to succeed. You know, I am quite familiar with the history of Florence and there were not only 'Florentines' in Florence."[46]

CHAPTER 9

THE EXISTENTIAL MITTERRAND

There is no force in the world, not philosophical, religious, state, or of money or capital in relation to which I am not completely free. And if I had one point of pride to show in my life, that would be it.

—François Mitterrand, 1993

De Gaulle existed. His acts created him.

—François Mitterrand, 1975

Tall cities, flat cities, lightning strikes where it will. I am relaxed among my contradictions. Beijing lies flat on a plain, like London or Marrakesh. I wouldn't want her any other way. In any city I feel myself emperor, or architect—which amounts to the same thing—I make judgments, I decide, I arbitrate, I convict, and in so doing am like my fellow citizens. Everyone turns his own taste into a general rule. But I temper this intolerance by a faithfulness in infidelity. I love the city where I am, if I love it. Once and for all.

—François Mitterrand, 1975

THE EXISTENTIAL MITTERRAND
WAS THE ESSENTIAL MITTERRAND

FRANÇOIS MITTERRAND WAS AN INTELLECTUAL if not a philosopher. By this I mean that he was an independent thinker who wanted—who craved—his own understanding of the world. He wanted to live and operate as a political man according to his own ideas. If not an original thinker neither was he a simple consumer of common sense or of rule books of maxims such as Thucydides, the Stoics, or Machiavelli. Nor can his career as leader of the Left be totally explained by picturing him as a blind avenger of a political grudge against de Gaulle and gaullism. Mitterrand's quality of mind cannot be denied even if he himself sometimes failed to live according to his ideas.

Here was a man, according to all who knew him, of deep curiosity about the world, someone who consciously wanted to experience everything he could. Mitterrand wanted to live by the idea that every instant is valuable, every experience is a chance for greater contact with the world. "Nothing is ever given to us," he once said. "A life is constructed at every moment. Effort is the law." Knowledge through the intellect is not enough. He comprehended more deeply whatever he had seen, questioned, touched. In his life he indeed experienced "far more of the world than most."

It may sound overblown to speak of such qualities in a political leader. But even the French biographies, despite all their criticisms, make similar points. "The strength of his personality," says the veteran French commentator Alain Duhamel, "his capacity to charm, the richness of his culture, his physical courage, his intellectual audacity, his exceptional stubbornness, make up an uncommon being even among his colleagues."[1] For a man with Duhamel's stake in the world of Paris criticism, this catalog of François Mitterrand's better sides shows intellectual courage. It would sound naive (or American) without the level-headed author's credentials as a skeptic. Franz-Olivier Giesbert, for three decades a top journalist and editor of *Le Figaro,* author of three books about Mitterrand, and himself of Franco-American origins, portrays a Mitterrand as the essence of France: "alternately or at the same time a pétainist and a résistant, a socialist and a liberal, a Catholic and a secular, a centralizer and a provincial, authoritarian and tolerant, François Mitterrand was an embodiment of the complexities of France."[2] Mitterrand, for Giesbert, was an exploit in himself.

But Mitterrand was more than an assorted collection of various pieces of "Frenchness," let alone a *summum* of stereotypes of the French with no character of his own. He was anything but a caricature, although he was so easy to caricaturize.

Like many people in public life he had a philosophical bent but little time. The career he chose, as opposed to other lives that might have been, meant two things. His worldview coalesced progressively over a lifetime and remained eclectic rather than finished. Second, he took the practitioner's inevitable intellectual shortcuts, picking up his philosophy piecemeal. However, his two unfinished historical projects and his polemical but substantial *Coup d 'état permanent* showed he had both the talent and the taste for serious history or constitutional law writing.

Mitterrand's political and moral ideas are to be found scattered in his various writings, interviews, and speeches. He was not well organized for research, and his writings often took a diary form, a paragraph or page set down late at night. He criticized himself for "scribbling ideas or impressions on little bits of paper" that he had difficulty sorting out or finding when he needed them.

Many of his political and moral ideas were mainstays of leaders the world over—the Realists and the Stoics or derivative writers appear often in his books. Most of his other sources were French. Among these were familiar major figures such as his initial intellectual passion, Pascal, and then Stendhal, Chateaubriand, and Lamartine. Others were lesser French authors, such as the provincialist Jules Renard and above all the family friend François Mauriac. The latter's books were full of small wisdom about human nature, how to live, and how to be nonconformist, but in a seductive rather than an offensive way, thus to be admired rather than resented. From traces in his own books, it is evident that Mitterrand read only modestly in foreign literature and then only in French translation.

What he took from his sources was usually a thought he agreed with and might have written himself out of his own experience. His "philosophy" was not very original, and, as said, was an eclectic accumulation rather than a system of thought. What *was* original in Mitterrand, however, was his own life, a work of art he created and lived as intensely as possible. Because it is the nature of daily personal relations, of life in common as it is, this meant imposing his own will on circumstances if not always on others. But of course for Mitterrand the political man and the social man it clearly meant imposing his will, his "agency," on the will of others.

How can we understand this compelling combination of freedom and imposition of one's will on others? Was Mitterrand just another power-hungry politician, just another alpha male lining up the ducks in his social world? Many people thought so of him, but not those closest to him. The people who knew him best were attracted to him, not subjected by him. And this was not simple seductiveness or charm. The attraction arose because they believed that however much he imposed on others, François Mitterrand was living an arduous, thought-through, fascinating life whose example might enrich their own lives if they could learn the secret of his own willpower and determination. Ironically, the key to Mitterrand's makeup was not some great mystery impossible to find. The secret was there all the time, in full view like Edgar Allan Poe's purloined letter, so obvious that it remained unnoticed.

◆   ◆   ◆

Getting behind caricatures and stereotypes to recognize a person's complexity is one thing. It is another to make a set of observations into a full concept, to take François Mitterrand seriously as a thinker, as someone who thought genuinely about the problems of existence and freedom. Although so many observers saw in him only a typical Machiavellian, Mitterrand was far from an ordinary politician, even a highly skilled ordinary one. Putting together writings, my own contacts with him, and the evidence provided by others, an "existential" Mitterrand emerges. The existential Mitterrand was the genuine Mitterrand.

◆   ◆   ◆

Mitterrand's intellectual and moral life, that of lapsed Catholic, Machiavellian and republican politician, and an ambiguous socialist, was, and had to be, because of its self-contradictions, a conscious refusal of all "systems" of thought. The life of absolute faith, of whatever kind, interested him intellectually and emotionally; but his own was agnostic and eclectic. He died not having resolved the puzzles of life, never having recovered his childhood faith nor finding any other certainty than the existentialist conclusion that life must create is own justifications. His own intellectual and moral values were therefore by nature against all absolutisms except the existentialist categorical imperative that each person has the moral responsibility to make one's own meanings in a universe with no transcendent meaning.

Faced with the fact of unresolvable contradictions at the personal level, Mitterrand's response was that "one had to live one's own contradictions" rather than to make a leap of faith to some global but unjustifiable intellectual or moral system. Thus his "socialism," for example, was not a trick. It was a partial and relative commitment, as it had to be. With relation to the church he became what Georges Duhamel called a "Christian agnostic." Mitterrand said that an agnostic was "not he who doesn't believe, but he who doesn't know if he believes." Of himself he added, "I don't see an antimony between faith in God and faith in man. . . . I'm thus closer to a spiritualist idea rather than a materialist one."[3] Or as he put it another time, "As a child I was a believer. Now truthfully I don't know. Let's say that given the lack of an explanation of the world my tendency is deist. I don't agree with those for whom everything is mere chance and necessity."[4] Deist, agnostic: sometimes the one and sometimes the other; better, both at the same time; best is to recognize that this particular distinction was not essential.

◆   ◆   ◆

Mitterrand, this chapter shows, had thoughtful, developed ideas of the human situation, of social relations and the nature of power in society and of course his abiding concern for his own autonomy in life. This passion for safeguarding his autonomy, the *libre arbiter,* was larger than his political life, it encompassed his political life. And it didn't require a total rejection of the rules of the French social and political game: There was so much to enjoy in the traditional French games, from power to oysters to mistresses and the three combined! Existential thoughts didn't prevent Sartre or Camus or de Beauvoir from libidinous lives. Why should Mitterrand have been any more pious?

The sources of Mitterrand's highly conscious and conceptualized passion for autonomy as a person and politician are in his character and personal development.

When did François Mitterrand quit living the truths of home—Catholic and "right-wing" if one wishes? He certainly began to have a larger view of the world in his Paris student days in the late 1930s. But World War II magnified his alienation from his *bien-pensant* family background and threw him into a world he could not have dreamed of.

Mitterrand was deeply marked by his firsthand experience of the concentration camps and death camps at the end of the war. Perhaps he did not, as later was said, accept that they were a unique evil in the history of mankind. Nevertheless the camps and the mass death of the war led Mitterrand to existentialist conclusions: God does not exist, at least in the Catholic sense; the world, existence, is thus "absurd," without any meaning external to itself, without meaning beyond that human beings themselves give to it.

After this point, finding a basis for a moral life is a new kind of problem for man, "the animal capable of conceiving problems," as the French thinker Raymond Aron defined us. It is not, faced with absurdity, necessary to deny the existence of God; it is enough to become agnostic.

To present François Mitterrand as an existentialist does not, given what was just said above, mean that suddenly a strict global explanation is being introduced where I have been arguing all along that the man's political, intellectual, and moral conceptions were a complex and somewhat incoherent set of ideas. Existentialist thinking itself is not a single coherent idea. Mitterrand, moreover, never claimed to be an existentialist, or even acknowledged particular existentialist influences. But if the evidence from his writings and interviews presented in this chapter is persuasive, it will be clear that an existentialist characterization fits him rather well.

MITTERRAND'S CONCEPTION OF THE SOCIAL CONTRACT

Mitterrand's formative milieu and its political culture, then his captivity as a German prisoner of war, gave him an immovable conception of society as necessarily a hierarchy: natural, unchangeable, and, unlike philosophies that luckily didn't have to account for Nazism and Stalinism, is composed of the stronger and the weaker. While at Vichy he published a revealing article that the then twenty-three-year-old author had first drafted en route by military train into Germany and imprisonment in 1940. It appeared in a revised form in the Pétainist, anti-Semitic journal *France, Revue de L'État Nouveau* (December 1942), the magazine started by Gabriel Jeantet, Mitterrand's main contact in Marshal Pétain's personal staff.[5] That there was a first draft version in 1940, which was revised in 1942 and then republished in 1977 in a collection of Mitterrand's articles, *Politique I,* tells us that Mitterrand thought this piece of permanent interest in his own development and that the pétainism of *France, Revue de L'État Nouveau,* did not mean that he felt every essay in it was a permanent stain on the author. In this article Mitterrand expresses a deep pessimism regarding the capacity of most people for freedom, and whether society can be based on equality and democracy.

"Pilgrimmage to Thuringia"—Thuringia was the prisoners' destination in Germany—is a diary-reverie, which would become a typical style for him. With remarkably little sense of self-pity the essay describes the men piling around and onto each other, human beings quickly learning, in a situation of no government among themselves, the rules of lack of space, food, water, and toilet facilities. These were the rules of an abbreviated social contract where comfort and existence itself were suddenly at the mercy of an enemy. "I was really astonished," wrote the young Sergeant Mitterrand

> at the ease with which men accustom themselves to the life of a herd of sheep. And these were the same men who, nourished by ideas of liberty and progress, had vaunted so much and so proudly their nature as individuals. . . . Like peasants . . . who surround their courtyard with high hedges the better to affirm their independence, they had lived in obscure territories, which they imagined bathed in light and bordered with walls, which they called their rights. They had self-esteem and thought well of themselves in advance. . . . I had expected revolt, or at the least some stupefaction. But I observed yet one more time that the play rarely touches its actors, that people are much like straw when faced with unhappiness or happiness; the greatest happiness gives a man migraine and the greatest unhappiness gets to him only through the small things that are lacking in a meal, or bread which gets stale. And thus each one—having given up without apparent despair his privileges of another century, having in an instant accepted to become successors of the suffering crowds, the wandering crowds—obeyed the ancient unavoidable lot of the masses pushed by obscure forces, immediately familiar with their fate. They began by cutting thin slices of break and they shared out somberly the can of paté for six people with that somewhat solemn attitude of the age-old French (*des gens de chez nous*).

In this passage, whose precision of language, concept, and insight into the French political culture reminds one of Tocqueville's *Old Regime,* the young Mitterrand seems to be observing a people, his own, not really suited to liberty under pressure. The French as a whole, on the model of the French peasant, tended to confuse liberty with independence: Mitterrand, like Tocqueville, Balzac, and so many others, emphasizes how the peasant surrounded his land with a high hedge in order to be "free."

His own difference, his activist, voluntarist drive, the "revolt" of a man attached to freedom, was demonstrated in Mitterrand's escape attempts. In his well-known book *Just and Unjust Wars,* political theorist Michael Walzer notes that according to the accepted rules of war, "Prisoners of war have a right to try to escape—they cannot be punished for the attempt—but if they kill a guard in order to escape, the killing is not an act of war; it is murder. For they committed themselves to stop fighting, gave up their right to kill, when they surrendered."[6] Most prisoners may dream about escape, but few actually try it. Escape attempts are efforts full of danger and discomfort compared with the quiet life of survival as a well-behaved prisoner.

Perhaps without realizing it, Mitterrand, in his negative assessment of his comrades and his implicitly positive assessment of his own unexplainable urge to freedom verified soon in his actions, was developing an existentialist consciousness. What you do is who you are. Life is a mysterious, absurd gift to each person, with no meaning beyond those created through one's own choices. Choice, it goes without saying, is far different from impulse. To act on impulse is not to be free; it is anarchy at the personal level. Only conscious, rational choices are authentic acts of freedom. Thus most people are not free because they do not choose to be. They are, or become indifferent to the possibility of their own freedom. Thoughtless obedience to the law and common sense values can be disguises for "inauthenticity," which is the refusal to take responsibility for the individual's capacity to live by free choice. Mitterrand's brother-in-law Roger Gouze, Danielle's sister's husband, confirmed that "The Second World War distanced him from the [Mitterrand] family's Catholicism and led him toward agnosticism," adding that meeting Danielle's anti-clerical, freemason, and socialist family in 1943-44 worked strongly in the same direction.[7]

Is there not enough evidence of Mitterrand's existentialist turn, an unplanned, eclectic change that came upon the captive soldier, so recently a deeply religious student in Angoulême and at the "104" in Paris? It seems highly likely. The loss of Catholic faith, a new absurdist conception of the "meaninglessness" of existence (existence, Jean-Paul Sartre wrote, is not the work of some "necessary causal being. . . . But no necessary being can explain existence . . . it is absolute and consequently perfect gratuitousness"[8]), the conclusion that human choice alone creates meaning—these ideas were in the air and many intellectually curious young French people found them congenial, even unavoidable. Sartre's *Nausea* was published in 1938, *Being and Nothingness* in 1943, *No Exit* in 1944. *Les Temps Modernes,* the famous journal whose editorial committee was a kind of Who's Who of existentialist thinking, had been launched. At the war's end Mitterrand in 1945-1946 wrote his editorials for the POW journal *Libres* "in a sad office in the rue du Croissant [the street where Socialist leader Jean Jaurès was assassinated in August 1914]. But he was intelligent enough to envy the articles, on similar themes and also often in substance, but so much more sober and accomplished, being written for the newspaper *Combat* a few steps away by Albert Camus."[9] It would be surprising if Mitterrand had not been, like most of his political generation at the time, a regular reader of *Combat,* the Resistance newspaper par excellence. If all this is not definitive proof of an existentialist "conversion" in Mitterrand's thinking, it is strongly suggestive of a large influence in his outlook.

In a 1969 book, *Ma Part de Vérité,* Mitterrand gave another, rather different account of his wartime discovery of the social contract:

> On a hillside in Hesse, with thirty thousand [captured prisoners] thrown together in disorder, everything recommenced at zero. At noon the Germans had us brought basins of rutabaga soup and hunks of bread, as if to say you guys figure it out for the day. At first there was the reign of the strongest, a government by knife. Those who snapped up the basins served themselves first and it was a good idea to await their extreme goodness for a bit of dirty water in order to survive. From the effect of what moment of consciousness did the mass overthrow this absolute power? After all, the knife is the knife, a simple principle to maintain an established order. But that didn't last three months. You had to have seen the new delegates, designated one didn't know how, cut the black bread in six slices to near-perfect equality, under the wide-open control of universal suffrage. A rare and instructive spectacle. *I was present at the birth of the social contract.*[10] [Emphasis in original.]

This optimistic text of 1969 must be read in one sense as proof of Mitterrand's leftward movement toward the Socialist party, burnishing his credentials for leadership of the PS. However there is a declarative directness and simplicity here which must impress any reader. The state of nature "didn't last three months"—but what were those two-plus months like to live? And then came the designation of new delegates, "one didn't know how," leading to a regime of law and equal rights born of a social contract. Two points seem important. Here is justification for Mitterrand's conviction that institutions are the basis of civilized society, a theme of chapter seven above. Second is justification of the special role of the "delegate," someone like himself. This leader arises or is chosen "one didn't know how." This is simultaneously a sense of responsibility for the group and a justification for bending the rules for oneself. In sum this is Mitterrand exactly, caught out in his own words.

A 1972 interview again spoke of the importance of his prisoner of war days in the development of his ideas of human nature and the social contract:

> My great awakening was captivity. I had been promoted to junior officer. A lieutenant and myself found ourselves the only officers in a work unit (*kommando*). It was a very, very hard work unit. I fortunately found in it a lot of friendship. I became acquainted with having nothing, I came to know solidarity. I also discovered, by the way, that . . . I possessed a very good capacity to survive.

The danger in this experience is the [illusion of a] classless society. We were all in uniform, all bent to the same work and the same German discipline. Thus we could imagine utopia. Why is it that things couldn't be like that in regular life? Certain comrades fell into this skewed idea. That communitarian life marked me deeply. I, by nature so profoundly individualist, I took pleasure in it.

But the main shock was that I suddenly became conscious that the natural hierarchy, meaning moral and physical, of the society in which I found myself, that of the prison camps, had nothing at all to do with the hierarchy I had known during my whole youth. The *notaire* and the professor threw themselves on their stomachs to grab up cigarette butts which the Germans laughingly threw them. I saw junior officers do the same. There was born in me the doubt, which has only intensified, about the value of a society which is not tested from time to time. The hierarchy of medals, of diplomas, of money, is worth nothing. The scale of true values is to be found elsewhere.[11]

Mitterrand's anti-bourgeois attitudes, his disdain for those who want comfort above all, seems to have had a right-wing as well as a left-wing origin: The idea that a society should be "tested from time to time" will sound manly to some, worrisome to others. And the idea that in "the natural hierarchy" solidarity is one of the "true values" can also seem right-wing or left-wing. All together, the proper conclusion is that Mitterrand's rejection of bourgeois society had roots in both sides of his political experience, the right-wing youth and the left-wing socialist.

ORIGINS OF POLITICS, FREEDOM, AND AUTHENTICITY

Proust's famous questionnaire has amused the literati for a century. François Mitterrand at eighteen years old, thanks to a vacation girlfriend, left posterity his own responses, which she held as a keepsake for sixty years. It was August 1935. He and his brother Robert were teased into playing the game by a seventeen-year-old girl who was on holiday in the same neighborhood at the seaside property of her grandparents at La Panne, Belgium. The Mitterrand brothers were staying at a neighbors' place. Young François's answers were sometimes revealing:

1. Motto: "Nothing will surprise me" ("ne s'etonner de rien")
2. Most marked characteristic: "Frankness"
3. Trait most deplored in others: "Obsequiousness"

4. Most admired person: [General] "Lyautey"
5. Favorite poet: "Baudelaire"
6. Favorite writer: "Pascal"
7. Favorite musician: "J. S. Bach"
8. Favorite flower: "Any one . . . but not in a vase. . . ."
9. Favorite color: "Gray"
10. Favorite pleasure: "The theater"
11. Greatest dislike: "Stupid people and bad taste"
12. What I want to become: "Everything or nothing"[12]

The vainglorious ambition and conformist cultural tastes of the young François could easily be mocked. His "hero"—Lyautey, a general—and his poet, writer, and musician are entirely conventional. De Gaulle once said "Eisenhower was the equivalent of our Lyautey."[13]

The future Mitterrand, however, is clearly visible in the motto he assigns himself: *ne s'etonner de rien,* meaning to be completely worldly and urbane, knowledgeable, and thus implicitly tolerant or at least understanding of human nature's infinite possibilities, not only of good but of evil and amoralism. It is Rabelais's *Nilum humanum*: "Nothing human is alien to me." The sentiment also prefigures an existential, free-thinker's life, one influenced later by Freemason thinking. Several of Mitterrand's close associates over the years were Masons, for example Charles Hernu and Robert Badinter. He never joined himself, perhaps because Masonry was politically controversial, perhaps because after his fervent Catholic background he refused any system of values.

POLITICS AS A PROFESSION
AND THE CONQUERING OF TIMIDITY

His public image of a poised, serene, often arrogant French president notwithstanding, François Mitterrand was haunted all his life by an underlying timidity. Far from being incidental or a bit of folklore in his biography, this characteristic timidity is a key to understanding his political style and his social personality.

The attraction to power and to office cannot be taken as a given; it needs to be explained. Everyone wants power, it is commonly said. But in fact many people do not want power and office; others find they are too diffident to try. And even were it so, the important questions would be what kind of power, in what ways, and for what ends.

By the end of his adolescence and going up to Paris, the young Mitterrand already had ambitions and wanted to be a leader. For a young Frenchman of his time and his culture, even for a provincial as opposed to a Parisian, this was common. His home town of Jarnac and the surrounding Charente produced more than their share of public figures. A law education or a political career were common roads to consider, although Mitterrand we saw earlier also had literary tastes and ambitions. In the France of his time politicians still were often literary men as well (Georges Clemenceau, Léon Blum), and literary men often were politically *engagé* (Emile Zola, François Mauriac).

What was the attraction for François Mitterrand to political power and public office? Why make a political life?

The answer is obviously plural. Power is one thing. Someone who doesn't seek to exercise power, influence, and authority is not, strictly speaking, a political person. But power is not all that a politician seeks in a career. For Mitterrand the political profession was also a solution to a serious problem in his personal development. It was a way to deal with a timidity so severe that it was a social handicap. To gain power, to become master in his relationships was one way of dealing with this timidity.

Anecdotes recalled by friends and family portray a boy who wanted to become "either pope or emperor," but Mitterrand's grasp for authority over others, for the superior position, arose in the first place as a conquest of his timidity, as a personal struggle for self-confidence. Mitterrand was, in the French phrase, *un grand timide*. He often told the story of failing the oral part of his first *baccalaureat* exam at Poitiers because he was so intimidated by the circumstances that he could hardly speak. Mitterrand's brothers and sisters remembered a summer vacation at the seaside in Normandy during which the young François spent afternoons hiding behind a sand dune, trying to work up courage to sell hello to an American girl there with her family. "It took me a long time to dominate" this timidity, he said. "I trained myself by an act of will to overcome a timidity that was almost morbid."[14] A letter of July 22, 1942, presumably written from Vichy, shows a continuing battle with a diffidence that made human contact, not to say intimacy, a heavy burden for him. The twenty-five-year-old Mitterrand worried about his "lack of life, [his] lack of the quality of sympathy [with others]." Thus he "speaks more easily of things than of people," adding:

> I have a great strength of indifference, which becomes a weakness, misery, when love comes over me. It is banal to notice, but many people can't get through to me. But this matters little. How can I deal with this timidity, this standing back, which is like a hidden secret distancing me from those who reach me?[15]

If Mitterrand himself did not admit so readily to this characteristic timidity and diffidence as a young person, its genuineness might need more substantiation. The real question is how did he deal with it? How, and why, did the timid interior Mitterrand become the man who would be king?

"My interior strength and tranquillity," Mitterrand said, "have not wavered, because nothing that is deep in me has ever changed."[16] I believe his diffidence, his timidity, is to be included here. That is, Mitterrand the Machiavellian, the elected monarch, conquered his diffidence anew every day. Mitterrand told another interviewer, "I live inside myself. Nothing basic in me has ever changed." The next question came quickly: "Are you haughty or timid?" Mitterrand replied equally rapid fire: "Both! As Jules Renard said, 'Be modest. It's the type of haughtiness that displeases the least.'"[17] Clearly, Mitterrand had thought over the subjects of haughtiness and timidity before.

Mitterrand's psychological insight was to understand the nature of his timidity early on. His strength was to devise ways to keep it from dominating his life, not to say his future. But even as president, the underlying diffidence remained, especially in certain personal relations. Listen to one of his last Élysée palace assistants: "[Mitterrand] always had trouble establishing contact with someone. When you talked to him, it took several minutes for him to begin to 'unfreeze.' For a long time I understood as distance what was in fact only timidity."[18] Such confirming evidence about so surprising a character trait over a lifetime is difficult to deny.

But different responses to timidity are possible. Some individuals may live inwardly, isolated from others because that is the situation, even if unsatisfactory, that causes the least pain. Others, to the contrary, engage their timidity, emerging armored and disguised. In this case there are usually two kinds of disguise. The first is arrogance or bully-behavior. The second is to create a facade of authority and imperiousness that, by winning respect or fear, reverses the outward situation while never quite eliminating the internal timidity of which it is the symptom and the coping strategy. Each response is an artifice creating personalities, masking basic character. Both have the minimal purpose of diluting timidity, squelching its tides, enabling social life by minimizing the pain of encounter. And since politics requires a certain combativity, it is a particularly favorable social field for diffident natures to create personality, to invent themselves, by creating a role they "play" like an actor.

This personality or role is, as I said, artificial compared to the genuineness and spontaneity of love or hate. Arrogance or authority is an emotional artifice, but responsibility in politics or professional life, at least for the diffident, requires just such a useful facade, suppressing distressing anxiety in the service of some other value—success, power, justice, helpfulness. In this sense political leaders tend to be "false." They create a comfortable persona and an artificial distance that is part of their effect on others, of their prestige. This prestige serves as self-protection, to protect the persona that is the tool of their trade. Machiavelli's *Prince* is the classic description of the whole artifice of autocratic leadership, and de Gaulle in his time as a war college professor analyzed various characteristics of military leadership such as "the prestige of silence" and the need for "distance" to reinforce authority.[19] The Shakespeare biographer A. L. Rowse, drawing from the Bard's immense insight into the political, described "those people who do not give themselves away, who do not bare their hearts, but are cold and unmoved and leave it to others to do so, they are the types who remain in control of themselves and of others: they inherit the earth. This is, in fact, the governing, political type; poets do not belong to it."[20] In François Mitterrand's case his enduring diffidence tempered the remarkable leadership persona he developed, because his internal fragility was so well protected by external imperiousness—impassiveness, magisterial authority, sudden audacity, regular disdain, and even occasional cruelty in human relations that is natural to the Shakespearean "governing, political type." Mitterrand's desire to dominate others, to control relationships, to impose his will on others, to operate by reciprocity rather than spontaneity even in friendship, derived thus not from an innate self-confidence but from a great innate diffidence that had to be conquered.

When one begins with this understanding of Mitterrand, other well-known and often-described psychological traits, some quite contradictory, become less puzzling.

Given the great game of the sexes that Mitterrand found so irresistible, women not surprisingly often perceived Mitterrand's real character more readily than men. The following extraordinary account of him is by Cristina Forsne, who was a mistress and then regular companion of the aging Mitterrand for the last fifteen years of his life (more of this "third woman" in the next chapter):

> He was not a skittish man, but on the contrary very curious about those around him and most of the time in good humor. But François Mitterrand was timid. Timid, stubborn and ambitious. Like so many timid people, he had learned to hide it by imposing a sort of set of rules on other people. As long as one respected it, he successfully hid his timidity. Otherwise, he seemed lost, like a little boy. . . . A sudden candor in his eyes, and a desire to rapidly camouflage what had been a moment uncovered. But thanks to his tenacious willpower, those around him rarely breached his defenses. On the contrary, everyone took on the role which had been assigned. This was as true for his family as for his "longtime

friends," as journalists called them. The result, for him, was a great solitariness.
. . . He was described as a cynic, an intriguer, a man of the darkness, a diabolical
person, a Florentine. For him, all that was absurd. As he spoke to me of his view
of the world, things were clear, coherent and if the different facets [of his
personality] had been better perceived, anyone would have seen the uncomplicated man he was. What seemed contradictory on the surface was really a thirst
for life and an insatiable curiosity for the ways people behaved. François
Mitterrand considered humanity like a puppet theater. He didn't pull the strings,
but didn't intervene either to correct false steps. He let people struggle, rivalries
be pursued, won or lost. . . . He learned from, made use himself of what happened
to others. And what others considered as his favoritism [of some particular
people] . . . in fact enriched his comprehension of humanity.[21]

All of this is an explanation, for example, of why the 1981 presidential
campaign slogan—Mitterrand as *la force tranquille,* the man of "quiet strength"—
was so successful. At the time many commentators mocked the slogan, which had
been invented by the advertising man Jacques Séguéla (Mitterrand was using a
professional public relations advisor for the first time in an election campaign), even
though public opinion clearly found it attractive. Mitterrand, the slogan intimated,
had matured, he was strong and ready, above all he had mastered himself (i.e., the
old worries about him could be put to rest) and he could be trusted to govern the
country, to deal with the Communists, to combine some new Socialist ideas with
traditional French values. The montage over the campaign slogan showed Mitterrand's calm, determined face against—what diabolical Machiavellianism for the
leader of the Left!—a backdrop of a church and a rural village.

The artfulness of Mitterrand's political personality can be shown in
another way. According to the stereotype of him as the formal, solemn, typical
French president, François Mitterrand was a man of state—humorless, even
incapable of laughter. Americans, for example, often perceived him this way, as
a sort of half-pint de Gaulle or second-rate Bonaparte.

The reality was that the solemn facade was a permanent effort for a
man interested in everything, very much in need of distraction, and with a
susceptibility to laughter he had to fight, as we'll see below. Mitterrand's own
sense of humor was clever rather than gross—mordant, satirical, sarcastic, a
sardonic hammer at times that had been fashioned to intimidate and put people
in their place. To endure the intimidating wit of *le president* was a familiar
aspect of dealing with him, whether his own associates, the political
professionals, journalists who were constantly rebuked for "not doing their
homework," and family, not least of all Danielle Mitterrand and their sons
Jean-Christophe and Gilbert.

Hardly known at all, on the other hand, was Mitterrand's susceptibility to the *fou rire,* the uncontrollable belly laugh. He carefully avoided this in public for obviously the president had to keep his dignity. But there was also a particular aesthetic embarrassment attached to it, another expression of diffidence. Mitterrand unfortunately had a very bad dentition—flawed, badly spaced, discolored front teeth plus vampirish incisors. Because his canine teeth were unusually large and long, a simple smile on his part could have a threatening look to it. Aged sixty-four and already a three-time presidential candidate, Mitterrand had his vampirish incisors filed down in 1980 at Jacques Séguéla's insistence, creating a softened image. The "man of quiet strength" couldn't look wolfish! Before that Mitterrand rarely smiled in public.[22] Mitterrand began as well to follow Séguéla's advice on how to dress to maximum effect in the campaign. It was a royal change to tailored suits, somewhat like Louis XIV deciding to dress up in order to dazzle the court.

But in family gatherings he could let down this particular mask. Roger Hanin, the French actor and presidential brother-in-law, who was married to Danielle Mitterrand's sister Christine Gouze-Rénal, had responsibility for telling amusing stories at the dinner table. Repeated over and over again, these jokes and family lore always broke Mitterrand up into uncontrollable laughter complete with tears. To hide the unattractiveness of his dentition and the horsy look it gave his face, Mitterrand had acquired the habit of hiding behind his napkin, held fast up to his face while he laughed helplessly. (See photo section.) I witnessed this extraordinary departure from character as a guest at Latche, and another account is in Georges-Marc Benamou's 1996 memoir: "It was the moment for funny stories, those you tell in family reunions . . . the stories which come at the end of the meal, those five or six stories which the president was known to like, which he always asked for and knew by heart, which he accompanied silently himself and which provoked uncontrolled outbreaks of silent laughing which he did hidden behind his napkin. [Roger] Hanin thus got up to respond to a pretended 'general request.'"[23]

Hubert Védrine adds an even more unsuspected version of presidents dropping the mask when he tells of Egyptian leader Hosni Mubarak's private visits to Paris (just as Mitterrand vacationed on the Upper Nile, with Mubarak's hospitality, every New Year's week). Mubarak would talk informally of Egypt and the Middle East situation, always including a story about Muammar Gadhafi in which the revolutionary Libyan leader was outmaneuvered or shown up as a peasant. Mitterrand "would laugh until tears came to his eyes, putting his napkin in front of his mouth. Never before," concludes Védrine, "had one seen such a relationship between French and Egyptian leaders."[24] And the French people rarely saw their president in any other role than that of the solemn public man.

The exceptions—the annual hike up Solutré mountain or Mitterrand dressed shockingly in peasant clothes for interviews with Giesbert for *Le Figaro* as death came close—were staged with his full knowledge that a camera would be playing its own part in the comedy. Mitterrand had once said to me in this regard, "I never fabricate my image." Naturally this false claim, this *peché mignon*, was itself part of the image.

THE SECRET OF
THE SPHINX: THE WILL TO DARE

Even as an opposition leader before he became president, François Mitterrand never wore a watch and rarely carried a wallet, unusual behavior for a democratic politician whose desire is to please. It was as if to say to all the others, "those who deal with me, *they* will have to think of time and money." Mitterrand was famous for his tardiness, but this was separately planned, another part of his artifice, not a matter of carrying a watch since anyone could have told him the time.

Mitterrand, with his tardiness, his attitude about paying his own way, and other such tricks put burdens on others that he himself wouldn't have accepted from someone else. But others did not have to accept Mitterrand's imperious habits, his sense of time and his tabs. Why was Mitterrand allowed to behave in this way? First because he dared do it, and second because to be associated with him offered compensations sufficient for others to accept the role he designed for them. In exchange, people could be associated with his prestige and possibly gain his favors.

But why did they conform, why did they allow him to create his particular "system of power," as he had called de Gaulle's behavior with others? Because they chose to, in order to be of the Mitterrand clan or to get ahead. But the fact is that no other French Left leader could succeed at the sort of game that Mitterrand played, at having it both ways: to be leader while also a nonconformist. The Socialists resented and criticized, when they finally dared to at the end of his term, Mitterrand's unconventional habits and past and his seigniorial political style. Mitterrand's particular intelligence was psychological capacity. He was not necessarily more intelligent or clever than all the others, but his psychological insight, self-motivation, and, above all, determination—including the ability to play the waiting game—were superb. Thus Mitterrand's *nilum humanum* and his gift for seeing through others' motives made him almost impossible to surprise with bad behavior, or good for that matter.

The French novelist and conservative commentator Jean d'Ormesson said of Mitterrand that "At the end of his life, those who detested him detested him less than at the beginning. And those who loved him liked him less than at the beginning.[25] He was exactly right about both the former and latter. Mitterrand had provoked extremes of resentment and admiration, and at the end some of the energy had been pumped out of the one and the other.

And rather than apologizing for his audacity or inflecting it, Mitterrand went on being himself until the end, the commanding character he had forged out of and against his timidity. Mitterrand lived a sort of life that, in its nonconformism and daring, politicians normally could not afford politically, or most of all psychologically. Not apologizing for this strategy and personality was part of an overall integrity that was not some conventional morality of honesty but a successful life lived existentially in its various parts according to one's own values.[26] Like him or not, François Mitterrand *a réussi sa vie,* as the French say: He made of his life a success.

Mitterrand literally took for granted many associates, especially among the Socialists who saw him most. Once he had seen their limits and knew they wouldn't cause him difficulty they ceased to interest him, in the sense of having to reckon with them, politically or socially. Those who resisted were the ones in whom, naturally, he was most interested. They were the ones whom it would be profitable to win over or negotiate or intimidate or outfox. Some of his aides, plausibly enough, complained that Mitterrand spent more time trying to convince his adversaries than in discussions with his own people.

THE CENTRALITY OF FRIENDSHIP:
AN EXISTENTIAL CREDO

In Mitterrand's life the political man and the social man overlapped, which is precisely why his personal relations, his idea of friendship as well as his significant involvements with women, were matters of alliance and reciprocity rather than love. Mitterrand had thought deeply, even philosophically, about friendship, which he practiced diligently. It is far from sure (at least after Béatrice) that he understood love so well or would again risk its potentially disastrous outcomes. Mitterrand, thus easier than most politicians, brought women into the political, strategic alliance, the great network of his political ambition and the friendship of his personal life. As with many political men, François Mitterrand's personal and family life was not so distinct or different from his public life. But unlike many political men who have no real personal life, Mitterrand knew how to be alone, knew how to take pleasure in reading, and did have intellectual and cultural interests which required solitude.

"Adventure, you see, not games—I'm not a gambler, whatever anyone says," Mitterrand told an biographer in 1966. "That's what gives you a reason to live. To escape the [Gestapo], and better yet to help a friend escape them! It was [in the Resistance], even more than in the camps, where my religion of friendship was born."[27] An existential morality of friendship had become Mitterrand's substitute for religion. It is plausible to see this idea of a "religion of friendship" as a transformed concept of "brothers" in the Church, i.e., the Marist brothers at Angoulême and at the "104" who had educated him and for whom he had had such esteem. Masonic ideas were conceivably also involved in Mitterrand's thinking, of course an overdetermined concept whose most intimate referent, men in combat who would die for each other, was his POW and Resistance comrades.

Mitterrand's religion of friendship as a moral code became legendary and for good reason. Friendship was at the center of a rich and dense personal life seemingly of more depth than his marriage, though it gives one no pleasure to say this.

Skeptics did not deny Mitterrand's devotion to friends but insisted it was strictly amoral, basically a mutual aid society that knew no moral bounds.[28] This is one of those absolute dismissals of Mitterrand-as-scoundrel that needs to be recognized as based on something other than facts.

Mitterrand's friendship had to have a moral basis because, among other things, it purposefully excluded many people who might have been useful to him and involved keeping or defending other individuals who were dangerous to him. This religion of friendship was based on a principle of reciprocity, a "Do unto others" the moral pedigree of which flows naturally from a Catholic background and was a mixture of conventional and unconventional moral rules. This was Mitterrand's moral solution to the loss of his church Catholicism. Yet it was also a moral solution that an existentialist agnostic could believe wholeheartedly. As for socialism, "I don't make it my bible," he once said, indicating something about socialism but also about a bible: Mitterrand was anti-dogmatic; he refused the very tendency to total systems of thought.[29]

Mitterrand's commitment to friends, loyalty to associates, relationships with all sorts of people all out of proportion to their potential political importance for him, was deeply, even fiercely, felt. And morality led him—a man who could at other times be so ungenerous and dismissive of other people— to take great pains to fulfill an obligation or to repay a debt.

There are innumerable instances of Mitterrand's long cultivation of friendships out of a shared past, of which we have already detailed many. His resistance comrades were one set of such friends: Ginette and Jean Munier, Roger-Patrice Pelat, and Bernard Finifter, who were the armed hands of the

"Morland" network while Mitterrand worked sabotage operations along with arranging the parachuting of supplies and intelligence.[30] Marguerite Donnadieu-Antelme-Duras was another permanent friendship. Mitterrand's unfailing telephone call to Georges Dayan's wife, Paule, commemorating his passing in 1979, was just one sign of a friendship that included making her a permanent part of his entourage in the Socialist party. Georges's brother Jean was another such friend. Jean Riboud the industrialist and other friends who had passed on joined Mitterrand's "departed ones," whom he thought of, he said, each night. "Before I go to bed and begin to read, when I am in peace, I like at that moment to think back on certain far-off episodes, or else to remember certain faces that are no longer with me. Really, there is not a day when I don't think of the people whom I have loved in my life."[31] Mitterrand found it difficult to let go of his friends, and he "accompanied them to the end," at their side, even as president, in their death throes. For example when Jean Chevrier, owner of the Vieux Morvan hotel in Château-Chinon, where Mitterrand the deputy had stayed so often, was in prolonged decline, "the president visited him at least twice a week." According to Giesbert, more than a few friends died in his arms.[32]

All together we see very early on several of the apparently contradictory psychological traits in his makeup which would baffle so many later observers.

ON THE DESIRE FOR POWER

But what, after all this talk of diffidence and reciprocity, does one say about François Mitterrand's thirst for power, the "instrumentalism" vis-à-vis others that so many commentators thought the central value in his character?

In *La Paille et Le Grain* (1975) Mitterrand wrote with grandiloquence, "In every city I feel myself emperor or architect, I decide, I render judgments, and I am the arbiter."[33] Is this, as it seems, a Bonapartist temperament revealing itself behind a republican mask? The young Mitterrand indeed was sometimes nicknamed "the emperor" or "Bonaparte." Yet, particularly an American observer of France might interpret this apparent grandiloquence not as a Bonapartist or de Gaulle–like leaning, but a Whitmanesque or Emersonian sentiment, a celebration of self. Mitterrand's whole life was a dare, a fight with diffidence and then a creative struggle to become himself, a "will to will." His writing can seem Emersonian as well as existentialist. To quote again from above, "There is no force in the world, nor any philosophical, religious, state power, or of money, of capital, in relation to which I am not completely free. And if there were one source of pride to take in my life, it would be that."[34] In this the cosmopolitanism of Mitterrand appears starkly in contrast with the French provincialism of de Gaulle's single idea: service to France.

Thus an existential outlook became, after surmounting the culture of Jarnac and his idolization of Pétain in 1940-1942, François Mitterrand's way to live in the world. What mattered to Mitterrand was no longer eternal truths and duties (Catholicism), nor the hope of a savior (Marshal Pétain). What mattered was "truth for me." Authority over others was not, as I said, natural to Mitterrand. Explaining its origins, or at least some of them, leads to a richer understanding of a man perceived by so many others as a *bête du pouvoir,* a pure power-seeker.

CONCLUSION:
POWER AND AUTONOMY

A last question arises from the preceding discussion: How did Mitterrand's desire for power fit with his more basic desire for autonomy, to safeguard his own freedom? Power and freedom are not the same thing and can be contradictory. Exercising power is also a set of restraints; the free man may exclude himself from power. To philosophize is a solitary but free activity; to be an office-holder is to be chained to the wheel.

Mitterrand's concept of autonomy was not first of all a morality but an *aesthetic.* We have emphasized how often he was wrongly thought of as amoral, wrong not because he had no moral values but because, as an agnostic and eclectic, he displayed no recognizable moral system. What I am calling his existentialist outlook was expressed simply by George Steiner as the "example of trying to live rationally, day in, day out," to live one's life as a permanent exercise of conscious choice.

So the judgment of Mitterrand by censors is wrong when they argue he began in amorality and ended in amorality. This was not an amoral man. He began in amorality and, through an impressive intellectual evolution, ended in moralities of friendship, of reciprocity, of "ardent republicanism," and in a belief that, however strong his own passion for autonomy, social and political institutions are necessary to avoid anarchy, the rule of the strong and the beasts. François Mitterrand was, in sum, a much more intellectual man and complex public figure than the stereotypes of him; all his shortcomings and mistakes don't change this.

The life of political power is on this account a choice, perhaps even a habit, but not an addiction.

Without this understanding, several defining events in Mitterrand's presidency are misperceived. For example Mitterrand's skillful working of the first cohabitation in 1986-1988 with Jacques Chirac depended on *not* being committed to staying in office at any price, on a willingness to resign if necessary, putting his office at stake in the political-constitutional struggle. The general view at the beginning in 1986 was that, because Mitterrand and Chirac were two such "beasts of power" presidential and prime ministerial authority were on a collision course. Cohabitation would not last the two years until the next election, it was figured, but no one could say, given the two combatants, how it was most likely to end. Would the termination be a constitutional chess game or a political clash? Would the consequence be a presidential resignation or dissolution by the president and new parliamentary elections? In the event, what happened was that the "hedgehog" Chirac was outfoxed by Mitterrand. And part of Mitterrand's foxiness was his greater detachment from the goal of keeping power at any cost. And while part of this detachment was the president's greater responsibility for the system as opposed to the partisan politics natural to the prime minister, the defining aspect was Mitterrand's knowing many things, as the fox does, rather than the single big thing, power, that the hedgehog sees.

What Jean Lacouture wrote of André Malraux applies rather well to François Mitterrand, although my French colleague may well resist my use of his words here: "What was intolerable for [others] was the eruption of talent, of audacity, of non-conformism and of disinterestedness—yes, this time one could speak of disinterestedness in the case of Malraux—in this little universe bleating with moist and fruitful servility."[35] Comparing Mitterrand and Malraux would lead to useful insights: the different balances between political and literary ambitions mentioned above; the nonconformism and the fabrication of a facade; the taste for the exotic and the love of home; the temptation by risky business.

In the end François Mitterrand's adopted existential outlook justified a self-generated moral system of a lapsed Catholic. In its nonconformism and post-faith character it naturally seemed immoral, or amoral, to many people. Making bad into worse, François Mitterrand didn't even try to be hypocritical about it, to pay the usual tribute of vice to virtue. He just talked as little as possible about his personal morality; this was French, not American politics.

Machiavelli's advice to the prince about doing evil is often misunderstood. He did not recommend that the prince always do evil, only to do as much evil as is necessary to the main purpose of maintaining the state and his own power. Likewise Mitterrand's attitude to conventional moral values was not deliberately to transgress—lying or corruption with no scruples. It was to take the liberties necessary to his purposes, given his own moral values.

As president of France, there were limits, republican-constitutional, legal, and self-imposed, that Mitterrand respected, deeply so even if not with absolute fidelity. As a man, the same was true of his existential engagement with life, deeply committed if not always true to his idea. And what, finally, did it mean that he left an example but no philosophical statement, only the bits and pieces we have quoted? It was Sartre himself who once said, "Existentialism must be lived to be really sincere. To live as an existentialist means to be ready to pay for this view and not merely to lay it down in books."[36]

CHAPTER 10

MITTERRAND AND THE HUMAN COMEDY

We must take care to observe how advantageous it is to a man to speak when he pleases, to choose his own subject, to break off or change the conversation with a magisterial authority, and to defend himself against the objections of others by a shake of the head, by a smile, or by silence, in front of an assembly that is tremulous with reverence and respect. —Montaigne, *Essays*

Despotism corrupts the man who submits to it much more than the man who imposes it. In absolute monarchies the king may often have great virtues, but the courtiers are always vile.

—Alexis de Tocqueville, *Democracy in America*

We know a thousand times better the mechanisms of "monogamous sexual love" than those of the monogamous devotion to a cause or a leader. There are in this world millions of aging Swanns, whose Odette is called, in the East, Stalin, Mao or Tito, in the South, Fidel Castro, Mobotu or Sankara and, in the West, Mitterrand, Mme. Thatcher or Nixon. No Proust deigns to ponder their cases, as if the *res publica* was not worthy of the microsurgeons of grief.

—Régis Debray, *Loués Soient Nos Neigneurs: Une Education Politique*

> Comedy purifies pathos . . . and pathos invigorates comedy.
>
> —Emmanuel Mounier, *Existentialist Philosophies*

MITTERRAND AND
THE RULES OF THE FRENCH GAME

THE DIRECTOR JEAN RENOIR'S CLASSIC 1939 FILM *La Règle du Jeu (Rules of the Game)* was a vivid, devastating study of a decadent French society, that of the "twenty-years crisis" interwar years. *Rules of the Game* still belongs in any French studies course, and it could have been remade in the 1980s, changing the background and the *enjeu,* the stake, but with the same method.

Had Jean Renoir remade the film, the central issue would not have been class and class conflict, yesterday's fetish; the story would dissect the social and personal obsession of the past two decades, that is, identity. The struggle for individual freedom and "agency," and for minority group rights, recognition, and respect—the interpersonal aspects of identity—these would have been at issue, yet another sign, by the way, of the decline of the old Left's hold on French political culture.

And the "players" in this imagined remake of *Rules of the Game*? The protagonist would be, as before, not a hero but an anti-hero, more Machiavellian than moralistic, a humanist rather than a conformist. But he would also have an existential consciousness, an awareness of the relativity, even the "absurdity," in an existential sense, of what Jules Michelet called "France as a religion" (read de Gaulle's "certain idea of France"), along with the ambiguities of his own will to freedom and identity. This protagonist would be a genuinely representative Frenchman, not the cardboard coq Frenchman embodied ten years ago by a Jean-Marie Le Pen or twenty years ago by the Communist leader Georges Marchais, but a complex individual, something like François Mitterrand (the reader will have already guessed). And the new Jean Renoir would doubtless distill the film into a single moment, as in *Rules of the Game,* when the reactionary, cardboard Le Pen exclaims of Mitterrand, "That man is not defending France, you see! And French identity, mon cher ami, it's being lost!" In some ways, France is, despite all the changes, still the country where "The more things change, the more they stay the same."

◆ ◆ ◆

In understanding the slippery subject of "leadership" it is vital, as Montesquieu, Tocqueville, and Régis Debray agree, to observe followers, that is, the planets and asteroids as well as the stars. Exclusive focus on leaders to study leadership is, of course, understandable. The leader in any field is more than the star of a show, he or she is the center of what Honoré de Balzac's epic series of novels termed "la comédie humaine" of nineteenth-century French life. The literal English translation is no good because lacking context it fails to convey the artistic intent of a literary fresco of human types and characters in society, the idea that a sociology of human society can be depicted novelistically, as a spectacle, a kind of theater in the manner of Molière's "La comédie francaise."

We want therefore to look at the human comedy that surrounded François Mitterrand. Of course Mitterrand was a man of high, and, in many ways, arrogant ambition, centered on himself. We need only listen to the following: *"Madame Bovary* is for me obviously the most important novel about French society. But what bothers me about nineteenth century characters is their occasional lack of reach. Look at the poverty of Julien Sorel's ambition. He has the modest idea of success that Stendhal, Consul at Civitavecchia, had for himself. Stendhal much admired Chateaubriand for being ambassador to Rome. . . ."[1]

But Mitterrand, while centered on himself, was not merely so. He both required and delighted in the human comedy of which he, naturally, was the focus and prime moving part. Mitterrand was the head of a clan, both in the political and social sense, as well as the titular head, less successful, of an ephemeral generation, the "Mitterrand generation" of French Socialists and of left-wing voters and sympathizers in the 1970s and 1980s, the *peuple de gauche* in French political life.

Understanding Mitterrand and the human comedy thus requires some account both of him as seen by others and others as seen through his own eyes. Of necessity only a sketch; interested readers will have to be francophone to go further. The result for an American audience can only be a selective glimpse of the Mitterrand clan with its various garrulous networks, the life's work of a man who made friendship into an art form, a "religion" that in a way replaced his lapsed Catholicism. Milking the human comedy was essential to François Mitterrand's success as a political leader, in a style which, especially on his arrival in the presidency, recalls the technique of John F. Kennedy. It was life in the Aristotelian sense, that man is by nature a social and thus a political animal, since the two are indivisible.

❖   ❖   ❖

Mitterrand could be rude and cruel with associates, but he had a sense of proportion and propriety about his own stature. He behaved as an excellent colleague with other world leaders—with Helmut Kohl, Ronald Reagan, George Bush, Margaret Thatcher, Mikhail Gorbachev, and others. And though famous for a regalian disdain for the informal "tu"—for example his icy and non-socialist chastening of a local party secretary who asked if they couldn't say *tu*: "Si vous voulez"—Mitterrand gave himself up quite well to the Group of Seven's habit of using first names within the peer group. But at home he was the star of the show, the gaullien "republican Prince," the "elected monarch," the center of the political-social whirl. He claimed to disdain it but obviously he relished all the "poisons and delights" of the French game.

Other facets added to his political character, derived not from power calculations but from ideas of the highest importance of friendship and the loyalty of friends, of cultural interests and—a Mitterrand subject par excellence—his relations with women. Intellectually and sentimentally, François Mitterrand was a kind of political Balzac. He delected the human comedy, needed—and thrived on—vast interconnecting networks of friendships, political groupings, interests, and curiosities.

The man Mitterrand was motivated, in politics as in society, by means as much as by ends. Playing political and social games meant permanent, widespread deployment of "seduction" in several guises. He loved to ensnare or overawe men into his political and friendship networks, and he loved to seduce or overawe women. Mitterrand had various sorts of complicit relations. With women there was his wife Danielle and his longtime companion, Anne Pingeot, the mother of his daughter Mazarine. There were also significant love affairs and affairs of affection along the way, of shorter or longer duration, including a "day companion" at the Élysée, to be discussed later; then innumerable encounters, the one-night stands of a sex-fixated politician on the road. To say Mitterrand loved the means as much and sometimes more than the end is to say he loved life ultimately more than he loved power. This was partly an existential worldview as outlined in the previous chapter, and partly sheer humanistic curiosity and desire for the experiences possible in life.

For François Mitterrand the play was the thing. His existentialist consciousness led directly to this conclusion. And with regard to women, we can speculate whether his passion for seduction rather than love was the lasting effect of his crushing rejection by "Béatrice" as a young man. Not to be vulnerable, "not to be surprised by anything": That was best. This befit the very reflexive man whose credo was to "always expect betrayal in politics" and that "nothing in politics is ever permanently won or lost."

◆ ◆ ◆

The French journalist Serge July's excellent 1986 book *Les Années Mitterrand: Histoire baroque d'une normalisation inachevée* (The Mitterrand Years: Baroque History of a Normalization as Yet Incomplete) already had some critical distance on the fact that his presidency involved "normalization," a generally disparaging term for what otherwise is called consensus or political legitimacy.[2]

July argued that the Mitterrand presidency, despite its left-wing Socialist beginning, was by 1986 adding to the "normalization" of French politics, to the decline of political-ideological intensity and the rise of the consensus-orientation that French historians Furet, Julliard, and Rosanvallon called "the Re-centered Republic."

That François Mitterrand was not a sectarian leftist and that his political network was far more diverse socially, culturally, economically, politically, ideologically, and geographically than perceived by French opinion or by foreigners who knew him only in his Socialist incarnation, was made flesh in a rare coming together of these otherwise compartmentalized relationships at Mitterrand's first "Bastille Day" Élysée garden party. July's is a marvelous description of the July 14, 1981, crowd as the "life's work" of a man seen as a loner in the 1960s (after the Observatory affair) and as an adventurer attempting the alliance of Cain and Abel in the 1970s. This first "family portrait" of *la Mitterrandie* showed a man who had, away from public view, become a "godfather of a family of loyalties":

> July 14, 1981, on the rolling lawn of the Élysée palace garden, spread out a crowd in large part inhabituated to the place, triumphant: This was the Mitterrand crowd. He contemplated it amorously because it was the masterwork of a life. There were writers, journalists, big business types, top government people, small business entrepreneurs, political people, some well-known people, others unknown, left-wing men and women but others openly right-wing and many others who had never asked themselves the question.
>
> This crowd has only a single catalyzing agent, which was neither French-style socialism, not the conjoined succession to Jean Jaurès and Léon Blum but a personal and unique relationship, sometimes having lasted already a long time, with the man whose complexion seemed vitrified by marbled pride. Among these various relationships there are not two alike. But each, with time, ended up cross-cutting each other on one geometric center: the president. A half-century of a life at once intellectual, worldly, romantic, warrior or political which Mitterrand cultivated and still cultivates like a seducer who is indefatigable but also religiously loyal. . . . In the "management" of these relations, it is never politics or ideas which get first place but a daily administration of loyalty and shared pleasure which do not accept the least betrayal.[3]

The Mitterrand network, said July, "plunges its roots into France as a whole, into all age groups," contrary to what much of France and certainly many foreign policy establishments abroad thought of him. July condensed the idea into an epigram: Mitterrand, he wrote, *est un orfèvre en hommes,* "Mitterrand is a master goldsmith in human relations." His friendships or relationships with conservatives, with Catholics, with cultural figures, with far-Right industrialists, with bankers, even with businessmen like Marcel Dassault whose company the Socialist program planned to nationalize, showed that. Mitterrand remained versatile as he had always been; neither the Observatory affair nor his alliance with the Communists had cut him off from the bourgeois and business worlds. Mitterrand had live contacts in the French bourgeois industrial class (the Schlumbergers, the Ribouds, the Bouygues), closer than his ties to trade union organizations even after he became the leader of the Left. He was also well traveled among the political elites in many countries (African countries from his Fourth Republic experience, Scandinavia, Israel and Arab countries both), and knew leaders of several African countries especially well, such as Félix Houphouët-Boigny, with whom he had sat in the Fourth Republic parliament, before national independence in Africa.

Mitterrand's network was, in the effusive words of one political aide, a "republican family." He was a natural clan as well as political leader, and to associate with his ambition and his successes was to feel part of a great adventure, to have one's chance of a lifetime, all opposite to the 1960s image of the post-Observatory affair loner. There are several stories on record of the exact moments when Mitterrand tempted or lured his allies into his network of power: "With a team of [a few hundred] dedicated people," Mitterrand would say, "we can win the country." Pierre Mauroy, Charles Hernu, and Roland Dumas are but three cases in point.

To do a good job in opposition to the government is a respectable role, but sometimes it is less than a full-time job. Mitterrand in any case had many interests outside politics, we already saw above, which he followed up intensely while in the opposition, but also, to a degree that surprised or disgusted political commentators, while he was president. He was not much in interested in painting (unlike Georges Pompidou) or even music. He showed some interest in theater but above all Mitterrand was interested in books. The writer Paul Guimard and lawyer/foreign minister Roland Dumas were often with him on book-hunting expeditions to his favorite stores, rare bookstores, or literary haunts such as Le Divan at St. Germain des Prés. Guimard's description of Mitterrand's literary tastes is hardly one that could be made of many French (or other) political men:

What was striking about Mitterrand's taste was three things that didn't always go together: a taste for the text; a passion for rare editions; and a great desire to meet the authors. That was how we met. When he liked a book he had to meet the author. . . . His tastes? Everyone knows that for him the summit of the art was a combination of the descriptions of Chateaubriand with the incisiveness of Pascal. That he admired Retz and St. Simon. That the nineteenth century was familiar territory, with a tender spot for Lamartine, a bit folksy, linked to Cluny and Milly, that is the home of [his wife] Danielle and of the Solutré mountain, but also with a taste for Stendhal and Benjamin Constant. As for the twentieth century, for him it was above all the [Nouvelle Revue Française] school—Valéry, Gide, Claudel. . . . But he wasn't much taken with Proust. Mauriac, Giono, Bernanos were his references. . . . And don't forget poetry. He adored poetry, he could recite hundreds of poems by heart—St. John Perse for example, but also Aragon. And toward the end of his life he discovered Artaud. . . . And this says nothing of the Russian novel, his passion for Dostoyevsky giving way little by little to his admiration for Tolstoy.[4]

This would be quite a letter of recommendation for a graduate student in literature, and hardly what one would expect from the professional politician, let alone the stereotype of Mitterrand as a man driven by the desire for power, more or less helpless in front of his own ambition.

Without neglecting his political and diplomatic functions he realized his dreams. He was always in search of nature, of history, of art. . . . His [political trips] were punctuated with detours. He went off to all points of the globe, with no sense of distance and time. If he suddenly remembered a place or an exposition he wanted to see, we left within the hour. . . . How many times were his secretaries trying to find him! He had left without saying anything to anybody. . . . I knew moments of incomparable happiness travelling the world at his side. Canadian maple forests burning with autumn colors; Bayreuth, temple of Wagnerian music; . . . Returning [from Egypt], he had to stop at Athens. He had heard that a researcher had discovered the tomb of Philip II of Macedonia, father of Alexander the Great. We took a plane the next day at dawn to the site.[5]

The author of this description of an avidly curious man is Christine Deviers-Joncour, and she is talking not of François Mitterrand but of his longtime friend, minister of foreign affairs, later president of the constitutional council, Roland Dumas. Whether or not Mitterrand, Dumas, and others were hip-deep in corruption (discussed elsewhere in this book), the Mitterrand "clan" was led by attractive men of large talents and charm. Dumas, for example, was also an amateur opera tenor and linguist.

Mitterrand attracted and long kept associated with him a group of gifted men and women, even the stereotypical Parisian polymath type. He was not afraid of colleagues with talent, partly because he was a sort of polymath himself and partly because it was more interesting for him. He was an avid player in the human comedy not only as a chef d'orchestre but as a participant. Mitterrand, said the historian François Furet, should be compared to the Third Republic founder Adolphe Thiers, "Because from Thiers, Mitterrand has the life at once bourgeois and bohemian, the pride of owing nothing to anything other than his own talent, the genius for adjustments to circumstances and to regimes. He has the same passion for trying to please, the same type of eloquence and the same capacity for the waiting game."[6] Not France's hero, as we said at the beginning of this study, but France's representative man.

Mitterrand was not, it is clear, as obsessed with getting and keeping power as people thought. Certainly his ambitiousness was immense, but too much else in his life nuances the stereotype of the single-minded power obsessive. He was interested in too many other things besides politics, and he spent much time on these other things. If where you spend your time is much of who you are, then it was as if for Mitterrand life was too full to be contained in politics, as if there were satisfactions other than winning. The American-style unbuttoned public elation, the V-signs, winks, and jumping up and down of election-night victories was not his way; he reminded associates at such moments that winning meant greater responsibilities and heavier burdens. His comment to aides, on learning of his first presidential victory, was "Do you realize what we're in for?"

Election evenings, including his first presidential victory, were usually spent partly reading in bed alone in the small, spare room number 10 in the Hotel du Vieux Morvan, which he had long occupied in his rural electoral district at Chateau-Chinon in the Nièvre. Its owners, Jean and Ginette Chevrier, had become part of the Mitterrand clan. The evening of his presidential reelection victory in 1988 the two families, the Mitterrands and the Chevriers, were at Ginette Chevrier's nearby house without Jean, who had died. The couple had sold the hotel a few years earlier but Mitterrand kept to his religion of friendship.

◆   ◆   ◆

As is the case with full-time politicians, much of his social life was also his political life, and vice versa. Mitterrand used contacts with others to stay in touch with the "real world," and to enrich his knowledge of other people. Guests always thought that they were observing him, which was of course true. But the least of his associates or guests might not have realized that Mitterrand was also observing them. He amused himself but also enriched himself intellectually and even emotionally with the human comedy. In political situations, he was playing a strategic or tactical game. "A true political man," said one close observer, a journalist, woman, companion, "he rapidly picked up in what way people might be useful to him. And he never confused the opinion he had of this one or that one with the role somebody might play. . . . Thus he distinguished morality and utility."[7]

One British reviewer of Jean Lacouture's 1998 Mitterrand biography finds "his overall judgment kind, possibly too kind," adding

> Yes, Mitterrand was talented, courageous, romantic, cultured, passionate, eloquent, audacious, brilliant at strategy and a charmer of women. But he could also be—especially later in life—petty, mean, obsessive, arrogant, vindictive, cynical, cruel, an inveterate liar, an almost sadistic schemer who loved to divide and rule, even among his own friends. . . . It could not have been simply Mitterrand's ambition and self-confidence which provoked such hearty loathing and suspicion around him through a scandal-scented life.[8]

Exactly so—the Machiavellian republican can get too comfortably into character on either side, with gratuitous cruelties and vindictiveness indeed growing later in life. It is almost a law of the species, and King Lear is its greatest depiction. But the founding political value in Mitterrand's mature personality was, we saw earlier, the duty of freedom, of choice, of agency, the result of our common existential predicament. This meant, among other things, a rejection of conformity, sometimes diving into pettiness and cruelty.

Within his entourage, his political-social network of family, friends, associates, hangers-on, and political courtesans, the rule was reciprocal loyalty. If people were loyal to him, he would be loyal to them and debts of friendship were repaid. Even critics recognized that Mitterrand, even as president, defended his friends and allies, sometimes to the point of damage to himself. Friendship could be a higher value than success to him, and perhaps it was also a higher value than love. Yet with the courtiers and sycophants Mitterrand could play the game of imperial power with perfect pitch, inciting others to humiliate themselves.

Mitterrand should be categorized as one of those rare Frenchmen who, to make use of Tocqueville's well-known distinction in The Old Regime, loved freedom more than equality. But his freedom was not a Millian or Tocquevillean liberty in which one's freedom is limited at the point where it infringes on that of others. It was an existentialist struggle of will and sovereignty. He could use others whereas they could not dispose of him, manipulate others while not being himself manipulated. But there was apparently contradictory behavior, his acts of generosity and taking large unnecessary trouble for others—especially the friends he tended to in sickness or approaching death—were not acts of politeness but of existential friendship;[9] on the other hand were Mitterrand's innumerable acts of presumption, for example finessing countless restaurant checks: "Well, you pay now and we'll settle up later on." Later on, of course, never came. He often asked for inconveniencing indulgences. Sometimes the inconvenienced subordinates were women who were former lovers. He might say "Drive me to X" (a long way). Or he might ask a subordinate who had traveled on the campaign plane to a provincial rally, "I have a guest coming back with me. Would you mind giving her your seat in the plane and taking the train back to Paris?"

François Mitterrand embraced the moral result of putting his freedom, his own willpower first: inequality, taking advantage of others unless successfully resisted. Mitterrand's moral stance was that everyone had the right to freedom, to seek to impose his will. But in the nature of things, some would lose. In this way, Mitterrand's conquest of his own timidity was the founding act of his freedom, an exercise of existential will. His idea of *equality* was eminently political, that is a matter of equal rights. But his idea of *liberty* was, in the usage of the French thinker Emmanuel Mounier, basically "personalistic."

Mitterrand, unlike de Gaulle, never referred to himself in the third person and spoke of the presidency as *la fonction,* "the office" or "job," emphasizing that the president's authority was limited and his only for a legally stipulated time. But like de Gaulle, Mitterrand enthusiastically performed the ceremonial aspects of being head of state, not only the high political ceremonies but the local openings of public buildings, monuments, and bridges in the provinces he had had so much pleasure in traveling and knowing. This "bondage" to the tedious ceremonial side of the state was for him another act of freedom because he chose it willingly. The sacrifice of time and mental energy was part of the duties of the presidency; public showings of the presidential flag, these ceremonial occasions, reinvigorated legitimacy—the legitimacy of the presidency and his own legitimacy as president.

Mitterrand was in fact a past master at submitting to boredom and concealing the effort, a particular challenge for someone of his temperament and intellect. Imagine how often, in twenty-three years of opposition, he gave the same speech, met the same sort of people, sat through meetings with identical agendas! Imagine how often, as president for fourteen long years, he presided at the same ceremonies, cut similar ribbons of opening, was asked the same questions. Four years, let alone eight, is quite enough for an American president!

THE PRESIDENT WHO DARED
TO HAVE CONTROVERSIAL FRIENDS:
ERNST JÜNGER AND MARGUERITE DURAS

Mitterrand's occasional visits to the controversial German writer-philosopher Ernst Jünger, who died in February 1998 at the age of 102, puzzled commentators. However, like many of his assiduous friendships and "surprising" traditional stops at the homes of old friends in his electoral district, the Jünger connection was genuine intellectual curiosity.

Jünger, described in an obituary by the American journalist David Binder, was "an aloof warrior-author regarded as one of Germany's most controversial and contradictory writers."[10] President Richard von Weisaecker, West Germany's moral conscience, and Chancellor Kohl together came to wish him well on his hundredth birthday, despite Jünger's earlier reputation as a Nazi apologist.

In World War I, Jünger had shown what his commanding general called "ruthless bravery." He had been wounded at least seven times and was awarded the Knights Cross of the House of Hohenzollern and also the Pour le Mérite medal, imperial Germany's highest award, of which he was believed to be the last living recipient. During Mitterrand's years of struggle with cancer between 1993 and 1995, he made a couple of helicopter visits to Jünger's home, apparently to discuss death and the existence of God with the German philosopher. But Jünger, in his late nineties by this time, gave frustrating answers to journalists' questions about the nature of their discussions: "He asked me about the afterlife," said Jünger, "and I told him I knew nothing about it, that it was impossible to know about it." Mitterrand had been fascinated by Jünger's writings, among them "Mantrana," which had been translated into French by Pierre Morel, a Mitterrand foreign policy aide, later ambassador to Russia and China. Mantrana is a series of short texts and maxims, often evocations of death and the afterlife. A philosophical textual "game of dominoes" is played, by adding one to another. Mitterrand was very taken with Jünger's ideas, quoting passages by heart in conversations, according to Morel.[11] Despite and because of his existentialist outlook, Mitterrand had an intense curiosity about the nature of death and fervently, as said already, kept in memory those who has passed on, those he affectionately called *mes morts:* "The people I have loved who are dead, I have always thought of them each evening . . . a kind of meditation in which I find them again."[12]

In the 1930s, Jünger became a darling of radical nationalist movements, including the Nazi party, with such warrior books as *Storm of Steel: From the Diary of a German Storm-Troop Officer on the Western Front; Combat;* and *Fire and Blood.* He didn't join the Nazis. He refused a parliamentary nomination in 1927 and also, after they were in power, membership in the Nazified German Academy. But his relationship with the Third Reich turned out to be unfortunately ambiguous. His *Marble Cliffs* (1939) was anti-Nazi, yet Jünger returned to uniform to serve Hitler's government. During World War II he served as a captain mostly in headquarters in occupied Paris, associating with French cultural luminaries such as Jean Cocteau, Sacha Guitry, Céline, Picasso, Georges Braque, and Montherlant. His *Gardens and Roads,* describing the Paris cultural scene, was published in both German and French in 1942. Jünger's ties with the German officers involved in the failed July 29, 1944, plot to kill Hitler led to summary dismissal from the German army. Then the Allied occupation government banned Jünger, labeled a "militarist," from publishing for four years after the war's end. Later books, such as *Radiations* and *Heliopolis,* had an anti-militarist, anti-Nazi tone. In 1950 he began a self-imposed exile in a forester's house on a baronial estate near Wilfingen in Upper Swabia.

Jünger was absorbed intellectually by death and heroism, by nihilist and end-of-the-world ideas. Like Mitterrand, he was a passionate observer of nature. He assembled a 40,000-piece collection of beetles and insects from Africa, the Middle East, and Asia. In 1970, reaffirming the range of his interests and his ability to surprise, he published *Approaches, Drugs and the Buzz,* about experiments with LSD and mescaline, and in 1985 there appeared a critically acclaimed detective story, *Dangerous Encounters.* One of Mitterrand aides Jacques Attali's controversial books, *A History of Time,* contained a multitude of pages plagiarized from a work by Jünger, which Mitterrand presumably had put in his hands. Jünger's works even received an enthusiastic review by the German Nobel laureate Heinrich Böll, himself a pacifist.

Jünger's return to public sympathy came in the 1980s when the city of Frankfurt, against protests, awarded him its Goethe Prize. And in 1984 he, with other prestigious guests, was invited to join François Mitterrand and Helmut Kohl at the emotional reconciliation ceremony at Verdun. Jünger made a decisive renunciation of his youthful warrior ideology as "a calamitous mistake."

It is apparent why Ernst Jünger interested Mitterrand. Their pasts had common points, including the connection of service to regimes they later disavowed. But it was both the subjects and the controversy of Jünger's views that appealed to Mitterrand, especially his spiritualist speculations which the intellectually voracious French president found of renewed relevance when his own mortality came into close view.

Marguerite Duras, internationally known author of *La Douleur* and *The Lover,* was another controversial friend. Duras was mentioned in the story of Mitterrand's Vichy and Resistance years. To keep in contact with her even as president meant many things to him. Duras was another living proof of his Resistance activity, and she was controversial, like Ernst Jünger and Mitterrand himself. Duras had lived and lived passionately in a dangerous time, adding danger to danger. Her liaison with the French Gestapo informant whom she hoped would enable her deported husband, Robert Antelme, to get free was "inexplicable" in terms of conventional morality. Duras, like Jünger and like François Mitterrand, had lived a daring existence and had passed through times of trouble, exacerbated by questionable personal behavior.

Asked to recall how he first met Marguerite Duras, President Mitterrand said:

> It was in 1943. She was a very young woman, very pretty, a bit Eurasian, with a charm she used all the time. You have to imagine Margarite Donnadieu [her original name], with that delicacy of a bird that was distinctive to her. [She] already had that rather dominating temperament which is now so familiar, in charge of her little world . . . and we accepted her because we loved her. Since then I have known all the periods of her life, this path which has led her to deepen, to improve, to simplify. I don't see any break in her biography.

Of her writing Mitterrand praised her as one who went right to the essential, not losing time in filling up pages. But overall "in Marguerite Duras it is really an attitude toward life which is interesting and which attracts one." Duras had said of Mitterrand in 1981 that "There is in him a basic doubt, a repugnance for power." Asked for a response he replied:

> I don't respond. If she describes me that way it must be that there is something true in it. . . . When she might make me angry instead she makes me laugh. She is very peremptory and I take her as she is. Sometimes some of her opinions make me laugh and I tell her. But I never argue with her. . . . For the last few months she has decided she doesn't want to come to the Élysée, its some idea she has about it, she just doesn't want to. On my part it is difficult to continue, though I'd like to, with the life of friendship and camaraderie which I had with many people. But we really had a lot of dinners that ended up late into the evening![13]

In a sense Duras's past was a validation of, or at least a companion to Mitterrand's, and it was a witness to the times from which one could exit honorably through humanism, talent, and authenticity.

THE MACHIAVELLIAN REPUBLICAN AT HOME

The Machiavellian republican is a less contradictory, more banal politician than it might seem. By this I mean that all or most democratic politicians could be called Machiavellian republicans, playing a combination of the Prince's game and the democratic republican game, albeit not with all the Machiavellian attributes of the gaullien French presidency or a politician of such skill as a Mitterrand.

Mitterrand, as if following Machiavelli's advice to the Prince, would have liked to be both feared and loved, but knew that if he had to choose, it was better to be feared than loved. Cristina Forsne's spirited memoir of her part of life with "François" describes the ambience of "soft terror" Mitterrand established around himself, dominating the behavior of political associates, business guests, friends, and even his own family. At his country home at Latche, Mitterrand, like a "Scoutmaster," says Forsne, presided over "days built of rituals." When Mitterrand suddenly decided, "everyone had to leave for the ritual walk in the forest" without failing to "stop to admire the bees, producers of the [breakfast] honey." A particularly great honor was "participation in the planting of the hundred oak trees which François Mitterrand had decided would be part of his heritage." Mitterrand, "dressed like a South-West French peasant—corduroy pants, cotton jacket, boots and well-worn fisherman's hat—loaded his companion for the day with the various knives, shovels and pots necessary, and led off the march, his walking stick well in hand."[14]

Comparing Mitterrand's average looks and stature with the huge control over others he produced, Forsne posed one of the basic questions about the man: "And I ask myself, one more time, how was [Mitterrand] able to attach so many people to himself?"[15] The answer is more than a power of seduction and less than any threat he could pose to life and limb, unlike a real-life Bourbon king or Bonapartist emperor. What Mitterrand offered was the chance to be part of the great man's entourage, to be part of his great adventure, to participate in the exercise of power, to touch glory, ultimately to give meaning to one's own life—and, in all this, and not least of all, to be led, to be organized.

Very many people have dreams of glory, but few are really serious. Mitterrand, despite his bohemian side, was an extraordinarily determined organizer of his networks. More than a few French leaders, it goes without saying, were trying the same game at the same time, and it was an education in leadership to observe how the hierarchy formed in particular among

Socialist leaders, how a Michel Rocard, or a Pierre Mauroy, or a Jack Lang, or a Jean-Pierre Chevènement became in Mitterrand's presence obviously a follower rather than a leader.

The fox knows many things; the hedgehog knows one big thing. The philosopher Isaiah Berlin wrote of Tolstoy that he "was by nature a fox, but believed in being a hedgehog."[16] Was François Mitterrand a hedgehog or a fox, or both, or someone who had lost his way? Or was Mitterrand, a man of so many interests, not a super-fox after all? Georges Kiejman, a longtime associate, quipped to this writer that "Probably there were things Mitterrand hid even from himself!" In any case it is wrong to read Mitterrand's motives only through one's own eyes or one's own main concern, for example, to say that the Socialist experiment failed because Mitterrand was never truly a socialist or that Mitterrand named Edith Cresson prime minister in 1991 because they had once been lovers. Such an earnest, sincere Mitterrand would never have gotten very far in politics. As a different Mitterrand friend, Maurice Faure, said, "It's when he's sincere that he is the least effective!"[17]

Thus we can explain why Mitterrand's moments of sincerity, often naive or even bumbling, were wrongly perceived as falseness when they were in fact the interior man being, for once, himself. When Mitterrand was faced with some dilemma, others almost always thought that his goal had to be the one not evident and his means had to be triply complex. Yet he was talking truth when he told a biographer "I'm always presented as a convoluted character cooking up convoluted schemes. But in reality what people think of as my maneuvering is nothing other than a great simplicity. I am always a man who tries to go straight to the essential."[18]

His "Florentine" reputation helped him, of course, precisely because people disbelieved what he said or the evidence of their own eyes. Women, who often recognize male vulnerability, fragility, and goals better than men themselves, generally understood François Mitterrand's personality and character better than male commentators who invented a stream of metaphors—God, the sphinx, Uncle—in vain attempts to capture the essence of the man. "François Mitterrand," Cristina Forsne writes, "was a much more banal man than the one described" in media accounts. "For me, he was far from the exceptional being that people thought, far from the complicated man that one depicted. I've known other men who resembled him, and what is exceptional is that he became president of the Republic."[19] Forsne is talking about daily life when she had him to herself. This was, after all, a man who already had one legal wife, two families, and a rich menu of other mistresses and companions!

MITTERRAND NAMES
FRANCE'S FIRST WOMAN PRIME MINISTER

François Mitterrand's choices of prime ministers were always overdetermined, always the result of more reasons than necessary to justify them. But a primary logic was discernable. The first prime minister in 1981, Pierre Mauroy, was above all else the man of the "Union of the Left," the Socialist most likely to be able to hold the Communists in the alliance and to keep the Socialists together in the process. The next three Socialist prime ministers were named each for different reasons. Laurent Fabius in 1984 was to be the man of modernizing and mainstreaming Socialist policy after the Socialist experiment's failure. In 1988 Michel Rocard had finally to be given his chance or else the Rocard wing of the Socialist party would feel permanently rebuffed by Mitterrand. Edith Cresson in 1991 had the task of redynamizing the Socialist government, moving it back to the left after what we perceived as the lackluster Rocard years.

At the same time the Fabius-Rocard-Cresson succession had another logic: nonconformism. Fabius was Jewish and, at thirty-seven years old, France's youngest ever prime minister. Michel Rocard was a Protestant. Edith Cresson was the first woman prime minister in France's history. No doubt Mitterrand, the breaker of taboos, took pleasure in the symmetry in nonconformism of these appointments. But the Cresson nomination in May 1991 was also bound up with a personal relationship with Mitterrand, which multiplied its complications. Rumors, almost certainly founded, alleged that she had been romantically linked to Mitterrand for a time in the 1960s. She aggressively shrugged off questions about it as the fate of women who climb the ladder in politics, that her critics believe "that everything is decided in the boudoir."[20] But the taint was real enough, abetted by Mitterrand's own reputation.

Born on January 27, 1934, into a well-to-do but left-wing family—her father was a senior civil servant—Edith Cresson became a left-wing activist at thirty-one years old, upon meeting the 1965 presidential candidate François Mitterrand. She was appreciated by him for her drive and intelligence, as well as because she was an attractive woman. She gradually became a permanent member of his entourage and ultimately a government minister. Married with two children, she had a degree in business and a doctorate in demography, and she spoke good English. Like Margaret Thatcher, to whom Mrs. Cresson was sometimes compared, she was no feminist but argued that women are as capable as men. "Men are irreplaceable," she said with typical candor, "in only one area—one's private life."[21]

Just as in 1984 he had given France its youngest prime minister in Laurent Fabius, so now he was giving France its first woman prime minister. It looked good, would go down in the history books, and would distract public attention from the Rocard government's difficulties, which included party finance corruption scandals as well as an economic slowdown. It was doubtful, given the Socialist government's minority position in parliament, that Cresson would find it any easier than Rocard to pass bills there. But she could lead Mitterrand's tack to the Left on social issues, including women's issues and ethnic and religious inclusion issues, and hopefully reverse an ideologically dismaying increase in income inequalities and unemployment. On issues of European integration, both national French development and Europe's interest in the Uruguay Round, Cresson's mission was a French-led "European Community nationalist" charge, tough and protectionist. She would be the bad cop to Mitterrand's good cop, attempting to reassert French diplomatic leadership within the European Community at a time when German leadership was forced to formulate economic policy with the problems of German reunification as the pre-eminent point of reference. As she had done as Minister of Foreign Trade, she would stigmatize Japanese trade practices, emphasizing less the American challenge, and more the common interest of the United States and European countries in joining forces against the Japanese. In this division of labor President Mitterrand would make the inevitable compromises and concessions, getting leverage from warning foreigners about his protectionist lobbies at home. Edith Cresson, said *The Economist,* "is a protectionist, a believer in the French 'national' (i.e., producer) interest long before she is a believer in the rights of French consumers to buy the best that the world can offer. If Fortress Europe is to be built, Mrs. Cresson will be there with a cement mixer."[22] Cresson called especially for European industrial alliances in electronics and automobiles to fend off the competitive threat from Japan. She blocked a proposed investment by Japanese NEC in Bull, the French computer maker. But France sought to divert Japan's protest at Mrs. Cresson's attacks, saying Tokyo had a trade dispute with Europe as a whole rather than with the French.

Cresson's appointment seemed a milestone for French women, who, one remembers, did not obtain even the right to vote until 1945. "There are three places where women have always been excluded," she said, "the military, religion and politics. I would say that today, it is still in politics where they have the least access."[23] Women held just 31 of the 577 seats in the National Assembly, and there had been just 4 women in Rocard's 35-member cabinet. Cresson named five women to her government, including Labor Minister Martine Aubry, Minister for Cooperation and Development Edwige Avice, Youth and Sports Minister Frédérique Bredin, and two junior ministers.[24]

Despite the gossip about her past with President Mitterrand, few commentators said, at first, that Edith Cresson was simply unqualified for the job of prime minister or inexperienced in politics. Besides his reputation as a ladies man, Mitterrand had unquestionably increased the number of women in substantial government positions and even had supported a one-third quota system inside the Socialist party. Cresson's nomination as prime minister seemed plausible on the merits. Successively as minister of agriculture, minister for tourism and trade, minister of trade and industry, and minister for European affairs she had not always been successful but there was never any question of her overall abilities. Among her defects were impatience and a lack of tact, diplomacy or willingness to conciliate—whether with French farmers or Japanese business/government collusion—and a protectionist economic nationalism. She wasn't a gaullist, but she displayed, or tried to, the gaullien concern for French national interests. Nevertheless, wrote a woman political journalist about the Cresson experiment, "Everything reinforced the sense that Cresson, underneath her air of decisiveness, was in reality a dominated women, in the most traditional way."[25] Meaning what? The fact that they had once been romantically linked was common knowledge. Cresson had first worked as a volunteer secretary in Mitterrand's shoestring 1965 campaign. The student Hubert Védrine remembered when Mitterrrand came to speak at Sciences-Po' or at other meetings, he merrily "arrived in a Fiat 600 driven by Edith Cresson."[26]

Although now, in 1991, seventy-five years old, Mitterrand's past with Cresson had not faded from memory. The sharpest denunciation was provided by a former *Le Monde* journalist and outraged former political advisor and speech writer for Pierre Mauroy. It appears in an "open letter" to the "Mitterrand generation which is missing the Boat," a particular warning directed to Isabelle Thomas, who had been a mediatized lycée student leader in the fall 1986 anti-government demonstrations. Soon thereafter she accepted a job offer from Mitterrand to become a policy aide to the president for education, culture, and youth problems. She then became a Socialist candidate for Parliament in a bad district, and lost. Here was the advice of a wizened member of the Mitterrand/Mauroy team:

> Dear Isabelle Thomas,
> You were the Joan of Arc of the [student leaders] of 1986. . . . And now you have started a political career. . . . Your fragility is still apparent. . . . The head of state, an interested charmer, doesn't he whisper in your ear? . . . Are you still naive enough or already blind enough to believe that he is interested in your future? . . . I would like to tell you a story, which has the merit of being true. . . . Contrary to what you think, you have not made use of François Mitterrand. Mitterrand in fact for a long time already has accustomed the group of his "friends" to unforeseen

feminine incursions. . . . From the time of the [FGDS] in the 60s, its leaders still remember the day when "the President" . . . arrived late for a meeting he was supposed to chair. . . . What marked the memory of this group of males was a sudden transgression symbolized by the attractive well-sculpted creature who accompanied their leader. They haven't forgotten the opulent auburn hair or the generously proportioned bosom. The young woman, silent, sat in a corner, in the background. . . . François Mitterrand sat down and took over the chair. . . . No one dared speak of the intruder. . . . Finally [Mitterrand] explained. The leadership of the FGDS grouping had come to seem "too masculine" to him. . . . And one of his women friends, whom he had asked to come with him, was available. No one else in the room knew who she was. No one made a sound. She was co-opted unanimously to the leadership of what was then called the "noncommunist Left." Thus began the political career of Edith Cresson.[27]

Edith Cresson's nomination as prime minister was inevitably tainted by this past relationship. Certainly a past intimacy should not exclude a person from appointment to a high governmental position, and wasn't Mitterrand once again usefully breaking a taboo? But if justice must not only be justice, but have the appearance of justice, then in practical terms another woman, without the encumbrance of a past with Mitterrand, would have been a better trailblazer.

Matters were only complicated when Cresson took as her principal advisor a man who soon appeared to insiders as a sort of Svengali, having extraordinary sway over the new prime minister. Abel Farnoux gave the appearance, with no apparent objection from her, of dominating rather than advising the head of government. Farnoux "didn't change his mode of relating to Edith Cresson," from when she had been minister for European affairs and then in the private sector, forgetting that she had become prime minister.

> [Behavior that] had already surprised more than one visitor [when she had been] Minister of European Affairs now fed harmful and unnecessary rumors. Farnoux, without the least hesitation, showed up at will in the head of government's office, even if she was in a meeting with a visitor. He addressed her in the familiar [tu] form, interrupted the conversation, or joined it, then left, sometimes only to come back. . . . At lunches where he was very often present, he would take the floor and not give it back. He talked in the place of the prime minister, who let him do so indulgently. . . . The press started to speak of a "guru" or "father image," a sort of "mysterious" influence of Abel on Edith.[28]

Possibly Cresson's use of Abel Farnoux had everything to do with Mitterrand. After all, why would France's first woman prime minister, conscious of her place in history, adopt such an omnipresent advisor as this man? Perhaps her idea was precisely to put some distance between her and Mitterrand. Perhaps the idea was that Farnoux, rather than making her appear a dominated woman, would be a rampart against domination of her prime ministership by Mitterrand. Edith Cresson was, in sum, short on Machiavellian insight.

This all too visible, controversial relationship with Farnoux, plus the evidence or supposition about her relationship with François Mitterrand, allowed the media soon to allege that hidden behind her strong, decisive exterior was a teleprompted woman who had, not on her own merit, been named prime minister of France. This critical image was devastatingly reinforced by the popular nightly political television satire, the *Bébette Show* (The Little Animals Show), in which puppets, animal caricatures of political leaders (Mitterrand as a Frog, Baymond Barre as a Bear, etc.) conducted a nightly mockery of the government. It was natural for the new prime minister to be caricatured, but in this situation the effect was devastating. "Amabotte" (roughly translated as "At My Boot," was the character chosen to represent Cresson. Amabotte's boot-licking slavishness to the Frog was an image that unfortunately stuck to her.

Cresson wanted to believe that being the prime minister ipso facto settled any questions of who was in charge, and the gap between what she and others perceived was enormous. Thus she didn't hide Farnoux's unusual role in her government. For her, it was a matter of letting the truth be perceived as such. For others, however, it was a double mistake: a lack of political gravitas, of the capacity to be genuinely in charge, and her lack of political public relations acumen. Cresson unfortunately alleged a "Vichyite pattern" of "rumor and secret denunciation."[29] The political class as a whole was out to destroy her prime ministership, thus to nullify Mitterrand's breaking of misogynist taboo at the top of the French state. And by destroying her, she said, these adversaries (mainly competitors in the Socialist party) were out to get Mitterrand himself. "Fundamentally," she said, "they played on the fact that I am a woman, and a woman, in this country where the elites believe themselves to be advanced, doesn't have the right to be chosen by the president of the Republic, doesn't have the right to have a special advisor. They never would have acted like that with the advisor of a male head of government."[30]

Mitterrand defended Cresson for months, taking a tough line especially with the Rocardian Socialists who had been outraged when the president unceremoniously dumped Michel Rocard for Cresson: "What bothered the Socialists so much? They criticized me for letting Rocard go? I had let him govern, but at a certain moment I thought we were going to fall into a chasm. What did the Socialists have to say? They considered Edith to be illegitimate, sure. . . . But in the name of what did they judge her thus? Why were they opposed to her? They complicated her job unnecessarily, and it was already objectively very difficult."[31]

But Mitterrand found Cresson's lack of political savvy, the criticism and shortcomings of her job as prime minister, to be finally too much. In a wrenching moment (they were after all "old friends" and Mitterrand had given her a considerable honor in the beginning), the president let go of the Cresson experiment in a bitter finish; in its way it was a bit like having had to abandon the socialist experiment *en catastrophe,* out of control. Cresson was replaced with Pierre Bérégovoy despite an intense and personal battle she fought behind closed doors with Mitterrand to keep her post. At the end she sent a harsh letter of resignation to him, alleging that he hadn't stood up for her against the injustices of her intransigent adversaries. Mitterrand, in a break with tradition, did not make public the entire contents of the prime minister's letter. Cresson, ever refusing to the play the game, sent a copy to *Le Monde.*[32] Mitterrand had not resisted the Socialist party seigneurs, the party "barons" and "elephants"; he had let her be pushed out, a personal as well as political betrayal. She had felt he would do whatever was necessary against the opposition and the criticism she faced. She told her entourage that she was disgusted with "that guy" *(ce type),* a colloquialism again suggesting a personal relationship.

Did François Mitterrand, as Cresson obviously thought, have the courage to appoint her but not the courage to see the struggle through against opponents? Or was Edith Cresson, whatever the misogyny she faced, unable to recognize her own shortcomings as a leader, blaming Mitterrand and Socialist party adversaries instead? Did she think, falsely, that her past with Mitterrand made her politically safe? And what made Mitterrand overestimate the woman he selected to break the taboo in France against a female prime minister? All these issues were no doubt involved.

Edith Cresson's resignation was not only a farewell to office, it was a good-bye to François Mitterrand, whom she avoided thereafter. At Mitterrand's insistence the Balladur cohabitation government in 1993 named her to a European Commission position. They met only once thereafter, on an official occasion, and she decided to attend—reconciliation beyond the tomb—Mitterrand's funeral mass. It cannot be said that France's first woman prime minister had a passage uncomplicated by the fact that she was female.

"MITTERRAND BY NIGHT"

Beyond the case of Edith Cresson, in François Mitterrand's relations with women in politics, were the women politicians first or women first? This is a harder question than his reputation would allow. Mitterrand certainly used his political renown to find girlfriends for an evening, to gain access to women. But Mitterrand also made the careers of more than several women in politics, some (at least) of whom were not former lovers.

In a larger view Mitterrand's political relationships with women were clearly but one version—adjusted to "la difference"—of his relationships with people in politics generally. Mitterrand treated woman and men, adjusted for the "difference," similarly, whether in politics or in private life. Politically, if Mitterrand was a Machiavellian republican, then on the personal level he was a Machiavellian existentialist. He surely took advantage of numerous women in the traditional manner of the man of power. But on the other hand with the important women in his life, the permanent relationships, there seems to have been reciprocity. He seems to have conceded to his wife, companions, or other serious women friends the freedoms, sexual and otherwise, he took for himself, despite a strong penchant for jealousy and control. (For example, Paris gossip had Mitterrand sighted on Sunday strolls along the quai together with Danielle and her "exercise coach," who for a time roomed in the rue de Bièvre house.) How this affected him or whether his women would have preferred a different life with him, as a conventional couple, is another matter. His explanation (and that of Dumas according to Christine Deviers-Joncour) resembled Sartre's with de Beauvoir: that women should seize their existential freedom to live as authentic beings rather than dependent on a man; that they are, like men, free to live as they choose, so long as it is authentic. If such women suffered from such men, this resulted from free choice; and very few women, so said the men, quit them.[33]

One Mitterrand chief of staff reports a spirited conversation with him about faithfulness in a couple, in which a government minister—a loyalist and a man about town himself—objected that these things were different for him, "because you, in any case, Mr. President, are profoundly amoral." Mitterrand's response was not to send a bolt of lightning or to launch an elaborate discussion of the meanings of morality, but to say, "And I hope you are not one of those men who permit themselves every liberty but would not tolerate one single second that a woman allows herself the same?"[34] Some women, French and American, will think that this is an astute line which, given male-female differences, is a trap.

The American novelist William Styron, a valued foreign invitee in Mitterrand's entourage, tells this story in a *New Yorker* magazine essay on American puritanism in the Clinton sex scandals:

> In May of 1981, on the day of François Mitterrand's inaugural, I stood amid a
> small circle of people gathered near the new President in the lush garden of the

Élysée Palace. Mitterrand had a fondness for writers, and I, along with Arthur Miller and Carlos Fuentes, had been invited to the occasion. The sunny weather was almost perfect; the historic nature of the moment caused people to speak in excited, mildly alcoholic murmurs, and Mitterrand himself rocked back and forth on his heels, wearing his new grandeur with a look of numb surprise. But mainly I recall a subtle and hovering eroticism. Sex drifted on the air like perfume. Several of the admirers surrounding Mitterrand were lovely young women in their spring dresses; as they left his side, one by one, each twittered, "A bientôt, François!" A French journalist I knew, standing next to me, whispered amiably, "And you can bet they will be back soon."[35]

Styron adds to the above, "Mitterrand had a slew of girlfriends. Everybody knew about it and nobody gave a damn, least of all the members of the press who had been aware for years." French political culture was very different from the American, and journalists didn't want to jeopardize their access or jobs by breaking ranks. Styron judges that "Mitterrand had a character that was deeply flawed—many Frenchmen still hate him—but his Presidency was creative and illustrious." A Mitterrand biographer adds a complementary anecdote, full of irony: "Reading a DGSE [secret service] report one day on Gorbachev's sex life, the president exclaimed in horror, 'It's really scandalous that there should be reports on such subjects!'"[36] In ribald moments Mitterrand avowed that such high-level carnal advantages were in themselves "reason enough" to be in power.

THE PRESIDENT'S "SECOND" FAMILY

A *Paris-Match* long-range camera lens finally revealed in fall 1994 what most of the French political class had known for years: François Mitterrand had a natural, out-of-wedlock daughter, called Mazarine. Her mother was Anne Pingeot, a museum curator who oversaw nineteenth-century sculpture at the Musée d'Orsay, whose relationship with Mitterrand went back more than twenty years.

Mitterrand and Anne first met in passing in the early 1960s but didn't become involved until 1969. She was the daughter of a Clermont-Ferrand industrialist, Pierre Pingeot, an acquaintance Mitterrand encountered often on the golf course at Hossegor. Although Anne was much younger (again a younger woman), and although François was married, there was an obvious romantic attachment between the two, which the Pingeot family seems to have accepted or perhaps just couldn't prevent. Of course at the first meeting François Mitterrand had been still the man of the Observatory affair whereas at the end of the 1960s he was the French Left's unchallenged leader. Anne was a serious, successful student, who would become a recognized art historian.

Born December 18, 1974 at Avignon, Mazarine was legally recognized only ten years later, in 1984, by then President François Mitterrand. The notarized act of recognition specified, however, that this new status for Mitterrand's daughter would not be revealed until after his death.[37] Legal recognition probably was connected to the fact that Mazarine's safety had become an issue for Mitterrand from the time of his election. Her existence was known fairly widely in the Paris milieu and she could easily become a target for kidnapping or other damage. There was a particular watch on the writer and eccentric Jean-Édern Hallier, whose novels Mitterrand in the 1970s had praised in the *Nouvel Observateur* magazine (still a fresh literary interest) but who later turned violently against him. In 1984 he intended to publish a story on the secret of Mazarine, and the Élysée's "anti-terrorist cell" overheard conversations threatening a kidnapping. They had to be taken seriously even though Hallier was somewhat of a crackpot.[38] Mazarine and Anne Pingeot had bodyguards from 1981 on, and moved from their small rue Jacob apartment in the sixth arrondissement into a government building on the Quai Branley near the Eiffel Tower. Protecting them became part of the duties of the Élysée anti-terrorist cell.

When *Paris-Match* published its photos of the president and his daughter in 1994, Mitterrand had in any case already begun to disclose his paternity. Confronted with a journalist's question in 1993 as to whether it was true he had an illegitimate daughter, Mitterrand replied sharply, "Yes it's true, and so what? It's none of the public's business." This was an answer an American president could only dream of! Then in October 1994 Mazarine attended a state dinner with her father in honor of the Emperor of Japan, and she accompanied Mitterrand on a visit to South Africa where she was introduced to Nelson Mandela.

Although the public didn't know it, President Mitterrand often, at times almost always, went home at night to Anne, Quai Branly, not to Danielle in their house in the rue de Bièvre across from Notre Dame Cathedral. Under the circumstances did it make sense to refer to Anne Pingeot as Mitterrand's "mistress" or was she his common-law wife, and more his wife than the woman he had legally married long ago? Had that legal marriage not been turned over the years into a shield against questioning of Mitterrand's moralities? But then was not his still regular if truncated family life with Danielle, her sister and their brother-in-law, the two sons and their families also a genuine family life? Did Mitterrand not in fact have two families, a social arrangement that would not cause comment in certain other societies? And did it matter whether, as was rumored, Anne Pingeot had originally given birth against Mitterrand's wishes, that this arrangement had not been planned by Mitterrand?

For years in any case they had owned a modest country house together in Gordes, near a real estate agency that François, with financial help from friends, had set up for her in the 1970s. One well-informed biographer described the different roles that each played: "Danielle, that was the real Left, an activist. Anne was the world of arts, an aesthete. For three decades, François Mitterrand lived between these two women. . . . That's his nature. He is an equilibrist. . . . He compartmentalized. Christmas with Anne; New Year's Day with Danielle. He kept groups of people separate: Roussel, Grossouvre, Badinter, that was with Anne. Lang, Bergé, Kiejman, that was with Danielle. Only a few, such as Charasse or Dumas, were part of both circles."[39]

From the middle of his first term many of his "home" weekends were taken with Anne and Mazarine at the Château de Souze-la-Briche, a state property whose twenty rooms and 246 hectares of woods were at the president's call. In 1988 Mazarine, then thirteen years old, wanted to follow her father's campaign for reelection as president. How to keep her safe? How to mask what was going on? A Club of Young Friends of François Mitterrand was set up, chaperoned usually by the lawyer-friend Charles Salzman, and run logistically in the campaign by Jean Glavany. In this group Mazarine traveled the country incognito attending her father's campaign meetings for several weeks. Glavany tells the story of how, at a huge rally at Paris-Le Bourget, she maneuvered a place center aisle so she could hand him a rose as he left the stadium, "with 60,000 people looking on but not seeing."[40]

The "second family" gradually became Mitterrand's priority during his second term—and Mazarine became the special focus of his affection. The president lived most of his family life, as said, with Anne and Mazarine, going home at night regularly to their Quai Branly presidential annex apartment.[41] After leaving office and terminally ill, Mitterrand moved to a separate, austere apartment in the avenue Frédéric-Le-Play, near the École militaire, the Seine, and the Eiffel Tower. He could suffer his illness in his own way, and with alternating visits by his two families. Mazarine became more than ever at this moment the most cherished person in his life, and she alone had a bedroom in the Frédéric-le-Play apartment, to be nearest to her father, the one who might divert his attention from the pain.

Images of the "two families" together at Mitterrand's funeral affected an international public and many Americans. They believed this to be "very French," but this wasn't French at all. It was an error to assume that Mitterrand had been open about Anne and Mazarine all along, that, as some said, he was an open bigamist or polygamist. He had kept the matter private and made it open only as, over the years, his affection for Mazarine grew far beyond what he had expected and he wanted publicly and against the grain of French bourgeois morality to recognize her and legitimize her status. In France as in other countries some men will father and discretely support children born out of wedlock. But a "second family" was to break a taboo, despite the false impression foreigners still have of the assumed "sophistication" of the French in attitudes toward marriage and family. The issue for Mitterrand had, in other words, not been the desire to make Anne Pingeot into a second wife but Mazarine into a true daughter. Mitterrand's testament gave Mazarine the rights and control of his entire literary legacy, emphasizing her special personality and place in his life and providing her an official economic inheritance.[42]

Danielle Mitterrand behaved stoically as she had for so long, saying that she had known about Mazarine's existence almost from the beginning (her sister Christine Gouze was cowardly deputized by François to tell her), and that she had accepted the girl completely. "There was no decision to take," she said, "because she was François's daughter." But of course there had been a "decision" to take on her part and she was telling public opinion not to think her a victim, that she took responsibility for her situation and in any case it was not, just as François had said, a public matter.

In a rare television interview after François's death, Danielle finally said what everyone had supposed, "Yes, François was a great *séducteur* [ladies' man]; I had to live with it." The French journalist Sylvie-Pierre Brosselette had put it another way, "To be loved interested him less, it would seem, than seduction itself."

Danielle Mitterrand's militant leftist views often exasperated François, although some of her contacts were useful. She was a friend of Salvador Allende's widow, Hortenzia, who was often an official Élysée guest. And she also in the 1980s became friends with Liu Shaoqi's much-esteemed wife, Wang Guangmei. But Danielle was officially denounced by the Turkish government over private visits by her to Turkish Kurdistan, and for her public advocacy of aid and human rights for the Kurds. One characteristic episode during the last presidential year occurred when she "dropped by" the Élysée palace to lobby her husband, who would see Fidel Castro later that day, to commit to a visit to Cuba. "If only after leaving office," she pleaded her case to the very sick man, in order to cheer the Cuban people and to show opposition to the U.S. embargo. Mitterrand asked her sardonically if she didn't have something to add about Cuban political prisoners.[43]

Since her husband's death she has continued her human rights activism. As president of her own human rights foundation, France-Libertés, she attended the celebrated international Zaptista rebel conference called by Subcommandante Marcos in July 1996 in Chiapas, Mexico, and she has made many other such trips. Her memoir, *En Toutes Libertés* (Liberty in All Its Forms), now two volumes, talks little of her relationship with François.[44] Suffice it to say that Danielle, although nearly silent, was clearly hurt by her husband's life with other women. But she chose not to discuss their personal life in public. One American commentator wrote after her husband's death that "She remains an exasperatingly innocent woman. She is melancholy, wistful, unrealistic—a Lady Bountiful visiting the Cubans and the Kurds and the Tibetans, all of whose causes she has championed and patronized."[45] The focus on her innocence was well taken. After a married life so far from what she might have expected, she clearly remained in love with, and fascinated by, François Mitterrand. Anne Pingeot, for her part, has said little or nothing in public of her life with Mitterrand.

Extravagantly, there was also the third woman in Mitterrand's life during his presidency, the Swedish journalist Cristina Forsne. Their intimate relationship, at first sexually charged but easing into companionship as François aged and became ill, lasted almost the entire fourteen years of his presidency. It began with an interview, soon after which she moved to Paris, becoming a regular lunch or dinner partner in the Élysée. She accompanied him on several foreign trips, camouflaged by a "beard," who pretended to be her escort. Mitterrand, as said above, greatly enjoyed her spirited company; she had no hope of becoming the first woman in his life and so was frank and teasing with him. She had considerable psychological insight, especially into his own character, perhaps more than either of his "two wives." With her, François was able to drop the mask and he could remember what it was like to have a normal conversation. She provided a down-to-earth female intellectual/political/sensual companionship that Danielle, the idealist, could not. Cristina's "buckaroo behavior," as one aide put it, worried Mitterrand's entourage, but it all ended well enough, although it was rumored she had wanted to have a child by him. She published a quick memoir, informally titled *François* to show their intimacy, which appeared first in Swedish in 1996, then in French in 1997.[46] The book was criticized by Roland Dumas and other Mitterrand associates for errors and its tone of self-importance. But no one denied the story of their long relationship.

The French people forgave Mitterrand these "sins," perhaps, foreigners will say, because they are sophisticated and amoral, perhaps because their Catholic traditions teach that sins can be forgiven, or perhaps because it was not their business. Unlike the situation in American political culture or British political tradition, neither Mitterrand nor the French in general believe that the head of state's function is to be a grand moral example to the people. In contrast to the weight put on the necks of recent American presidents by public prudishness and prurience, abetted by the American media, François Mitterrand did not have to moralize or discuss his private life (let alone his sexual life) to do his job. If Mitterrand was reproached by some of the French people for his morality, at least as many respected a double life discreetly done.[47] Mitterrand was surprised in 1994-1995, making an arduous round of political good-bye appearances urged on him by Roland Dumas and others because "one doesn't just depart without saying goodbye," that he seemed, in spite of all the controversies surrounding him, to have become genuinely liked by the mass of French people, especially in the provinces. One could not say about Mitterrand as it was said about de Gaulle, that he "loved France but despised the French."

Mitterrand as already said, offended and infuriated critics by rarely admitting a mistake or offering an apology. Yet he was not the first Fifth Republic president to operate in this manner. And the reason was not that he thought himself infallible—the Observatory affair was always a useful reminder of that—but because in French political culture to do either is perceived as weakness and, in the French Machiavellian republic, has been perceived as an invitation not just to criticism but to defection, betrayal, and revolt. An old proverb says that "When an oak falls, everyone becomes a woodcutter." In contemporary American political culture, on the other hand, constant apology has become politically correct "sensitivity." Not to be quick to apologize, even hypocritically, is, for an American leader today perceived as a character flaw.

DEATH

Mitterrand answered the first existentialist question, whether to commit suicide, in a characteristic way: The worst thing he said when asked if he feared death, "is not death but no longer to be alive." Such valuing of this life on its own merit was clearly enough a denial by this lapsed Catholic of the idea of an afterlife. Death is the end of life, thus the end of all possibility of a moral, authentic life, the end of all possibilities. All Mitterrand wanted was that his self-orchestrated, private death would still matter, that he would will to the end and "not die amidst indifference." He wanted desperately to matter even in death, because it would be his last conscious moment of mattering.

Mitterrand's agony was worse than all but a narrow group of family and intimate associates were allowed to see. Georges Benamou, a young journalist, was taken on to put Mitterrand's memoirs into some kind of order and to write the story of Mitterrand's last days. Their work together began in 1993 when Mitterrand first thought he might be close to the end. Benamou's *The Last Mitterrand* is the report of someone allowed to witness almost all of the last difficulties, the last agonies.[48] It was, on one hand, a contemporary cancer story like all the others; the worst is the constant pain, unendurable even for the willpower of a François Mitterrand, who complained constantly as he faded in and out of awareness. But it is also a story of a kind of victory over a usually more efficient illness. However much his capacity to function as president was diminished, François Mitterrand finished his second term.

Mitterrand's home life in his last two years as president was divided mainly between the Élysée and the Quai de Branly apartment of Anne and Mazarine Pingeot. His time with Danielle and the first family was limited usually to Sunday dinners at their house in the Rue de Bièvre. Mitterrand became the prey of the media, hoping for some revealing glimpse of a preeminent sick man who had by necessity become a virtual recluse.

In the last months Mitterrand arrived at the "office," on days when he didn't remain in bed at home Quai de Branly, about 9:30 A.M. He took the elevator up to the second floor where the presidential offices are located, and went over only the most pressing appointments and papers with his secretaries and then closed himself in his Élysée bedroom. Except for a minimum of paper work and meetings with others, such as the weekly Wednesday cabinet meetings with the Balladur government and greeting foreign guests, he saw only a few aides, especially Anne Lauvergeon, his assistant chief of staff, Michel Charasse, and Christian Dufour, and he often ate lunch alone, although sometimes his sister Geneviève or his brother-in-law Roger Hanin kept him company. Cristina Forsne returned to Sweden in order not to complicate the situation even more.

Mitterrand's capacity even to initial documents became limited, and administration slowed sharply. But cohabitation with a conservative government, Hubert Védrine said, suddenly was a blessing because it put so much presidential power into the prime minister's office that "It suits us fine. The Matignon people are of good will. It would be easy for [prime minister] Balladur and [his chief of staff Nicholas] Bazir to short-circuit us. But oddly they are playing fair."[49]

Mitterrand's appearance in the human comedy neared its appointed end. He came to dread the weekly council of ministers' meetings and other unavoidable encounters such as the national defense council or visits by heads of state. Every time he shook a hand it was, he said, as if his counterpart was taking his pulse, hoping perversely for some personal scoop to gossip around Paris. At meetings he had to sit upright for hours, constantly worried he might experience some physical failure which, through ministerial leaks, would feed media speculation about whether the last days had not arrived. At one council of ministers meeting Mitterrand suddenly lost his voice (the cancer in the last weeks of 1994 reached his vocal cords), couldn't finish a sentence and had to go dramatically silent. His body was, in effect, dying bit by bit. Often among family and friends he fell asleep at the end of a sentence, or his attention wandered sitting right in front of another person.

In his last televised New Year's Eve greetings to the country Mitterrand added a calculated spiritual touch: "Next year it will be my successor who will express his good wishes to you. From where I will be at that moment, I will listen to him with a heart full of thanks to the French people who have confided their destiny to me for such a long time. . . . I believe in *les forces de l'esprit* [the forces of the spirit] and I will not leave you."[50]

François Mitterrand died in his sleep early in the morning of January 8, 1996, by his own decision to stop the medication that had been keeping him alive. Death came in the rather small, third-floor, state-owned apartment, avenue Frédéric-le-Play, in the eighth arrondissement, where he lived after leaving office between his two families. His doctor Jean-Pierre Tarot first alerted Anne and Mazarine Pingeot, who came immediately for a last moment with the body before Dr. Tarot gave the news to Danielle Mitterrand and their sons.

MITTERRAND'S "LAST SECRET," DR. GUBLER'S REVELATION

François Mitterrand's "last secret" was the stunning posthumous revelation by his former physician that a metastasized prostate cancer had been diagnosed, not when it was announced in 1992 at the first of two operations, but already in November 1981. That is, Mitterrand had been faced with this disastrous medical report only a few months after arriving in power, at the very beginning of his fourteen-year presidency.

Mitterrand decided his illness was to be a "state secret." He ordered his doctor, Claude Gubler, to conspire with him, directly contrary to his "republican" promise to be the first French president to publish regular medical bulletins. Mitterrand's cancer was to be treated as a reason of state lie, necessary for the good of the state. The prognosis then was an average survival of three months to three years, but, remarkably, François Mitterrand's cancer went into remission and he went eleven years before surgery was required, fourteen before it carried him away.

Gubler's book was published in January 1996, not even two weeks after Mitterrand's death. It was a coincidence according to the doctor. He said he had wanted Mitterrand to respond, that he wanted a debate on medical and political ethics. Forty thousand copies of *Le Grand Sécret* were sold in two weeks before a temporary injunction won by Mitterrand's family took it off the shelves.

In France Claude Gubler has been widely condemned for revealing Mitterrand's illness, as a violation of the doctor's ethic of medical confidentiality. For eleven years he signed false medical reports, although he could have resigned, until 1992 when the first of Mitterrand's two prostate operations was the occasion for the president to reveal that he had a cancer, although he still did not disclose when it first had been diagnosed. Gubler's action has been unjustly disdained in France, as merely publicity seeking and self-enrichment. He has had his medical license and other professional privileges revoked.

In France there is still no law concerning presidential medical fitness, but there is the precedent of President Georges Pompidou's shocking, unexpected death in 1974. Hiding such a grave illness, not just for a while but right up to the end when death hit public opinion as a total surprise, left a question mark in French politics. What guidelines must a president respect in a democracy concerning health reports to the public?

In the 1974 presidential campaign necessitated by Pompidou's death, Valéry Giscard d'Estaing, running against François Mitterrand, promised accountability, saying that if elected he would make regular and full disclosures of medical examinations. He didn't follow through and rumors regularly circulated of his "fragility," that he was ill with depression and/or other problems.[51] In 1981 Mitterrand promised accountability against Giscard's failure to honor his word, assuring that a left-wing president could be relied on to honor the people's right to transparent government.

How to balance the ethic of medical confidentiality against the public's right to information about the health of its leaders, especially when the politician himself has made a promise of disclosure? Dr. Gubler readily admitted, in a medical ethics inquiry in June 1996, that his late disclosure had violated the medical obligation of confidentiality. He claimed that, caught between two codes of honor, he had finally if belatedly chosen the higher good by bringing the issue to public debate, making repentance for having signed false medical bulletins, albeit under presidential order to hide a "state secret," twice a year for a decade.

What should the good doctor have done in the Mitterrand case? The social and political circumstances cannot be ignored. The diagnosis of cancer was first made in late 1981, soon after Mitterrand took office. The Socialist experiment had already begun to get out of control. Because Mitterrand was so crucial to the political situation, because no other conceivable leader could successfully have replaced him, it made sense that to announce his illness at that point literally risked destabilizing French politics domestically, and perhaps the European situation then approaching the tensest period of the Euromissile crisis.

Plausibly a "state secret" was at issue, grounds for invoking reason of state calculations. But the problem for Gubler was that the first decision to keep silent was a special constraint, since a later revelation would have raised the question of why the doctor had kept silent in the first place. It was a situation clearly beyond

Gubler's responsibilities as a mere general physician, especially one with no previous experience or training in the legal aspects of his unexpected role.

But is the burden of proof really on Dr. Gubler? He kept his silence for long years, respecting Mitterrand's injunction, revealing "Mitterrand's last secret" only after his president had left office. What is surprising is that the French courts and media questioned the propriety of Mitterrand's own action so little. The legal decisions against Gubler had more to do with invasion of the Mitterrand family privacy, the French emphasis, than with questions of medical ethics in government.

But what if Mitterrand's responsibility, rather than Dr. Gubler's, is the focus? Did the president's behavior not violate what in America is called "the public's right to know" about vital matters concerning its top governmental leader? The answer is almost without question in the affirmative. We must naturally first take into account the difference between the French and American experience, the fact that French public opinion's right to know as a routine matter of governance has just been evolving in the past few decades. But even then, Mitterrand's unambiguous promise to the French electorate of regular, honest disclosure of his health set a clear standard. To go back on such a promise could only have been justified on reason of state grounds, which is of course what happened.

But even then, should Mitterrand, given the three-month to three-year prognosis of survival, have resigned immediately in November 1981, when the diagnosis was made, or at least announced his illness (it was after all a metastasized, advanced cancer), whether because of his "republican values" promise to public opinion or just the memory of the trauma of President Pompidou's "sudden" death? Or should we say that with a prognosis of "normal" hope of up to three years' survival, he was correct not to resign immediately, yet nonetheless wrong to hide this sword of Damocles now suspended over his presidency? Or, given his promise, was his moral responsibility not merely to reveal his illness but to put in place a standing advisory group—medical and governmental—to ascertain his competency? But would he not therein—back to the risky political situation he had created—have weakened the "union of the Left," the socialist experiment and NATO's united front in the Euromissile crisis, compromising French and European political stability at a particularly dangerous moment?

And what should be said of President Mitterrand's "order" to Gubler to consider his illness a "state secret"? Mitterrand had bound himself to issue honest medical bulletins, and he may, in American terms, have abused his office, committed an abuse of presidential power, in swearing Gubler to a state secret, making him a co-conspirator against his will.[52] But was such presidential authority, such wide discretion, not an established tradition of the French

Machiavellian Fifth Republic, one which Mitterrand had every right to claim as the successor to de Gaulle, Pompidou, and Giscard d'Estaing?

Was Mitterrand's solution a corrupt one? In fact he had broken his republican promise to inform the citizens about his health. But his decision to declare the diagnosis of his illness a "state secret" was a successful Machiavellian move. The end here justified the means for Mitterrand the Machiavellian, although he had originally intended, sincerely, to behave with democratic accountability in this matter. This was an act, in Mitterrand's calculation, to be judged on its success—and effective it was, not just in keeping him in office but in avoiding a dangerous political destabilization. Had the cancer progressed quickly, Mitterrand would have had to resign, like it or not.

Was Dr. Gubler's revelation of the president's lie a crime, an invasion of family privacy, or a service to the future of the republic? Each did what he had to do, with the rules for this situation still very much to be defined in contemporary democracies, as the 1982 near-fatal assassination of President Ronald Reagan showed in the American case and as the grotesque perseverence of President Yeltsin showed in the Russian case. Here the questions can only be posed. They await answers by specialists of medical ethics and constitutional law and still other fields.

In his last months in 1994 to 1995 on the rare occasions when a timorous press asked whether he would resign because of illness, the president stonily responded that he would certainly resign if necessary, but only if he was no longer able to carry out the duties of office, only if "the pain became too much," a refrain of terminal cancer patients everywhere. Mitterrand's decision to try to finish out his term had many motivations—the pain had not yet extinguished all desires for this world. But at the center of his determination to stay was the concern to stay intellectually in charge of his life, to be existentially free until death took, as it inevitably would, his last and most vital possession, his power of will.

After Mitterrand's death many commentators tried to explain why some French people, especially Socialist politicians and voters, had resented him at the end, especially violently at the personal level. Criticism of his policies was much more muted than how people felt about Mitterrand as a person.

Perhaps the issue was anger that Mitterrand had had it so many different ways. He had been president without having to relinquish his extravagant private life; he had been reelected without having to stop lying; he had delected the French *comédie humaine* without being overthrown by it. For those whose primary feeling toward Mitterrand was *ressentiment,* the issue was presumptuousness, the taking of advantage, which the presidential existentialist saw no reason not to do. Mitterrand, many people felt, had not sacrificed, paid enough for the privilege of being president. At most he complained about the cage of constraints a leader inhabits, but for him the bars of this cage were jello and escape was easy. The French presidential palace is far from the bubble in which an American president lives.

At the same time, surely the resentment and dislike of Mitterrand's playing of the human comedy was homage to an actor of uncanny skills and psychological insight. Mitterrand really was far and away the master politician of his generation.

CHAPTER 11

MITTERRAND *AGONISTES:* VICHY YET A LAST TIME (FALL 1994)

Vichy was a *pétaudière* [a mass of confusion]. It is wrong to imagine
it as a Nazi regime. It wasn't the way one describes it today.

—François Mitterrand, 1994

Fortune appears sometimes purposely to wait for the last year of our
lives in order to show us that she can overthrow in one moment what
she has taken long years to build.

—Montaigne, *Essais*

VICHY AS HISTORY

VICHY YET A LAST TIME. François Mitterrand's right-wing youth and Vichy past
was a moot issue until it was resurrected, albeit for the first time in such detail,
in the last year of his presidency.

A detailed and complex account was published by the journalist Pierre Péan
in September 1994. The dying president had to face up to his wartime record once

again, fifty years after the facts. Péan's book, *Une Jeunesse Française: François Mitterrand 1934-47,* came to benign, disculpatory conclusions about Mitterrand's World War II record, but it nevertheless launched a last great firestorm over the controversial path of France's representative man. For a few weeks in fall 1994 Montaigne's warning about fortune's capacity to destroy a life even at the end seemed about to apply to the mortally ill French president. Had François Mitterrand, according to a Latin maxim, "lived too long by just one day"?

Chapter 3 told the factual story of Mitterrand's wartime record. In this chapter the 1994 debate is the focus—the context of young Mitterrand's choices, the nature of Vichy, the significance of historical context, and the accounting of moral responsibility. François Mitterrand's "trial" in fall 1994 was a historical and moral lesson for the French as a nation, it was a contribution to French self-understanding.

The publication of *A French Youth* provoked widespread instances of condemnation of Mitterrand. The accusation was obvious: Finally caught out by Pierre Péan for having worked at Vichy in 1942-1943, François Mitterrand must have been a fascist or at least a collaborator. All sorts of mysteries and unanswered questions about Mitterrand, past and present, seemed suddenly to be clarified. He must have been, as long rumored, a member of the Cagoule and Action française. No matter that Péan's book, quite to the contrary, showed that Mitterrand had never joined either organization. Because of family milieu he did know members of both groups and he was surrounded with conservative and extreme Right types all through his formative years. And as a student in Paris, he had, as chapter 3 noted, joined the National Volunteers, the youth organization of Colonal de la Roque's Croix de feu, for a short time. But Péan showed he was never deeply involved and never joined the more extreme organizations.[1] Some critics further misused the Péan book as "proof" of President Mitterrand's protective attitude toward former Vichy police chief René Bousquet in the 1980s; of Vichyite morality in sending presidential wreaths on several occasions to decorate Marshal Pétain's grave; and of "ordering" justice ministers and investigating magistrates to slow down investigations into cases concerning suspected war criminals in the hope that death would defeat justice.

Had François Mitterrand, like Kurt Waldheim, escaped scrutiny for decades only to be caught out near the end of his life? Péan's book, in any case, made no such damning judgments about Mitterrand's World War II record and said nothing about his presidency. The 1994 "indictment" of François Mitterrand as a Vichyite, a collaborationist, or a fascist rested on a misuse of misunderstood evidence. But one lie doesn't efface another. In the 1994 debate there was much justifiable discomfort about episodes in Mitterrand's past and criticism about his lack of candor and/or lying.

But why had Mitterrand chosen to engage himself so much with Péan? Why did the president supply him with all sorts of documents and letters so as to make *A French Youth* a kind of authorized story? When Péan originally approached Mitterrand, research for the book was already advanced and his attitude toward the president was not particularly friendly. He had already dug far deeper than any other researcher had done and would publish in any case. Mitterrand surely wanted to cut his losses and influence Péan's interpretations. And since there were in fact no treasonous skeletons in Mitterrand's World War II closet, better to get the whole story out while he could still fight for his own version of events rather than rely on historians when he was gone.

Yet why had Mitterrand never told his Vichy story completely before? Surely one reason was to avoid handing adversaries an easy crack in his armor. Husbanding his image and ensuring his electability remained paramount. "It would be an exaggeration to say that the early life of President François Mitterrand was a state secret," one veteran foreign journalist observed dryly, "but as long as he was a politician with another election ahead of him, he ensured that an aura of mystery surrounded the years before he emerged as a Socialist leader."[2] Not a gaullist and thus not immunized by de Gaulle's own legitimacy (unlike Prime Ministers Michel Debré and Maurice Couve de Murville, who had both, we saw earlier, also worked at Vichy before going into the Resistance), Mitterrand, all along his road to power and in power, risked major political damage if the story came out. But now, at the end of his role in the play, he could afford disclosure. In fact, he needed it for the next stage in his ambition, his place in history. For decades, prudence had meant secrecy; now prudence needed disclosure.

Finally there was the comparison of Mitterrand as France's man and de Gaulle as France's hero, in a parallel suggested by Stanley Hoffmann:

> Another [explanation for Mitterrand's disclosure] is both political and psychological. His contribution to Péan may be his own last public settlement of accounts with de Gaulle. . . . The story revealed by Péan is indeed that of a *jeunesse française,* far more typical of the average Frenchman, even of the average non-Communist *résistant,* than the story of Charles de Gaulle. Wasn't this [Péan] book a way of exorcising the ghost of the great man, telling the French: He was an exception, he wasn't really like us, but you, my friends, were very much like me?[3]

VICHY IN REALITY

The Vichy regime headed by Pétain has become a blurred stereotype in popular memory, dark and totally unredeemed, just as the Resistance is absolutely pure, its total opposite. De Gaulle's exterior Free France movement and the interior

Resistance were France's band of heroes in World War II; Vichy was France's evil. If Vichy was evil, its officials must have been all tainted. This "normal" conception of Vichy rules in our thoughts, it is our point of departure for any specific analysis of a historical issue. We cannot always and continually be rethinking our mental abbreviations.

But when such approximations are the basis for history and intellectual inquiry, they impose the consequences of their unexamined and often faulty assumptions. Simple good sense, not common sense, should indicate that not every gaullist was a hero, that not every Vichy civil servant was a "Vichyite," meaning a coward or a bureaucratic assassin. The Resistance was made of good and bad people, efficient and disorganized people, those dedicated to an ideal and those out for adventure. Likewise Vichy was not a cunningly engineered monolithic bloc but a jerry-built operation in which commingled collaborators, fascists, artists of revenge, and former Third Republic government civil servants continuing to do their jobs, which they really believed to be patriotic duty, and also, of course, opportunists and simple survivors. To insist on this need for distinctions and the analysis of individual responsibility is not—and far from it—to assert that Vichy and Free France were equivalent. The various Resistance movements were no place for fascists and collaborators; Vichy was no sweet home for anti-German, anti-Nazi patriots.

Vichy's complexities are in fact many, if we make an effort to sort them out. Some Vichy officials were anti-Semitic but also anti-fascist; others were collaborators but neither pro-fascist nor anti-Semitic. Still others were intensely pro-German while yet others were anti-German, and both the pro- and the anti-German Vichyites thought of themselves as French patriots. And among those who were pro-German, some idolized the invaders while others were merely resigned to unavoidable German dominance, appeasers who saw only the defeatist strategy of saving France's place in what looked to be a permanently German Europe. Still other Vichyites acted primarily in a spirit of revenge at the national level. Their motivation, as in France's defeat in the Franco-Prussian war of 1870, was to wield power at Vichy as a continuation of France's historic domestic revolutions and counterrevolutions, blindly to continue the Franco-French secular civil war of Left and Right, of Red and Black, of class egotism and class struggle. These people sought to use France's defeat by Germany, certainly unwanted but perhaps useful, to destroy old enemies. In the 1930s there were anti-parliamentarist, anti-republican fascists and Bonapartists, Monarchists, and other authoritarians. Beyond what divided them, nearly all believed that the parliamentary regime, the Third Republic—*la Gueuse,* the "slut," they called it—was responsible for France's historic decline.

French decline had been both a cause and result of Germany's rise, so the best French policy, they wrongly reasoned, was accommodation to the new irresistibly strong Germany. This was the core of the "Vichy syndrome." In that syndrome, in other words, anti-Semitism was often only one part of a general French defeatism.

VICHY AND THE JEWS

The infamous October 3, 1940, Vichy Jewish Statute was, to take an early and indicative guide, Vichy's own idea. In the historian Robert O. Paxton's words, from a short text written at the time of the 1997-1999 trial of Maurice Papon, where he was called as an expert witness: "In 1940, the Nazis wanted only to dump German Jews into unoccupied France. Yet the Vichy Government went further and registered its Jews, excluded them from jobs and forced many foreign Jews into camps. By 1942, when the Nazis began their extermination program, the French Jews were vulnerable. . . . Vichy France was the only Western European country under Nazi occupation that enacted its own measures against Jews."[4] The French historian Marc Ferro emphasizes that the Vichy Jewish Statute, officially the "Raphaël Alibert Law," was even harsher than a model law the Germans had drafted just a few days earlier as a guide for the Pétainist legislation. This law defined a Jew by race not religion, as anyone having three Jewish grandparents, or only two if a spouse was Jewish also. It banned Jews from the civil service, from teaching (Marshal Pétain, who took a personal role in drafting this law, insisted that Jews be banned from teaching as well as from the court system), and from the military command structure. In liberal professions Jews were subject to a *numerus clausus,* a quota limit. No Jew could be editor of a newspaper or write in the press, other than scientific journals, or work in positions of responsibility in the theater, radio, or cinema. "But by decree," the insidious possiblity of individual salvation, "exceptions could be made for Jews who 'had rendered exceptional service to the French State.'"[5]

The Pétaino-gaullism of the French people in 1940 to 1942 was the popular belief that despite all signs to the contrary (e.g., de Gaulle denounced the anti-Jewish measures), Pétain and de Gaulle were somehow secretly working together. This is another obstacle against seeing Vichy as a monolithic operation. In a situation of this magnitude and danger, there was much, the French supposed, that they "didn't know," an idea that helped them to go on. The French historian Philippe Burrin's summary of the different situations among the French is persuasive:

Total rejection of the occupiers was bound to be no more than marginal: A few French left for England to join de Gaulle; others moved clandestinely to the free zone where a new government, itself the product of the defeat and occupation, imposed its law. But for the vast majority there seemed no alternative but to submit, to bow before the triumphant force and adjust one's behaviour accordingly. Even those determined to resist had to appear, despite secret defiance, to compromise in the interests of their underground activities, as they waited for a superior force to bring liberation to reset the clock. Accommodation was forced upon the French people, who had to choose the least of all evils and make concessions that might or might not prove compromising.[6]

But what would be the meaning of "accommodation"? In this word's ambiguities were contained the dangers and the agonies of wagering lives, freedom, patrimonies. Burrin emphasizes the degrees of shadow in "the vast grey area that was the dominant shade in any picture of those dark years":

As a substantial minority saw it, it was hopeless to calculate and stick to a minimum degree of compromise. The kind of accommodation deliberately chosen by this minority was indulgent toward the [conquerors], sympathetic to certain aspects of their ideology and politics, desirous of agreement or *entente,* offering to be of service or even to enter their service. Some simply judged it opportune to adapt in this way at a time when the enemy's victory appeared too extensive to be reversed. As they saw it, the French had to resign themselves to living on German time. Still others believed it now indispensable to reach lasting agreement with yesterday's enemy. In their view, it was positively good for France to embrace the German power.[7]

Thus it is clear—even this basic distinction will surprise many Americans and perhaps a few French—that *Frenchmen could have been simultaneously for Pétain and anti-German.* And from these initially pro-Pétain/anti-German ranks came many résistants, including some of the best. Among them was the young François Mitterrand, who, we saw in chapter 3, was more of a *maréchaliste,* someone who admired and had hope in Pétain, the Hero of Verdun, than a *pétainiste,* someone who accepted and propagandized the Vichyite ideology of the reactionary National Revolution for France's salvation.

On the other hand, Burrin rightly warns against letting the making of distinctions run beyond reason, seeing Vichy's policies and people *only* as shades of gray. "There can be no question," he says, "of dissolving . . . collaboration within the general category of 'accommodation.' [Collaboration] was, so to speak, accommodation raised to the level of politics."[8] His language is somewhat ambiguous; his point is not. Collaboration, whatever the variations within it and however much its origins are those of accommodation, was more than accommodation. Collaboration was consciously working with the enemy on his terms and was condemnable, a national disaster.

Certainly the Vichy government became a political cesspool populated by collaborators, fascists, and Nazi sympathizers. From the beginning it was a "revenge of the old elites" against the "red" France of the 1930s, against republicans, Socialists, Communists, and the Popular Front government.[9] But others went to Vichy, took jobs there, because it was simply France's new government.

"Why," Burrin asks, "was there no massive, immediate rejection of the armistice, no hostility towards the government that signed it, no opposition to the policies that it introduced? Why such indecision regarding the occupying power. . . . It is understandable that defeat came as a shock, the behavior of the Germans as a surprise. But what about all the idolatry of the aged Marshal, the tendency to hope for a rapid return to normality . . . ?"[10] Even Marshal Pétain himself, Burrin implies, was at first more a *maréchaliste* than a *pétainiste* and collaborator. When Pétain declared on October 30, 1940, following his famous first meeting with Hitler, "I am today setting out along the road of collaboration," he did not mean to say "I am today setting out along the road of disaster" or "the road of betrayal."[11] Even Pétain did not imagine in those first months what he would choose to do or be convinced and compelled to do, acts for which he would be tried and condemned to death at war's end. Burrin's warning is useful: " . . . at the end of the road, it was quite natural to think that there had been clear and constricting choices to be made right from the start," whereas "Any history of this period should take into account just how opaque the future was. . . . In the summer of 1940, the French had no way of foreseeing the four years through which they were about to live."[12] Jean-Paul Sartre imagined the existential reality in *Nausea:* "And we have the impression that [our protagonist] lived all the details of that night like annunciations. . . . We forget that the future was not yet there."[13] Each human act is in a sense a new beginning, and no matter what the conditioning by previous acts, the possibility of a different beginning is never absent. This means that neither cowardice nor collaboration, nor even heroism is necessarily permanent.

EVALUATING MITTERRAND'S VICHY TIME

"François Mitterrand came from a provincial, Catholic and conservative background which in a general way predestined him to support the regime of Marshal Pétain; one must remember that in 1940-1942 the majority of the

French were *pétainistes*."[14] This judgment, although the opinion of a friend not free of controversy himself, suggests that Mitterrand's initial reaction to sign up at Vichy is not the most important thing. "What is important is what he became in going to the end of his conscience, to the end of what he was. His break with Vichy and his entry into the Resistance attest to a conversion all the more meritorious in that, coming from the background that he did, it required a lot of intellectual courage to rip himself away from this conformist thinking and much physical courage to chose the discomfort and risks of clandestine life."[15]

Thus Mitterrand should not be a priori reproached, let alone indicted, for having worked at Vichy during part of the war. Not all Vichy's work was collaborationist, and, as said before, many later résistants in the interior or with de Gaulle's Free France, not to mention many honorable postwar democratic leaders who didn't join the Resistance, also worked there. Questions about Mitterrand's Vichy time must concern specific acts and allegiances.

De Gaulle's *War Memoirs* mention Mitterrand once, in discussing the influence of de Gaulle's rival, General Henri Giraud, among former Vichy cadres. The passage doesn't reproach Mitterrand for his Giraudist sympathies. De Gaulle just lists him among "a series of couriers and *chargés de mission* who came and went between Algiers and metropolitan France—Pierre Guillain de Bénouville, Maurice Bourgès-Maunoury, François Closon, Louis Mangin, General Brisac, Colonel Zeller, Gaston Defferre, François Mitterrand, my nephew Michel Cailliau, and others."[16] Thus in the middle 1950s, when de Gaulle wrote his memoirs, nothing marked Mitterrand out for opprobrium. To the contrary, the list in which his name appears is and remains a recommendation of merit.

Two items especially—the photo of Mitterrand with Pétain and the *francisque* medal—symbolized the case against Mitterrand's Vichy past in the 1994 controversy. The photo, as said in chapter 3, was taken on October 15, 1942, and shows Mitterrand being received by Marshal Pétain. The third man in the photo was Marcel Barrois. Barrois was deported one year later as a résistant and died in April 1944 on the train taking him to Buchenwald. Taken out of context, this snapshot of course appears to condemn young Mitterrand as a "man of Vichy." In fact, however, the photo implies more what Mitterrand might have become, not what he did become. Fifty years later Mitterrand recalled "those twenty minutes" inside Pétain's headquarters at the Hôtel du Parc: "Pétain received us along with representatives of other social policy administrations . . . concerning a campaign to collect warm clothes. . . ."[17] Perhaps Mitterrand told the truth, perhaps not.

He was apparently tempted episodically by *pétainisme,* as indicated in a surprising private letter written in April 1942 to Marie-Claire Sarrazin, the distant cousin to whom he had developed a strong attachment after the break with Béatrice. Péan calls this Mitterrand's most intense expression of pétainist sentiments. Mitterrand wrote to "Clo" that France needs men "linked by the same faith" to survive its current ordeal:

> In France we need to be able to organize militias [*des milices*] which will enable us to wait out the end of the Germano-Russian struggle without fear for its consequences—whether Germany or Russia wins. If we are strong enough in our will, they will leave us be. That is why I don't share the worry about the government change. [Pierre] Laval is surely determined to get us out of our bad situation. If his method seems bad, do we know for sure what it is? If it allows us to endure it will be good. . . .[18]

In sum, François Mitterrand might, despite certain protections of his education and instincts, have conceivably become a true "man of Vichy"—who among us can be absolutely sure of what we will do under the pressure of circumstances? Which Jew becomes a camp guard of his fellow Jews rather than his brother's keeper? Which Frenchman (or German) hides or saves Jews, thereby putting himself at risk? The fact is that, for whatever combination of reasons, at least some of which were praiseworthy, Mitterrand did not become a "man of Vichy."

The second scandalous item was the *francisque* medal, the Vichy regime's highest civilian decoration. According to the rules, Mitterrand had to nominate himself, which he did in February or March 1943, requesting two friends, prewar rightist friends then important Vichy officials, to sponsor the nomination. What, it was said in 1994, could be more conclusive evidence of true Vichyism?

Jean Védrine was a comrade who also received the medal and also became a Resistance cadre. He had originally been more *pétainist,* more a believer in the National Revolution ideology than Mitterrand. He and several other sources interviewed by Péan testified that anti-German and Resistance networks at Vichy were using the *francisque* as camouflage, seconding each other's nominations for it. This explains why Mitterrand and other emerging Resistors asked to be nominated, and at a time, in early 1943, when even an opportunist—*especially* an opportunist—would have been cautious because the war was turning. Jean Védrine was number 2172 to receive the medal, Mitterrand, number 2202. Védrine's sponsors were Maurice Pinot and Paul Racine, while Mitterrand's were Simon Arbellot and Gabriel Jeantet. The well-known writer Paul Morand was number 2203, and Jean Védrine and Pierre Chigot were the sponsors for André Magne, number 2247, and Pierre Coursol, number 2307. Given that all these men were soon in the Resistance, it is quite plausible that the camouflage did have a purpose. Nonetheless, after the war Mitterrand was archly reproached with "having worn both the *francisque* and the Medal of the Resistance," by de Gaulle himself at one point.[19] The *francisque* was given to Mitterrand for his work at the Commissariat for POWs, not for reasons that could be called collaborationist.

Mitterrand's defense of his Vichy job was straightforward.[20] To disparage all the résistants who arrived in 1942 and 1943 by comparing them to de Gaulle and the few résistants of the first hour in 1940-1941 is unfair. And in Mitterrand's specific case remember that he himself had been a German prisoner of war until December 1941. To the extent that Mitterrand's courage was ever questioned, more than enough evidence accumulated—in the Battle of France, during his imprisonment, at Vichy, and in the Resistance—to demonstrate this man was no coward. During his missions to London and Algiers at the end of 1943 he could have obviously stayed safely abroad. Instead he returned to France, where several times "Morland" narrowly escaped the Gestapo. He took more risks than almost all French people and nearly all members of the political class. Seen in this light, Mitterrand's comportment, far from being treasonous or cowardly, can seem exemplary, as outrageous as critics will find the word.

Mitterrand's transit at Vichy is attested in another way by citing courageous men, including several subsequent prominent gaullist leaders, who had, like him, worked at Vichy before joining the Resistance. De Gaulle's foreign minister and second prime minister, Maurice Couve de Murville, was an important finance ministry official at Vichy from August 1940 until he went to Algiers in March 1943. Michel Debré, de Gaulle's first prime minister and later defense minister, in 1942 was named a council of state lawyer by the Vichy justice minister. Alexandre Parodi was a Vichy legal official before becoming one of de Gaulle's Free France lieutenants and putting together the temporary "Secretaries-General Government" at the Liberation. Parodi had rejoined the Resistance after his brother was executed by the Germans in 1942. Even Jacques Chaban-Delmas, prime minister under Georges Pompidou from 1969 to 1971 and a Compagnon de la Libération, recipient of the highest Free France decoration, had in 1941 and 1942 worked at the Vichy ministry for industrial production. Chaban's charismatic presence on national occasions, clad in his battered Resistance trench coat, became a familiar sign of patriotism over four decades on the Left as well as on the Right. His "social gaullist" profile made him sympathetic to the Left (one of his advisors from 1969 to 1971 was Jacques Delors), and his endorsement mattered a lot in questions of Resistance bona fides. It was thus significant that Chaban, who had known Mitterrand well in the Resistance, repeatedly vouched for his friend's integrity.[21]

THE WORRY ABOUT BANALIZING VICHY

Another issue in the 1994 controversy was the worry that destigmatizing the mere act of working at Vichy comforts partial rehabilitation of the Vichy regime's evils and its leaders. The inevitable result, it was argued, will be a "banalization" of Vichy, like the attempted "banalization" of the uniqueness of the Holocaust by some German scholars in the *Historikerstreit,* the historian's controversy of the 1980s. But if the task is to fight against forgetting, who is to be held accountable today for Vichy's crimes? France? All the French? The French state? The French nation? The French republic? Or, surely, certain individual people whose guilt had, or has, to be determined in each case? "And also, who must point the finger at them officially, and above all, *how,"* say French historians Eric Conan and Henry Rousso, "by what proceeding, since so many people believe that the guilty have never been brought to account?"[22]

Mitterrand's controversial response was to disculpate the "republic," that is, to separate the republic from the Vichy regime, which he said was not the true France. While the guilty men of Vichy should be held accountable, it is wrong to say the French, as a nation or a people were guilty, because the true French state was the republic that had been ousted by Vichy. Here is Mitterrand from a speech:

> Across all its history the Republic constantly had a totally open attitude which considered that the rights of citizens should apply to any person recognized as a citizen, and in particular French Jews. Therefore don't ask this Republic to render accounts! It fulfilled its duty . . . this Republic which for two centuries during which various republican regimes came and went, passed laws ensuring equality and citizenship. It was the Republic which decided that the Algerian Jews should no longer be considered a sort of inferior race. . . . The Republic always was the [government] which extended its hand to avoid racial segregation. So let us not ask the Republic to justify itself! But in 1940 there was a "French State," the Vichy regime. That was not the Republic. And from that "French State" we must ask for accounts to be rendered, I obviously agree. . . . I totally share the sense of those who want me to [condemn the Vichy regime], but the Resistance, the de Gaulle government, then the Fourth Republic and the following one, were founded on a rejection of this "French State." We must be clear about it.

A few days later, at the fiftieth anniversary commemoration of the Vel' d'Hiv dragnet, Mitterrand's respected justice minister Robert Badinter, himself a Jew and later president of the judicial Constitutional Council (1986-1995), endorsed Mitterrand's view: "the Republic cannot be considered accountable for the crimes committed by the men of Vichy, who were its enemies. . . ."[23] But the commemoration committee, which had summoned Mitterrand to speak out as president of the country, was infuriated. Since any legal French government is "the French state" at that moment, what it does "in the name of France," legitimately or not, implies that the French people had and still have a responsibility not for the crimes but for assuming the nation's past, for accepting this responsibility of history, and for continuing to search out and call to account any remaining perpetrators of crimes. This matter, they said, cannot be let go. And in any case even innocent French people, those who had no responsibility and no guilt, must, like the German people of 1933 to 1945, acknowledge that crimes were committed by the government of their nation and in their name.

Mitterrand was caught conceptually as well as politically and morally by his attempt to separate the republic from Vichy. Not in a solemn state declaration but in passing references in newspaper interviews, in September 1994 the president finally said grimly that the Vichy regime was "fundamentally condemnable." It was as if he were doing his duty as president, but keeping his personal view to himself.

To be clear, there is no evidence that François Mitterrand was ever anti-Semitic or acted out of anti-Semitism, even though many among his family and friends were involved with anti-Semitic, fascist groups. Mitterrand told Péan in weak explanation of his attitude in 1942: "I didn't think about the anti-Semitism of Vichy . . . and I didn't implement the legislation of the day or the measures being taken."[24] This of course is some sort of implicit avowal. Mitterrand could hardly have been unaware in 1942-1943 of widespread anti-Semitism in France, including the Vel' d'Hiv dragnet, as well as of Vichy's still-operative 1940 discriminatory Jewish statute. And in the 1994 presidential interviews, it was morally wrong even if legally correct to make use of Vichy's own distinction between French and non-French Jews; this amounts to justifying sending foreign Jews back to Germany from 1940 to 1942 before Vichy began itself to deport French Jews.

THE PROBLEM OF RENÉ BOUSQUET

And then there was Mitterrand's long political friendship with René Bousquet, the most explosive issue because, alone, it extended into his presidency.

Bousquet had been a genuine "man of Vichy" but a complicated case of guilt to ferret out. In 1942-1943 he had been Vichy's civilian police chief. His responsibility for crimes in this regard was crystal clear at war's end, and he was tried and convicted by the French High Court on this accusation. But further war guilt remained hidden for three decades. Until 1978 it was not known, or even alleged, that René Bousquet himself had been in charge of the infamous Vel' d'Hiv operation, the first French dragnet of Jews for deportation in July 1942. His responsibility for this heinous act of Nazi collaboration surfaced in two stages. He was first accused inconclusively in 1978 by a controversial source, another former Vichy collaborator speaking from his own longtime hideout in Spain. Then came a mass of corroborating evidence presented by Nazi hunters in 1983. How had Bousquet stayed free so long? How, with his war record, had he been accepted into French society and business circles? What was the nature of his relationship with François Mitterrand, and why did Mitterrand not break off their contacts until 1986?

Bousquet in the late 1930s had been a rising star in the prefectoral corps, the powerful Paris-appointed, nonelected "governors" of French departments. A dedicated career civil servant (the old French combination of ambition and service to the state seen as a calling), Bousquet accepted France's defeat in 1940 and, like most prefects, it must be stressed, made the switch from the Third Republic to the Vichy regime. Even a defeated France, *especially* a defeated France (so they told themselves), needed its government administration.

In spring 1942 Pierre Laval offered Bousquet the job as Vichy's chief of police. The mere fact that he had received such an offer from Vichy's most notorious collaborating politician indicates that Bousquet had, in the interim, taken a very bad road. For Pierre Laval to show such confidence in Bousquet means that he had become totally implicated in the apparatus of French collaboration with the Nazis. During 1942-1943 he was nothing less than the secretary general, the administrative head, of the Vichy regime's police, one of the key men, a central official, in Vichy's collaboration policy. But moral, political, and legal mitigation concerning René Bousquet arose from the fact that in 1943-1944 he had unquestionably helped the French Resistance, for which he had received leniency from the High Court. This leniency had enabled him to live his postwar life as a man with a hidden past. After four years' investigation of his case, Bousquet was convicted in 1949 of collaboration as the Vichy chief of police, but then absolved by the Court because of service rendered to the Resistance. He was sentenced to five years loss of civil and political rights but pardoned at the same time.

In 1978, however, Bousquet was accused in an interview in *L'Express,* given clandestinely by Louis Darquier de Pellepoix, former Vichy commissioner for Jewish questions. It was Darquier who first said Bousquet had organized the Vel' d'Hiv dragnet. By 1983 the Nazi hunter Serge Klarsfeld had unearthed the evidence showing that, unknown to the 1949 Court, Bousquet had indeed been the organizer on the Vichy side of the Vel' d'Hiv operation.

The Vel' d'Hiv operation, July 16-17, 1942, had long signified both Vichy's complicity and its autonomous responsibility in the war against the Jews. It had been the first French dragnet of French Jews—12,884 people, "foreign and stateless Jews," meaning French Jews who had been stripped of their nationality and foreign Jews who had fled to France and were being handed back to the Nazis. It followed an agreement made a few days earlier between Bousquet, as secretary general of the Vichy police, and Karl Oberg, head of the SS and the German police in occupied France. As early as May 1941 Vichy police dragnets had begun looking for Jewish males who could be arrested as "terrorists," but at that point women, children, and old people were targeted as well. Entire families were deported by Vichy under the Bousquet-Oberg agreement, as part of the "Final Solution" policy that had been launched at the beginning of 1942 in Western Nazi-occupied territories. [25]

By 1983 René Bousquet had not yet been indicted, but Klarsfeld's evidence showed that Darquier de Pellepoix's accusation in 1978 was almost certainly true. [26] For reasons to be determined, François Mitterrand, however, continued to see Bousquet in the period between 1983 and 1986. After that, apparently as a response to protests by Jewish groups and others over various war crimes cases and other World War II–related issues, Mitterrand quietly ceased all contact with him.

By that point a new trial of Bousquet was almost certain. The statute of limitations had passed on war crimes legally defined. But he could be charged with crimes against humanity, due to a de Gaulle–era legislative provision of 1964 written to keep open the prosecution of Nazis and collaborators in the French Penal Code. In the late 1980s Mitterrand's justice ministry was the first to make use of the crimes-against-humanity charge, despite the president's advice, "orders" said his critics, against new trials for World War II offenses. Mitterrand argued that new trials would do more damage to "national reconciliation" in a nation still divided than was merited by "a tardy justice meted out to a few old men for acts committed half a century ago." Like Presidents Pompidou and Giscard d'Estaing before him, his view—a utilitarian argument—was that the nation would benefit not to have "civic peace" torn up by new trials. Mitterrand denied obstructing justice with his advice to justice ministry officials to go slow in getting Bousquet to trial. His advice did not constitute an order, and his personal control over the process was far from total. The Bousquet case moved toward trial, albeit slowly. Was Mitterrand responsible, or was the slowness rather a deliberateness typical in such matters? Later, in 1984, Mitterrand denied having "protected" René Bousquet:

> It is an issue of trying to pacify the quarrels which divide the French. It's time to end the permanent civil war among the French. . . . I have always believed that my duty as president of the Republic was to work to calm national conflicts. For example it was me who, in the most difficult of circumstances, made the decision to amnesty the generals who had made the putch in Algiers [against de Gaulle in 1962]. . . . It's true that I gave advice to the ministers involved to slow down these sorts of trials . . . in order to avoid reigniting national divisions.[27]

For perspective one notes that altogether four crimes against humanity cases arose during Mitterrand's presidency. Klaus Barbie, the first, was kidnapped and extradited from Bolivia in an operation mounted directly by the Mitterrand Élysée, as part of his new Middle East and Israel policy.[28] Barbie, the "Butcher of Lyon," was convicted in a 1987 trial with worldwide publicity. Paul Touvier, who had been protected and hid for decades by church organizations, was tried, convicted, and sentenced in April 1994 to life in prison. René Bousquet himself was finally indicted in March 1991 after eight years of investigation. But he was then assassinated, apparently by a deranged rather than politically motivated individual, on June 8, 1993, just as final investigation was winding up with the trial imminent. The fourth case was that of Maurice Papon, who came to trial in 1997 and was convicted in 1998.

Mitterrand's long association with Bousquet was without the slightest doubt shocking.[29] Among other things, editorial endorsement and financial support from Bousquet's *La Dépêche du Midi* newspaper for Mitterrand's electoral campaigns had been significant over the years. The gaullist minister and electoral advisor Roger Frey in the 1965 presidential campaign emphasized to de Gaulle that one of Mitterrand's biggest electoral supporters was René Bousquet—"And who is supporting [Mitterrand] most actively in the shadows? Bousquet! . . . There's a lot to say about him!"[30] Bousquet had already partially financed Mitterrand's trip to China in 1960. Some of Bousquet's associates going back to Vichy days, in particular Jean-Paul Martin, were in Mitterrand's Fourth Republic staff. Was Bousquet giving money to Mitterrand for possible protection if his own story ever came out? It is likely. Did Mitterrand therefore protect Bousquet after Klarsfeld's evidence was made public in 1983? It is possible. But then why did Mitterrand break off with Bousquet in 1986 when the latter was not indicted until 1991?

For Mitterrand to have manipulated his justice ministry to repay Bousquet's political and electoral finance support would have been a crime. But it does not make sense that a master Machiavellian such as Mitterrand would put himself in such danger, even for a longtime supporter. But what could have been so damaging at that point that Mitterrand would risk himself to keep it hidden? Mitterrand's own Vichy past was already on the record, if not all the details of it. The most likely answer is that Mitterrand, like everyone else, had not known that Bousquet had been responsible for the Vel' d'Hiv roundup, that he heard of the possibility first in the 1978 Darquier de Pellepoix interview, before he was president. The source was tainted, disdained at the time by him as by almost everyone else. But then as president in 1983 he had to deal with Klarsfeld's solid evidence.

Mitterrand, his defenders said, was singled out in the 1994 controversy about Bousquet because he was president. Numbers of French political and business leaders also had been friendly with René Bousquet for years, and he had done favors for many of them. None of them was now confronted as Mitterrand was. Bousquet's high Vichy positions had long been known to all; his 1949 condemnation by the High Court was specifically for having accepted the job as Vichy police chief. After his absolution for helping the Resistance, he was soon accepted in French business and political circles, and he sat on numerous boards of directors that included influential, vigilant French Jews such as the industrialist Antoine Veil, husband of the politician, government minister, and former European Parliament president Simone Veil. Bousquet's 1949 punishment was generally seen as a slap on the wrist combined with a pat on the back. His responsibility in the Vel' d'Hiv roundup was still hidden.

In retrospect, Mitterrand surely would have rather done entirely without Bousquet. But by 1983 there was a long connection based on Bousquet's campaign support going back at least to when Mitterrand was most alone, at the mercy of a few contributors in his first presidential campaign in 1965. Perhaps Mitterrand justified his benevolence by invoking the necessary presumption of innocence that applies even in such a case. But a president's ethics must be wider and deeper than those of a private individual; they must answer to the nation's sense of right and wrong, not instead of, but larger than legality. A president is never merely an associate in political business or a political friend, and there are no set rules governing all situations. A president's hard decisions are always contestable because their reasons cross-cut each other morally and politically.

Finally, the fact that Bousquet's acquaintance became a tar baby for Mitterrand after 1983 underscores one of two conclusions, either Mitterrand's republican courage in defying an overwrought public opinion or his Machiavellianism. Serge Klarsfeld's forceful evidence was made public in 1983. If Mitterrand was an amoral Machiavellian, he never would have placed himself in danger in order to protect Bousquet—why risk his own legitimacy and reputation in history for Bousquet? Or else, Mitterrand was given to quixotic gestures of loyalty to friends and associates, and in that case he was no pure Machiavellian. Those who think that Mitterrand was a cynic can't have it both ways. His entire postwar past—four decades in two republics—is, in any case, evidence that he was not protecting Bousquet out of Vichyism. The one other possibility would be blackmail concerning Mitterrand's Vichy time, and no researcher has turned up evidence that Bousquet knew something still secret that could have enabled him to blackmail Mitterrand.

Thus, the reasons Mitterrand continued to see Bousquet between 1983 and 1986 were, if not praiseworthy, less sinister than the 1994 suspicions of Vichyite complicity. Klarsfeld's new evidence implicating Bousquet became public, as said above, in 1983. But final investigation was not completed and a lawsuit actually filed by him until 1986. Here is one accounting for the 1983-1986 Mitterrand-Bousquet contacts. Second, Mitterrand's sheer stubbornness, his determination to maintain his freedom of decision and independence against what he saw as conformist critics, surely played a part. Third, did the sometimes sentimental, humanist François Mitterrand see in René Bousquet a man who might, but for the grace of God, have been himself, and applied the *nihil humanum?* "During troubled times," he had told Pierre Péan, "moreover when you are young, it is difficult to choose . . . I managed to come out all right. It is unfair to judge people by mistakes that can be explained by the atmosphere of the times."

Against Mitterrand's policy is the fact that Bousquet had committed terrible crimes, gotten away with them, and was hardly a man, until he came under suspicion again in 1978 and 1983, to evoke sympathy. He was a successful businessman with large political influence who dined at the table of the president of his country. He had perpetrated gross, inhuman fraud.

The most banal answer may, fortunately and unfortunately, be the correct one—fortunately because it dispels the suspicion of lingering Vichyite sympathies in Mitterrand, unfortunately because it underlines yet again his manipulative, opportunist character. For three years beginning in 1983, Mitterrand became increasingly focused on the 1986 elections. After the collapse of the socialist experiment in 1983, the Socialist party looked to be routed electorally in parliament in 1986. If a 1986 repudiation of the Socialists, and thus Mitterrand, couldn't be avoided, Mitterrand wanted obviously to minimize its size. He pulled out all the stops, even (as we saw above) getting the Socialist parliamentary majority to change the electoral law to proportional representation, which would reduce the size of a conservative victory but also balloon the number of National Front deputics.

Was Mitterrand between 1983 and 1986 therefore using Bousquet, rather than the reverse, to milk his assets again for electoral purposes? Does this explain why Mitterrand, having come under fierce new criticism about Bousquet in 1986, dropped him even though he had still not yet been indicted despite Klarsfeld's lawsuit against him?

The sequence and motives are plausible. In Franz-Olivier Giesbert's words, "in Mitterrand's series of networks there was a 'Bousquet' network just as there was a 'Resistance' network and a 'Convention of Republican Institutions' network."[31] The Bousquet channel was built on three foundations: anti-gaullism (the *Dépeche du Midi* newspaper he owned was, according to Mitterrand, "one of the few dailies favorable to us during the de Gaulle period . . . I wrote editorials in it"); on camaraderie (the former Vichy police chief was, writes Giesbert, a *bon convive,* a hale fellow well met, which appealed to Mitterrand); and on his positions at the Bank of Indochina and the *Dépeche du Midi,* where Bousquet's influence, Mitterrand said, "determined whether there would be blue sky or rain." Mitterrand's estimate that they had met "at least ten or twelve times" was certainly not true, concerning a significant relationship that lasted thirty-nine years. "I knew that Bousquet had collaborated but I gave him the benefit of the doubt. When it was proven that he had committed crimes, I stopped seeing him. That was in 1986. But before, there was insufficient reason to flee from him." The Bousquet affair, somewhat like the Observatory affair, had turned into a series of progressive explanations by Mitterrand, often internally contradictory. "After sowing so much ambiguity," comments Giesbert, "he harvested doubt."[32]

MITTERRAND AND THE CASE OF MAURICE PAPON

Having pleaded "national reconciliation" as a reason to influence Bousquet's legal process, Mitterrand was led to do the same for the gaullist notable and former Vichy prefect Maurice Papon.

Maurice Papon's was the fourth war crimes case to arise during in Mitterrand's presidency and the one that went on beyond Mitterrand's departure. A Resistance figure and later a high gaullist party official and government minister in the Fifth Republic, Papon had also been investigated for years. Evidence against him first surfaced in 1981, when he was a minister of the Giscard d'Estaing government. He finally was brought to trial in October 1997 in Bordeaux, where he had been Vichy's prefect from 1942-1944. Eighty-seven years old, an arrogant, clear-headed Papon, although in fragile health, quickly denied all responsibility, appearing not at all the sort of "poor old man" Mitterrand had counseled against putting on trial. After a few weeks, however, Papon's health collapsed and the trial continued irregularly, with the possibility always in the air that death would intervene before a verdict by the law.

Papon's trial and verdict showed that it can be possible to determine guilt and assign responsibility sometimes long after the fact. His persistent line of defense was that as secretary general of the Gironde Prefecture, the regional administrative arm of the Vichy state in the Bordeaux area, he was subordinate to the prefect, Maurice Sabatier (long dead). He had, Papon repeatedly asserted, no authority over the policy to make arrests. His clear signature on numerous written orders to the police, including those authorizing the deportation to Nazi death camps of more than 1,500 Jews from Bordeaux, were, he asserted, a matter of form: "When you find a signature like this, there's no doubt that I am relaying a decision of the Prefect."[33] When the judge asked him about the files kept by the Gironde Region prefecture's Office of Jewish Questions—used by the Germans to choose their victims in 1942-1943 for deportation to the Drancy transit camp and Auschwitz—Papon replied shamelessly that "They were a force for good. The files helped prove that a given person should be exempted because of his ancestry, or another for some other reason." Creating and using the files related to Papon's "duty," legally defined as a French official, in that most of the Jews deported from Bordeaux during the war, about 6,000 in all, were foreign-born, not French.[34] In Papon's explanation, the seizures of factories and valuables from Jews "was a way of guaranteeing that they could eventually be returned to their rightful owners."

As opposed to his arguments that disobedience was impossible at his level, witnesses cited numerous cases to the contrary, cases of high Vichy officials evading Gestapo orders or turning them to some advantage. Papon's defenses were totally dismantled in weeks of testimony and he was found guilty of complicity in crimes against humanity, on two counts of having helped organized the arrest and deportation of Jews from Bordeaux. He was acquitted of the third count, complicity in their murder at Auschwitz. He was sentenced on April 2, 1998 to ten years in prison.[35]

Papon refused to accept the verdict and sentence and appealed to the Cour de Cassation, France's highest appeals court. But the day before his hearing he fled the county, which under French law meant that his conviction was inviolate. He wrote a letter saying that the only "honorable course was exile," even for a man ninety years old. He added grandiloquently that exile was "a choice that had been made by some of the most noted men of history." His intention, he said, was to ask the European Court of Human Rights to take his case and to condemn French justice for what he called a long list of illegal acts in investigating and trying his case.

Papon was located ten days later in a hotel in Gstaad, Switzerland, registered under the name and passport of a Resistance comrade, Robert de la Rochefoucault. The Swiss government lost no time in expelling him. Under intense pressures concerning Swiss behavior in World War II–related issues it had every interest in getting rid of Papon immediately. Papon was quickly taken to the prison at Fresnes where he is now serving his sentence.

Robert Paxton's comment on the Papon case and the other French cases discussed here goes against conventional views:

> It was remarkable enough that Papon was tried at all. France and Germany are the only major World War II belligerents to have tried any of their own citizens for crimes against humanity for acts committed in that war. The often-expressed American view that the French won't confront the dark side of their response to Nazi occupation has been false for thirty years.[36]

Paxton adds that François Mitterrand "quietly obstructed any judicial probing of similarly sinuous pasts" (referring, one supposes, to Touvier and Bousquet), and that Papon's case had been stalled by his friends for sixteen years.[37] Of the three cases, only that of Bousquet relates specifically to Mitterrand, as we have seen. The Touvier and Papon cases involved conservative governments as much or more than Mitterrand's administration.

THE YOUNG GENERATION
AND THE NATIONAL MEMORY OF VICHY

Paxton points out that the future of Vichy in French memory is that, "As for trials, there is nobody left to charge." As such, "There remains only pedagogy." This is a fundamental point in my judgment.

Papon's trial was supposed to teach young French people about Vichy, and historians were given an unusually prominent place in it. Jurors, and through them the nation, had to be given an explanation of how the Vichy regime fit into French history. But "in the end, Papon's trial could not teach the clear, simple, and unanimously agreed-upon history lesson that many advocates of prosecution had hoped for. . . . Instead of the morality play of good versus evil that Papon's trial was expected to produce, intermediate shadings appeared. The 'Vichyite resister,' a type made notorious by the revelations about François Mitterrand, reappeared in the person of Maurice Papon."[38] Paxton's comparison of Papon and Mitterrand seems tenuous at best. Papon is a proven perpetrator of crimes against humanity. The notion of the "Vichyite resister," which could indeed group the two of them, seems quite secondary.

Demographic change also amplified the shock of the Péan book. By 1994 the great majority of French people had been born after the war, more or less half after de Gaulle's resignation in 1969. The younger generations had not learned much about Vichy, either in school or in the media. Mitterrand's electoral campaigns avoided discussion of his past—the good and the bad—because everywhere there were possible traps. Young people had been taught the simple lesson that the Resistance had been good and Vichy was evil, so the "revelation" that the president of the country had worked at Vichy was electrifying at first.

The Israeli historian Zeev Sternhell claimed to see a "new, more demanding . . . pugnacious . . . sensitive [French] generation" in the fall 1994 controversy, but the episode lasted only a few weeks. Opinion polls indicated the French people were little affected by the polemic. Mitterrand's own cohabitation ratings had gone up in the previous few months (along with Prime Minister Edouard Balladur's, to be sure), and there was no sudden drop in the approval rating of the president or a rise in those who believed Mitterrand was lying or had done something very bad. His overall ratings stayed over 50 percent, and a large majority (80 percent) said they did not think he had been covering up racist or treasonous behavior. Did this express the people's absolution of Mitterrand? Or was it popular indifference or confusion, particularly among young people, the "normalized" French generations, for whom the whole episode was a battle of old men about long-ago, if terrible doings in which everyone was probably guilty? Surely both. In opinion polls only a small minority thought the president was a particularly bad man. The sense that a despicable crime had been discovered in the presidency waned rapidly, and matters were relegated to vitriolic skirmishes among intellectuals and journalists. Such a situation would have been inconceivable in the old daggers-always-drawn French political culture of the 1960s and 1970s.

The weakness of Mitterrand's defense by his Socialist party associates was a last noteworthy episode of the 1994 controversy. Lionel Jospin, now prime minister, said limply that "one could have wished for a rather different past" for a left-wing president. Laurent Fabius said that if the accusation were true that President Mitterrand had knowingly dealt with and protected René Bousquet, "That would be a serious problem." In fact, the knives were drawn in the Socialist party in fall 1994 as the Mitterrand era entered a *fin de regne;* some of the harshest reproaches of Mitterrand arose, not surprisingly, from disappointed friends.*

Why was François Mitterrand so little defended, even attacked, by his own people? By 1994 criticism of Mitterrand, once unthinkable, had become

---

* In December 1999, Elie Wiesel's *And the Sea Is Never Full: Memoirs, 1969-* (Knopf, 1999) was published, including a chapter called "François Mitterrand and Jewish Memory," pp. 311-42. Wiesel's friendship with Mitterrand from 1980 on is described, including disappointment over alleged manipulation and lies on Mitterrand's part in producing and publishing their *Memoir in Two Voices.*

acceptable, even a cause for mutual proofs of courage inside the party. It was time for a Jospin and a Fabius to step away from him. Other Socialists remained silent. Mitterrand observed this with detachment, even if the personal and political turning of coats sometimes enraged him. On the other hand, the new first secretary of the party, Henri Emanuelli, spoke out against "those who give lessons" and "witch hunts." A few deputies, such as the controversial young Julian Dray, himself Jewish, defended Mitterrand publicly. Cutting criticisms were made by longtime associates such as Gilles Martinet, a veteran Socialist journalist who had long had tense relations with Mitterrand. It was joked that the president had named Martinet ambassador to Italy in 1981 as a way to get him out of Paris. After years of courtesan behavior and being intimidated by Mitterrand, many Socialist leaders were now striking poses of independence. Their goal "was not so much to demolish the target . . . as to reinvent a virginity for the archer. At bottom one felt they had so loved Mitterrand . . . that they wanted to wash themselves of this weakness. And everyone knows that an effect of emotional balance is that the more one has loved the more one is capable of hating."[39]

Yet there was a genuine repugnance, especially in the middle ranks of party activists and among people who had known no other president but Mitterrand. They felt betrayed by him, about Vichy certainly, but now, crystallized by this "revelation," about the entire experience of the so-called Mitterrand generation. Most had known little or nothing of the Vichy story, and suddenly they were presented with evidence indicating that their leader had deceived them all along, not only about Vichy but also about socialism and the U-turn in the Socialist experiment of 1983.

An entire Socialist generation had worked enthusiastically for Mitterrand and for his presidential ambition, because he embodied their hopes. If François Mitterrand was a fraud it meant that their own political engagement was blackened as well. It was not the suspicion that he had been a secret fascist—patently unjustified—but the idea that their *own* political activism now seemed, not a lie but a charade manipulated by a Machiavellian that affected people so deeply. A Chinese proverb says that "Where there is a will to condemn, there is evidence."

Paradoxically the exposé and controversy was also a last service Mitterrand rendered to the Socialist party he had refounded a quarter century earlier. Demystifying the sphinx, killing the father, allowed the Socialists to get out from under Mitterrand's sway. It liberated party leaders finally to see the arrival of normalization after years of mesmerization by a dominant leader. At the end of the 1990s the Socialist party could become, it had to become, a party of normal politicians seeking their turn in office, a party that offers candidates and programs but has abandoned the pretension that its unique mission, consecrated by two centuries of French revolution, is to "change society." Mitterrand's suffering so much Socialist repudiation without public counterattack displayed forbearance that kept the party together. Much sooner than expected, given predictions that Mitterrand was leaving the party an "orphan," a new prime minister, Lionel Jospin, was produced, less talented and versatile but also less controversial and more honest.

MITTERRAND, VICHY, AND JEWISH QUESTIONS

What is not in doubt is the adult Mitterrand's philo-Semitism after the war, a four-decades-long commitment. No French political leader had stronger ties to Jews as friends (Georges Dayan), as political colleagues (Shimon Peres), and as government colleagues and aides (Prime Minister Laurent Fabius and others too numerous to mention), or commitments to the existence and security of the state of Israel. For two decades Mitterrand held these views prominently against the policy of Fifth Republic conservative governments and commonly held views in the Quai d'Orsay.

As president, Mitterrand made many specific gestures of solidarity with France's Jews and with Israel. He reacted immediately on August 9, 1982, to a terrorist machine-gun attack at the well-known Goldenberg's restaurant, located in the rue des Rosiers in the Marais Jewish district.[40] Mitterrand arrived but a few hours after the attack, soon followed by Prime Minister Pierre Mauroy. The president went to the closeby synagogue in the rue Pavée with Gaston Defferre to mark their solidarity with France's Jewish community, although there he was greeted by a group of protestors who blamed him for having endorsed the idea of a Palestinian homeland. Yet Mitterrand's gesture of solidarity was widely appreciated and was compared with President Giscard d'Estaing's failure to do likewise at the Rue Copernic synagogue after a terrorist bombing in October 1980.

"The essential point," writes French journalist and author Georges Benamou, "was that . . . [Mitterrand] had always considered the issue of the deportation of French Jews as an abstract question, or worse, as a strictly Jewish question. . . . He was sensitized to the *Vel' d'Hiv* raid, but . . . considered it as if it were a gigantic police accident, a colossal dirty act . . . just another vicious trick of the French Right. . . ." This would explain how Mitterrand might have understood René Bousquet's role—not that of a monster who wanted a part in killing all the Jews but a latter-day pogromist, still a torturer of Jews but not a genocidal maniac. "In truth," says Benamou, "François Mitterrand didn't believe in the uniqueness of the Holocaust, in spite of his . . . 'friendship for the Jewish people.'"[41] I believe this is exactly right. A humanist existentialism carried Mitterrand into territory where the uniqueness of any evil act, even the Holocaust, was reclaimed into the all-too-human possibilities of human nature. This may be a profoundly mistaken view but it is not an anti-Semitic one. Mitterrand again asserted the right to an independent judgment about the Holocaust when he told Elie Wiesel, "I conduct myself toward the Jewish people as I believe it is useful, honest and just to do. . . . [Before and today as president] I contributed to rendering justice, but not more than that."[42]

Mitterrand, says Benamou, resembled "a reader of Renan who, like the historian, believed he had liberated himself of his prejudices," and that for him was the essential.[43] Mitterrand thus had always been literally *indifferent* to "the Jewish question" in the sense of a unique instance of prejudice; while he had a blind spot, he also was immune to anti-Semitism. This was "a positive point," Benamou adds, "when one considers the milieu he was raised in."

But Mitterrand, in his Renan-like elevation of view, failed to recognize an instance of evil unique in its combination of conception, scope, and the horrors of its execution. He "never took the measure of the Jewish drama, he remained a man of the nineteenth century, meaning a man who considered that the greatest tragedy of all time was Verdun, those thousands of square kilometers plowed under by bombs, that territory seeded with human bones. And having said this, it becomes clearer still how Mitterrand could have so revered, at least for a time, Marshal Philippe Pétain, the 'Hero of Verdun,' of France's survival and victory in World War I."[44] For Mitterrand anti-Semitism was one of a whole category of group prejudices, where race, religion, and ethnicity block a humanist approach to each individual. To understand the Holocaust as a unique evil in history could have seemed to Mitterrand as a kind of unjustified "Judeo-centrism"—a view that, however displeasing, has nothing to do with anti-Semitism.

Mitterrand's attitude about Jewish questions, in World War II or as French president, in no way proves that he was "just like the men of Vichy." And paradoxically his reputation in history may benefit from the 1994 ordeal, as one otherwise harsh critic courageously pointed out:[45]

> By taking responsibility for his own history . . . and insisting on its commonplace character, Mitterrand is in a curious way acting as a true President of the French nation. He was representative of many in his attitudes before and during the war and he was typical of many in the way he rebuilt his contacts and revised his biography after the war. In his insistence on putting his own life in . . . context . . . he is offering France the occasion to . . . be at

peace with the collective past. . . . As a contribution to civic peace in France, this gesture is not to be underestimated.

The Anglo-American historian Tony Judt's observation holds good.

The enduring lesson of the 1994 exhumation and "trial" of François Mitterrand's Vichy past has to do not so much with either guilt or innocence but with the rules for telling the difference. It is a lesson in historiography, in the alignment of historical memory with historical facts. Paul Thibaud, a résistant of undoubted credentials and longtime editor of the Christian democratic revue *Esprit*—as well as a tough critic of Mitterrand—defined the methodological error in question: "It was rather logical that by considering our history to be a sack of cowardly acts which must be emptied, the result was finally to tarnish those who had opposed this cowardice."[46]

EPILOGUE TO VICHY:
AN AGNOSTIC PRESIDENT AND A JEWISH CARDINAL

François Mitterrand's reputation as an "elusive" character reflected partly things he did and partly what he was. In particular, the gap seemed great between his right-wing origins and his left-wing policies. Some opponents were frustrated, others offended. How could he become a leftist so late in life and get away with it? No one ended up totally admiring the man; his accusers, the various Zolas of 1954, 1959, 1994, and other moments, sometimes were correct. But Mitterrand consistently escaped definition by any single epithet; he was larger than any of the nicknames hung on him.

A glaring example: Clashing totally with the mistaken view of him as anti-Semitic was his reputation among Arab governments as "France's Jewish president." Mitterrand's Middle Eastern policy, contrary to the stereotype of a French government perpetually inclined toward the Arab states because of France's need for oil supplies, was fundamentally sympathetic to Israel. Mitterrand had wanted his first state visit to be to Israel. "His intention," writes Hubert Védrine, "was to quickly make his first foreign visit there so that the rebalancing of [French] policy be achieved."[47] In May 1981 he reassured Arab ambassadors in Paris and sent emissaries to Riyadh and other Arab capitals with his message: "Justice for the peoples, security for states." In July 1981 Mitterrand annulled a notorious Raymond Barre directive of 1977 that organized French business acceptance of the boycott of Israel decreed by the Arab League. But rebalancing France's Middle Eastern diplomacy was frustrated because on June 7, 1981 the Menachem Begin government's raid destroyed the Iraqi nuclear site at Tamuz, killing a French technician in the process. Mitterrand tempered his protest—"We condemn the raid, not Israel"—but decided to postpone his Tel Aviv trip and go to Saudi Arabia first. Afterward, despite Mitterrand's intentions, the conservative Begin government was a difficult partner.

The Israeli visit finally took place in March 1982, when Mitterrand made his remarkable speech to the Knesset—a "masterpiece of Mitterrandian farsightedness, tact and courage" according to Hubert Védrine—emphasizing Israel's right to security but calling for a homeland for the Palestinians, "which for the Palestinians can, at the appropriate time, mean a State. . . . Because it is impossible to ask anyone to renounce their identity, nor to speak in their place."[48] An unpopular position among Western states at the time, it was violently rejected by the Begin and Shamir governments in Israel. Yet Mitterrand's 1982 policy, pressuring the Palestine Liberation Organization (PLO) regarding Israel's security while acknowledging a Palestinian right to some form of a state, foresaw the Oslo agreement reached ten years later between the Yitzhak Rabin government and Yasir Arafat's PLO.

With regard to Lebanon, Mitterrand pursued a traditional policy as patron of the Maronite Christian minority, but the French government no longer had the resources to make its will prevail in the Lebanese civil war, where the big power was now Syria. Menachem Begin had lied to him, Mitterrand felt, about the "limited aims" of the Israeli incursion into southern Lebanon on June 6, 1982, which, as conceived by defense minister Ariel Sharon, had the goal of eliminating Arafat's organization. Mitterrand thus was caught between his pro-Israel and pro-Palestinian and Lebanese policies, and he was further suspected by conservative Israelis and Americans of trying to reintroduce the Soviets back into the Middle East peace process. Beyond the dilemmas of policy in the Middle East, however, no knowledgeable government leader doubted Mitterrand's strong sentiments about the security of Israel as a state and about the Jews as a people.

◆　◆　◆

Cardinal Archbishop Jean-Marie Lustiger of Paris began life a Jew. Born in 1926, Aaron Lustiger was the son of Polish Jewish parents. At the age of thirteen, in 1939, the teenaged Lustiger was baptized as a Roman Catholic in Nazi-occupied Poland. The timing of this conversion indicates an all-too-familiar story of 1933 to 1945, a matter of desperate parents trying to save their children from anti-Semitism and its deadly consequences. Aaron Lustiger escaped with his life, but his mother died at Auschwitz, and several other family members perished in the Holocaust as well, there or at other camps.

Half a century later, in 1994, a man—now Cardinal Jean-Marie Lustiger of France, Archbishop of Paris—arrived in the state of Israel, invited to a special symposium, a discussion-debate scheduled on the Day of Remembrance of the Six Million Jews who perished in the Shoah. The Day of Remembrance, April 27, specifically commemorates the liberation of the death camps; readers will remember that in 1945 François Mitterrand had been a representative of the French Provisional Government with the delegation that had opened Dachau and Lanzberg.

But the French Cardinal Lustiger arrived on Israeli soil to a storm of controversy, criticized—publicly, bitterly—by several Orthodox rabbis and government officials because of his 1939 conversion. The loudest voice of outrage was that of Israel Meir Lau, Grand Rabbi of Israel, the Ashkenzic leader. Rabbi Lau was himself a Buchenwald survivor, a witness among witnesses, who, in repeated sermons and interviews, castigated the adolescent Lustiger's conversion. By saving himself at the cost of his heritage, said the grand rabbi, Aaron Lustiger had "betrayed his people and his faith during the most difficult and darkest of periods." Had Lustiger been a model for how young Jews should behave in the face of persecution, "not one Jew would be left in the world to say Kaddish," the Hebrew mourner's prayer for the dead.[49] A collective truth, surely, but could it be hung around the neck of individuals?

Many Israelis thought it a scandal that Lustiger should be welcomed in this way by Israel's highest religious officials. However, others, and not only the Orthodox, considered the reproach to be just.

Lustiger replied that his conversion to Catholicism had been genuine and authentic, resulting from "a spiritual awakening," a profound personal crisis that came on him while attending a Catholic school his Jewish parents had found for him at the start of World War II. He pointed out that he had reaffirmed his conversion later on, after the war, once the danger was past. It was not merely a way to hide from the Nazis, although he understood it might look like that.

Lustiger was to give an address on "The Silence of God" during the Genocide. Israeli critics demanded that he speak about the silence of the Catholic church. A minority among the participants wanted him invited, in a spirit of reconciliation, to the ceremony at the memorial of Yad Vashem. The invitation was not extended, however, and the Cardinal-Archbishop of Paris decided to attend as an individual, one face in a crowd.

Lustiger always emphasized that despite conversion he had never repudiated his Jewish origins; in Israel he spoke of "we Jews" and signed guest books "Aaron Jean-Marie Lustiger." He made a plea for humanistic understanding beyond the boundaries of churches, beyond religious formalism: "To say that I am no longer a Jew," he contended, "is like denying my father and mother, my grandfathers and grandmothers. . . . I am as Jewish as all the other members of my family who were butchered in Auschwitz or in other camps."

The grand rabbi could not agree. Nor would he remain silent. To him Lustiger was a traitor to his faith and, the very worst moral condemnation he could have made, an image of the extinction of the Jewish people.

Who was right, who was wrong? Who was intolerant, who was defending what could not be compromised? The Grand Rabbi's logic was implacable. But the weight of the charge, above all given the circumstances, is impossible to put on the conscience of any single person. To teach a human lesson ought not to require the actual sacrifice of the son, especially someone else's innocent son. The story serves as well or better. Myth can be stronger than fact.

We have here two exemplary "men of France": Aaron Jean-Marie Lustiger and François Mitterrand, the political man and the religious man, whose itineraries and intersecting paths in French history since the 1930s form a metaphor for an era.

What is the lesson to come away with? That to begin life in one place and end up in another is not in itself proof of bad faith, let alone lack of honor. Shifts of character or camp are not necessarily cowardice. Neither those who remain steadfast nor those who change, nor those who are forced into unwanted situations in which they must struggle for survival or freedom, are ipso facto virtuous.

And societies, peoples, nations themselves can change, can behave differently at different moments in time. Fin-de-siècle France was a cultural garden that also produced the black flower of the Dreyfus affair. Vichy, which condemned Free France and slandered résistants as Jews and Communists, was in turn condemned by the Resistance and buried by it. Which was the "true" French nation—the splendid France of Renoir and Manet, or the sinister France of Pétain and Laval? The France that was anti-Semitic or the French people who protected Jews and peopled the Resistance? Any adequate historical understanding is complex, just as obscurantist complexity can be immoral.

The conclusion is not that judgments are impossible but that convincing judgments are always nuanced. Individuals are responsible for their own actions, not for where, or what, they happened to be born. Individual actions and responsibilities need always to be understood in context. Sometimes nothing is more ambiguous than the obvious, whether Aaron Lustiger's conversion away from Judaism or François Mitterrand's winding road from the Right to become the French Left's man.

The second lesson is the symbolism in a coincidence. At François Mitterrand's death in January 1996, naturally it was the Cardinal-Archbishop of Paris, Aaron Jean-Marie Lustiger, who officiated the national mass at Notre

Dame Cathedral. It was a case of the converted eulogizing the agnostic; a Polish Jew by origin leading the nation's Catholic adieu to a president very French by birth, education, experience, and culture. This was a stunning symbol of the human truth that we are hurled into consciousness and that we must make our own meaning out of it.

CHAPTER 12

CONCLUSION: LEGACIES

Every itinerary is necessarily made up of a series of reactions to accidental circumstances, following out a fundamental orientation.

—Simon Leys

Worldly wisdom teaches that it is better for reputation to fail conventionally than to succeed unconventionally.

—John Maynard Keynes

The young of bears and dogs show their natural dispositions. But men, falling immediately under the sway of custom, opinion, and law, easily change or assume disguises. Yet it is difficult to overcome the natural bent.

—Montaigne

THE RELUCTANT PEDAGOGUE
AND THE REPUTATION OF "DIRTY HANDS"

FRANÇOIS MITTERRAND'S POLITICAL CAREER was a series of maneuvers, exploits, and battles. His very personality was a continuing controversy. The most important lessons his political biography leaves us with, however, concern not his policy successes and failures but a certain perspective on leadership in contemporary democracy.

Democratic leadership, in our times as in all times, cannot avoid some degree of Machiavellian behavior. Especially true in foreign affairs, this denaturing of democracy is also true domestically, as anyone who reads a newspaper knows from the constant supply of scandals and manipulations. The French Fifth Republic from de Gaulle through Mitterrand was, as I have emphasized, an extreme instance of the institutionalized Machiavellian democratic presidency, an ambiguous and shifting balance of Machiavellianism and republican democracy.

Because of excessive institutional power and prestige, the French president is permanently tempted by a splendid aloofness. This is not only a matter of decision-making but a lack of concern with the consultation and education of public opinion. The failure to tie the French presidency to the wheel of accountability was exacerbated by the personalities of de Gaulle, Pompidou, Giscard d'Estaing, and Mitterrand (Georges Pompidou least of the four), not to mention the historical disdain of public opinion by the French political class. French institutions plus personalities plus the historic elitism of the political class: The result was a gulf, sometimes an abyss, separating the government from the people, from public opinion, from the electorate.

De Gaulle was repudiated by the people in May 1968 and Valéry Giscard d'Estaing was voted out of office in 1981. Georges Pompidou's foreshortened term was inconclusive. What is to be said about François Mitterrand, who after all finished two full seven-year terms in office, even ending with higher opinion poll ratings than when he began?

On leaving office Mitterrand's legacy seemed not less positive but more ambiguous than that of any of the others. His changeability, his "succession of sincerities," was complicated by the fact that he communicated with the people no better than his predecessors. François Mitterrand was what I would call a reluctant pedagogue, insufficient in the teaching aspect of democratic leadership. The consequences were real, if not immediately dramatic: repeated missed chances and public uncertainty about who he really was. But Mitterrand's reasons were at least characteristic of the man as we have come to know him deeper.

◆   ◆   ◆

A democratic leader, to be successful in moral and human as well as in policy terms, must do more than merely govern. He or she must be at least somewhat open and candid on a personal level, and an effective espouser of the theory and practice of democratic republican government. In the French Fifth Republic Charles de Gaulle's pedagogical style, lofty as it was, did, without question, reach and convince public opinion, especially during his first term to 1965 and especially in crisis situations. In return, the French people were by and large enthusiastic about the Fifth Republic in its first years and proud that with de Gaulle at the helm France counted, at least until into his second term when routinized times no longer suited a style that had in any case grown wearying. The events of May 1968 were totally unexpected until, after they had occurred, everyone said they had been "inevitable."

De Gaulle's aloofness and his concern with "France" rather than the French were denounced as insufferably monarchical and archaic. Georges Pompidou, with his peasant affability and his endorsement of the goal of prosperity ("French people, enrich yourselves!"), seemed a return to basic realities and a release from de Gaulle's emphasis on duty, dignity, and France's place in the world.

Valéry Giscard d'Estaing, by contrast, was tone-deaf to public opinion. Obsessed in American fashion with opinion polls, trying to tell the French what polls said they wanted to hear ("France wants to be governed in the center"), he was inept or blind to his own limits as a democratic communicator. His elitist style was suited to pretentious and intimidating presentations, talking down to the people as a *grande école* professor talks to students. Thus the bite in Mitterrand's memorable retort in a presidential debate with Giscard: "Remember that you are not the professor here, and I am not your student."

The point is that Fifth Republic presidents have underestimated the need and difficulty of genuinely republican pedagogy, of democratic teaching about how hard and how satisfying democracy is in public policy. Tony Judt aptly described Richard Nixon's similar problems as "the inability of Nixon . . . to grasp that in a democracy the government is not only obliged but is also well-advised to give a running account of what it is doing and why, if it wishes to retain public confidence and support."[1] Nixon was, not surprisingly, an immense admirer of de Gaulle. But no heroic leader himself, Nixon ended up excessively Machiavellian and not enough of a republican. He lost track of how much the prince, who may talk a great deal, is by nature an anti-pedagogue; the prince is not a teacher but a sophist, a liar, a dissembler. He is naturally wary of public opinion, has only the goal of turning it to his advantage.

François Mitterrand's is certainly the most convoluted, the most exotic case of the Fifth Republic's four presidents. His combination of republican, Machiavellian, and existentialist conceptions produced in him, I believe, a characteristic and quasi-philosophical *aversion* to the role of political teacher and conversational partner with democratic opinion.

A leader may refuse the pedagogical role but, as just mentioned, the result will be uncertainty in public opinion about his intentions, about his character, and even about his successes. A democratic leader who does good things for the people without their consultation and consent is, despite elections, not so different from an enlightened despot. The democratic leader must both inform and seek consent, even when doing good. Self-government cannot be done *for* the people, only *by and with* the people. A confused, contested reputation results whenever pedagogy is refused, which is not the same thing as neglecting public relations or "spin." In such a case what is genuine is public opinion, its ability to think for itself. When a leader does not make his own case repeatedly in his or her most genuine style, the result is not the worst case scenario but a public dialogue that is left too much in the hands of adversaries, exaggerators, and demagogues.

This point is central to the problem of François Mitterrand's contested reputation. By concluding on the issue of political pedagogy, this study explains—the crucial missing explanation—how a leader of such talents, battles, and achievements as Mitterrand could have departed after so long in office with a reputation so uncertain among his own people.

Why was Mitterrand, the political talent of his generation, such a reluctant pedagogue? Critics would say it was because, especially in the periods of scandals and above all after the sudden eruption of controversy about his Vichy past, that he had just been hiding as always, that he had never ceased to be a "man of Vichy," the focus of the "Observatory affair," and the betrayer of socialism. His entire political career, so they said, was a fraud wrapped in an enigma embodied in his sphinxlike facade. But by now we have seen in detail that such a view is completely untenable.

A better explanation of Mitterrand's relative indifference to the role of teacher of the democracy comes out of two subjects discussed above: French institutions and his moralities. It is not an obvious account, but the combination of long observation, all the books about him, and my own contacts with him give me confidence that it is true.

First, institutions: Any French Fifth Republic president is much more protected, by the constitution, the rules, and by political culture, from public scrutiny than is any American president. Beginning with de Gaulle, the Fifth Republic president was intentionally supposed to be above partisan politics, the "guarantee" and the "arbiter" of national life, a very conscious reference to the collapses of 1958 and 1940. The French president, despite his part in actual government, is not obliged institutionally to answer questions publicly every week like a British (or French) prime minister. Nor is the French president expected to give full press conferences with regularity or to be available for "photo-ops" at anywhere near the American president's schedule. François Mitterrand in any case used the institutional protections of the presidential office (as had his predecessors) to regulate and even to avoid the media, for whom he had overall little respect.

An exception to this was the remarkable series of press conferences held by President Mitterrand from November 1990 to January 1991 during the crisis with Saddam Hussein and Iraq leading up to the Gulf war. There were six full-scale press conferences in two months, which prepared the French people for the conclusion that France's government had tried all diplomatic means to avoid war and that, finally, France's military participation with her allies in "Operation Desert Storm" was responsible policy. After that, Hubert Védrine noted, Mitterrand's staff pleaded with him to give more frequent press conferences. The Gulf war exercises in republican pedagogy had been very successful in winning public support for a good cause, and Mitterrand seemed to accustom himself more than ever to give and take with journalists.

Mitterrand didn't follow his aides' advice to have more press conferences and to give greater access to journalists. His methods remained largely the behind-closed-doors policymaking of the past, for example, the Euromissile crisis and the March 1983 decision on monetary policy, which in effect abandoned the socialist experiment.

These grave decisions were never explained to the public or even to the president's Socialist and Communist supporters. They were just announced, decisions from on high, the voice of the French state upon which the media could comment in a monologue. Julius W. Friend rightly says of this, "Mitterrand may or may not have believed deeply in the policies of 1981, but it is beside the point to attack him for possible insincerity. Mauroy, in longevity and sincerity more socialist than he, also advocated the policies that led away from the socialism of 1981-1982. Mitterrand can be more justly criticized for having tiptoed away from these early policies, for never really apologizing or explaining why they went wrong."[2] In spite of the benefits of being able to act without rendering accounts, a price had to be paid in public support. It is difficult for citizens to like or to support over an extended period a leader they don't feel they know.

But Julius Friend is even more correct than he realizes in pleading the significance of what Mitterrand did in 1981, whether he had believed sincerely in socialism at the time or not. This was not just any set of policies, it was to be, finally after a century of struggle, the attempt at "socialism." And this was no amorphous coalition government, it was the French Socialists and Communists who would finally test their utopian goals but also settle historical accounts with each other. And it was François Mitterrand, believer or make-believer, who had made all this possible by reviving the Socialist party and then winning the presidency. We are certainly not talking about Moses leading the Hebrews to the Promised Land, but the ideological thrill and hope that passed through the

French Left in May-June 1981 was very real. Even sophisticated semicynical Parisian Socialists gave in to their hidden desire to believe that the working class would ascend to heaven. Among the French Communist rank and file, if rarely the top leaders, honest hopes were much higher.

So what is the conclusion about Mitterrand in 1981? He had perceived a historic role to play in France as uniter of the French Left. De Gaulle had had the other, bigger one in rallying the French people at large, then keeping the French Right and Center firmly with him. Whether or not Mitterrand genuinely believed in socialism in the strong, ideological meaning of a totally different kind of society, he was in 1981 the historic unifier and only conceivable government leader of the French Left. In uniting the Left, accepting the gaullist institutions, trying socialism, and veering toward the mainstream after his radical program failed, Mitterrand was a maker of legitimacy in French politics and society. Franz-Olivier Giesbert's judgment of the man is right on target: "He knew the vanity of things, but couldn't resist the desire to try to make history, a very French malady."[3] Mitterrand is seen once again as simultaneously France's representative man and France's most controversial politician.

The second reason for Mitterrand's reluctance to be a political teacher was, as I said, more personal and philosophical. Even as president he remained steeped in his existentialist conception of the individual's autonomy and independence.

Values are learned and confirmed from experience, out of one's own life. To the extent that values are teachable, Mitterrand believed, they are best learned by example. The voice of government, which tries to teach, can easily turn into propaganda and indoctrination—like the catechism of the Catholic church or the ideology of Vichy from which Mitterrand had separated, or the doctrine of the Communist party that Mitterrand disdained and had always combated. Mitterrand could not in good faith have tried a de Gaulle–like or American-style presidency. In existentialist terms it would have been "bad faith," violating his own "authenticity" and the respect he owed others as individuals in the existentialist predicament.

But inescapably in politics, public opinion is also to be manipulated, to be "spun." Yet Mitterrand clearly did not believe the president's role was to decree political truths from on high, truths that were always complex, not reducible to memorable slogans, let alone sound bites. Here was another aspect of his refusal of de Gaulle as a model. According to Mitterrand's high regard for parliamentary government, he always believed the institutionalized representative organizations of society—the political parties and the other intermediate organizations such as labor unions—should have responsibility for the continuing education and definition of pluralist interests and values which make up public debate. Remember young Mitterrand's public accusation of Vichy's new Minister for prisoners of war at the rally in July 1943: "Whom do you represent? You don't represent us!" Representation, not the enunciation of truths: This was Mitterrand's conception of public opinion.

Mitterrand's brilliant Machiavellianism plus his existentialist ethics did make of him an idiosyncratic politician. He was singular at the same time that he was very French. It is no wonder the French people found him so hard to figure out. It just makes sense that public opinion, which thrives on the familiar, would struggle with the exotic Mitterrand. What is most remarkable then is that such a man made it to the top at all, let alone remained there for so long, while remaining true to his conception of self.

When Mitterrand finally started to open up and explain his past and his policies, it was near the end of his presidency and he seemed to be trying only to justify himself. He largely failed because it was too late, he was too ill, and he was too old for a new specialty as democratic communicator.

That the French people should have known so little about a president with such a controversial past no doubt seems incomprehensible to Americans, who know if anything too much about too much of their leaders' private lives and great thoughts. The large number of biographical interviews Mitterrand gave, while quite ill, in the last year of his presidency left the reasonable impression, after so long a silence, that he was trying above all else to influence his place in the history books. In sum this pedagogical weakness, this inattention to teaching, was a fundamental lack in Mitterrand's presidency and his greatest personal shortcoming as France's leader.

His greatest single *policy* failure, among several, was a record of punitive rates (finally at 12-13 percent) of unemployment. This unemployment aggravated a sense of dislocation, resentment, and demoralization in a French society pressured economically, socially, and culturally. But unemployment can be understood, if not necessarily justified, as the price paid for some other good thing: for the advances in European integration, for the strong franc/low inflation policy, and thus the solid Franco-German partnership.

It makes no sense to believe that Mitterrand *wanted* high unemployment or that he wasn't affected by it in a human sense as well as in terms of his own responsibility and reputation. And in terms of sincerity and good faith, Mitterrand's very agonizing over abandoning socialist policies was a proof of authenticity in his concern for the degree of social damage a government can legitimately inflict on society. But having said all this, it was still a mistake not to go to the people with an account of lessons learned in the socialist experiment. Mitterrand obviously thought the accounting would be too damaging, perhaps even that his French Left supporters could never accept this account from him on their behalf. There was still a question of his legitimacy as leader of the Left at that point.

Another crucial moment when Mitterrand evaded public opinion was German reunification. Hubert Védrine asserts that Mitterrand's hesitations were justifiable—that French policy was right to seek guarantees from the Bonn government—yet his public presentation, such as it was, seemed wrapped in "an excess of worry and too many precautions."[4] The French people were right to be puzzled: If communism was collapsing and the division of Europe ending, why should German unification provoke such anxiety in French policy and among France's top leaders? French young people especially, with less historical memory, couldn't fathom such *angst* about a country they had always been taught was France's strict partner in European peace and integration.

The drama was, despite his denials of it, precisely that François Mitterrand wasn't sure what France's policy should be, but not because he was anti-German, nor because he was indecisive. France's national interests were complex and the situation was rapidly evolving. The stakes were very high and France, in its unique position geopolitically next to Germany, had to deal with diametrically opposed U.S. and British positions as well as a collapsing Soviet Union. The French couldn't manage events yet they would have to live permanently with the consequences of a new Germany, including permanent changes disadvantageous to France's strategic situation.

"Every statesman," Henry Kissinger says, "must attempt to reconcile what is considered just with what is considered possible. What is considered just depends on the domestic structure of his state; what is possible depends on its resources, geographic position and determination, and on the resources, determination and domestic structure of other states."[5] The term "hesitations" is exactly right to describe Mitterrand's search for the right combination of the just and the possible. Another French leader might have announced that France was, like the United States, full speed ahead for German unification. But would that French leader not have been condemned for unjustified blind faith, for gambling with France's national interest and the European equilibrium, for giving France's unqualified blessing just when German leaders realized they had to give guarantees for the future? Would it not have been said, in such a case, that a French president should have played a waiting game, "hesitated," and bargained for more German guarantees?

We already imagined an alternative French policy regarding German unification.[6] The de Gaulle of 1940 and 1958, not of 1968, might have intuited the futility of trying to delay German unification because collapse in East Germany, people suddenly free and voting with their feet, was making rapid, total unification unavoidable. It could be announced to the French people that this was a great victory for France, it was what the French had wanted continuously since Yalta, a victory (just like the Resistance) for *them*. To the contrary, Mitterrand, first in his "hesitations" and then in pretending he had none, then in making the best of it, was an agile French leader doing what he could.

Mitterrand's hesitations about German unification were the true expression of France's political class taken as a whole. Of course the opposition leader Jacques Chirac quickly applauded the prospect of imminent German unification. But had *he* been French president at the time, the weight of history, his own bureaucracy, other countries such as Poland and Czechoslovakia that were counting on France, might have necessitated a policy equally as cautious and reticent as Mitterrand's. To tell the truth, probably even a de Gaulle would have hesitated.

How does this relate to democratic leadership? Had Mitterrand launched a genuine public debate about German unification he might, contrary to the above, have learned that the French people were not as worried as he was, and that therefore, as a president who takes public opinion into account, he should think again about his own position. In any case in a public debate the French people would have seen better the fraught connections between German unification and the European equilibrium, thus understanding the puzzling reluctance of François Mitterrand to support Germany's unification, particularly since the French *bête noire*, Margaret Thatcher, was so ill-disposed.

Hubert Védrine says that among Mitterrand's advisors there were some who saw that the pedagogical need regarding German unification was not being met:

> Of course the president never stopped talking. No week passed without an interview, a press talk or a reaction to some event. But at no moment did [the president] address himself to the French on the theme, "My fellow citizens, here is what is going on, here is what I am doing in your name." . . . Even his "Good luck to the Germans!" came late, in October 1990.

Védrine, along with former conservative foreign minister Jean-François Poncet and others thought that "while Mitterrand did the right thing, he did not manage well the symbolic dimension of unification. And he didn't ask [Mitterrand's foreign minister] Roland Dumas, who was quite capable, to do it either." Mitterrand, later recalling his Gulf war press conferences, agreed: "If only I had done that kind of communication during German reunification!"

Védrine says that Mitterrand thought it impossible to get across "the requisite mixture of friendship, confidence and precautions. To try it would have provoked complications which then would have themselves required managing." Put another way, this failure showed the limits of another Mitterrand axiom: "One emerges from ambiguity only to one's own detriment."[7]

The concept of "managing the symbolic dimension of unification" is bureaucratic jargon for a kind of public relations. What Mitterrand did in the Gulf war press conferences was not, in any case, merely the managing of symbols but real education. He talked frankly to the media and to the people about the strategic situation, why he was persisting in French diplomatic efforts until the last possible moment, even if others didn't understand or agree: If there was to be war, the responsibility for it would be with Saddam Hussein. He discussed the alternatives for France, for the United States and the allies, and above all for Saddam, giving a convincing explanation of why the choice of war or peace was his, not the allies'. These were extraordinary occasions for public opinion insight into the strategy and diplomacy of war and peace, the true beliefs of leaders at their most crucial moments. It was much more than "managing symbolism," though it was that, too. And it is not always better to act decisively, risking a huge mistake, rather than to test possibilities, to play a waiting game.

True enough, but Mitterrand and the French had had decades of post–World War II experience with West German partners in the "Franco-German couple." West Germany's leaders and the West German people who were going to control reunified Germany had for four decades shown a commitment to stability and liberal democracy. Mitterrand might have swallowed his hesitations because they concerned the long term and announced his confidence in Kohl even if he was unsure. He could have embraced German unification in order to stand with France's best allies—the Germans and the Americans—and to win over French critics. Nevertheless, Mitterrand's worries were true to his view of circumstances and the changing European equilibrium, a statesman eyeing the long term.

Mitterrand in his way was a "conviction politician" like Margaret Thatcher; the difference was in the nature of their convictions. Thatcher proceeded from a narrow set of substantive convictions about the nature of politics, economics, and society. She (and everyone else) knew, even though she sometimes could be flexible, what her position would be as a question arose. Mitterrand's policies may have seemed to be changeable, but even de Gaulle was capable of radical revisions, as on Algeria. Naturally Mitterrand may have been wrong in the dangers he perceived. But he felt they were genuine.

There was a big difference between the simplicity of a Thatcher or a Reagan and the complexity and ambiguity of the various roles assumed by Mitterrand. Ernst Jünger said: "There is much truth in what is invisible and much illusion in the visible. When someone thus says 'I believe only what I see,' he believes at once too little and too much."[8] French public opinion learned too little from Mitterrand's example because it was too complex—there were too many "faces," they sometimes clashed, and each face was ambiguous in itself. So the people respected the man as president, the sum of his presidential roles— Mitterrand was "somebody" and France "counted" because of him—but their understanding of him was frustrated intentionally by him.

Finally, Mitterrand caused more damage to the pedagogical role of the president because he hid so much, almost all, of his unconventional private life from the people, and not only the semilibertine, two-family, and Mitterrand-by-night aspects. The people to some extent deserve to know truly the person to whom they are confiding leadership of the government. This does not mean, contrary to the American example, that the voters have a right to know private details of a president's personal life. But some knowledge of Mitterrand's wide interests and talents would have dissuaded the image of an opportunist totally absorbed in political power. Some of the confusion about his character, thus about his presidential motives, would have been cleared up had he given public opinion more access to his personal life, not to seek approval but as part of the obligation involved in asking for the job of president. But this merging of politics and private life was precisely what Mitterrand rejected. It explains Jacques Chirac's eulogy that Mitterrand's greatest work was his life, not his political career.[9]

The pedagogical role of the French president, like any other function of the office, needs an institutional context, not yet created. The lack of a French presidential duty to report to the people on the "state of the union" is but one instance. A permanent scrutiny and countervoice to limit abuse of the function is another. In the United States the president's natural tendency to give only the best possible version of his policies and intentions is balanced by a vigorous congressional oversight role and a demanding investigative press. The American president's role as educator is not a free ride exactly because it is so open to abuse, and in fact congressional and mass media scrutiny of the presidency has often seemed inquisitorial. But the U.S. presidency has the resources to challenge scrutiny in return and sometimes wins battles or succeeds in "criticizing the criticism." The French republican monarch role would be disastrous in the American context where an adversarial press, representing public opinion, asks hard questions and fights presidential intimidation tooth and nail. A gaullist imperiousness would be rejected by Congress, the media, and public opinion alike. By contrast, Mitterrand often "won" an interview, but he wasn't often liked for it.

François Mitterrand, here recalling a Third Republic president, excelled at polishing symbols of the republic, if not at explanation of them. He did, despite his character, identify deeply with the French people and France, and he did take seriously the symbolic tasks of commemorations and ceremonies because respect for institutions and the state, he knew, requires ritual, solemnity, and, with luck, the patriotism that they can inspire. He understood that symbols were a renewal and prolonging of the nation's historical memory. One thinks of the 1981 inaugural ceremony at the Pantheon; the new image of Paris and France in the Pyramid in the Louvre; the famous photograph of Helmut Kohl, the giant German, and Mitterrand, the small Frenchman, at the Verdun monument, hands joined in homage to the war dead of both nations, a memory of the "three wars in a single man's lifetime," in de Gaulle's phrase. This photograph symbolized the fact that the French Left is capable of statesmanship, of governing in France's national interest and Europe's wider interest. De Gaulle, and the de Gaulle/Adenauer couple, are, after Mitterrand/Helmut Kohl, not the only ones in the history of Franco-German reconciliation.

The French people, despite their uncertainty in estimating him, were not indifferent to Mitterrand, the fate he once said he feared most, "to die amidst indifference." In the first year after his death some 360,000 people visited his tomb in Jarnac, and five years later he remains a subject of intense discussion, with an entire generation having grown up knowing only him as president.

MITTERRAND AND
"THE PROBLEM OF DIRTY HANDS"

Jean-Paul Sartre's play *Les Mains Sales* is an obvious way to move from discussing the flaw misperceiving Mitterrand's teaching obligation to concluding on the question of his "dirty hands": how much, if at all, the French president was especially corrupt in office.

The political theorist Michael Walzer has distilled the problem in a famous article called, "Political Action: The Problem of Dirty Hands," which discusses *Les Mains Sales*.[10] Sartre's character, Hörderer, a Communist leader, tries to justify the horrors in which he has participated: "I have dirty hands right up to the elbows. I've plunged them in filth and blood. Do you think you can govern innocently?"

Walzer's answer is at first to agree. No, he says, it is not possible to govern innocently, not even for the best of leaders. How can this be so? Doing the right thing in utilitarian terms, says Walzer, may "leave the man who does it guilty of a moral wrong. The innocent [leader], afterwards, is no longer innocent. If on the other hand he remains innocent . . . he not only fails to do the right thing (in utilitarian terms), he may also fail to measure up to the duties of his office (which imposes on him a considerable responsibility for consequences and outcomes)."[11]

The dilemma of "dirty hands," says Walzer, "derives from an effort to refuse 'absolutism' without denying the reality of the moral dilemma." The politician is singled out, unlike "the other entrepreneurs in an open society, who hustle, lie, intrigue, wear masks, smile and are villains," for three reasons. First, the politician acts, or claims to act on our behalf, in our name. Second, the politician rules over us, "and the pleasures of ruling are much greater than the pleasures of being ruled. The politician has, or pretends to have, a kind of confidence in his own judgment that the rest of us know to be presumptuous in any man." The politician with dirty hands is typically the liar, not the killer. And third, politicians "can do no good themselves unless they win the struggle, which they are unlikely to do unless they are willing and able to use the necessary means. So we are suspicious even of the best of winners. No one succeeds in politics," Walzer concludes, "without getting his hands dirty."

The moral dilemma is that "sometimes it is right to try to succeed, and then it must also be right to get one's hands dirty. But one's hands get dirty from doing what it is wrong to do. And how can it be wrong to do what is right? Or, how can we get our hands dirty by doing what we ought to do?"[12]

Looking at the comparisons, it is hard to argue that Mitterrand's tenure was significantly more or significantly less corrupt than his predecessor or successors. At the time the finance scandal engulfing the Socialist party seemed to be unique, and the corporate insider scandals of his associates and friends, especially Patrice Pelat, were made out to be his own particular fault. But the various scandals surrounding President Jacques Chirac seem to be, if anything, worse. Even Helmut Kohl, the "chancellor of German unification," had to resign in January 2000 as honorary chairman of the German CDU party. "Mr. Kohl's image as a statesman," commented a leading American newspaper, "is rapidly degenerating into that of a corrupt and arrogant machine boss." What is more, "The Kohl affair is a reminder that the United States is not the only advanced democracy where the insatiable demands of campaign finance threaten to undermine democracy. Since the reckless fund-raising of the 1996 American presidential campaign, France, Spain, Italy and Britain have all been rocked by fund-raising scandals."[13] Not even a mention of Mitterrand by name in all this, and he would have been very glad to know he was proven wrong in his prediction of permanent damage.

Changing the electoral law for the 1986 elections was also portrayed as a, perhaps the, summum of corruption, because it would increase the size of the National Front's representation in parliament (which it did). But over a decade later the FN has faded politically and split internally, despite a majority electoral system reestablished already in 1988. Today some of the same critics argue that France now needs a proportional representation voting system (i.e., the "guilty" 1986 system) because the majority system of voting disadvantages the French Ecologists, especially in comparison with the German Greens who have many more parliamentary seats with an only slightly larger electorate.

With respect to the matter of lying, of which his French counterparts thought him especially guilty, it is difficult to judge, because there are distinctions: important lies versus unimportant lies; lies in partisan politics versus reliability as a partner in international affairs; and the fact that, as Walzer says, some lying, some dirty hands, may be necessary to doing good. Did Mitterrand lie when he claimed to be a socialist convert? If so, was it a lie that did more good than harm?

I would judge that François Mitterrand was both more and less guilty than the comparisons we have set up. He was no doubt guilty of gluttony in lying, of the sin of overindulgence. He often told unimportant lies for no particular gain, seemingly just to amuse himself. Yet his word as France's representative in international relations was respected, as we saw, and France "counted" in important situations with Mitterrand at the helm.

Walzer's distinctive conclusion is to give us three ways of thinking about dirty hands: the neoclassical, the Protestant, and the Catholic perspective. Machiavelli is the best representative of the neoclassical outlook. The end, for Machiavelli, justifies the means, and a politician must learn how to do wrong, harm, evil, "how not to be good," in order to succeed. Sometimes "when the act accuses," he wrote in the *Discourses,* "the result excuses." This does not mean, however, that bad means are really good; if they were good, Machiavelli would not have to justify learning how not to be good.

The second tradition, Protestant thinking, is exemplified by Max Weber and his essay "Politics as a Vocation," his famous exposition of how "the good man with dirty hands is a hero still, but he is a tragic hero." With full consciousness of what he is doing, the politician "does bad in order to do good, and surrenders his soul." Thus this kind of political man fixes the prices he pays for acting in this world: the loss of his soul.

Walzer's most important, third, model of facing the dirty hands dilemma is the Catholic tradition, and, given Mitterrand's deeply Catholic background, it is the most pertinent here. In this view the politician with dirty hands does not lose his soul irrevocably. In committing a determinate wrong "he must pay a determinate penalty." So doing wrong in order to do what is right (or what one thinks is right) is to violate a set of rules. It is to go beyond a moral or legal limit in order to do what one believes one should or must do, and "to acknowledge responsibility for the violation by accepting punishment or doing penance."[14]

Since in most cases of dirty hands moral rules are broken for reasons of state, only the doer himself can provide a punishment. Thus a good leader deals with (but doesn't resolve) the problem of dirty hands by *conscience.* He feels guilty for the wrong done, even though the end was good. It is a kind of commission of sin and absolution, although the sinner and the confessor/absolver are the same person. Thus we know the good leader who has dirty hands by his conscience: "Here is the moral politician; it is by his dirty hands that we know him. If he were a moral man and nothing else, his hands would not be dirty; if he were a politician and nothing else, he would pretend that they were clean. We don't want to be ruled by men who have lost their souls."[15] The politician's guilty conscience proves his own humanity.

If Mitterrand, a lapsed Catholic, had an existentialist consciousness, a Catholic conclusion about his reaction to dirty hands, with its idea of a universal external morality, is probably not adequate. Yet it still makes sense to ask whether François Mitterrand was "sorry" for his wrongs, sorry in his own terms.

Did Mitterrand at least "die sorry" for his political mistakes and his personal cruelties? Even at the end of my thinking, I'm not certain. We can't get at the matter directly. But it is significant that he was reproached by many French politicians and intellectuals for never apologizing for mistakes, never recognizing errors or owning up to his major policy reversals, especially the abandonment of socialism in 1982-1983. But then again, had Mitterrand apologized to the satisfaction of some critics, others would immediately have said these apologies were false. In any case it seems hardly likely that the man was "sorry" in a general sense of strict Catholic conscience for his lying, his mistakes, errors, and for what one has to call his personal corruption, even if it turns out to have been not so egregious. But, without making a sense of guilt his general rule, he was surely sorry about specific acts or results. First would be the human costs of high unemployment due, at least in part, to his European integration policy: By what right did he do so much damage to the lives of so many others, even for a good cause? Second would be what happened or did not happen on his watch as France's president in developing country situations, especially in Africa and above all in Rwanda. Finally, were such specific instances as the Portuguese photographer's accidental death in the *Rainbow Warrior* incident. Was the French president not responsible in a general way for what his government subordinates did or did not do?

Let us say that probably in his private moments, alone with his conscience, he was sorry—or that he struggled to remember what it once had been to be sorry. This was a republican prince who had had such a long, arduous career as a man with a mask! He was permitted, and chose, to last too long in the highest office of the republic. And his own illness, especially near the end, was too full of pain for him to remember the times without pain, the time before he had caused pain and become guilty. In this sense, too, de Gaulle's famous comment about his former superior Marshal Pétain applies to Mitterrand: "Old age is a shipwreck!" The scandal is not only that no one gets out alive but that so much damage is done in dying.

Mitterrand will not be remembered for his personal moral example. But the French president, I have stressed, is not asked to be a moral role model in the American model. He is expected to embody national dignity, seriousness, and French prestige, all of which Mitterrand did with aplomb, showing in the process that the French Left could stand stead for France as well as the Right.

Otherwise Mitterrand's presidency will be remembered, ultimately, for his unconventional achievements—a dissipater of illusions, a maker of legitimacy, a transgressor of taboos, all of which are worthy enterprises.

THE MITTERRAND ERA IN FRENCH HISTORY

In response to Elie Wiesel's question as to how Mitterrand judged his own record, Mitterrand answered, unusually modestly: "Being by nature someone never satisfied, I believe that I have ended up far below my ambitions. And generally speaking I tend to credit the criticisms which are made of me even if my adversaries are wrong to condemn my achievements en bloc and without appeal. My opinion is more mixed, of course, it is wrong I think to denigrate everything [I have done]." In this response one first of all gets a sense of how widely and severely Mitterrand was criticized in the last period. Speaking then to Wiesel's hope for a more spiritual or humanistic thought, Mitterrand said he hoped historians would credit his "faith in humanity's destiny, in France's destiny, and in the construction of Europe." For all the boilerplate, this was surely sincere. For certain of his actions Mitterrand claimed credit: first of all for abolishing the death penalty, then decentralization of the French state, his defense, at least rhetorically, of oppressed peoples and minorities, and, finally, his great role in advancing European integration. "I believe those things are part of a balance sheet of which I could be proud," he concluded, "if I had the propensity for pride." He confirmed again that the punitive French unemployment rate, although "the malady is not French [but international] in its origin," was his biggest regret. He concluded with Willy Brandt's self-evaluation: "I did what I could." But he added, "if anguish is allowed to dominate [a leader's thoughts], the power-holder lives in a condition of irresolution. It is a very noble sentiment to be anguished by the consequences of the decisions which are to be taken, but this can become a continuing self-frustration."[16]

François Mitterrand is surely an extraordinarily complex and self-aware case study in the eternal problem of the politician's dirty hands. But Mitterrand's career shows also that any theoretical conception such as Walzer's is only a beginning, never an end, to analysis. "A life is a whole," said Mitterrand in another of his Stoic ideas, "One can't judge a man until after his death."[17] Mitterrand the Stoic was also Mitterrand pleading his case to history.

◆　◆　◆

Mitterrand's fundamental orientation certainly evolved over time and in reaction to circumstances, including the personal crisis that resulted from the Observatory affair. He was neither an unequivocal rightest nor leftist. Was Mitterrand then a centrist after all? Yes and no. If we take the long view, his presidency did produce a recentered, deradicalized republic, as various French writers called it. But the Union of the Left, an alliance with the Communists during the cold war, surely cannot be called a centrist policy. Was Mitterrand's socialist experiment in 1981 the work of a centrist politician? Was abolition of the death penalty on taking power in 1981 (France was late to do so among European Community countries) the act of a centrist? "Centrist" in Mitterrand's case means simultaneously a "radical centrism" in the beginning and a long-term centrism by default, in the sense that almost any politician who governs for so long heads for realism, which means, more or less according to circumstances, the center.

"Worldly wisdom teaches that it is better for reputation to fail conventionally than to succeed unconventionally." Is not François Mitterrand a convincing case in point of Keynes's maxim? The time is here for a new look at the fact that Mitterrand's achievements were often not what he had promised; he many times failed at what he said was his goal, yet succeeded in ways he never could have, had he said what wanted to do. He failed at socialism but resolved the Communist problem and made the Socialist party into a responsible, strong European social democratic party, the permanent alternative governing party in France. He failed to reform the Fifth Republic's constitution and institutions as thoroughly as he had promised; but in fact he completed their legitimation by getting the Left to accept the overpowerful presidency and cohabitation. He didn't want cohabitation but made it a success, part of his hidden agenda of institution-building and making legitimacy. He had said as an opposition politician that "Europe will be socialist or it won't be," but ended up building the capitalist single integrated market and setting up the Single European Currency framework.

Mitterrand's presidency came at the end of a period in French development when clearing away old debris and abandoning old hypocrisies were as important as new projects, and he was an exceptional leader for the job. It seems a striking paradox, otherwise, that the man who led the Socialist-Communist Left to government ended by presiding over the disillusionment of the left-wing socialist myth. Mitterrand was more certain than Mikhail Gorbachev of where he wanted to go.

Making legitimacy, the French Left's acceptance of the Fifth Republic's institutions, was also an unconventional achievement. Accepting the gaullist presidency or cohabitation, for example, could not have been proclaimed in a party program because it never would have passed. Under Mitterrand the French Left tiptoed into legitimacy as it tiptoed away from socialism.

The considerable forward movement in European integration is on the other hand François Mitterrand's most significant positive achievement. He helped reinvigorate France's leadership in the whole European movement and especially in the specific Single European Act (1987) and Maastricht treaties (1991). But European integration was a long-term perspective within which Mitterrand was, in the short and medium term, consciously paying high prices at home, especially the unemployment rate. This kind of balance sheet, policymaking for the long term, also indicates an unconventional leader. Keynes really was correct to say that, for reputation, failure in conventional patterns may look better than an unconventional success.

Mitterrand's presidency came at a time not entirely of his choosing (he thought he was too old, sixty-five, when he finally was elected; he had planned on 1976, which would have been the end of Pompidou's term) and at a time when launching the French Left's socialist experiment was complicated by all the aspects of exhaustion and crisis of the "end of French exceptionalism."

Mitterrand was, as he said, the "last of the great French presidents," meaning the last president to wield the full powers of the gaullist Machiavellian republican presidency of the Fifth Republic. He was also, by historical circumstance, the last president of the long period of French exceptionalism. His presidency did not cause, though it coincided with and in certain respects finished up, the end of a centuries long period. The historian François Furet's statement of the late 1970s that "The French Revolution is finally over" indicated the end of French exceptionalism in which François Mitterrand took office. In this sense, Mitterrand's presidency was a bridge between past and future. He was an exceptional leader at a time when France was ceasing to be an exception.

Stanley Hoffmann has made the same point in a different way, speaking in terms of French identity: "The *malaise* about identity results more from domestic politics [than from France's international position]. . . . Over time, the French search for distinctiveness and autonomy may transfer its focus from France to a Europe in which France will continue to play an important role. Thus, at last, France would become an 'ordinary' European nation, encased in a highly original Community. An unromantic prospect, but a likely fate."[18]

"[N]o policy can combine all advantages." So says Henry Kissinger concerning diplomatic strategies at the Congress of Vienna of 1815.[19] Kissinger could have added that no strategy can accomplish all of its goals—especially when they are as many, as varied, as contradictory, and as opposed by trends in other countries and international forces as were Mitterrand's on arrival in office in 1981.

Mitterrand's great dilemma in 1981, he said repeatedly, would be "the necessity of taking care of everything at once": the first governmental *alternance* in the Fifth Republic; the first left-wing government since the Popular Front; the first Socialist domination of the Communists; the Euromissile crisis; the huge financial risks of his domestic socialist program; the threat of its breaking up the Common Market and the European Monetary System; the permanent threat that the Communists would dessert the government in order to sabotage the Socialists, and still more. He had to fail somewhere, and surely in more than one place. Looking dispassionately in retrospect, it is apparent that a leader of rare talents was required in order not to make *more* mess in the first few years, to survive the initial disasters in order to reach the calmer waters of 1984 and beyond.

As for his political itinerary, the fact that after beginning on the Right François Mitterrand ended up a genuine man of the Left has importance beyond the issue of what remains of the old Left after communism's collapse and the demise of "socialism" as a concept and an ideal. It is key to understanding how Mitterrand was able to sustain France's rank as a nation, capable, if not guaranteed, of a continuing important international role—just as de Gaulle, entering from the Right, did in his time. Mitterrand was elected as the first leftist president of the Fifth Republic but became president of all the French—itself an important legacy coming from the Left, a more significant achievement than it appears to be today, when the titanic Left-Right and intra-Left struggles in France are receding into the lore of history. And against a history of shaky European left-wing attitudes in east-west relations and defense and security issues, Mitterrand's own policies, showing that a Socialist French president could be solid on both counts, were crucial. He served as a nonconformist example of political courage for Socialist leaders in other countries in the 1980s (Spain, Portugal) and took security worries off the agenda of those who believed the Left was disqualified from running western governments. As for Mitterrand's suspicion of American policy, whether this was a gaullist attitude alone or something more deeply French needs a nuanced answer:

The powerful nationalism motivating Mitterrand and so many of the French is certainly antecedent to de Gaulle. However, de Gaulle turned up a flame that was burning very low after the defeat of 1940. Incarnating French nationalism, he inculcated a new pride of country in his contemporaries and the following generations. His institutions allowed new scope for the ambitions (and resentments) of French national sensibility. Once he had passed that way, much French nationalism had a *gaullien* tone. But essentially Mitterrand was acting as a Frenchman of his cultural background and political generation who would have behaved as he did had he never heard of de Gaulle.[20]

Mitterrand's European policies were much more than mere nationalism and more than simply a rejection of gaullism. They had the vision of a statesman and did not merely undo de Gaulle's *Europe des patries* intergovernmentalist conception but extended its underlying idea, a gaullien conception of the national interest, in ways de Gaulle himself, thirty years on and in very different circumstances, might have approved as being in France's national interest.

Even if his record of success and failure was mixed (so was de Gaulle's, remember), and even if his practical policies preserved national sovereignty in much EU business by seeking an increased role for the European Council, François Mitterrand was undoubtedly a "European" in the strong sense. He had in mind federalist structures in a "little Europe" as the core ultimate goal, even with a looser European Confederation surrounding it. However communism's collapse and the "return to Europe" of Central and East Central European countries meant that the European Union would expand and that Mitterrand's "little Europe" ideas were null or would have to be seriously reformulated. But this was neither Mitterrand's "mistake," nor could he have avoided either German unification or EU expansion. Conditions change and statesmen adjust, or not. The Maastricht Treaty's programs for Monetary Union and Political Union, conceived with Helmut Kohl, were Mitterrand's adjustment. Decried as too impractical to be realized, to the end of his term of office and into Jacques Chirac's, the advent of the Single European Currency, the euro, is one posthumous vindication of Mitterrand's daring and his ability to recoup. *The Economist* magazine in October 1999 commented, "One can already see the wisdom of the pact made a decade ago between President François Mitterrand of France and Chancellor Helmut Kohl of Germany to bind a united Germany more tightly into Europe through monetary union. This Germany has big political options not available to other countries, such as a sphere of interests in Central and Eastern Europe and a strong bilateral relationship with Russia. Even when latent, these may give Germany a distinct view of the world and of its own interests which is bound to tug at its EU loyalties from time to time."[21]

In general, the record shows that Mitterrand masterfully served not only French but European interests, a record of genuine statesmanship even allowing for weak spots, achievements which if not historic are on the historical scale.[22] Wanting to make history has not only the benefits of aiming high but also their costs, and the desire to make history also raises the stakes. "He knew the vanity of things," Gresbert wrote, "but couldn't resist the desire to try to make History, a very French malady."[23] Again and again François Mitterrand is representative of France and French leadership.

Helmut Kohl was arguably the most successful European politician of the second half of the twentieth century, partly because his country had so much more to gain in its policies than did a "satisfied" country such as France. Kohl was the chancellor of the great positive achievements of Germany's peaceful unification and introduction of the European single currency. But in choosing to run again in 1998, Kohl risked much that he had built, and his reputation was diminished by his not knowing when to go. The first fault did not apply to Mitterrand, because he was too sick even to think of running again in 1995 (as the French constitution permits). Fixed terms for leaders are a good thing, although for plausible reasons a parliamentary system allows leaders, as Mrs. Thatcher said, "to go on and on." Absent the American presidential two-term limit, Ronald Reagan might have run and won in 1988, becoming a disaster in a third term. That François Mitterrand did not groom a clear successor is sometimes counted as a lapse and attributed to the corruption of power, the supposed impossibility to give it up willingly. I do think Mitterrand was partial to certain possible successors, but he knew more clearly whom he did not want than whom he did. The strong impression left by Mitterrand's relative inaction on a successor is, in any case, that he believed power must be taken, should be won in a struggle and not received.

In terms of German unification, in truth Mitterrand lacked not so much confidence in Germany but rather in a certain geopolitical *imagination,* the imagination necessary to conceive what a world other than Yalta Europe might be. Had Mitterrand seen clearly enough the potential structures of a post-Yalta Europe (which he had never expected to see) he might have sponsored German unification from the beginning, rather than late and with "hesitations." He could have spoken for Kohl's intentions internationally and welcomed East Germany and the East German people into the west and into the European Union.

But international trends are not kind to French strategic vision these days. French policymakers themselves see over and over that the secular trends, those long-term trends that can hardly be affected by national decisions and willpower, are not favorable to France. In demographic terms, Eric Hobsbawm reminds us that the French Revolution "occurred in the most powerful and populous state of Europe (leaving Russia apart). In 1789 something like one European out of every five was a Frenchman."[24] The Old Regime and the Napoleonic First Empire, the France of 1680, 1792, and 1806 or 1812, whose armies could sweep Europe and even assault Moscow, were the most feared in Europe.

Who fears the French today, and why would they? Geopolitically, France's demography leads straight to pessimistic forecasts of French international influence, not to speak of France's incapacity to rescue Rwanda even in theory; and more pessimism about how much France, on its own, will count thirty or fifty years from now. Although it is improbable that the low birth rates of the period from 1975 to 2000 will continue, France's population, sixty million in the year 2000, will decline in absolute terms by 25 or 30 percent in the next half century, with the same outlook for France's European partner countries. France today represents only about 1 percent of world population. In fifty years the French will constitute only 0.5 percent. Hubert Védrine notes the French predicament was felt keenly in Mitterrand's team: "No secular world trend on any level—diplomatic, commercial, military, cultural, linguistic—is intrinsically favorable to [France]," meaning that "it is not enough to summon willpower. A convincing idea must guide [French strategy and] today it can only come out of a positive resolution of the France-Germany-Europe equation."[25] Thus Mitterrand's speech to a European Forum in 1990 exhorting the French had an undertone of anxiety:

> One must accept things as they are; what use is served by complaining about them? . . . In France, one must be capable of living next door to a dynamic Germany which is a peaceful conqueror. . . . Well, why not? . . . If Germany grows, France will too. . . . Why should France think a priori that it won't be capable of keeping pace, or even taking the lead? Why can't it conquer markets too? Why should France be defeated in advance? . . . The development of Germany is an incentive to do better. . . . The greatness of each of the two countries must be accompanied by the greatness of the other. . . . We are the ones who asked for [European integration], France and Germany together.[26]

◆   ◆   ◆

Was François Mitterrand, his complexity understood, a "great" president or not? What is "great"? What is the standard?

Mitterrand was not a political genius, perhaps not a great president, but still he was an exceptional president, a remarkable and innovative one. And, like de Gaulle, he was a president as remarkable for what he was as for what he did, although neither Americans nor even the French themselves are sufficiently aware. And we have seen the reasons for this. As pointed out already, some of the French confusion about Mitterrand is in part a confusion about themselves as a people and about their history. Mitterrand was very representative.

And Mitterrand did not, contrary to what critics at the end said, leave the Socialist party an orphan. He knew it was vainglorious to anoint a successor. "When I was made leader," he said, "[the PS] had just won 5 percent in the presidential election. [Now] it has become the alternative governing party. [In the future] Sometimes it will govern, and sometimes it will be the main opposition party."[27] This, not hand-picking a successor, was the important thing. Lionel Jospin emerged on his own as the successor, as head of the party and Socialist prime minister, even if he wasn't a genuine successor to Mitterrand.

The French Communists have accepted permanent junior partner status on the Left. This is not surprising after the Soviet Union's collapse, but it was a major change in its time. For example, after the unexpected 1997 Socialist parliamentary victory, Lionel Jospin told the Communists: "It is not for us to accept conditions posed by the Communists to obtain their entry into the government, but the contrary. I am not against their presence in the government, but it must be the basis of clear principles, and in due course. . . . It is the PS, the majority of the majority, which will fix the line, not the contrary."[28] This was an echo of Mitterrand's refusal of Communist intimidation in the 1970s, except that he was the only Socialist leader remotely capable of it at the time.

On the other hand, Mitterrand's vision of human relations was based in this world, founded, as I've said, on reciprocity and friendship. The classic social democratic moral tone was, on the other hand, one of generosity. In this and in other important ways Mitterrand can be said to have acted "for" the true-blue ideological French Socialists but he was never really "of" them ethically. His own brand of socialism was a choice rather than a tradition. Compared to Pierre Mauroy's "lyrical" and generous social democracy, to Jean-Pierre Chevènement and Pierre Joxe's Marxist-inspired democratic socialism, and to Michel Rocard's "second left" modernistic socialism, it was fundamentally eclectic, intrinsically less ideological or a matter of the heart. Thus is explained the perpetual conflicts about whether François Mitterrand was "really" a socialist. Given the varieties of socialism, there could be no final answer; given the results of Mitterrand's political struggle as contrasted with other potential Socialist leaders, his socialism, if not the real thing according to one or another party faction, was indeed the real thing according to the tests of popular support and practical acts.

Mitterrand's record of achievements (and failures) in French political life bears comparison with Margaret Thatcher's "revolutionary" reshaping of British politics and her three parliamentary electoral victories. In the 1980s he, Margaret Thatcher, and Helmut Kohl constituted a European "little Big Three" during that turning point decade in European history.

In Mitterrand's example, the French learned how to avoid becoming a people whose last defense was delusion. The French have understood that their interest is not to be the last of the 1960s-style gaullist Mohicans. An absolutely intransigent defense of national sovereignty, despite occasional blockades of borders by French truckers and the refusal of British beef exports by French authorities, makes no sense.

On the other hand, Mitterrand's presidency failed, crucially, to narrow inequalities in French society. A Socialist had to be sensitive on this point. To the contrary, socioeconomic inequalities increased drastically. But a remarkable aspect of this failure is that the French people, and French unions, didn't react more strongly, as if they now accepted the neoliberal assumption that the state could no longer be held responsible for everything—even in France.

Was Mitterrand a cynic? "[G]reat tasks are rarely achieved by cynics," writes Henry Kissinger of Winston Churchill.[29] Successful politicians have to care, and caring involves desire and ambition. Jean Monnet observed that "all people of great achievement are ambitious. But the key question is whether they are ambitious to 'be' or to 'do.'" Statesmanship, he said, combines insight and courage. "Insight defines a society's freedom of action, while courage enables the statesman to act on his convictions before they are generally understood. Great statesmen operate on the outer margin of their society's capabilities; weak statesmen tend to be overwhelmed by events."

François Mitterrand's record on this standard is mixed; but the mixture is rich on the positive side.

◆   ◆   ◆

This book has been more a study in politics than a biography or a history. It has considered the life and times of a quintessentially French political man. To the extent that my analysis is successful as history, the representativeness and richness of the case is the reason. So far from being a French sphinx, Mitterrand's character was, in this book's view, complex but not confounding.

Mitterrand was not first of all a rightist, a democratic republican, a leftist, or a socialist. He was foremost a political man, a French political man, a person of ambition who wanted responsibility and had ideas about what must be done. He would have been a political man in almost any regime with the caveat that when he was faced with a bad regime, collaborationist Vichy, he deserted to become an adversary. But all politics is in a true sense "local" politics, and even global politics has a "local" nature—local at any given spot. This book shows that politics has to be learned, compared, understood in local contexts, here meaning the nation-state and, increasingly, the regional level. Political study is sterile when it is place-neutral. In world politics today, national "local" leaders and governments interact increasingly with each other; the national becomes simultaneously the local and the regional; the region becomes globalized and decentralized.

De Gaulle's legacies made possible Mitterrand's legacies. The former's abandonment of empire eliminated the vicious struggles over decolonization from French domestic politics. His creation of a directly elected, nationally legitimate presidency became a fait accompli that Mitterrand and the Left, contrary to their promises, accepted after their great victory in 1981.

Mitterrand once said that, unlike Clemenceau or de Gaulle, he was denied the very possibility of greatness, because "I didn't have a war. I can't be compared to Clemenceau. He, he faced circumstances, such as war, which made his glory." Another journalist said to him: "One could think that you would say, 'I had bad luck: Clemenceau had his war, de Gaulle also. I only had the Gulf war—not much.'" To which Mitterrand replied, "You know it is quite tolerable not to have to face grand catastrophes."[30] How seriously is this to be taken? I cannot help but think that François Mitterrand, reproaching himself for it, pondered the lack of a grand catastrophe in relation to his place in history.

Mitterrand leaves France an example of the existential potential of *la volonté*, of the individual's capacity to forge a destiny and to give existence a moral meaning even as an agnostic. Hubert Védrine aptly saw in François Mitterrand a classic example of "the French will to will." This French idea, no longer much in fashion, of a special "French will to will," of French determination, intellectuality, and courage, goes back in French history to its great legends—to Vercingétorix, to Joan of Arc, Napoleon, and others. But it is also part of existentialist thinking. Jean-Paul Sartre said that man "will be what he makes of himself. . . . He is what he wills and as he conceives himself after existing—as he wills to be after that leap towards existence."[31]

The French medieval historian Georges Duby, who died in 1997, put the purpose of historiography in compatible terms, terms of encouragement of the will to will: "Why write History," he asked, "if it is not to aid our contemporaries to keep confident about their future and better to face the difficulties which they meet every day?"[32] Or, in the Italian philosopher Benedetto Croce's words, some men combine "a pessimism of the intellect tempered by an optimism of the will." Mitterrand, like de Gaulle, quit this life with doubts as well as hopes for his people, *les gens de chez nous,* and his country.

THE LAST FRENCH
PRESIDENT AND FRANCE'S FUTURE

François Mitterrand will have been the last "heroic" Fifth Republic president: the last in the *gaullien* mode with the gaullist republic's exaggerated tendency toward elected monarchy. In the future, even with a favorable parliamentary majority, French presidents will be less politically powerful and more institutionally accountable as France becomes, through the dual motor of national evolution and European integration, more a rule of law state and less a reason of state regime. For better and worse, France will be more globalized and less provincial. The battle for the French language, for example, is basically a lost cause, even in the European Union itself. Future French presidents, barring the exception that proves the rule, will have to speak English, as Giscard and Helmut Schmidt did in blazing a new road already in the 1970s, and as Jacques Chirac and Gerhard Schröder do today. The fact that Britain's prime minister Tony Blair speaks passable French is an accident. A conversation between Chirac, Schröder, and Blair will of necessity be in English.

The old France is, like every advanced country, being internationalized and globalized, thus it is disappearing—the end of French exceptionalism— even as a new France is being made. The old French have more or less gracefully reconciled their sterile and sterilizing conflicts prior to leaving the stage. Given what the American journalist Thomas Friedman calls the problem of "the Lexus and the Olive Tree," there was really no way to go on successfully with the old French games as if the rest of the world didn't exist.

The French are becoming French-and-European, and they are achieving a post-colonialist, internet-based, e-commerce awareness not only of global threat to them, but of global opportunities for them. The "Hexagon," the geography-based image of a six-sided France taught to schoolchildren, is no longer big enough for success. Disastrous "Vichy" as symbol and reality of French history is going the way of heroic "Verdun." French reactions to German unification in 1989 and the Soviet Union's collapse in 1991 will soon be the benchmark of "historical" judgments. In France as everywhere else it will soon be said that an anachronistic politician is "a hopeless man of the twentieth century."

◆　◆　◆

Mitterrand's talent, seen in perspective, was well-suited to the institution-building that, so far, is called European integration. His achievement, even vis-à-vis de Gaulle's long shadow, is that his European legacy stands on its own, a mark of pride for the French Left as for himself. Supported by de Gaulle's edifice and standing on de Gaulle's shoulders, Mitterrand's legacy is marked with his own beginnings, his own shifts, and his unquestionable points of originality. As left-wing leader and as president Mitterrand took the French national interest not so much in a radical new direction but rather in a plausible extension of the historic path of French policy debates. To ask what de Gaulle would do is no longer a convincing method of analysis even among the neo-gaullists.

As Pierre Morel says, the essence of Mitterrand's diplomacy, like de Gaulle's, was care for the European equilibrium. It was not integration for its own sake. If Mitterrand was the "last" French president as I have defined it, he, along with Valéry Giscard d'Estaing, was France's first "Franco-European" president. In a rough-and-ready definition this means a French president who accepts European Council meetings based on majority voting as normal and who asks for the floor rather than demands it.

Mitterrand's legacies are far from homogeneous, but he ranks among the exceptional leaders of our time. His domestic success was to clarify French politics by winning the last national battles of what historians call Europe's "long" nineteenth (1789-1914) and "short" twentieth (1914-1989) centuries. French politics has become less exotic, and Mitterrand, the departed exotic, was much responsible for the change. In that respect his legacy is a normalization that has been criticized as too much consensus. But it cleared the decks to face the real problems of French society at the new century.

The Mitterrand presidency internationally was a culmination of secular French and European trends. The French today are less comfortably ensconced than ever before in contemplation of their exciting history, less self-confident as a people in their "Frenchness," and more uncertain as a national power. France alone, *la France seule,* no longer is an attractive image for French young people thinking about their future. It can only be a trap, as in the contemporary far Right's slogan, "France for the French."

The old self-sufficiency, the smug satisfaction in what is "French," plays less well even at home. And these dilemmas will worsen with the new century—problems of declining demography, racism, xenophobia, and national identity—unless "Europe" becomes a sufficiently attractive and welcoming new élyséen mansion. From that perspective François Mitterrand's reputation as a solid bridge between the French past and future will improve with age.

NOTES

PREFACE

1. Daniel Halpern, "The Last Existentialist," *The New York Times Book Review,* December 19, 1999, p. 39.

CHAPTER 1

1. François Mitterrand, *Ici et Maintenant* (Paris: Fayard, 1980), pp. 242-43. This statement could have been signed by de Gaulle as well, although the latter probably was not much interested in Americans as people.
2. François Mitterrand, *La Paille et le Grain* (Paris: Flammarion, 1975), p. 139.
3. Ralph Waldo Emerson, "History," in *Self-Reliance and Other Essays* (Mineola, N.Y.: Dover, 1993), p. 6.
4. Henri Michaux, *Un Barbare en Asie* (Paris: Gallimard, 1967), p. 179.
5. The judgment is that of Friedrich von Gentz, long Metternich's closest associate, quoted in Henry Kissinger, *A World Restored: Metternich, Castlereagh and the Problems of Peace, 1812-1822* (Boston: Houghton Mifflin, 1957), pp. 11-12, from Heinrich von Srbik, *Metternich der Staatsmann und der Mensch,* 2 vols. (Munich: 1925), vol. 1, p. 144. The full comment was that Metternich was "Not a man of strong passions and of bold measures; not a genius but a great talent; cool, calm, imperturbable and calculator *par excellence.*" François Mitterrand had the capacity for strong passion and sometimes of bold measures, although a French journalist, Paul Fabra, regarding German unification and Soviet collapse, wrote a biting editorial entitled "Metternich-Mitterrand," arguing that the French president, like the Austrian diplomat was "always in favor of the status quo."

CHAPTER 2

1. Erik Erikson, *Young Man Luther: A Study in Psychoanalysis and History* (New York: Norton, 1958), p. 14.
2. Ibid., p. 23.
3. Interview, *L'Express,* no. 2245, July 21, 1994, p. 16. Compare a 1975 text describing the young Mitterrand's impression of de Gaulle in August 1944 at the first interim government meeting: "I still hear in my mind his monologue on that occasion. I listened, I observed, I admired. Having lived through many historic days whose memory I have lost, I have become stingy with such emotions. I was twenty-seven years old, had reserves of enthusiasm and a certain propensity to dramatize events. I also had reason to open my eyes wide. It was the beginning of an era, and it was General de Gaulle. I ask myself sometimes why that hour did not create more of a connection between myself and the man who was such a lesson for me." From Mitterrand, *Le Paille et le Grain,* op. cit., p. 137.

4. de Gaulle, *War Memoirs,* vol. 1, chap. 3, "Free France" (New York: Simon and Schuster, 1967), p. 81.

5. Ibid., pp. 82-3, emphasis mine. No better raconteur of "de Gaulle" ever existed than de Gaulle himself. In his 1930s books, *The Edge of the Sword* (New York: Greenwood Press, 1975) and *The Army of the Future* (Philadelphia, PA: Lippincott, 1941), written as a young professor at the French War College and Polytechnique, de Gaulle wrote stirringly about the nature of the modern army and of leadership in what were transparent versions of his concerns and himself. A high irony, he was at the time an assistant, and ghostwriter, for Philippe Pétain!

6. Hoffmann, op. cit., p. 236. He adds that "for de Gaulle the aim in life was not to realize a program, but to be a *caractère,* to have a firm identity."

7. See Pierre Péan, *Une Jeunesse Française: François Mitterrand, 1934-47* (Paris: Fayard, 1994), p. 149ff. This episode is more fully evoked in chapter 3 below.

8. See for example Lacouture, op. cit., I, p. 44.

9. The Communists also wanted Algeria to remain French, but for hypocritical "proletarian internationalist" reasons rather than the clearer rationale of colonialism. The PCF's policy, guided by the Soviets, foresaw Algerian independence only after the Communists came to power in Paris. Independence and socialism would then come "in a single step" in Algiers. Meantime the Algerian Communists would remain subordinated to the Paris Politburo, and through Paris, subordinate to Moscow strategy. In the 1950s the Algerian FLN thus needed emancipation not only from France but also from the Soviet Union, which explains why "socialist" Algeria was never a simple Soviet satellite.

10. See Catherine Nay, *Le noir et le rouge* (Paris: Grasset, 1984), p. 253. Nay's book is the most detailed biography on the Observatory affair. The entire press file on the Observatory affair is available on microfilm at the Institut d'Etudes Politiques (Paris), #FRA 59 (021), including material not used by others and also the important statements I have quoted along with them.

11. *The Times,* October 23, 1959, from IEP dossier.

12. *The Guardian,* October 30, 1959, IEP dossier.

13. *France-Observateur,* October 29, 1959, IEP dossier.

14. See Franz-Olivier Giesbert, *François Mitterrand, une vie* (Paris: Seuil, 1995), p. 187.

15. Nay, *Le Noir et le Rouge,* op. cit., 255-56.

16. *France-Observateur,* October 29, 1959, IEP dossier. In order to make the summary of events easier to understand, I have taken small liberties with chronology.

17. From *France-Observateur* weekly October 29, 1959, pp. 4-5ff. IEP dossier.

18. See *L'Express,* whose director Jean-Jacques Servan-Schreiber, and columnist, Françoise Giroud, had supported Mitterrand, and where he had published guest editorials. Taken from Nay, *Le noir,* op. cit., p. 257.

19. François Mauriac, "Bloc-notes," November 24 and 30, 1959, *L'Express,* quoted in Giesbert, op. cit., p. 193.

20. Mitterrand was a senator rather than a deputy at this time, having been defeated for the lower house in the gaullist landslide of November 1958. He won a Senate seat, from the Nièvre, in April 1959, then won back his National Assembly seat in 1962.

21. Jean Lacouture implicates Michel Debré personally more heavily both in the Bazooka affair and the entrapment of Mitterrand in the Observatory affair. The passion is high but the evidence is a bit short; yet if true the upshot would be grave, given Debré's importance in de Gaulle's return and the whole beginning of the Fifth Republic. See Lacouture, *Mitterrand,* op. cit., vol. 1, chap. 8.

22. *Le Monde,* November 25, 1959, p. 1.

23. Peyrefitte, *C'était de Gaulle* (Paris: Éditions de Fallois, Fayard, 1994, 1998), 2 vols., p. 601.

24. Peyrefitte, op. cit., p. 602. Peyrefitte says that in 1994 Roger Frey explicitly approved this summary of the conversation the two men had with de Gaulle that day, because of the points concerning Mitterrand and the institutions. Peyrefitte adds, "The General, with his instinct for the State, had just invented a sort of immunity for presidential candidates. Today this

Roman virtue seems to Frey and myself more explanatory than convincing." Another troubling aspect (see chapter 11) is Frey's affirmation that one of Mitterrand's biggest electoral supporters in 1965 was René Bousquet, with money and his *Dauphiné* regional newspaper—"And who is supporting [Mitterrand] the most actively in the shadows? Bousquet! There's a lot to say about him!" Even if Bousquet's support were no longer as important to a president as it had been to a struggling candidate in the early 1960s, Mitterrand's attitude toward Bousquet in the 1980s would perhaps have been affected by loyalty or repaying debts.

25. Roland Dumas, *Le Fil et le Pelote: Mémoires* (Paris: Plon, 1996), p. 136.
26. *Lettre Ouverte aux Hommes Politiques* (Paris: Albin Michel, 1976), reprinted also in Jean Montaldo, *Lettre Ouverte d'un "Chien" a François Mitterrand au nom de la Liberté d'aboyer* (Paris: Albin Michel, 1993), pp. 47-50.
27. Nay, *Le Noir et le Rouge*, op. cit., p. 262. Other intimate friends, such as Michèle Cotta, confirmed to this writer in interviews that years later "Mitterrand would still get to tears whenever the subject of the Observatory affair came up" and that he appeared psychologically pushed to the edge at the time. Georges Dayan apparently told Giesbert what he had told Nay (*François Mitterrand*, p. 192). Mitterrand's wife, Danielle, told him it was "the most difficult moment of his career." (Ibid.) Lacouture's new biography reconfirms that Rousselet "remains convinced that [Mitterrand] was capable of any act" (*Mitterrand*, op. cit. vol. 1, p. 233n). This evidence justifies interpretation of the experience as an identity crisis.
28. Nay, *Le Noir et le Rouge*, op. cit., p. 263.
29. Cayrol, *François Mitterrand, 1945-67* (Paris: PFNSP, 1967), p. 87.
30. In Lacouture, *Mitterrand: Une Histoire de Français,* vol. 1 (Paris: Seuil, 1998), p. 257.

CHAPTER 3

1. Taken from Anonymous, *Mémoires pour Servir à l'Histoire de Ma Vie* (Paris: Editions Bartillat, 1997), p. 11.
2. See Alain Peyrefitte, *C'était de Gaulle* (Paris: Editions de Fallois, Fayard, 1994, 1998), vol. 2, pp. 578-81. Serge July, editor of the left-wing newspaper *Libération* and an anti-de Gaulle veteran of May 1968, lumped the two together: "[Mitterrand] shares with de Gaulle the same volcanic pride of a Rastignac gone up to Paris to impose his own order on it . . ." De Gaulle was from the northern city of Lille. See his *Les Années Mitterrand Histoire Baroque d'une Normalisation Inachevée* (Paris: Grasset, 1986), p. 24. Catherine Nay disagreed: "The young François . . . was no Eugène de Rastignac of Balzac lore. . . . If it ever occurred to him to throw down Rastignac's challenge to the capital—'It's now between the two of us!'— Mitterrand had no notion of courting the rich, getting introductions to the powerful, or marrying into money." However, she does note that Mitterrand had four letters of recommendation from his family to influential people, the best known and most useful being François Mauriac, a friend of his mother and uncle. Mitterrand told her in an interview, "Only . . . François Mauriac, as it happens, spoke to me about myself and my future. The other three waxed eloquent about themselves, so I only went back to see him." Nay, *Le Rouge et le Noir*, op. cit., pp. 37-8.
3. See David Robin Watson, *Georges Clemenceau: A Political Biography* (New York: David McKay Company: 1974), p. 15.
4. Nay, *Le Noir et le Rouge*, op. cit., p. 17, and Lacouture, *Mitterrand: Une Histoire de Français,* op. cit., vol. 1, pp. 15-18.
5. From an interview in *L'Expansion*, August 15, 1972, p. 48.
6. Lacouture, *Mitterrand: Une Histoire de Français,* op. cit., vol. 1, p. 19.
7. Pierre Péan, *Une jeunesse française: François Mitterrand, 1934-1947* (Paris: Fayard, 1994), pp. 20-21.
8. Péan, op. cit., pp. 9-25.

9. Péan, op. cit., pp. 49-51. François Mitterrand's report on this special lecture concerning Ethiopia was found by Péan in the files of the Cent-Quatre hostel.

10. From Péan, op. cit., pp. 51-52.

11. The novelist and gadfly writer Jean-Édern Hallier alleged in print that Mitterrand had joined the Cagoule organization, saying that a former member, Raymond Abelio, had given him the only existing copy of the full list of the membership. See *L'Idiot International,* May 16, 1991, p. 3. Giesbert quotes the most recognized historian of the Cagoule, Philippe Bourdre: "Much imagination would be necessary, or bad faith, to imagine François Mitterrand as a terrorist bomber or active militant in the secret organization; but there remains to explain what is obviously a continuous link in the 1930s to [Cagoule] activists." Giesbert, op. cit., p. 51. Péan's book gives a similar explanation.

12. See Jacques Nobécourt, *Le Colonel de la Rocque, 1885-1946: Ou les Pièges du National-isme Chrétien* (Paris: Fayard, 1996).Nobecourt underlines the differences between the "national" and patriotic de la Rocque and the seriously fascist groups.

13. See Péan, op. cit., pp. 84-5.

14. From Robert Mitterrand, *Frère de quelqu'un* (Paris: Robert Laffont, 1988), quoted in Péan, op. cit., p. 95.

15. Marie-Louise Terrasse, under the stage name of Catherine Langeais, became one of France's first and most popular television "presenters"—the announcer appearing after the evening news to detail the evening's program.

16. Péan, op cit., pp. 85-86.

17. Ibid., pp. 97-98.

18. Ibid., pp. 98-99.

19. From Mitterrand, *Mémoires Interrompus* with Georges-Marc Benamou (Paris: Odile Jacob, 1996), op cit., pp. 9-10.

20. Mitterrand told the story in *Mémoirs Interrompus,* op cit., pp. 10-11: "I let them carry me. Then Italian planes surged in and machine-gunned our human column. Everyone jumped into the ditches on the side of the road, including my buddy, who, since he couldn't take me with him, left me with these good words: 'Don't worry, I'll be back.' I lay there, immobile, my face raised to the sky, following the planes diving on our road and leaving their carpet of bullets." Mitterrand recounts that his group went first to Esnes-en-Argonne, then to a train in the spa of Vittel. But the Germans had already encircled the entire Lorraine. He finally was hospitalized at Bruyêres, in the Vosges Mountains. The Germans arrived on June 18, and he was captured and transferred to a hospital in Lunéville, then to the prisoners' camp nearby.

21. Ibid., p. 18.

22. Ibid., p. 16.

23. François Mitterrand with Elie Wiesel, *Mémoires à deux voix* (Paris: Odile Jacob, 1995), p. 195.

24. From Péan, op. cit., pp. 128-29. The article from *France, Revue de l'État Nouveau* is reprinted in François Mitterrand, *Politique I* (Paris: Fayard, 1977). That Mitterrand in 1977 would reprint an article from a Pétainist magazine, albeit a POW magazine, indicates that he didn't think it was particularly incriminating. A fellow prisoner interviewed by Péan is quoted as saying "We were all Pétainists. We were devoted to the Marshal. For us, he was the grandfather. De Gaulle and the Marshal both were serving France" (p. 145).

25. Péan, op. cit., pp. 160ff.

26. Some critics believe the story of three Mitterrand escapes is fanciful. One version is that there were only two attempts. Another is that Mitterrand's return to France was not an escape at all, but the result of being put on a list of civil servants the Vichy government asked the Germans to return. This author knows of no evidence for these hypotheses and much corroboration of the three escapes.

27. In Péan's account, Mitterrand's brother Robert came to meet him. Finding him so thin and exhausted, Robert convinced him to go to the Lévy-Despases, who had a large house near the citadel of the town. Mitterrand had been to dances at their home in Paris before the war.

Coincidences abound: The eldest Lévy-Despas son, Guy, attended Amherst College, this writer's institution, as a special student in 1939-1940. He had been in the United States when the war broke out, and this was a safe solution for him. Upon completing his Amherst year, however, Guy Lévy-Despas went to Canada where he enlisted in the Royal Canadian Air Force. He was commissioned and went into active service in May 1941, with the flying name "Carlet." In July 1941, Lévy-Despas shot down three enemy aircraft, but later that month his own plane was shot down. He was twenty when killed in action. In November 1975, on the occasion of an address at Amherst, François Mitterrand was shown the stone put up by fellow students in memory of Guy Lévy-Despas, whom Mitterrand had, of course, never met.

28. Mitterrand's brother Robert said that François knew about Marie-Louise's change of heart. Refusal to accept the rupture of his great love was the real reason that, at the end of 1941, François remained so determined to attempt escape again after two failures.

29. In Giesbert, *François Mitterrand*, p. 40, including above quotations. Marie-Louise had fallen in love with a young and handsome Pole, Antoine Gordowski. They were soon married and had two children, Marie-Elisabeth and Jean-Michel. In a second marriage Marie-Louise, now known as Catherine Langeais, married the journalist Pierre Sabbagh.

30. Marie-Louise Terrasse/Catherine Langeais, French television personality and François Mitterrand's ex-fiancée, died on April 23, 1998.

31. See Ronald Tiersky, *French Communism, 1920-1972* (New York: Columbia University Press, 1974), chap.5.

32. One of them was the young Georges Marchais, who from 1968 was the French Communist party leader and thus the leading PCF negotiator with Mitterrand during the Union of the Left period. In this neo-Stalinist Communist leader, the list of concealed wartime pasts of major French politicians had another surprising case. Until the 1980s, Marchais successfully hid his time as a worker in Third Reich Germany. He was even accused then of having gone as a voluntary, rather than as a conscripted, worker. This secret was kept from French public opinion and his own party, except for the internal "control commission" that kept the infamous biographies all members were required to write. Naturally the Soviets also knew, and thus had a leash on him. Marchais never joined the Resistance and entered the Communist party through the Communist-dominated CGT trade union organization shortly after the war.

33. Péan, op. cit., p. 198.

34. Ibid., pp. 198-99.

35. Ibid., p. 141.

36. Ibid., p. 193, who cites Jean-Albert Roussel as the source of this information.

37. Ibid.

38. Eric Hobsbawm, *The Age of Extremes: A History of the World, 1914-1991* (New York: Pantheon Books, 1994), pp. 123-24.

39. Eugen Weber, "A Question of Conscience," *The New York Times Book Review,* June 30, 1996, p. 12, a review of Brian Moore's novel, *The Statement* (New York: Dutton, 1996), a *roman à clef* based on the cases of three French war criminals, Paul Touvier, René Bousquet, and Maurice Papon.

40. Nay, *Le Noir et le Rouge,* op. cit., p. 78.

41. Quoted in Péan, op. cit., p. 171.

42. Nay, *Le Noir et le Rouge,* op. cit., p. 78.

43. Péan, op. cit., p. 193-95. In 1986, inaugurating a monument to Antoine Mauduit, President Mitterrand said, "I have not met five people in my life with such a magnetic personality."

44. Péan reproduces a Mitterrand letter about the meeting, dated June 11, 1942, which strikes an unusually military tone: "Friday evening I plan to leave for Montmaur, in the Hautes-Alpes, where a meeting of ex-prisoners is to take place. I would like to see the creation and organization of a solid movement come out of it. I will emphasize a few main ideas: 1) A mass of men can only be led by a few; 2) these must be exempt from answering to that mass;

3) the leaders must operate as they see fit, which for our part will be our conscience and our will to succeed." Ibid., p. 194.

45.   Ibid., p. 288.

46.   Ibid., p. 295.

47.   Ibid., p. 294ff. Péan's chapter on the *francisque* controversy, pp. 287-95, reproduces a long letter by Simon Arbellot in defense of Mitterrand's argument that this was part of a résistant's double game. Péan also gives a list of seventeen *francisque* awards (including Maurice Pinot, Henri Guitton, and Jean Védrine) to men who were Mitterrand's Vichy coworkers and also résistants.

48.   Philippe Burrin writes that "By recalling Laval. . . . Pétain testified to his desire to press on with the policy of collaboration. Or, at least, he recognized that he could think of no alterative." Laval now had the extraordinary powers he had demanded of Pétain. "As head of government, he now appointed his ministers and assumed direction of governmental policy. As a security measure, he himself took on Internal Affairs, Foreign Affairs and Information." Burrin, *La France à l'heure allemande* (Paris: Seuil, 1995), p. 145.

49.   Giesbert, *François Mitterrand*, op. cit., p. 63.

50.   Péan, op. cit., p. 298.

51.   See an annex to ibid., six historically dramatic single-spaced pages, dated November 23, 1943, titled "Interrogation of Pepe and Monier," The record is said to concern "two men who have latterly been working together in a GIRAUDIST organization in France." The two men are named: Commandant DU PASSAGE, Pierre, aka Pepe, aka du Tertre, Pierre François aka LAURENT, and, François MITTERRAND, aka MONIER, François Jacques, aka MORLAND, François, aka LAROCHE, Jacques André.

52.   Quoted in Péan, op. cit., pp. 309-10.

53.   In 1975 Mitterrand wrote that "The unusual personality of Free France's chief both attracted and repelled me. I believed that our resistance to the Nazis inside France, with its constant risk of torture and death, differed sharply from resistance carried out from abroad. Thus I did not grant the [gaullists] their self-annointed pre-eminence. I questioned whether the word 'resistance' was really applicable to the struggle carried on from London or Algiers." Mitterrand, *Ma Part de Vérité: De la Rupture à l'Unité* (Paris: Fayard, 1969), p. 25-7. This conflict between the metropolitan and the exterior Resistance movements was a point of principle in Mitterrand's mind, of which he never let go.

54.   See Nay, *Le Noir et le Rouge*, op. cit., pp. 93-94. The "document" in question was a letter from the controversial Michel Calliau, de Gaulle's nephew and Mitterrand's rival in organizing the returned-POW movements. Maurice Pinot, interviewed by Nay, recalled: "[Mitterrand] told me of the difficulties of his trip. . . . We were recognized and we were going to get funds and weapons. But Mitterrand told me the General had received him badly, heaping scorn on the demand of former POWs to be grouped into a specific Resistance movement. 'Why not the hairdressers and cooks?' de Gaulle reportedly asked." Nay, *Le Noir et le Rouge*, op cit., p. 95.

55.   Péan, op. cit., p. 364ff. Freney was subsequently a repeated witness for the integrity of François Mitterrand's war record. See Freney's memoir, *La Nuit Finira* (Paris: Plon, 1983).

56.   See Jean-Claude Baker and Chris Chase, *Josephine: The Hungry Heart* (New York: Random House, 1993), chaps. 26-29.

57.   Another chance encounter of significance occurred in London. Trying for days to negotiate a way back to France, Mitterrand met and became friends with a young Communist named Waldeck Rochet, who asked him to carry a letter to his mother back in France. The son of peasants, Waldeck Rochet ended up leader of the French Communist party in the mid-1960s, the successor to Maurice Thorez. In 1965 this old connection, maintained off and on despite the cold war's problems, proved crucial in negotiating Communist acceptance of François Mitterrand as the united Left's presidential candidate.

58.   Péan, op. cit., pp. 375-76.

59. From François Mitterrand, *Les Prisonniers de Guerre devant la Politique* (Paris: Éditions du Rond-Point, 1945), quoted in Péan, op. cit., pp. 368-9.

60. In Nay, *Le Noir et le Rouge*, op. cit., p. 90.

61. Ibid.

62. Ibid., p. 91.

63. After Mitterrand's death in January 1996, it was to be expected that momentos, letters, and other objects belonging to him would surface. The first to be sold at auction seems to have been a lover's short story that he wrote in 1940, called "Premier accord," ("First Link" or "First Connection," meaning "First Love Affair"). Surely not by coincidence, the title of his daughter Mazarine's first book is *Premier roman* (First Novel) (Paris: Odile Jacob, 1998).

64. As Péan notes, these details are taken from Marguerite Duras's book, *La Douleur* (Paris: P.O.L., 1985). Duras claimed she found the manuscript only years later and that she had "no memory of having written it." Péan, op. cit., p. 454fn.

65. Ibid., p. 457.

66. Ibid., p. 471.

67. The above events are summarized from Ibid., pp. 459-474. The double love affair and two children are discussed on p. 473. Paulette Delval was in love with him, Mascolo said to Péan; but Paulette claimed her affair with Mascolo was to try to save her husband (p. 470).

68. From *L'Autre Journal*, 1985, as quoted in Giesbert, op. cit., p. 94.

69. See Giesbert, *François Mitterrand*, op. cit., p. 94, from *La Douleur.*

70. Patrice Pelat agreed: "At that time François looked like a tango dancer." Quotations from Nay, *Le Noir et le Rouge*, op. cit., pp. 133-34.

71. They had three sons. After the deceased Pascal, Jean-Christophe was born in December 1946, and Gilbert in February 1949.

72. Péan, op. cit., pp. 396ff. Nay, *Le Noir et le Rouge*, op. cit., p. 119, reproduces a letter from Michel Calliau of December 8, 1943, to his uncle, de Gaulle: "Miteran [*sic*], in his German camp, after a brilliant war, was a leader of a Pétainist circle. . . . Back in France he went to work for the Commissariat for POWs, put in charge of propaganda, in which direction you can well guess. . . . Now he is an active member of the 'Legion,' and close to Armand Petitjean, very *Action française*. . . . I wonder how he got sent to London." (signed) VERGENNES (Michel Charrette), i.e., Michel Calliau.

73. Edgar Morin recalled: "From the first contacts, the Communist party, via the central committee with which I was in secret contact, asked me to introduce a third movement, the Communist movement [into the gaullist/Pin'Mitt" fusion]. This movement didn't exist. It was me who [set up a facade]. . . . If I hadn't been there, if I hadn't penetrated the Gaullist movement, there would have been only two Resistance movements to fuse." Péan, op. cit., pp. 398-99.

74. See Tiersky, *French Communism,* chaps. 5-6.

75. On recognizing him at a reception for the temporary "secretaries general" ministers— Mitterrand was at the end of the line because he was the youngest—de Gaulle looked at him and said sardonically, "So, you again . . . !" But it was not all bad to have such a reputation— even, or especially, with someone so used to courtiers as de Gaulle.

76. See Peyrefitte, *C'était de Gaulle,* op. cit., vol. 2, pp. 579-80. De Gaulle had earlier described this scene himself at the end of his *War Memoirs,* in the chapter titled "Disunity," but without saying who the insubordinate, rudely disciplined official was. But in a presidential campaign television interview on December 10, 1965, de Gaulle retold the story, this time naming Mitterrand, who was now his opponent in the run-off ballot.

77. Péan, op. cit., pp. 512-15.

CHAPTER 4

1. Lacouture, *Mitterrand,* op. cit., p. 120.

2. Recounted in ibid., vol. 1, p. 83.

3. Ibid., p. 111.
4. Ibid., p. 110.
5. Northcutt, op. cit., p. 34.
6. Mitterrand, *Politique I,* op. cit., p. 370.
7. See Jean Daniel and Jean Lacouture, *Le Citoyen Mendès France* (Paris: Seuil, 1992), and François Stasse, *Le Morale de L'Histoire: Mitterrand - Mendès France, 1943-1982* (Paris: Seuil, 1992).
8. Northcutt, op. cit., p. 46.
9. Lacouture, *Mitterrand,* op. cit., vol. 1, p. 170.
10. Daniel and Lacouture, op. cit., pp. 14-15
11. Roland Cayrol, *François Mitterrand, 1945-67* (Paris: PFNSP, 1967), p. 20.
12. This surely was one reason that Mendès France was so quick to defend Mitterrand in the Observatory affair in 1959, although with less justification as it turned out.
13. Northcutt, op. cit., p. 47.
14. Mendès said later of Mitterrand, "No one knew better the deputies . . . their secret ambitions and confidential dealings. He knew everything and everybody and played parliament like an expert." In Denis MacShane, *François Mitterrand: A Political Odyssey* (London: Quartet Books, 1982), p. 66. And in 1974 he said, "I was completely ignorant of the parliamentary world . . . from the beginning Mitterrand instructed me" (Giesbert, op. cit., p.119). Who do these accounts compliment, or indict, most? They seem the stereotypes of Mendès the Pure and Mitterrand the Manipulator.
15. Nay, *Le Noir et le Rouge,* op. cit., p. 143.
16. Northcutt, op. cit., p. 48.
17. Mitterrand's progressivism was reformist, not revolutionary. In the early 1950s he perceived that having his own network of African allies would be useful, and he swayed the Democratic African Rally, or RDA, away from its links with the French Communist party. The RDA consisted of a group of noteworthy African deputies in the French National Assembly: its leader was Félix Houphouët-Boigny, a doctor from the Ivory Coast. Other leaders were Sékou Touré (as Guinée's president in 1958, he was the only one to reject de Gaulle's "Community" proposition), Diori Hamni, Léon M'ba, and Modibo Keita. The RDA made the Pleven-Mitterrand UDSR party its partner, angering the Communists. Northcutt, op. cit., pp. 50-51.
18. Lacouture, *Mitterrand,* vol. 1, op. cit., pp. 154-55.
19. Ibid., p. 193.
20. Daniel and Lacouture, op. cit., pp. 26-27. Mitterrand's versatile personality and reputation had been delineated in another way when *Elle* magazine asked its readers in October 1951 to name the most attractive men in French public life (movie actors excluded). Mitterrand, *"le beau François"* rated high on the list, next to Maurice Druon, Jacques Chaban-Delmas, Albert Camus, Hubert de Givenchy, and Hervé Alfand.
21. The PSA soon renamed itself the Unified Socialist Party (PSU). It did attract a core of talent and was in the forefront of the May 1968 events. In 1969 its young leader, Michel Rocard, ran for president (getting 2 percent of the vote) in the election provoked by de Gaulle's resignation. In the mid-1970s the PSU and Rocard, along with the CFDT Socialist trade union movement, merged into the new Socialist party led by François Mitterrand.
22. *L'Express,* February 23, 1961, in Lacouture, *Mitterrand,* op. cit., vol. 1, p. 199.
23. As for the elaboration of French Communist strategy, the PCF through secret channels was still very much under Moscow's sway and financial support, at this time.
24. Mitterrand, *Ma Part de Vérité,* op. cit., p. 68.
25. Serge July, "François Mitterrand: Une histoire française," *Le Monde,* January 9, 1996, p. 5.
26. Mitterrand the candidate in 1965 was described with verve by one French author: "It was this Mitterrand who, forty-nine years old, survivor of the stalags, of Vichy, of the MRNPG network, [many] times minister, deputy for twenty years, three years a senator, mayor of the town of Chateau-Chinon, president of the Nièvre General Council, author of several books

of various quality, episodic lawyer at the Paris Bar, married, father of two boys, rich in adventures of good and doubtful types, voracious reader, incisive orator, a man always walking and rarely alone, an indefatigable seducer, a bon vivant in a hurry, a meticulous gardener—and indicted for six years for an infraction which the government justice department has avoided bringing to court—this is the man who entered the competition against General de Gaulle." See Lacouture, *Mitterrand,* op. cit., vol. 1, p. 258.

27. See Tiersky, *French Communism, 1920-1972* (New York: Columbia University Press, 1974), chap. 7.

28. July, *Les Années Mitterrand,* op. cit., p. 24.

29. In Northcutt, op. cit., p. 2.

30. Mitterrand, *Ma Part de Vérité,* op. cit., cited in Nay, *Le Noir et le Rouge,* op. cit., pp. 70-1.

31. See Annie Kriegel, *The French Communists: Portrait of a People* (Chicago: University of Chicago Press, 1972). Georges Lavau, *A Quoi Sert le Parti Communiste Français?* (Paris: Seuil, 1981); and Tiersky, *French Communism,* op. cit.

32. Raymond Aron, *La Révolution Introuvable* (Paris: Calmann-Levy, 1968).

33. Similar points are made by Hubert Védrine, including the French Right's realization of its interest in good relations with Moscow: "This was the epoque when prestigious artists and men of culture rallied 'the Party,' when the weight of communist and marxist ideas made themselves felt far outside the PCF, of Socialists who made a psychological complex of a [Communists] political engagement 'more advanced' than their own, of intellectuals fascinated by the messianic ambition of the fatherland of the Revolution and the project of creating a New Man. Léon Blum, it is true, denounced the 'psychic dependence' regarding the USSR. But the [cold war] socialist left defined itself in a self-denying way: it was the *non communist* left. [U]ntil François Mitterrand overturned the game . . . a part of the French Right . . .saw the advantage it could get, given its willingness to dine with the devil, from the PCF's dependence on the USSR. In order to trap the French Communist party domestically and to disqualify the Left as a whole, why not, in the name of realism, or of economic interests . . . have good relations with the master of the Kremlin?" See Védrine, *Les Mondes de François Mitterrand: A L'Élysée 1981-1995* (Paris: Fayard, 1996), pp. 94-95.

34. Aron, *Plaidoyer, pour l'Europe décadent* (Paris: Robert Laffont, 1984), p.384-85. Aron refers to a PCF-inspired clause in the program that "when the workers of a business express the desire for nationalization, and in accord with the government," any business can be brought up for nationalization. The Communists and the Socialist Marxist left hoped this could be an extensible tool. Mitterrand, who was interested more in getting a joint program than in any particular point, assumed he and the Socialists would keep control or, if not, that the government would be ousted or paralyzed. See also Jean-François Revel's *The Totalitarian Temptation* (Garden City, NJ: Doubleday, 1977), a best-seller English translation of *La tentation Totalitaire* (Paris: 1976).

35. Aron, *Plaidoyer,* pp. 383-84.

36. Quoted in Tiersky, "French Communism, Eurocommunism and Soviet Power," in R. Tökes, ed., *Eurocommunism and Detente* (New York: New York University Press, 1978), p. 164.

37. Quoted from an April 1976 interview in Giesbert, op. cit., p. 300.

38. Ibid., p. 301.

39. In Mitterrand, *Ici et Maintenant,* op. cit., p. 50.

40. Albert Du Roy and Robert Schneider, *Le Roman de la Rose: D'Épinay à L'Élysée* (Paris: Seuil, 1982), p. 225.

41. Giesbert, *François Mitterrand,* op. cit., p. 336.

42. Mitterrand, *la Paille et le Grain,* op. cit., p. 268.

CHAPTER 5

1. Julius W. Friend, *The Long Presidency: France in the Mitterrand Years, 1981-1995* (Boulder, CO: Westview Press, 1997), p. 201.

2. Jacques Attali, *Verbatim,* vol. 1 (Paris: Fayard, 1993), pp. 46-7.
3. Mitterrand's "blue teletype" letter to Ronald Reagan is reproduced in ibid., pp. 44-45. Bush's advocacy for Mitterrand in the Reagan administration began a cordial relationship of considerable importance during the Bush presidency, 1988-1992, during the Gulf War among other crises. See George Bush and Brent Scowcroft, *A World Transformed* (New York: Knopf, 1998). Mitterrand saw Bush as European-oriented by background and education.
4. Attali, op. cit. vol. 1, p. 47.
5. Védrine, op. cit., p. 184.
6. The following section follows Peter Hall, "The Socialist Experiment of François Mitterrand," chapter 8 in his *Governing the Economy: The Politics of State Intervention in Britain and France* (New York: Oxford University Press, 1986), pp. 193ff. A good French account is Pierre Favier and Michel Martin-Roland, *La Décennie Mitterrand,* vol. 1, *Les Ruptures (1981-84)* (Paris: Seuil, 1990), and the raw material in Attali, op. cit.
7. Attali, op. cit., vol. 1, p. 52.
8. Lester Thurow, *Head to Head, The Coming Economic Battle among Japan, Europe, and America,* vol. 1, (New York: Warner Books, Inc., 1993), p. 73.
9. Hall, op. cit., p. 195.
10. Interview in the *Témoignage Chrétien* newspaper, quoted in ibid., translation adapted.
11. Ibid., p. 197.
12. Ibid., pp. 197-98.
13. Eric Aeschiman and Pascal Riché, *La Guerre de Sept Ans: Histoire Secrète du Franc Fort, 1989-1996* (Paris: Calmann-Lévy, 1996), pp. 27-8.
14. *L'Expansion* magazine, April 8, 1983, p. 8.
15. The expression "night visitors" was the title of the classic film by Marcel Carné. In it, the "night visitors" Dominique and Gilles are wandering minstrels sent by the devil to a chateau with the mission of "creating despair." See Aeischermann and Riché, op. cit., p. 27.
16. Hall, op. cit., p. 203.
17. The following section relies on Favier and Martin-Rolland, op. cit., vol. 1, pp. 160-68.
18. Ibid., p. 168.
19. The following section is based on Ronald Tiersky, *France in the New Europe: Changing Yet Steadfast* (Belmont, CA: Wadsworth, 1994), pp. 74-6.
20. See Ronald Tiersky, "Ambivalence Yet Again Unresolved," in William E. Griffith, ed., *The European Left: Italy, France, and Spain* (Lexington, MA: Lexington Books, 1979), pp. 49-80.
21. See Catherine Grémion and Jean-Pierre Worms, "La corruption, bon ou mauvais procès fait à la décentralisation?," in Martha Zuber, ed., *États de la Corruption: Politics, Morals and Corruption in France,* special issue of *French Politics and Society* II, no. 4 (fall 1993), pp. 47-64.
22. Aeschiman and Riché, op. cit., p. 171-73.
23. In an interview with Franz-Olivier Giesbert, *Le Figaro,* September 8, 1994, pp. 1-4.
24. Daniel Singer, *Is Socialism Doomed? The Meaning of Mitterrand* (New York: Oxford University Press, 1988), p. 204.
25. Laure Adler, *L'Année des Adieux* (Paris: Flammarion, 1995), pp. 196-98.
26. Ibid.
27. Quoted in Robert Schneider, *Les Dernieres Années* (Paris: Seuil, 1994), p. 11, from the June 30, 1993 issue of *Charlie-Hebo.*
28. Albert Camus, *La Chute,* quoted in Claude Gubler, *Le Grand Secret* (Paris: Plon, 1996), epigram.

CHAPTER 6

1. Part of this section is taken from Tiersky, "France in the New Europe," op. cit., and *France*

in the *New Europe: Changing yet Steadfast* (Belmont, CA: Wadsworth, 1994), chapter 9.

2. Charles de Gaulle, *Memoirs of Hope,* vol. 1 (New York: Simon and Schuster, 1971), pp. 177-8.

3. Ronald Tiersky, *French Communism,* pp. 207-8.

4. These points are the basis of François Mitterrand's posthumous short book on Franco-German relations, *De l'Allemagne, de la France* (Paris: Odile Jacob, 1996).

5. Helmut Kohl, from *Die Zeit,* March 9, 1990, quoted in Renata Fritsch-Bournazel, *Europe and German Unification* (New York: St. Martin's Press, 1992) p. 179.

6. Védrine, op. cit., p. 755.

7. See Zbigniew Brzezinski's well-known article, "The Myth and the Reality of Yalta," *Foreign Affairs,* winter 1984-1985.

8. Védrine, op. cit., p. 470.

9. See my concluding chapter in Ronald Tiersky, ed., *Europe Today* (Boulder, Co: Rowman and Littlefeld, 1999).

10. From Mitterrand's first presidential interview, by James Reston, the *New York Times,* June 4, 1981, p. 1. During the 1970s the American Embassy not surprisingly did little to make Mitterrand feel welcome, at least at high levels. Mitterrand's anti-capitalist, seemingly anti-American "union of the Left" rhetoric had a small cost. At lower levels, however, a series of often excellent political section people kept in close touch with Socialists and a few Communist officials.

11. Schmidt and Giscard d'Estaing had developed a close working relationship. They had launched the industrialized country summit meetings (G-5, then G-6, then G-7). They negotiated the European parliament's election by universal suffrage. In 1978 they created the European Monetary System, precursor of the Single European Currency of today. Schmidt did, however, reproach Giscard d'Estaing his "near-silence" about the Soviet SS-20 missiles. See Védrine, op. cit., p. 128.

12. Brzezinski, op. cit., p. 290.

13. Richard Loewenthal, "The German Problem Transformed," *Foreign Affairs* (1985), p. 314. Loewenthal added a warning to German neutralists and pacifists: "But the German peace movement is likely to have a constructive effect only if it is presented as an expression not just of unique German interests, but of a common and vital interest of all Europeans." On the Euromissile crisis a superb analysis in English is Josef Joffe, *The Limited Partnership: Europe, the United States, and the Burdens of Alliance* (Cambridge, MA: Ballinger, 1987).

14. Mitterrand had already given an indication of a willingness to act decisively when in April 1980 (before being elected) he supported the Carter administration's attempt to free American embassy hostages in Tehran at the beginning of the Iranian revolution. This was an unpopular position in France. He was criticized inside his own party, and, of course, by the French Communists.

15. Védrine, op. cit., p. 130.

16. Védrine, in Alain Finklekraut, Pierre Hassner, and Hubert Védrine, "François Mitterrand face aux bouleversments du monde," *Commentaire,* 79 (fall 1997), p. 647.

17. Joffe, op. cit., p. 83; Mitterrand quotation from pp. 36-37.

18. Mitterrand quoted in Favier and Rolland, op. cit., vol. 1, p. 267.

19. Védrine, *Les mondes,* op. cit., p. 236.

20. In a 1997 interview, quoted in Lacouture, op. cit., vol. 2, p. 147.

21. At the next central committee meeting, Georges Marchais on best behavior declared "There is no disagreement between Mitterrand and us on foreign policy," replying to Anicet Le Pors, a Communist government minister, who wanted the party to denounce Mitterrand's "Atlanticist speech." Le Pors was criticized also by the Politburo foreign policy specialist, Maxime Gremetz, who said, "You're trying to outflank us on our left." Mitterrand's diplomacy thus had the extra advantage of sowing discord inside the Communist party councils. See Favier and Martin-Rolland, op. cit., vol. 1, 270.

22. Henry Kissinger, *Diplomacy* (New York: Simon and Schuster, 1995), p. 777.

23. See George Ross, *Jacques Delors and European Integration* (New York: Oxford University Press, 1995); and Charles Grant, *Delors: Inside the House that Jacques Built* (London: Nicholas Brealing Publishing, 1994).

24. *Le Monde,* June 25, 1996, p.8.

25. But strong right-wing "historic Gaullist" dissent continued led by Pasqua. Séguin, feeling politically exposed, resigned in early 1999 as leader of the neo-gaullist RPR party. In the June 1999 European elections the minority Pasqua "Euroskeptic" list came first among several groups, including the main gaullist RPR movement, which lost badly in a deeply split French Right. Pasqua still wants the Amsterdam treaty put to a referendum.

    French Euroskepticism is, as in other countries, not a Left-Right but a cross-cutting issue, featuring but not linking the Pasqua neo-gaullists, the xenophobe extreme-Right National Front, the French Communist party, an anti-globalization wing of the Greens and the "Hunters" protest movement. This group could never unite to form a government. The French pro-Europe consensus is thus unlikely to be threatened even if agreement within it is sometimes superficial.

26. See Mitterrand, *De L'Allemagne, de la France,* op. cit.

27. Védrine, *Les mondes,* op. cit., p. 436.

28. The speaker was François Bujon de l'Estang, French Ambassador to the United States, in a personal interview, December 1996. Of course what the General would have done is itself not so simple. Another possible de Gaulle-like reaction was Margaret Thatcher's outright opposition to German unification. Her *Memoirs* are clear and deserve quotation here: "If there is one instance in which a foreign policy I pursued met with unambiguous failure, it was my policy on German reunification. . . . This policy was to encourage democracy in East Germany while slowing down the country's reunification with West Germany." The policy failed, she says, "But was the policy wrong?" Rapid unification would be "economically disastrous [in Germany] and would "spread to the rest of the European Community via the Bundesbank's high interest rates and the ERM. . . . There is now a German state so large and dominant that it cannot be easily fitted into the new architecture of Europe. . . . Arriving prematurely as it did, a united Germany has tended to encourage three unwelcome developments: the rush to European federalism as a way of tying down Gulliver; the maintenance of a Franco-German bloc for the same purpose; and the gradual withdrawal of the U.S. from Europe on the assumption that a German-led federal Europe will be both stable and capable of looking after its own defense." (p. 814). Only a joint Anglo-French front could have diverted German unification. "Once it was decided that East Germany could join the EC without detailed negotiations . . . there was little we could do to slow down reunification via the Community's institutions." The "Four Powers" framework could have been useful, until the United States and soon the Soviets too ceased to regard it "as anything other than a talking shop for discussing the details of reunification." The CSCE could work against unagreed border changes but not against reunification itself. "So the last and best hope seemed the creation of a solid Anglo-French political axis which would ensure that at each stage of reunification—and in future economic and political developments—the Germans did not have things all their own way."

    According to Thatcher, Mitterrand "was still more concerned than I was" about the German problem. "He complained that the Germans treated any talk of caution as criticism of themselves. . . ." "[Mitterrand] made the wrong decision for France," concludes Thatcher, but she admits that this "refected his basic unwillingness to change the direction of his whole foreign policy," and "that his judgment that there was nothing we could do to halt German reunification turned out to be right" (pp. 796-98). But what, one wonders, would Thatcher's policy have been had she been not British prime minister but president of *France?* "I [had] many disputes with President Mitterrand . . . but I never forgot . . . his personal support . . . throughout the Falklands crisis," she added. Geography, in other words, counts still!

29. This vision "anchored in the past" was a classic French view that deserves restating. The following, written before Mitterrand became president, indicates why the French constantly

worry about Soviet interests and attitudes, and how, in a Europe-centered view, French ideas about alliance with the United States are ambivalent, less than totally satisfying to Americans: "I have long believed that good relations with Russia must be a constant of French diplomacy and, surely, also a constant of our security. Extrapolating, one observes over the centuries a French search for the eastern alliance which would serve as a counterweight to our nearby continental adversaries (NB: in French diplomacy this is called the *alliance de revers* strategy). At one time it was Austria-Hungary, at another it was Spain or Prussia, and, on the seas, it was Great Britain. I never was shocked at this. On the contrary I find it excellent that the French Third Republic—you can imagine the circumstances, at the end of the last century—negotiated with the Emperor of All the Russias. . . . French foreign policy must have the greatest concern for Russian interests. . . . But this desire for a European equilibrium, guaranteed by a good relationship with our eastern ally, must not go to the point of renouncing France's basic interests. Whenever there is a threat from the [eastern] side, it is absolutely normal to seek guarantees of our security elsewhere." "Elsewhere" means the United States and NATO. For Mitterrand, as for de Gaulle and other French leaders, the danger that the Americans would one day return to isolationism, would leave Europe of their own accord, was "natural," that is, geopolitically realistic or even inevitable. France, Germany, Russia, and Great Britain are fated to deal with each other in proximity. Mitterrand, *La Paille*, p. 4.

30. Védrine, in Samy Cohen, ed., *Mitterrand et la Sortie de la Guerre Froide* (Paris: PUF, 1998), p. 432.
31. W. R. Smyser, *From Yalta to Berlin: The Cold War Struggle over Germany* (New York: St. Martin's Press, 1999), pp. 375-76ff.
32. Védrine, *Les mondes*, op. cit., p. 457.
33. Teltschik, op. cit., pp. 244-5.
34. Védrine, *Les mondes*, op. cit., pp. 562 and 567.
35. Ibid., p. 470.
36. Ibid., p. 472.
37. See Élisabeth Guigou, *Pour les Européens* (Paris: Flammarion, 1994).
38. See Védrine, *Les mondes*, op. cit., p. 560.
39. Mitterrand quoted in Giesbert, *Dying without God* (New York: Araco Publishers, 1998), p. 88.
40. I discuss the Gulf war and Bosnia in *France in the New Europe* and "Mitterrand's Legacies," op. cit.
41. Bush in George Bush and Brent Scowcroft, *A World Transformed,* op. cit., p. 376.
42. Védrine, *Les mondes*, op. cit., p. 529.
43. Bush and Scowcroft, op. cit., p. 383.
44. Ibid., p. 76.
45. See Védrine, *Les mondes*, op. cit., p. 641-42 passim. In 1999 Bernard Kouchner was named director of UN operations for rebuilding Kosovo as a European Union protectorate.
46. See this author's conclusion, in Tiersky, ed., *Europe Today* (Lanham, MD: Rowan and Littlefield, 1999).
47. Yaneyev's letter was in fact sent to many leaders. Later, when Gorbachev's memoir *The Coup* appeared, there was a new turn. In an undercorrected foreign edition, Gorbachev spoke of "disappointment"—still a "painful memory" he said—that Mitterrand did not telephone him as soon as possible after his liberation, as opposed to George Bush's quick reaction. In other language editions the pertinent sentence did not appear. Gorbachev unconvincingly denied, in a fence-mending meeting with Mitterrand, that he had ever written the sentence. Mitterrand of course pretended to believe him. It was small potatoes, but a large question, for both, of saving political face.
48. Quoted in Védrine, *Les mondes,* op. cit., p. 636.
49. Védrine, ibid., pp. 638-39. "Then let us be realists and speak frankly"! Mitterrand restates almost word for word Thucydides's dialogue of the Athenian generals talking to the Melian

magistrates. The difference is Mitterrand's goal is not empire but some peaceful outcome. More generally, here, as in the other international developments and crises discussed in this chapter, right or wrong in his policies, Mitterrand had a statesman's view of international politics.

50. Samy Cohen, ed., *Mitterrand et la Sortie de la Guerre Froide,* op. cit., is a summary of French debate.

51. From Philippe Delmas, *De la Prochaine Guerre avec L'Allemagne* (Paris: Odile Jacob, 1999) pp. 192-94.

52. *The Economist,* September 23, 1995, pp. 14-15.

53. C. Fred Bergsten, "Clash of the Titans," *Foreign Affairs* 78, no. 2 (March-April 1999), p. 34.

54. Mitterrand's own staff in internal memos criticized how African policy had slid back to old ways. A harshly self-critical memorandum written by Erik Arnoult, an aide to foreign minister Roland Dumas, stimulated the speech at La Baule. See Attali, *Vérbatim III* (Paris: Fayard, 1993), p. 472, and Védrine, *Les mondes,* op. cit., p. 693. For several years a special advisor for Africa at the Élysée was Jean-Christophe Mitterrand, the president's eldest son. Christophe was unkindly nicknamed "Papa-m'a-dit . . ." ("Dad said to me . . .") by African leaders, and his competence, business propriety, and the nepotism in the appointment were cause of criticism.

55. See especially the work of Jean Bayart, *The Criminalization of the State in Africa* (Bloomington: Indiana University Press, 1999).

56. "One of the direct effects of the Somalia disaster was America's failure (along with other countries) to support and reinforce the United Nations peacekeeping force in Rwanda that could have limited a true genocide in 1994." Joseph S. Nye, Jr., "Redefining the National Interest," *Foreign Affairs* (July/August 1999), p. 32.

57. *The New York Times,* December 20, 1998, p. 17.

58. Védrine, *Les mondes,* op. cit., p. 703.

59. Alan J. Kuperman, "Rwanda in Retrospect," *Foreign Affairs* (January-February 2000), p. 94 and passim. for points made below.

60. But in the accounting of François Mitterrand's and the French government's responsibility for Rwanda, it is demagogic to report as fact, as one otherwise estimable reporter does, that "the late French president François Mitterrand said of Rwanda in 1994, 'In such countries, genocide is not too important.'" Philip Gourevitch, in *The New Yorker* magazine, April 26-May 3, 1999, p. 39. This alleged remark retools the image of François Mitterrand as totally heartless and cynical, which is obviously disproven. Gourevitch should have specified the circumstances of the supposed quotation and, in so grave a matter, given the French original. For example, if Mitterrand had said, in French, *pas très important,* this would have meant "not too large in scope," that is, ethnic/tribal fighting in Africa rarely produces vast numbers of deaths. It would not have meant, as in Gourevitch's odd-sounding translation, that genocide in sub-Saharan Africa is "not too important," that is, not of much consequence, with the accompanying undertone of racism on Mitterrand's part.

61. See Védrine, *Les mondes,* op. cit., p.570.

CHAPTER 7

1. André Laurens, editor-in-chief of *Le Monde,* September 11-12, 1994, p. 9.

2. Pierre Nora, *Les lieux de mémoire* (Paris: Gallimard). Quotations from *Le Point,* #1256, October 12, 1996, p. 108. In 1964 André Malraux gave a moving speech on the transfer to the Pantheon of the remains of Jean Moulin. Nora comments that this speech, amounting to a celebration of national unity, is Malraux's first claim to join the others in the Pantheon.

3. Charles de Gaulle, *War Memories,* op. cit., vol. 3, p. 781-83.

4. Cf. *Ordinary Stalinism,* pp. 155-57ff.

5. Of all the books and speeches of PCF "dissidents" in this period, the most outstanding is Henri Fiszbin, *Les Bouches S'Ouvrent* (Paris: Grasset, 1980). Fiszbin, who was no less than

secretary of the PCF's crucial Paris organization, details the working of "democratic centralism," its written and unwritten rules, the reasons why the Communists (himself included) believed in it for so long, and why the "consensus" in the party about the trustworthiness of its leadership was ruined by the "Marchais group's" trickery at the top. The interested English-language reader should consult Tiersky, *Ordinary Stalinism,* op. cit., chap. 6.

6. See Tiersky, *Ordinary Stalinism,* op. cit., pp. 155-61.

7. Bush in Bush and Scowcroft, op. cit., pp. 75-76.

8. Ten years later on March 24, 1993, when the Socialist Bérégovoy government would be ousted a few days later, Mitterrand talked of the new problem of the Communists' weakness. The lesson of the devastatingly bad first ballot, he said, was that he had not sufficiently gauged "the repercussion which the collapse of the communist world would have on the leftwing vote. This collapse is a good thing in itself because a priori it is a victory for democracy. But it deprived the leftwing [parties] of necessary votes. . . . The left has become a minority because, the PCF being weakened by the collapse of the East, all the weight of electoral expectations was put onto the PS." Mitterrand added that "We should have looked for the means to survive," adding a self-criticism: "I reproach myself with not having imposed on the [Socialist party] rebels the electoral law change I had suggested. I should have obliged the government, even changed the government if necessary. I should have done it. It was the key to everything." In other words, with the Communist vote down to 10 percent and the Socialist vote between 20 and 25 percent, left-wing candidates can be eliminated in the first round of the two-ballot voting, leaving two center and rightist candidates in the runoff ballot. See Mitterrand, *Les Forces de L'Esprit,* Roland Dumas, ed., (Paris: Fayard, 1998), pp. 24-25.

9. This is Fareed Zakaria's point, *The New York Times Magazine,* November 1, 1998, p. 47.

10. Jack Hayward in Hayward, ed., *De Gaulle to Mitterrand.* In *Presidential Power in France* (New York: New York University Press, 1993), pp. 31-32.

11. *Le Monde,* July 2, 1981, p. 1. De Gaulle, to justify rejecting the June 1940 armistice (thus the Third Republic's right to speak for France), created the distinction between a legal or "republican legitimacy" and a deeper legitimacy, which he sometimes called "French legitimacy" or "historical legitimacy." The Third Republic government could legally accept an armistice with the Third Reich and German rule, and the Vichy regime had some legal standing, but both were illegitimate. De Gaulle's task in 1958 was to make the two forms or principles of legitimacy, coincide again.

12. Hayward, op. cit., p. 32.

13. Ibid., pp. 30-31.

14. "Whether he is reticently anti-partisan like de Gaulle, covertly partisan like Pompidou, pseudo-consensual like Giscard or overtly partisan like Mitterrand, the presidential states-man seems impelled to act like a republican sovereign. . . . [But altogether] the practical problem of converting the permanently subversive constituent power of the nation into the sole legitimate basis of political authority has been resolved. The sheer difficulty of this achievement accounts for the obsessive urge to tinker with its institutions that characterizes the French political class in the intervals between its electoral struggles for power, indicative of a congenital reluctance to accept that the centrepiece of their institutions should be the instrument of reform rather than its object." This perceptive analysis is by Hayward in ibid., 34.

15. Presidential archives.

16. *Le Monde,* September 16, 1981, p. 1.

17. These points enunciated by Mitterrand were requoted in the newspaper *Libération,* June 9, 1997, p. 4, just as the Lionel Jospin Socialist government prepared to begin the third cohabitation, with conservative president Jacques Chirac.

18. Védrine, *Les mondes,* op. cit., p. 398.

19. Elie Wiesel, *And the Sea Is Never Full: Memoirs, 1969-* (New York: Knopf, 1999), p. 316.

20. Interview with the author.
21. See *The Economist*, March 5, 1994, p. 57-58.
22. See the U.S. government publication, FBIS-WEU-93-057, March 26, 1993, pp. 52-53.
23. Jean-Marie Colombani, *Le Monde*, July 16, 1993, pp. 1, 7.
24. Thomas Ferenczi, in *Le Monde*, April 11-12, 1993, p. 1.
25. From a France-2 Television network interview, June 22, 1993.
26. Pascal Boniface, *Contre Le Révisionnisme Nucléaire* (Paris: Éllipses, 1994), p. 9.
27. Ibid., p. 10.
28. *Liberation*, October 28, 1994, p. 11.
29. Benamou, op. cit., p. 145.
30. Harvey C. Mansfield, Jr., *Taming The Prince: The Ambivalence of Modern Executive Power* (New York: The Free Press, 1989).
31. Alan Ehrenhalt, *The New York Times*, December 20, 1998, p. 13.
32. *La Paille et Le Grain*, op. cit., p. 63.

CHAPTER 8

1. Mitterrand's retort to Socialist leaders at the 1979 Metz congress, responding to complaints about his "authoritarian" leadership style. See Giesbert, *Le President*, op. cit., p. 56.
2. From an apocryphal anonymous "memoir," *Mémoires pour Servir à L'Histoire de Ma Vie*, op. cit., p. 255.
3. From Mitterrand, *La Paille et Le Grain: Chronicle* (The Wheat and The Chaff: A Chronicle) (Paris: Flammarion, 1975), p. 55.
4. Claude Nicolet, *L'Idée Républicaine en France: Essai D'Histoire Critique* (Paris: Gallimard, 1982).
5. See ibid., p. 415.
6. Samy Cohen, in Cohen, op. cit., p. 372-77.
7. Ibid., p. 377.
8. Mitterrand, *Le Coup D'État Permanent* (Paris: Plon, 1964; reissued Paris: Julliard, 1984), p. 274.
9. See the historical fresco in Nicolet, op. cit.
10. "Parce que je suis amoureux de Paris," *Le Nouvel Observateur*, December 14, 1984, p. 69, as quoted in Eric Cahm, "Mitterrand's *Grands Projets:* Monuments to a Man or Monuments to an Age?" in Mairi Maclean, ed., *The Mitterrand Years: Legacy and Evaluation* (London: Macmillan, 1998), p. 263.
11. Giscard d'Estaing "only had three incomplete projects to his credit" (ibid., p. 264), but that is three more than an American president would have and in any case, Giscard figured in many other ways in the architecture and appearance of Paris.
12. Ibid., p. 265.
13. Malraux's status as culture minister benefited from his own literary reputation and his renown as a traveler-archaeologist (early on he illegally swept out historical treasures from Cambodia), as a camp follower (but his novels about the Chinese revolution had the benefit of only about a month actually spent in that country), and as a revolutionary fighter (in the Spanish Civil War). Despite the esteem de Gaulle gave him, Malraux failed to get the Finance Ministry evicted from a wing of the Louvre museum where it had been "temporarily" ensconced, a transfer that waited a quarter century for the Mitterrand-Jack Lang duo to accomplish. See D. Looseley, ed., *The Politics of Fun: Cultural Policy and Debate in Contemporary France* (Oxford: Berg, 1997).
14. No other Mitterrand aide played the courtier better than Lang (though rivaled by Jacques Attali). Lang inveigled himself into countless "photo opportunities" and travels with Mitterrand. Lang also had an international agenda, and in the archives consulted by this writer is a note in preparation for a trip to the United States in which he implores Mitterrand to give him "some message" to carry, "for example to President Reagan."

15. Harrison, op. cit., p. 202, from Maryvonne de Saint Pulgen, *La Syndrome de L'Opera* (Paris: Gallimard, 1991).

16. Martin Harrison, "The President, Cultural Projects and Broadcasting Policy," in Hayward, ed., *De Gaulle to Mitterrand: Presidential Power in France* (New York: New York University Press, 1993), p. 202.

17. Harrison, op. cit., pp. 202-3.

18. Margaret Thatcher, *Memoirs: The Downing Street Years,* (New York: HarperCollins, 1993); Helmut Kohl, *Ich Wollte Deutschland's Einheit* (Berlin: Propyläen, 1996); and Bush and Scowcroft, *A World Transformed,* op cit.

19. This section is based on Tiersky, *France in The New Europe: Changing Yet Steadfast* (Belmont, CA: Wadsworth, 1994), pp. 115-16.

20. After Mitterrand had passed on there appeared, in 1966, a revelation that Charles Hernu had been on the Soviet payroll in the 1950s and 1960s, writing reports on the French political scene. He supposedly was not passing government secrets (he was in the opposition), but writing even anodyne political reports was potentially compromising since the Soviets knew he might be blackmailed later. If the report was true, the bon vivant Hernu probably did it for money, not out of Soviet sympathies. He himself had died when the allegation surfaced, but no one denied its truth, even if no one made very much of it either. If true, Hernu seems to have gotten off the Soviet payroll in the 1970s.

It seems unlikely that Hernu's vulnerability influenced his actions as defense minister from 1981 to 1985. He acted a strongly anti-Soviet role and was the key advisor in convincing Mitterrand to give up his earlier promise to do away with France's nuclear deterrent if elected. Conceivably Hernu had even been a double agent. It is possible that Hernu never told Mitterrand about his past (whichever version is true, the Soviet connection or the double agent).

21. Giesbert, op. cit., p. 473.

22. Attali, op. cit., pp. 785-86. Given the controversy over the accuracy of Attali's quotations, this should be taken as only a summary of Mitterrand's remarks.

23. Attali, op. cit., p. 43. Three years later Attali records the same Mitterrand sentiment (p. 60): "We're going to lose the [coming] elections. Even a proportional representation system won't avoid defeat. And in case I am against proportional representation but I'll be forced into it by the Socialist [party]. In any case the electoral law should be changed from time to time."

24. Mitterrand, *Les Forces de L'Esprit: Messages pour Demain* (Paris: Fayard, 1998), pp. 24-25.

25. Friend, *Long Presidency,* op. cit., p. 130ff, which provides a good summary of the scandals discussed in this section.

26. Friend, *Long Presidency,* op. cit., p. 132.

27. The following section depends heavily on ibid., pp. 132-36; Favier and Martin-Roland, op. cit., vol. 3, pp. 307-25; and also Antoine Gaudino, *L'Enquête Impossible* (Paris: Albin Michel, 1990).

28. Friend, *Long Presidency,* op. cit., p. 133.

29. Giesbert, *François Mitterrand,* op. cit., p. 610.

30. See Christine Deviers-Joncour, *La Putain de La République* (Paris: Calmann-Lévy, 1998).

31. The Crédit Lyonnais branch, located at the Place Maubert, was Mitterrand's as well. Dumas had bought an entire building in the same street as Mitterrand's, the narrow rue de Bièvre built over the old Bièvre stream, which still empties underground into the Seine.

32. See the *Financial Times,* February 11, 2000, p. 2.

33. Jean Montaldo, *Mitterrand et Les 40 Voleurs* (Paris: Albin Michel, 1994).

34. The above quotes are all from Lacouture, *Mitterrand,* vol. 2, pp. 280-82. See also Favier and Martin-Rolland, op. cit., vol. 2, pp. 677-85 passim; Giesbert, op. cit., pp. 526-33; and in English, Northcutt, op. cit., pp. 260-61.

35. *The Economist,* November 28, 1998, p. 20.

36. The following paragraphs have confirming sources in nearly all the books on Mitterrand but they come particularly from my own interviews with him.

37. See Robert Schneider, *La Haine Tranquille.* (Paris: Seuil, 1992).

38. See *La Revue du Droit Public,* no. 5-6 (1998), and the commentary in *Le Monde,* November 21 and 22, 1998.

39. See Favier and Martin-Roland, op. cit., vol. 3, p. 533.

40. *Le Monde,* November 21, 1998, p. 1.

41. Brosselette, ibid., p. 9

42. *Essays,* p. 351.

43. Alistair Cole, *François Mitterrand: A Study in Political Leadership* (London: Routledge, 1994), pp. 168-69.

44. See Lacouture, *Mitterrand,* op. cit., vol. 1, 160-61.

45. On March 30, 1993, the Socialist party, and its government, led by Prime Minister Pierre Bérégovoy, were badly beaten at the legislative elections. Barely a month later, on May 1, Bérégovoy used his chauffeur's weapon to commit suicide, at Nevers near the canal, in his parliamentary district. Bérégovoy had fallen into a deep depression, provoked by a sense of failure and responsibility for the defeat combined with a media scandal about a $200,000 interest-free loan he had received from Roger-Patrice Pelat. The loan allowed a man whose income had never been excessive to buy a modest apartment in an upscale neighborhood. Bérégovoy felt that revelation of the loan, which the media portrayed as another major scandal of financial corruption in the Mitterrand entourage, was a great stain on his honor.

   Bérégovoy also felt that he was being unfairly criticized by his own Socialist comrades, that his "strong franc" policy as finance minister in the 1980s was being indicted. His wife Gilberte said she had found a small card in his briefcase, on which was scribbled a phrase from Clémenceau: "My party has abandoned me, my friends have abandoned me, I am a dead man." She tried to dissuade Mitterrand from attending her husband's funeral, but the president imposed himself because he wanted to counterattack. Mitterrand spoke with extreme bitterness, saying that French journalists had "delivered the honor of a man up to the dogs."

   The investigative and sensationalist journalist Jean Montaldo seized on this to write a second book of allegations of corruption, *Lettre Ouverte D'Un Chien* (Open Letter from A Dog) (1993) after his first, *Mitterrand and The Forty Thieves.*

   The principal informant for the second book was François de Grossouvre, another Mitterrand crony who was given jobs and an office in the Élysée. De Grossouvre also committed suicide, alleging betrayal on the part of Mitterrand. The evidence indicates he also took his life in the throes of psychological illness. Dark allegations of Mitterrandian "responsibility" for these two sad deaths seem unfounded.

46. Quoted in Giesbert, *François Mitterrand,* op cit., p. 560.

CHAPTER 9

1. Alain Duhamel, *Portrait D'Un Artiste,* op. cit.; See also Jean Glavany, *Mitterrand, Jospin et Nous,* op. cit., p. 96.

2. Giesbert, *François Mitterrand,* op. cit., p. 731.

3. In Roger Gouze, *Mitterrand par Mitterrand,* pp. 132-3.

4. Giesbert, *François Mitterrand,* op. cit., p. 20.

5. The little essay is reproduced verbatim in a 1994 book by three young French journalists about Mitterrand's right-wing youth. Mitterrand included the piece in his collected essays, *Politique I,* op. cit., though, probably in a second-thought about political acceptability he abbreviated the magazine's provocative name to *France,* no. 5. The long quotation below is taken from *La Main Droite,* pp. 235-36.

6. Michael Walzer, *Just and Unjust Wars: A Moral Argument with Historical Illustrations,* 2nd ed. (New York: Basic Books, 1992), p. 46.

7. Roger Gouze, op. cit., pp. 132ff.

8. Sartre, *Nausea*, op. cit., p. 188.

9. Lacouture, I, pp. 110-11. Tony Judt says, "His essays in the postwar paper *Combat* had given him, in Raymond Aron's words, a singular prestige; it was Camus whose conclusions set the moral tone of the Resistance generation as it faced the dilemmas and disappointments of the Fourth Republic and whose many readers had 'formed the habit (said Aron) of getting their daily thought from him.'" See Judt, *The Burden of Responsibility: Blum, Camus, Aron and The French Twentieth Century,* p. 88.

10. Péan, op. cit., pp. 124-25.

11. From a Mitterrand interview with the journalist Roger Prioret, in *L'Expansion,* no. 54 (July-August 1972), quoted in Péan, op. cit., pp. 155-56.

12. From *Paris-Match,* January 25, 1996 (special issue on Mitterrand's death), pp. 76-77. The young girl, who preferred to remain anonymous, had kept the notebook in which François and others had written their answers, and the pages reproduced are certainly in Mitterrand's handwriting, which changed very little from that time to his maturity.

13. In Peyrefitte, op. cit., p. 374.

14. From Mitterrand, *La Paille et Le Grain,* in Nay, *Le noir et le rouge,* op. cit., p. 48.

15. Péan, op. cit., p. 215.

16. From an interview June 28, 1983, where Mitterrand was asked, at a crucial period we have seen, whether he felt as strong, tranquil, and serene as before becoming president. Quoted in Nay, op. cit., p. 141.

17. Roger Gouze, *Mitterrand par Mitterrand* (Paris: Le Cherche Midi Editeur, 1994), pp. 150-51. Gouze is Mitterrand's brother-in-law, the brother of Mitterrand's wife Danielle.

18. In Giesbert, op. cit., p. 718. Anne Lauvergeon confirmed and elaborated on this in a personal conversation with this author June 25, 1997.

19. De Gaulle, *The Edge of the Sword.*

20. A. L. Rowse, *William Shakespeare: A Biography* (New York: Harper & Row, 1963), p. 180.

21. Mitterrand's regular "daytime companion" during his presidency was a Swedish journalist. See Cristina Forsne, *François* (Paris: Editions de Seuil, 1997) pp. 32-3, a translation from the Swedish original published by Fischer & Co., Stockholm, 1996.

22. See Giesbert, *François Mitterrand,* pp. 329ff.

23. Georges-Marc Benamou, *Le Dernier Mitterrand* (Paris: Plon, 1996), p. 30.

24. Hubert Védrine, *Les mondes,* op. cit., p. 315.

25. *Le Figaro,* January 9, 1996, p. 1. See also Giesbert, op. cit., p. 731.

26. In this own way he was following de Gaulle's example: "Never give the impression that you are ashamed of yourself . . ."in Peyrefitte, op. cit., p. 86.

27. In Lacouture, *Mitterrand,* op. cit., vol. 1, p. 82.

28. For example Giesbert, *François Mitterrand,* op. cit., pp. 731-35.

29. Nay, *Le Noir et le Rouge,* op. cit., p. 53.

30. Lacouture, *Mitterrand,* op. cit., vol. 1, p. 82. On August 20, 1944, with Paris still in German hands, Mitterrand, pistol in hand, and Jean Munier together "liberated" the commissariat for prisoners-of-war from which Maurice Pinot had been evicted by Laval. They held it sporadically for the next few days until the August 25 arrival of Leclerc and de Gaulle (p. 103).

31. Giesbert, *François Mitterrand,* op. cit., p. 668.

32. Ibid., p. 670.

33. All quotes from Catherine Nay, *Le noir et le rouge,* op. cit., p. 50.

34. Quoted in Giesbert, *François Mitterrand,* op. cit.

35. Jean Lacouture, *Malraux: Une Vie dans Le Siecle, 1901-1976* (Paris: Seuil, 1976), p. 77

36. Walter Kaufmann, *Existentialism* (New York: Penguin, 1975), p. 47.

CHAPTER 10

1. See Nay, *Le Noir,* which uses this revelatory quotation as its epigram.
2. Serge July, *Les Années Mitterrand,* op. cit. Franz-Olivier Giesbert's *Le President.* (Paris: Editions du Seuil, 1990) also uses this method of defining Mitterrand by his relationship to others.
3. July, op. cit., pp. 19-20. Maurice Faure, a centrist crony from the Fourth Republic, emphasized how, or perhaps why, Mitterrand compartmentalized his friendships: "He mixes his friendships so little and compartmentalizes them such that one wonders if he's not afraid that they might somehow meet up and, thus, constitute his portrait." In Giesbert, op. cit., p. 513.
4. Lacouture, *Mitterrand,* op. cit., vol. 1., pp. 236-37.
5. Deviers-Joncour, op. cit., pp. 95-96.
6. Quoted from *L'Express,* January 11, 1996 in Giesbert, op. cit., p. 732.
7. Forsne, op. cit., p. 34.
8. *The Economist,* "The Economist Review," November 14, 1998, p. 4.
9. Mitterrand's closest friend, Georges Dayan, died on May 28, 1979, unexpectedly during a heart operation. "Every May 28, Irène Dayan [his wife] received from Mitterrand a letter, a telegram or flowers—except in 1994 when, two days after the painful anniversary, Mitterrand, struggling against his own illness wrote to excuse himself 'for having failed at the most elementary of signs of affection and loyalty.'" In Lacouture, *Mitterrand,* op. cit., vol. 1, p. 366, from a letter shown to him by Irène Dayan.
10. David Binder, *The New York Times,* February 18, 1998, p. D22.
11. Ernst Jünger, *Mantrana* (Paris: La Délitante, 1984), p. 43; trans. Pierre Morel.
12. In Giesbert, op. cit., p. 729, from a March 13, 1995, interview.
13. Nicole Leibowitz, "Mitterrand: 'Pourquoi j'aime Marguerite,'" in *Le Nouvel Observateur,* January 9-15, 1994, p. 11.
14. Forsne, op. cit., pp. 27-29.
15. Ibid., p. 9.
16. Isaiah Berlin, *The Hedgehog and the Fox: An Essay on Tolstoy's View of History.*
17. In Giesbert, op. cit., p. 670.
18. Ibid., p. 734, from an interview with Mitterrand, September 18, 1988.
19. Forsne, op. cit., p. 11; *Elle* magazine (January 1997), p. 5.
20. *The Washington Post,* May 17, 1991, p. A19.
21. *The Economist,* May 18, 1991, p. 52.
22. Ibid., p. 13.
23. *The New York Times,* May 16, 1991, p. A3.
24. Legislative amendments ending discrimination against gays and lesbians were also a notable feature of the first few years of the Mitterrand-Mauroy governments. Internal memos and other records show the François Mitterrand himself was a very active force in amending civil and penal codes, as his humanist philosophy would have predicted. The result was, not special rights for homosexuals, but a legal indifference to sexual orientation in the laws of the republic. For example, the age of legal consent, which had been 18 years for homosexuals and 15 years for heterosexuals was made the same. Mitterrand believed this legal indifference, which in context amounted to a pro-gay policy, to be a simple matter of the universal equality of citizen in the French republic tradition going back to the Great Revolution. See Frédéric Martel, *The Pink and the Black: Homosexuals in France Since 1968* (Stanford: CA: Stanford University Press, 1999), trans. by Jane Marie Todd.
25. Elisabeth Schemla, *Edith Cresson. La Femme Piegée,* p. 189 and *passim.*
26. Védrine, *Les mondes,* op. cit., p. 15.
27. Thierry Pfister, *Lettre Ouverte À La Génération Mitterrand, Qui Marche À Coté de Ses Pompes* (Paris: Albin Michel, 1988) pp. 195-98. The same facts, a bit less explicit, are related in Marie-Thérèse Guichard, *Le Président Qui Aimait Les Femmes* (Paris: Robert Laffont, 1993), pp. 124-46.

28. Schemla, op. cit., pp. 188-89.

29. Ibid., p. 190.

30. Ibid., p. 191.

31. Ibid., p. 113, from an interview with Mitterrand, November 13, 1992.

32. See ibid., op. cit., p. 318ff.

33. Few of the women involved with Mitterrand, Dumas, and others have discussed the "rules of the Mitterrand game" in memoirs or with the press. Danielle Mitterrand in her two volumes of memoirs avoids the subject. A few exceptions are Forsne, op. cit., passim and Deviers-Joncour, op. cit., passim., and esp. pp. 120ff.

34. Glavany, op. cit., p. 119. Elisabeth Badinter's *L'Un Est L'Autre* (Paris: Editions Odile Jacob, 1986) was a good example of the kinds of attitudes of the Mitterrand group, especially the women. It was translated in the United States as *The Unopposite Sex: The End of the Gender Battle* (New York: Harper & Row, 1989), a title that renders more clearly its message.

35. *The New Yorker* magazine, November 13, 1998, William Styron, p. 33. See also Styron "Introduction" to Franz-Olivier Giesbert, *Dying without God*, op. cit.

36. Giesbert, *Le President*, p. 123. No worse than President Valéry Giscard d'Estaing, of whom one Socialist deputy sighed that he had a "military discipline" in conducting his extramarital affairs.

37. The existence of Mazarine was reported in the November 10, 1994, edition of *Paris-Match*. Philippe Alexandre, normally a fierce critic of Mitterrand, presented the whole story in *Plaidoyer Impossible pour Un Vieux Président Abondonné Par Les Siens* (Paris: Albin Michel, 1994.). See also Giesbert, *François*, pp. 716-21. The goal of protecting François Mitterrand's private life by learning what certain journalists were planning to do with information about it was one of the reasons for illegal telephone tapping by the so-called Élysée cell.

38. See Jean-Marie Pontaut and Jerome Dupuis, *Les Oreilles du President* (Paris: Fayard, 1996). Hallier's tract was titled *L'Honneur Perdu de François Mitterrand* (Paris: Editions du Rocher/Les Belles Lettres, 1992).

39. Giesbert, *François*, p. 719.

40. Glavany, op. cit., pp. 113-15.

41. Former president Giscard d'Estaing—who used the presidential office for all sorts of sport and who departed office by a back gate with crowds chanting at him "Give us back our diamonds"—said hypocritically in a television interview that "What truly shocks me is that a state apartment was provided for this woman, and for this young girl, as a sort of privilege, going against all the norms" See Glavany, op. cit., pp. 115-16, who notes that a president has a right to a government apartment besides the Élysée. Mitterrand owned his house in rue de Bièvre with his wife Danielle, so he could legally use the Quai Branly apartment with Anne and Mazarine, who needed a protected situation.

42. See Giesbert, *François*, p. 729.

43. Ibid., p. 719.

44. Danielle Mitterrand, *En Toutes Libertés* (Paris: Editions Ramsay, 1996.)

45. Adam Gopnik, "Elvis in the Elysée," *The New Yorker*, June 3, 1996, p. 44.

46. Forsne, *François*, op. cit.

47. By contrast, President Bill Clinton's clumsy moral problems in the Monica Lewinsky scandal were put differently by some Americans: "Having a con man at the helm is bad, but for some men having [an incompetent] is even worse. . . ." Walter Kirn in *Time* magazine, September 21, 1998, p. 38.

48. Benamou, op. cit.

49. Védrine, *Les mondes*, op. cit., p. 56-57. Balladur had coincidentally been Georges Pompidou's chief of staff during his illness in 1972 to 1974.

50. In Mitterrand, *Les Forces de L'Esprit*, op. cit., p. 51.

51. Thus Giscard's revelation in a memoir that Helmut Schmidt had collapsed during a private Élysée meeting, and that the French president had cradled the German Chancellor, was another instance of what people saw as the former's hypocrisy.

52. Gubler poses the interesting question whether foreign secret services had diagnosed Mitterrand's illness. The CIA, for example, followed the evolution of Leonid Brezhnev's illness through various sorts of information gathering, including surreptitious collection of the Soviet leader's urine, for testing, during an American trip. The CIA also knew the exact nature of Pompidou's illness, of which Washington circles were better informed than Paris. Gubler details funny yet grave and desperate tricks on foreign trips by the president, such as watching over combs and brushes to collect hairs, following the president in foreign bathrooms presumably to prevent tests of Mitterrand's excretions, and improvising intravenous systems to deliver medications, once hooked up with a coat hanger onto the top of a door (pp. 43-46).

CHAPTER 11

1. See Péan, op. cit., 180ff.
2. Alain Riding, *International Herald Tribune,* September 3-4, 1994, p. 2.
3. Stanley Hoffmann, in *French Politics and Society,* Symposium on Mitterrand's Vichy past, p. 9.
4. *The New York Times,* October 16, 1997, p. A35.
5. Ferro, *Pétain,* p. 241ff.
6. Philippe Burrin, *France under the Germans: Collaboration and Compromise* (New York: The Free Press, 1996), pp. 1-2, first published as *La France à L'Heure Allemande, 1940-1944,* op. cit.
7. Ibid., pp. 2-3.
8. Ibid., p. 2.
9. See Stanley Hoffmann, *Decline or Renewal?*
10. Ibid., p. 32
11. Of a similar but far from identical situation—Metternich's policy for Austrian adaptation after 1809 to Napoleonic French supremacy—Henry Kissinger assessed Metternich's policy, "a policy which today we would call 'collaboration.'" "It is a policy which can only be carried out by a state certain of its moral strength or overwhelmed by the consciousness of moral impotence. It is a policy which places peculiar strain on the domestic principles of obligation for it can never be legitimized by its real motives. Its success depends on the appearance of sincerity, on the ability, as Metternich once said, of seeming the dupe without being it. To show one's purpose is to court disaster; to succeed too completely is to invite disintegration. In such periods the knave and the hero, the traitor and the statesman are distinguished, not by their acts, but by their motives. At what stage collaboration damages the national substance, at what point it becomes an excuse for the easy way out, these are questions that can be resolved only by people who have lived through the ordeal, not by abstract speculation." Kissinger, op. cit., p. 20. In other words, if either Pétain or the French people had been different, Vichy's collaboration need not have been what it became.
12. Burrin, op. cit., p.4. And why did de Gaulle commute Pétain's death sentence? Himself sentenced, *in absentia,* to death by Vichy's justice for treason, would he, had he been captured, have escaped execution? Was de Gaulle's clemency recognition of the inhumaneness of executing a senile old man, or a last recognition of one military man to another for the Hero of Verdun in World War I? Or was it rather a calculation of postwar French interest, of *raison d'état?* Would Pétain's execution not have provoked a violent reaction in French opinion? As usual, there were more than enough reasons to arrive at a particular decision.
13. Jean-Paul Sartre, *Nausea,* op. cit., p. 63.
14. Roland Dumas, *Gala* magazine (December 1996), p. 39.
15. Ibid.

16. De Gaulle, *War Memoirs,* op. cit., p. 494.

17. Lacouture, *Mitterrand,* vol. 1, op. cit., p. 68.

18. In Péan, op. cit., pp. 187-88, quoted also in Lacouture, *Mitterrand,* op. cit., vol. 1, p. 60, who makes more of this single letter than it would seem to merit.

19. Peyrefitte, *C'était de Gaulle,* vol. 2, p. 107. When in the 1950s Mitterrand spoke in parliament, from the conservative benches he was greeted with cries of "Francisque! Francisque!" and "Pesquet! Pesquet!" Giesbert, op. cit., p. 200.

20. See "Mitterrand Aides Reply in Vichy Debate," in *French Politics and Society.*

21. To make a comparison: The writer, intellectual, and revolutionary adventurer André Malraux, later de Gaulle's close comrade and culture minister, had literally to reinvent himself in World War II, having been, in the 1930s, a left-wing fighter close to the Chinese Communists and the Spanish Republican movements. At the beginning of World War II he was close to the Communist movement and an ardent anti-fascist. At the war's end he was an anti-Communist and a gaullist. He joined the Resistance only in 1944, when he became a freedom fighter in the Alsace-Lorraine brigade. In fact, Malraux was known from the 1940s to the 1960s rather for his "deafening silences."

22. Eric Conan and Henry Rousso, *Vichy, Un Passé qui Ne Passe Pas* (Paris: Fayard, 1994), p. 46.

23. Mitterrand is quoted from *Le Monde,* July 16, 1992, in Conan and Rousso, op. cit., pp. 41-42, Badinter is quoted on p. 45. Mitterrand's and Badinter's attempt, clear enough but unsuccessful, to distinguish the French Republic from the Vichy State as "true" and "false" expressions of "France" is an example of the relativism which existentialist thinking can engender. Isaiah Berlin gave the general principle: For existentialists "the ends of action are not discovered, but are created by individuals or cultures or nations as works of art" *(The Proper Study of Mankind* [New York: Farrar, Straus, and Giroux, 1997], p. 70). Francois Mitterrand's general embrace of "institutions," detailed in chapter 7, was a way of solving this problem; it even "explains" his penchant to accept Vichy. But another reason (there were many; another overdetermined decision) was necessary to explain why he then rejected Vichy.

24. Jews could be interned by the government prefects, and already in the spring of 1941 about 40,000 Jews were in camps. See Conan and Rousso, op. cit., pp. 241-42.

25. Ibid., p. 33.

26. Darquier hated Bousquet, who resigned in December 1943 as Vichy's chief of police, to be replaced by Joseph Darnard, who had founded the "Milice." Giesbert, *François* (p. 709) quotes from an April 20, 1944, editorial in which Darquier wrote bizarrely that "Bousquet is a democrat-political type of the worst kind, a judeophile and an anglophile. . . . We are aware of the continuous treason of this dishonest man." Bousquet, from a kind of house arrest in Germany, aided the Resistance by interfering with Gestapo orders for arrests in France.

27. Interview with television broadcaster Jean-Pierre Elkabbach, Antenne 2 television, text reprinted in *Le Figaro,* September 13, 1994, p. 8.

28. Jacques Attali reports that Régis Debray and Serge Klarsfeld coordinated the effort to get Barbie arrested and extradited. The German government had first asked for extradition in May 1982; now France joined the request. Klarsfeld had the idea that the Bolivians should deliver Barbie to Cayenne, where the French would take him into custody. Barbie was arrested on January 26, 1983 in La Paz and a French military plane took him from Cayenne to France, where he was put in the Lyons prison, at the site of his crimes. Attali, *Verbatim,* op. cit., vol. 1, pp. 386-87, 392-93.

29. In *Vichy France: Old Guard and New Order, 1940-44* (New York: Columbia University Press, 1972), Robert O. Paxton gave this account of Bousquet: "At his trial, René Bousquet, prefect of the Marne in 1940 and later Laval's chief of police, defended his efforts to restore France's 'armature' in the summer of 1940. He didn't touch politics, he asserted in a typical French civil servant's conception. Insisting that it was 'not heroic to flee' the country, he said

one had to work with the Germans 'to restore the necessary order for survival.'" (p. 16). Bousquet got an agreement from SS General Karl Oberg, head of security in France beginning June 1, 1942, guaranteeing the sovereignty of French administration and the independence of French police in the Occupied Zone, "in contrast," so the agreement went, "to the preceding period." Paxton comments that "French police were supposedly given full independence in matters of internal order and French citizens charged with crimes, even political crimes, would be dealt with by French authorities. The French police would not be required to take any role in designating hostages or to take part in any actions that went beyond the armistice." Paxton says "René Bousquet seems at the time to have regarded this agreement as at least a partial victory [when] in fact, greater independence for the French police in the Occupied Zone meant a larger role in measures against the Resistance and an entering wedge for German police measures in the unoccupied zone" (pp. 295-97). In fall 1942 the French police rounded up 8,000 to 10,000 foreign Jews in the unoccupied zone for deportation. Moreover "Heydrich had apparently been convinced by his experience in Czechoslovakia that local police cooperated more willingly when given some measure of independence." Finally "After the total occupation of France on 11 November 1942, the decision to continue the Vichy regime meant that French officials would continue to struggle for autonomy. René Bousquet engaged in new conversations on police powers in November with a 'firm will to maintain and safeguard the principle of French government sovereignty.' An agreement on 2 April 1943 between Bousquet and General Oberg divided police responsibilities in the formerly unoccupied zone along the same lines as the agreement of July 1942 in the Occupied Zone. The French police were solely responsible for French citizens charged with all crimes except direct actions against the German forces. German police, however, could intervene wherever they felt their security was threatened. That security became perilous during 1943, and while the French police arrested some 9,000 persons that year for 'Gaullism, Marxism, or hostility to the regime,' the German police arrested 35,000. Bousquet seemed too lukewarm to the Germans, and after Pétain had made one more effort in December 1943 to get rid of Laval they forced Pétain to accept Joseph Darnand as police chief on 15 December 1943" (p. 297).

30. Peyrefitte, op. cit., vol. 2, p. 601.
31. Giesbert, *François,* p. 710.
32. Ibid., pp. 712-13. Contrary to Mitterrand's explanation here, in 1986 Bousquet only became the object of Klarsfeld's lawsuit, which was not in itself a proof of guilt let alone an official indictment, which came only in 1991.
33. *The New York Times,* December 8, 1997, p. A8.
34. The initial indifference of Nazi officials to Vichy's willingness to collaborate is well documented, a German attitude that changed after Hitler ordered the attack on the Soviet Union, straining Third Reich capacities in the western area. The collaboration of Vichy's police force, authorized under the Oberg-Bousquet summer 1942 agreements in exchange for the basically fictitious French policy autonomy, made the dragnet and deportation of Jews from France much less difficult. In Robert Paxton's testimony at the Papon trial, "From the time Jews expelled from other countries began to arrive, the Vichy authorities were consternated by what to do with these refugees." Sending them back to Germany, despite growing knowledge of what was happening to the Jews there, was the Vichy authority's answer. *Le Nouvel Observateur,* November 6-12, 1997, p. 94. Overall almost 75,000 of the 330,000 Jews living in France were deported, a statistic that shows simultaneously the great crime against these French Jews and that numbers of French Catholics must have protected Jews.
35. See Robert O. Paxton's summary account, "The Trial of Maurice Papon," in *The New York Review of Books,* December 16, 1999, pp. 32-38.
36. Ibid., p. 32.
37. Ibid.
38. Ibid., p. 38.

39. Jean Glavany, *Mitterrand, Jospin et Nous* (Paris: Grasset, 1998), pp. 51-52.
40. See Favier and Martin-Rolland, op. cit., vol. 1, p. 303.
41. Benamou, op. cit., p. 193.
42. Quoted in Attali, *Verbatim* I, p. 691, op. cit., from Mitterrand and Wiesel, *Memoir À Deux Voix.*
43. Benamou, op. cit., pp. 193ff. The following section is based on this source.
44. Ibid. p. 196ff.
45. *New York Review of Books,* November 3, 1994, p. 12.
46. In "La République et ses heros. Le gaullisme pendant et après la guerre," p. 65, cited in Conan and Rousso, op. cit., p. 231.
47. Hubert Védrine, *Les Mondes,* op. cit., p. 310ff.
48. Ibid., p. 311.
49. See the *New York Times,* April 28, 1995, p. A4.

CHAPTER 12

1. Tony Judt, *The New York Review of Books,* August 13, 1998, p. 55.
2. Friend, *Long Presidency,* op. cit., p. 258.
3. Giesbert, op. cit., p. 12.
4. In Cohen, ed., op. cit., p. 433.
5. Kissinger, *Diplomacy,* op. cit., p. 5.
6. See pages 183-184 and note 28, page 410.
7. See Védrine, *Les mondes,* op. cit., pp. 455-56, including the dictum. One French journalist critical of Védrine's account as trying to pass off Mitterrand's mistakes as "a simple communications problem" is Pierre Haski, "Mitterrand et la réunification de l'Allemagne," in Cohen, ed., op. cit., p. 12.
8. Jünger, op. cit., p. 29.
9. See *Le Monde,* January 10, 1996, p. 1.
10. Michael Walzer, "Political Action: The Problem of Dirty Hands," in Marshall Cohen, Thomas Nagel, and Thomas Scanlon, *War and Moral Responsibility* (Princeton, NJ: Princeton University Press, 1974), pp. 62-82.
11. Ibid., p. 63, including the quotation from *Les Main Sales.*
12. Ibid., pp. 65-66.
13. The *New York Times,* January 20, 2000, p. A18. The "Flick" party finance scandal in the 1980s has to be added to the list of comparisons as well.
14. Ibid., p. 80.
15. Ibid., pp. 79, 70.
16. Mitterrand and Wiesel, op. cit., pp. 205-206, 217, 204.
17. Giesbert, op. cit., p. 731.
18. Stanley Hoffmann, "French Dilemmas and Strategies in the New Europe," Harvard Center for European Studies, Working Paper #38, 1992, pp. 34-35. See also Tiersky, *France in the New Europe,* op. cit., chaps. 9-10.
19. Kissinger, *Diplomacy,* op. cit., p. 110
20. Friend, *Long Presidency,* op. cit., p. 263.
21. *The Economist,* Survey on Europe, October 23, 1999, p. 6.
22. My initial assessment was Tiersky, "Mitterrand's Legacies," *Foreign Affairs,* 74, no. 1 (January-February 1995).
23. Giesbert, op. cit., p. 12.
24. Eric Hobsbawm, *The Age of Revolution: 1789-1848* (Cleveland: The World Publishing Co., 1962), p. 54.
25. Védrine, *Les mondes,* op. cit., p. 760.
26. Mitterrand from *European Affairs* 4 (Winter 1990), p. 37.
27. Mitterrand, *Le Figaro,* September 9, 1994, p. 1.

28. From Jospin's election night speech, in *Paris-Match,* June 12, 1997, p. 62.
29. *The New York Times Book Review,* July 16, 1995, p. 7, Kissinger review of *Churchill: The Unruly Giant* (New York: The French Press, 1995).
30. Interview by Giesbert, *Le Figaro,* September 8, 1994, p. 2.
31. Jean-Paul Sartre, *Existentialism and Humanism* (London: Methuen, 1948), p. 28.
32. Georges Duby, *An 1000 An 2000* (Paris: Les Éditions Textuel, 1995), p. 9.

BIBLIOGRAPHY

Adler, Laure, *L'année des adieux* (Paris: Flammarion, 1995).

Aeschimann, Eric and Pascal Riché, *La guerre de sept ans: Histoire secrète du franc fort, 1989-1996* (Paris: Calmann-Levy, 1996).

Anon., *Mémoires pour servir à l'histoire de ma vie* (Paris: Éditions Bartillat, 1997).

Aron, Raymond, *Memoirs: Fifty Years of Political Reflection* (New York: Holmes and Meier, 1990).

————, *In Defense of Decadent Europe* (South Bend, IN: Gateway, 1977).

————, *The Elusive Revolution: The Anatomy of a Student Revolt* (New York: Praeger, 1969).

Attali, Jacques, *Verbatim,* 3 vols., *I: 1981-1986* (Paris: Fayard, 1993); *II: 1986-1988* (Paris: Fayard, 1995); *III: 1988-1991* (Paris: Fayard, 1995).

Badinter, Elisabeth, *L'un est l'autre* (Paris: Odile Jacob, 1986).

Barbier, Christophe, *Les dernières jours de François Mitterrand* (Paris: Grasset, 1998).

Barzini, Luigi, *The Europeans* (New York: Simon and Schuster, 1983).

Bayart, Jean-François, *The State in Africa: The Politics of the Belly* (New York: Longman, 1993).

Bell, David S. and Byron Criddle, *The French Socialist Party: Resurgence and Victory* (Oxford: Oxford University Press, 1984).

————, *The French Communist Party in the Fifth Republic* (Oxford: The Clarendon Press, 1994).

Benamou, Georges-Marc, *Le dernier Mitterrand* (Paris: Plon, 1996).

Bergsten, C. Fred, "Clash of the Titans," *Foreign Affairs,* March-April 1999, 78 (2), pp. 20-34.

Berlin, Isaiah, *The Hedgehog and the Fox: An essay on Tolstoy's View of History* (New York: Simon and Schuster, 1970).

Bloch, Marc, *Strange defeat: A State of Evidence,* written in 1940 (New York: Norton, 1968).

Bloch-Lainé, François and Claude Gruson, *Hauts fonctionnaires sous l'occupation* (Paris: Odile Jacob, 1997).

Boniface, Pascal, *Contre la révisionnisme nucléaire* (Paris: Ellipses, 1994).

Burrin, Philippe, *La France à l'heure allemande, 1940-1944* (Paris: Seuil, 1993), trans. as *France under the Germans: Collaboration and Compromise* (New York: The Free Press, 1996).

Bush, George, and Brent Scowcroft, *A World Transformed* (New York: Knopf, 1998).

Cadiot, Jean-Michel, *Mitterrand et les communistes: Les dessous d'un marriage de raison* (Paris: Ramsay, 1994).

Carle, Françoise, *Les archives du président* (Paris: Éditions du Rocher, 1998).

Chapman, Herrick, Mark Kesselman and Martin Schain, *A Century of Organized Labour in France: A Union Movement for the Twenty-first Century?* (New York: St. Martin's Press, 1998).

Cayrol, Roland, *François Mitterrand, 1945-67* (Paris: PFNSP, 1967).

Charasse, Michel, *55, rue du Faubourg St. Honoré* (Paris: Grasset, 1996).

Chaslin, F., *Les paris de François Mitterrand: Histoire des grands projets architecturaux* (Paris: Gallimard, 1985).

Clark, Alan, "François Mitterrand and the Idea of Europe," in Brian Nelson, David Roberts and Walter Veit, eds., *The Idea of Europe: Problems of National and Transnational Identity* (New York: Berg, 1992).

Claude, Henri, *Mitterrand ou l'atlanticisme masqué* (Paris: Messidor, 1982).

Cohen, Samy, ed., *Mitterrand et la sortie de la guerre froide* (Paris: PUF, 1998).

Cole, Alistair, *François Mitterrand: A Study in Political Leadership* (London: Routledge, 1994).

Collard, Sue, "Mission impossible: Les chantiers du Président," *French Cultural Studies* (1992), pp. 97-132.

Conan, Eric, and Henry Rousso, *Vichy, Un Passé qui Ne Passe Pas* (Paris: Fayard, 1994).

Le Crapouillot (summer 1981). "Le vrai Mitterrand."

Le Crapouillot (fall 1982). "Mitterrand: L'état de disgrace."

Czerny, Philip G. and Schain, Martin, eds., *Socialism, the State, and Public Policy in France* (New York: Methuen, 1985).

Daley, Anthony, ed., *The Mitterrand Era: Policy Alternatives and Political Mobilization in France* (New York: New York University Press, 1995).

Daniel, Jean, *L'ère des ruptures* (Paris: Grasset, 1979).

———, *Les réligions d'un président. Regards sur les aventures du mitterrandisme* (Paris: Grasset, 1988).

———, and Jean Lacouture, *Le citoyen Mendès France* (Paris: Seuil, 1992).

Debray, Régis, *Loués soient nos seigneurs: Une éducation politique* (Paris: Gallimard, 1996).

Delmas, Philippe, *De la prochaine guerre avec l'Allemagne* (Paris: Odile Jacob, 1999).

Deviers-Joncour, Christine, *La putain de la République* (Paris: Calmann-Lévy, 1998).

Diekman, Kai and Ralf Georg Reuth, *Helmut Kohl: Ich wollte Deutschlands einheit* (Berlin: Propylaeen Verlag, 1996).

Doherty, Elizabeth, *Playing by the rules: The Mitterrand Government and the International Economy, 1981-83* (Boulder, CO: Westview Press, 1997).

Duby, Georges, *An 1000, An 2000* (Paris: Les Editions Textuel, 1995).

Duhamel, Alain, *De Gaulle-Mitterrand: La marque et la trace* (Paris: Flammarion, 1991).

———, *Portrait d'un artiste* (Paris: Flammarion, 1997).

Dumas, Roland, *Le fil et la pelote: Mémoires* (Paris: Plon, 1996).

———, ed., *Les Forces de L'Esprit* (Paris: Fayard, 1998).

Duras, Marguerite, *Un parcours: 1943-1993* (Paris: Gallimard, 1997). Collected works, including *La Douleur*.

Du Roy, Albert and Robert Schneider, *Le Roman de la rose. D'Épinay à l'Élysée* (Paris: Seuil, 1982).

Ehrmann, Henry W. and Martin A. Schain, *Politics in France,* 5th ed. (New York: HarperCollins Publishers, 1992).

Fabius, Laurent, *Les blessures de la vérité* (Paris: Flammarion, 1995).

Faux, Emmanuel, Thomas Legrand and Gilles Perez, *La main droite de Dieu: Enquête sur François Mitterrand et l'extrême droite* (Paris: Seuil, 1994).

Favier, Pierre and Michel Martin-Roland, La décennie Mitterrand, 3 vols. *I. Les ruptures (1981-84)* (Paris: Seuil, 1990); *II. Les épreuves* (Paris: Seuil, 1991); *III. Les défis* (Paris: Seuil, 1996).

Figueras, André, *Mitterrand dévoilé* (Paris: A. Figueras, 1980).

Finklekraut, Alain, Pierre Hassner and Hubert Védrine, "François Mitterrand face aux bouleversements du monde," *Commentaire,* 79 (fall 1997), pp. 645-55.

Fitoussi, Jean-Paul, *Le débat interdit: Monnaie, Europe, Pauvreté* (Paris: Arléa, 1995).

Flynn, Gregory, ed., *The New France in the New Europe* (Boulder, CO: Westview Press, 1995).

Forrester, Viviane, *L'horreur économique* (Paris: Fayard, 1996).

Forsne, Cristina, *François* (Paris: Seuil, 1997), trans. from the Swedish.

Freney, Henri, *La Nuit Finira* (Paris: Plon, 1983).

Friend, Julius W., *The Linchpin: French-German Relations, 1950-1990* (New York: The Center for Strategic and International Studies, 1991).

———, *The Long Presidency: France in the Mitterrand Years, 1981-1995* (Boulder, CO: Westview Press, 1997).

Froment, Pascal, *René Bousquet* (Paris: Stock, 1994).

Fumaroli, Marc, *L'état culturel. Essai sur une réligion moderne* (Paris: PUF, 1991).

Gaudino, Antoine, *L'Enquete Impossible* (Paris: Albin Michel, 1990).

de Gaulle, Charles, *War Memoirs* (New York: Simon and Schuster, 1960).

———, *Memoirs of Hope* (New York: Simon and Schuster, 1971).

Giesbert, Franz-Olivier, *François Mitterrand, une vie* (Paris: Seuil, 1995). An updated, collated version of *François Mitterrand ou la tentation de l'histoire* (1977) and *Le Président* (1990).

———, *Dying without God: François Mitterrand's Meditations on Living and Dying* (New York: Arcade Publishers, 1998), introduction by William Styron.

Glavany, Jean, *Mitterrand, Jospin et Nous* (Paris: Grasset, 1998).

Golsan, Richard J., ed., *Memory, the Holocaust, and French Justice: The Bousquet and Touvier Affairs* (Hanover, NH: University Press of New England, 1995).

Goodman, John B. Monetary *Sovereignty: The Politics of Central Banking in Western Europe* (Ithaca, N.Y.: Cornell University Press, 1992).

Gordon, Philip H., *A Certain Idea of France: French Security Policy and the Gaullist Legacy* (Princeton: Princeton University Press, 1993).

Guéhenno, Jean Marie, *La fin de la démocratie* (Paris: Flammarion, 1993).

Guichard, Marie-Thérèse, *Le président qui aimait les femmes* (Paris: Robert Laffont, 1993).

Hall, Peter A., *Governing the Economy: The Politics of State Intervention in Britain and France* (New York: Oxford University Press, 1986).

Hallier, Jean-Édern, *La force d'âme; suivi de l'honneur perdu de François Mitterrand* (Paris: Belles Lettres, 1992).

Hayward, Jack, ed., *De Gaulle to Mitterrand: Presidential Power in France* (New York: New York University Press, 1993).

Hobsbawm, Eric, *The Age of Extremes: A History of the World, 1914-1991* (New York: Pantheon Books, 1994)

———, *The Age of Revolution, 1789-1848* (Cleveland: The World Publishing Co., 1962).

Hoffmann, Stanley, *Decline or Renewal? France since the 1930s* (New York: Viking Press, 1974).

Jessel, Jacques, *La double défaite de Mitterrand* (Paris: Albin Michel, 1992).

Joffe, Josef, *The Limited Partnership: Europe, the United States, and the Burdens of Alliance* (Cambridge, MA: Ballinger, 1987).

Jouve, Pierre and Ali Magoudi, *Mitterrand: Portrait total* (Paris: Carrer, 1986), 19 hours of interviews edited into TF1 documentary, Jan. 27, 1987.

Judt, Tony, *Past Imperfect: French Intellectuals, 1945-1957* (Berkeley: University of California Press, 1993).

Judt, Tony, *The Burden of Responsibility: Blum, Camus, Aron and the French Twentieth Century* (Chicago: University of Chicago Press, 1999).

July, Serge, *Les années Mitterrand. Histoire baroque d'une normalisation inachevée* (Paris: Grasset, 1986).

———, *Le salon des artistes* (Paris: Grasset, 1989).

Jünger, Ernst, *Mantrana* (Paris: La Delirante, 1984). trans. Pierre Morel.

Kissinger, Henry, *A World Restored: Metternich, Castelreagh and the Problems of the Peace, 1812-1822* (Boston: Houghton Mifflin, 1957).

———, *Diplomacy* (New York: Simon and Schuster, 1995).

Kriegel, Annie, *Les communistes françois,* 2nd ed. (Paris: Seuil, 1970), first ed. trans. as *The French Communists: Portrait of a People* (Chicago: University of Chicago Press, 1972).

Kuperman, Alan J., "Rwanda in Retrospect," *Foreign Affairs,* 79 (1), January-February 2000, pp. 94-119.

Lacouture, Jean, *Pierre Mendès France* (New York: Holmes & Meier, 1984). Trans. George Holoch.

Lacouture, Jean, *Mitterrand: Une histoire de français,* 2 vols. (Paris: Seuil, 1998).

Laughlan, John, *The Death of Politics: France under Mitterrand* (London: Michael Joseph, 1994).

Lavau, Georges, *À Quoi sert le Parti communiste français?* (Paris: Fayard, 1981).

Loewenthal, Richard, "The German Problem Transformed," *Foreign Affairs,* Winter 1984-85.

Looseley, D., ed., *The Politics of Fun: Cultural Policy and Debate in Contemporary France* (Oxford: Berg, 1997).

Machiavelli, Niccolo, *The Prince* (London: Penguin Books, 1961), trans. George Bull.

Maclean, Mairi, *The Mitterrand Years: Legacy and Evaluation* (New York: St. Martin's, 1998).

MacShane, Denis, *François Mitterrand: A Political Odyssey* (London: Quartet Books, 1982).

Manceron, Claude et Bernard Pingaud, *François Mitterrand: L'homme, les idées, le programme* (Paris: Flammarion, 1981).

Marrus, Michael R. and Robert Paxton, *Vichy France and the Jews* (New York: Basic Books, 1981).

Mény, Yves, *La Corruption de la Republique* (Paris: Fayard, 1992).

Mitterrand, Danielle, *En toutes libertés* (Paris: Ramsey, 1996).

Mitterrand, François, *Les prisonniers de guerre devant la politique* (Paris: Éditions du Rond-Point, 1945).

———, *Aux frontières de l'union française* (Paris: Julliard, 1953).

———, *Présence française et abandon* (Paris: Plon, 1957).

———, *La Chine du défi* (Paris: Julliard, 1961).

———, *Le coup d'état permanent* (Paris: Plon, 1964), reissued (Paris: Julliard, 1984).

———, *Ma part de vérité: De la rupture à l'unité* (Paris: Fayard, 1969).

———, *Un socialisme du possible* (Paris: Seuil, 1971).

———, *La rose au poigne* (Paris: Flammarion, 1973).

———, *La paille et le grain* (Paris: Flammarion, 1975).

———, *Politique I* (Paris: Fayard, 1977); *Politique II* (Paris: Fayard, 1981).

———, *François Mitterrand et la crise du Golfe: Discours et messages, 9 aout 1990-16 janvier 1991* (Paris: Todlage, 1991).

———, *L'abeille et l'architecte* (Paris: Flammarion, 1978).

———, *Ici et maintenant* (Paris: Fayard, 1980).

———, *Réflexions sur la politique extérieure de la France: Introduction à vingt-cinq discours, 1981-85* (Paris: Fayard, 1986).

———, *Lettre à tous les français* (Paris: Parti socialiste, 1988).

———, with Élie Wiesel, *Mémoire à deux voix* (Paris: Odile Jacob, 1995).

———, *Il faut laisser le temps au temps: les mots de François Mitterrand,* Michel Martin-Roland, ed. (Paris: Editions hors Collection, 1995).

———, with Georges-Marc Benamou, *Mémoires interrompus* (Paris: Odile Jacob, 1996).

———, *De l'Allemagne, de la France* (Paris: Odile Jacob, 1996).

———, *Les forces de l'esprit. Messages pour demain,* Roland Dumas, ed. (Paris: Fayard, 1998).

Mitterrand, Robert, *Frère de quelqu'un* (Paris: Robert Laffont, 1988).

Montaldo, Jean, *Lettre ouverte d'un "chien" à François Mitterrand, au nom de la liberté d'aboyer* (Paris: Albin Michel, 1993).

———, *Mitterrand et les 40 voleurs* (Paris: Albin Michel, 1994).

Moore, Brian, *The Statement* (New York: Dutton, 1996), the novelized version of Paul Touvier's life.

Morin, Edgar, *Autocritique* (Paris: Seuil, 1970).

Nay, Catherine, *Le noir et le rouge, ou l'histoire d'une ambition* (Paris: Grasset, 1984), trans. *The Black and the Red: Francois Mitterrand, the Story of an Ambition.*

———, *Les sept Mitterrand ou les métamorphoses d'un septennat* (Paris: Grasset, 1988).

Nicolet, Claude, *L'idée républicaine en France: Essai d'histoire critique* (Paris: Gallimard, 1982).

Nobécourt, Jacques, *Le Colonel de la Rocque, 1885-1946: ou les pièges du nationalisme chrétien* (Paris: Fayard, 1996).

Northcutt, Wayne, *Mitterrand: A Political Biography* (New York: Holmes & Meier, 1992).

Ory, Pascal, *L'aventure culturel française, 1945-1989* (Paris: Plon, 1990),

Paxton, Robert O., *Vichy France: Old Guard and New Order* (New York: Columbia University Press, 1972).

Péan, Pierre, *Une jeunesse française: François Mitterrand, 1934-1947* (Paris: Fayard, 1994).

Peyrefitte, Alain, *C'était de Gaulle,* 2 vols., Eds. de Fallois (Paris: Fayard, 1994, 1998).

Pfister, Thierry, *Lettre ouverte à la génération Mitterrand qui marche à coté de ses pompes* (Paris: Albin Michel, 1988).

———, *La vie quotidienne à Matignon au temps de l'union de la gauche* (Paris: Hachette, 1985).

———, *Dans les coulisses du pouvoir: La comédie de la cohabitation* (Paris: Albin Michel, 1986).

Picard, Michel and Julie Montagard, *Danielle Mitterrand, Portrait* (Paris: Editions Ramsey, 1982).

Pierre-Brossolette, Sylvie, *Paroles de président. Carnets sécrets* (Paris: Plon, 1996).

Pingeot, Mazarine, *Premier Roman* (Paris: Odile Jacob, 1998).

Plenel, Edwy, *Les mots volés* (Paris: Stock, 1997).

Poirier, Lucien, *La crise des fondements* (Paris: Economica, 1994).

Ponteau, Jean-Maire and Jerôme Dupuis, *Les oreilles du président* (Paris: Albin Michel, 1996).

Programme commun de gouvernement, French Socialist and Communist parties (Paris: Éditions sociales, 1972).

Rondeau, Daniel, *Mitterrand et nous* (Paris: Grasset, 1994).

Ross, Georges, *Jacques Delors and European Integration* (New York: Oxford University Press, 1995).

————, Stanley Hoffmann and Sylvia Malzacher, *The Mitterrand Experiment: Continuity and Change in Modern France* (New York: Oxford University Press, 1987).

Rowse, A. L., *William Shakespeare: A Biography* (New York: Harper & Row, 1963).

Sartre, Jean-Paul, *La nausée* (Paris: Gallimard, 1938).

————, *Existentialism and Humanism* (London: Methuen, 1948).

Schemla, Elisabeth, Edith Cresson, *La femme piégée* (Paris: Flammarion, 1993).

Schnapper, Dominique, *L'Europe des immigrés: Essai sur les politiques d'immigration* (Paris: François Bourin, 1992).

————, *La communauté des citoyens: Sur l'idée moderne de nation* (Paris: Gallimard, 1994).

Schneider, Robert, *La haine tranquille* (Paris: Seuil, 1992).

————, *Les dernières années* (Paris: Seuil, 1994).

Singer, Daniel, *Is Socialism Doomed? The Meaning of Mitterrand* (New York: Oxford University Press, 1988).

Stasse, François, *La morale de l'histoire: Mitterrand-Mendès France, 1943-1982* (Paris: Seuil, 1992).

Styron, William, see Franz-Olivier Giesbert, *Dying without God.*

Tertrais, Bruno, *L'arme nucléaire après la guerre froide: L'Alliance atlantique, l'Europe et l'avenir de la dissuasion* (Paris: Economica, 1994).

Tiersky, Ronald, *French Communism, 1920-1972* (New York: Columbia University Press, 1974).

————, "Ambivalence Yet Again Unresolved: The French Left, 1972-1978," in William E. Griffith, *The European Left: Italy, France, and Spain* (Lexington, Ma.: Lexington Books, 1979) pp.49-80.

————, *Ordinary Stalinism: Democratic Centralism and the Question of Communist Political Development* (Winchester, MA: Allen & Unwin, 1985).

————, "France in the New Europe," *Foreign Affairs,* 71(2) spring 1992, 131-46.

————, *France in the New Europe: Changing Yet Steadfast* (Belmont, Ca.: Wadsworth, 1994).

————, "France, the CFSP and NATO," in Pierre Laurent ed., *State of the European Union,* vol. IV (Boulder, CO: Lynne Rienner Publishers, 1998), pp. 179-190.

————, "Mitterrand's Legacies," *Foreign Affairs,* 74(1), January-February 1995, pp. 112-121.

————, "Mitterrand's Legacy and French Security Policy" (Washington D.C.: National Defense University 1995).

————, with Philippe Burrin, Jean-Marie Domenach, Stanley Hoffmann, Dominique Moisi and Robert O. Paxton, "Élysée Replies to Questions About Mitterrand's Wartime Record," *French Politics and Society,* spring 1995.

Tocqueville, Alexis de, *The Old Regime and the French Revolution* (New York: Doubleday Anchor Books, 1983), trans. Stuart Gilbert.

Védrine, Hubert, *Les mondes de François Mitterrand: À l'Élysée 1981-1995* (Paris: Fayard,1996).

Vidal, Gore, *Palimpsest: A Memoir* (New York: Penguin Books, 1995).

Walzer, Michael, "Political Action: The Problem of Dirty Hands," in Marshall Cohen, Thomas Nagel and Thomas Scanlong, *War and Moral Responsibility* (Princeton, N.J.: Princeton University Press, 1974).

————, *Just and Unjust Wars: A Moral Argument With Historical Illustrations* (New York: Basic Books, 1992), 2nd. ed.

Wiesel, Elie, *And the Sea Is Never Full: Memoirs, 1969-* (New York: Knopf, 1999).

Zorghibe, Charles, *De Gaulle, Mitterrand, et l'esprit de la constitution* (Paris: Hachette Pluriel, 1991).

Zuber, Martha, ed., *États de la corruption: Politics, Morals, and Corruption in France.* Special issue of *French Politics and Society,* 11(4), fall 1993.

INDEX

About the Author

Ronald Tiersky is Joseph B. Eastman Professor of Politics at Amherst College. He is author of *France in the New Europe* and *Ordinary Stalinism*. He is editor of *Euro-skepticism: A Reader* and *Europe Today: National Politics, European Integration, and European Security*. He is general editor of Rowman & Littlefield's Europe Today series.